James,
thank you for all
the great times and
conversations with food.
Hope you and your family
enjoy some of these ideas
Happy B-day.
Kelly. "2017"

MAN MADE MEALS

STEVEN RAICHLEN
MAN MADE MEALS

THE ESSENTIAL COOKBOOK FOR GUYS

WORKMAN PUBLISHING, NEW YORK

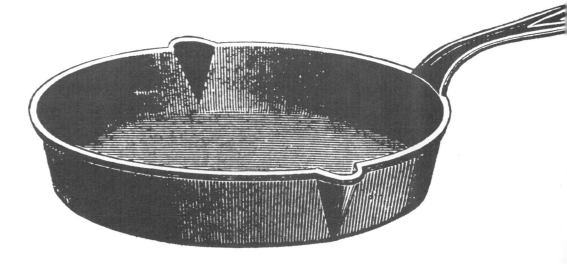

BARBECUE! BIBLE is a registered trademark of Steven Raichlen and Workman Publishing Co., Inc. WORKMAN is a registered trademark of Workman Publishing Co., Inc.

Library of Congress Cataloging-in-Publication Data is available.

ISBN: 978-0-7611-6644-3

Cover and interior design by Jean-Marc Troadec
Cover photograph by Jeffery Salter
Food photography by Lucy Schaeffer
Food styling by Chris Lanier
Prop styling by Sara Abalan
Additional thank-yous and photography credits on page 631.

Steven Raichlen is available for select speaking engagements. Please contact speakersbureau@workman.com.

Workman books are available at special discounts when purchased in bulk for premiums and sales promotions as well as for fund-raising or educational use. Special editions or book excerpts can also be created to specification. For details, contact the special sales director at the address below, or send an email to specialmarkets@workman.com.

WORKMAN PUBLISHING CO., INC.
225 VARICK STREET
NEW YORK, NY 10014-4381

workman.com

Printed in the United States of America
First printing April 2014

10 9 8 7 6 5 4 3 2 1

In memory of Peter Workman
Publisher. Mentor. Friend.

ACKNOWLEDGMENTS

This book came to life at a meeting with Peter Workman at the offices of Workman Publishing. Prophetically, my longtime editor, Suzanne Rafer, was away on jury duty. So it was just us guys. Having taught millions of men how to grill, Peter reasoned, we should do a book to teach them other forms of cooking. And being Peter Workman, he wanted a *big* book, full of big-flavored food and actionable information.

The idea struck a chord, for while most people know me for the Barbecue! Bible cookbook series, I have a background in classic French cuisine (and French literature, but that's another story). And so *Man Made Meals* came to life.

Peter passed away before publication. I've tried to infuse the book with his big-hearted spirit. We miss him. No one will ever completely fill his shoes, but other longtime Workmanites are steering his ship to new horizons.

The most gratifying aspect of writing a book is thanking the people who helped make it possible. First, my extraordinary editor, Suzanne Rafer, who never met a manuscript she couldn't improve. (This year marks two decades of working together.) Production editor Carol White, copy editor Barbara Mateer, and assistant editor Erin Klabunde made sure I dotted my i's and crossed my t's. Barbara Peragine and Julie Primavera herded the manuscript through production.

Art director Jean-Marc Troadec came up with the handsome cover and page design. Photo director Anne Kerman, photographer Lucy Schaeffer, food stylist Chris Lanier, and prop stylist Sara Abalan filled the book with hunger-inducing photos.

On the digital side, Andrea Fleck-Nisbet, Kate Travers, and Julia Langer Warren masterminded the website (barbecuebible.com). Selina Meere, Courtney Greenhalgh, and Jessica Wiener use publicity and marketing to help spread the gospel of guy cooking far and wide, as does international sales director Kristina Peterson. Walter Weintz, Page Edmunds, Jenny Mandel, Pat Upton, and a great sales team keep the sales engine humming.

My assistant and friend Nancy Loseke assisted in all matters editorial and culinary. Stepdaughter and dietician Betsy provided nutritional advice, while stepson Jake provided the perspective of a Brooklyn chef restaurateur. Son-in-law Gabriel rocked the bar shaker. Ella, Mia, and Julian reminded us of what *really* matters in life. Barbara kept me focused, organized, and on message, while juggling the challenging roles of being my in-house editor, *consigliere*, and wife. As always, all good that happens to me starts with her.

Finally, a big thanks to all you guys out there who expanded my world from the grill to the kitchen. It's back to smoking and grilling in the next book—I promise.

Steven Raichlen
Miami, Florida

CONTENTS

HOW TO COOK LIKE A PRO

Call it culinary literacy for men. Or simply what every guy should know about cooking. There are certain tasks involving food a man should know how to do without hesitation: shuck an oyster and steam a lobster, for example; grill a steak; roast a rack of lamb; and cook up a pot of kick-ass chili. Every well-informed male should know the proper way to stir a martini, carve a turkey, smoke ribs, make pancakes for his kids, and clinch a romantic dinner with a rich chocolate dessert. But, first and foremost, a guy should know how to get himself dinner (or any meal) on the table without having to rely on take-out.

You should know how to execute kitchen tasks with confidence, aplomb, and—I dare say—showmanship. The act should not only assuage your hunger and bring you respect but should give you satisfaction and pleasure.

This book will show you how. Step by step, I'm going to teach you everything you need to know about cooking: starting with the basics, like how to read a recipe, navigate the stove, and stock the fridge and pantry. I'm going to teach you how to prepare great meals for yourself, your buddies, your girlfriend or wife, your immediate or extended family, and how to throw a killer cocktail party.

I'm going to teach you how to stew, roast, braise, sauté, and flambé like a professional, and of course, how to fire up a grill and smoker. I'll show you the proper way to choose and wield a knife, heat a wok, handle a cocktail shaker, and how to maximize the use of your kitchen no matter its size.

A quick word about what you *won't* find in *Man Made Meals*. I'm *not* going to tell you how to cook a pot roast on your car engine or poach a whole salmon in your dishwasher. This book is about the cool, smart things guys can do to make really great-tasting food—without sensationalism or weirdness for the sake of shock value. Nor will you find in these pages doughnuts, sushi, or cupcakes. Sure, you can make doughnuts or sushi at home, but the pros do it better at bakeries and restaurants. As for cupcakes, they aren't really guy food.

Whether you're single or married, in college or retired, on a budget or on the board of directors, you have the right, need, and desire to eat well. This book will help you do it. Part cookbook, part textbook, part technical manual, and part guidebook to the world of male cooking, *Man Made Meals* is a gospel of great eats—filled with indispensable skills, cool tools, engaging stories, actionable information, and a terrific repertory of big-flavored, foolproof dishes. We're going to have fun. We're going to kick butt. And by the time we're done, you'll definitely know your way around the kitchen.

◄ This book is about the cool, smart things guys can do to make really great-tasting food.

THE MEN WHO COOK MANIFESTO

This book is based on ten simple principles.

1 | Knowledge is power. The best way to eat well is to cook well. And the more you know about ingredients and fundamental cooking techniques, the better you'll perform in the kitchen. Knowledge coupled with practice brings competence, and competence in the kitchen brings pleasure.

2 | You live in the best time in history to cook and eat well. Never have there been better ingredients from more geographically diverse sources at your metaphorical fingertips—within a short walk or drive to your local food market or with a tap of the screen. This book tells you what you need to know: where to order the best prosciutto (hint: not necessarily from Italy); what to look for when buying lobsters; and whether Kobe-style beef is really worth the price. And of course, such essential basics as how to fry an egg, build a quesadilla, grill a steak, and cook vegetables.

3 | You don't need to know how to cook everything. Mastery of a few dozen iconic dishes and principles will serve you better than a cursory knowledge of every recipe in a food magazine.

4 | You hunger for flavor. For most guys, bolder equals better. This book will tell you how to make food that explodes with flavor—whether you're preparing the Skillet Creole Shrimp on page 426 or the spice-crusted whole beef tenderloin on page 250. I'll show you how to make food with personality, soul, and even a touch of genius.

5 | How you cook matters as much as what you cook. Flames. Smoke. Sharp implements. Blowtorches. High-tech gear and power tools. And of course, alcohol. We guys love this stuff. This book will teach you how to cook with attitude, edge, and style.

6 | You want what you eat to be good for you *and* the planet. Sure, there's a time for nachos and fried turkeys (I cover both). But on a daily basis, most of us want what we eat to be healthy—and respectful of the environment. This book will help you to shop locally and green and to cook in a way that's friendly to your heart and waistline. Hey, if you think buffalo wings are great fried in vats of hot oil, wait until you taste them roasted or smoke-roasted (see page 207).

7 | You understand the importance of quality. Often the difference between a merely adequate dish and a masterpiece boils down to the raw materials. This book will tell you how to select the best salt, olive oil, heritage pork, and other ingredients to make your food explode with flavor. Or as a sage once observed: Better to eat a prime dry-aged steak once or twice a month than factory beef 24/7.

8 | You know the value of money. Cooking needn't cost a fortune to ring up pleasure. Indeed, some of the most popular guy dishes—wings,

▶ I promise you, we'll keep it simple.

brisket, short ribs—originated to make inexpensive cuts of meat palatable. I'll show you how to extract the richest flavors from the humblest cuts. However, there are times when it makes sense to spend more on ingredients or tools—when buying dry-cured ham or organic meats or a knife, for example—and I'll show you how to reap the best return on your investment.

9 | You appreciate speed and simplicity. Most guy food is simple. Steaks. Chops. Burgers. So, I promise you, we'll keep it simple. Even when a dish is unavoidably complicated or time-consuming (and some, like chili and pot roast, are), I'll show you how to prepare it without breaking a sweat—and of course using as few pots and pans as possible.

10 | You see the big picture. A successful meal involves a lot more than simply what you cook and put on the plate. The cocktails, wine, table setting, music, and the choreography of the evening go a long way toward making a meal unforgettable. And so does knowing how to stay organized—from shopping to clean-up.

GETTING STARTED—WHAT IS COOKING?

I have in my personal library about two thousand cookbooks—thirty of which I've written. Small potatoes next to the more than seven hundred cookbooks published each year. So you might think that cooking is *really* complicated.

It's not. All the world's cooking can be accomplished using five basic processes: gathering, cutting, mixing, seasoning, and transforming by heat, cold, or chemical reaction. Five—that's it. Master them and you'll rule the kitchen.

1 | Gathering Any meal starts with procuring the ingredients. In the old days, men hunted and fished while our spouses gathered the plant foods. For chefs today, gathering is as important as any cooking method or seasoning. I'm not suggesting you set off to pry barnacles off sea rocks, but I cannot emphasize enough that great cooking begins at the market. You know the old saying: You can't make a silk purse out of a sow's ear. Your food will be only as good as the ingredients you start with.

2 | Cutting Lest you ever doubt the machismo of cooking, consider the tools a chef holds most dear: his knives. Two million years ago or more—even before the discovery of fire—a distant human ancestor called *Homo habilis* ("handy man," literally) contrived to strike two flint stones together to give one of them a sharp edge for cutting. It turns out we taught ourselves butchering skills long before we mastered fire.

Most food in the wild comes in a form too large, tough, or otherwise incommodious to consume as is. Cutting enables us to remove the inedible parts and reduce food to a size we can fit in our mouths. Cutting embraces good knifesmanship (slicing, chopping, mincing, and so on), and it also includes peeling, grating, blending, and pureeing in a food processor.

3 | Mixing Once you gather and cut your food, you need to mix it with other ingredients to make it palatable and, even more important, interesting. To transform it by the power of your imagination. Eating a strawberry isn't imaginative. Dipping it in sour cream, then brown sugar transforms it into dessert.

Mixing includes stirring (which you do with a spoon), whisking (which you do with a whisk), folding (which you do with a spatula), beating (which you do in a mixer), and kneading (which you do to dough—in a food processor, mixer, or best of all, by hand).

4 | Seasoning What separates man from beast? There are art, religion, commerce, and opposable thumbs. But I'd argue that our most primal difference is cooking. All animals eat to live—but only man modifies his food to suit his aesthetics. A bear eats salmon raw. Man dips raw salmon in soy sauce spiced with wasabi. A lion devours red meat. Man chops it with anchovies and capers to make Steak Tartare (page 267). An ape eats a banana. Man may eat a banana, but it isn't cuisine until he sprinkles it with sugar, caramelizes it with a blowtorch, and flambés it with rum (see Deconstructed Bananas Foster on page 564).

So what constitutes a seasoning? Salt and pepper are seasonings. Olive oil and lemon juice are seasonings. Ditto for the Asian triad: ginger, garlic, and scallions. A rub is a seasoning composed of salt, herbs, and spices that you massage into raw meat before cooking, hence the term *rub*. A marinade is a wet seasoning, as are herb butters, glazes, and sauces. Seasonings enable you to give food ethnic identity. Season a neutral chicken breast with soy sauce, sesame oil, and mirin (sweet rice wine), for example, and you get Japanese teriyaki. Slather it with a ferocious paste of Scotch bonnet chiles, allspice, onions, garlic, and so on, and it becomes Jamaican jerk. Season it with turmeric, cumin, and coriander, and it transports you to Morocco.

Men and women often cook differently and a generous—even profligate—use of seasonings is one of the defining virtues of our gender.

5 | Transformation by heat, cold, or chemical reaction Notice I didn't say cooking. Cooking implies heat and heat is certainly one way—the most popular by far—to transform otherwise inedible or unpalatable ingredients into food. Grilling, roasting, braising, simmering, and frying are examples of how we cook with heat. Chilling can be equally transformative: Think of ice cream, for example, or the tongue-coating lusciousness vodka acquires when frozen in a block of ice (see page 597).

But many foods require neither heat nor cold to make them delicious. Think gravlax, which is Scandinavian-style salmon cured with salt, sugar, and dill under a weight. Or *crudo* (Italian "sashimi")—raw fish seasoned with lemon juice, herbs, and olive oil. In these dishes, as well as the Peruvian Ceviche (page 363), the salt or citrus juice causes a chemical reaction that "cooks" the fish in the sense of altering its texture and taste.

◄ All animals eat to live—but only man modifies his food to suit his aesthetics.

UNLEASHING YOUR INNER CHEF

Chefs cook differently than the rest of us. For starters, they cook for pay, which means they have to prepare a *lot* more food in a *lot* less time under a *lot* more pressure than we civilians do at home. They also have to cook night after night, balancing creativity with consistency.

This book aims to turn you into a proficient home cook, not a professional chef. But there's a lot we can learn from chefs. Not just recipes, but how to *think* like a chef.

1 LET THE MARKET DETERMINE YOUR MENU Every day, Grand Central Oyster Bar chef Sandy Ingber goes to New York's Fulton Fish Market at 3 a.m. He doesn't finish writing his menu until two hours before lunchtime. The next time you go food shopping, try doing it without a complete shopping list. Buy the seafood or produce or whatever else looks best and let your menu evolve from your purchases. Notice I said *complete* shopping list: Of course you'll want to bring a list of staples you may need—mayonnaise, eggs, flour, and the like—to keep your pantry stocked and ready for action.

2 SHOP LOCAL, COOK SEASONAL In this age of instant gratification and international air freight, we can now eat raspberries from South America in January and asparagus pretty much year round. In the process, we've lost a connection with our local food purveyors and the annual rhythm of eating seasonal foods at their peak. Shop at your local farmers' market, basing your meals on what's in season where *you* live. Celebrate truly seasonal foods, like soft shell crabs in June or Nantucket bay scallops in November. Eat something else when they're not in season.

3 THINK PROCESS, NOT RECIPE When a chef prepares a dish, he's thinking process, not recipe. He knows how to grill a steak or sauté a fish fillet because he's done it a thousand times. The rub, marinade, or sauce may vary daily, but the technique remains the same. As your culinary repertory grows, concentrate on techniques. The recipes will follow.

4 LEARN TO MULTITASK If you've ever stepped into a professional kitchen, you've witnessed organized chaos. A chef works on a dozen dishes at once—prepping some, cooking others, planning ahead for the next meal. Likewise, a chef never walks through the kitchen empty-handed. When he carries a dirty pot to the dishwasher, he returns with a fresh ingredient he'll need in the near future.

5 COOK WITH THE END IN MIND Even if you're cooking just for yourself and a friend, you may want to make a salad, main course, and starch or dessert. And you'll want these dishes to be ready more or less simultaneously when you sit down for dinner. So you may need to start with Belgian Beer Brownies (page 569) for dessert, which need an hour to cool, then make your Quinoa Pilaf (page 489), which takes thirty minutes to cook. You might not sauté the Tapas Bar Shrimp main course (page 422) until everyone is seated for dinner.

6 START WITH YOUR *MISE EN PLACE* *Mise en place* (pronounced *meez en plahs*) is French for setup, and it makes all the difference between you controlling the cooking process and it controlling you. Basically, this means assembling and prepping all your ingredients *before* you start cooking (chopping the onions, measuring the wine, and so on). This may seem like an extra and unnecessary step, but it actually helps you cook faster.

7 CLEAN UP AS YOU GO ALONG It's easier to cook in a neat kitchen and a lot faster to clean up afterward.

8 DON'T BE AFRAID OF HIGH HEAT Professional stoves burn hotter than home models, and chefs tend to work over a higher heat than most guys do at home. Not only does this speed up the cooking process—essential when you're in a hurry—but the high heat caramelizes animal proteins and plant sugars, intensifying the flavor.

9 PUMP UP THE FLAVOR Chefs have a heavy hand with salt, pepper, and butter. They believe the food should be fully and properly seasoned *before* it reaches the table. Season your food like you mean it. But note: As a corollary to this principle, it's also a good idea to season food incrementally; that is, add salt and pepper gradually at several stages along the cooking process. This makes you less likely to overseason at the end.

10 BROWN IS BEAUTIFUL For most foods, maximum flavor lies at the razor's edge between cooked and burnt. When a recipe instructs you to brown an ingredient (beef, chicken, fish fillets), use high heat to achieve a dark brown color just shy of burnt. Food that looks anemic will taste anemic, too.

11 START WITH A HOT PAN AND DON'T CROWD IT The best way to brown your ingredients properly is to start with a hot pan. That means heating the empty pan over high heat then swirling in the butter, oil, or bacon fat. Similarly, when browning multiple pieces of food, leave at least one inch of space between the pieces. Work in multiple batches as necessary, reheating the pan between each: When you crowd the pan, food stews rather than browns.

12 TASTE, TASTE, TASTE The only way to make great-tasting food is to taste it often. Keep a mug of tasting spoons next to the stove for this purpose. Or taste from a finger dipped in the pot—but only when no one can see you.

THE MAJOR COOKING METHODS

F irst, the bad news. There are close to thirty different methods of cooking (including all the grilling methods), and no man can consider himself kitchen literate without at least a rudimentary knowledge of all of them.

Now the good news. There are close to thirty different methods of cooking, and you probably have experience with many of them already. You certainly know how to boil water to cook spaghetti. I bet you know how to simmer a stew, fry a sunny-side-up egg, bake a potato, and panfry a pork chop. You likely know how to roast, braise, and broil, and I imagine you know your way around a grill. (I hope so.)

The easiest way to keep all these methods straight is to think about where you do them: in a dish, on the stove, in the oven, outdoors, or in a specialized piece of equipment.

IN A DISH OR JAR

We start with the no-cook methods, so called because they require no heat. Pickling, curing, and marinating so completely transform the texture and taste of foods that they are in effect "cooked" even without fire or heat.

Pickling | Uses salt and beneficent bacteria to initiate a fermentation process that turns cucumbers into pickles, soybeans, and other grains into miso, and ground pork and spices into dry-cured sausages.

Marinating | What do ceviche (page 363) and *lomi-lomi* (page 365) have in common? Both are raw animal proteins that are "cooked" by the addition of lime juice, vinegar, or a strongly acidic marinade. Note: Don't confuse *cooking* marinades with *flavoring* marinades—the latter a wet mix of flavorings used to season raw food

before conventional cooking on the grill, stove, or in the oven.

Curing | Curing uses salt, sugar, and sometimes pressure to turn raw salmon fillets into Jewish-style lox or Scandinavian gravlax.

ON THE STOVE

Generally done in a pot or skillet, stovetop cooking methods include boiling, steaming, simmering, panfrying, stewing, sautéing, stir-frying, deep-frying, griddling, and flame-charring. In some parts of the world (especially Africa and Asia), people don't have ovens, so most of the cooking is done on the stove or on a burner.

Boiling | Cooking in lots of rapidly boiling water over high heat. Boiling is how you cook pasta, beans, grains, and many vegetables.

Steaming | Similar to boiling, only you use less water and do the cooking in the hot steam that rises from the boiling water. Two foods we commonly steam are lobster and broccoli.

Simmering | Cooking soups, chili, and other wet dishes over low heat so that bubbles just barely break the surface. Boiling toughens meat (then softens it), while simmering keeps it tender from the start.

Stewing | Resembles simmering in that the dish is cooked over low heat but is generally used for stewing chunks of meat, poultry, or seafood.

Panfrying | Cooking thin, flat, tender foods in a little fat in a skillet or frying pan. The operative words when panfrying are *thin* and *quick cooking*—as in eggs, fish fillets, cutlets, thin-cut pork chops, and grilled cheese—and *little*—as in a tablespoon or two of melted butter or olive oil.

▶ The operative words when panfrying are *thin* and *quick cooking*.

Sautéing | Another variation on panfrying, but generally done with small pieces of food, like sliced mushrooms or diced chicken. If you've ever watched a chef flick a skillet with his wrist, sending the ingredients skyward (ideally to have them return to the pan), you've witnessed sautéing.

Stir-frying | This Asian version of sautéing or panfrying is done in a wide bowl-shaped steel pan called a wok. The ingredients are cut into small pieces and cooked over high heat in a precise sequence: aromatics first, then protein, then vegetables, and finally, the sauce and thickeners. One of the virtues of stir-frying is its speed: The whole cooking process takes five to ten minutes. (For detailed instructions on stir-frying, see page 439.)

Deep-frying | Resembles boiling, except that instead of water, you cook the foods in hot vegetable oil (or lard) at least several inches deep. Deep-frying locks in moisture and gives food a crisp crust. (Think fried chicken and french fries.) The secret to deep-frying is to use plenty of oil and work over heat high enough to maintain a consistent temperature of 350° to 400°F.

Griddling | The Spanish call it a *plancha*. Argentineans call it a *champa*. The short-order cook at your local diner calls it a griddle and uses it to fry eggs, bacon, and hash browns. Similar to panfrying, griddling involves cooking foods on a heated flat metal surface with just a little oil or butter. You get a slightly more roasted flavor than with panfrying, which makes griddling (cooking *a la plancha*) great for seafood.

Flame-charring | The most dramatic stovetop cooking method, used primarily for eggplants and poblano or bell peppers. You place these directly on a gas or electric burner (no pan needed) and roast them until charred and black all over. This burns the skin, which you don't want to eat anyway (scrape it off with a paring knife), imparting an extraordinary smoke flavor. One of my favorite flame-charred dishes is *Rajas* (roasted poblanos; see page 200).

IN THE OVEN

The oven is the box beneath your stove, and you use it not just for storing unwanted cookware but for roasting, baking, braising, broiling, and drying. Most stovetop cooking requires constant attention (especially panfrying and stir-frying). With the exception of broiling, oven-cooking methods require only minimal supervision.

Roasting | A dry-heat method for cooking prime rib, pork shoulder, roast chicken, and other large hunks of meats. (Also great for root vegetables.) Generally done in an open pan at a medium to medium-high temperature (350° to 450°F) for a cooking time measured in hours. Done properly, roasting gives you a crusty brown exterior and moist tender meat in the center.

Baking | Similar to roasting, but used for breads and baked goods. You "roast" meat but "bake" corn bread (page 514) or biscuits (page 517).

Braising | One of my all-time favorite cooking methods because it combines the flavor-intensifying properties of roasting with the humidifying effects of stewing. Simply defined, braising involves cooking meat (or seafood or vegetables) with liquid and flavorings in a covered pot. The tight-fitting lid helps lock in and concentrate the flavor, while the liquid keeps the food from drying out or burning. Braising is generally done at a low heat (250° to 300°F) for intervals that can last three to five hours. As long as you use enough liquid (check it from time to time), it's virtually impossible to burn braised food. And although the outcome is similar to stewing, braising is easier and gives you richer flavors. Think of it as the original "set it and forget it" cooking method.

(*continued on page 14*)

◄ You use the oven not just for storing unwanted cookware.

GRILLING AND SMOKING

Repeat after me: Grilling is not gender specific. But chances are, if there's live-fire cooking to be done outdoors and your hostess hasn't expressly laid claim to the grill, the tongs will devolve to you. Grilling taps into the primeval male urge to make and manage fire, and it generally involves two other beloved guy entities: sharp knives and alcohol.

That means you need to be comfortable lighting and operating a grill (and maybe even a smoker), and you'll need at least a passing familiarity with the five techniques of live-fire cooking, namely:

- Direct grilling
- Indirect grilling
- Smoking
- Spit-roasting
- "Caveman" grilling, aka cooking in the embers

Don't worry: I've had decades of experience teaching guys these techniques. This stuff isn't complicated, but you do need to master some basic techniques.

FIRST, THE GRILLS

Grills come in three basic models: gas-fired, charcoal-burning, and wood-burning.

CHARCOAL GRILLS | If I had to pick only one grill for you to buy, it would be a 22½-inch *charcoal kettle grill*, first, because charcoal gives you the primal thrill of playing around with fire, and, second, because it's well-suited to all five methods of live-fire cooking. (A gas grill is not.) Limited in outdoor space? Consider a smaller, widely available, and eminently affordable charcoal grill popular in Asia: a *hibachi*.

GAS GRILLS | These have the advantage of push-button ignition and turn-of-a-knob heat control, which explains why nearly 70 percent of American households have one. You want a model with at least two burners (so you can indirect grill); ideally three, four, or even six burners. Gas grills are good for direct and indirect grilling, and spit-roasting. Not so good for smoking or caveman grilling.

WOOD-BURNING GRILLS | (which burn logs), **SMOKERS** (which cook "low and slow"—at a low heat for a long time using wood smoke for flavor and heat transfer), and **KAMADO COOKERS** (egg-shaped, thick-walled ceramic grills epitomized by the Big Green Egg), and others are beyond the scope of this book, but are definitely worth investigating. To learn more about them, check out some of my more specialized books, such as *How to Grill*, *The Barbecue! Bible*, or *Planet Barbecue!*

NEXT, THE ACCESSORIES

There are six I consider essential:

- Chimney starter (for lighting a charcoal grill)
- Stiff wire grill brush (for cleaning the grill grate)
- Long-handled spring-loaded tongs (for turning the food and oiling the grate)
- Pair of heavy suede grill gloves (for handling the chimney and other hot items)
- Instant-read thermometer for checking doneness
- Fire extinguisher (not that *you'll* ever need it, but better safe than sorry)

LIGHTING THE GRILL

TO LIGHT A CHARCOAL GRILL | Invest in a chimney starter (an upright metal cylinder or box with a horizontal partition in the middle and a heatproof handle). Place a crumpled sheet of newspaper or a paraffin firestarter at the bottom and fill to the top with charcoal. Place the chimney on the bottom grate of your grill and light the paper: The chimney's upright design guarantees even ignition in 15 to 20 minutes—which is about the same amount of time it takes to preheat a gas grill. Empty the charcoal into the grill. Note: I personally prefer cleaner-burning natural lump charcoal (jagged chunks of carbonized wood) to briquettes (which contain coal dust, borax, and petroleum binders). But the latter have their partisans, as briquettes burn longer and more evenly than lump charcoal.

TO LIGHT A GAS GRILL | Open the grill lid (this is *very* important, otherwise you may get a potentially explosive buildup of propane). Make sure your propane cylinder is full (or sufficiently full—at least a quarter cylinder) and open the valve. Turn on the burner (some manufacturers specify which burner to use for start-up) by rotating the knob, then press the igniter button. You'll hear a clicking noise. A whoosh or flame will indicate ignition, but hold your hand about 3 inches above the burner for 30 seconds to make sure it's really on. One by one, turn on the remaining burners. If ignition fails the first time, shut off all the burners, air the grill out for at least 5 minutes, then relight. Note: Always keep an extra full cylinder on hand. There's nothing worse than running out of propane halfway through cooking dinner.

PREPPING THE GRILL

No, that salmon skin burned onto the grate from last week's grill session does not add flavor, at least not in a good way. (A general rule at the grill and in the kitchen: If your spouse says something is disgusting, it probably is.) To grill well, you need to start with a clean hot grate and keep it properly lubricated (oiled) to prevent sticking. Follow these four simple steps and you'll grill like a pro every time.

(continued on the next page)

(continued from the previous page)

1 KEEP IT HOT Preheat your grill to high—what I call a "2- to 3-Mississippi fire." Hold your hand 3 inches above the grate and start counting. If the heat forces you to move your hand after 2 to 3 seconds, you've got a hot fire.

2 KEEP IT CLEAN Brush the bars of the grate clean with a stiff wire brush. Put some muscle behind it. It's much easier to clean the grate when it's hot than when it's cold.

3 KEEP IT LUBRICATED Oil the grate with a paper towel folded into a tight pad, dipped into a small bowl of vegetable oil, and drawn across the bars of the grate at the end of tongs. This prevents sticking and helps give you well-defined grill marks. It also cleans any debris from the grate before you put the food on.

4 DON'T FORGET TO BRUSH, CLEAN, AND OIL THE GRILL GRATE *after* you're done grilling, while the grill is still hot.

THE FIVE METHODS OF LIVE-FIRE COOKING

Master these and you'll rule the grill.

DIRECT GRILLING | Cooking food directly over the fire. Used for small, tender, quick-cooking foods like steaks, burgers, chicken breasts, shish kebabs, fish fillets, vegetables, and more. Direct grilling is generally done over high heat (450° to 600°F) and the cooking time is measured in minutes.

INDIRECT GRILLING | Cooking the food next to, not directly over, the fire at a moderate heat (325° to 400°F) with the grill lid closed. Used for larger cuts of meat, like prime rib, whole chickens and turkeys, whole fish, and/or fatty foods, like baby back pork ribs. To indirect grill on a charcoal grill, rake the coals into mounds at opposite sides of the grill; on a gas grill, light one burner on a two-burner grill; the outside burners or front and rear burners on a grill with 3 or more burners, and cook the food over the unlit part of the grill. Note: *Smoke-roasting* involves indirect grilling with soaked hardwood chips tossed onto the coals or added to your grill's smoker box to generate wood smoke.

SMOKING | Similar to indirect grilling in that the food is cooked next to, not directly over, the fire with the grill or smoker lid closed. But smoking is generally done at a lower temperature (225° to 250°F) for a longer period (4 to 16 hours depending on the cut of meat), and it always involves hardwood chips, chunks, or logs to create a smoke flavor. Foods that are typically smoked include beef brisket, pork shoulder, spareribs, baby backs, and more.

SPIT-ROASTING | Cooking foods on a rotisserie next to (not directly over) the heat source. Spit-roasting is well-suited to cylindrical or fatty foods, like whole chickens, duck, beef rib roasts, and pork roasts.

CAVEMAN-STYLE GRILLING | The most primal (and eye-popping) method of cooking. Roasting steaks, tubers, peppers, onions, eggplants, and other vegetables directly on the hot embers of a charcoal or wood fire.

SOME OTHER USEFUL GRILLING TECHNIQUES

BUILDING A "THREE-ZONE" FIRE | This configures your fire in such a way that you have a hot zone for searing, a medium zone for cooking, and a cool or safety zone where you can move the food to dodge flare-ups or keep it warm without further cooking. On a charcoal grill, mound the coals in a double layer in the back third of your grill to create a hot zone. Mound coals in a single layer in the center of the grill to create a moderate or medium zone. Keep the front third of your grill coal-free to create a cool or safety zone. On a gas grill, set one burner on high, one on medium, and leave one off. (On a two-burner gas grill, the warming rack serves as your safety zone.)

TO SMOKE ON A CHARCOAL GRILL | Soak 1 to 2 cups of hardwood chips in water for 30 minutes, then drain well, and toss on the coals. Soaking makes the chips smolder, not catch fire, generating clouds of flavorful wood smoke.

TO SMOKE ON A GAS GRILL | In a word, don't. Gas grills do a notoriously poor job of smoking—even if they have dedicated smoker boxes. (The smoke escapes out the wide vents in the back of the grill before it has a chance to flavor the meat.) If you're a diehard gas griller and you *really* want food with a smoke flavor, invest in an inexpensive charcoal grill.

TO COOK A WHOLE MEAL ON THE GRILL

▶ First, direct grill a platter of vegetables (brush with olive oil and season with salt and pepper) several hours or even a day before the meal. Grilled vegetables taste great at room temperature, especially when dressed with a simple vinaigrette.

▶ Next, indirect grill or smoke a large hunk of animal protein, like a beef tenderloin (page 250), turkey, or a pork shoulder (page 275). You can do this several hours ahead (the meat needs to rest before serving), then carve it as everyone watches.

▶ Once the party starts, direct grill the appetizer, like the garlic bread or bruschetta on pages 513 and 511. Serve the bread slices hot off the grill to the crowd that invariably gathers.

▶ After dinner, build up your fire and direct grill dessert. S'mores come to mind (roast the marshmallows over the coals). So do peach halves brushed with melted butter and crusted with cinnamon sugar. Again, urge everyone to gather around the grill to participate.

(*continued from page 9*)

Broiling | Most ovens are equipped with an electric or gas heating element at the top that functions like an inverted grill. Place steaks, chops, fish fillets, or other quick-cooking foods a couple of inches under the broiler and cook them as you would on a grill. Broilers don't get as hot as most grills, but you don't lose any juices to the fire.

Drying | You can also use your oven for drying foods, like sliced fruit, beef for jerky, or tomatoes. Set the temperature as low as it will go (150° to 180°F) and prop the oven door slightly open with the handle of a wooden spoon so excess moisture can escape. Drying generally takes four to six hours or as long as overnight.

OUTDOORS

This brings us to the part of home where I like to cook best. Direct grilling, indirect grilling, caveman grilling, spit-roasting, and smoking are all done outdoors. For specifics, see the box on page 10.

ALTERNATE COOKING METHODS

These modern cooking methods range from low-tech (contact grills à la George Foreman) to high-tech (sous vide).

Contact grill | Looks like an oversize waffle iron with two ridged, nonstick, electrically heated plates connected by a hinge at the back. The ridges give you "grill" marks, while the dual heat sources (from top and bottom) keep cooking times brief. A contact grill is great for making panini and grilled sandwiches. Few models get hot enough to properly sear burgers or steaks. The George Foreman may be the best-known contact grill, but Breville and VillaWare get higher marks for grill marks.

Microwave | Cooks food from the inside out by bombarding it with electromagnetic waves. A microwave is useful for popping popcorn, "baking" potatoes, "frying" bacon, reheating soups and leftovers, defrosting frozen foods, and even scrambling eggs in a microwave-safe cup or bowl. It's not particularly good for roasting meat. For the record, I've never owned a microwave.

Slow cooker | Another one of those "set it and forget it" cooking methods, you cook in a heavy ceramic or metal vessel equipped with a heating element (like a Crock-Pot). This allows you to braise without an oven. Some apartment-bound barbecue buffs swear by it for making pulled pork.

Sous vide | Cooking food in a vacuum-sealed plastic pouch at extremely low temperatures (145°F for short ribs) for a period that can last several days. Popular with the molecular and Modernist cuisine crowd, sous vide allows you to cook food to precise internal temperatures while retaining most of the food's natural juices. I'm a live-fire roasting and grilling sort of guy, so I'm not a huge partisan, but I have had some amazing sous-vide ribs, and a growing number of chefs and home cooks swear by it.

▶ For the record, I've never owned a microwave.

WHAT YOU NEED TO OUTFIT YOUR KITCHEN: THE ESSENTIAL TOOLS

A kitchen full of costly cookware won't necessarily make you a great cook, but the right tools make any task easier and more pleasurable. Sure, as you become more accomplished in the kitchen, you'll want to add more equipment, but if you're just getting started, happily you don't need to purchase the entire inventory of Williams-Sonoma. At a minimum, here's what you *do* need.

Measuring cups and spoons | Cooking is part art and part chemistry. For the latter you need  a set of nesting measuring cups for dry ingredients and a standard 2-cup measuring cup for liquid ingredients. For small amounts, you'll need a set of nesting measuring spoons. Buy sturdy metal ones; they're less likely to break or to warp in the dishwasher.

A *santoku* knife | Knives come in an awe-inspiring array of sizes and shapes, with a variety of functions (you can read all about knives on page 19). If you buy only one knife, make it an 8-inch *santoku*, a Japanese-style knife that looks like a slender cleaver tapering to a point at the end. This knife is long enough for chopping, agile enough for trimming, and has a wide blade that's useful for crushing garlic and transferring chopped onions and other ingredients from the cutting board to a bowl or pan. You can buy a good one without spending a fortune.

Speaking of knives, you'll also need a cutting board—I personally prefer a wooden one about 15 by 20 inches. Why wooden? For me it feels better to chop on.

A vegetable peeler | I like the control afforded by a vegetable peeler with a fixed blade to peelers with swivel blades. Either way, nothing beats a vegetable peeler for cutting paper-thin strips of lemon and orange zest for martinis, Manhattans, and old-fashioneds—not to mention the more mundane tasks of peeling potatoes, carrots, cucumbers, and such.

A grater | Essential for reducing cheese to shreds and aromatic roots (for example, ginger and horseradish) to flavorful dust. Use a box grater for cheese and a **Microplane** (it looks like a woodworker's rasp or a turbocharged nail file) for citrus zest and whole nutmeg.

Mixing bowls | You'll want one or two sturdy stainless steel bowls that are about 12 inches  across to use for mixing and marinating and one or two 10-inch glass bowls you can use for both mixing and serving (salads, for example, or popcorn). It's also worth investing in a few small (5-inch) bowls for holding prepped ingredients.

 **A food processor** | Do you absolutely need one? No. But grating, chopping, slicing, pureeing, and even kneading dough take a heck of a lot longer without one. I guess you do need one.

◄ If you buy only one knife, make it an 8-inch *santoku*.

On the Shelves

(see page 18 for an identification key)

On the Shelves Key

1	3-quart saucepan	13	Box grater	24	10- and 12-inch cast-iron skillets
2	10-inch frying pans	14	2-cup measuring cup	25	Meat thermometer
3	Dutch oven	15	Baking sheet	26	2-quart saucepan
4	Cutting board	16	Coffee mugs	27	Kitchen blowtorch
5	Potato masher	17	French press coffee maker	28	Cast-iron loaf pan and platter
6	Whisk	18	Blender	29	Dry measuring cups
7	Wooden spoon and fork	19	Dutch oven	30	Food processor
8	Colander	20	Wire cooling racks	31	Salt mill and pepper mill
9	Spatter shield	21	Ladles, spatula, strainer, measuring spoons	32	Stockpot
10	Spoons and forks (for tasting)	22	Bar glasses, shaker	33	Roasting pan with rack
11	Dish towels	23	Strainer, tongs, jigger	34	Immersion blender
12	Mixing bowls				

▶ You can buy a good knife without spending a fortune.

Hand tools | You need five.

▶ **A whisk** for blending batters, sauces, and salad dressings—look for a 10- to 12-inch whisk.

▶ **A wooden spoon** with a handle that's 12 to 16 inches long; use for stirring soups and stews.

▶ **Kitchen tongs** that are 10 to 12 inches long; handy for turning steaks, chops, and pasta, among many other foods.

▶ **A silicon or rubber spatula** for scraping batters and other wet mixtures out of bowls and jars.

▶ **A metal or plastic spatula** (with a wide flat head) for turning over foods like fried eggs and quesadillas. Note: With nonstick skillets use plastic spatulas so you don't scratch the coating.

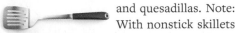

A skillet | The pan you will use the most. I'm partial to my 10-inch Lodge cast-iron skillet,  but a lot of guys swear by a 10-inch nonstick skillet, especially for cooking foods like omelets and frittatas that are prone to sticking. If you opt for nonstick, choose a skillet with an oven-safe handle. Eventually, you'll want both. Note: If you cook for lots of people, bump the skillet size up to 12 inches. As you round out your gear, pick up a small (6- to 8-inch) skillet or two for fried eggs and omelets (although they certainly can be made in a 10-inch skillet).

Saucepans | You'll want a basic 3-quart saucepan (one that is 10 inches across)—maybe  even two—for making soups and steaming vegetables. Choose the thickest-walled copper, stainless steel, or anodized aluminum pot you can find (thick walls spread the heat evenly). As your kitchen battery grows, add a 2-quart saucepan or two for simmering sauces.

A stockpot | And as you climb the ladder of culinary enlightenment, you'll want to invest in  a really big pot, also known as a stockpot. Look for one that is at least 8 inches tall and 10 inches across—preferably larger. It should be able to hold 6 to 8 quarts. Use for boiling pasta, brining chicken, making stovetop shrimp boils, and of course, making stock. Look for the thickest gauge stainless steel you can find.

A Dutch oven | A large wide heavy pot used for stews and braises. Choose one with at least a 7-quart capacity. It should be 6 to 8 inches deep and 12 to 14 inches across if round, 16 inches long if oval.

A colander | Useful for draining noodles and vegetables and rinsing lettuce. Buy one large enough to accommodate one pound of cooked pasta; it should be 10 to 12 inches across. A **strainer** has a fine mesh and handle and is useful for making sauces and cocktails. If you eat a lot of salad (and you should), invest in a **salad spinner**, which you could think of as a strainer on a centrifuge.

A baking sheet | Not just for baking, but also for setting up your *mise en place* (see page 7), moving  ingredients, transferring cooked steaks, chops, and the like. Buy nonstick baking sheets with raised sides—you'll want two or three. I buy mine at a restaurant supply house (better quality and price).

A roasting pan | If you're like most guys, you're going to cook a lot of large hunks of meat. The  best way to do this is in a deep rectangular pan, ideally 12 by 16 inches and 4 inches deep. It should be thick-walled (aluminum gives you the best bang for the buck) and nonstick, which facilitates easy clean-up. If it comes with a wire roasting rack, so much the better. While you're at it, invest in a **baking dish**, a smaller glass or ceramic version of a roasting pan, which you'll need for baking things like mac and cheese (page 460) and brownies (page 569). A good size is 9 by 13 inches.

An instant-read thermometer | The only truly accurate way to tell when a roast is done  is to use an instant-read thermometer.

WHAT YOU NEED TO KNOW ABOUT KNIVES

The first knife I ever bought was a Sabatier filleting knife from the E. Dehillerin cookware shop in Paris. (Think world's coolest hardware store, only for chefs.) The carbon steel, which discolored after the first use, made it the ugliest blade in my knife block. But I've never since owned a knife that was easier to sharpen, more dexterous to use, or felt better in my hand. Lessons learned?

▸ Buy a knife for its functionality, not just beauty.

▸ Make sure it feels comfortable in *your* hand.

In the Equipment Drawer
(see facing page for an identification key)

1   2   3   4   5   6   7   8   9   10   11

12   13   14   15   16   17

18   19

20   21   22   23   24   25   26   27   28   29   30   31   32   33

Knives come in an almost limitless selection of shapes, sizes, and metals. Your local cookware merchant wants you to buy all of them, so you may be surprised to learn that you really need only two knives to do 90 percent of your cutting, with two or three more knives for specialized tasks.

A paring knife | A stiff-bladed knife with a short (3- to 4-inch) stubby blade used for carving vegetables and trimming and boning meats. Depending on what you're cutting, you use the front half of the blade for slicing and the back half for paring (trimming).

A chef's knife | This is what most people mean when they think of a kitchen knife: a wide (1½ to 2½ inches at the widest point of the blade), medium long (8- to 12-inch), stiff-bladed knife primarily used for chopping. Chef's knives are thicker and heavier than most knives; their heft helps push through the ingredients you're chopping. The part of the knife you use most is the back half of the blade.

If you can buy only one knife Make it a *santoku*, a Japanese knife with the pointed end of  a paring knife and the flat blade of a chef's knife. (See page 15.)

SPECIALIZED KNIVES

A bread knife or serrated knife has a long, slender, nontapered blade with deeply  scalloped serrations that cut cleanly through crusts, bread, and ripe tomatoes without tearing them.

A slicing knife has a long (12- to 14-inch), razor-sharp, slender blade designed for carving smoked salmon, ham, leg of lamb, prime rib, and other large roasts.

While you're at it, pick up a **carving fork**—armed with two long tines and a sturdy handle. Use it to steady turkey, prime rib, and other roasts as you carve, and for maneuvering individual slices of meat onto waiting plates.

◀ You really only need two knives to do **90 percent** of your cutting.

Key to the Equipment Drawer

1 Ladle
2 Metal spatula
3 Slotted and kitchen spoons
4 Meat fork
5 Rubber spatula
6 Basting brush
7 Nesting measuring spoons
8 Potato masher
9 Whisk
10 Wooden spoon

11 Wooden spatula
12 Strainer
13 Can opener
14 Vegetable peeler
15 Cocktail jigger
16 Hawthorn cocktail strainer
17 Ice tongs
18 Nesting measuring cups
19 Meat thermometer
20 Cleaver
21 Carving knife
22 Serrated bread knife

23 Chef's knife
24 *Santoku* knife
25 Fillet knife
26 Paring knife
27 Oyster knife
28 Carving fork
29 Sharpening steel
30 Microplane grater
31 Kitchen tongs
32 Instant-read thermometer
33 Kitchen shears

REALLY COOL TOOLS

Forget about that Japanese drop-forged *santoku* knife or gleaming copper saucepan from Paris. Enter the realm of extreme cuisine, where cookware meets power tools. Here are five cool tools to help take your cooking over the top.

BLOWTORCH | When it comes to impressing your pals (why else stage a dinner party?), few tools beat a blowtorch. Sprinkle bananas with sugar and melt it to a shatteringly crisp candy crust (see page 564). Blast raw salmon with fire to give sashimi the smoky overtones of bacon. One good blowtorch brand sold at hardware stores everywhere is BernzOmatic. Note: You want the blue cylinder, which contains propane, not the yellow one (which contains toxic methyl acetylene-propadiene gas).

IMMERSION BLENDER | Chef slang for this tool says it all: weed-whacker. Imagine a blender turned inside out—that is, a shaft with a fast spinning propeller at the end. Plunge it into boiled vegetables and broth to make creamy soups and purees. Zap pan juices and butter to make those foams that top avant-garde food everywhere. More powerful than a blender and easier to clean. One good brand is KitchenAid.

SMOKE GUN | It looks like a pistol-shaped hair dryer. If you love smoked foods but don't have access to a smoker, it's the answer to your prayers. Chefs use it for smoking everything from soups to strawberries and even bartenders get in the act, smoking Bloody Marys (page 569) and Manhattans. Load it with the hardwood sawdust of your choice, plug it in, and shoot smoke at whatever needs flavorizing. To smoke cocktails, soups (see the gazpacho on page 125), and other liquids, attach the rubber hose to the smoker and place the other end in the liquid. Two good manufacturers are Aladin and PolyScience.

SOUS-VIDE IMMERSION CIRCULATOR | Call it the greatest culinary technological leap forward since the microwave. Or call it an exorbitantly priced Crock-Pot. Sous vide is the process of cooking foods in vacuum-sealed pouches at controlled low temperatures for durations often measured in days. Its partisans maintain that it makes the moistest ribs, the most succulent steaks, the most perfectly cooked chicken. Detractors say it turns meats into hospital food. Love it or hate it (I remain skeptical), immersion circulators are found in the kitchens of some of the world's most serious chefs. PolyScience manufactures a home version that costs less than $1,000.

WHIPPING SIPHON | No, it's not just a nitrous oxide delivery device (although we've all tried *that* at some point). While it turns out awesome whipped cream (no elbow grease required), futuristic-minded chefs use it to make everything from turbocharged soups to soufflé-like scrambled eggs. One good brand is ISI.

A fillet knife looks like a miniature slicer with a thin blade flexible enough to follow the  contours of a fish skeleton. But don't stop there. The narrow width of the blade of a fillet knife makes it ideal for cutting through onions and other root vegetables.

A cleaver is a large, flat, and homicidal-looking cutting tool designed for cleaving through bones,  joints, and gristle. It is also useful for smashing garlic. Cleavers are available in two styles: the thick heavy cleavers favored by Western butchers and the thin rectangular cleavers of Asia.

An oyster knife is a short stubby knife with a thick stiff blade (and often a metal guard that 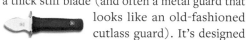 looks like an old-fashioned cutlass guard). It's designed specifically for shucking oysters and should not be confused with a clam knife, which looks like a sturdy butter knife.

WHAT TO LOOK FOR WHEN BUYING A KNIFE

Knives come in a variety of materials, each with advantages and drawbacks. The two easiest to recommend are carbon steel and stainless steel. Carbon steel is soft and easy to sharpen, but the blade discolors easily. Stainless steel keeps its shine forever, but is harder to sharpen and keep sharp.

Forged blades are made with heated hammered steel that is tempered by being plunged in cold water. (A good knife maker does this multiple times.) This gives the blade strength and flexibility, but of course, it adds to the price.

Stamped blades are cut from a sheet of metal like cookies from dough. This produces a thinner, lighter, less expensive blade, but stamped knives don't hold a sharp edge as long as forged blades.

When buying a knife, in addition to the blade, examine the bolster, tang, and grip. The bolster is the flared metal collar that separates the blade from the grip. It protects your hand from the rear edge of the blade and should fit comfortably into the crux of your thumb and forefinger.

The tang is the part of the blade that extends into the grip. In good knives, it runs the full length and width of the grip for greater strength. (If you examine the butt of the knife handle, you should see the metal tang sandwiched between the two halves of the grip.) Cheap knives have a thin rod-like tang that can bend or wiggle loose with heavy use. You want a full tang for a chef's knife; a rod-shaped tang is OK for a paring knife.

The knife grip (the handle) can be made of wood or high-impact plastic. Make sure the grip is firmly attached, often with rivets. The best grip for you is highly personal: It should feel comfortable in your hand.

HOW TO TEST DRIVE A KNIVE

1 | Hold the knife in your hand: Does it feel solid and well-balanced? Rock the blade on a cutting board, moving the handle up and down, as you would when chopping. Does the blade move easily?

2 | Test the knife. Some kitchenware shops keep produce on hand for just that purpose. So, if possible, use the knife to slice a tomato. A sharp well-proportioned blade will glide through the skin. A poorly designed knife will slide off to one side or simply crease the skin. Next, try slicing a carrot. A good knife will produce thin, even vertical slices. A poorly ground or off-balance blade will veer off to one side.

3 | Finally, check out the craftsmanship: Does the knife look well made?

HOW TO STORE AND SHARPEN A KNIFE

The best knife in the world won't cut forever if you don't store and maintain it properly. Store your knives in wooden knife blocks or on magnetized holders that keep the blades separate. The

◄ Store your knives in wooden knife blocks or on magnetized holders that keep the blades separate.

worst place to store knives is piled in a kitchen drawer where the blades can hit one another and nick the blades. (Sound familiar?) If you must store your knives in a drawer, protect them with plastic sheaths, which are available at kitchenware stores.

To sharpen a knife effectively you need to understand the structure of the edge. It actually has two parts. First there is the bevel, produced by grinding away a narrow strip of metal on either side of the blade. Atop this bevel sits a thin ridge of microscopic metal flakes, which act like saw teeth. This is the part that does the actual cutting. With prolonged use these flakes become bent or misaligned, or they wear off.

A sharpening steel is a metal rod with finely etched parallel ridges or a roughened surface. You use it for realigning, i.e., "truing," a knife's edge. (The actual sharpening is done on a whetstone.) When you draw a knife's edge down the length of a honing steel you're not actually sharpening the edge, you're straightening the metal teeth. Hold the knife at about a 15-degree angle to the steel. Draw the blade along the steel toward or away from you in a smooth clean stroke. Move the knife to the other side and repeat the motion. Three or four strokes per side will do it. Repeat this each time you use the knife. Do not do this over the food or cutting board.

Eventually, the tiny metal teeth wear away and the knife will remain dull no matter how much you use the steel. When this happens, you need to sharpen (regrind) the bevel edge. Use a whetstone or an electric knife sharpener. Better yet, do as chefs do: Once or twice a year, have your knives professionally sharpened. Many cookware shops do this on their premises or can recommend a competent professional.

SOME FINAL KNIFE WISDOM

1 | Chefs say that you're more likely to cut yourself with a dull knife than a sharp one. The reason? You need to exert more pressure to cut with a dull knife. But you can do plenty of damage with a sharp knife, too. Always be conscious of where your hand is in relation to the knife blade.

2 | It's also said that if you use another person's chef's knife, it will cut you. There's a kernel of truth here, too, as each knife has a different balance and center of gravity that it takes time to get used to.

3 | For ease in slicing, pull the blade toward you in one continuous stroke as you cut. This allows the tiny metal flakes on the edge of the knife to cut through the meat or vegetables. A lot of guys saw back and forth when they cut, but a single motion will achieve the same effect with a lot less work.

4 | When chopping round vegetables, like potatoes or carrots, cut a thin slice off the bottom or side before you start. This steadies the vegetable on the cutting board so it doesn't roll around when you cut it.

5 | You can use the flat part of the blade to transfer chopped vegetables from the cutting board to the pot or bowl. This is a lot easier than picking them up with your hands. It is considered bad form to scrape a cutting board with the sharp edge and it is hard on your knife.

6 | Use the right knife for the job. It makes no more sense to dice a small shallot with a large chef's knife than it does to try to chop a big bunch of basil with a paring knife.

7 | Always be mindful as you cut—especially if you like having ten fingers.

8 | Never put knives in the sink, especially in a sink filled with suds—it's a trip to the emergency room waiting to happen.

9 | Never wash knives in a dishwasher. Debris can fly around when the washer is in use, nicking the blades, invading the seams, and dulling the look of the handles.

10 | Carbon steel knives react with acidic foods like tomatoes, citrus fruits, and the like. Wash and dry carbon steel knives promptly if you are working with these foods.

▶ Once or twice a year, have your knives professionally sharpened.

A WORD ABOUT THE BASIC INGREDIENTS (HOW TO STOCK YOUR PANTRY)

Throughout these pages, you'll learn how to use both familiar and esoteric ingredients. The unusual ones will be explained in the Shop section of each recipe. Here are the basic ingredients you'll always want to have on hand so you can whip up a stellar dish at a moment's notice.

Bread crumbs | Essential for crusting fish fillets and chicken breasts and for topping gratins and other vegetable dishes, mac and cheese, and salads. Bread crumbs are easy to make from scratch and infinitely better than commercial ones. (On page 459, I'll tell you how to make them.)

Brown sugar | Made by mixing molasses with granulated sugar. More molasses creates dark brown sugar; less makes light brown sugar. Dark brown sugar has a more pronounced flavor, but unless otherwise specified, the two are interchangeable.

Butter | There once was a time when butter was salted to preserve it. So, unsalted butter, theoretically, was fresher. This is no longer the case. Most chefs prefer unsalted butter to give them greater control over the final seasoning of a dish. But for your purposes, unless otherwise specified, the two are interchangeable.

Eggs | Use large eggs—preferably farm-raised or organic.

Flour | Unless otherwise called for, you want to use unbleached all-purpose white flour. Unbleached? Some manufacturers bleach their flour with peroxides and chlorine—supposedly to produce lighter, finer-textured baked goods. I'll pass. Self-rising flour, which is used to make biscuits, contains baking powder and salt. Whole wheat flour is ground from the whole wheat berry, containing the nutrient- and fiber-rich bran, germ, and endosperm. Note: Straight whole wheat flour makes for leaden batters and bread doughs, but mixed with all-purpose flour in a 1-to-2 or 1-to-3 ratio, it gives you great flavor and health benefits too.

Milk | Unless otherwise indicated, depending on your fat preference, you can use whole, low-fat, or skim (fat-free) milk for the recipes in this book. Preferably the milk will be organic.

Mustard | There are hundreds of mustards to choose from, ranging from strong-tasting bright-yellow ballpark-style mustard to sweet honey mustard or spicy jalapeño mustard. My default is Dijon mustard, which is made with white wine and no or minimal sweeteners.

Olive oil | The oil I use more than any other—as a fat for sautéing, as a flavoring for salad dressings and marinades, and to drizzle over everything from roasted peppers (page 200) to Skillet Rib Steak (page 231). Always use extra virgin olive oil. See page 168 for a full discussion of this essential ingredient.

Paprika | A rust-colored spice made from ground dried Hungarian or Spanish peppers and available in sweet (mild), hot, and smoked varieties. One good brand for both sweet and hot paprikas is Szeged from Hungary (available at most supermarkets).

Pepper | The fruit of this tropical flowering vine is the world's most popular spice. Yes, it adds heat, but more important, it adds flavor. Black pepper is the most aromatic. White pepper (black

◄ Bread crumbs are easy to make from scratch and infinitely better than commercial ones.

peppercorns with the outside skins removed) is milder. Green peppercorns—made by brining or pickling the fresh fruit—have an herbal heat that goes great in steak au poivre (page 238). For the best results, use freshly ground pepper. You can grind it in a peppermill (you know—those wooden grinders brandished by waiters at steakhouses), but if you use as much pepper as I do, you may want to pre-grind fistfuls in an electric spice mill every week or so and store it in a sealed jar.

Salt | The most essential seasoning (not to mention an essential part of a human being's chemical makeup). Salt comes from two main sources: evaporated seawater or mined mineral beds. I prefer coarse sea salt—coarse, because the crystals dissolve slowly, and from the sea, because it contains dozens of flavor-enhancing trace elements. Some chefs swear by the purity of kosher salt, which is mined and also comes in slowly dissolving coarse crystals. On page 227, you'll find an in-depth discussion of salt.

Sugar | When a recipe calls simply for sugar that means granulated white sugar.

Vegetable oil | Used for deep-frying and pan-frying and as an ingredient in salad dressings, like French vinaigrette. My go-to vegetable oil is canola, which has a mild flavor and high smoke point (this means you can heat canola oil to 400°F before it begins to burn). Peanut oil also has a high smoke point, but a lot of people have peanut allergies, so I tend to avoid it.

▶ For the best results, use freshly ground pepper.

FLAVOR BOOSTERS FROM A TO Z

One hallmark of guy food is our enthusiasm for (make that obsession with) flavor. We crave the fiery bite of chipotle peppers and hot sauce. We hunger for big-flavored condiments like olive paste and miso (even if we're not quite sure what they are). Here's an A to Z guide to some of my personal favorite flavor boosters.

Anchovies | Tiny salt-cured fish bursting with briny umami flavors (for a description of umami, see page 28). Mandatory for an authentic Caesar Salad (page 163) and *bagna cauda* (Anchovy Hot Tub, page 204). Anchovies are surprisingly good paired with steak. My favorite anchovies come packed in oil in flat cans. Read more about anchovies on page 203.

Bacon | It's hard to imagine guy food without cured smoked pork belly, aka bacon. Look for thick-sliced artisanal bacon, which means it's been smoked with real wood in a smokehouse. (Most inexpensive supermarket bacon is injected with liquid smoke.) One good nationally available brand is Nueske's.

Capers | The salty pickled buds of shrubs in the nasturtium family, capers come large and small (the latter, sometimes called nonpareil, are more desirable). Capers also come salt-cured, but for me, pickled have a more complex flavor. Caper berries (the plant's fruit) are sold with the stems attached—munch on them as you would olives, or use them to garnish gazpacho (page 125) or a Bloody Mary (page 594). Caper juice works wonders in marinara sauce.

Dijon mustard | You slather it on hot dogs and sandwiches, of course, but mustard makes just about every savory dish taste better, from salad dressings to mac and cheese to planked salmon. Dijon mustard, enriched with white wine and mercifully free of sweeteners, has a much more refined flavor than American ballpark-style mustard. My go-to brand is Maille.

Espresso | Not just for drinking, although we certainly do that every morning. Ground espresso beans make a great rub for pork and other meats (see Coffee-Crusted Pork Tenderloins with Redeye Gravy on page 281). A shot of brewed espresso is just the thing for invigorating a barbecue sauce.

Fish sauce | A malodorous brown condiment made from fermented anchovies and used like soy sauce in Southeast Asia. Fish sauce is loaded with umami flavors (see page 28) and it tastes a *lot* better than it smells (or sounds). My favorite brand is Red Boat (redboatfishsauce .com). Note: There's a special version of Red Boat fish sauce that's aged in barrels previously used for bourbon. Awesome.

Garlic chips | Garlic is endlessly versatile. For complete instructions on how to work with garlic, see page 129. Thais, Malaysians, and Burmese raise the bulb to another level by frying paper-thin slices of fresh garlic in hot oil to make aromatic, crunchy, golden-brown garlic chips. Sprinkle them over satés, noodle dishes, and salads.

Hot sauce | On any given day I have at least a dozen different varieties of hot sauce open in my refrigerator—Cholula from Mexico (flavored with pequin peppers and árbol chiles), Nando's Peri-Peri from South Africa (essential for *peri-peri* chicken), fiery Scotch bonnet–based Matouk's from Trinidad, garlicky Sriracha from Thailand, and Tabasco sauce from Louisiana (which is aged in oak barrels). There are literally thousands of hot sauces around the world and I, for one, can't get enough of them.

Ice cream | Melted, it makes a fine sauce for chocolate pudding (page 568) and other desserts. Add vanilla extract, nutmeg, cinnamon, and bourbon to melted vanilla ice cream and you've got terrific holiday eggnog.

Jalapeño peppers | Once considered exotic, today as commonplace as bell peppers, jalapeños have become America's workhorse chile when a bright grassy gentle heat is required. Smoke fresh jalapeños and pack them in a vinegary sauce called *adobo* and you get fiery, smoky chipotle peppers—one of your best flavor allies in the kitchen (and one of the rare foods that tastes best when canned).

Kimchi | Spicy Korean pickles—especially pickled napa cabbage and daikon radish (the two most common). Kimchi is essential for Korean Beef Tacos (page 244) and makes an intriguing addition to a Bloody Mary (page 594).

Liquid smoke | There's no substitute for real wood smoke from a charcoal-burning grill or smoker, of course, but liquid smoke—a natural distilled product made from real wood—comes in handy if you live in an apartment with no access to an outdoor grill. Use liquid smoke sparingly—a drop or two in a braising liquid, beef stew, or barbecue sauce goes a long way.

Miso | A sweet-salty protein-rich paste made from cultured (fermented) soybeans and other grains. Native to Japan, but now manufactured in the United States, miso comes in white (*shiro*—made with soybeans and rice); in red (*aka*—farmhouse-style and high in salt); made with barley (*mugi*—brown and earthy flavored); and *hatcho*-style (pure soybean and aged for up to three years in cedar vats). Add miso to vegetable soups and Asian-style salad dressings or mix it with mayonnaise to make a killer sauce.

Nutmeg | Once prized as a cure for bubonic plague (and just about anything else that ailed you), nutmeg is the fragrant, egg-shaped seed of a tropical tree native to Indonesia. Grate it fresh (use a Microplane) over eggnog and other cocktails, apple and pumpkin pies, mashed potatoes, roasted onions, and other savory dishes for an unexpected musky sweetness.

◄ I have at least a dozen different varieties of hot sauce open in my refrigerator.

Olive paste | A puree of black or green olives—often with capers and anchovies—native to Provence, where it goes by the name of tapenade. (Italy and Spain also have versions.) You can buy commercial versions or make your own (see page 313). Great on bruschetta (grilled garlic bread, page 511), chicken breasts, rack of lamb, and deviled eggs.

Pimentón | This smoked paprika from Spain is a great way to add smoke to dishes not easily cooked on a grill (scrambled eggs, for example). Also works wonders on pork and chicken. For extra smoky barbecue substitute *pimentón* for the paprika in your favorite rub (see Raichlen's Rub #2 on page 531). Like paprika, *pimentón* is available both sweet and hot. Two good brands are La Dalia and Santa Domingo.

Quince paste | A jelly so thick you can slice it with a knife, quince paste is made from a yellow fruit that looks and tastes like a cross between an apple and a pear. Traditionally served on a cheese tray, quince paste is also delicious sliced and cooked in a grilled cheese sandwich (see page 71) or stirred into homemade barbecue sauce.

Roquefort | A sheep's milk cheese from the southwest of France inoculated with a special mold that gives it greenish veins and a salty, tangy, and almost metallic (in a good way) flavor. Blue cheese dressing becomes extraordinary when you add it. Roquefort also goes great on steak and grilled bread. Alternative blues to Roquefort include Gorgonzola, a cow's milk cheese from northern Italy; Stilton, a cow's milk cheese from England; Cabrales, a Spanish cheese made from a mixture of cow's, goat's, and sheep's milk; the Californian blue Port Reyes; and Maytag blue from Iowa. Warning: When buying blue cheese (as with all cheese) you get what you pay for: The difference between genuine Roquefort and cheap domestic blue is like the difference between lodging at a swank hotel versus couch surfing.

Saffron | The fragrant stigmas of a Spanish crocus that add a vivid orange color and intensely aromatic flavor to Mediterranean specialties ranging from French bouillabaisse to risotto Milanese. Buy the threads, not the powder—they're expensive, but a little goes a long way.

Sesame oil | One of the mainstays of Japanese and Korean cooking and one of my go-to ingredients when an extra flavor is required. Be sure to buy toasted sesame oil, which has a rich, nutty flavor. (Avoid the bland untoasted oils.)

Tamari | One of the dozens of types of soy sauces used as a flavoring and condiment from Japan to China to Southeast Asia—and I trust, in your kitchen. Tamari has less salt and a richer flavor that regular soy sauce. While we're on the subject, you might want to pick up a bottle of *kejap manis*, a sweet molasses-thick soy sauce from Indonesia. Yes, it gave us the name ketchup.

Umami | Less an ingredient than a state of mind. The Japanese call it the "fifth taste" (after sweet, sour, salty, and bitter), and it refers to a family of earthy, meaty, salty ingredients high in glutamic acid that make food taste luscious and satisfying in your mouth. Umami flavorings include fish sauce, miso, beef stock, mushrooms, tomatoes, caramelized onions, roasted vegetables, and Parmesan cheese. To get a better idea of what I mean, try the L.A. Burger on page 106.

Vinegar | The word *vinegar* literally means "sour wine," although you can buy vinegars made from rice (used in sushi rice and Japanese salad dressings), malt (sprinkled by the English on fish and chips), cider, and boiled-down grape juice. The last, better known as balsamic vinegar (*aceto balsamico*), is a specialty of Modena, Italy, where it's aged in successively smaller barrels of oak, cherry, mulberry, and other woods to concentrate the sweetness and flavor, producing a sweet-sour vinegar with the complex taste of wine. But don't overlook true wine vinegar, the forthright acidity of which punches up salad dressings, relishes, soups, and stews.

Wasabi | The spicy green paste you dissolve in soy sauce to serve with sushi. It possesses a peppery, mustardy flavor designed to blast open your sinuses. True wasabi comes from a root in the Brassicaceae family of plants, which includes cabbage and horseradish. One commercial grower in the Pacific Northwest sells the fresh root online at wasabia.com. Most of what passes for wasabi at American sushi restaurants is actually a spicy powder made from powdered horseradish, mustard seed, and green food coloring. Pleasant, but it's *not* wasabi.

XO sauce | One of the dozens of Chinese chile pastes you'll find in my refrigerator, XO is flavored with dried shrimp, scallops, and fish; chiles; garlic; and onion. Think hot and salty, with loads of umami flavors. Despite the name, this Cantonese condiment contains no cognac.

Yuzu | A small intensely aromatic Japanese citrus fruit that will make you think simultaneously of lemon juice, grapefruit, and perfume. It's the souring agent in *ponzu* sauce (soy sauce and rice vinegar are the other key ingredients), and if you've ever dined at one of the Nobu restaurants, it's prominent in the signature hamachi *tiradito* (thin slices of raw yellowtail marinated in yuzu juice with Peruvian chile). Yuzu is available bottled and frozen at Asian markets and natural foods stores.

Zest | The shiny outer rind of a lemon, lime, orange, grapefruit, or other citrus fruit. It contains the fruit's aromatic oils but no acidity, and it brightens every dish to which it's added. Some examples you'll find in this book: beef stew (see page 254) and barbecue sauce (see page 537). Whenever something tastes boring or flat, my go-to fix is a dose of grated lemon zest. Use a Microplane to grate it (see page 15) and take only the oil-rich outer rind, not the bitter white pith beneath it.

◄ Whenever something tastes boring or flat, my go-to fix is a dose of grated lemon zest.

HOW TO PLAN A MENU

Cooking is more than creating killer dishes. You also need to know how to assemble and sequence them in a harmonious whole. Many factors go into planning a menu, starting with the occasion—weeknight dinner, tailgating party, or Thanksgiving feast. Next, there's the theme of the meal: tapas spread or weekend barbecue, for example, or Sunday brunch or sandwiches for your weekly poker game. You also need to think about the flavor profile: Do you want a fusion menu (combining multiple ethnic flavors) or a meal that has a strong sense of a particular place (like a Tex-Mex taco party or Cajun shrimp boil)? Finally, you should take into consideration how much time you have available, how hard you want to work, and what you're willing to spend.

Planning a menu is a little like creating a playlist. It's not enough to put one great song after another. You want them to set the mood over a period of time and create a coherent ambience.

It's called "menu planning" for a reason | A meal should have a beginning, middle, and end. This can be as simple as marinated olives to start with, followed by a roast chicken and baked potato, and finally, a fruit salsa for dessert. Or as regal as a prime rib dinner complete with martinis, anchovy toasts, salad, Yorkshire pudding, and a rich chocolate finale. When planning a menu, think not innings or quarters, but whole ballgame.

You eat with all your senses | A great meal plays to all the senses: sight, smell, and taste, of course, but also touch (i.e., temperature and texture) and sound (the pop of a champagne cork or sizzle of flambéed *saganaki*, page 198, not to mention that music on your playlist). As you plan your menu, blend colors, textures, and tastes.

Think health and nutrition | Nachos, buffalo wings, and thick juicy burgers are quintessential guy foods. But most of us also care about the health consequences of what we eat. And, typically, so do the people you invite for dinner. When planning a menu, wow with flavor, not just fat, and pair proteins with plenty of plant-based foods. Whenever possible, serve whole wheat, whole grains, and colorful vegetables.

Make your life easy | Build your menu around a large hunk of meat that's forgiving in terms of split-second timing. You can cook a pork shoulder, brisket, or ribs hours before serving. The same holds true for braises and stews—in fact, these rib-sticking dishes often taste better made the day before and reheated just before serving. Likewise, grilled or roasted vegetables

▶ The best way to impress your company is to *be* good company.

can be prepared well ahead and served at room temperature.

But be mindful of your guests' needs | Nothing stops a dinner party in its tracks faster than the guest who announces he's a vegan as you proudly present the roasted pork loin. Or your freshly baked biscuits to your—surprise— gluten-free sister-in-law. Or your almond-crusted chicken breast to your girlfriend's nut-allergic mother. Best to ask the invitees in advance if they have any food limitations or dislikes.

Make sure you're a guest at your own party | The purpose of any meal is pleasure, and you can't enjoy a party if it requires *you* to be a line chef. For large groups, serve punch or sangria, not custom cocktails. Build your menu on a mix of quick and slower-cooking dishes. Keep last-minute cooking to a minimum. Reduce stress by sticking to dishes you've made successfully at least once before. And augment the homemade fare with thoughtfully curated store-bought items, like Spanish ham, farmhouse cheeses, and bread or dessert from an artisanal bakery. The best way to impress your company is to *be* good company, and you can't do that if your menu is too ambitious.

MODERN HUNTING AND GATHERING

Great cooking begins with shopping. The good news is that there has never been an age when so much great food was so readily available.

Here's what you need to know to be a modern day hunter-gatherer:

▶ Start with a shopping list. Keep a dedicated pad, notebook, or file on your phone or laptop in one spot in the kitchen and add to it on an ongoing basis.

▶ Add an item when you run low, not when you run out.

▶ Organize your shopping list in categories— meat, produce, dairy, packaged goods, alcohol, and so on—acccording to your supermarket's layout. This reduces the chance of forgetting something and cuts down on time spent in the store.

- Do not forget to bring your list with you when you go shopping. I repeat—do not forget to bring your list when you go shopping.

- Take a pencil or pen with you. Cross off each item as you put it in your basket. This seems obvious, but failure to do this can leave you with three bottles of soy sauce.

- Don't be *too* organized. Some of my best meals come from items I purchase spontaneously that weren't on the list.

HOW TO USE A RECIPE

As you set out to accomplish great things in the kitchen, recipes are your marching orders. A good recipe tells you what ingredients you'll need; how to combine, cook, and serve them; and how much time to allow for each step. It should tell you where to source any exotic ingredients and suggest reasonable substitutes if you can't find them. It lets you know what equipment you'll need, how many people you'll be able to feed, and when you can pause in the preparation process. Ideally, the recipe will also tell you why the finished dish is one you'll want to make and also something about the history and culture of the dish—information that's useful for story-telling, bragging rights, and interesting table talk. So how do you use a recipe?

- First, read it from start to finish. I repeat, read it from start to finish. There's nothing worse than starting a recipe you plan to serve for dinner in a few hours—only to find the words "refrigerate overnight" in the last sentence.

- Do your setup (you may have heard the French term for this: *mise en place*). Our word "recipe" comes from the Latin verb *recipe* (pronounced "ray-keep-ay")—literally "to take" (as in "take some of this, take some of that"). In the Middle Ages, pharmacists wrote their medicinal formulas the same way, abbreviating *recipe* as Rx. (How's that for table talk?) So the next step in using any recipe is "taking" *all* the ingredients you need from the shelf, pantry, or refrigerator and assembling them on the counter *before* you start cooking. If you're feeling particularly virtuous, measure them out ahead of time. I don't always pre-measure (except when I'm on television), but I try to have all the ingredients on the work counter.

- Better ingredients mean better results. Period. Choose sea or kosher salt over cheap table salt, freshly ground black pepper over preground canned, fresh herbs over dried (except for oregano and rosemary), spices that are still potent (purchased within the last six months or so), and heirloom or vine-ripened tomatoes.

- Make common sense substitutions. Don't have scotch bonnet chiles? Use habaneros or jalapeños. Most recipes are forgiving if you stay within a broad register of flavors.

- Know when to measure and when to eyeball. Measure carefully when making cocktails and baking (as in the pancakes on page 59 or brownies on page 569). You can be more spontaneous when dosing out hot sauce or mustard.

- The standard measures for most recipes are cups, tablespoons, and teaspoons. (A quick FYI: There are 3 teaspoons in a tablespoon and 16 tablespoons in a cup.) Use a set of nesting

◄ If a recipe is like a pharmaceutical formula, it's also like a musical score.

measuring cups and measuring spoons to measure dry ingredients. Dip the correct size cup or spoon into the flour or sugar, then scrape off any excess with the back of a knife—the idea is to have a *level* cup or tablespoon. Use a standard liquid measuring cup (typically glass and large enough to hold 2 cups of liquid) to measure liquids. Meats and seafood are generally measured in pounds or ounces.

► Which brings us to the mystical words "season to taste." Here's where the soul comes into your cooking—where chemistry becomes art. Add salt or pepper to *your* taste; a splash of vinegar to sharpen a sauce or a pinch of sugar to mellow it. Wield the cayenne or hot sauce like you mean it, adding as much as you and your guests can comfortably bear. In the final reckoning, a cook's most important tools are his taste buds.

► Last but certainly not least, make a game plan. Think about how much overall time you need and what needs to happen when. There's no shame in jotting down a simple timetable.

If a recipe is like a pharmaceutical formula, it's also like a musical score. You follow it to reproduce a pleasing melody, but it doesn't become music until you add soul.

All this may sound elementary. It *is* elementary, but using a recipe correctly invariably saves time and produces better results.

Measuring Flour or Sugar

1 Dip the measuring cup in the bag of flour or sugar, and take out a generous scoopful.

2 Scrape the top of the measuring cup with the back of a knife to remove the excess flour or sugar, leaving exactly 1 cup.

Man Made Meals:
THE RECIPES

BREAKFAST

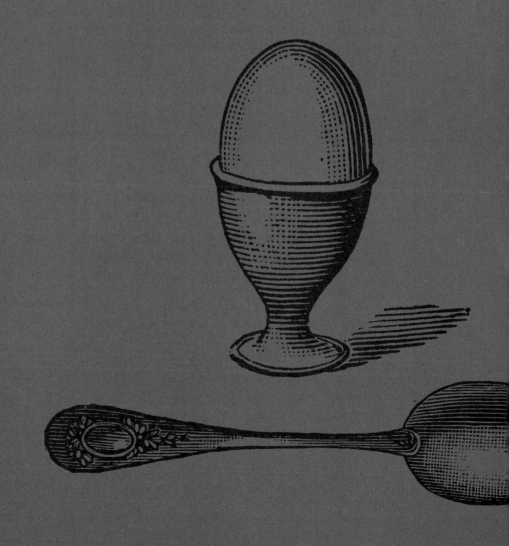

My father wasn't much of a cook. Few men of his generation were. But he excelled at making pancakes. He'd cook them every Saturday morning, and if he used a mix (sold in a clever cylindrical measuring cup to which you'd add milk, oil, and egg to the indicated levels), we weren't sophisticated enough to care. It was male bonding at its best—a son and his dad in the kitchen— and I looked forward to it all week.

Men don't have a monopoly on breakfast, of course, but this first meal of the day gives us a unique opportunity to shine. When a woman makes breakfast, it's a morning meal. When a guy does breakfast, it becomes an event. You'll know what I mean—if you don't already—the first time you cook breakfast for a date that began the previous evening. Or for your wife on Mother's Day. Or for your kids pretty much any time you have the opportunity. There's a lot to master in the following chapter, so pay attention. Breakfast may just be the most important meal of the day.

SCRAMBLED EGGS AND CREAM CHEESE

Scrambled eggs may seem rudimentary, but for at least three of the Food Dudes interviewed for this book, this simple dish represented their initiation into the art of cooking—and a technique all men should master. I'll never forget how one of my mentors, a Parisian chef named Fernand Chambrette, turned what's a three-minute American breakfast into a half-hour ritual that involved slooooooooow cooking the eggs with black truffles chopped fine as dust over a pan of gently simmering water (aka a double boiler), producing a scramble with the creamy consistency of hollandaise sauce. Not that you need a double boiler or truffles, because great scrambled eggs require little more than a bowl, wooden spoon, and frying pan. And 5 minutes of preparation time. The trick is to add cream cheese (that's how my wife, Barbara, does it), giving the eggs an incredible airy, creamy consistency. Even the most kitchen-impaired guy can do it. **Serves 1; can be multiplied as desired**

SHOP In the best of all worlds you'd use farm eggs and organic cream cheese.

GEAR Your basic kitchen gear including a large (10- to 12-inch) skillet (preferably nonstick)

WHAT ELSE Whipped cream cheese melts quicker than cream cheese in block form, but don't make a special trip to the store if all you have is the latter.

TIME 5 minutes

2 large eggs

1 tablespoon milk

Coarse salt (kosher or sea) and freshly ground white or black pepper

3 tablespoons whipped cream cheese

1 tablespoon butter or extra virgin olive oil

Crack the eggs into a mixing bowl. Add the milk, season with salt and pepper to taste, and whisk to mix. Place the cream cheese and butter in a large skillet and melt over medium-low heat, tilting the pan to coat the bottom evenly. Add the eggs and cook, stirring with a rubber spatula, until thick and creamy, 2 to 4 minutes. Dig in.

Cracking and Separating Eggs

TO CRACK AN EGG

▶ You may have done this a thousand times, but in case you're a neophyte, here's how to crack and separate an egg.

1 Hold the egg horizontally between your thumb and forefinger.

2 Tap the egg firmly against the edge of a bowl or skillet to make a clean crack in the middle of the shell on the bottom.

3 Pry the halves of the shell apart with your thumbs, letting the egg slide into the bowl. If you see any loose pieces of shell or blood spots, fish them out with one of the eggshell halves.

4 If you're so inclined, use the tine of a fork or the edge of an eggshell to fish out the chalaza (white filament). I seldom bother. If you're careful, the fork won't break the yolk.

TO SEPARATE AN EGG

1 Working over a bowl, crack the egg as described on the facing page.

2 Carefully let the egg white spill into the bowl, leaving the yolk in one half of the eggshell.

3 Gently transfer the yolk to the other half shell, spilling more of the egg white into the bowl. Do this once or twice more until all of the egg white is in the bowl. Take care not to break the yolk.

4 When working with multiple eggs, separate each white into a small bowl and make sure it is yolk-free before adding it to the other whites.

◄ Yes, farm eggs cost more than supermarket eggs, but the flavor and texture are eminently worth the price.

EGGS

It used to be that eggs were eggs. Today, you face a confounding selection: brown eggs or white; "natural" eggs or ones from cage-free chickens; eggs from hens fed grain or a diet enhanced with omega-3 fatty acids.

It's enough to make you hang up your skillet and boil a pot of oatmeal (well, if you'd like some oatmeal, there's a recipe that uses a blowtorch on page 65). Here's an egg scorecard to help you identify the players.

FARM EGGS | Raised by a local farmer, these eggs are recognizable by their lack of uniformity (they may be large or small; blue-shelled, tan, or white), their lurid orange yolks, and their rich flavor. Yes, they cost more than supermarket eggs, but the flavor and texture are eminently worth the price—whatever their color or size.

ORGANIC EGGS | These come from hens raised on certified organic feed in smaller flocks that have some access to the outdoors. (Believe me, you don't want to know how the chickens that lay eggs in factories are raised.)

BROWN EGGS AND WHITE EGGS | Brown eggs come from chickens with reddish feathers; white eggs come from chickens with white feathers.

Brown eggs may cost slightly more, but there's no appreciable difference in texture, flavor, or health benefits.

EGGS FROM CAGE-FREE CHICKENS | Cage-free hens are raised in large pens, not tiny cages, so they have more freedom of movement. There are no guaranteed nutritional benefits, but the chickens are raised more humanely than hens that are confined to typical factory cages.

EGGS FROM FREE-RANGE OR FREE-ROAMING CHICKENS | This, too, means the hens are raised in enclosures, not tiny factory cages, ideally with access to the outdoors. Again, no extra nutritional benefits are guaranteed, but the chickens are raised more humanely.

EGGS FROM PASTURED CHICKENS | A new designation that refers to eggs from hens raised outdoors in portable enclosures that are moved often so the chickens can scratch and feed outdoors. Local farms are your best source for these eggs. (Note: There's no third-party inspection to ensure this actually happens, so find a farmer or store you trust.)

HORMONE-FREE EGGS | An empty marketing term, as the FDA (Food and Drug

Administration) permits no egg-laying hen to be treated with hormones.

NATURAL EGGS | Another empty marketing term; the FDA does not specify what constitutes "natural."

OMEGA-3 EGGS | These eggs come from hens fed a diet of flaxseeds or other foods high in omega-3 fatty acids (you know, those healthful compounds found in salmon, mackerel, and other oily fish).

GRAIN-FED HEN EGGS | These come from hens fed solely on grains (not the fish meal and other animal by-products typically fed to factory egg layers). I don't know about you, but I'd rather not eat eggs or chickens raised on fish meal.

PASTEURIZED EGGS | Eggs processed using a technology developed by National Pasteurized Eggs, Inc., of Lansing, Illinois, to kill salmonella and other bacteria. These are recommended for Caesar salads (page 163), homemade mayonnaise (page 543),

sunny-side up eggs, and other preparations that call for raw or lightly cooked eggs. Look for a red "P" on the carton and on the eggshells.

FERTILE EGGS | These eggs contain a tiny blood spot—the embryo. They may be farm or organic eggs and are more perishable than nonfertile eggs.

AND WHAT ABOUT EGG SIZES | They range from small to jumbo. Does size matter? No, but note: All the recipes in this book call for "large" eggs.

MODERNIST SCRAMBLED EGGS
WITH MANCHEGO CHEESE

SHOP Use organic or farm eggs and Spanish Manchego cheese or another firm aromatic cheese, like cave-aged Gruyère.

GEAR Your basic kitchen gear including a saucepan and a large (10- to 12-inch) skillet

WHAT ELSE Myhrvold scrambles his eggs at precisely 164°F in a combi oven (a special multifunction high-tech oven). You can achieve a similar result by cooking the eggs over a pan of barely simmering water. Serve the eggs with the brioche toast points on page 218.

TIME about 10 minutes

For food visionary Nathan Myhrvold (read about him on page 52), the secret to great scrambled eggs is to use three yolks but only two whites—a ratio that dramatically improves the texture. Here's the way to raise scrambled eggs to the level of art. **Serves 1; can be multiplied as desired**

3 large eggs

1 ounce Manchego, aged Gruyère, or other aromatic cheese, cut into ¼-inch dice or coarsely grated

Coarse salt (kosher or sea) and freshly ground white or black pepper

1 tablespoon salted butter

1 Crack 2 of the eggs into a mixing bowl. Separate the third egg (see page 39) and add the yolk to the mixing bowl. (Discard the egg white or set it aside for another use, such as the frittata on page 55.) Whisk the eggs well, about 1 minute. Stir in the cheese and season with salt (just a little) and pepper to taste.

2 Pour water to a depth of 1 inch into a skillet and let come to a bare simmer over low heat.

3 Place the butter in a saucepan that's sitting in the skillet with the hot water. Once the butter has melted, add the egg and cheese mixture and cook, whisking continuously, until the eggs thicken and the cheese melts, about 5 minutes. Proper scrambled eggs should be soft and creamy—almost like cream of wheat. If you're accustomed to the usual dry, chewy curds, these will come as a revelation.

4 Taste for seasoning, adding more salt and pepper as necessary. Dig in.

JOSE'S FRIED EGGS

What's your go-to dish when you're by yourself? For Spanish-born super-star chef José Andrés it's eggs fried in garlic-scented olive oil and served with Spanish ham and toast. Now, there are fried eggs and there are *fried eggs*, and José's owe their extraordinary texture—softly crisp on the outside and melting and oozing when you cut into them—to a technique pioneered by the magiste-rial twentieth-century French chef Fernand Point. Namely, you tilt the skillet to pool the oil at one edge so the egg poaches in the hot oil while you spoon more hot oil over the egg, frying it on all sides. (You can read about José Andrés on page 134.) **Serves 1; can be multiplied as desired**

For the eggs
¼ cup extra virgin olive oil, preferably Spanish

1 clove garlic, peeled and lightly flattened with the side of a knife (see page 129)

2 large eggs

Coarse salt (kosher or sea) and freshly ground black pepper

For serving (optional)
2 thin slices Spanish ham (see above)

2 slices country-style bread

1 Heat the olive oil in a large skillet over medium-high heat until shimmering, about 1 minute. Add the garlic clove (when the oil is heated to the proper temperature bubbles will dance around the garlic clove). If you don't see bubbles, keep heating until you do, but don't let garlic turn dark brown or it will be bitter. Cook the garlic until fragrant, about 1 minute, then using a slotted spoon, remove and dis-card it. (You discard it because it would burn by the time you cook 2 eggs. You just want the garlic to flavor the oil.)

2 Tilt the skillet so the oil pools on one side of the pan. Gently slip 1 egg into the pool of oil. Fry the egg until the white is crisp and lightly browned around the edge but the inside remains soft, 1 to 2 minutes. As the egg fries, use a metal spoon to spoon the oil over the top, so the egg fries on both sides. Carefully transfer the egg to drain on a plate lined with a paper towel. Fry the second egg the same way. Season both with salt and pepper to taste.

3 If you are frying the ham, gently arrange the slices in the hot oil and fry the ham over

SHOP This dish is simplicity itself, but unless you use fresh organic eggs from your local farmers' market and fruity Spanish olive oil, you won't get the full effect. Authentic Spanish ham, called *jamón serrano* or *jamón ibérico* (see page 608), can be purchased from specialty food markets or online from tienda.com.

GEAR Your basic kitchen gear including a large (10- to 12-inch) skillet (preferably nonstick) plus a plate lined with a paper towel

WHAT ELSE For the best results, fry the eggs one at a time. José serves the ham raw and the bread toasted, but I like to fry both in the olive oil (the ham crisps like bacon).

TIME about 5 minutes

medium heat until crisp, about 1 minute per side. Using tongs or a fork, remove the ham from the skillet, letting any excess oil drain back into the pan, and transfer the ham to the paper towel–lined plate to drain.

4 If you are frying the bread, pour off all but 2 tablespoons of the oil from the skillet. Add the bread slices to the skillet and fry over medium heat until browned on both sides, 30 seconds to 1 minute per side.

5 Transfer the eggs and the ham and toast, if serving, to a warm plate and dig in.

Variation
American-Style Fried Eggs

Want to keep it really simple? To make eggs sunny-side up, place 1 tablespoon of extra virgin olive oil or butter in a skillet and heat the oil or melt the butter over high heat until it sizzles, 20 seconds. Then crack in the eggs. Fry the eggs until they are crisp at the edges and browned on the bottoms, 2 to 3 minutes, depending on whether you like your eggs really runny or a little more set.

If you prefer your eggs over easy, carefully turn them with a spatula after they have cooked for 2 minutes and fry them on the second side until done to your taste, 1 to 2 minutes longer.

CYCLOPS EGGS

SHOP Buy fresh farm eggs if you can—as much for their flavor and safety as for the supernatural orange of their yolks. White bread or whole wheat—you choose. To up the ante, use brioche.

GEAR Your basic kitchen gear including a large (10- to 12-inch) skillet

WHAT ELSE Tradition calls for cooking the eggs in butter, but you can mix the butter with the healthier olive oil or use olive oil on its own.

TIME about 5 minutes

There's a scene in the dystopian movie *V for Vendetta* when the manly but tenderhearted protagonist (don't we all want to be manly and tenderhearted?) prepares breakfast for the tough but vulnerable Evey, played by Natalie Portman. With biohazard-scarred hands, he gently tears the center out of a slice of bread and places the piece of bread in a hot skillet. He cracks an egg in the hole in the center and fries the whole shebang in butter, turning it effortlessly without rupturing the yolk. It's an edible love letter from a hideously maimed freedom fighter, and it melts Evey's heart. Reason enough to try it yourself, not to mention the fact that for untold generations of Englishmen and Boy Scouts, eggs in the hole or eggs on a raft (other names for these Cyclops Eggs) are the perfect breakfast: eggs, toast, and butter all rolled into one. **Serves 1; can be multiplied as desired**

2 large eggs

2 slices white bread

3 tablespoons butter, 3 tablespoons extra
virgin olive oil, or a combination of the
two

Coarse salt (kosher or sea) and freshly
ground black pepper

2 teaspoons minced fresh chives or
scallions (optional)

1 Crack each egg into a separate cup, taking care not to break the yolk.

2 Using a paring knife or the rim of a drinking glass, cut a 2-inch circle in the center of each slice of bread to make a hole in the center. Set aside the circles of bread.

3 Place half the butter and/or olive oil in a large skillet and cook over medium heat until the butter melts or the olive oil is hot, 20 to 40 seconds. Tilt the skillet to coat the bottom evenly. (To test the temperature of the fat, dip in a bread circle—bubbles will dance around it.) Add the bread slices to the skillet with the 2-inch cutouts next to them, and cook until the bottoms start to brown, about 1 minute. Place a pea-size piece of butter or ½ teaspoon of olive oil in the center of the hole in each slice of bread.

4 When this butter melts or the oil is hot, pour an egg into each hole. Continue cooking the bread and eggs until they are browned on the bottom, 1 to 2 minutes. If the bread starts to dry out or burn, place a couple of pea-size pieces of butter or drizzles of oil at the edge of the bread and tilt the pan so the butter slides under the bread.

5 Slide a spatula under each slice of bread to lift it, then place a pea-size piece of butter underneath or drizzle in a little oil into the pan. Gently turn over the slices of bread with the eggs and the bread circles. Cook the second side until the bread is browned and the yolks are cooked to taste, 1 to 2 minutes. Add more butter or oil as needed.

6 Transfer the eggs with the bread cutouts to a warm plate. Season with salt and pepper to taste and sprinkle with chives or scallions, if using.

BAKED EGGS

ere's a dish so simple it makes fried eggs seem complicated. It's called baked eggs ("shirred eggs" in gourmet speak), and if you can crack an egg and turn on your oven, you're in business. Note: I often cook the eggs on a grill set up for indirect grilling. (My gas grill preheats faster than my oven.) Besides, it's always a good day when you get to barbecue for breakfast. **Serves 1; can be multiplied as desired**

1½ tablespoons butter or extra virgin olive oil

2 large eggs

1 tablespoon heavy (whipping) cream

¼ cup (about 1 ounce) freshly grated Parmigiano Reggiano, Gouda, cheddar, or other cheese

1 tablespoon bread crumbs, preferably made from scratch (page 459)

Toast, for serving

1 Preheat the oven to 400°F.

2 Grease a small baking dish or ovenproof skillet with ½ tablespoon of the butter or olive oil. Crack the eggs into the baking dish or skillet and pour the cream over them. Sprinkle the cheese and bread crumbs on top, then dot the eggs with the remaining 1 tablespoon of butter or oil.

3 Bake the eggs until the bread crumbs are browned and the eggs are just set, 6 to 10 minutes. The yolks should remain a little runny in the center. (They will jiggle when you gently tap the side of the baking dish.) Serve with toast.

Variations

Before baking the eggs, top them with fried and crumbled bacon, prosciutto that has been crisped and crumbled (see Step 1 of Eggs Fra Diavolo on page 56), *Rajas* (strips of roasted peeled poblano peppers, see page 200), and/or slivered fresh basil leaves or other fresh herbs.

SHOP You probably have everything you need in your refrigerator, but if you do make a special shopping trip for this dish, try to find farm eggs and real Parmigiano Reggiano cheese.

GEAR You have several options for baking dishes. Easiest is a small baking dish—3½ to 4 inches across and 1 inch deep. Another option, a ramekin, is a small straight-sided ovenproof ceramic or glass bowl.

WHAT ELSE Need an easy brunch dish? Bake eight or ten eggs in a large ovenproof skillet. Upscale appetizer or late-night pick-me-up? Serve the baked eggs with sour cream and salmon caviar spooned on top. You see the possibilities.

TIME about 10 minutes

YOUR BASIC OMELET

SHOP Buy farm eggs when possible.

GEAR Your basic kitchen gear including a small (6-inch) skillet or omelet pan

WHAT ELSE Ham, cheese (the usual suspects: cheddar, Gruyère, pepper Jack), mushrooms, diced tomatoes, sautéed onions, caviar, and diced cooked lobster: All have been used to embellish omelets, but make sure you master a simple egg omelet first.

TIME about 10 minutes

Every man should know how to make an omelet. Not that you have to go to the extreme taken by Charles Blondin. In 1859, the aerial acrobat stretched a rope across Niagara Falls, wheeled a cook stove across it, and fried an omelet 160 feet above the water. No, the task will be easier for you. You will take two eggs and beat them vigorously with three tablespoons of cream or milk. You'll cook them in a skillet in sizzling hot butter. You'll perform a couple of time-honored gestures with a fork and you'll wind up with a dish that's quick enough for breakfast, yet substantial enough for dinner. It shouldn't take you more than ten minutes from start to finish, and when you do it right, the center of the omelet will be as creamy as scrambled eggs, with an exterior you can cut and eat with a knife and fork. (See pages 50 and 51 for a visual guide.) **Serves 1; can be multiplied as desired**

2 large eggs

3 tablespoons heavy (whipping) cream, half-and-half, or milk

Coarse salt (kosher or sea) and freshly ground black pepper

1½ tablespoons butter

1 Crack the eggs into a small mixing bowl. Add the cream, season the eggs with salt and pepper to taste, and beat well with a whisk or fork to mix, about 1 minute.

2 Melt the butter in a small skillet over high heat and cook until the sizzling subsides, about 30 seconds; tilt the skillet to coat the bottom evenly.

3 Add the beaten eggs and cook, shaking and tilting the skillet to set the eggs on the bottom, about 15 seconds. Using a fork (hold it in one hand almost parallel to the bottom of the pan), stir the omelet to mix the cooked and raw parts while simultaneously continuing to gently shake the skillet to keep the omelet from sticking. Do this for about 15 seconds. Stop stirring the omelet and continue shaking the skillet for about 15 seconds longer.

4 *Finishing the omelet, with a rubber spatula:* Use a spatula to lift the edge of the omelet. Slide the omelet to the far edge of the pan and using the spatula, flip the omelet over onto itself. Roll it over one more time and let it cook about 30 seconds longer. It should be set on the outside, but still creamy and a little wet inside. Invert the omelet onto a plate for serving; it should be oblong-shaped.

Finishing the omelet using a pan flip: Tilt the skillet handle upward, holding it toward the end, and gently tap it with the other hand to move the omelet to the far edge of the pan. Now flick your wrist to roll the omelet back into the pan uncooked side down. Cook the omelet until it is set on the second side but still creamy—even a little wet—in the center, about 30 seconds longer. Remove it from the pan as noted in the spatula method.

Variations

Herb and cheese omelet: Beat 2 tablespoons of chopped fresh basil, chives, parsley, cilantro, and/or other herbs into the eggs. Coarsely grate ¼ cup (1 ounce) of Gruyère, cheddar, pepper Jack, or other cheese. Sprinkle the cheese over the omelet once you're done stirring the eggs, but before you fold it.

Pepper, ham, and cheese omelet (sometimes called a Western omelet): Dice ½ poblano or bell pepper and 1 ounce of cooked, smoked, or cured ham (about ¼ cup diced). Grate ¼ cup (1 ounce) of cheddar cheese. Melt the butter (or heat the olive oil) in a skillet over high heat, add the pepper and ham, and let brown for about 3 minutes. Add the eggs and cook the omelet as described above. Sprinkle the cheese over the omelet once you're done stirring the eggs, but before you fold it.

Mushroom-shallot omelet: Wipe 3 ounces of mushrooms clean with a damp paper towel and trim the stems. Cut the mushrooms into slices or ½-inch chunks. Mince 1 shallot. Melt 1 tablespoon of butter in a skillet over medium heat. Add the shallot and cook until lightly browned, about 3 minutes. Increase the heat to high, add the mushrooms, and cook until lightly browned and the liquid exuded by the mushrooms is mostly evaporated dry, about 3 minutes. Transfer the mushroom mixture to a plate. Add another tablespoon of butter to the skillet. Cook the omelet as described above. Spoon the mushroom mixture in the center of the omelet once you're done stirring, but before you fold it.

Two Ways to Make an Omelet

SPATULA METHOD

1. Melt the butter in an omelet pan over high heat until sizzling.

2 When the sizzling subsides, add the beaten egg and cook for 15 seconds.

3 Stir the omelet with a fork to mix the cooked and raw parts while simultaneously shaking the pan to keep the omelet from sticking.

4 Use a rubber spatula to loosen the edges of the omelet from the pan, then raise the pan handle to slide the omelet to the far edge.

5 Using the spatula and starting at the far end, fold the omelet into a roll.

6 Tilt the pan to tip the cooked omelet onto a plate.

1 Melt the butter in an omelet pan over high heat until sizzling.

2 When the sizzling subsides, add the beaten egg and cook for 15 seconds.

3 Stir the omelet with a fork to mix the cooked and raw parts while simultaneously shaking the pan to keep the omelet from sticking.

4 Raise the pan handle by the end and gently tap it to slide the omelet to the far edge of the pan.

5 Flick your wrist to invert the omelet.

6 Cook the other side with the pan tilted to give the omelet its trademark oblong shape.

NATHAN MYHRVOLD

He's the creator of a deconstructed, reconstructed thirty-hour hamburger. His barbecued baby back ribs involve a four-step process that includes smoking over hickory, poaching sous-vide, a bath in liquid nitrogen, and a plunge in a deep-fat fryer. He's the ultimate food geek—a man so obsessed with the science of cooking, he installed a machine shop next to his kitchen so he could cut pots, pans, woks, grills, and even whole ovens in half and glue Pyrex glass on the front, the better to observe what *really* happens when you cook foods using traditional methods. The result is the most ambitious cookbook ever written: a stunning five-volume treatise on cooking and food science called *Modernist Cuisine*. When I visited Nathan Myhrvold in his lab on the outskirts of Seattle (formerly a Harley-Davidson repair center) he served me pastrami-spiced short ribs—some of the most extraordinary ribs I've ever tasted in my life.

Inventor, entrepreneur, tech wizard, and amateur paleontologist, Myhrvold found his passion for cooking early. One day when he was nine years old, he announced to his family that he would cook Thanksgiving dinner. He spent weeks poring over cookbooks at the Santa Monica Public Library and, when the holiday arrived, he turned out turkey with all the proverbial trimmings, including baked yams flambéed with pyromaniacal zeal. The food prodigy went on to acquire a PhD in mathematical physics by the age of twenty-three and become chief technology officer for Microsoft, not to mention becoming an amateur paleontologist with a *T. rex* skeleton in his living room. More recently, he founded Intellectual Ventures, a company that holds more than 30,000 patents. (Myhrvold himself holds more than one hundred.) Over the years, Myhrvold trained as a chef in France and competed—and triumphed—at the Memphis in May World Championship Barbecue Cooking Contest. His winning dish? Smoked pasta with Vidalia onion cream sauce.

What's the most recent dish you've cooked?
This morning, I made scrambled eggs from *Modernist Cuisine* for breakfast. The secret is to use three eggs, but discard one of the whites. The extra yolk gives you an incomparably creamy texture. It also helps to cook the eggs at precisely 164°F in a combi oven for exactly twenty minutes. [You'll find Myhrvold's scrambled egg recipe on page 42.]

What's your go-to seduction dish?

I've been married a long time, but if memory serves, it isn't a particular dish that's seductive, but the fact that you—the guy—know how to cook.

Three dishes every guy should know how to make?

Like I told my sons when they went off to college, every man should know how to grill a steak, roast a chicken, and make scrambled eggs. (The eggs in the event you're lucky enough to make her breakfast the next morning.)

> ▶ The key to great pizza is transferring a lot of heat to the crust in a hurry.

Three ingredients you can't live without?

Salt

Salted butter (I like the flavor and cooking properties of a French butter called Plugra.)

Mozzarella di bufala (buffalo milk mozzarella)

Three tools you can't live without?

A digital scale: It's a lot more accurate than cups and tablespoons for measuring.

An instant-read thermometer

A pressure cooker: It's great for making stock—it extracts the flavor from the bones much faster. It's great for cooking seeds to make dishes like pine nut risotto. For that matter, it's great for cooking conventional risotto.

Three more tools you can't live without?

A combi oven: The single most versatile oven ever invented. It enables you to steam at a low temperature, roast at a high heat, and everything in between.

A sous-vide water bath: It allows you to cook foods, housed in airtight plastic bags, with great precision at incredibly low temperatures for a long time. For example, you can cook a steak to a perfect rare temperature of 125°F with no danger of overcooking it.

A BernzOmatic blowtorch: The self-lighting torch that costs fairly little, yet nothing beats it for browning that sous-vide steak.

What are the three most important things to keep in mind if you're just starting out in the kitchen?

Understand how heat moves through food. If you double the thickness of a steak, for example, it takes up to four times as long to cook. So to cook the steak through without burning the exterior, you need to lower the heat. If you're just starting out, it's best to cook relatively thin pieces of meat. Once you've mastered a particular thickness for a cut of meat, stick with it.

When making pizza at home, preheat the oven as hot as it will go and in it preheat a thick metal plate for baking the pizza. The key to great pizza is transferring a lot of heat to the crust in a hurry. Roll out the dough as thinly as possible.

Practice a dish multiple times, keeping all of the variables the same. What a lot of guys forget is that professional chefs cook the same dish over and over, so of course they get it right.

What are the three most common mistakes guys make in the kitchen?

Overcooking pasta: It should have a little chew to it. You don't want it falling apart.

Overcooking fish: The FDA recommends you cook it to 145°F, which is too low to kill any bacteria, but way too high to preserve the pristine flavor and texture. I shoot for 113°F. That's what's so brilliant about sashimi and sushi—you can't overcook them!

Comparing themselves to a chef in a restaurant: He's done it before. A lot. When you cook for company, make something you've prepared before.

Something unexpected you've learned over the years that really helps you up your game in the kitchen?

Always start with a *mise en place*. That's French for setup (see page 7). The French always prep and measure *all* their ingredients and line up the equipment ahead of time, so they can shoot through a recipe without having to stop to rummage for missing supplies.

What's your next project?

We're looking at taking the modernist approach to traditional guy dishes, like buffalo wings, pizza, and chili.

LAOTIAN OMELET

SHOP To be strictly authentic, you'd use bird's-eye chiles (also called Thai chiles), Southeast Asian chiles that are tiny in size but fierce. Look for them at Asian markets, but a commonplace jalapeño or serrano pepper will give you plenty of firepower, too.

GEAR Your basic kitchen gear including a small (6-inch) skillet or omelet pan, preferably nonstick

WHAT ELSE Fish sauce is a malodorous condiment made from fermented anchovies. It's available at Asian markets and well-stocked supermarkets, or substitute soy sauce.

TIME about 10 minutes

Consider this the ultimate morning wake-up: an omelet electrified with chiles, cilantro, and garlic. I first tried it in the French Colonial hill town of Luang Prabang on the Mekong River in northern Laos. (A must-visit destination to add to your places to see before you die list—be sure to book an elephant safari while you're there.) Any breakfast built on garlic and chiles wins in my book—especially when it takes all of ten minutes to prepare. **Serves 1; can be multiplied as desired**

2 bird's-eye chiles, or 1 jalapeño or serrano pepper

1 shallot, peeled, or 1 scallion, trimmed

1 clove garlic

⅓ to ½ bunch coarsely chopped fresh cilantro

2 large eggs

2 tablespoons heavy (whipping) cream, half-and-half, milk, or water

1 teaspoon Asian fish sauce, or soy sauce

Freshly ground black pepper

1½ tablespoons vegetable oil

1 Thinly slice the chiles or pepper, shallot or scallion (white and light green parts), and garlic crosswise. Coarsely chop enough cilantro to measure ¼ cup.

2 Crack the eggs into a small mixing bowl. Add the cream and fish sauce or soy sauce. Season with black pepper to taste, then beat the eggs with a whisk or fork until smooth.

3 Heat the oil in a small skillet over medium-high heat. Add the chiles, shallot, garlic, and cilantro and cook until just beginning to brown, about 2 minutes, stirring with a wooden spoon.

4 Add the beaten eggs and cook, shaking and tilting the skillet to set the eggs on the bottom, about 15 seconds. Using a fork (hold it in one hand almost parallel to the bottom of the pan), stir the omelet to mix the cooked and raw parts while simultaneously continuing to gently shake the skillet to keep the omelet from sticking. Do this for about 15 seconds. Stop stirring the omelet and continue shaking the skillet for about 15 seconds longer.

5 Finish the omelet using a spatula (see page 50) or a pan flip (see page 51): Tilt the skillet handle upward, holding it toward the end, and gently tap it beneath your hand to move the omelet to the far edge of the pan. Now flick your wrist to roll the omelet back into the pan uncooked side down. Cook the omelet until it is set on the second side but still creamy—even a little wet—in the center, about 30 seconds longer. Invert the omelet onto a plate for serving; it should be oblong-shaped.

FRITTATA
WITH SPRING VEGETABLES

Cross an omelet with a quiche and you get a frittata. Like the omelet, it's made with eggs, and like the quiche, it's baked in a pan and served in wedges. A frittata is easy to make and infinitely customizable (you can stuff it with just about anything). You start it on the stovetop, to brown the bottom, then finish it in the oven, which makes the timing a lot more forgiving than that of an omelet. In fact, unlike an omelet, you can make a frittata several hours ahead and reheat it or serve it at room temperature. **Serves 4 to 6**

3 tablespoons extra virgin olive oil or unsalted butter

1 bunch scallions, trimmed and thinly sliced crosswise

3 to 4 cups diced, sliced, or slivered vegetables, such as asparagus, zucchini, spinach leaves, Swiss chard, and/or kale (see Note)

2 to 3 tablespoons thinly slivered fresh herbs, such as basil, dill, tarragon, flat-leaf parsley, rosemary, sage, and/ or other herbs (optional)

8 large eggs

1¼ cups (about 5 ounces) freshly grated Parmigiano Reggiano or pecorino romano cheese

Coarse salt (kosher or sea) and freshly ground black pepper

SHOP Want to make a great frittata even better? Buy the eggs and vegetables at your local farmers' market.

GEAR Your basic kitchen gear including a large (10- to 12-inch) heavy skillet, preferably nonstick, with an ovenproof handle, a bamboo skewer, and a heatproof plate or platter at least 11 inches in diameter

WHAT ELSE Use this recipe as a blueprint. To make Spain's *tortilla española,* use sliced cooked potatoes and onions.

TIME about 20 minutes

1 Preheat the oven to 400°F.

2 Heat 2 tablespoons of olive oil or melt 2 tablespoons of butter in a large skillet over medium heat until sizzling. Add the scallions and cook until fragrant but not brown, 1 to 2 minutes. Increase the heat to high and add the remaining vegetables and the herbs, if using. Cook until the vegetables are limp and their juices have evaporated, 3 to 5 minutes.

3 Meanwhile, crack the eggs into a large mixing bowl and lightly beat them with a whisk or fork. Beat in 1 cup of grated cheese and season with salt and pepper to taste. Stir in the vegetable mixture.

4 Add the remaining 1 tablespoon of olive oil or butter to the skillet and heat over medium-high heat. Add the egg mixture and cook without stirring until the bottom starts to brown, about 2 minutes. (Lift an edge with a spatula to check.)

5 Place the skillet in the oven and cook the frittata until set and the top is lightly browned, 8 to 10 minutes. To test for doneness, insert a bamboo skewer into the center of the frittata; it should come out dry. Remove the skillet from the oven and let the frittata rest for 3 minutes. Run a paring knife around the inside of the skillet to loosen the frittata. Place a heatproof platter over the top of the skillet and invert both so that the frittata falls onto the platter. Or you can serve the frittata right out of the skillet. Either way, sprinkle the frittata with the remaining ¼ cup Parmesan and cut into wedges.

Note: Finely dice, slice, or sliver the vegetables. For example, if using asparagus, break off the fibrous stems and slice the stalks on the diagonal into ¼-inch-thick slices. Rinse and dry zucchini and cut it into ¼-inch dice. If you are using spinach, Swiss chard, or kale, rinse it and shake it dry. Remove and discard the stems or ribs, roll the leaves into a tight cylinder, and cut them crosswise into ¼-inch slivers.

EGGS FRA DIAVOLO
(POACHED IN SPICY MARINARA SAUCE)

SHOP Look for farm eggs when you can get them and imported canned San Marzano tomatoes for the sauce.

For most guys, eggs poached in marinara sauce do not a breakfast of champions make. For Italian American actor Stanley Tucci (read more about him on page 294), it's just another day at the stove. "What, you've never tasted eggs poached in marinara sauce?!" exclaimed the star of two major foodie movies: *Big Night*, which Tucci also directed and cowrote, and *Julie & Julia* (in which he played Julia Child's husband, Paul). Ruefully, I confessed I hadn't. "You can eat them for breakfast, lunch, or dinner," Stanley said. "My father used to make them when we were growing up: It's one of the great dishes of all time." Having prepared it several times since our interview, I can assure you that poaching eggs in marinara sauce is also one of the coolest cooking techniques of all time. **Serves 4**

2 tablespoons extra virgin olive oil

4 thin slices prosciutto

1 medium-size onion, finely chopped

1 rib celery, finely chopped

1 clove garlic, minced

2 sprigs fresh oregano, or 1 teaspoon dried oregano

½ teaspoon hot red pepper flakes

1 tablespoon tomato paste

1 can (28 ounces) peeled whole tomatoes with their juices, preferably San Marzano

8 fresh basil leaves, slivered

1 teaspoon sugar (optional)

Coarse salt (kosher or sea) and freshly ground black pepper

8 large eggs

1 chunk (2 ounces) pecorino romano or Parmigiano Reggiano cheese (optional), for grating

Garlic Bread (page 513) or French bread, for serving

GEAR Your basic kitchen gear including a large (10- to 12-inch) skillet, preferably not cast iron

WHAT ELSE Stanley likes to serve the eggs with prosciutto "bacon." But Eggs Fra Diavolo make a great vegetarian dish—just skip the first step. Instead, heat 2 tablespoons of extra virgin olive oil in a skillet over medium heat and proceed with Step 2.

TIME about 30 minutes

1 To make the prosciutto "bacon," heat the olive oil in a large skillet over medium heat. Dip an edge of a slice of the prosciutto in the oil; when the oil is hot enough, bubbles will dance around the prosciutto. Working in several batches as needed so you don't crowd the pan, cook the prosciutto until crisp, about 1 minute per side. Using tongs, lift each slice of prosciutto out of the skillet, letting the excess oil drip back into the skillet. Transfer the prosciutto to a paper towel-lined plate to drain.

2 Add the onion, celery, garlic, oregano, and hot pepper flakes to the skillet. Cook over medium heat until caramelized to a deep golden brown, 5 to 8 minutes. Reduce the heat as needed to keep the onions from burning.

Add the tomato paste and cook until fragrant, about 1 minute.

3 Coarsely chop the tomatoes. (You can do this right in the can, scissoring them with two knife blades.) Stir the tomatoes with their juices into the skillet. Add half of the slivered basil, then the sugar. Let the marinara sauce simmer gently over medium-low heat, about 10 to 15 minutes, stirring often. Taste for seasoning, adding salt and pepper as necessary; the sauce should be richly flavored.

4 Just before serving, let the marinara sauce come to a brisk simmer over medium-high heat. Crack 2 eggs, one at time, into small bowls, taking care not to break the yolks. Carefully pour the eggs into the sauce and poach until cooked, 2 to 3 minutes, spooning the sauce over them so the tops cook, too. Don't overcook the eggs; the yolks should remain runny. Using a slotted spoon, transfer the cooked eggs to a large shallow bowl. Repeat with the remaining eggs.

5 Return the poached eggs to the skillet with the sauce. Grate the cheese, if using, over the top. Crumble the prosciutto "bacon" on top. Sprinkle the remaining slivered basil over the eggs and serve them right out of the pan with a large spoon and with crusty bread for dipping.

BREAKFAST NACHOS

SHOP You know the drill: organic or farm eggs, sharp cheddar or Jack cheese, local veggies, and so on.

GEAR Your basic kitchen gear including a large (10- to 12-inch) skillet and a 9-by-13-inch baking pan (or another skillet)

WHAT ELSE The beauty of these breakfast nachos is that you can dress them up or down as much as you like. Add chili con carne for omnivores, roasted vegetables and beans for the meatless crowd.

TIME about 15 minutes

What makes a righteous brunch dish? It should be colorful enough to attract attention, flavorful enough for people to want seconds, customizable to suit varied tastes, and easy to make and to multiply when extra people drop by. Which brings us to these breakfast nachos, which you could think of as scrambled eggs and tortilla chips on steroids. A tip of the hat to my assistant, Nancy Loseke, who made breakfast nachos one morning during one of our test sessions. Now *that* got us going. **Serves 4; can be multiplied as desired**

For the nachos
3 cups tortilla chips

1½ cups (6 ounces) freshly grated cheddar cheese, Jack cheese, or pepper Jack cheese

2 tablespoons extra virgin olive oil

1 bunch scallions, trimmed and thinly sliced (keep white and green parts separate)

1 to 2 jalapeño peppers, thinly sliced crosswise (for milder nachos, remove the seeds)

¼ cup chopped fresh cilantro (optional)

6 large eggs

3 tablespoons heavy (whipping) cream, half-and-half, or milk

Coarse salt (kosher or sea) and freshly ground black pepper

1 cup beef chili (page 146), refried beans, or canned pinto beans or black beans, rinsed and drained

For serving
Sour cream

1 cup Pico de Gallo (page 210) or other favorite salsa, for serving

1 Preheat the oven to 400°F.

2 Arrange the tortilla chips in a single layer in the baking pan. Sprinkle ¾ cup of the cheese evenly over the chips.

3 Heat the olive oil in a large skillet over medium heat. Add the scallion whites, jalapeño(s), and cilantro, if using, to the skillet and cook until just beginning to brown, about 3 minutes.

4 Meanwhile, crack the eggs into a mixing bowl, add the cream, and beat to mix. Season with salt and pepper to taste. Add the eggs to the skillet and cook, whisking continually, until done to taste (I like mine soft), 1 to 2 minutes. Spoon the eggs evenly on top of the tortilla chips.

5 Spoon the chili or beans over the scrambled eggs. Sprinkle the remaining ¾ cup of cheese on top, followed by the scallion greens.

6 Bake the nachos in the oven until the cheese is melted and bubbling, 5 to 8 minutes. Serve the nachos with sour cream and Pico de Gallo on the side.

Variations

Before baking the nachos, top them with any of the following: *Rajas* (strips of roasted peeled poblano pepper, see page 200), slices of pickled jalapeño, thinly sliced black olives, diced sweet onion, and/or thinly sliced sautéed chorizo.

MADE-FROM-SCRATCH MULTIGRAIN PANCAKES

At some point you will find a little girl or boy at your breakfast table—your child or your girlfriend's, a niece, nephew, or grandchild. He or she will look at you expectantly with one desire: pancakes. If you're smart, you'll make the batter by hand, whisking theatrically. You'll spoon it with ceremony into a hot skillet, where pancakes will form in a puff of steam with a hiss of melted butter. They'll rise by some mystical alchemy that doesn't need to be understood to be appreciated.

If you get it right, the pancakes will be crisp at the edge, soft in the center, and as redolent of grain as freshly baked bread. **Makes 16 to 20 silver dollar pancakes, enough to serve 2 hungry guys or 4 people if a couple are kids**

For the pancake batter
¾ cup unbleached all-purpose white flour

2 tablespoons whole wheat flour or rye flour

2 tablespoons finely ground cornmeal or more whole wheat or rye flour

1 tablespoon sugar

1 teaspoon baking powder

½ teaspoon fine sea salt

1 cup buttermilk or whole or skim milk

1 large egg, lightly beaten with a fork

1 tablespoon extra virgin olive oil, vegetable oil, or melted butter

½ teaspoon pure vanilla extract

For the add-ins
(optional; add one or more)
2 tablespoons malted milk powder

1 cup fresh or frozen blueberries

1 ripe peach or banana, cut into ½-inch dice

½ cup coarsely chopped pecans or walnuts

1 teaspoon freshly grated lemon zest

¼ cup ricotta cheese

For cooking the pancakes
About 1 tablespoon extra virgin olive oil or canola oil or more butter

About 1 tablespoon butter

For serving the pancakes
Butter

Pure maple syrup

1 Make the pancake batter: Place the white and whole wheat or rye flour, cornmeal, if using, sugar, baking powder, and salt in a large mixing bowl and whisk to mix. Make a depression in the center of the flour mixture and add the buttermilk, egg, the 1 tablespoon oil or melted butter, and the vanilla extract. Whisk the ingredients into a smooth batter, working from the center outward. Whisk as little as possible—overwhisking will make the pancakes tough.

2 Whisk in any of the optional add-ins.

3 Make the pancakes: Melt ½ tablespoon butter in ½ tablespoon oil in a large skillet over medium heat. To test the temperature, add a few drops of pancake batter; when the skillet is hot enough, bubbles will dance around the drops of batter. Using a large soupspoon or small ladle, spoon in enough batter (about 2 tablespoons) to make silver dollar–size pancakes (about 2¼ inches across)—you should be able to fit 7 or 8 in the skillet at one time. Why such small pancakes? More buttery crust to each pancake. Try it and you'll never make big ones again.

4 Cook the pancakes until bubbles form on the tops and the bottoms are browned, 1 to 2 minutes. Carefully turn the pancakes (a fork works better for this size than a spatula) and cook until the second sides are browned, 1 to 2 minutes.

5 Add more butter and oil to the pan as needed and continue cooking pancakes until you have used all of the batter. Serve with maple syrup and more butter if desired. No, you won't get to sit down and eat with everyone else. You're not supposed to. The bonds you form with kids over pancakes are reward enough.

Variation
Waffles

Preheat a waffle iron. Melt 1 tablespoon of butter in 1 tablespoon of olive or canola oil in a small saucepan. Lightly brush the inside surfaces of the waffle iron with some of the butter mixture. Add about ¼ cup of batter to the center of the waffle iron (the amount varies with the size of your waffle iron), close the lid, and cook the waffle until it is puffed and browned. Don't try to open the waffle iron during the first 1 minute of cooking or the waffle will stick. As it cooks, the waffle will come loose. Pry loose with a fork and serve. Repeat with the remaining batter. The first waffle may stick a little but after cooking the first few waffles you probably won't need to grease the waffle iron again. Serve the waffles one by one as they emerge from the iron. Note: Any leftover waffles can be reheated in your toaster. As with the pancakes, this will serve 2 to 4.

MILE-HIGH PANCAKE

No, it's not from Denver—maybe from Holland or Germany. You can call it a pancake on steroids. It's cut from the same cloth as popovers and Yorkshire pudding, and it puffs up like a soufflé. In short, it's one of those infallible dishes that requires virtually no skill but makes you look like the genius you are—especially when you pull this towering golden, crusty, buttery pancake steaming hot out of the oven. Did I mention the mere five minutes of preparation time? Or the taste—transitioning from the toasty crunch of a popover to the custardy softness of an omelet in a single bite? It's that good. **Serves 1 or 2**

2 large eggs

½ cup milk

½ cup unbleached all-purpose white flour

½ teaspoon sugar

¼ teaspoon fine sea salt

2 tablespoons (¼ stick) butter

Cinnamon sugar (see Note) or confectioners' sugar, for serving

1 Preheat the oven to 450°F.

2 Crack the eggs into a mixing bowl and whisk to mix. Whisk in the milk, followed by the flour, sugar, and salt. Set the pancake batter aside.

3 Place the butter in a large ovenproof skillet and place in the oven. When the butter is melted and sizzling, 3 to 5 minutes, using a potholder, remove the skillet from the oven and tilt it to coat the bottom with butter. Add the pancake batter and immediately return the skillet to the oven.

4 Bake the pancake until it's dramatically puffed and golden brown, 20 to 25 minutes. Don't open the oven door for the first 15 minutes while the pancake bakes. If your oven has a light and a glass window in the door, you can check it without allowing heat to escape.

5 Serve the pancake at once sprinkled with cinnamon sugar or confectioners' sugar. If you are using confectioners' sugar, shake it onto the pancake through a strainer.

Note: To make cinnamon sugar, mix 1 cup granulated sugar with 4 teaspoons ground cinnamon. Store in a plastic canister or jar with a lid and use as called for.

SHOP Nothing special here, but when possible, use organic flour and dairy products.

GEAR Your basic kitchen gear including a large (10- to 12-inch) cast-iron or other ovenproof skillet.

WHAT ELSE Like many great dishes, this one is infinitely customizable: Sprinkle the pancake with confectioners' sugar or cinnamon sugar for breakfast. Drizzle maple syrup over it and add some walnuts. Or, top it with grated cheddar cheese and jalapeño peppers and serve it for brunch or lunch.

TIME about 25 minutes

BRIOCHE FRENCH TOAST

Pain perdu. Torrejas. French toast. Whatever you call it, bread slices soaked in an egg and milk batter, then panfried are one of the world's classic breakfasts. And there are at least three reasons you should know how to make it. French toast is quick enough to cook for yourself on a workday but impressive enough to wow overnight company when you make it the next morning. And, it's infinitely customizable, meaning you can make a dozen different breakfasts by varying the bread or flavoring or by stuffing it with fillings ranging from Nutella to sliced bananas (the Variations below have some suggestions). **Serves 2; can be multiplied as desired**

SHOP I like to make French toast with brioche—appropriately, a French loaf enriched with butter and eggs. (Buy it at a bakery or in the bakery section of your supermarket. Many, like Whole Foods, carry it.) Challah (Jewish egg bread) makes good French toast, too, as does a sturdy loaf of country-style white bread. The key is to buy a whole loaf, so you can cut thick slices.

GEAR Your basic kitchen gear including a baking pan and a large (10- to 12-inch) heavy skillet

WHAT ELSE For a really cool variation, make French toast waffles. Heat a waffle iron and brush both sides with melted butter. Add the slices of French toast and cook them until browned and crisp.

TIME 10 minutes

4 slices brioche (each about 1 inch thick)

1 large egg

1 cup milk

1 teaspoon pure vanilla extract and/or Grand Marnier

1 tablespoon each unsalted butter and olive or canola oil, or 2 tablespoons butter

Maple syrup or cinnamon sugar (see Note, page 63), for serving

1 Place the slices of brioche in a baking pan just large enough to hold them in one layer.

2 Combine the egg, milk, and vanilla in a mixing bowl and whisk or beat with a fork until smooth. Pour the egg mixture over the brioche and let it soak for 5 minutes, gently turning the slices with a spatula so the egg mixture is completely absorbed.

3 Melt the butter in the oil in a large skillet over medium-high heat until sizzling. Add the soaked brioche slices and panfry until browned on the bottom, 2 to 4 minutes. Using a spatula, turn the slices of brioche over and cook until the second side is browned and the French toast is cooked through, 2 to 4 minutes longer. Serve with maple syrup or cinnamon sugar.

Variations

Stuffed French toast: Using a paring knife, cut a deep pocket in the side of each slice of bread. Insert thinly sliced bananas, guava paste and cream cheese, spoonfuls of Nutella, or dulce de leche—you get the idea. Soak and panfry the slices of bread as described in the Brioche French Toast recipe.

Crusted French toast: Dip the soaked bread in a shallow bowl filled with slivered almonds, crushed cornflakes, or Rice Krispies. Panfry as described in the French toast recipe.

Monte Cristo deconstructed: French toast, fried eggs, ham, and cheese? The combination is called a Monte Cristo, and it sounds like the right amount of excess to me. Traditionally these ingredients are battered and deep-fried. My deconstructed version eliminates the deep-frying.

Make the French toast as described above. Add a little more butter or oil to the skillet in which you cooked the French toast and panfry until browned on both sides as many thin slices of smoked ham as you have slices of French toast. Place 1 slice of ham on top of each slice of French toast. Top the ham with thinly sliced cheddar, Jack, or Swiss cheese. Add a little more butter or oil to the skillet and fry as many eggs as you have slices of French toast. Slide the fried eggs on top of the French toast slices; the hot eggs will melt the cheese. That should hold you until lunch.

BLOWTORCH OATMEAL

You probably didn't buy this book to learn how to cook something as elemental as oatmeal. But even commonplace breakfast cereal is capable of gustatory greatness. The secret is to start with premium oats and borrow a tool from your workshop. Just before serving, you lightly sprinkle the oatmeal with sugar and burn it into a hard candy shell with a blowtorch. What results is the breakfast equivalent of crème brûlée. **Makes 4 cups (4 breakfasts' worth)**

1 cup steel-cut oats

¼ teaspoon fine sea salt

4 cups water

4 tablespoons granulated sugar or cinnamon sugar (see Note, page 63), for serving

Overnight oatmeal method: Place the oats, salt, and water in a large heavy saucepan and bring to a boil over medium-high heat, about 5 minutes, stirring occasionally. Once the mixture boils, remove the oatmeal from the heat and let it cool to room temperature uncovered (so as not to get condensation), then cover and refrigerate it overnight. If you plan to eat the oatmeal over several days, you may want to store it in a covered glass or plastic container with a lid. The next morning, place the quantity of oatmeal you want to serve in a saucepan. If it has thickened too much, add a little more water; you don't want it to stick to the bottom of the pan. Bring the oatmeal to a slow boil over medium heat.

Same-day oatmeal method: Place the oatmeal, salt, and water in a large saucepan and bring to a boil over high heat, stirring occasionally. Reduce the heat so the oatmeal simmers and cook until tender, 20 to 30 minutes, stirring occasionally. If you're not sharing it, transfer any extra to a glass or plastic container with a lid and refrigerate for another day.

To brûlée the oatmeal: Transfer the hot oatmeal to heatproof serving bowls, smoothing the top with the back of a spoon. Wait 2 minutes, then sprinkle the top of each serving of oatmeal with granulated sugar or cinnamon sugar (1 tablespoon per serving should do it. Light a blowtorch and aim the flame at the sugar to caramelize it; the sugar will bubble and brown, about 30 seconds. Let the oatmeal cool until the sugar hardens, about 1 minute, then dig in. (Before you take blowtorch to oatmeal, turn to page 566 for tips on the safe way to ignite food.)

SHOP No offense to Quaker, but the world's best oatmeal comes from Ireland—specifically from the more-than-two-century-old firm of John McCann's, which is recognizable by its signature white can. No flat, floury, mealy rolled oats these, but steel-cut grains you can sink your teeth into. (Steel-cut means less processing.) Yes, they require more cooking than a few seconds in the microwave, but the rich earthy grainy flavor is worth the effort, and I'll teach you a trick for speeding up the cooking.

GEAR Your basic kitchen gear including a large saucepan plus a kitchen or workshop blowtorch (see page 22)

WHAT ELSE This recipe was inspired by my physician, Alberto Mitrani, for whom steel-cut oatmeal is nothing short of a miracle drug. Steel-cut oats are loaded with fiber: soluble fiber, which helps lower cholesterol and blood sugar, and nonsoluble fiber, which keeps you feeling full and promotes weight loss. I precook the oatmeal in large batches so I always have some on hand.

TIME about 8 minutes cooking time using the overnight method; 20 to 30 minutes using the same-day method

GAME PLAN HASH

SHOP You don't need to, as the best hash is made with leftovers.

GEAR Your basic kitchen gear including a large (10- to 12-inch) heavy skillet

WHAT ELSE Some guys like their hash in large chunks, so you can taste the individual ingredients. Others prefer small dice, so the flavors merge into a whole. Tradition calls for hash to be topped with poached eggs, but I've always found fried eggs to have a better texture and flavor.

TIME 20 to 25 minutes

Leftovers resurrected. That's what hash (from the French word *hacher,* "to chop") is. And like a great many guy dishes, you can vary it to suit your taste or the ingredients you have on hand. Start with corned beef or pastrami or leftover steak. Sauté onions, shallots, or leeks. Add a little hot sauce or the whole volcano, and you've got comfort food for breakfast (or any time of day) you can call your own. So consider the following a game plan, not a recipe to be followed to the tablespoon. **Serves 2; can be multiplied as desired**

For the hash

2 tablespoons butter, extra virgin olive oil, or bacon fat, or more as needed

¾ cup aromatics, such as finely chopped onion, shallots, leek, scallions, celery, bell pepper, and/or jalapeño peppers

2 cups coarsely or finely diced leftover cooked steak, roast beef, corned beef, brisket, pastrami, pulled pork, venison, chicken, or turkey, or for a meatless hash, tofu or sautéed mushrooms

2 cups coarsely or finely diced cooked root vegetables, such as potatoes, sweet potatoes, yams, and/or cooked beets (the beets make a New England classic: red flannel hash)

¾ cup chicken or beef stock or water

2 tablespoons chopped fresh herbs (optional)

For the flavorings, any or all of the following

2 teaspoons Worcestershire sauce, or more to taste

2 teaspoons steak sauce, or more to taste

½ to 1 teaspoon hot sauce, or more to taste

Coarse salt (kosher or sea) and freshly ground black pepper

1 Heat 1 tablespoon of butter, oil, or bacon fat in a large skillet over medium heat until melted. Add the aromatics (see above list) and cook until browned, about 3 minutes, stirring with a wooden spoon.

2 Increase the heat to medium-high and add the remaining 1 tablespoon of butter, oil, or fat. Add the meat and the root vegetables (potatoes and/or beets) and cook until browned, 3 to 5 minutes.

3 Stir in the stock, 1 tablespoon of the herbs, if using, and the Worcestershire sauce, steak sauce, and/or hot sauce. Let the hash simmer briskly until some or all of the liquid is absorbed and the flavors have melded, 5 to 10 minutes. Reduce the heat as needed so the hash doesn't burn. Taste for seasoning, adding additional Worcestershire sauce, steak sauce, and/or hot sauce as necessary and salt and pepper to taste.

Some people like their hash soft, in which case, serve it before all the liquid has evaporated. Others (me included) like their hash crisp and brown, in which case, let all of the stock evaporate. Then, add a little more butter, oil, or fat and cook the hash until crusty, about 3 minutes longer.

4 Spoon the hash onto plates, sprinkling it with the remaining 1 tablespoon of herbs.

Variation

To serve the hash with eggs, wipe the skillet clean (or use a second skillet), add 1 more tablespoon of butter, oil, or bacon fat, and heat it over medium-high heat until almost smoking. Fry 2 eggs over medium-high heat until cooked to taste, 2 to 3 minutes. Then slide 1 egg on top of each serving of hash.

BACON THREE WAYS

In the beginning, there was bacon. In the middle and end, too. From breakfast bacon and eggs to a BLT for lunch to a bacon sundae for a dinner dessert (see page 553), bacon is the primordial guy food. Properly prepared, it will be crisp but not burnt, with a little chewy softness at the center. Ignore knowing how to cook bacon at your peril. **Serves 2 or 3; can be multiplied as desired**

½ pound thick-sliced artisanal bacon

You may be surprised to learn that most of the bacon sold at the supermarket has never seen the inside of a smokehouse. On the contrary, it's "smoke flavored" or smoke-injected—in other words, not for you. You want thick-sliced artisanal bacon, the kind you imagine your grandmother frying for breakfast (especially if she was Pennsylvania Dutch). One good nationally available brand is Nueske's from Wisconsin, which is cured the old-fashioned way and smoked over smoldering cherrywood.

GEAR Your basic kitchen gear including a large (10- to 12-inch) heavy skillet or a baking sheet and a wire rack, and a plate lined with paper towels. A mesh spatter shield to cover the skillet is optional.

WHAT ELSE There are two basic ways to cook bacon: in a skillet on the stove or on a baking sheet in the oven. The first requires a little more attention and the cooking may have to be done in batches; the latter is effortless, but takes a little longer. You can also cook bacon in a microwave oven. You'll find instructions for all three ways on this page.

TIME about 8 minutes per batch if you are frying the bacon; 15 minutes if you are baking it; 6 minutes in the microwave

Skillet method: Place as many of the slices of bacon as will fit in a single layer in a large heavy skillet. Top the skillet with a splatter guard, if using, and heat over medium heat. Fry the bacon until it is browned on the bottom, 3 to 5 minutes, then turn the slices and fry until browned on the second side, 3 to 4 minutes. Reduce the heat as needed; you don't want the bacon to burn. So why do you start the bacon in a cold skillet? It crisps better and is less likely to curl and burn.

Transfer the bacon to a plate lined with paper towels to drain for about 30 seconds (or drain it on a clean paper bag), and repeat the process with any remaining bacon, if frying in batches. Serve the bacon hot and crisp. Save the fat for cooking corn bread (page 514) and/or meatballs (page 463).

Baking sheet method: Preheat the oven to 375°F. To facilitate cleanup, line a baking sheet with parchment paper or aluminum foil. Place a wire rack on the baking sheet. Arrange the slices of bacon in a single layer on top of the rack. Bake the bacon until sizzling and browned, about 15 minutes to 20 minutes.

Microwave method: Place 4 to 6 slices of bacon in a single layer on a microwave-safe plate; make sure the slices don't overlap. Cover the bacon with a microwave-safe paper towel. Microwave the bacon on high power for about 3 minutes, then rotate the plate and microwave the bacon until it is cooked to your liking, about 3 minutes longer. (If your microwave has a built-in turntable, there is no need to rotate the plate.) Carefully remove the very hot plate from the microwave and transfer the bacon strips to a plate lined with paper towels to drain. Continue with the next batch of bacon until all the strips are cooked.

SANDWICHES, QUESADILLAS, BURGERS, AND HOT DOGS

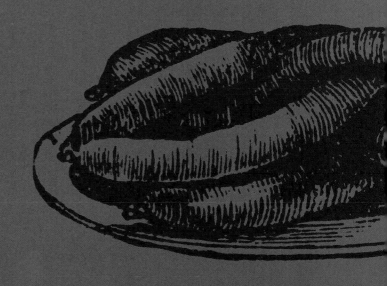

Of all the sandwiches named for people—the Reuben and the Dagwood to mention two—none has the name recognition of the sandwich itself. Did the concept of eating a slab of meat between two slices of bread really originate with the English nobleman John Montagu so he could spend more time at the card table? Or did the Fourth Earl of Sandwich, his official title, simply have a good spin doctor who celebrated Montagu's gambling-friendly convenience food in an eighteenth-century London guidebook? Either way, the sandwich has become one of the world's great guy foods, and any man in culinary good standing should know how to make a dozen or so from around the world.

The A-list includes the BLT (here, enhanced with arugula and avocado) and the *Chivito* (a jaw-stretching South American steak sandwich loaded with bacon, egg, cheese, and tomato). Along the way, you'll master such classics as the Maine lobster roll; a New Orleans muffuletta piled high with Italian soppressata, smoked ham, and provolone; and a Latin-inflected double pork *medianoche* from, unexpectedly, Montreal. Grilled cheese? I give you a basic recipe with five gooey variations to choose from. Egg salad? My version ups the ante with caramelized onion and curry. Tuna salad sandwich?

This one speaks French. Mexican quesadillas? The main recipe has five variations—I've got you covered.

Which brings us to burgers, brats, and hot dogs. For some guys, these define the American male diet. So if you're a newcomer to the culinary arts, you may want to read this part of the chapter carefully from beginning to end. The challenge? How to keep burgers luscious and moist while cooking them to a food-safe temperature. The solution? You'll find it in the Inside-Out Cheeseburger and the Swedish Meatball Sliders. Are there any Packers fans out there? Learn how an iconoclastic Yankee cooks bratwurst. And old dogs learn new tricks with my "Dear" Dog and "Hot" Dog twists on the commonplace frankfurter.

Sir John, wherever you are, thanks for the inspiration.

Your Basic
GRILLED CHEESE SANDWICH

Crusty melty guy food you can whip up in minutes? Or a soggy kitchen cliché? When it comes to making a world-class grilled cheese sandwich, the raw materials matter as much as the technique. Here are your basic marching orders: Customize to suit your taste. (That includes doubling or tripling the ingredients to make as many sandwiches as you crave.) **Makes 1 sandwich; can be multiplied as desired**

For the sandwich
2 slices bread, such as white, whole wheat, multigrain, rye, sourdough, brioche, or raisin bread

1 tablespoon butter, melted, or 1 tablespoon extra virgin olive oil

1 to 2 teaspoons mustard, such as Dijon, Meaux, English, German, honey mustard, or pepper mustard

2 ounces your choice of thinly sliced or coarsely grated cheese, such as cheddar, Gruyère, Emmentaler, or Comté, Jack, muenster, taleggio, mozzarella, Gouda, Edam, or Jarlsberg

For the add-ins (optional)
1 to 2 tablespoons condiment, such as chutney, pesto, piccalilli, Olive Relish (page 91), or prepared horseradish

Sliced tomato, pickle, avocado, roasted pepper, and/or sauerkraut

Crisply cooked bacon (page 67), Canadian bacon, cured ham, cooked ham, smoked ham, or prosciutto

Mushroom Hash (page 476) or grilled or pickled mushrooms

SHOP Like all simple dishes, a grilled cheese sandwich soars or sinks depending on the quality of the ingredients: Choose bakery bread, pedigreed cheese, and craft condiments.

GEAR Your basic kitchen gear including a large (10- to 12-inch) cast-iron or nonstick skillet plus a grill press (optional)

WHAT ELSE You have at least two options for cooking your grilled cheese sandwich: in a skillet (or on a griddle) or on a contact grill (or panini machine). For an extra crusty texture, cook the sandwich under a grill press (if not using a contact grill).

TIME about 10 minutes

GRILLED CHEESE

THE CHEESE | If your idea of cheese comes in plastic-wrapped single slices, it's time for an upgrade. The cheese in your sandwich should equal the quality of what you crave on a cheese tray. If you're in a hurry, put slices of cheese on the bread, but the cheese will melt more evenly if you grate it first. (This also makes it easier to use a blend of cheeses.) Grate the cheese on the coarse side of a box grater or use the large-holed shredding disk of a food processor.

THE FAT | A proper grilled cheese sandwich offers a contrast of textures, the buttery crisp crust giving way to a gooey cheesy center. You can't achieve that without greasing the skillet with butter and/or extra virgin olive oil. Mixing the butter with olive oil allows you to heat the butter to a higher temperature without burning it. To help both sides of the sandwich cook evenly, use a pastry brush to dab some of the melted butter or olive oil on the outside of the bread before putting the sandwich in the skillet.

THE PAN | There are several good options here. Despite the name, most grilled cheese sandwiches are made in a skillet or on a griddle. Cast iron works great because it spreads the heat evenly. Nonstick pans have the advantage of being, well, nonstick.

Because they cook simultaneously from the top and bottom, contact grills (think George Foreman) and panini machines also work well for making grilled cheese sandwiches. Yes, you can even use a barbecue grill; just oil the grate generously, work over medium heat, and don't allow anything to distract you.

THE HEAT | Many a grilled cheese sandwich has been wrecked by starting with a skillet that is too hot. Start cooking over medium heat and then lower the temperature as needed to prevent the bread from burning before the cheese melts. (Use a spatula to turn the sandwich over to brown both sides.) A great grilled cheese sandwich requires patience, which many of us guys have in short supply.

THE PRESS | Another way to obtain a properly crisp crust is to cook the grilled cheese sandwich under a weight. One good tool is a grill press, available at cookware shops.

ONE PARTING WORD OF ADVICE | Sometimes less is more. Sometimes more is more. You can make a killer grilled cheese sandwich with just: great bread, great cheese, and butter. You can take the same sandwich over the top with a wide range of condiments and garnishes. I've included several ideas to get you started (see page 73).

1 Place the slices of bread on a work surface. Brush the tops using half the melted butter or olive oil, if you are cooking the sandwich in a skillet, or use the full 1 tablespoon if you are cooking the sandwich in a contact grill. Turn the bread slices over and spread each slice with the mustard and any other condiment you desire.

2 Neatly and evenly arrange the sliced or grated cheese on top of the condiments on one of the slices of bread. Place any add-ins on top of the cheese. Place the second slice of bread, mustard side down, on top.

3 *If you are cooking the sandwich in a skillet:* Heat the remaining butter or oil in a cast-iron or nonstick skillet over medium heat. When the butter sizzles or the oil shimmers, add the cheese sandwich. (If you are cooking multiple sandwiches, leave at least 1 inch between them.) Cook the sandwich until the bottom is golden brown, 2 to 3 minutes. (Lift one corner of the sandwich with a spatula to check for doneness.) Using a spatula and taking care not to lose the filling, turn the sandwich over and cook the second side until golden brown, 2 to 3 minutes. Ideally, the cheese will be completely melted by the time the second side is browned. If the bread browns too quickly, reduce the heat. When the bread is browned and crisp and the cheese is melted, serve the sandwich at once.

If you are cooking the sandwich on a contact grill: Preheat the grill. When the grill is hot, place the sandwich in it and cook the sandwich until the bread is browned and crisp and the cheese is melted, 4 to 6 minutes. Serve the sandwich at once.

FIVE VARIATIONS ON A THEME OF GRILLED CHEESE

The directions that follow are for cooking the sandwiches in a skillet. If you make yours in a contact grill, brush the full amount of butter or olive oil on the outside of each sandwich. You won't need to save any for the grill surface. **All make 1 sandwich and can be multiplied as desired.**

PIMENTO CHEESE AND BACON

THE SOUTHERNER

White bread? Bacon? Pimento cheese? It's a grilled cheese sandwich channeled by the Deep South.

1 tablespoon butter, at room temperature

2 slices white sandwich bread

2 ounces (¼ cup) pimento cheese, at room temperature

2 slices bacon, cut in half crosswise and cooked crisp (page 67)

Spread butter on one side of each slice of bread, setting aside ½ tablespoon (1½ teaspoons) for the skillet. Turn the slices of bread over and spread the pimento cheese on the second side of each. Place the bacon on top of one of the cheese-covered slices. Place the second slice of bread, cheese side down, on top. Cook the sandwich as described in Step 3 of the basic recipe on page 73.

CHEDDAR AND BRATWURST

THE WISCONSINITE

For all you Cheeseheads out there, here's a sandwich made with Wisconsin cheddar and bratwurst. For a Polish twist, use kielbasa instead of bratwurst. A semmel roll has a thin, hard crust and soft crumb—if you live in Wisconsin, you will know where to find it; if not, use a kaiser roll.

1 tablespoon butter, at room temperature

1 to 2 teaspoons German-style mustard

1 kaiser or semmel roll, cut in half through the side, or 2 slices white sandwich bread

2 slices (2 ounces; cut ⅛ inch thick) Wisconsin cheddar cheese

1 smoked or cooked bratwurst (optional, see page 116), thinly sliced on the diagonal

Sweet pickle slices or sauerkraut

Spread ½ tablespoon (1½ teaspoons) of the butter on the outside of the roll, setting aside the remaining butter for the skillet. Spread the mustard on the inside of the roll. Add the cheddar, bratwurst, and pickle slices or sauerkraut. Cook the sandwich as described in Step 3 of the basic recipe on page 73. Note: If you use a roll, you may want to cook it under a sandwich press (or in a panini machine). Lower the heat as needed to melt the cheese without burning the bread.

MOZZARELLA, TOMATO, AND BASIL

THE CAPRESE

Think of this as Italy's famous salad in sandwich form. Focaccia and ciabatta are soft, puffy Italian breads—available now in the bakery sections of most natural foods supermarkets. The cheese should come packed in water or be wet with moisture. Avoid rubbery industrial mozzarella sold in vacuum-sealed plastic.

1 square (4 by 4 inches) focaccia or ciabatta, or 2 slices Italian bread

1 tablespoon extra virgin olive oil

4 fresh basil leaves, or 1 tablespoon store-bought pesto

2 ounces thinly sliced fresh mozzarella (if possible, the kind sold in water and still dripping with moisture)

3 thin slices luscious red ripe tomato

THE SEVEN TYPES OF
CHEESE

Cheese is made around the world and there are literally thousands to choose from.

FRESH CHEESES | All cheese starts by separating the curds (the milk solids) from the whey (the watery part). Fresh cheeses are soft, creamy, minimally processed fresh curds. The short list includes American cottage cheese and cream cheese, Indian *paneer*, and Italian ricotta, mozzarella, and mascarpone.

SOFT-RIPENED CHEESES | Made by spraying disks or cylinders of pressed curds with mold so they ripen from the outside in. The classics include French Brie, Camembert, and L'Explorateur.

WASHED RIND CHEESES | Aka "stinkers," this refers to a family of pungent cheeses that are washed repeatedly with beer, brine, salt water, brandy, cider, or other flavorful liquids during the aging process, which give them a moist rind, nose-blasting aroma, and toe-curlingly strong taste. These include French Epoisses and Reblochon, Belgian Chimay, and Red Hawk from California's Cowgirl Creamery. They also include brined cheeses, like Greek/Middle Eastern feta.

SEMIFIRM CHEESES | The largest category by far, these cheeses start with curds pressed into rectilinear or round forms, with firm waxy rinds and an incredible range of flavors—from mild to sharp, nutty to pungent, and everything in between. They include Alpine cheeses, like Emmentaler and Gruyère; English cheeses, like Cheshire and Cheddar; and Dutch cheeses, like Edam and Gouda.

HARD CHEESES | Made from cooked curds that are pressed under weights and aged for months or years to give them a firm consistency, hard cheeses are ideal for grating. Exemplars include Italian Parmigiano Reggiano and pecorino romano, Dutch aged Gouda, and American dry Jack.

BLUE CHEESES | These cheeses owe their blue/green veining to mold injected deep inside the cheese. This gives them a strong and unique salty tang. They include French Roquefort and Fourme d'Ambert, British Stilton, Italian Gorgonzola, Spanish Cabrales, and American Maytag Blue Cheese.

FLAVORED CHEESES | These are made by any of the above techniques and flavored with herbs, spices, chiles, fruit, even cocoa powder. Examples include the Dutch cumin-spiced Leiden or mustard seed-studded Beemster, Italian peppercorn provolone, American pepper Jack, and Vermont sage cheese.

If you are using focaccia or ciabatta, cut the bread in half through the side. Brush ½ tablespoon (1½ teaspoons) of the olive oil on the outside of the bread, setting the remainder aside for the skillet. If you are using basil leaves, arrange them on top of the inside of the bottom half of the focaccia or ciabatta. If you are using pesto, spread it on the insides of the bread. Arrange the mozzarella on the bottom half of the focaccia or ciabatta and top it with the tomato. Place the top half of the bread over the tomato. Cook the sandwich as described in Step 3 of the basic recipe on page 73.

MOZZARELLA, ANCHOVIES, AND HOT PEPPERS

THE SICILIAN

A high-testosterone grilled cheese sandwich from Southern Italy—pumped up with anchovies and hot peppers.

1 tablespoon extra virgin olive oil, preferably Sicilian

2 slices dense white sandwich bread

4 anchovy fillets

2 ounces thinly sliced fresh mozzarella cheese

2 pickled pepperoncini peppers, thinly sliced crosswise

Freshly ground black pepper

Brush the olive oil on one side of each slice of bread, setting ½ tablespoon (1½ teaspoons) aside for the skillet. Turn one slice of bread over and arrange the anchovies on top of it. Top the anchovies with the mozzarella followed by the pepperoncini. Season the sandwich with black pepper to taste. Place the second slice of bread, oiled side up, on top. Cook the sandwich as described in Step 3 of the basic recipe on page 73.

JARLSBERG CHEESE AND SMOKED SALMON
THE NORWEGIAN

Jarlsberg is a mild, sweet, nutty cheese you could think of as Norwegian Swiss. Use a cold-smoked fish, like Norwegian salmon.

1 tablespoon butter, melted

2 slices white sandwich bread

2 ounces thinly sliced Jarlsberg cheese

1 ounce thinly sliced smoked salmon

1 thin slice fresh lemon (optional), rind and seeds removed and discarded, lemon diced

Spread the butter on one side of each slice of bread, setting ½ tablespoon (1½ teaspoons) aside for the skillet. Turn one slice of bread over and place the Jarlsberg cheese on top. Top the cheese with the smoked salmon followed by the lemon, if using. Place the second slice of bread, buttered side up, on top. Cook the sandwich as described in Step 3 of the basic recipe on page 73.

YOUR BASIC QUESADILLA
(AND VARIATIONS)

SHOP Flour is the traditional tortilla for a quesadilla, but corn has a more interesting flavor. One good compromise: white corn tortillas.

GEAR Your basic kitchen gear. The traditional pan for cooking quesadillas is a sort of Mexican griddle called a *comal*. You can use a large (10- to 12-inch) cast-iron or nonstick skillet instead.

Grill cheese between tortillas instead of bread and you get a quesadilla. Mexico's take on the grilled cheese sandwich has long since conquered the rest of the Americas, where in typical fashion we've transformed it beyond recognition. I've eaten lobster quesadillas in the Bahamas, barbecued duck quesadillas in Las Vegas, and *huitlacoche* (Mexican "truffle"—black corn fungus) quesadillas in Denver. It's enough to make you hunger for the original quesadilla in its primal simplicity, which means cheese melted between tortillas with a whisper of jalapeño and perhaps some scallion or tomato. In the unlikely chance you've never made quesadillas before, here's how to do it.

The basic formula includes your choice of tortillas, such as wheat, white corn, or yellow corn, and cheese, such as Cotija (a sharp Mexican cheese), Jack, pepper Jack, cheddar, Gruyère, Gouda, or goat cheese. Embellishments range from fresh or pickled chile peppers or *rajas* (roasted poblano peppers) to fried garlic, caramelized onions, corn kernels, or sautéed mushrooms; and sour cream or *crema* (Mexican sour cream). **Makes 2 quesadillas**

WHAT ELSE Round or half-moon? Both are popular shapes for quesadillas. When using large flour tortillas, I like to fold them in half to make half-moons. The reason is simple: They're easier to turn. When using small corn tortillas, I make round quesadillas, with one tortilla on the bottom and one on the top. Corn tortillas break when you fold them in half and small circles are easier to turn.

In many parts of Mexico quesadillas are deep-fried, not panfried or grilled. As you can imagine, my kind of quesadilla is grilled. Lightly brush the outside of the quesadillas with melted butter or oil and grill them directly over a medium flame.

TIME about 10 minutes

For the quesadillas

2 flour tortillas (each 8 inches across— if using smaller corn tortillas, use 2 per quesadilla to make a sandwich without folding)

3 tablespoons sour cream (optional)

¾ cup (about 3 ounces) grated Jack, pepper Jack, or white cheddar cheese

1 tablespoon butter, at room temperature or vegetable oil

Your choice of store-bought or homemade salsa (optional; for recipes see pages 209 through 212), for serving

For the add-ins (optional)

1 fresh or pickled jalapeño pepper, thinly sliced (for milder quesadillas, remove the seeds)

1 scallion, trimmed, both white and green parts thinly sliced crosswise

3 tablespoons thinly sliced pitted olives

3 tablespoons diced fresh tomato

3 tablespoons chopped fresh cilantro

1 Place a tortilla on a work surface. Spread one half of the tortilla with half of the sour cream, if using. Sprinkle half of the grated cheese on top of the sour cream. Dot the cheese with half of the jalapeño, scallion, olives, tomato, and/or cilantro, if using. Fold the bare half of the tortilla over the filling. Repeat with the second tortilla.

2 Melt or heat ½ tablespoon (1½ teaspoons) butter or oil in a large skillet over medium heat. Swirl the skillet to coat the bottom. Add the quesadillas, taking care not to spill the filling.

Cook the quesadillas until browned on the bottom, 2 to 3 minutes.

3 Using a spatula, carefully turn the quesadillas over, adding the remaining butter or oil to the skillet. Continue cooking the quesadillas until the second side is browned and crisp and the cheese is melted, 2 to 3 minutes.

4 Serve the quesadillas whole as sandwiches or cut each into 4 wedges with a knife or pizza cutter to serve as an appetizer. If desired, serve salsa on the side for spooning or dipping.

Five Variations on a Quesadilla

Bacon cheddar quesadillas: Prepare the quesadillas as described in the basic recipe on page 78 using grated cheddar cheese and adding slices of fried bacon. (For extra extravagance, fry the bacon in the skillet you are going to use to cook the quesadillas, then brown the quesadillas in the bacon fat.)

Dutch ham and cheese quesadillas: Prepare the quesadillas as described in the basic recipe on page 78 using grated aged Gouda cheese or spiced Leiden cheese (a semi-firm cheese flavored with cumin seeds), diced smoked ham, and mustard.

Mango shrimp quesadillas: Prepare the quesadillas as described in the basic recipe on page 78 dividing ¼ cup each diced ripe mango and peeled and diced cooked shrimp between them. The dice should be about ¼ inch in size. These quesadillas are especially good made with grated Manchego cheese.

Chipotle chicken quesadillas: Prepare the quesadillas as described in the basic recipe on page 78 adding ¼ cup diced or thinly sliced cooked chicken and 1 to 2 teaspoons minced chipotle pepper. Grated Jack cheese is a good match here.

***Huitlacoche* (corn smut) quesadillas:** *Huitlacoche* is a black corn fungus sometimes called the Mexican truffle. (The flavor is more mushroomy than truffly.) You can buy it frozen or canned at Mexican markets and specialty food shops, or online at mexgrocer .com. Dice a peeled small onion and cook it in 1 tablespoon butter or oil in a large skillet over medium heat until golden brown, 4 minutes. Add 6 ounces (about ¾ cup) of diced or thinly sliced *huitlacoche* and cook it until the liquid has evaporated, 5 to 8 minutes. Place the *huitlacoche* mixture on the tortillas along with grated Jack or white cheddar cheese.

GREEN BLTS

SHOP A sandwich this simple lives and dies by the quality of the raw materials: bakery brioche, thick-sliced artisanal bacon, farm stand or heirloom tomatoes, and real mayonnaise (I prefer Hellmann's, which is known as Best Foods west of the Rockies). Note: Miracle Whip is not mayonnaise.

The BLT is one of the world's sandwich wonders—remarkable for its contrast of temperatures (hot bacon, cold lettuce), textures (crisp toast, moist tomatoes), and flavors (salty bacon, creamy mayonnaise). So the idea of trying to improve on it may smack of heresy. Well, don't burn me at the stake, but when I make a BLT, I like to use arugula in place of lettuce, brioche (French egg bread) instead of white bread, and pepper bacon to kick up the spice. And I add cool, creamy avocado to counterpoint the hot crunch of the bacon and toast. **Makes 2 sandwiches**

6 thick slices artisanal pepper bacon or regular bacon

4 slices brioche or country-style white bread

3 tablespoons mayonnaise, preferably Hellmann's

1 small bunch arugula, rinsed and patted dry with paper towels

1 large luscious red ripe tomato, thinly sliced crosswise

1 ripe avocado, cut in half, pitted, peeled, and thinly sliced

1 Place the slices of bacon in a single layer in a cold heavy large skillet and heat over medium heat. Cook the bacon until it is crisp and browned and most of the fat is rendered (melted out), about 6 minutes, turning it over with tongs once the first side is browned (after about 3 minutes). (For alternative methods for cooking bacon see page 67.) Transfer the bacon to a plate lined with paper towels to drain.

2 Toast the slices of brioche in a toaster until golden. Place the slices of toast on a clean dish towel (this keeps the steam from making them soggy). Spread each with some of the mayonnaise. Top 2 of the slices with arugula, then with slices of tomato, bacon, and avocado. Place the remaining 2 slices of brioche on top, mayonnaise side down, and cut the sandwiches in half on the diagonal before serving.

GEAR Your basic kitchen gear including a large (10- to 12-inch) skillet, a plate lined with paper towels, and a toaster or broiler

WHAT ELSE The ingredients for making a great BLT may be simple, but the execution is crucial. The bacon and toast must be hot; the greens and tomato cold. If you slice the avocado too far ahead of time, it will brown. Prep your veggies just before you start cooking the bacon.

TIME about 10 minutes

A BLT with Fried Egg and Cheese
SPANGLISH SANDWICH

Thomas Keller owns two of the top-ranked restaurants in the United States— The French Laundry and Per Se—plus a growing empire of Bouchon bistros and bakeries. He is, in other words, a chef's chef (you can read more about him on page 92). Yet, when asked about the quintessential guy dish, he names not a hunk of meat, but a sandwich—an everything-but-the-kitchen-sink combination of bacon, lettuce, tomato, melted cheese, fried egg, and *lots* of salt. Sound familiar? It will if you've seen the romantic comedy *Spanglish*, where Adam Sandler, playing the role of chef John Clasky and soon-to-be paramour of the lovely Flor Moreno (played by Spanish actress Paz Vega), prepares it after a hard night in the kitchen. In short, it's

SHOP You want a mild sourdough or country-style white bread, preferably oval in shape (so you get a larger sandwich). And artisanal bacon, ripe tomatoes, best-quality mayonnaise—perfection lies in the details.

GEAR Your basic kitchen gear including a large (10- to 12-inch) nonstick skillet, a plate lined with paper towels, plus a toaster oven or broiler

WHAT ELSE This sandwich is simple—that's the point—but it takes a certain choreography to get it right. You fry the bacon, then the egg, while simultaneously melting the cheese on one slice of bread in a toaster oven or under the broiler.

TIME about 15 minutes

3 slices artisanal bacon, such as Nueske's

2 thin slices Monterey Jack cheese (about 2 ounces)

2 slices sourdough or country-style white bread

1 tablespoon mayonnaise, preferably Hellmann's

4 thin slices luscious red ripe tomato

Coarse salt (kosher or sea; Keller uses Maldon salt from England)

1 teaspoon unsalted butter

1 large egg

2 Boston lettuce leaves, rinsed and patted dry with paper towels

1 Arrange the bacon in a single layer in a cold nonstick skillet and place it over medium heat. Cook the bacon until crisp and lightly browned, about 3 minutes. Transfer the bacon to a plate lined with paper towels to drain. Using a paper towel, wipe the remaining bacon fat out of the skillet.

2 Meanwhile, preheat a toaster oven or broiler to high (400°F).

3 Arrange the slices of cheese on top of 1 slice of bread. Place the cheese-topped slice of bread in the toaster oven or under the broiler and let it heat until the cheese melts, about 2 minutes.

4 Using a butter knife or spatula, spread the mayonnaise on one side of the second slice of bread. Top it with the bacon and the tomato slices. Sprinkle the tomatoes with a few grains of coarse salt.

5 Melt the butter in a large nonstick skillet over medium-high heat until it sizzles. Crack in the egg and cook it until it is set on both sides but the yolk is still runny, about 2 minutes on the first side and 1 minute in the second side (carefully slide a spatula under the egg to turn it over). Slide the egg on top of the tomatoes. Top the egg with the lettuce leaves.

6 By now, the cheese should be melted. Place the slice of bread with the cheese, cheese side down, on top of the lettuce. Place the sandwich on a plate and cut it in half crosswise with a serrated knife and watch the egg yolk ooze lasciviously over the other ingredients.

CURRIED EGG SALAD SANDWICHES

An egg salad sandwich is, well, an egg salad sandwich. Or so I felt until I tasted the smoked egg salad at the Auberge Shulamit in Rosh Pina, Israel. That set me to thinking about how you could infuse the commonplace egg salad sandwich with some excitement. The answer comes from India's playbook: caramelized onions and curry. (I'm not sure how far you want to take this, but for even more flavor, you can add chiles and chopped cilantro.) **Makes 2 sandwiches**

SHOP You probably know by now that I'm a big partisan of organic or farm-fresh eggs. As for curry powder, one good imported brand is Sun from India, but any curry powder will do the trick.

GEAR Your basic kitchen gear including a small saucepan, a large (10- to 12-inch) skillet, and a food processor or potato masher

WHAT ELSE I like egg salad on sliced whole wheat or multigrain bread, but for an Indian touch, you can buy ready-made *naan* (Indian flatbread) at most supermarkets (one readily available brand is 365 sold by Whole Foods). Warm the bread in the skillet in which you cooked the onions or in a toaster oven or toaster.

TIME about 15 minutes

4 large eggs

1 tablespoon butter or extra virgin olive oil

1 small onion, peeled and finely chopped

1 to 2 jalapeño peppers (optional), seeded and finely chopped (for a hotter egg salad, leave the seeds in)

1 teaspoon curry powder, or to taste

3 tablespoons mayonnaise, preferably Hellmann's

3 tablespoons chopped fresh cilantro (optional)

Coarse salt (kosher or sea) and freshly ground black pepper

4 slices whole wheat or multigrain bread, or 2 naans

1 Place the eggs in a small saucepan and add enough cold water to cover by 3 inches. Bring the water to a boil over high heat, then reduce the heat to medium and simmer the eggs until hard-cooked, 11 minutes (a few minutes longer if you live at a high altitude). Drain the water from the saucepan, then fill it with cold water to stop the eggs from cooking further. When the eggs have cooled slightly, crack and remove the shells (hard-cooked— aka hard-boiled—eggs peel more easily when warm). Return the peeled eggs to the cold water in the saucepan and let them cool completely, then drain. Cut each egg into quarters.

2 Melt the butter or heat the oil in a large skillet over medium heat. Add the butter or olive oil and cook until the butter melts or the oil is hot. Add the onion and jalapeño(s), if using, and cook until the onion has turned a deep golden brown, 6 to 8 minutes, stirring often with a wooden spoon. (You may need to reduce the heat as the onion darkens.) Stir the curry powder into the onion and cook until the curry powder is fragrant, about 1 minute. Let the onion mixture cool.

3 Place the onion mixture, egg quarters, mayonnaise, and cilantro, if using, in a food processor. Run the machine in short bursts to chop the eggs and just mix. Do not overprocess the egg salad; you want it to be a little chunky. Alternatively, mash the eggs with a potato masher (see mashed potatoes on page 497) or mash with the back of a fork. Season the egg salad with salt and black pepper to taste.

4 Spread the egg salad on 2 slices of bread and place the remaining 2 slices of bread on top. Or spread the egg salad on one side of each naan, folding the flatbread over to make a sandwich.

DOWN EAST LOBSTER ROLLS

SHOP When making lobster rolls, the best thing is to cook your own lobster (see page 429). If that's not an option, buy the lobster already cooked from your local fishmonger or seafood department.

GEAR Your basic kitchen gear including a rubber spatula and a large (10- to 12-inch) nonstick skillet

I f you live in coastal New England, lobster roll is a staple. It's a luxury anywhere else. Which may explain why Maine's most famous sandwich has turned up at some of the nation's trendiest tables from Los Angeles to Miami Beach. You might think a sandwich with three main ingredients (lobster, lettuce, bread) would need no special operating instructions, but the details matter: a hot butter-toasted bun, chilled fresh lobster, and a crisp Boston lettuce leaf (and it must be Boston). **Makes 2 lobster rolls**

12 ounces (1½ cups) cold cooked lobster meat, cut into bite-size chunks

3 to 4 tablespoons mayonnaise, preferably Hellmann's

½ teaspoon grated lemon zest (optional, see Glossary)

Freshly ground black pepper

2 split-top hot dog buns (see Note)

2 tablespoons (¼ stick) salted butter, melted

4 small Boston lettuce leaves, rinsed and patted dry with paper towels

1 Place the lobster, mayonnaise, and lemon zest (if using) in a mixing bowl and gently mix with a rubber spatula. Season with pepper to taste.

2 Open the buns, being careful not to break the "hinge" that holds the halves together, and lightly brush the insides and outsides with the melted butter. If using bakery hot dog buns, slice them through the tops with a serrated knife, stopping before you cut through the bottoms. Heat a large nonstick skillet over medium-high heat. Toast the buns cut sides down in the hot skillet until they are a light golden brown but still soft in the center, about 2 minutes. Turn the buns over and quickly toast the outside.

3 Place 2 lettuce leaves in each bun and fill the leaves with the lobster mixture. The lobster meat should tower over the edge of the bun. Cut each bun in half crosswise and serve while the buns are still warm.

Note: The traditional buns for lobster come split at the top and are baked touching, so there's a rough crumb on both sides—perfect for grilling. One popular brand of these rolls is Country Kitchen—sold in supermarkets in the northeast and online at FamousFoods.com. Hot dog rolls from your supermarket bakery will work just fine.

WHAT ELSE Some lost souls add celery or onion to lobster rolls in a misguided attempt to improve on the perfection of simplicity. Don't. Likewise, Miracle Whip has no place in a well-constructed lobster roll. Give me Hellmann's or switch my order to fried clams. The optional lemon zest is decidedly nontraditional, but I like the way it brightens the taste of the lobster. Note: To make a Down East crab roll, substitute 12 ounces of fresh lump crabmeat for the lobster.

TIME about 15 minutes

Provençal Tuna Sandwiches

PAN BAGNAT

Here's a little known fact about this global grilling explorer and relentless omnivore—a guy who munched termites in Thailand and grilled lambs' intestines in Uruguay: As a child, I was a notoriously finicky eater. For one inglorious nine-month period I ate *nothing* but Bumble Bee tuna sandwiches. So imagine my astonishment the first time I experienced *pan bagnat* on a beach in Nice on the Côte d'Azur. Here was a tuna sandwich that rams your taste buds with the force of an oncoming truck: the tuna dark and oily, its robust fish flavor reinforced by salty anchovies, briny olives, tangy capers, raw onion, bell pepper, and hard-cooked egg. In short, a tuna sandwich worthy of the designation "guy food." **Makes 2 sandwiches**

SHOP I like white Bumble Bee tuna as much as the next guy, and if you like your tuna mild, by all means use it. To get the full effect, you must use dark tuna packed in oil and preferably imported from France, Spain, or Italy. Ventresca, from the belly of the tuna, is especially rich. One good brand is Ortiz.

GEAR Your basic kitchen gear

WHAT ELSE The traditional bread for *pan bagnat* is a large round roll with the crisp crust and soft interior of a French bread. Eight-inch lengths of baguette or even kaiser rolls work just fine. The traditional seasoning for *pan bagnat* is a strong fruity olive oil from Provence.

TIME 15 minutes plus 11 minutes for cooking the eggs

2 large eggs

2 large round French rolls (crusty on the outside and soft inside), 2 pieces of French bread (each 8 inches long), or 2 kaiser rolls

4 Boston lettuce leaves, rinsed and patted dry with paper towels

1 can (5 to 6 ounces) tuna (ideally dark and packed in oil), drained and broken into chunks

1 luscious red ripe tomato, thinly sliced

1 green bell pepper, stemmed, seeded, and cut crosswise into thin rings

½ cup pitted black olives, preferably tiny nicoise or kalamata olives

6 to 8 drained anchovies

1 tablespoon drained capers

½ small mild red onion, thinly sliced

8 fresh basil leaves

2 tablespoons best-quality extra virgin olive oil

Coarse salt (kosher or sea) and freshly ground black pepper

1 Place the eggs in a small saucepan and enough cold water to cover by 3 inches. Bring to a boil over high heat, then reduce the heat to medium and let the eggs simmer until hard-cooked, 11 minutes (a few minutes longer if you live at a high altitude). Drain the water from the saucepan, then fill it with cold water to stop the eggs from cooking longer. When the eggs have cooled slightly, crack and remove the shells (hard-cooked—aka hard-boiled—eggs peel more easily when warm). Return the peeled eggs to the cold water and let them cool. Drain the cooled eggs well and thinly slice them crosswise.

2 Cut the rolls almost in half through the side and open like a book. Place 2 lettuce leaves on the bottom half of each roll. Pile the tuna on top, followed by the tomato slices, bell pepper rings, egg slices, olives, anchovies, capers, onion slices, and basil leaves, dividing them equally between the 2 sandwiches. Drizzle 1 tablespoon of olive oil over the filling of each sandwich and the top half of the roll. Season the fillings with salt (just a little: the olives, anchovies, and capers are salty) and pepper to taste, then close the sandwiches. Let the sandwiches sit for at least 10 minutes so the juices have a chance to soak into the bread. Then dig in (serve with plenty of napkins)!

PASTRAMI REUBEN

The Reuben is one of America's landmark sandwiches—a melting pot mash-up of Irish corned beef, Swiss cheese, German sauerkraut, Russian dressing, and Jewish rye bread—brought together in 1914, as one legend goes, by Arnold Reuben, who owned a restaurant on 58th Street in New York City. A well-made Reuben is a study in contrasts: salty and sweet (the meat and the Russian dressing), sweet and sour (the dressing and sauerkraut), crunchy and meaty (the pickles and the corned beef), and crisp and gooey (the buttered toast and melted cheese). And if you think a Reuben is good made with corned beef, wait until you try it with the garlicky, smoky pastrami I suggest here. **Makes 1 sandwich**

2 slices dark or marbled rye bread

1 tablespoon salted butter,
    at room temperature

3 tablespoons Russian Dressing
    (recipe follows, or use your favorite
    store-bought brand)

3 ounces lean pastrami beef, sliced
    paper-thin across the grain

2 ounces thinly sliced Gruyère or
    Emmentaler cheese

⅓ cup sauerkraut, drained and wrung dry

5 dill pickle slices

SHOP You'll want lean pastrami for this sandwich, sliced paper-thin to order (ask to sample the first slice). The traditional cheese for a Reuben is Emmentaler, but you'll get an even richer flavor if you use the tangy, smaller-holed Gruyère. Sauerkraut bought in bulk from a deli (or in a plastic bag in the cold cuts section of the supermarket) is always better than canned.

GEAR Your basic kitchen gear including a large (10- to 12-inch) cast-iron or nonstick skillet plus a grill press, a contact grill, or second heavy skillet

WHAT ELSE Sure, you could buy bottled Russian dressing, but in your refrigerator you probably have the ingredients to make the dressing from scratch.

TIME about 15 minutes

1 Butter the bread slices with ½ tablespoon (1½ teaspoons) of the butter. Place one slice buttered side down on a work surface. Spread the top with about 1½ tablespoons of the Russian dressing. Arrange the pastrami on top, followed by the cheese, sauerkraut, and dill pickle slices.

2 Spread the second slice of bread with the remaining 1½ tablespoons of Russian Dressing. Place the slice of bread, dressing side down and butter side up, on top of the pickles.

3 *If you are cooking the sandwich in a skillet:* Melt the remaining butter in a large cast-iron or nonstick skillet over medium heat. Add the sandwich and place a grill press or second heavy skillet on top. Cook the sandwich until the bread is brown and crisp, the cheese is melted, and the pastrami is hot, 2 to 3 minutes per side, carefully turning the sandwich over with a spatula. Reduce the heat as needed to keep the bread from browning too much before the cheese has melted.

If you are cooking the sandwich in a contact grill: Preheat the grill. When the grill is hot, place the sandwich in it and cook the sandwich until the bread is brown and crisp, the cheese is melted, and the pastrami is hot, 4 to 6 minutes.

4 Cut the sandwich in half and serve it at once.

Note: Put the leftover sauerkraut in a plastic container with a lid. It will keep indefinitely in the refrigerator and be at the ready for Reubens, hot dogs, and whatever else you enjoy with a side of kraut.

RUSSIAN DRESSING

A thoroughly American condiment despite the name, Russian dressing is made by combining mayonnaise with chili sauce or ketchup. (The chili sauce in question here is a sweet red condiment similar to ketchup. One widely available brand is Heinz.) This recipe makes more than you'll need for the Reuben sandwich on page 87, but it's good stuff to have in your refrigerator, where it will keep for at least a week. **Makes about 1 cup**

⅔ cup mayonnaise, preferably Hellmann's

¼ cup chili sauce or ketchup

3 tablespoons sweet pickle relish

Place the mayonnaise, chili sauce, and pickle relish in a bowl and stir or whisk to mix. The Russian Dressing can be refrigerated, covered, for up to 1 week.

▶ *Pastrami Reuben*

New Orleans's Hot Cold Cut Sandwiches
MUFFULETTAS
WITH OLIVE RELISH

SHOP Sure, you could buy your cold cuts and cheese at the supermarket, in which case you'll wind up with a perfectly pleasant muffuletta that could have been a contender. Take the time to source genuine Italian prosciutto, *coppa,* soppressata (wine-cured salami), and sharp provolone cheese aged at least one year, and you'll turn out a champ. Or go native and substitute tasso (spicy Cajun ham—see page 608) for the *coppa.*

GEAR Your basic kitchen gear including 2 pieces (each 12 by 18 inches) of parchment paper or aluminum foil and a large (10- to 12-inch) heavy skillet, plus a grill press, contact grill, or second heavy skillet

Hoagie. Grinder. Submarine. Hero. Wherever you live, whatever you call it, Italian cold cuts and cheese on bread make a sandwich of the utmost excellence. If I had to pick my favorite, it would be New Orleans's muffuletta. Born a century ago at the Central Grocery, the muffuletta combines the ancient art of Sicilian meat curing with America's spirit of overkill.   **Makes 2 sandwiches**

2 kaiser rolls

2 tablespoons extra virgin olive oil

3 ounces thinly sliced aged provolone cheese

2 ounces thinly sliced coppa, smoked ham, or tasso

A few paper-thin slices of sweet onion

½ cup Olive Relish (recipe follows), or more to taste

2 ounces thinly sliced prosciutto

2 ounces thinly sliced soppressata or Italian salami

1 Slice the kaiser rolls almost in half through the side. Brush the outside of the rolls with 1 tablespoon of the olive oil. Place the 2 pieces of parchment paper or aluminum foil on a work surface. Place a roll in the center of each piece and open the rolls up like a book. Brush the insides of the rolls with the remaining 1 tablespoon of olive oil. Place the provolone and *coppa* on the bottoms of the rolls, dividing them equally between the 2 rolls. Layer the onion, Olive Relish, prosciutto, and soppressata in that order on the top halves of the rolls. Leave the sandwiches open. Fold the parchment paper or foil over the sandwiches to enclose the filling.

2 *If you are cooking the sandwiches in a skillet:* Heat the skillet over medium heat. Arrange the wrapped sandwiches in the skillet with the bottoms of the rolls facing up and place a grill press or second heavy skillet on top of them. Cook the sandwiches 3 to 5 minutes; the meats should be sizzling and the cheese melted. Unwrap each sandwich and fold it closed. Place the unwrapped sandwiches back in the skillet, place the grill press or skillet on top of them, and cook the sandwiches until they are browned and crisped, 1 minute.

If you are cooking the sandwiches on a contact grill: Preheat the grill. When the grill is hot, place the wrapped sandwiches in it and cook them until the bread on the bottom starts to brown, the meats are sizzling, and the cheese is melted, 3 to 5 minutes. Unwrap each sandwich and fold it closed. Place the unwrapped sandwiches back in the grill and cook them until they are browned and crisped, and compressed, 1 minute.

3 Cut each sandwich in half and serve at once.

WHAT ELSE Ever wonder how New Orleans's sandwich kings manage to heat the filling of this thick sandwich through without burning the exterior? The answer is simple: They cook the sandwich open-faced long enough to sizzle the salami and melt the cheese. A piece of parchment paper (a heat-resistant paper with a nonstick coating available at cookware shops and most supermarkets) keeps the ingredients from sticking to the contact grill. Alternatively, you can use aluminum foil.

TIME about 20 minutes

OLIVE RELISH

A generous helping of this big-flavored relish—salty with olives and capers, fiery with hot pepper, tart with vinegar—is what distinguishes the muffuletta from commonplace hoagies or submarine sandwiches. This makes more relish than you need for two muffulettas. The relish is great spooned over just about everything, from grilled swordfish to roast chicken: I'm sure you won't have any trouble finding a use for any leftovers. **Makes about 1 cup**

½ cup pimiento-stuffed green olives

½ cup pitted black olives or kalamata olives

1 rib celery, coarsely chopped

1 clove garlic, peeled and coarsely chopped

2 tablespoons finely chopped fresh flat-leaf parsley

1 tablespoon drained capers

1 pickled hot pepper (pepperoncini), coarsely chopped, or ½ teaspoon hot red pepper flakes

½ teaspoon dried oregano

3 tablespoons extra virgin olive oil

1 tablespoon red wine vinegar, or more to taste

Freshly ground black pepper

Place the green and black olives and the celery, garlic, parsley, capers, hot pepper or pepper flakes, and oregano in a food processor. Running the machine in short bursts, coarsely chop the olive mixture (do not puree it). Add the olive oil and wine vinegar and pulse the machine just to mix. Taste for seasoning, adding more wine vinegar as necessary and black pepper to taste. The relish will keep for at least a week, covered and stored in the refrigerator.

THOMAS KELLER

The first time I met überchef Thomas Keller, it was over an ice cream cone. At least it looked like an ice cream cone. Actually, it was a sesame *tuile* (a wafer-thin "tile cookie") filled with astonishingly fresh salmon tartare topped with briny pearls of salmon roe. It was refined, whimsical, delicate, cerebral, and packed with flavor—in short, quintessential Keller. It's these qualities that have made his flagship restaurants The French Laundry, in the Napa Valley, and Per Se, in New York City, two of the most consistently top-rated dining establishments in the world. Yet, Keller's career began modestly enough as a line cook at The Dunes Club in Rhode Island. "My boss was a French chef named Roland Henin," Keller recalls. "He enlightened me why people cook, which when it boils down to it, is to nurture people."

Today, Keller presides over an empire that includes restaurants, bistros, bakeries, and food products. He remains as notorious for his dry sense of humor as for his fanatic attention to detail. He's the sort of chef who might serve a rack of rabbit with its bones impeccably frenched (scraped clean) so that it looks for all the world like a rack of lamb the size of a postage stamp. In the course of a meal at The French Laundry you might dine on "tongue and cheek" (incredibly delicate braised veal tongue and beef cheeks) and "oysters and pearls" (made with Malpeque oysters and osetra caviar). Dinner at The French Laundry or Per Se will set you back several hundred dollars per person and that's *before* wine, tax, and tip. But the meal will be so unforgettable and the experience so extraordinary, you may actually feel like you got a bargain. Keller sums up his philosophy this way: "Respect for food is respect for life, for who we are and what we do." Amen.

You'll find Keller's recipe for his *Spanglish* Sandwich on page 81.

Your first food memory?
Peanut butter.

First dish you ever cooked?
Hamburger Helper. Hey, I was thirteen years old.

Why is it important for men to know how to cook?
Cooking gives you a sense of self-confidence, self-sustainability, and individuality. It enables you to take care of yourself, which is one of the most essential human needs.

The ultimate guy dish?
The *Spanglish* Sandwich. Basically, it's a bacon, lettuce, and tomato sandwich

with fried egg and melted cheese. If you haven't seen the romantic comedy *Spanglish*, I recommend that you rent it.

What's your go-to dish when you're by yourself?

Well, I don't really cook at home. But I'm likely to eat something like quinoa with hummus. Maybe with cooked beans, avocados, or a can of tuna on top. I keep it pretty healthy.

What's your favorite seduction menu?

Simple and to the point. Champagne and caviar to start. Pasta and truffles. Some kind of chocolate for dessert. Most women find that if you extend yourself, if you can handle yourself in the kitchen, that's seductive enough in itself.

> ▶ Respect for food is respect for life, for who we are and what we do.

Three dishes every guy should know how to make?

A great sandwich.

A grilled steak.

A roast chicken. This isn't complicated, but you have to start with a really good bird and let it sit, uncovered, in the refrigerator for a day or two to dry out the skin. (This helps crisp the skin, which is the best part of any roast chicken.) It's also important to "temper" the bird, that is, let it come to room temperature before cooking. And roast it in a hot oven (425°F).

Three ingredients you can't live without?

Eggs.

Unsalted butter. Salt was once added to butter as a preservative. That isn't necessary today, of course, but, when cooking with butter, I like to add my own salt to taste.

Salt. At the restaurants we use non-iodized kosher salt for cooking. And Maldon salt from England for "finishing" (final seasoning). It's all sodium chloride, of course, but I like the flaky texture of the Maldon.

Three tools you can't live without?

A spoon.

A knife.

A palette knife (a long, slender metal spatula) for turning the food.

What are the three most important things to keep in mind if you're just starting out in the kitchen?

Think process, not recipe. Master the technique, not a particular dish. Once you learn the proper way to braise, roast, or sauté, you can use that method for pretty much anything. We tend to focus on recipes way too much.

Patience. You need it for cooking individual dishes and for your own development as a cook. Guys always want to accomplish more than we're actually ready for.

Practice. The more you cook, the better you get at it.

So what are the essential techniques every guy should know how to do?

Baking. Braising. Roasting. Sautéing. And as you well know, Steven, grilling. And, of course, how to cook an egg.

What are the three most common mistakes guys make in the kitchen?

Moving the food around too much. Let's say you're sautéing scallops. When you put them in the pan, let them stay in one spot. That way they'll develop a beautiful flavorful crust. If you keep moving them around, they'll stew rather than sear.

Don't try to be overly ambitious. It's better to do one dish really well than a whole menu poorly.

Don't be discouraged by failure. The first time you undertake a new recipe, your rate of failure is much higher. The best way you improve your cooking is repetition. And to learn from your mistakes.

Something unexpected you've learned over the years that really helps you up your game in the kitchen?

Pay attention to the details. For example, when we receive a fish shipment at one of my restaurants, we store the fish upright. That's the way it swims, and if you lay it on its side on ice with more ice on top, you wind up crushing the fillets.

Parting words of advice?

The hardest thing for me to learn was how to delegate. You don't always have to do everything yourself.

A Double Pork and Gruyère Cheese Sandwich

THE CUBANO AND ITS AMIGOS

SHOP This sandwich is simple, but it does require a bit of advance preparation. You need roast pork, for example, leftovers from the garlicky Porchetta (see page 277). Of course, a good supermarket or specialty store deli counter will have store-made roast pork on hand for the slicing.

For the ham, you can use the traditional cooked smoked ham or, for an offbeat touch, paper-thin slices of a Spanish cured ham like *jamón serrano* (see page 608). If you can find aromatic cave-aged Gruyère cheese, your Cubanos will be all the more flavorful. Cuban bread is baguette shaped, but with a softer crust than a French bread: the latter works just fine.

GEAR Your basic kitchen gear including a large (10- to 12-inch) heavy skillet, plus a grill press, contact grill, or second heavy skillet

WHAT ELSE If you bought a contact grill hoping it would turn out respectable steaks and burgers, then shelved it in disgust when it didn't, now's the time to dust it off. A contact grill works great for grilled sandwiches of all sorts.

TIME about 10 minutes

The Cubano may be the best pork sandwich south of the Carolinas. Take it from me: I know—I live in the sixth province of Cuba, which is sometimes known as Miami. The Cubano owes its distinction to a quadruple blast of flavor in the form of garlicky roast pork, smoked ham, pungent Gruyère cheese, and tangy pickles. Curiously, the best Cubano I ever tasted came not from the tropics but from a lively café in wintery Montreal called olive + gourmando. The secret? Two ingenious twists on the Cuban classic: They use cornichons (super-sour tiny French pickles) in place of dill pickles and add some smoky chipotle mayonnaise. **Makes 2 sandwiches**

2 pieces Cuban bread or French bread (each 8 inches long), or 2 hoagie rolls

2 tablespoons Dijon mustard

2 to 4 tablespoons Chipotle Cilantro Lime Mayonnaise (recipe follows) or regular mayonnaise

3 ounces thinly sliced roast pork

3 ounces thinly sliced smoked ham

3 ounces thinly sliced Gruyère cheese

8 cornichons, thinly sliced, or 8 dill pickle slices

1 tablespoon butter, melted or at room temperature

1 Slice the pieces of bread or rolls almost in half through the side, then open them up like a book. Spread one side of the inside of each with 1 tablespoon of mustard. Spread the other side with Chipotle Cilantro Lime Mayonnaise. Arrange the pork, ham, cheese, and pickle slices on top of the mustard and close up the sandwiches. Lightly brush or spread the outside of the sandwiches with half the butter (if cooking in a skillet) or all the butter if using a contact grill.

2 *If you are cooking the sandwiches in a skillet:* Melt the remaining ½ tablespoon (1½ teaspoons) butter in the skillet over medium heat. Add the sandwiches and place a grill press or second heavy skillet on top of them. Cook the sandwiches until the bread is browned, crisped, and compressed, the cheese is melted, and the filling is hot, 3 to 6 minutes per side. Reduce the heat as needed to keep the bread from browning too much before the cheese has melted.

If you are cooking the sandwiches on a contact grill: Preheat the grill. When the grill is hot, place the sandwiches in it and cook them until the bread is browned, crisped, and compressed, the cheese is melted, and the filling is hot, 4 to 6 minutes.

3 Cut each sandwich in half sharply on the diagonal and serve at once.

Variations

Medianoche ("midnighter" sandwiches): A Cubano's little brother, the *medianoche* was traditionally served after movies and shows let out in Havana. To make these, substitute 2 slightly sweet rolls like brioche or bakery hot dog buns for the bread in the Cubano. Add lettuce leaves and sliced tomato to the sandwich and cook the sandwiches as described in Step 2 on the facing page.

Pan con lechón (roast pork sandwiches with garlic and lime sauce): The third of the triumvirate of Cuban sandwiches found at sandwich shops throughout Miami is made with 2 pieces of Cuban or French bread, each about 8 inches long, or 2 hoagie rolls, 6 ounces of thinly sliced warm roast pork (see page 94), 1 small sweet onion, thinly sliced, and 3 to 4 tablespoons Mojo (Cuban garlic lime sauce, see page 432). Cut the pieces of bread or rolls almost in half through the side. Fill each with half of the roast pork and onion and douse generously with Mojo. Butter and grill the breads as described in Step 2 on page 164.

CHIPOTLE CILANTRO LIME MAYONNAISE

The chipotle (smoked jalapeño) is a Mexican chile, not Cuban, but its smoky heat goes great with the pork on this sandwich. For info on buying chipotles, see page 606. You'll use any leftover sauce quickly enough. **Makes ¾ cup**

⅔ cup mayonnaise, preferably Hellmann's

1 tablespoon minced canned chipotle pepper with its juice

3 tablespoons minced fresh cilantro leaves

1 tablespoon fresh lime juice

Place the mayonnaise, chipotle and its juice, cilantro, and lime juice in a bowl and whisk to mix. The chipotle mayonnaise can be refrigerated, covered, for at least a week.

TEN THINGS YOU NEED TO KNOW ABOUT

CHEESE

1 Cheese is one of the world's most diverse foods, and yet all cheese starts with just three ingredients: milk, salt, and bacteria. Depending on the source of the milk (from a cow, sheep, goat, buffalo, reindeer, yak—you name it), the bacteria, and the manufacturing and aging process, you get cheeses as varied as cheddar (an Anglo-American cow's milk cheese), Roquefort (a French sheep's milk blue cheese), Gjetost (a hard, sweet Norwegian goat cheese), and everything in between.

2 Some products called "cheese" are not cheese—aesthetically, biologically, or legally. The short list of these includes American cheese (epitomized by Velveeta) and Cheez Whiz. Cheese might be listed among their many other polysyllabic ingredients, but do not confuse these products with real cheese.

3 Cheese is incredibly versatile. You can serve it by itself as a starter or snack, first course, main dish, cheese course (of course), or dessert (think cheesecake). You can use it as a flavoring in a zillion rib-sticking dishes, from planked Camembert (page 200) to mac and cheese (page 460). Many varieties are great baked or panfried (try the *Queso Fundido*— Mexican Grilled Cheese—on page 199). Pasta without freshly grated Parmigiano Reggiano would be as unthinkable as a martini without vermouth.

4 There has never been a better time or place for a cheese lover than twenty-first-century America. Specialty food shops carry an astonishing assortment of domestic and imported cheeses. My local supermarket carries more international cheeses now than a specialty shop would have twenty years ago. And domestic cheesemakers everywhere are giving the French and Swiss a run for their money.

5 Like wine, cheese is highly regional and, as a general rule, the more precisely you can pinpoint its place of origin, the better the cheese will be. Brie from the French towns of Meaux or Melun will have more character and finesse than, say, a generic soft-ripened "Camembert" from Denmark—not that there aren't some great cheeses from Scandinavia.

6 In cheese, as in so much in life, you get what you pay for. Real Parmigiano Reggiano costs around twenty dollars a pound, but its unique texture (crunchy-creamy) and its extraordinary sweet-salty-milky flavor make it unique among grating cheeses. (It's pretty terrific eaten in chunks, too.) Look for the words "Parmigiano Reggiano" stamped into the rind. And choose chunks that have a relatively small ratio of rind to cheese. Finally, freshly grate your cheese with a Microplane (see page 15), on a box grater, or in a food processor. It will taste infinitely superior to pre-grated cheese.

7 Store cheese in the refrigerator wrapped in waxed paper, plastic wrap, or cheese paper (available at cheese shops), but serve the cheese at room temperature. Cheese at room temperature has a hundred more flavor nuances than cheese served cold and hard out of the fridge. Leave the cheese on a tray or platter covered with a clean cotton dish towel for an hour or so until it comes to room temperature.

8 When assembling a cheese tray, aim for a contrast of flavors, textures, colors, shapes, and intensity. Counterpoint the saltiness of a blue cheese, like English Stilton, with the nutty sweetness of an Alpine cheese, like Fribourg or Comté. Serve a soft, creamy cheese, like Camembert, next to a hard cheese, like pecorino romano. Provide relief from a malodorous cheese, like Epoisses (which is rinsed with brandy as it ages), with a mild cheese, like Italian taleggio (OK, it's not *too* mild). Then up the ante with some walnuts or Marcona almonds from Spain, dried apricots or prunes or other dried fruits, quince jelly or guava paste, mustard, cornichon pickles, and of course, some interesting bread and/or crackers.

9 Most cheeses taste best at room temperature, but some cheeses shine only when heated or grilled. The short list includes Greek (and Cypriot) Haloumi, which is traditionally flambéed with brandy to make saganaki (see page 198 for a recipe), and *provoleta,* which Argentineans melt and brown on the grill.

10 At some point you will look in the refrigerator drawer and discover that a chunk of cheese you forgot about is covered with blue-green mold. (Not a blue cheese, which is supposed to have channels of mold, but some other cheese.) And being a guy, you will wonder if you can still eat it. The answer is a qualified yes. Slice the moldy part off along with a quarter inch of unspoiled cheese beneath it, wiping your knife between cuts. Then taste a little piece. If it tastes like cheese, not mold, you're OK. But as with all foods, when in doubt, throw it out.

Uruguay's Amazing Steak and Egg Sandwich

CHIVITO

The *chivito* was the first thing I ate on my first trip to Uruguay and it foreshadowed the onslaught of red meat that would accompany my visit. ("We eat meat thirteen times a week," my guide confided, the fourteenth meal being fish for lunch on Friday.) Simply defined, the *chivito* is a steak sandwich—the way the Super Bowl, simply defined, is a football game. You start with thin-sliced steak and pile on bacon, eggs, cheese, lettuce, tomato, roasted peppers, and mayonnaise. It makes a Philly cheesesteak look downright anorexic. **Makes 2 sandwiches**

2 kaiser rolls

3 tablespoons mayonnaise, preferably Hellmann's

2 Boston lettuce leaves, rinsed and patted dry with paper towels

4 slices bacon, cut in half crosswise

2 beef steaks, each 3 to 4 ounces and cut or pounded ¼ inch thick

Coarse salt (kosher or sea) and freshly ground black pepper

2 slices Jack or mild cheddar cheese, each about 1 ounce

2 large eggs

1 luscious red ripe tomato, thinly sliced

2 large strips roasted red pepper (optional, page 200)

1 Cut the rolls almost in half through the side. Spread the cut sides of the rolls with the mayonnaise. Place a lettuce leaf on the bottom of each roll. Set the rolls aside while you cook the bacon, steak, and eggs.

2 Arrange the bacon in a single layer in a cold large skillet and heat over medium heat. Cook the bacon until it is crisp and browned,

3 minutes per side. Transfer the bacon to a plate lined with paper towels to drain. Leave the bacon fat in the skillet.

3 Season the steaks with salt and black pepper to taste. Heat the skillet over high heat. Add the steaks to the skillet and cook until done to taste, 2 minutes per side for medium.

SHOP There are lots of options for the steak: for example, rib eye (my favorite), sirloin, or top or bottom round. What's essential is that the steak be pounded or thinly sliced so that it's ¼ inch thick. (Ask the butcher to cut thin slices on a meat slicer or pound it yourself between 2 sheets of plastic wrap with the bottom of a heavy skillet.) In Uruguay *chivito* comes on a soft, slightly sweet roll. A kaiser roll or hoagie roll gets you in the ballpark.

GEAR Your basic kitchen gear including a large (10- to 12-inch) skillet and a plate lined with paper towels

WHAT ELSE Opinions vary widely in Uruguay as to what constitutes a proper *chivito*. Some people use ham instead of bacon, others hard-boiled eggs instead of fried. Grilled onions and/or roasted peppers turn up on many versions, and it's worth noting that in Uruguay, the beef would be grass-fed (see page 225) and cooked to medium.

TIME about 20 minutes

4 Place the steaks on the rolls, and top them with the bacon and cheese. Leave the fat in the skillet.

5 Once again, heat the skillet, this time over medium-high heat. Crack the eggs into the skillet and cook until the whites are crisp and browned on the bottom and edges, 2 minutes on the first side, 1 minute on the second side, carefully turning them with a spatula. Slide the eggs into the sandwiches on top of the cheese.

6 Top each egg with slices of tomato and a strip of red pepper, if using, and season the sandwiches with a little more salt and black pepper. Close the sandwiches and cut them in half before serving.

A NEW PB&J

SHOP If you live near a great Asian market you can buy *nam prik* (Thai chili jam) ready made. Otherwise, use a good Thai sweet chili sauce, like Mae Ploy, which is available at most supermarkets.

GEAR Your basic kitchen gear including a small (6-inch) skillet, a slotted spoon, and a plate lined with paper towels, if you are frying the shallots

WHAT ELSE Thais often turbocharge their food with fried shallots or garlic. If you're in a hurry, you can skip Step 1. But the sandwich will taste much more interesting if you include the shallot. If you have the time, the crunch and flavor of the shallots will take your sandwich to a new level.

TIME 15 minutes (5 minutes without the shallots)

I never liked PB&Js—too sweet, too sticky. And so it remained until I had a meal in Bangkok that included both satés (Thai kebabs with peanut sauce) and *nam prik* (a Thai condiment loosely translated as chili jam). This gave me the idea for a PB&J you could actually serve with a straight face to a grown man, a sandwich that pairs nutty peanut butter with sweet, subtly hot chili sauce or jam, plus fried shallots for crunch. **Makes 2 sandwiches**

¼ cup canola oil

1 shallot or 3 cloves garlic, peeled and thinly sliced crosswise

4 slices whole wheat bread

6 tablespoons peanut butter (I prefer chunky)

4 to 6 tablespoons Thai chili jam or sweet chili sauce

1 Heat the oil in a small skillet over medium-high heat. Add the shallot or garlic slices and cook until golden brown and crisp, 1 to 2 minutes, taking care they don't burn. Using a slotted spoon, transfer the shallot or garlic to a plate lined with towels to drain. The shallot or garlic can be fried several hours ahead to this stage. Simply leave it on the paper towels at room temperature till you're ready to use it.

2 Spread 2 of the slices of bread with the peanut butter. Spread the chili jam on top of the peanut butter. Sprinkle the fried shallots or garlic over the chili jam. Top with the remaining bread slices to make sandwiches. Cut the sandwiches in halves or quarters and serve.

THE UR-BURGER

The perfect burger. Platonic idea? Or beef patty that actually exists? If you start with the right meat, patty shape, and bun and keep the flavorings subordinate to the beef, any burger has the potential for greatness. In the following pages you'll find some favorites. We start with the Ur-Burger (from the German word *ur* for original, fundamental, or basic), which you can customize to taste. **Makes 4 burgers**

1½ to 2 pounds ground beef, well chilled

Coarse salt (kosher or sea) and freshly ground black pepper

3 tablespoons plus 1 teaspoon salted butter, at room temperature

4 freshly baked hamburger buns or brioche rolls

"Secret Sauce" for Burgers (page 542) or your condiments of choice

4 Boston or Bibb lettuce or 8 arugula leaves, rinsed and patted dry with paper towels

1 luscious red ripe tomato, thinly sliced

Your choice of embellishments for the burgers (see page 107 for suggestions)

1 Divide the beef into 4 equal portions. Shape each portion into a patty about 1 inch thick and slightly larger in diameter than the buns (lightly wet your hands with cold water before handling the meat). Work with a light touch, handling the meat as little as possible. Make a slight depression in the center of the patties; they should be slightly concave. You can form the burgers up to 6 hours ahead. Arrange the burgers on a plate lined with plastic wrap and

SHOP My dream ground meat mix combines ground sirloin (40 percent), chuck (40 percent), and brisket (20 percent). Make friends with your local butcher and ask him to custom-grind it for you. Brioche rolls (French egg bread) make great buns. Add ripe heirloom tomato and leaf lettuce or arugula. Perfection lies in the details.

GEAR Your basic kitchen gear including a large (10- to 12-inch) cast-iron or nonstick skillet and an instant-read thermometer

WHAT ELSE I prefer my burgers hot off the grill (surprise), and on page 113 you'll find instructions for grilling burgers. But apartment dwellers without grill access can take comfort in the knowledge that many an iconic burger (California's In-N-Out Burger and Umami Burger to name two) is cooked on a griddle, and you can achieve the same result using a skillet.

TIME about 20 minutes

cover them with more plastic wrap. Refrigerate the burgers until you are ready to cook them.

2 Just before cooking, generously season the burgers on both sides with salt and pepper, turning them gently.

3 Melt 1 tablespoon of the butter in a large skillet over medium-high heat. Add the burgers, spacing them 2 inches apart. Cook the burgers until the bottoms are browned, 3 to 5 minutes. Using a spatula, gently turn the burgers over and continue cooking them until done to taste, about 5 minutes more for medium. To test for doneness, insert an instant-read thermometer through the side of a burger. When the burger is cooked to medium the thermometer will register 160°F.

4 Transfer the burgers to a warm plate. Place a tiny pat of butter (about 1 teaspoon) on top of each burger and let the burgers rest for 1 to 2 minutes. (Chefs call this "tempering" the meat and it helps produce juicier burgers.)

5 Meanwhile, spread the insides of the buns with the remaining 1 tablespoon of butter. Pour off the fat from the skillet and wipe it clean with paper towels. Toast the buns, cut sides down, in the skillet over medium-high heat until golden, 1 to 2 minutes. You may need to work in several batches.

6 To assemble the burgers, spread the buns with "Secret Sauce," if using, or whatever condiment(s) you prefer. Place a burger on top of the sauce and top it with a lettuce leaf and a tomato slice and any embellishments you like. Add the top of the bun and dig in.

Burgers Under the Broiler

If you prefer broiling your burgers, prepare the Ur-Burger through Step 2. Preheat the broiler to high. Place the burgers on a broiler pan 1 to 2 inches below the heating element. Broil the burgers until they are sizzling and browned on to top, about 4 minutes. Gently turn the burgers over with a spatula and continue broiling them until done to taste, 4 to 6 minutes more for medium. To test for doneness insert an instant-read thermometer through the side of a burger. When the burger is cooked to medium, the thermometer will register 160°F. Pick up the Ur-Burger recipe at Step 4. Toast the buns under the broiler, cut sides up, 1 to 2 minutes.

BURGERS

The burger is so ubiquitous, so iconic, so seamlessly integrated into the American diet, you may wonder what I could possibly tell you that you don't already know. The basic principle—a cooked patty of ground beef on a bun—can be mastered in ten minutes, and unlike other guy foods (chili or brisket, for example), a neophyte can make an excellent burger the first time he tries it. So what makes an extraordinary burger? Here are the ten steps you need to become a master.

1 BUY THE RIGHT MEAT: A few years ago, celebrity butcher Pat LaFrieda developed a marquee blend of ground chuck, short rib, and brisket. Others upped the ante (and the price) by grinding wagyu or Kobe-style beef. Prime beef may give you a richer mouthfeel, but as far as I'm concerned, USDA Choice makes a fine burger.

2 SAY NO TO PINK SLIME: Where you buy your meat is as important as what you buy. In the best of all worlds you'd buy it from a trusted butcher who grinds the beef daily or you would grind it yourself. If you shop at a supermarket, ask for beef ground on the premises that day from domestically sourced beef. Avoid frozen preformed patties from multinational corporations. These are the geniuses who brought us

"pink slime"—ammonia-treated patties formed from industrial and sometimes trash cuts of meat that may have originated in multiple countries. Yes, in a single burger. Cheap, yes, but believe me, you pay in the long run.

3 FAT IS BEAUTIFUL: You need at least 15 percent and as much as 22 percent fat to give you the buttery rich mouthfeel one associates with a great burger. My target ratio is 18 percent.

4 AVOID CROSS-CONTAMINATION: Wash your hands well with soap before and after handling ground beef. Never put cooked burgers on a plate that held raw—use a fresh plate. Never cut lettuce, tomatoes, or other vegetables on a cutting board you used for raw meat; use a clean cutting board. Keep burgers refrigerated until you're ready to cook them.

5 SIZE AND SHAPE MATTER: The size and shape of a burger also influence its texture and taste.
- To shape the burgers, lightly wet your hands with cold water and divide the meat into equal-size portions, then shape each into a thick patty.
- Use 6 ounces of beef per burger at a minimum—8 ounces for a burger that really fills out a bun.

▶ The patty should be thick (about 1 inch), with a slight depression in the center because it will rise more here than at the edge when you cook it.

▶ Handle the burger meat with a light touch: If you are mixing in flavorings, use a wooden spoon, not your fingers. (You don't want to heat the meat with the warmth of your hands.)

▶ Place the burgers on a plate lined with plastic wrap (this prevents sticking). Cover them with plastic wrap (this prevents oxidation) and refrigerate them until you are ready to cook. You can make the burgers up to six hours ahead.

6 SEASON LIKE YOU MEAN IT: I season my burgers with salt—large crystals of sea salt or *fleur de sel* (see page 227)—right before cooking so the salt dissolves on the meat slowly and crunches under your teeth. And freshly ground black pepper, which has a brighter, profoundly more intense flavor than the preground spice sold in cans. I don't go for the "kitchen sink" approach—adding chopped onions, peppers, steak sauce, hot sauce, or any or all of a dozen other flavorings (that's what meat loaf is for). I like to keep the focus on the primal flavor of the beef.

7 GRILL OR SKILLET? As you might imagine, my preferred cooking method is grilling. The high dry heat of the grill sears the meat, melts out some of the fat, and imparts a charred smoky crust you just can't get in a skillet. This is not to say that some of the world's great burgers aren't cooked in a skillet or on a flattop griddle. For indoor cooks, unless you have an industrial-strength broiler, I'd stick with a skillet. The contact grill runs a very distant fourth (sorry, George)—it just doesn't get hot enough to sear the meat properly.

8 TAKE ITS TEMPERATURE: When I was growing up, we routinely ate raw hamburger meat. To do so today would be gastrointestinal suicide. To be safe, you should cook hamburgers to medium (160°F). Insert the probe of an instant-read thermometer through the side of the burger (you won't get an accurate reading through the top). This may be more well-done than you like your burger, but that's what it takes to be safe.

9 DON'T FORGET THE BUN: You wouldn't hang a Rembrandt in a plastic picture frame. Likewise, you shouldn't serve your craft burger on an anemic factory bun. Buy freshly baked buns from an artisanal bakery or your supermarket bakery (my local supermarket makes excellent buns). For the ultimate burger, use buttered and toasted or grilled brioche buns (made from an egg and butter-enriched dough).

10 LESS IS MORE: When it comes to garnishing burgers, I'm of the "less is more" school. Lettuce leaves? Yes. (Placed under the burger, they keep it from making the bun soggy.) Sliced tomato? Yes, but only when you can use really luscious ripe tomatoes. I like the occasional slice of melted cheddar or provolone cheese on a burger and I rarely say no to bacon. But when you start with good meat and cook it right, you don't really need a lot of enhancements. Ketchup or mustard? Oddly, I'm a mayonnaise guy, but use any condiment in moderation.

L.A. BURGER

SHOP The only esoteric ingredient here is Umami Ketchup, which has a deeper, richer flavor than the conventional red stuff. (It contains anchovies and soy sauce.) You can order on line here: umami.com/shop.

GEAR Your basic kitchen gear including a large (10- to 12-inch) nonstick skillet, an instant-read thermometer, and a nonstick baking sheet

WHAT ELSE For a strictly authentic Umami Burger, you'd make Parmesan Crisps (page 108) and Roasted Tomatoes (page 505). If you are pressed for time, shave Parmesan cheese on top of the burgers and add raw tomatoes instead. You will still get plenty of umami taste from the caramelized onion and shiitakes.

TIME about 30 minutes— longer if making Parmesan Crisps and Roasted Tomatoes

It's one of the most satisfying burgers you'll ever sink your teeth into. And if you live in car-centric Los Angeles, it just may be the best thing to happen to the burger since the drive-in. Brainchild of literature student turned wine consultant and restaurateur Adam Fleischman, Umami Burger is a fast-food joint with an existential philosophy—based on what the Japanese call the "fifth taste." Umami embraces the earthy, meaty flavors associated with foods high in glutamic acids, such as mushrooms (especially shiitakes), cheese (especially Parmesan), tomatoes (roasted), caramelized onions and shallots, and the Asian seasoning called monosodium glutamate (MSG), which was originally extracted from seaweed. (For more on umami, see page 28.) It's also a burger emporium with style, offering craft beers and wines from small vineyards. A bite of the L.A. Burger plays pinball on your taste buds, possessing flavors far deeper and more soulful than you ever thought possible for a burger—especially one cooked on a griddle. When in L.A., eat there. The home version is a little involved, but the results are worth it. **Makes 4 burgers**

3 to 4 tablespoons butter, at room temperature

6 ounces shiitake mushrooms, wiped clean with a damp paper towel and stemmed

1 medium-size onion, peeled and thinly sliced

1½ to 2 pounds ground beef

Coarse salt (kosher or sea) and freshly ground black pepper

4 hamburger buns

Umami Ketchup (see Shop on this page), or ¼ cup ketchup mixed with 2 teaspoons Asian fish sauce or soy sauce

3 ounces Parmesan cheese or 4 Parmesan Crisps (recipe follows)

4 slices ripe tomato, or 4 Roasted Tomato halves (see page 505)

1 Melt 1 tablespoon of the butter in a large nonstick skillet over medium heat. Add the mushrooms and cook them until they are soft in the center and a little crisp on the edges, 3 to 5 minutes per side. Using a slotted spoon, transfer the mushrooms to a plate.

2 Add 1 tablespoon of the butter and the onion to the skillet and cook the onion until it is a dark golden brown, 8 to 12 minutes. Reduce the heat as needed so the onion doesn't burn. Transfer the onion to the plate with the mushrooms. Set the skillet aside. (The mushrooms and onions can remain at room temperature for an hour or so.)

3 Divide the beef into 4 equal portions. Shape each portion into a patty about 1 inch thick and slightly larger in diameter than the buns (lightly wet your hands with cold water before handling the meat). Work with a light touch, handling the meat as little as possible. Make a slight depression in the center of the patties; they should be slightly concave. You can form the burgers up to 6 hours ahead. Arrange the burgers on a plate lined with plastic wrap and cover them with more plastic wrap. Refrigerate the burgers until you are ready to cook them.

4 Just before cooking, generously season the burgers on both sides with salt and pepper, turning them gently.

5 If you're cooking the burgers right after preparing the mushrooms and onions, you may still have enough butter left in the skillet. If not, melt 1 tablespoon of the butter in the skillet over medium-high heat. Add the burgers, spacing them 2 inches apart. Cook the burgers until the bottoms are browned, 3 to 5 minutes. Using a spatula, gently turn the burgers over and continue cooking them until done to taste, about 5 minutes more for medium. To test for doneness, insert an instant-read meat thermometer through the side of a burger. When the burger is cooked to medium the thermometer will register 160°F. (To cook the burgers under the broiler, follow the directions in the box on page 103. To grill them, see the box on page 113.)

6 Transfer the burgers to a warm plate and let them rest for 1 to 2 minutes.

7 Meanwhile, spread the buns with about 1 tablespoon of butter. If you've cooked the burgers in a skillet, pour off the fat from the skillet and wipe it clean with paper towels. Toast the buns cut side down in the skillet over medium-high heat until golden, about 2 minutes. (If you cooked the burgers under

Embellishments for Making a Great Burger Better

Some people would argue that a simple grilled ground beef patty on a bun is perfection itself. The rest of us like to dress up our burgers with a wide range of condiments and garnishes. Here are some of the classics:

▸ Dill or sweet pickle slices

▸ Sweet onion, like a Vidalia or Walla Walla, sliced ¼ inch thick; the onion can be raw or sautéed

▸ A slice of thick smokehouse bacon, cut in half crosswise and cooked until crisp (see page 67 for how to cook bacon)

▸ Sliced mushrooms—sautéed or grilled

▸ An egg fried in butter (you'll find instructions for frying eggs on page 44)

▸ A slice of smoked ham (about 1 ounce), browned in butter or on the grill

Or, for the perennial favorite cheeseburger, place a slice (about 1 ounce) of aged cheddar, Gruyère, pepper Jack, Roquefort, or any other cheese you like on top of the burger right after you turn it over and let it melt while the second side cooks.

the broiler, toast the buns under the broiler, cut sides up, until golden, 1 to 2 minutes; if you grilled the burgers, grill the buns cut sides down, for about 1 minute.)

8 To assemble the burgers, spread the buns with the Umami Ketchup. Spoon the mushrooms and onion on the bottoms of the buns and top them with the burgers. Using a vegetable peeler, shave the Parmesan on top of the burgers or place a Parmesan Crisp on top of each, followed by a slice of tomato and the top of the bun. One bite and you'll *definitely* understand the concept of umami.

PARMESAN CRISPS

Parmesan Crisps are ridiculously easy to make and unbelievably flavorful (think potato chip made from cheese), but you must use real Parmigiano Reggiano cheese. It also helps to line your baking sheet with parchment paper. At very least use a nonstick baking sheet. **Makes 8 crisps**

1 cup (about 4 ounces) finely freshly
    grated Parmigiano Reggiano cheese

1 Preheat the oven to 400°F. Line a nonstick baking sheet with parchment paper, if using.

2 Spoon the cheese in eight 2-tablespoon mounds on the baking sheet, spacing the mounds about 4 inches apart. Gently flatten each mound of cheese with the back of the spoon.

3 Bake the crisps until they have spread out and are golden and crisp, 3 to 5 minutes. Let the crisps cool slightly on the baking sheet, then, using a spatula, slide them onto a wire rack to cool completely. Once cool, store the crisps in an airtight container until ready to use but try to eat within a day or two.

INSIDE-OUT CHEESEBURGER

I created this killer burger a few years ago in my ongoing effort to make a hamburger that would stay moist even when you cook it to a safe temperature. The solution was to turn a conventional cheeseburger inside out—namely, fold the cheese (now coarsely grated) into the ground beef. The cheese melts as the burger cooks, delivering a luxurious mouthfeel. Customize the cheeseburger by using the cheese you like best. **Makes 4 burgers**

SHOP See the notes on buying ground beef on page 104. As for the cheese, a firm cheese will be easiest to grate.

GEAR Your basic kitchen gear including a large (10- to 12-inch) skillet and a box grater or rotary grater (like a Moulinex—available at cookware shops and a very handy piece of equipment to own, especially if you eat a lot of pasta—or Inside-Out Cheeseburgers).

WHAT ELSE I've kept the garnishes simple here to keep the focus on the cheese. For additional embellishments, see page 107.

TIME about 15 minutes

1½ to 2 pounds ground beef, well-chilled

4 ounces cheese of your choice (see below for suggestions)

Coarse salt (kosher or sea) and freshly ground black pepper

2 tablespoons butter

4 hamburger buns or kaiser rolls, split

4 Boston or Bibb lettuce leaves, rinsed and patted dry with paper towels

1 luscious red ripe tomato, sliced

Your choice of embellishments for the burgers (see page 107 for suggestions)

1 Place the beef in a mixing bowl. If the cheese has a rind, remove it. Using a box grater or rotary grater, coarsely grate the cheese into the bowl with the beef (you can also grate the cheese in a food processor). Using a wooden spoon, mix the cheese well into the ground beef.

2 Divide the beef into 4 equal portions. Shape each portion into a patty about 1 inch thick and slightly larger in diameter than the buns (lightly wet your hands with cold water before handling the meat). Work with a light touch, handling the meat as little as possible. Make a slight depression in the center of the patties; they should be slightly concave. You can form the burgers up to 6 hours ahead. Arrange the burgers on a plate lined with plastic wrap and cover them with more plastic wrap. Refrigerate the burgers until you are ready to cook them.

3 Just before cooking, season the cheeseburgers on both sides with salt and pepper. You'll need less salt than for a plain burger, as many cheeses are already quite salty.

4 Melt 1 tablespoon of the butter in a large skillet over medium-high heat. Add the burgers, spacing them 2 inches apart. Cook the burgers until the bottoms are browned, 3 to 5 minutes. Using a spatula, gently turn the burgers over and continue cooking them until done to taste, about 5 minutes more for medium. To test for doneness, insert an instant-read meat thermometer through the side of a burger. When the burger is cooked to medium the thermometer will register 160°F. (To cook the burgers, under the broiler, follow the directions in the box on page 103. To grill them, see the box on page 113.)

5 Transfer the burgers to a warm plate and let them rest for 1 to 2 minutes. Meanwhile, butter the buns with the remaining tablespoon of butter. Pour off the fat from the skillet and wipe it clean with paper towels. Toast the buns, cut sides down, in the skillet over medium-high heat until golden, about 2 minutes. (If you cooked the burgers under the broiler, toast the buns under the broiler, cut sides up, until golden, 1 to 2 minutes; if you grilled the burgers, grill the buns, cut sides down, for about 1 minute.)

6 To assemble the burgers, place a lettuce leaf on the bottom of each bun. Place a burger on top and top it with some tomato slices and any embellishments you like. Add the top of the bun and serve at once.

BARBECUE PORK BURGER

SHOP You want ground pork that is 15 to 20 percent fat, not pork sausage, which can contain as much as 30 percent fat.

GEAR Your basic kitchen gear including a large (10- to 12-inch) cast-iron skillet

Y ou could think of this smoky burger as pulled pork in a hurry. The rub provides the barbecue flavor with crumbled bacon standing in for the "brownies," the shards of crisp roast pork skin that distinguish superior Carolina-style pulled pork. For the full Southern effect, pile on sweet pickles, barbecue sauce, and some coleslaw. **Makes 4 burgers**

4 slices bacon

1½ to 2 pounds lean ground pork,
    well-chilled

1 tablespoon of your favorite barbecue rub

½ teaspoon liquid smoke (optional)

2 tablespoons butter,
    at room temperature

4 hamburger buns, split

Sliced sweet pickles

Southern Mustard Slaw
    (optional; page 178)

Your favorite of barbecue sauce,
    such as Dark and Stormy Barbecue
    Sauce (page 537), for serving

WHAT ELSE On page 285 you'll find instructions for making a homemade Raichlen's Rub #1, and on page 537 you'll find the Dark and Stormy Barbecue Sauce. Alternatively, you can use your favorite store-bought brands of rub and barbecue sauce.

Liquid smoke is a natural ingredient made from real wood smoke. A few drops will intensify the barbecue effect in the burgers; just don't overdo it.

TIME about 20 minutes

1 Place the slices of bacon in a cold cast-iron skillet and heat over medium heat. Cook the bacon until it is crisp and browned, 3 minutes per side, turning it over with tongs once the first side is browned. Transfer the bacon to a cutting board to cool, then finely chop it and place it in a mixing bowl. Discard the bacon fat or cool it, transfer it to a jar with a lid, and refrigerate it for another use (bacon fat makes everything taste better).

2 Add the pork to the mixing bowl with the bacon. Add the barbecue rub and liquid smoke, if using, and stir with a wooden spoon to mix. Divide the pork into 4 equal portions. Shape each portion into a patty, about 1 inch thick and slightly larger in diameter than the buns (lightly wet your hands with cold water before handling the meat). Work with a light touch, handling the meat as little as possible. Make a slight depression in the center of the patties; they should be slightly concave. You can form the burgers up to 6 hours ahead. Arrange the burgers on a plate lined with plastic wrap and cover them with more plastic wrap. Refrigerate the burgers until you are ready to cook them.

3 Melt 1 tablespoon of the butter in a large skillet over medium-high heat. Add the burgers, spacing them 2 inches apart. Cook the burgers until the bottoms are browned, 3 to 5 minutes. Using a spatula, gently turn the burgers over and continue cooking them until done to taste, about 5 minutes more for medium. To test for doneness, insert an instant-read meat thermometer through the side of a burger. When the burger is cooked to medium the thermometer will register 160°F. (To cook the burgers under the broiler, follow the directions in the box on page 103. To grill them, see the box on page 113.)

4 Transfer the burgers to a warm plate and let them rest for 1 to 2 minutes.

5 Meanwhile, butter the buns with the remaining tablespoon of butter. Pour off the fat from the skillet and wipe it clean with paper towels. Toast the buns, cut sides down, in the skillet over medium-high heat until golden, about 2 minutes. (If you cooked the burgers under the broiler, toast the buns under the broiler, cut sides up, until golden, 1 to 2 minutes; if you grilled the burgers, grill the buns, cut sides down, for about 1 minute.)

6 Line the toasted buns with sliced pickles. Place the burgers on top and top them with the slaw, if using, and barbecue sauce. Add the top of the bun and serve at once.

TEX-MEX TURKEY BURGERS

SHOP Ground turkey comes in many grades, some quite lean and others shockingly fatty. Look for ground turkey white meat with 5 to 10 percent fat and read the label carefully if you buy it prepackaged.

Jicama is a Mexican root vegetable that has the moist fresh crunch of a radish and tastes like a cross between potato and apple. You'll find it in the produce section of most supermarkets.

GEAR Your basic kitchen gear including a large (10- to 12-inch) skillet and tongs

WHAT ELSE To jazz up the burgers further (not that they need it), pile on some *rajas* (roasted poblano pepper strips) and/or sour cream (full or low fat).

TIME about 20 minutes

The turkey burger arose in an effort to enjoy the lusciousness of a hamburger with the clean conscience that comes with eating low-cholesterol and low-fat meat. These turkey burgers light up your mouth with chile powder, jalapeño pepper, and cilantro. In keeping with the Tex-Mex theme, serve the burgers on flour tortillas along with avocado and slivered jicama. **Makes 4 burgers**

1½ to 2 pounds lean ground turkey, well-chilled

¼ cup chopped fresh cilantro

1 to 2 jalapeño peppers, seeded and minced (for hotter burgers, leave the seeds in)

1 scallion, both white and green parts, trimmed and minced

1 tablespoon pure chile powder, preferably ancho chile powder

½ teaspoon ground cumin

Coarse salt (kosher or sea)

1 tablespoon olive oil

4 flour tortillas (8 inches in diameter)

1 cup Pico de Gallo (page 210), Salsa Chipotle (page 211), or your favorite salsa (optional)

8 ounces jicama (optional), peeled and cut into matchstick slivers

1 avocado (optional), peeled, seeded, and diced

½ cup Rajas (optional; page 200)

Sour cream (optional)

1 Place the turkey, cilantro, jalapeño(s), scallion, chile powder, and cumin in a mixing bowl and, using a wooden spoon, stir to mix.

2 Divide the turkey into 4 equal portions. Shape each portion into a patty about 1 inch thick (lightly wet your hands with cold water before handling the meat). Work with a light touch, handling the meat as little as possible. Make a slight depression in the center of the patties; they should be slightly concave. You can form the burgers up to 6 hours ahead. Arrange the burgers on a plate lined with plastic wrap and cover them with more plastic wrap. Refrigerate the burgers until you are ready to cook them.

3 Just before cooking, generously season the burgers on both sides with salt, turning them gently.

4 Heat the olive oil in a large skillet over medium-high heat. Add the burgers, spacing them 2 inches apart. Cook the burgers until the bottoms are browned, 3 to 5 minutes. Using a spatula, gently turn the burgers over and continue cooking them until done to taste, about 5 minutes more for medium. To test for doneness, insert an instant-read thermometer through the side of a burger. When the burger is cooked to medium the thermometer will register 165°F. (To cook the burgers, under the broiler, follow the directions in the box on page 103. To grill them, see the box on page 113.)

5 Transfer the burgers to a warm plate and let rest for 1 to 2 minutes.

6 Meanwhile, wipe out the skillet and use it to warm the tortillas over medium heat until pliable, about 10 seconds per side. Use tongs to turn them. (If you cooked the burgers under the broiler or on the grill, warm the tortillas in either one for about 10 seconds per side.)

7 To serve, place a burger on one side of each tortilla. Spoon some salsa over each burger, if using, and top the burgers with jicama, avocado, and/or *Rajas* and sour cream, if desired. Fold the bare halves of the tortillas over the burgers and serve.

Burgers on the Grill

Yes, great burgers can be made stovetop, But no, that doesn't mean I've forsaken grilling burgers for panfrying. In fact, I would be falling short if I didn't include some tips for cooking the burgers on the grill.

Set up the grill for direct grilling and preheat it to high (see page 10). In a perfect world you'd grill over a wood fire. When working on a charcoal or gas grill, you can add a couple handfuls of soaked, drained hardwood chips to generate optional wood smoke.

When ready to cook, brush and oil the grill grate. Arrange the burgers on the hot grate and grill them until the bottoms are browned, 3 to 5 minutes. Using a spatula, gently turn the burgers over. However, *never* press the burgers with the spatula; you'll force out the flavorful juices. Continue grilling the burgers until cooked to taste, 3 minutes more for rare beef burgers, 5 minutes more for medium. Unless you're absolutely sure about the purity of your meat, cook beef burgers to medium—160°F. Turkey burgers will brown on the first side after about 4 minutes and take about 5 minutes more to be done through; they should be cooked to at least 165°F. Insert an instant-read thermometer through the side of the burger to verify the internal temperature of the burgers. Grill the buns, cut sides down, until golden, about 1 minute.

SWEDISH MEATBALL SLIDERS

SHOP Tradition calls for ground beef in addition to the pork, but veal gives you more refinement. It's your call— buy what's available.

GEAR Your basic kitchen gear including a large (10- to 12-inch) nonstick skillet, a broiler, or a contact grill

WHAT ELSE There are several options for cooking the sliders: in a skillet (the traditional way), under the broiler, or even on a contact grill.

TIME about 30 minutes

Noomi Rapace. Stieg Larsson. The Volvo. Sweden has given the world a lot of cultural enrichment, yet what I appreciate most is the *köttbullar*, the Swedish meatball. Pork and veal make it rich; ginger and allspice make it fragrant. And I'm about to show you a thoroughly un-Nordic way to cook and serve it: slider style on a potato bun. I've taken a few other liberties with the traditional recipe, including a Nordic-style lemon and dill sauce. **Makes 12 sliders; serves 4**

1 slice white bread, crusts removed

¼ cup half-and-half or milk

12 ounces ground pork, well-chilled

12 ounces ground veal or beef, well-chilled

1 large egg, beaten

1 shallot, peeled and minced

1 tablespoon finely grated peeled fresh ginger, or 1 teaspoon ground ginger

¼ teaspoon ground allspice

¼ teaspoon ground or freshly grated nutmeg

1½ teaspoons coarse salt (kosher or sea)

½ teaspoon freshly ground black pepper

About 2 tablespoons (¼ stick) butter, or about 2 tablespoons extra virgin olive oil

12 potato rolls or Parker House rolls, sliced in half (see Note)

Arugula leaves (optional), rinsed and patted dry with paper towels

Lemon-Dill Sour Cream Sauce (recipe follows)

1 Make the sliders: Place the white bread in a large mixing bowl. Pour the half-and-half over it and let soak until soft, about 5 minutes. Pour off any unabsorbed half-and-half (save it for cereal), then gently squeeze the bread with your fingers to wring out any excess liquid. Return the squeezed bread to the bowl.

2 Add the pork, veal, egg, shallot, ginger, allspice, nutmeg, salt, and pepper to the bread. Wet your hands with cold water and knead the ingredients together with your fingers, making sure the bread and other ingredients are well distributed throughout the meat. (Sure, you could use a wooden spoon, but your hands are more efficient.) If you have time, refrigerate the meatball mixture for about 30 minutes; it will be easier to shape.

3 Divide the meat mixture into 12 equal portions. Roll each into a ball and flatten these to form patties that are ½ inch thick. Arrange the patties on a plate lined with plastic wrap and cover them with more plastic wrap. Refrigerate the patties until you are ready to cook them. You can make the patties several hours ahead.

4 Heat 1 tablespoon of butter or olive oil in a nonstick skillet over medium-high heat. Add the sliders and cook them until browned on the outside and cooked through, 3 to 4 minutes per side. Work in several batches if needed so you don't crowd the skillet.

To cook the sliders under the broiler, follow the direction in the box on page 103; they'll need 3 to 4 minutes per side. To grill them, see the box on page 113; they'll also need 3 to 4 minutes per side.

5 Lightly butter or oil the cut sides of the rolls. If you have cooked the sliders in a skillet, toast the rolls, cut sides down, in the skillet over medium-high heat until golden, 1 to 2 minutes (add butter or oil to the skillet as needed, although you probably won't need to).

If you cooked the burgers under the broiler, toast the rolls under the broiler, cut sides up, until golden, 1 to 2 minutes.

If you cooked the burgers on a contact grill, place the rolls cut side down on the grill, close the cover, and grill until golden, for 1 minute.

6 To serve, place some arugula leaves, if using, on the bottom half of each roll. Top each roll with a slider and a spoonful of the Lemon-Dill Sour Cream Sauce. Add the top of the roll and serve at once. Bet you can't eat just one.

Note: Both potato and Parker House rolls are soft and puffy. They're available fresh at bakeries and packaged in the bakery section of your supermarket.

LEMON-DILL SOUR CREAM SAUCE

This sour cream sauce is a staple of Scandinavian cooking. To get the full effect, you must use fresh dill and grate the lemon zest fresh. Have it ready before you prepare the burgers. **Makes about ¾ cup**

⅓ cup sour cream

⅓ cup mayonnaise, preferably Hellmann's

1 tablespoon Dijon mustard

2 tablespoons minced fresh dill

1 teaspoon grated lemon zest (see Note)

Coarse salt (kosher or sea) and freshly ground black pepper

Place the sour cream, mayonnaise, mustard, dill, and lemon zest in a mixing bowl and whisk to mix. Season the sauce generously with salt and pepper to taste; it should be highly seasoned. Refrigerate the sauce, covered, until ready to serve. It will keep for several hours.

Note: The zest is the oil-rich outer rind of the lemon. Grate it with a Microplane (see page 15), being careful to grate only the yellow rind, not the bitter white pith underneath.

A NEW WAY WITH BRATWURST

SHOP For brats, it's hard to beat the Johnsonville brand.

GEAR Your basic kitchen gear plus a charcoal or gas grill, hardwood chips, and an instant-read thermometer. (Optional: Soak 1½ cups hickory or other hardwood chips in cold water to cover for 30 minutes and drain.)

WHAT ELSE So what about our apartment-dwelling friends who lack access to a grill? In the variations on page 117 you'll find a cool method for oven roasting bratwurst: Crisp casing. Succulent meat. The only thing missing is the wood smoke.

TIME 40 minutes (but not all of it spent cooking)

Cooking bratwurst on the grill is a bit like attempting to barbecue dynamite. Potentially incendiary, to say the least. Which doesn't stop legions of guys from building blast-furnace fires and incinerating their brats in some strange sacrifice to the God of Tailgating. If you do choose to direct-grill your bratwurst, work over a moderate fire and leave yourself a large flame-free safety zone where you can move the brats in the event of flare-ups. But I have an even better option—indirect grill the brats, that is, cook them next to, not directly over, the fire with the grill lid closed. Indirect grilling offers several advantages over conventional direct grilling: You avoid the grease fires traditionally associated with grilled brats; the casing comes out crackling crisp and the brat meat supernaturally moist. And if you're so inclined, you can toss soaked hardwood chips on the coals (or in your gas grill's smoker box), adding an extra dimension of flavor in the form of wood smoke. **Makes 12 bratwursts; serves 4 to 6**

12 fresh (uncooked) bratwursts

Semmel, kaiser, or other hard rolls

Melted butter (optional)

German-style mustard

Drained sauerkraut

1 Set up the grill for indirect grilling and preheat it to medium (see page 10).

2 When ready to cook, arrange the bratwursts on the grill grate away from the heat and over the drip pan. If using wood chips, toss them on the coals or place them in the smoker box of your gas grill.

3 Cook the bratwursts until the casings are browned and the sausages are cooked through, about 30 minutes. Because you are grilling using the indirect method, there is no need to turn the brats. When done the brats will be golden brown and plump with sizzling juices. To check for doneness, insert an instant-read thermometer in one end of a brat toward the center; the internal temperature should be at least 160°F.

4 Transfer the bratwursts to a platter or serve them hot off the grill. If you're so inclined, split the rolls in half, brush the insides with melted butter, and lightly toast them, cut sides down, on the grill, about 1 minute (place the rolls directly over the fire). Serve the brats on the rolls with mustard and sauerkraut.

Variations

Oven-roasted bratwursts: With the oven method you have the opportunity to roast the bratwursts with onion and garlic, adding extra flavor from the outside in. Preheat the oven to 400°F. Arrange 12 brats in a single layer in a roasting pan. Drizzle 1 tablespoon of olive oil or butter over them and gently stir to coat. Stir in 1 onion cut into 6 wedges and 2 unpeeled garlic cloves. Roast the bratwursts until the casings are browned and the sausages are cooked through, 30 to 40 minutes, turning with tongs as needed. To check for doneness, insert an instant-read thermometer in one end of a brat toward the center; the internal temperature should be at least 160°F.

Transfer the brats to a platter. If you're so inclined, split semmel or kaiser rolls in half, brush the insides with melted butter, and lightly toast them in the oven, cut sides down in the roasting pan for 2 to 3 minutes.

Serve the brats on the rolls with mustard, sauerkraut, and the roasted onion and garlic (squeeze the garlic cloves out of their skins).

Italian sausage and peppers: Oven-roasting gives you terrific Italian sausage and peppers. Follow the directions for the oven-roasted bratwursts, substituting sweet or hot Italian sausage for the brats. In addition to the onion and garlic, add 2 or 3 slivered red, yellow, and green bell peppers. Stir the sausages a few times as they roast. Spectacular color and taste.

A GUY'S BEST FRIEND

HOT DOGS

My cousin, David Raichlen, is an anthropology professor at the University of Arizona by day and a smoke-obsessed pit master nights and weekends. So when Dave has a new food find for me in Tucson, I can't climb into his pickup truck fast enough. During my last visit, Dave introduced me to a cross-cultural food phenomenon taking southern Arizona by storm: the Sonoran hot dog. Our destination? El Güero Canelo (loosely translated as The Mulatto), where the humble hot dog comes cooked, wrapped in bacon, and jammed onto a soft sweet roll under a deluge of stewed beans, grilled green onions, and jalapeños, radishes, cucumbers, mayo, and three different salsas. Sound excessive? You bet! Hot dogs are like that: prone to excess.

Consider the samba dog—lavished with hard-boiled quail eggs and pepper-onion-olive relish—served as a late-night snack in Rio de Janeiro. Closer to home, I created a truly "hot" hot dog for *Barbecue University*—a knockwurst split lengthwise, stuffed with sliced jalapeños and pepper Jack cheese, tied into a tube and grilled (see page 121). For other must-try dogs, see page 120.

If cooking isn't rocket science, hot dogs are barely cooking. Here are five tips to help you put on the dog.

1   THE HOT DOG ITSELF: Sure you can buy Kobe beef hot dogs and even franks stuffed with foie gras. For me, the best store-bought hot dog out there is Hebrew National, with the perfect ratio of salt to spice.

2   THE COOKING METHOD: For me, not surprisingly, nothing beats a screaming-hot grill. Grill the hot dogs until the casings blister and brown, two minutes per side, six to eight minutes in all, turning them with tongs. One variation on this theme is to cut the dog almost in half lengthwise, then open it and grill it cut side down and opened flat (even better under a grill press), giving it a quarter turn half way through to apply a handsome crosshatch of grill marks. Grill the second side the same way. The beauty of this method: You expose even more surface area to the smoke and fire.

3   INDOOR COOKING METHODS: Don't have access to a grill? Don't worry. Brown the dogs in a cast-iron skillet or grill pan (the split method above works wonders here also). Or, cook the hot dogs under the broiler. Again, the idea is to brown and blister the casing.

4   A METHOD NOT TO USE: Boiling or simmering. Sorry to all the "dirty water dog" devotees, but boiling gives you no texture contrast between the casing and the meat.

5   THE BUN: Butter the inside and toast it until crisp on the grill, in a skillet, or in your toaster oven. No arguments.

THE "DEAR" DOG

This is a true story. My grandfather, Sam Raichlen (known to all by his nickname "Dear"), loved food like a man possessed. The short list of his favorites included, lox and eggs, *gribenes* (chicken fat cracklings), and his mother-in-law's chocolate roll. (For him, that chocolate roll was, perhaps, my great-grandmother's sole virtue.) As much as anyone in my family, it was Dear who inspired me to become a food writer. But as my grandfather lay on his deathbed, his last food request, uttered with some of the last words he spoke on earth, was for a hot dog.

The Raichlen frank, you see, was no ordinary hot dog. It started with all-beef hot dogs, which my grandfather sliced lengthwise nearly in half. He opened them up like a book and seared them in a skillet, browning the inside as well as the exterior. (More crust equals more flavor.) He browned a few bologna slices as well, wrapping them around the hot dogs. He buttered and toasted the buns (we kept Jewish, not kosher), which he slathered with spicy mustard, and piled sauerkraut and pickles high on top. Now *that* was a hot dog, and you can understand how it might be a dying man's last craving. **Makes 8 hot dogs**

SHOP There is only one hot dog in our pantheon: Hebrew National. And use fresh bakery hot dog buns when they are available.

GEAR Your basic kitchen gear including a large (10- to 12-inch) skillet, a plate lined with paper towels, plus a grill press (optional)

WHAT ELSE For a cosmopolitan touch, substitute Italian mortadella for the bologna.

TIME about 15 minutes

8 hot dogs

3 tablespoons butter, at room temperature

8 thin slices of bologna

8 hot dog buns, split lengthwise

Spicy brown mustard, Dijon mustard, or horseradish mustard

About 2 cups drained sauerkraut

Dill pickle slices, sweet pickle slices, or, why not, pickled jalapeños

1 Carefully slice each hot dog almost in half lengthwise, cutting to but not through the bottom casing. Gently open up the hot dogs as you would a book so that they lay flat. Set the hot dogs aside.

MUST-TRY HOT DOGS

Born in Frankfurt, Germany, the hot dog has become a food of the world, adopted and customized by every culture that eats it.

BRAZILIAN *TURBINADO* | A "jet-propelled" hot dog heaped with mashed potatoes, crunchy shoestring potatoes, bacon bits, mayonnaise, and tomato-onion salsa.

CHICAGO DOG | A Vienna-brand all-beef hot dog served on a poppy seed bun with chopped raw onions, sliced tomatoes, sport peppers (pickled peppers in Chicagoese), dill pickle spears (or cucumbers), neon-green pickle relish, and a sprinkle of celery salt. *Never* ask for ketchup.

CHILEAN *COMPLETO* | The name says it all—a hot dog on a soft bun piled with tomatoes, avocado, sauerkraut, and a scandalous amount of mayonnaise.

CINCINNATI *CROQUE MADAME* DOG | A specialty of the Senate restaurant on Vine Street, where all-beef hot dogs wrapped in Black Forest ham come on brioche with poached eggs and béchamel sauce.

COLOMBIAN *PERROS CALIENTES* | Hot dogs drenched with salsa, pineapple sauce, mayonnaise, mustard, ketchup, shredded lettuce, and crushed potato chips. Bad dogs.

CONEY ISLAND DOG | Naturally, this beef and pork hot dog could hail only from . . . lower Michigan. Topped with beanless chili, yellow mustard, and diced yellow onions.

ICELANDIC DOG | A lamb, pork, and beef hot dog lavished with rémoulade sauce (a tartarlike sauce enriched with horseradish, and pickles), mustard, ketchup, and French fried onions. If you are in Reykjavik, try it at Bæjarins Beztu Pylsur.

NEW YORK SYSTEM WIENERS | Part of Rhode Island's food culture since the early 1900s (and another instance of a hot dog hijacking a name from somewhere else). To order this veal and pork dog like a local, ask for it "up the arm," which requires the cook to balance the steamed buns on his forearm as he adds onions, celery salt, mustard, and cumin-scented meat sauce.

SEATTLE DOG | A Japanese-style hot dog topped with soba noodles, teriyaki onions, pickled ginger, nori seaweed, bonito flakes, and/or wasabi cream. Order it from Nikaido's, a pushcart in downtown Seattle.

SWEDISH *TUNNBRÖDSRULLE* | Don't pass judgment on this improbable assemblage until you've stumbled out of a Stockholm bar at closing time in need of alcohol-absorbing sustenance. It starts with a soft tortilla-like wrap, *tunnbröd*, to which are added hot dogs, mashed potatoes, shrimp salad sloppy with mayo, onions, shredded lettuce, and squiggles of ketchup and mustard.

WEST HOLLYWOOD OKI'S DOG | A Pico Boulevard legend supposedly inspired by a hot dog stand in Okinawa. We're talking two hot dogs wrapped in a large flour tortilla, burrito style, with chili and pastrami.

2 Melt 1 tablespoon of butter in a large skillet over medium-high heat. Add the bologna slices and cook until browned, about 2 minutes per side, working in batches if necessary. Transfer the bologna to a plate lined with paper towels to drain.

3 Add the hot dogs to the skillet, cut side down and cook until crusty and browned on both sides, about 3 minutes per side, working in batches, if necessary. Place a grill press on top of the dogs if you have one or use a second heavy skillet. Transfer each batch of hot dogs to a platter as they are done. Pour off all but about 1 tablespoon of fat from the skillet.

4 Lightly brush the insides of each hot dog bun with the remaining butter. Toast the buns buttered side down in the skillet over medium heat until golden brown, 1 minute.

5 To serve, slather each bun with mustard. Place a slice of bologna in each bun, then add a hot dog and some sauerkraut and pickle slices.

THE "HOT" DOG

Here's a hot dog that really is hot—stuffed with fresh jalapeño peppers and pepper Jack cheese. **Makes 8 knockout knockwursts**

For the hot dogs
8 knockwursts

4 jalapeño peppers, thinly sliced crosswise, or 32 slices drained jarred pickled jalapeño peppers

8 ounces pepper Jack cheese, thinly sliced (1 inch wide by 4 to 5 inches long)

8 hot dog buns, split lengthwise

2 to 3 tablespoons butter, at room temperature

Jalapeño mustard, horseradish mustard, or Dijon mustard

For serving (optional)
Grilled or sautéed onions

Rajas (roasted poblano pepper strips, page 200)

Pico de Gallo (page 210) or Salsa Chipotle (page 211)

SHOP You can certainly use a conventional hot dog, but a fat dog, like knockwurst, is easier to stuff. Look for it in the deli case.

GEAR Your basic kitchen gear plus cotton butcher's string and a charcoal or gas grill

WHAT ELSE Just how hot you take these dogs depends on your capsaicin tolerance. I call for fresh jalapeños, but a sadist might use bird's-eye chiles, scotch bonnets, or even ghost peppers.

TIME 20 minutes

1 Set up the grill for direct grilling and preheat to high (see page 10).

2 Carefully slice each knockwurst almost in half lengthwise, cutting to but not through the far edge. Gently open up the knockwursts as you would a book so that they lie flat.

3 Stuff each knockwurst with jalapeño and pepper Jack cheese slices. Using butcher's string, tie each knockwurst closed in 3 places.

4 When ready to cook, brush and oil the grill grate. Arrange the knockwursts on the grill grate (balance them, cut side up, lengthwise between the bars of the grate).

Grill the bottom and both sides of the knockwursts until browned and the cheese is melted, about 2 minutes per side (6 minutes in all), turning with tongs. Transfer the knockwursts to a platter.

5 Lightly brush the inside of each hot dog bun with the butter. Toast the buns buttered sides down on the grill, 1 to 2 minutes. Watch carefully as buttered buns can burn easily.

6 To serve, snip the strings off the knockwursts. Slather the toasted buns with jalapeño mustard and place the knockwursts in the buns. Top the knockwursts with onions, *rajas*, or salsa as desired.

SOUP
AND CHILI

Soup—it's liquid comfort on a cold winter day, and relief, not just for a hangover, but also for the common cold. And a reminder that while man does not live by bread alone, he can survive exceedingly well on bread dunked in a brimming bowl of soup. In fact, modern soup originated as the medieval *sop*—a slice of stale bread softened with broth.

This chapter is all about liquid sustenance. Cold soups, like gazpacho, you can make in fifteen minutes. Hot soups, like Mexico's fiery chile-lime soup and a rib-sticking Cheddar beer soup from England. Being a part-time New Englander, I'll show you how to make classic clam chowder and oyster stew the way they prepare it at the Grand Central Oyster Bar in Manhattan. And because every man should know how to cook up a pot of chili, I'll give you three to choose from: traditional meat, fiery New Mexican chili *verde*, and a bean chili for meatless Mondays.

Soups and chilis. Because sometimes the best comfort foods come ladled from a pot.

BASIC GAZPACHO

If you've never made soup before—if you've never cooked *anything* before— gazpacho (aka liquid salad) is a great place to start. You can prepare it in minutes and it requires no heat or cooking. It's supremely refreshing in summertime, which is the best time to make it because that's when the tomatoes and other ingredients are in peak season. Note: Gazpacho lends itself to several killer variations, including adding vodka, clams, or wood smoke. **Serves 4; can be multiplied as desired**

4 luscious red ripe tomatoes (about 2 pounds)

1 medium-size cucumber

1 small onion, peeled and coarsely chopped (about 2/3 cup)

1/2 green bell pepper, stemmed, seeded, and coarsely chopped

1/2 red bell pepper, stemmed, seeded, and coarsely chopped

1 clove garlic, peeled and coarsely chopped

3 tablespoons best-quality extra virgin olive oil, plus more for drizzling

1 to 2 tablespoons red wine vinegar (or sherry vinegar), or to taste

Coarse salt (kosher or sea) and freshly ground black pepper

1 tablespoon chopped fresh chives or scallion greens

SHOP Gazpacho lives or dies by the quality of the tomatoes. Ideally, they'll come from your garden or a local farm stand and will *never* have seen the interior of a refrigerator. (Refrigerating tomatoes harms a tomato's texture and flavor.) For onion, try to find a sweet variety, like Vidalia, Walla Walla, or Maui.

GEAR Your basic kitchen gear including a blender, immersion blender, or food processor

WHAT ELSE If you choose to make the smoked variation (see page 126), you'll need a smoking gun.

TIME about 15 minutes

1 Remove the stem ends from the tomatoes and cut the tomatoes into 1-inch pieces. Peel the cucumber, cut it in half lengthwise, and scrape out the seeds with a spoon. Cut the cucumber into 1-inch pieces.

2 Place the tomatoes, cucumber, onion, green and red bell peppers, garlic, olive oil, wine vinegar, and salt and pepper (start with 1 teaspoon of the former and 1/2 teaspoon of the latter) in a blender and blend until smooth,

adding 1/2 cup of cold water, or enough to obtain a thick puree. *If you are using an immersion blender,* place the ingredients in a large deep pot or bowl and puree them. *If you are using a food processor,* puree the tomatoes, cucumber, onion, bell peppers, and garlic first, then add the water, olive oil, and wine vinegar.

3 Taste the gazpacho for seasoning, adding salt, pepper, or more vinegar as necessary; the gazpacho should be intensely flavorful, with the acidity of the vinegar balancing the sweetness of the vegetables.

4 Pour the gazpacho into bowls or mugs. Drizzle a little oil over each serving. Sprinkle with chopped chives and dig in. The virtue of gazpacho is its freshness. Try to serve within 1 hour of preparing. It won't taste as good the next day.

Variations

Bloody gazpacho: Serve the gazpacho in bar glasses, adding a shot of iced vodka or pepper vodka to each.

Clam or oyster gazpacho: Shuck a dozen or so littleneck clams or oysters, working over a bowl to catch the juices (see pages 398 and 409). Make the gazpacho as described, substituting the clam juices or ½ cup of bottled clam broth for the ½ cup of water. Slide 3 shucked clams or oysters into each serving.

Smoked gazpacho: For this futuristic gazpacho you get to use a really cool tool from the world of molecular cuisine: a smoke gun. It looks like a hair dryer: You load it with hickory, oak, or another hardwood sawdust and fire the smoke at the food (or in this case through a rubber hose into the soup). If you think traditional gazpacho is refreshing, just wait until you experience it smoked.

To smoke the gazpacho using a smoke gun, load the smoke gun following the manufacturer's instructions. Immerse the rubber smoking tube in the gazpacho and smoke the soup for 3 to 5 minutes (cover with plastic wrap to hold in the smoke). Remove the tube and re-blend the gazpacho to mix in the smoke flavor.

Don't have a smoke gun? Add ½ teaspoon of liquid smoke to the soup.

GARLIC SOUP

SHOP *Pimentón* is Spanish smoked paprika (see page 28)—available at your local supermarket or natural foods store (or through amazon.com). Two good brands are Santo Domingo and La Dahlia. I generally use sweet *pimentón*, although hot *pimentón* would certainly wake you up.

There once was a party animal from Toledo (Spain, not Ohio) who overindulged in a night of barhopping. To jolt himself back to life the next morning, he made a rouse-the-dead breakfast of fried garlic, salty ham, smoky paprika, and an egg poached in chicken broth. Thus was born Spain's gutsy *sopa de ajo*, garlic soup, or so the story goes, although its roots were likely more prosaic. Like many guy classics, it likely began as a poor man's attempt to resuscitate stale bread with garlic and water. Whatever its origins, garlic soup should be part of your repertoire as an eye-opening breakfast or brunch dish, light lunch, or supper starter. It doesn't hurt that you can whip it up in minutes. Here's how San Sebastián–born chef Jon Gonzalez made it at a Miami tapas bar called Xixón. **Serves 1; can be multiplied as desired**

GEAR Your basic kitchen gear including a small (6- to 8-inch) skillet or shallow saucepan

WHAT ELSE In its original form, *sopa de ajo* likely would have been made with water. But chicken stock gives it considerably more depth of flavor. On page 549 you'll find instructions for making stock from scratch (and why you should do it).

TIME about 10 minutes

1 tablespoon extra virgin olive oil, preferably Spanish

2 slices (½ inch thick) country-style or French bread, cut into ½-inch cubes

2 to 4 cloves garlic (dose your poison to taste), peeled and thinly sliced crosswise

1 ounce jamón serrano (Spanish ham) or cooked ham, cut into matchstick slivers

½ teaspoon pimentón or sweet paprika

1 cup chicken stock (preferably homemade, page 549, or use a good no- or low-sodium store-bought brand)

Coarse salt (kosher or sea) and freshly ground black pepper

1 large egg (preferably organic)

1 Heat the olive oil in a small skillet over medium-high heat. Add the bread cubes and cook until golden brown, 1 to 2 minutes, stirring with a wooden spoon. Add the garlic and ham and cook until the garlic just begins to brown, 1 to 2 minutes. Do not let the garlic burn or it will become bitter.

2 Stir in the sweet *pimentón* and chicken stock and boil for 2 minutes (long enough to absorb the garlic flavor). Season with salt and pepper to taste; the soup should be highly seasoned.

3 Crack the egg into a small bowl, being careful not to break the yolk. Slide the egg into the soup. Adjust the heat to medium so the liquid is just simmering and poach the egg in the soup until it is just set, 2 to 3 minutes, spooning the hot broth over the egg to cook the top. Ladle the soup into a soup bowl, taking care not to break the egg, and dig in. Note that Garlic soup is best made in one fell swoop right before serving. Its virtue lies in its spontaneity.

How to Make Garlic Chips

Fried garlic chips are great in salads, on fish and pork chops, in Asian peanut sauce, as a garnish for soups, and just about any other way you can think of. Try to make them within an hour or so of serving.

To make garlic chips, peel and trim six to eight cloves of garlic, then cut them crosswise into paper-thin slices. (Cool tool: A safety-edged razor blade works well for this.) Pour vegetable oil to a depth of ½ inch in a small skillet; you will need about ½ cup. Heat the oil over medium heat. This takes a minute or two depending on your stove. When the oil is hot enough, bubbles will dance around a slice of garlic dropped in it after a few seconds.

Add all the garlic slices to the oil and cook them until golden brown, 1 to 2 minutes, stirring with a slotted spoon or fork. Once the garlic slices are golden brown, use a slotted spoon to immediately remove them from the skillet and transfer them to a plate lined with paper towels to drain. Watch the garlic carefully as it cooks—do not let the chips burn. Save the oil; it will have a mild garlic flavor and you can use it for future sautés. Store the garlic chips on the paper towel or in a small bowl and try to use within an hour or two of frying. Garlic oil will keep several hours at room temp or several days if refrigerated.

HOW TO PEEL, CHOP, MINCE, AND COOK
GARLIC

As you cook your way through this book, you'll use a lot of garlic. So you need to know how to choose and handle it. But first a little chemistry lesson that explains what makes garlic so pungent. When garlic cells are ruptured by cutting or pounding, they release a compound called alliinase. When alliinase mixes with oxygen, it forms a mild form of hydrochloric acid—that's what "irritates" (make that stimulates) your eyes and nasal passages. The finer you chop garlic, the more of this compound is released.

For a mild garlic flavor, use whole peeled cloves. For a more pronounced flavor, lightly crush the cloves with the side of a cleaver or chef's knife or coarsely chop them. For a strong garlic flavor, finely chop or mince the garlic. Raw garlic tastes stronger than cooked garlic, and when browned, garlic acquires a toasted nutty flavor with its pungency greatly reduced. But, take care not to burn garlic or it will taste bitter.

HOW TO BUY GARLIC | Garlic comes in "heads"—roundish clusters of cloves (the basic unit of garlic—not the spice—a dozen or so to a head). Look for firm clean plump heavy heads free of shriveling or brown spots and with no green sprouting at the top.

HOW *NOT* TO BUY GARLIC | Pre-chopped and packed in oil. The stuff has a ghastly flavor and gives me indigestion. Some markets sell pre-peeled whole cloves of garlic. These are OK for high-frequency users, but spoil more quickly than fresh. I personally always start with whole fresh heads.

HOW TO SEPARATE GARLIC CLOVES | When ready to cook, press down on the head with the heel of your hand to separate the cloves. Gently pull apart the individual cloves with your fingers.

HOW TO PEEL GARLIC CLOVES: METHOD #1 | Gently crush the clove with the side of a cleaver or a chef's knife. Press just hard enough to break the skin that covers the garlic but not so that hard you smash the garlic. Slip off the skin with your fingers.

METHOD #2 | Place the cloves in a covered jar and shake like crazy for 20 seconds. This knocks the skins right off the cloves.

HOW TO TRIM GARLIC | Using a paring knife, cut off the woody stem end of the garlic clove. If the clove has a green shoot running its length, cut the clove in half lengthwise and, using the tip of the knife, remove it.

HOW TO GET THE GARLIC SMELL OFF YOUR HANDS | When it comes to garlic, one man's odor is another's cologne. The best way to keep the garlic smell off your hands is to wear latex gloves when handling. Otherwise, wash your fingers with liquid soap, then with baking soda and water.

Working with Garlic

1 Press down on the head with the heel of your palm to separate it into cloves.

2 Gently press on a clove with the side of your knife blade to break and loosen the skin.

3 Pull the skin off a garlic clove with your fingers.

4 Cut the garlic clove crosswise into ¼-inch-thick slices.

5 Or, use the side of the knife to smash the clove. Have the edge angled down toward the cutting board so you don't cut yourself and push down on it with the side of your fist.

6 To chop or mince the clove, rock the knife blade up and down on the sliced or smashed clove until you get the right size pieces.

BEER SOUP
WITH CHEDDAR AND STOUT

SHOP To be strictly authentic use Guinness stout and a sharp British Cheddar like Dorset Drum or Quickes. But an American cheddar, like Tillamook, paired with an American stout, like Rise Up Stout by Maryland's Evolution Brewing Company, make an excellent soup, too.

GEAR Your basic kitchen gear including a large heavy saucepan and a blender or immersion blender

WHAT ELSE Want to make a quick cheese fondue? Bring 2 cups of stout, ale, or white wine to a boil in a heavy saucepan rubbed with a cut clove of garlic. Mix 1 pound of grated cheese with 3 tablespoons of flour, then stir the mixture into the boiling liquid. Add 1 tablespoon of Dijon or English prepared mustard and season with salt and pepper to taste. Use bread cubes or vegetables for dipping into the melted cheese.

TIME about 30 minutes

Beer and cheese have been staples of the English diet since Anglo-Saxon times (remember *Beowulf*—the action movie based on the equally action-packed epic poem you studied in English lit class in college?) and likely before. Both result from fermentation; add a third fermented food, bread (that's what yeast does to dough), and you get the traditional ploughman's lunch. Think of this thick, creamy beer soup as fondue you eat with a spoon, with an interesting yin-yang of bitter stout and sharp cheddar flavors. **Serves 4**

3 tablespoons butter

1 bunch scallions, trimmed, white and green parts finely chopped

2 carrots, trimmed, peeled, and finely chopped

2 ribs celery, finely chopped

3 tablespoons unbleached all-purpose flour

1 bottle (12 ounces) Guinness or other stout

2 cups chicken stock (preferably homemade, page 549, or use a good no- or low-sodium store-bought brand)

½ cup half-and-half, milk, or heavy (whipping) cream

4 cups (about 1 pound) freshly and coarsely grated sharp cheddar cheese, preferably English

1 tablespoon English or Dijon mustard

1 to 2 teaspoons Worcestershire sauce

Coarse salt (kosher or sea) and freshly ground black pepper

1 Melt the butter in a large saucepan over medium heat. Set 2 tablespoons of the scallion greens aside for serving. Add the remaining scallions and the carrots and celery to the pan and cook until just beginning to brown, about 4 minutes, stirring with a wooden spoon. Stir in the flour and cook until blended, about 1 minute.

2 Gradually whisk in the stout; the mixture will foam and thicken. Whisk in the chicken stock and half-and-half. Let the soup simmer until the vegetables are very soft and the soup is richly flavored, about 10 minutes. Puree the soup with an immersion blender (see page 22) or in a blender. Or for a chunky beer soup, leave the vegetable pieces whole. Safety tip: When pureeing soup in a blender, work in small batches (don't fill the blender bowl more than halfway). Place the lid on tightly and cover it with a clean dishcloth, using the latter to hold the lid firmly in place. Return the soup to the saucepan.

3 Just before serving, let the soup come to a gentle simmer, then whisk in the cheese, mustard, and Worcestershire sauce (start with 1 teaspoon and adjust to taste). Season with salt and pepper to taste; the soup should be highly seasoned. Let the soup simmer until the cheese is melted, about 3 minutes. Serve in bowls with the remaining scallion greens sprinkled on top.

CHILE-LIME CHICKEN SOUP

Electrifying. What else do you call a soup the main ingredients of which are chiles, garlic, and lime juice? *Sopa de lima* (lime soup), as it's known in the Yucatán, has been prescribed for everything from hangover relief (jalapeños to clear your head) to a cure for the common cold (the lime juice blasts you with vitamin C, while the garlic serves as an antiseptic). Medicinal virtues aside, this is about the most flavorful chicken soup you'll ever taste, and it even has "noodles" in the form of slivered flash-fried tortillas. Great on a cold day and it could almost rouse the dead. **Serves 4 as a starter, 2 as a light main course**

SHOP To get the vivifying effect of this soup, you must use freshly squeezed lime juice, so stock up on limes.

GEAR Your basic kitchen gear including a medium-size saucepan, plus a citrus press or reamer for squeezing the lime juice

WHAT ELSE If you happen to have leftover chicken (from the roast chicken on page 327, for example), use it here in place of the chicken breast.

TIME about 20 minutes

1 whole skinless, boneless chicken breast (12 to 14 ounces)

2 corn tortillas (6 inches each)

¼ cup vegetable oil, such as canola or extra virgin olive oil

4 cloves garlic, peeled and thinly sliced crosswise

4 to 8 jalapeño peppers, thinly sliced crosswise

4 cups chicken stock (ideally homemade, page 549) or use a good no- or low-sodium store-bought brand

1 large ripe tomato, seeded and cut into ¼-inch dice

½ cup coarsely chopped fresh cilantro

⅓ cup fresh lime juice (from 2 limes), or more to taste

Coarse salt (kosher or sea) and freshly ground black pepper

1 Cut the chicken breast into matchstick slivers. The easiest way to do this is to thinly slice the breast crosswise against the grain, then cut each slice into slivers. Set the chicken aside.

2 Cut each tortilla in half, then stack the halves and cut them crosswise into ⅛-inch strips.

3 Heat the oil in a medium-size saucepan over medium heat. To check if the oil is the right temperature, dip a tortilla strip in it. Bubbles will dance around it after a few seconds. Stir in the tortilla strips and cook until golden brown, about 1 minute. Using a slotted spoon, transfer the tortilla strips to paper towels to drain.

4 Add the garlic and jalapeño slices to the hot oil and cook until lightly browned, 1 to 2 minutes. Stir in the slivered chicken and the chicken broth and let simmer gently until the chicken is cooked through, about 5 minutes. The soup can be prepared several hours ahead to this stage. Cool in the pan, cover, and refrigerate.

5 Shortly before serving, place the soup over high heat and let come to a boil. Stir in the diced tomato, cilantro, and lime juice and cook just until the soup boils again, about 1 minute. Season with salt and pepper to taste; the soup should be highly seasoned.

6 Ladle the soup into bowls. Top each with the fried tortilla strips and dig in.

Working with Tomatoes

HOW TO SEED A TOMATO

1 Cut the tomato in half crosswise (if it were a globe, you'd cut through the equator).

2 Hold a half in your hand and gently squeeze out the seeds and liquid.

3 Use a spoon handle to scrape out any remaining seeds.

HOW TO CHOP A TOMATO

1 Cut the tomato in half crosswise, then cut each half into ½-inch-wide slices.

2 Pile up the slices and cut widthwise to obtain ½-inch strips.

3 Cut the strips crosswise to dice the tomatoes.

JOSE ANDRES

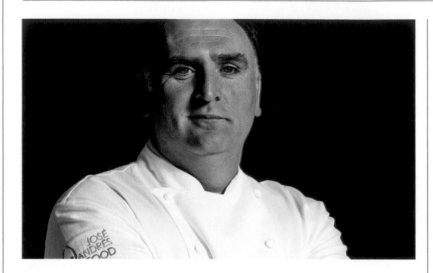

The first time I met José Andrés was at his intimate tasting bar-restaurant—minibar—in Washington, D.C., where mojitos come in aerosol cans to be sprayed on your tongue and Philly-inspired "cheesesteaks" consist of crystal-crisp pastry shells filled with Parmesan foam and grilled beef. On average, it takes three months to get a reservation.

The next time was at his *nuevo latino*–themed Café Atlántico, where the irrepressible chef stopped us midmeal (literally) to drive us to Crystal City to experience his newly opened Mexican restaurant, Oyamel Cocina Mexicana. I've since eaten dozens of José's meals in Los Angeles, Las Vegas, and Miami, and what always strikes me is the authenticity of his flavors and the bravura with which they're served.

Born in Asturias, Spain, in 1969, José Ramón Andrés trained with the legendary Ferran Adrià at the Catalonian temple of molecular cuisine El Bulli. He then moved to Washington, D.C., to open his first restaurant, a tapas bar called Jaleo. As a TV host, he stars on both sides of the Atlantic with the wildly successful *Vamos a Cocinar* on Spanish national television and a twenty-six-part *Made in Spain* show on PBS. Over the years, José has received

a James Beard Foundation Outstanding Chef award, was named one of the *GQ* magazine Men of the Year, was awarded Spain's Order of Arts and Letters, and was named Chairman Emeritus for his hunger relief work with D.C. Central Kitchen. A proponent of molecular cuisine (the specialty of his flagship restaurant é in Las Vegas), José has the distinction of being one of the few chefs ever to teach a culinary physics course at Harvard University. You've got to love this guy. I do.

Why should a man know how to cook?
If you want to lead the tribe, you have to be able to feed the tribe. Since prehistoric times, this has been the essence of leadership.

What's your favorite seduction dish?
Much to my wife's chagrin, I don't like to cook for two people. It's the same amount of work to cook for two as it is to cook for twenty-four. I guess I'm a show-off.

What's your go-to dish when you're by yourself?
One dish I return to is a tomato and mayonnaise sandwich. You start with good country bread and slather it with

homemade mayonnaise. You need an amazing July or August tomato that ripened on the vine and has never seen the inside of a refrigerator. Add sea salt and freshly ground black pepper and a drizzle of extra virgin olive oil. *That's* something I can eat again and again.

What are three dishes every guy should know how to make?

Paella: It's something every man in Valencia knows how to do, and once you understand how it works, you can make it for two or two hundred. It's important for men to know how to cook for large numbers of people.

Stew: I grew up in Asturias, Spain, where every Sunday, my father or one of my uncles would make a stew like *fabada* (bean and meat stew) or *marmitako*, a fish stew made with bonito (similar to tuna), wine, and potatoes.

A whole baby lamb, goat, pig, or rabbit cooked *a la estaca*—on a stake: You open the animal like a book and impale it upright on a stake in front of a campfire, using wooden cross braces to hold it open. You roast it for two and a half to three hours (less for rabbit), rotating the stake often to cook both sides. Even if you don't have anything—pots, pans, or a kitchen—you can always cook on a campfire.

Three ingredients you can't live without?

Spanish olive oil: You can use it to fry, poach, sear, grill, sauté, dress a salad, and make mayonnaise.

Jamón ibérico (Spanish ham): Other families have a dog as a pet; we have a whole ibérico ham. The hogs feed on acorns, which produce an incredibly sweet meat. With ham I can feed anyone any time.

White truffles: A while ago I won a poker game and I used my earnings to buy these aromatic fungi from northern Italy. Shave truffles over pasta, risotto, eggs, toast—you name it. When truffle season is over in late November, I get really depressed.

Three tools you can't live without?

An Evo: It's a round gas-fired *plancha* [griddle—see page 9] designed for outdoor use. I keep one in my garage. When it comes to grilling cheese or searing fish, shrimp, or scallops, nothing can beat it—not even a grill.

A Microplane: The Microplane gives you much finer, more sophisticated shavings than a box grater or even a truffle slicer. I use it to shave everything from Parmesan cheese to white truffles. Freeze a slice of watermelon and shave it with a Microplane to make an incredible *granita* (frozen dessert).

A juicer: It gives me orange juice for breakfast and fresh lemon and lime juice for cocktails. When you bring a girl home for the first time, show her a fresh peach and tell her to smell it. Then juice it into champagne glasses. Open a bottle of champagne in a very manly manner and add it to the peach juice. If you don't get lucky that night, you're hopeless.

What are the most important things to keep in mind if you're just starting out in the kitchen?

You will cut and burn yourself. Man up. It comes with the territory.

You will rarely succeed the first time you try a dish. Learn from your failures.

Learn to cook with three or four pans at a time. You'll look like a culinary god.

As you start to become competent in the kitchen, your children will become your toughest critics.

What are the three most common mistakes guys make in the kitchen?

We overbuy. When most men shop, we're still thinking like hunter-gatherers from fifty thousand years ago.

We oversalt.

We overestimate our talents in the kitchen. We think that cooking is not an exact science, which it is, and that anything we cook will be amazing, which it will not.

Something you've learned over the years that really helps you up your game in the kitchen?

When it comes to cooking, we men tend to think about the tangibles: ingredients, techniques, equipment. But what *really* matters are the intangibles: how to control the fire; how much wood to add or gas to use; how to keep the frying pan at the right temperature for five or ten minutes, or however long you need it.

The other overlooked element is tempo—how to cook the diverse parts of a meal using diverse methods and still have everything come out at the right time.

What else?

Send a message to Congress. Right now our laws are written to benefit big corporations. They need to be rewritten to help us feed our families and communities better. And vote for women. If we had more women in Congress, you can bet we'd do a better job feeding our country.

Parting words of advice?

Master the art of making tapas and cocktails well and you'll rule the world!

BEAN SOUP THREE WAYS

Consider bean soup: Robust. Rib sticking. A welcome starter when it's cold or raw outside and substantial enough for a simple main course when you don't feel like doing a lot of cooking. You might think that bean soups require lengthy cooking, but thanks to organic low-sodium canned beans, you're looking at fifteen minutes of preparation time. We're talking about soups with deep soulful flavors and plenty of protein.

The basic formula is simple: If you're carnivorous, start with some chorizo, kielbasa, Italian sausage, or ham. Meat lover or not, you'll brown a member of the allium family—onion, scallions, shallots, ramps, or leeks—and add whatever bean you like—white, black, navy, kidney, chickpea—you name it. Stir in some chicken, beef, or vegetable broth. Greens like kale, collard greens, Swiss chard, and spinach add color, nutrients, and flavor. And to finish the soup: freshly grated cheese—Parmigiano Reggiano, pecorino romano, cheddar, Jack, pepper Jack— you get the idea. Whichever options you choose, the result will be substantially more than the sum of the parts.

SHOP You'd be amazed (and appalled) by how much sodium is found in many popular canned bean brands. For the best taste and health, buy an organic low- or no-sodium brand.

GEAR Your basic kitchen gear including a box grater and a large saucepan

WHAT ELSE Most canned beans come packed in a thick, starchy liquid. I like to rinse and drain the beans so I get pure bean flavor.

WHITE BEAN, KALE, AND KIELBASA SOUP

A Tuscan-inspired soup with a Polish twist, this soulful soup is made with kielbasa (garlicky smoked sausage). To stay strictly Italian, use fresh sweet or spicy Italian sausage (you'll need to cook it a little longer). For a Portuguese version, use a paprika- and garlic-flavored sausage called *linguiça*. **Serves 4**

TIME about 15 minutes prep, plus 15 minutes cooking time

1 bunch kale (black kale—see page 165—is great) or collard greens

1 large leek or 1 bunch scallions

1 tablespoon extra virgin olive oil

8 ounces kielbasa (garlicky cooked Polish sausage) or fresh Italian sausage (mild or spicy), thinly sliced crosswise

1 can (15 ounces) white beans, such as cannellini or navy beans, rinsed and drained

3 cups chicken stock (preferably homemade, page 549, or use a good no- or low-sodium store-bought brand)

Coarse salt (kosher or sea) and freshly ground black pepper

1 to 2 ounces ($\frac{1}{4}$ to $\frac{1}{2}$ cup) freshly grated Parmigiano Reggiano cheese

1 Rinse the kale, shake it dry, and cut out and discard the tough center stems. Roll the leaves lengthwise into a tight tube and cut them crosswise into $\frac{1}{4}$-inch slices (this is the easiest way I know to cut kale). Set the kale aside.

2 If you are using a leek, clean as described in the box below and thinly slice it crosswise. If you are using scallions, trim off and discard the roots and any wilted green parts, then thinly slice the scallions crosswise. Set the leek or scallions aside.

3 Heat the olive oil in large heavy saucepan over medium heat. Add the kielbasa and cook until browned, 2 to 3 minutes, stirring with a wooden spoon. (If you are using fresh sausage, cook it until all traces of pink are gone, 4 to 5 minutes, stirring and chopping the sausage with a wooden spoon.) Leave the sausage in the pan but pour off and discard all but about 1½ tablespoons of the fat.

4 Add the leeks or scallions to the sausage and cook over medium heat until wilted and lightly browned, about 3 minutes. Add the kale to the pan and cook it until wilted and about a quarter of its original volume, about 3 minutes.

5 Stir in the beans and chicken stock. Let come to a boil, then reduce the heat and let the soup simmer until it is richly flavored and the kale is tender, 10 to 15 minutes. Taste for seasoning, adding salt and pepper as necessary; the soup should be highly seasoned.

6 Ladle the soup into bowls. Grate the Parmigiano Reggiano on top.

To Clean a Leek

Leeks are often sandy and must be cleaned before you chop them. To do this, cut off and discard the leek's dark green leaves but keep the white and light green parts. Make four lengthwise cuts through the leek up to but not through the root end. Plunge the leek up and down in a large bowl of cold water (like you would a plumber's helper) to remove the grit. Change the water as needed until it's grit free. Shake the leek dry, then thinly slice it crosswise. Cut off and discard the furry root end.

BLACK BEAN CHORIZO SOUP

re's the quintessential soup of the Spanish Caribbean and Latin America—rich with Spanish-style chorizo sausage and pungent with cumin and cilantro. Note: If you're one of the 10 percent of the population for whom cilantro tastes like soap, not wonderfully aromatic, you're probably allergic to it. Substitute flat-leaf parsley instead. **Serves 4**

TIME about 15 minutes prep, plus 15 minutes cooking time

1 tablespoon extra virgin olive oil

8 ounces precooked chorizo or linguiça sausage, thinly sliced crosswise (see Note)

1 medium-size onion, peeled and finely chopped

1 clove garlic, peeled and minced

1 teaspoon ground cumin

½ cup chopped fresh cilantro

1 can (15 ounces) black beans, rinsed and drained

3 cups chicken stock (preferably homemade, page 549, or use a good no- or low-sodium store-bought brand)

Coarse salt (kosher or sea) and freshly ground black pepper

1 to 2 ounces Manchego, Jack, or cheddar cheese, coarsely grated (¼ to ½ cup)

1 Heat the olive oil in a large heavy saucepan over medium heat. Add the chorizo and cook until browned, about 3 minutes, stirring with a wooden spoon. Depending on the sausage, you may get a lot or a little rendered fat; pour off and discard all but about 1½ tablespoons.

2 Add the onion, garlic, and cumin and cook over medium heat until browned, about 3 minutes. Stir in most of the cilantro (save 2 tablespoons for the end), black beans, and chicken stock. Let come to a boil, then reduce the heat and let the soup simmer until richly flavored, 10 to 15 minutes. Taste for seasoning, adding salt and pepper as necessary; the soup should be highly seasoned. The soup can be made ahead to this point. Cool to room temperature, transfer to a storage container with a lid, and refrigerate until serving. It will keep for up to 2 days. Reheat in a saucepan over medium heat.

3 Ladle the soup into bowls and top it with the remaining 2 tablespoons of cilantro. Sprinkle the cheese on top.

Note: For a vegetarian version, simply omit the meat and substitute a vegetable broth (a good store-bought brand) for the chicken broth. You'll still get protein from the beans.

SOUP AND CHILI 139

CHICKPEA LAMB SOUP WITH NORTH AFRICAN SPICES

TIME about 15 minutes prep, plus 15 minutes cooking time

Here's how bean soup is made in North Africa—loaded with lamb, chickpeas, and spinach and scented with cinnamon, cumin, coriander, and ginger. If you're the sort of guy who enjoys ferreting out exotic ingredients, use a spicy North African–style lamb sausage called *merguez*. (You can find it at select Whole Foods, halal butchers, or online at dartagnan.com.) But ground or diced lamb will give you plenty of flavor, too. **Serves 4**

1 bunch or 1 package (10 ounces) fresh spinach

8 ounces merguez (fresh lamb sausage, casing removed), ground lamb, or lamb shoulder meat (see Note)

1 tablespoon extra virgin olive oil

1 medium-size onion, peeled and thinly sliced crosswise

1 piece (1 inch) fresh ginger, peeled and finely chopped

2 teaspoons sweet or hot paprika

½ teaspoon ground cumin

½ teaspoon ground coriander

¼ teaspoon ground cinnamon

1 can (15 ounces) chickpeas (garbanzo beans), rinsed and drained

3 cups chicken stock (preferably homemade, page 549, or use a good no- or low-sodium store-bought brand)

⅓ cup chopped fresh cilantro or flat-leaf parsley (optional)

1 large ripe tomato, stemmed and cut into ½-inch dice with its juices

Coarse salt (kosher or sea) and freshly ground black pepper

1 Stem the spinach and wash well in a large bowl in cold water. (Change the water as needed until there's no more grit at the bottom.) Drain the spinach well and thinly slice. Set aside. If you are using lamb shoulder meat, chop it or cut it into ¼-inch dice.

2 Heat the olive oil in a large heavy saucepan over medium heat. Add the *merquez* or ground or diced lamb and cook until browned, about 3 minutes, stirring with a wooden spoon. Pour off and discard all but about 1½ tablespoons of the fat.

3 Add the onion and ginger and cook over medium heat until browned, about 3 minutes. Stir in the paprika, cumin, coriander, and cinnamon and cook until fragrant, about 1 minute.

4 Stir in the chickpeas, chicken stock, and all but 2 tablespoons of the cilantro, if using. Let the soup come to a boil, then reduce the heat and let simmer until richly flavored, 10 to 15 minutes. Stir in the tomato and spinach for the last 5 minutes of cooking. Taste for seasoning, adding salt and pepper as necessary; the soup should be highly seasoned.

5 Ladle the soup into bowls and top with the remaining cilantro, if desired.

Note: For a vegetarian version, simply omit the lamb and substitute a vegetable broth for the chicken stock. You'll still get plenty of protein from the beans.

How to Mince Herbs

1 Strip the leaves from the thicker stems by gently sliding your thumb and index finger down the length of each stem. Pick off any thinner stems, if desired.

2 Gather the leaves up in a tight pile all facing the same direction and start chopping by rocking your knife back and forth over the pile.

3 Keep gathering the pile as tight as possible as you continue chopping the leaves. Change the direction of the knife slightly with each chop.

4 When done, your herbs will be reduced to a pile of fragrant dust-size bits.

LUMBERJACK SOUP
(SPLIT PEA SOUP WITH COUNTRY HAM)

SHOP Dried green split peas can be bought by the pound in plastic bags or in bulk at your local natural foods store.

GEAR Your basic kitchen gear including a large saucepan

WHAT ELSE Split peas typically come in 1-pound bags, so this recipe makes a rather large batch—enough soup to feed 8. Freeze the excess in 2-cup containers so you always have some on hand.

TIME about 45 minutes

Once popular with the woodsmen of rural Quebec and Maine, this split pea puree has everything you want in a soup: rib-sticking richness, a creamy finish, a smoky ham flavor that just won't quit, and an ingredient list that won't break the bank. It takes a little longer to make than the previous soups because you start with dried split peas. (Not that you spend most of that time cooking—on the contrary.) Like most bean soups, it's good the day you make it and even better the next day or two (store in the refrigerator). Note: The soup will thicken overnight, so you need to loosen it up with more stock or a cup of milk as you reheat it. **Serves 8**

---

2 tablespoons extra virgin olive oil or butter

1 large onion, peeled and finely chopped

12 ounces (¾ cup) diced smoked ham, Smithfield ham, or ham steak

1 pound dried green split peas

4 carrots, peeled and cut crosswise into ½-inch slices

1 cup milk or half-and-half

7 cups chicken stock (preferably homemade, page 549, or use a good no- or low-sodium store-bought brand) or water, or more as needed

1 bay leaf

Coarse salt (kosher or sea) and freshly ground black pepper

---

1 Heat the olive oil in a large heavy saucepan over medium heat until shimmering. Add the onion and ham and cook until lightly browned, about 4 minutes.

2 Stir in the split peas, carrots, milk, chicken stock, and bay leaf. Let the soup come gradually to a boil, then reduce the heat to medium-low and let the soup simmer gently, stirring often, until the peas are soft and the soup is thick and creamy, 30 to 40 minutes. If the soup gets too thick, add additional stock or water. Just before serving, discard the bay leaf and taste for seasoning, adding salt and pepper as necessary; the soup should be highly seasoned.

3 For a coarse soup (the way I like it), serve as is. For a creamy soup, puree in batches in a blender or right in the saucepan with an immersion blender. Serve at once. Leftover split pea soup will keep in the refrigerator for several days (let it cool to room temperature first), transfer it to a plastic container with a lid, and refrigerate. Reheat in a saucepan over low heat, adding additional stock or water as needed to thin.

CLAM CHOWDER

A half millennium ago or so, Breton fishermen from the west coast of France (the same guys reputed to have "discovered" North America decades before Columbus) cooked fish stew in a heavy cast-iron pot called a *chaudière*. That's the origin of the creamy-smoky-briny soup we New Englanders call chowder. You can make it with clams. You can make it with fish. You can make it white, red, or even meatless (see the Corn Chowder on page 144). If you've never tasted chowder made from scratch, you're in for a revelation. **Serves 4**

2 thick slices artisanal bacon, cut crosswise into ¼-inch slivers

1 medium-size onion, peeled and finely chopped

2 tablespoons unbleached all-purpose flour

2 cups bottled clam broth or juice or chicken stock

2 cups half-and-half

½ teaspoon fresh thyme (optional)

1 pound potatoes, peeled and cut into ¾-inch cubes

24 littleneck or cherrystone clams in the shell or 12 quahogs (large chowder clams), enough for 1 cup shucked clam meat with juices

Freshly ground black pepper and, if needed, a whisper of coarse salt (kosher or sea)

1 tablespoon minced fresh chives or trimmed green scallion tops

SHOP In the best of all worlds you'd use freshly shucked clams, and on page 409, you'll find instructions for shucking. Here's one shortcut: Ask your fishmonger to shuck the clams for you. (My fish guy does it for an extra $1 a pound.) Here's another: Use smoked clams or canned clams. (Shhh—I didn't mention the latter.) To intensify the clam flavor, use bottled clam broth (sometimes called clam juice), which is available near the canned tuna fish in your supermarket.

For spuds, I like thin-skinned red or white fingerling potatoes. The latter are small, stubby, finger-shaped potatoes. You can find them at the farmers' market as well as the supermarket.

GEAR Your basic kitchen gear including a large heavy saucepan plus a clam-shucking knife

1 Cook the bacon in a large heavy saucepan over medium heat until the fat starts to melt, about 1 minute. Add the onion and cook until it and the bacon are lightly browned, about 3 minutes, stirring often. Stir in the flour and cook until sizzling but not brown, about 1 minute, stirring often.

WHAT ELSE Some
New Yorkers (but not my
editor, Suzanne Rafer) and
Rhode Islanders like a clear
chowder with tomatoes.
If you subscribe to this
particular heresy, add water
in place of the half-and-half,
plus a couple of diced ripe
tomatoes.

For step-by-step
instructions for shucking
claims, see page 409.

TIME about 30 minutes

2 Stir in the clam broth and half-and-half and let gradually come to a boil over medium-high heat, scraping the bottom of the pan with a spoon to prevent sticking. The liquid will thicken slightly. Add the fresh thyme (if using) and potatoes, reduce the heat to medium, and let simmer gently until tender (they will be easy to pierce with a fork), 8 to 10 minutes. Set aside while you prepare the clams. (The chowder can be prepared ahead to this stage, cooled to room temperature, and refrigerated, covered, in the saucepan, for up to 3 days. Reheat it over medium heat.)

3 Scrub the clam shells. Working over a large bowl, shuck the clams. You should have about 1 cup of meat and juices. If you are using littlenecks or cherrystones, you can leave the clams whole. Cut larger clams into ¼-inch dice.

4 Shortly before serving, stir in the clams with their juices. Let simmer over medium heat just long enough to cook the clams, 1 to 2 minutes. This is the secret to my chowder—not to overcook the clams. Season the chowder with plenty of pepper. You probably won't need salt as the clams are quite salty, but add it as necessary. Ladle the chowder into bowls and sprinkle the chives on top.

Variations

Fish chowder or smoked fish chowder: Prepare the chowder as described on page 143, substituting 1 pound of diced uncooked fish for the clams. Which fish? Haddock, halibut, cod, snapper, salmon, smoked salmon, finnan haddie (smoked haddock)—whatever looks best.

Corn chowder: Prepare the chowder as described on page 143, substituting 1 cup of grilled corn kernels (from 2 or 3 ears of corn) for the clams (see page 503 for how to grill corn). For a vegetarian corn chowder, substitute ½ cup each diced red bell pepper and celery for the bacon and 1½ tablespoons olive oil for the bacon fat. Use 2 cups of vegetable stock (page 550) in place of the clam juice.

OYSTER STEW

Back when bars doubled as men's clubs, with spittoons under the counters and sawdust on the floors, the steam kettle was a fixture of ingenuity and beauty. Ingenious, because by circulating hot steam between the kettle walls rather than having a direct flame under the pot, you could cook delicate foods, like oyster stew, without curdling the broth or toughening the shellfish. Beautiful because the barmen of the day spent hours polishing the metal until it shone mirror-bright. You can still find such steam kettles today at vintage restaurants like the Grand Central Oyster Bar in New York City. This recipe for soulful oyster stew—all briny bivalves, butter, and half-and-half—comes from the Oyster Bar. Rest assured: no steam kettle needed for my version. **Serves 2; can be multiplied as desired**

1 cup bottled clam broth

2 tablespoons (¼ stick) unsalted butter

1 teaspoon Worcestershire sauce

½ teaspoon celery salt (or sea salt—but celery salt adds more flavor)

12 shucked oysters with their juices (about 1 cup)

1¼ cups half-and-half

2 slices white bread, toasted and buttered

Sweet paprika (preferably Hungarian, see page 25), for sprinkling

Oyster crackers (optional), for serving

1 Pour water to a depth of 2 inches in the bottom of the large saucepan. Bring the water to a boil over high heat.

2 Place the clam broth, butter, Worcestershire sauce, and celery salt in a smaller saucepan and float it in the larger pan. Reduce the heat to medium.

3 Once the butter has melted, 1 to 2 minutes, add the oysters with their juices and cook until the oysters are just barely poached

(cooked—the oysters will start to firm up), about 30 seconds, stirring constantly.

4 Add the half-and-half and cook until hot but not boiling, about 2 minutes.

5 Place a slice of toast in each of 2 wide shallow soup bowls. Using a slotted spoon, place 6 oysters on top of each slice of toast. Ladle in the broth. Sprinkle paprika over the oyster stew, top it with oyster crackers, if desired, and dig in.

Variation

Oyster pan roast: Prepare the preceding oyster stew, adding ¼ cup of Heinz chili sauce to each serving when you add the oysters.

SHOP For convenience I call for shucked oysters here (available by the pint at fish markets and supermarkets), but the purist can certainly buy and shuck oysters in the shell (see page 398 for instructions on how to shuck oysters). You'll find bottled clam broth, sometimes called clam juice, near the canned tuna fish in the supermarket.

GEAR Your basic kitchen gear including 2 heavy saucepans, one slightly larger than the other

WHAT ELSE So what's the difference between oyster stew and oyster "pan roast"? In a nutshell, oyster pan roast is oyster stew with a shot of chili sauce (you'll find this variation below)—a distinction in search of a difference.

TIME about 15 minutes (a little longer if you shuck the oysters yourself)

A GUY'S BEST FRIEND

CHILI

(OR, THE TEN STEPS TO CHILI ENLIGHTENMENT)

First, a bit of heresy: There's no such thing as a single pot of perfect chili. Texans prefer all-beef chili—ideally, with meat cubed rather than ground—and points are deducted for adding beans and other fillers. In New Mexico it's the chile peppers that matter and some versions don't even contain meat. The world's strangest chili may be Cincinnati "five-way": layers of spaghetti, cinnamon-scented ground beef chili, onions, kidney beans, and grated orange cheese. Of course, if you're one of the legions of Cincinnatians who jam to the popular chili parlor chain, Skyline, there's nothing the least bit odd about this singular combination.

Then there's the question of the proper accompaniments: sour cream, grated cheddar or Jack cheese, and chopped scallions, at a minimum. Diced tomatoes cool things off, and avocados and sliced black olives add a Tex-Mex border touch. Crackers (for example, saltines) belong on the side in most of the country, but for me, chili isn't complete without corn bread.

John Jepson of Merced, California, knows a thing or two about chili. A former International Chili Society grand championship winner, Jepson once bested 137 state and regional champions in front of 30,000 spectators to take home a $25,000 prize. So what's it take to become the world chili champ?

First, a lot of practice. Jepson started cooking chili more than thirty years ago, competing in more than a dozen competitions each year. Then, there's feedback. Jepson takes notes on every batch of chili he makes. He even reviews the judges' notes to learn what worked and what didn't. Finally, there are the chiles. Jepson uses a blend of mild and fiery New Mexican chili powders, with a little California Anaheim chile for sweetness.

Here's what else chili champ John Jepson wants you to know about cooking the perfect bowl of red:

1 KEEP IT PURE Chili con carne should be just that: beef and chiles and/or chile powder. No beans. No fillers. No pasta (sorry, Cincinnati).

2 CHOOSE THE RIGHT MEAT Jepson uses a lean, flavorful, triangular-shaped cut of sirloin called tri-tip. If you live west of the Rockies, you'll find it at your local supermarket. East Coasters may need to special order it from the butcher (or substitute a top sirloin or tenderloin tips). Jepson cuts the beef into ¼-inch cubes, which he says produces a better consistency than ground.

3 USE THE RIGHT POT For decades Jepson has cooked his chili in a thick-walled, multilayered stainless steel pot. Thick-walled so the heat spreads evenly, and multilayered (with a copper insert) to prevent scorching. Stainless steel, because while cast-iron Dutch ovens have cowboy romance, Jepson believes they impart a metallic taste to the chili. A large heavy stainless steel pot should serve you well.

4 FOLLOW THE PROPER SEQUENCE Brown the meat first. Then add the broth. (Jepson uses a mix of beef and chicken broths to achieve a more complex flavor.) Finally add the chile powders, tomatoes, and other seasonings.

5 ADD THE CHILE POWDERS IN SMALL BATCHES Mixing in the chile powders gradually as the chili cooks gives you control and lets you season the chili to taste. You can always add more chile powder, but you can't take it away.

6 USE ONION POWDER AND GARLIC POWDER You might be surprised by Jepson's preference for dried onion and garlic rather than fresh. The flavor of fresh onion and garlic varies too widely from region to region, Jepson

maintains. Onion and garlic powders give consistent results wherever you cook your chili.

7 TAKE IT EASY WITH THE TOMATO You need a little tomato (Jepson adds no more than two ounces per pound of meat), but too much will alter the flavor of the other ingredients.

8 AVOID THE WEIRD STUFF Jepson spurns achiote (annatto seeds), cinnamon, cocoa powder, and other offbeat flavorings used by innovators to try to make their chili different from the next guy's.

9 MAKE IT HOT BUT NOT INFLAMMATORY Jepson would describe his chili as "three alarm"—hot enough to be interesting, but not so fiery you shy away from seconds. Your ultimate goal is balance. The chili should be intensely flavorful, but no one flavor should predominate.

10 STUDY BEFORE YOU START The International Chili Society website, chilicookoff.com, features the winning chili recipes from the last forty-five years! And remember, you don't need to win: When you make chili, the most important thing is to have fun.

The recipe for John Jepson's championship chili can be found at: chilicookoff.com. Click on Recipes.

BEEF AND PORK CHILI

Our first chili takes an ecumenical approach, featuring both beef and pork—meats both diced and ground—two kinds of beans, plus plenty of chile powder, poblano pepper, and jalapeño to crank up the heat. Don't be deterred by the long ingredient list—you probably have most of the aromatics in your kitchen already. And despite the lengthy instructions, you can make it from start to finish in 1 hour. **Serves 8**

SHOP Use a pure chile powder rather than a blend, and preferably one ground from ancho chiles.

GEAR Your basic kitchen gear including a large heavy pot like a Dutch oven

WHAT ELSE You may be surprised to see the addition of bittersweet chocolate to this chili—a combination that may sound bizarre until you stop to think that the Aztecs made their hot chocolate with cocoa beans and chiles. (Montezuma allegedly consumed fifty cups a day.) Of course, like most chili, the flavor actually improves if you prepare it several hours or even days ahead.

TIME 1 to 1½ hours

2 tablespoons extra virgin olive oil

1 pound beef tenderloin tips, cut into ¼- to ½-inch dice

2 pounds lean ground beef or bison

¼ pound ground pork

1 large onion, peeled and finely chopped

1 poblano pepper, seeded and finely chopped

1 to 3 fresh jalapeño peppers, seeded and finely chopped

2 cloves garlic, peeled and minced

⅓ cup pure chile powder, or more to taste

2 teaspoons ground cumin

1 teaspoon freshly ground black pepper

1 teaspoon dried oregano

½ teaspoon ground cinnamon

2 quarts beef or chicken stock, preferably homemade (page 549)

1 bottle (12 ounces) beer, light or dark

1 can (8 ounces) tomato sauce, preferably organic

2 cans (about 15 ounces each) pinto beans, preferably organic and low sodium, rinsed and drained in a colander

2 cans (about 15 ounces each) kidney beans, preferably organic and low sodium, rinsed and drained in a colander

1 tablespoon (packed) dark brown sugar, or more to taste

1 to 3 teaspoons Tabasco sauce

1 ounce bittersweet chocolate, such as Baker's (the budget choice) or Scharffen Berger (if you're feeling flush)

Coarse salt (kosher or sea)

Fixings—see What to Serve with Chili (page 150)

1 Heat the oil in a Dutch oven over high heat. Add the diced tenderloin and cook until browned on all sides, 4 to 6 minutes, stirring often. Work in several batches as needed so you don't overcrowd the pan. Transfer the browned tenderloin to a large platter.

2 Working in 2 or 3 batches, add the ground beef and pork and brown over high heat, about 4 minutes per batch. Transfer the ground meat to the platter and pour off all but about 2 tablespoons of fat from the Dutch oven.

3 Add the onion, poblano, jalapeños, and garlic, reduce the heat to medium-high, and cook until lightly browned, about 4 minutes. Stir in the chile powder, cumin, black pepper, oregano, and cinnamon. Cook until fragrant, about 2 minutes.

4 Stir in the stock, beer, and tomato sauce. Let the chili simmer gently over medium heat until the tenderloin cubes are very tender and the chili is richly flavored, 30 to 40 minutes, stirring from time to time. (Reduce the heat as needed to maintain a gentle simmer.)

5 Stir in the pinto and kidney beans, brown sugar, Tabasco sauce, and chocolate. Let the chili simmer gently until thick and even more richly flavored, 5 minutes. Taste for seasoning, adding salt to taste and more brown sugar, chile powder, cumin, and/or Tabasco sauce as necessary; the chili should be highly seasoned.

6 You can serve the chili now or let the flavors develop for a few hours or even days in the refrigerator (let cool to room temperature, cover the Dutch oven, and refrigerate. Reheat over medium heat). Serve the fixings alongside.

What to Serve with Chili

What to put on your chili is as idiosyncratic as how you make your pot o' red to begin with. Grated cheese, sour cream, and scallions are mandatory. Other fixings are limited only by your imagination.

► Tortilla chips
► Sour cream
► Coarsely grated cheddar cheese (orange or white)
► Coarsely grated pepperjack cheese
► Finely chopped scallions or green onions
► Chopped ripe tomatoes
► Finely diced sweet onion
► Peeled diced jicama
► Thinly sliced fresh or pickled jalapeño chiles
► Thinly sliced or pitted black olives
► Stemmed chopped fresh cilantro

The PB&J Corn Bread on page 514 goes great with any sort of chili.

New Mexican Green Chili

CHILI VERDE

The email came early one morning in August. "We've got some real firebombs—how many pounds do you want?" The scorchers in question were Hatch chiles from New Mexico—offered by my go-to guy for exotic produce, Robert Schueller of Melissa's. I ordered a case of the crop of tongue-blistering chiles from New Mexico's Hatch Valley. With a grassy aroma and all-business bite, these chiles don't have the sadistic burn of a habanero pepper, but a slow fire that makes you want to eat more. And more. Which brings me to the second chili in our roster—chili *verde,* New Mexican green chili. It should certainly be part of your chili recipe collection and it will definitely wake people up at your next tailgate or Super Bowl party. **Serves 6 to 8**

For the Chili Verde
24 Hatch or other New Mexican chiles

1 pound tomatillos, husks removed (slip them off with your fingers), fruit rinsed to remove stickiness

3 cups chicken stock (preferably homemade, page 549, or use a good no- or low-sodium store-bought brand), or more as needed

¾ cup chopped fresh cilantro

3 pounds boneless pork shoulder or boneless country-style ribs

Coarse salt (kosher or sea) and freshly ground black pepper

2 tablespoons vegetable oil

1 large onion, peeled and finely chopped

2 cloves garlic, peeled and finely chopped

1 teaspoon ground cumin, or more to taste

1 teaspoon dried oregano, preferably Mexican (see Shop note), or more to taste

1 tablespoon masa harina (optional) or yellow cornmeal

For serving (optional)
Freshly fried or good-quality store-bought totopos (tortilla chips, see page 220), or fresh corn tortillas

Fixings—see What to Serve with Chili (page 150)

SHOP Fresh Hatch chiles are in season from mid-August to late September. One good mail-order source is Melissa's (melissas.com). If Hatch chiles are unavailable, you can substitute poblanos, Anaheims, or another New Mexican chile.

Tomatillos are green tomato-like fruits with a papery husk; most supermarkets carry them. Masa harina, the optional thickener, is a corn flour used for making tortillas. Mexican markets and most supermarkets carry it. Mexican oregano can be found in the ethnic section of some supermarkets or online at amazon.com. It is related to lemon verbena and is more robust than Mediterranean oregano, which belongs to the mint family. But in such a richly flavored dish as chili *verde*, you won't likely notice a big difference.

GEAR Your basic kitchen gear including a food processor or blender and a large heavy pot like a Dutch oven

WHAT ELSE If you live in the Southwest, you can probably buy freshly roasted Hatch or other New Mexican chiles at your local farmers' market when they are in season. (Farmers roast the chiles in cylindrical wire baskets using industrial-strength blowtorches.) If you can find the roasted chiles fresh or frozen, omit the grilling or flame-charring in Steps 1 and 2.

TIME about 1 hour prep, plus 3 hours cooking time

1 If you are roasting the chiles and tomatillos on the grill, set it up for direct grilling and preheat it to high.

2 When the grill is hot, place the chiles and tomatillos on the hot grate and roast them until the skins are darkly browned on all sides, turning with tongs so they char evenly, 8 to 12 minutes. Or you can roast the chiles and tomatillos under a broiler or directly on a gas or electric stove burner. (Lay them right on the burner.) See Burn This (page 485).

3 Let the chiles and tomatillos cool. Using a paring knife, scrape the charred skin off the chiles. Note: If you have sensitive skin, wear latex gloves. Remove the stems and seeds. Pull the stems off the tomatillos. Coarsely chop the chiles and tomatillos and place them in a food processor or blender. Add the chicken stock and ½ cup of the cilantro (if making the chili a day in advance, store the remaining cilantro in an unsealed plastic bag in the refrigerator). Process or blend the ingredients until they form a slightly chunky puree. Set the chile-tomatillo puree aside.

4 Cut the pork into 1-inch cubes. Don't worry about trimming the pork too much; some fat is good. Generously season the pork on all sides with salt and pepper.

5 Heat the oil in a Dutch oven or large saucepan over high heat. Working in 2 or 3 batches so as not to crowd the pan, add the pork cubes in a single layer and cook until browned all over, 6 to 8 minutes per batch, stirring with a wooden spoon. As you work, transfer the browned pork to a platter. Pour off and discard all but about 2 tablespoons of the fat.

6 Add the onion, garlic, cumin, and oregano to the pot, reduce the heat to medium-high, and cook until browned and fragrant, about 4 minutes. Return the pork to the pot. Stir in the chile-tomatillo puree.

7 Lower the heat to medium-low or low and gently simmer the chili *verde*, covered, until the pork is very tender, 2½ to 3 hours, stirring occasionally. (You can also cook the chili in a 275°F oven.) If the chili is too soupy, uncover the saucepan for the last 30 minutes of cooking to let some of the excess liquid evaporate. If desired, you can also stir in a spoonful of masa harina to thicken the chili. (Sprinkle it over the top, then stir.) If the chili is too thick, add additional chicken broth ½ cup at a time. You're looking for a consistency somewhere between soup and stew—thick but pourable. Taste for seasoning, adding more salt, pepper, cumin, and/or oregano as necessary; the mixture should be highly seasoned. Serve now or cool the chili to room temperature, cover the pot, and store in the refrigerator overnight. About 30 minutes before serving, reheat the chili over medium heat.

8 Serve the chili *verde* in large shallow bowls with some of the remaining ¼ cup of cilantro sprinkled on top of each. Serve the *totopos* (chips) and any of the other fixings, if desired, on the side.

CHILI SANS CARNE

Every man should know how to make a killer meatless chili. A chili to serve to his vegetarian pals or a girlfriend; to trim the fat in his own diet and boost the health value of the iconic American bowl of red. This one delivers plenty of smoke and fire in the form of chipotle chiles (smoked jalapeños) and smoked cheddar cheese. With three different beans (black, red, and pinto) for texture and protein, I doubt you'll miss the meat. **Serves 6 to 8**

2 tablespoons extra virgin olive oil

1 poblano pepper or small green bell pepper, stemmed, seeded, and diced

1 large onion, peeled and finely chopped

2 cloves garlic, peeled and minced

1 tablespoon pure chile powder, such as ancho chile powder, or smoked paprika

1 teaspoon ground cumin

1 teaspoon dried oregano, preferably Mexican

½ cup dark beer, preferably Mexican

1 can (about 15 ounces) black beans, preferably organic and low-sodium, rinsed and drained

1 can (about 15 ounces) small red kidney beans, preferably organic and low-sodium, rinsed and drained

1 can (about 15 ounces) pinto beans, preferably organic and low-sodium, rinsed and drained

1 can (28 ounces) peeled tomatoes, chopped with their juices (see Note)

1 to 2 chipotle chiles in adobo sauce, minced, with 1 tablespoon can juices

2 cups homemade vegetable stock (page 550; or use a good store-bought brand)

Coarse salt (kosher or sea) and freshly ground black pepper

Hot sauce (optional)

2 tablespoons masa harina or yellow cornmeal (optional)

Fixings—see What to Serve with Chili (page 150)

SHOP Buy canned chipotles; they give you tangy adobo sauce in addition to the smoked jalapeños. And buy smoked cheddar cheese for serving.

GEAR Your basic kitchen gear including a box grater and a large saucepan

WHAT ELSE For extra flavor, when sweet corn is in season, grill 1 to 2 ears (see page 503 for instructions), cut the kernels off the cobs, and add them to the chili at the same time that you add the beans.

TIME about 30 minutes

1 Heat the oil in a large heavy saucepan over medium heat. Add the poblano and onion and cook until darkly browned, 4 to 6 minutes, stirring often with a wooden spoon. Add the garlic after the poblano and onion have cooked for about 2 minutes. Do not let the garlic burn or it will turn bitter.

2 Stir in the chile powder, cumin, and oregano, and cook until fragrant, about 30 seconds. Add the beer, increase the heat to high, and bring to a boil. Stir in the black beans, kidney beans, pinto beans, tomatoes, and chipotles with the adobo sauce, and vegetable stock, and season with salt and black pepper to taste.

3 Let the chili simmer gently until thick and richly flavored, about 20 minutes, stirring from time to time with a wooden spoon. If the chili starts to dry out, add a little water. For an even spicier chili, add a spoonful of your favorite hot sauce. For a thicker chili, sprinkle the masa harina over the top, then stir it in, and let the chili simmer for about 5 minutes longer. Taste for seasoning, adding salt or pepper as necessary; the chili should be highly seasoned. The chili will keep for several days in the refrigerator. Cool it to room temperature and transfer it to a storage container with a lid. Reheat it in the saucepan over medium heat.

4 Serve the chili in bowls with the fixings on the side for spooning on top.

Note: You can chop the tomatoes right in the can using two knives and a scissor motion.

SALAD

Salad may not be the first dish you think of when it comes to guy food. But some of the world's most famous salads were created by guys—the Cobb (supposedly named for 1930s Hollywood Brown Derby restaurant owner Robert Cobb), for example, or the Caesar salad, created by Tijuana restaurateur Caesar Cardini. On page 163 you'll find the classic Caesar, plus updated versions made with grilled lettuce or kale.

But don't stop there. In the following pages you'll learn how to make a salad for every season, from a summery tomato corn salad to a winter salad of endive, walnuts, and olives. Potato salad goes upscale with a warm bacon dressing, and bean salad gets the South American gaucho treatment. You'll discover five versions of coleslaw, and seven dressings you shake in a Ball jar. Salad. Because even the most confirmed carnivore craves a salad every once in a while.

CRAZY SALAD

You probably know Oliver Platt for his acting roles in films and TV series as diverse as *Casanova* and *The Bronx Is Burning*. What you may not know is that he has a fanatical obsession with cooking—particularly what he calls icebox cooking. He explains: "You have five hungry people waiting for dinner. You forgot to go to the store. The power is out. Your kids are drumming their fingers. The bad guys are coming over the hill. So you open the fridge and start pulling out ingredients: a not-too-overripe pear, a lump of cheese, and a package of walnuts. You've got some raisins. And there's a ripe avocado that's been sitting on the counter. You put these all in a bowl and season the hell out of them with salt and rice vinegar. Now *that's* how you make a salad." **Serves 4**

SHOP You can replicate this salad exactly. It's delicious. But, the spirit of this recipe is to use what you already have on hand, so use it as a template.

GEAR Your basic kitchen gear plus a salad spinner and salad bowl

WHAT ELSE Platt loves vinegar. Not just the obvious balsamic vinegar and wine vinegar. But rice vinegar. Sherry vinegar. Fig vinegar. Use salt, yes salt, to balance the acidity—it cuts the sharpness without making your salad overly sweet.

TIME 10 to 15 minutes

For the greens

1 head of lettuce, such as Boston, Bibb, romaine, or iceberg, broken into leaves, rinsed, and spun dry or patted dry with paper towels (see page 159)

Any or all of the following

1 ripe avocado

1 apple (Platt likes Fujis)

1 Asian pear or ripe Anjou or Bosc pear

¼ cup walnuts or almonds (whole, halves, slivered—it's your choice)

¼ cup raisins or dried cranberries

½ cup coarsely grated full-flavored cheese, such as pecorino romano, feta, cheddar, or Gruyère

3 tablespoons extra virgin olive oil

1 to 2 tablespoons rice vinegar, fig vinegar, balsamic vinegar, or cider or distilled white vinegar

Coarse salt (kosher or sea) and freshly ground black pepper

1 Tear the lettuce into bite-size pieces and place them in a large salad bowl. Peel and pit the avocado, cut it into ½-inch dice, and add it to the bowl. Remove and discard the cores from the apple and pear. Cut the fruit into ½-inch dice and add it to the bowl. Add the walnuts, raisins, and cheese to the bowl.

2 Just before serving pour the olive oil and vinegar over the salad and toss to mix. Season the salad with salt and pepper to taste; it should be highly seasoned.

SALAD

When I was growing up, lettuce pretty much meant iceberg. Today, a guy at a market faces a staggering selection of salad greens. This may confuse you, but ultimately it's good news, because never has it been easier to assemble an interesting salad.

KNOW YOUR MACHE FROM YOUR MIZUNA | There are five major types of salad greens. If one green is good, a blend is usually better.

▸ Head lettuces: These are the round mild-flavored lettuces like iceberg, butter, and Boston lettuce.

▸ Leaf lettuces: These grow from a single stalk and include crunchy romaine, mild mâche (also called lamb's lettuce), red-tinged oak leaf, and the lettuces with jagged edges like frisée.

▸ Bitter greens: These greens, which include red- and white-leafed radicchio (and its flat-leafed cousin, Treviso), escarole, endive, curly endive, chicory, and dandelion greens, have a pleasantly bitter taste. Use them sparingly in mixed salads the way you'd add a few drops of bitters to a cocktail.

▸ Spicy greens: These peppery greens include arugula (called rocket in the United Kingdom), watercress, peppercress, upland cress, mustard greens, and mizuna (a small jagged-leafed Asian green).

▸ Vegetable greens: The leaves (usually baby) of plants we normally eat as vegetables, such as spinach, bok choy, kale, collards, and beet greens also make awesome salads.

TEAR, DON'T CUT | Once you get the lettuce home, tear off and discard any bruised or damaged outer leaves. For head lettuces, break the leaves off the core, discarding the latter. For leaf lettuces, tear off any tough stems. Note, I say *tear*. Cutting lettuce leaves with a knife bruises the edges of the lettuce leaves. The exception here is iceberg lettuce, which you cut in quarters with a chef's knife, then slice the core off each wedge.

KEEP IT CLEAN | Rinse the lettuce leaves in a large bowl (or a salad spinner bowl) filled with cold water. Don't overcrowd the bowl. Gently agitate the leaves with your fingers to dislodge any dirt. Transfer the leaves to a colander (or a salad spinner basket), then pour off the sandy water. (I'm sure this goes without saying, but don't pour the dirty water back over the lettuce.) Continue rinsing and draining the leaves until the water runs clean.

STORE IT MOIST | The best way to store lettuce is rinsed but not dried. Place it in a colander or the basket of a salad spinner and let drain for 1 minute. Loosely cover the top with damp paper towels. Do not store the lettuce in a sealed plastic bag or it will start to smell funky. Refrigerated, lettuce will keep this way for 3 days.

SPIN IT DRY | Just before preparing the salad, gently shake the lettuce in a colander, then pat dry with paper towels. Or spin the lettuce dry in a salad spinner. Wet salad dilutes the dressing.

PUT IT ALL TOGETHER | There are two schools of thought when it comes to assembling a salad. The French keep it simple: lettuce leaves of a single variety and a simple vinaigrette dressing. We Americans go for mixed salads with varied colors, textures, and flavors. Add vegetables, such as tomatoes, cucumbers, radishes, diced avocado—any of your favorites. Add nuts (walnuts, pine nuts, pistachios), croutons, and/or bread crumbs for crunch. Add raisins, currants, dried cranberries, or other dried fruits for sweetness. Add anchovies, hard-cooked eggs (grated or sliced), or grilled shrimp, chicken, or steak for protein. And of course don't forget the dressing. You get the idea.

SAVE THE LEFTOVERS | Don't. Leftover salad gets soggy. Try not to make more salad than you can eat at a single meal.

BLT SALAD

If the BLT ranks as one of the world's great sandwiches, imagine what the combination can do for a salad. It's one of the rare occasions when iceberg lettuce works better than a designer green like arugula. To make a red-blooded American twist on the ubiquitous Italian bruschetta you can spoon the salad on toasted slices of French bread instead of mixing croutons with the greens. Salad is good for you. Bacon is about to make it taste better. **Serves 4 to 6**

4 slices bacon, cut crosswise into ½-inch slivers

4 slices French bread, cut into ½-inch cubes (about 1½ cups)

1 tablespoon extra virgin olive oil or butter (optional)

2 tablespoons mayonnaise, preferably Hellmann's

2 tablespoons buttermilk, heavy (whipping) cream, or half-and-half

1 tablespoon distilled white vinegar or rice vinegar

1 small or ½ large head iceberg lettuce

2 large or 4 medium-size luscious red ripe tomatoes

Coarse salt (kosher or sea) and freshly ground black pepper

SHOP You know the drill: ripe heirloom tomatoes and thick-sliced smokehouse bacon. Baguettes from an artisanal bakery. Excellence lies in the details.

GEAR Your basic kitchen gear including a large (10- to 12-inch) skillet, slotted spoon, and a plate lined with paper towels, plus a salad bowl

WHAT ELSE For the best results, make your croutons from scratch. If you were sensible, you'd toast the bread with extra virgin olive oil or melted butter. But you're not sensible and neither am I, so we'll use the fat from the bacon and keep it between us. Of course, to save time, you could use store-bought croutons, but let's pretend I didn't say that.

TIME about 20 minutes

1 Place the bacon in a cold heavy large skillet and heat over medium heat. Cook the bacon until it is crisp, browned, and most of the fat has rendered (melted out), 4 to 6 minutes, stirring often. Using a slotted spoon, transfer the bacon to a plate lined with paper towels to drain. Leave the bacon fat in the skillet.

2 Add the bread cubes to the bacon fat and cook over medium heat until well browned, stirring often, 5 to 8 minutes. If bacon fat sounds excessive (or there isn't quite enough, say 1½ tablespoons), wipe out the skillet, add the olive oil or butter and toast the bread cubes

in that. Do not let the bread cubes burn. Using a slotted spoon, transfer the bread cubes to the plate with the bacon.

Simple Green Salad

Every man should know how to make a simple green salad: Rinse, dry, and tear up a head of Boston lettuce. Not more than 30 minutes before serving, place the lettuce in a salad bowl with three to four tablespoons of Mustard Shallot Vinaigrette (page 182). Not more than 5 minutes before serving, toss the lettuce to coat with dressing: Now you know how to make a simple green salad.

3 Place the mayonnaise, buttermilk, and vinegar in a salad bowl and whisk to mix. Set the dressing aside.

4 If you are using a whole head of lettuce, cut it in half. Remove and discard the core and coarsely chop the lettuce. You should have about 4 cups. Remove and discard the stem ends of the tomatoes, then dice the tomatoes.

Place the lettuce, tomatoes, croutons, and bacon in a large bowl but don't toss until serving.

5 Just before serving, gently toss the salad with the dressing (use the slotted spoon or a rubber spatula). Season the salad with salt and lots of pepper to taste; remember, the bacon is salty already.

Variation
BLT Salad Bruschetta

Prepare the BLT Salad, omitting the croutons, but do not toss the salad. Cut 8 slices of French bread sharply on the diagonal and about ½-inch thick, and brush the bread on both sides with bacon fat or olive oil. Bake the slices of bread in a 350°F oven or toaster oven until crisp and golden brown, about 5 minutes per side, or brown the bread slices on the grill. Lightly spread each piece of toast with some mayonnaise. Toss the salad and spoon it onto the toasts.

COLLARD GREEN SALAD
WITH SMASHED CROUTONS

SHOP Because you're eating them raw, you want the youngest, most tender collard greens you can find. Look for baby or young collard greens at your local farmers' market. You could substitute kale, mustard greens, or even a bitter lettuce, like escarole.

GEAR Your basic kitchen gear plus a pastry brush and a salad bowl

"I'm always hunting down the croutons in a salad," observes Jon Shook, co-owner of the restaurants Animal, Son of a Gun, and Trois Mec in Los Angeles (you'll find an interview with Jon and his partner, Vinny Dotolo, on page 320). Jon likes to smash the croutons before adding them to a salad so you get a little crunch in each bite. Combine this with young collard greens, sweet dried currants, salty Parmesan, and tangy lemon, and you get a simple salad that knocks it out of the park with taste. **Serves 4**

4 slices (½ inch thick) French bread or white bread

¼ cup extra virgin olive oil

1 bunch young collard greens or kale

1 clove garlic (optional), cut in half crosswise

Juice of 1 lemon (2 to 3 tablespoons)

¼ cup dried currants, raisins, cranberries, or cherries

½ cup freshly grated Parmigiano Reggiano cheese (about 2 ounces)

Coarse salt (kosher or sea) and freshly grated black pepper

WHAT ELSE To cut or tear? Cut sturdy greens like collards or kale with a knife after first removing the tough center stems. Tear tender lettuces like romaine, butter or Boston lettuce, escarole, or frisée with your fingers.

TIME about 20 minutes

1 Preheat the oven or toaster oven to 400°F.

2 Using a pastry brush, lightly brush the slices of bread with olive oil on both sides; you'll need about 1½ tablespoons of oil. Arrange the bread on a rimmed baking sheet and bake until the slices are golden brown and crisp, 3 to 5 minutes per side. Transfer the slices of bread to a wire rack to cool or prop them at an angle against the edge of the baking sheet; the idea is to let the bread cool without letting steam form underneath it. The bread can be toasted up to 1 hour ahead.

3 Rinse the collard greens and shake or spin them dry. Using a paring knife, cut the tough stem out of each leaf. Roll the collard greens lengthwise into a cigar-shaped tube, then thinly slice them crosswise into ¼-inch ribbons.

4 Rub the inside of a salad bowl with the cut side of the garlic, if using. Add the collard greens, separating the ribbons with your fingers. Add the remaining 2½ tablespoons of olive oil and the lemon juice and currants but don't toss the salad until the last minute.

5 Just before serving, crumble the toasted bread slices over the salad and toss it. Add the Parmigiano Reggiano. Season the salad with salt and pepper like you mean it.

CAESAR SALAD

Eighty years plus have passed since Tijuana restaurateur Caesar Cardini first tossed romaine lettuce leaves with mashed anchovies, garlic, lemon juice, pecorino romano cheese, and a coddled (soft-boiled) egg to make a salad now so commonplace you find it at fast food restaurants. In the process, the Caesar

For lettuce, you'll save time and effort if you buy hearts of romaine (preferably organic, as always). As for the cheese—and here's another way your Caesar will differ from the hackneyed salad bar versions—you must use genuine pecorino romano, a sharp salty grating cheese from Italy that owes its pungent bite to sheep's milk. For anchovies, I like the oil-cured kind sold in flat cans.

GEAR Your basic kitchen gear plus a salad spinner and a large salad bowl, preferably wooden

WHAT ELSE Because there are so many issues with consuming raw eggs, I now use egg-based mayonnaise to emulsify (bind) the dressing. The rich umami flavors of anchovy and cheese remain the same.

TIME about 20 minutes

salad has lost the theatrics that made it so remarkable to begin with, especially its ceremonial preparation at tableside. Well, maybe you want to resurrect the tradition and make it as retro performance art, or maybe you just want to enjoy a classic Caesar the way people did it before it became a commodity. No bottled dressing required—or allowed. **Serves 4**

For the croutons and salad

4 slices (½ inch thick) French bread, cut sharply on the diagonal

2 tablespoons (¼ stick) butter, melted, or 2 tablespoons extra virgin olive oil

4 romaine lettuce hearts (the inside portion of the lettuce heads), or 1 whole head of romaine lettuce

For the salad dressing

1 clove garlic, peeled and minced

2 anchovy fillets, coarsely chopped, plus 4 to 8 anchovy fillets for serving

2 teaspoons Dijon mustard

2 tablespoons mayonnaise, preferably Hellmann's

1 tablespoon fresh lemon juice, or more to taste

1 teaspoon Worcestershire sauce

3 tablespoons extra virgin olive oil

Coarse salt (kosher or sea) and freshly ground black pepper

¾ cup (3 ounces) freshly finely grated pecorino romano cheese

1 Make the croutons and prepare the salad: Preheat a toaster oven, oven, or grill to 400°F.

2 Lightly brush the slices of bread on both sides with the butter or the 2 tablespoons of olive oil. Bake or grill the bread until lightly browned and crisp, 3 to 5 minutes per side. Watch carefully, especially if you are toasting the bread on a grill. Transfer the toasted bread to a wire rack to cool. You can make the toasts several hours ahead.

3 Break the romaine lettuce leaves off the stem(s). Rinse the leaves in a bowl of cold water, changing the water as needed, then spin them dry or pat them dry with paper

towels. (Skip washing if you start with hearts of romaine.) Tear the lettuce into pieces that are about 2 inches. You can rinse the romaine several hours ahead; store it in the refrigerator loosely covered with a damp paper towel.

4 Just before serving, make the salad dressing, preferably at the table: Place the garlic and the 2 chopped anchovy fillets in the bottom of a salad bowl, and using the back of a spoon, mash them into a paste. Using a whisk, gradually whisk in the mustard, mayonnaise, lemon juice, Worcestershire sauce, and 3 tablespoons of olive oil; the dressing should be smooth and creamy. Season the dressing with salt and pepper to taste.

5 Add the torn romaine leaves to the salad bowl. Crumble the toasts in large pieces over the lettuce. Gently toss to mix. Sprinkle the salad with ½ cup of the pecorino romano and gently toss again to mix.

6 Transfer the salad to 4 plates and drape 1 or 2 anchovy fillets over each serving. Sprinkle the remaining ¼ cup of pecorino romano evenly over the salads and dig in.

Variation
Black Kale Caesar

Want a change of pace? A few months ago, when making Caesar salad, I took to replacing the traditional romaine lettuce with the dark crinkly leaves of black kale. In addition to its considerable nutritional benefits (megadoses of calcium, iron, and so on), kale has a terrific texture and flavor—at once crunchy and chewy, earthy and aromatic. The rich umami flavors of anchovy and pecorino romano in the salad remain the same.

Black kale, sometimes called dinosaur kale (cool name), Tuscan kale, *lacinato* kale, or *cavolo nero*, has long slender corrugated dark green leaves and an earthy mineral-like flavor. Look for it in your natural foods market and choose young small bunches. Alternatively, you can use regular kale or collard greens (again, the younger, the better).

Prepare the Caesar salad as described on page 163, substituting a 12- to 16-ounce bunch of black kale for the romaine. Cut out and discard the tough center stems of the kale before cutting it into 2-inch pieces.

STALE BREAD SALAD

Frugality is one of the core values of professional chefs, and that holds true whether you're Thomas Keller (read about him on page 92) or the guy running your local diner. Respect for food means you don't waste it. This brings us to a salad popular around the Mediterranean. Italians call it panzanella; in the Middle East it's known as fattoush. I call it one of the best ways I know to resuscitate stale bread. If you want to cook like a pro, this simple salad should be in your repertory. Add an antipasto platter—sliced prosciutto and some cheese—and you've got a great summer picnic or supper. **Serves 4**

SHOP The usual: luscious vine-ripened tomatoes, fresh basil, flat-leaf parsley—the only thing you *shouldn't* buy fresh is the bread.

GEAR Your basic kitchen gear plus a large salad bowl

WHAT ELSE Panzanella
is traditionally made with
stale white Italian bread,
but there's no reason you
couldn't use whole wheat or
multigrain. (So what does
"stale" mean? You'll know it
when you taste it: Stale bread
is dry and hard.) This recipe
is a broad guide: Don't panic
if you don't have all of the
ingredients on hand.

TIME about 20 minutes

8 cups stale bread cubes (1-inch cubes; cut from ½ to 1 loaf, depending on the size of the loaf)

2 large juicy ripe tomatoes, cut into ½-inch dice, with their juices

1 large cucumber, peeled and cut into ½-inch dice (seeded or not—your choice)

1 small red onion, peeled and finely chopped

2 ribs celery, thinly sliced on the diagonal

½ cup chopped pitted kalamata or other black olives

¼ cup coarsely chopped fresh flat-leaf parsley

12 fresh basil leaves, coarsely chopped

1 tablespoon capers with their brine

3 tablespoons extra virgin olive oil

1 tablespoon red wine vinegar, or more to taste

Coarse salt (kosher or sea) and freshly ground black pepper

Place the bread cubes in a large salad bowl. Stir in the tomatoes with their juices, followed by the cucumber, onion, celery, olives, parsley, basil, capers, olive oil, and wine vinegar. Let the salad stand until the juices soften the bread, about 10 minutes. Just before serving, stir the salad again. Taste for seasoning, adding more wine vinegar as necessary, and salt and pepper to taste; the salad should be highly seasoned.

Variation
Fattoush (Pita Bread Salad)

Suppose your stale bread is pita. Make a popular Middle Eastern salad called fattoush. Substitute 4 medium pitas for the bread (tear them into 2-inch pieces), 3 or 4 scallions for the red onion, ¼ cup chopped fresh mint for the basil, and a couple tablespoons of fresh lemon juice for the vinegar. Halve a pomegranate, break the halves into pieces, pry out the seeds, and add them to the salad (yes, you eat the seeds) in place of the capers and olives. If you live near a Middle Eastern market, pick up a bottle of pomegranate molasses and drizzle a tablespoon or so over the pita bread salad. Once you taste this intense sweet-sour condiment, made by boiling down fresh pomegranate juice, it will become one of your secret weapons in the kitchen.

HOT POTATO SALAD

Every guy should have a killer potato salad in his lineup. You could go the traditional cold mayonnaise-mustard route (and you'll find instructions for that potato salad on page 170). But for my money, the best potato salad comes from Germany. Assemble it hot, the bacon blasts it with smoke flavor and vinegar invigorates your taste buds. **Serves 4**

1½ pounds fingerling or Yukon Gold potatoes

Coarse salt (kosher or sea)

4 slices (¼ pound) bacon, cut crosswise into ¼-inch slivers

4 scallions, trimmed and thinly sliced crosswise, 2 tablespoons of the green parts reserved for serving

1 to 2 tablespoons extra virgin olive oil (optional)

3 tablespoons red wine vinegar, or to taste

1 tablespoon Dijon mustard

1 tablespoon sugar, or to taste

Freshly ground black pepper

1 Scrub the potatoes, cutting any larger ones in half so all of the pieces are more or less the same size (about 1½ inches long). Place the potatoes in a large saucepan and add cold water to cover by 3 inches. Season with a good dose of salt. Let the potatoes come to a boil over high heat, then reduce the heat and simmer until tender, 15 to 25 minutes, depending on their size. Drain the potatoes in a colander, then return them to the saucepan and cover the pan to keep warm.

2 Meanwhile, place the bacon in a large skillet and cook over medium heat until browned and crisp, 3 to 4 minutes, stirring often with a wooden spoon. After about 1½ minutes, add the scallions and brown them along with the bacon. (At this point, the health-conscious among us may wish to pour off a tablespoon or two of the bacon fat, replacing it with an equal amount of extra virgin olive oil.)

3 Stir in the wine vinegar, mustard, and sugar and let come to a boil over high heat, about 1 minute. Pour the vinegar mixture over the potatoes and stir gently to mix. Season the potato salad with salt and pepper to taste. Transfer the salad to a platter or bowl and serve warm with the reserved scallion greens sprinkled on top.

SHOP This is a great place to use those organic fingerling potatoes (miniature potatoes the size of your thumb) you see at your local farmers' market and supermarkets like Whole Foods. For color, pick a mix of white, red, and purple potatoes. As for the bacon, you'll get the best flavor from an artisanal smokehouse bacon from a local farm or from a national company like Nueske's.

GEAR Your basic kitchen gear including a large saucepan for cooking the potatoes, a colander, and a large (10- to 12-inch) skillet for the bacon

WHAT ELSE Bacon fat tastes good. Bacon fat has a rich mouthfeel. But bacon fat won't always endear you to your cardiologist. To lighten this salad, you could replace some or all of the bacon fat with extra virgin olive oil.

Warm or room-temperature potato salad might seem like a formula for food poisoning. It's not. That's because this salad doesn't contain mayonnaise. If you make the mayonnaise-based potato salad on page 170, you must keep it chilled at all times.

TIME about 30 minutes

WHAT YOU NEED TO KNOW ABOUT
OLIVE OIL

Olive oil ranks among the two or three most important ingredients in your kitchen—second perhaps only to salt. In the course of a week you'll toss it on salad, drizzle it on bread, pour it over pasta and T-bone steaks, use it for marinating all manner of meats and seafood, heat it in a skillet to sauté shrimp or a chicken cutlet, and use it for basting pretty much anything you put on the grill.

Olive oil also happens to be one of the rare fats that's actually good for you. Moderate consumption has been shown to boost your HDL (the "good" cholesterol) levels, while cutting LDL (the bad).

Back when I was learning to cook, you didn't question an olive oil's virginity. Today, there are hundreds of varieties of olive oil to choose from, among them extra virgin, organic, single estate, and cold-pressed. A decent bottle of olive oil can cost as much as a good bottle of wine and is every bit as challenging to select. So how do you know which olive oil is the right one for you? Here are ten things every man should know about olive oil.

1   Always buy olive oil labeled extra virgin. This identifies olive oils that have satisfied all of the International Olive Council (IOC) standards for excellence and means that the oil has a low level of acidity—0.8 percent or less (acidity interferes with the flavor).

2   Look for harvest dates or "use by" dates on the front or back label (sometimes the date is printed vertically). Both are an indication of the freshness of the olive oil. Unlike wine, olive oil does not improve with age—on the contrary, it should be consumed as close to the harvest date as possible. So, here's the calendar: Mediterranean olive oils are pressed from October through January; oils from the southern hemisphere (for example Chile, Australia, and South Africa) are freshest during the summer months up north. Time your purchases accordingly.

3   Chile? South Africa? Doesn't the best olive oil come from Tuscany? Yes, Italians make some great olive oil, but because the demand outstrips the supply, many olive oils that are labeled as bottled in Italy actually are made from olives grown elsewhere. Some of the best Mediterranean olive oils—and best values—come from Portugal, Spain, and Greece. Elsewhere look for oils from Chile and California (buy Californian olive oil after the harvest in October and November) and, from the southern hemisphere, try olive oils from Australia and New Zealand.

4 "Unfiltered oils" are just that—sold with a trace of sediment at the bottom. They are neither superior nor inferior to filtered oils; it's a matter of personal taste. (Don't worry if you see sediment in your olive oil—it occurs naturally.)

5 "Cold-pressed" olive oils are extracted by mechanical means at temperatures generally less than 80°F. Since virtually all olive oils are cold-pressed these days, the term doesn't necessarily mean a better oil.

6 The olive variety matters, too. Olive oils are made from Spanish arbequina olives, French picholine, Greek koroneiki, and Chilean racimo verde. In fact, nearly three hundred varieties of olives are cultivated worldwide. Each olive brings its own unique flavor to the oil. Take notes on the ones you like. "Organic" olive oils vary widely in quality (not to mention what it takes to qualify to be labeled as such). Most of the world's best olive oils are *not* organic. Like wines, the best olive oils come from specific estates and are labeled "estate pressed." This means that the time between harvest and pressing is likely a matter of hours, not days.

7 The bottle is also a factor. Buy olive oils that come in dark green or brown bottles; clear bottles let in more light, which degrades the oil. Avoid bottles that have languished on the retail shelf long enough to gather dust. Conversely, the color of the olive oil itself is an unreliable predictor of flavor; superior oils can range in color from pale golden yellow to vivid green.

8 Never buy olive oils labeled "light." They are generally inferior oils that fell short of IOC standards and have had their flavor and color chemically stripped. And they still have one hundred calories per tablespoon.

9 Unless you go through a lot of olive oil, buy small bottles or tins—open olive oil will deteriorate over time, developing an unpleasant flavor. Store your olive oil in a cool, dark place, never on or next to the stovetop.

10 Like wine, olive oil is a highly personal taste. Some people like tongue-blasting peppery oils from Tuscany and others prefer fruity oils from Greece that recall the olives they come from. Here are a few of my favorites: California Olive Ranch (American); Lucini or Barbera (Italian); Merula (Spanish); and TerraMater (Chilean).

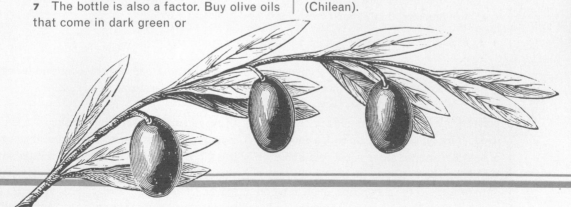

COLD POTATO SALAD
(WITH MUSTARD AND MAYO)

SHOP Cornichons are miniature vinegary French pickles: You'll find them at gourmet shops.

GEAR Your basic kitchen gear including a large saucepan

WHAT ELSE Because this salad contains mayonnaise, you must keep it chilled at all times. Especially at that outdoor picnic when it's 90 degrees in the shade.

TIME about 30 minutes

This mayonnaise- and mustard-based potato salad is probably more like the spud salad you grew up with. Conventional wisdom insists you use waxy thin-skinned potatoes (see box on page 496) on account of their reduced starch levels. But I've made awesome potato salad with leftover baked potatoes. What gives you the edge are the tangy pickles, capers, olives, and mustardy sauce. **Serves 4**

1½ pounds waxy thin-skinned potatoes, like Yukon Gold potatoes

Coarse salt (kosher or sea)

3 tablespoons mayonnaise, preferably Hellmann's

2 tablespoons sour cream

1 tablespoon Dijon style mustard, or to taste

2 teaspoons red wine vinegar, or to taste

3 scallions, both white and green parts, trimmed and thinly sliced crosswise

½ cup sliced pitted black or green olives

2 tablespoons slivered celery leaves (optional)

2 tablespoons diced pickles, such as French cornichons or dill pickles

1 tablespoon drained capers

2 hard-boiled eggs, peeled and sliced crosswise (optional)

Freshly ground black pepper

Smoked or sweet paprika for sprinkling

1 Scrub the potatoes, cutting any larger ones in half so all of the pieces are more or less the same size (about 1½ inches long). Place the potatoes in a large saucepan and add cold water to cover by 3 inches. Season with a good dose of salt. Let the potatoes come to a boil over high heat, then reduce the heat and simmer until tender, 15 to 25 minutes, depending on the size of the potatoes. Use a fork to test for doneness; it should pierce the potatoes easily.

Drain the potatoes in a colander and let cool to room temperature.

2 Meanwhile, make the dressing: Place the mayonnaise, sour cream, mustard, and vinegar in a large mixing bowl and whisk to mix. Add the cooled potatoes, scallions, olives, celery leaves (if using), pickles, capers, and eggs (if using). Fold (stir) gently just to mix with a rubber spatula. (Don't over-stir or you'll break up the potatoes.) Cover and refrigerate until serving time. (The salad will keep for up to 24 hours.)

3 Just before serving, fold the salad again, adding salt, pepper, and more vinegar if needed. Sprinkle with the smoked paprika and dig in.

GAUCHO BEAN SALAD

This salad often accompanies wood-grilled meats in Argentina and Uruguay. You might recognize it as a cousin of the American three-bean salad, but with one key difference: It contains no sugar. This makes it especially well-suited to grilled beef. If you do a lot of tailgating, you need a bean salad in your repertory. This one is for grown-ups. **Serves 6 to 8**

1 can (about 15 ounces) pinto beans, preferably organic and low-sodium

1 can (about 15 ounces) small kidney beans, preferably organic and low-sodium, or another can of pinto beans

1 medium-size sweet onion, peeled and finely diced (about ¾ cup)

1 poblano pepper or green bell pepper, or 2 jalapeño peppers, stemmed, seeded, and finely diced

1 large luscious red ripe tomato, finely diced, with its juices

½ cup coarsely chopped fresh flat-leaf parsley

1 teaspoon dried oregano

1 teaspoon hot red pepper flakes, or to taste

3 to 4 tablespoons extra virgin olive oil

1½ tablespoons red wine vinegar, or more to taste

Coarse salt (kosher or sea) and freshly ground black pepper

1 Drain the beans in a colander, rinse them well with cold water, and drain them again.

2 Transfer the beans to a mixing bowl. Stir in the onion, poblano pepper, tomato, parsley, oregano, hot pepper flakes, olive oil, and wine vinegar. Taste for seasoning, adding more vinegar as necessary and salt and black pepper to taste; the salad should be highly seasoned. Any leftover salad will keep, covered, in the refrigerator for at least 3 days.

SHOP In South America they use a small dark rectangular bean called *poroto,* which has a nutty, earthy flavor. Here I use pinto or kidney beans or a mix of both.

GEAR Your basic kitchen gear including a colander and mixing bowl

WHAT ELSE It's not traditional, but for extra flavor you could grill or smoke the onion, pepper, and tomato before adding them to the salad. Roast them until the skins are completely charred, then scrape the skins off (see the instructions on page 506).

TIME about 15 minutes

MICHAEL POLLAN

> ► If the ingredient list on the package has a lot of polysyllabic chemicals . . . don't buy it.

He's an activist journalist who costarred in the documentary *Food, Inc.* (If you haven't seen it, download it ASAP.) He's a bestselling author whose books, like *The Omnivore's Dilemma*, *Food Rules: An Eater's Manual*, *In Defense of Food*, and *Cooked*, have revolutionized the way Americans think about food. A respected journalism professor at the University of California, Berkeley, he writes cover stories for *The New York Times* Sunday magazine; his interests are wide-ranging enough to include essays on forsaking your front lawn (which he deems ecologically unsustainable) and on marijuana from the plant's point of view. (You'll find the latter in his book *The Botany of Desire*.) His name is Michael Pollan, and if the words *locavore* and *sustainability* are part of your vocabulary, if you make a concerted effort to patronize farmers' markets and eat grass-fed beef, if you scrupulously avoid industrial agricultural products and livestock raised on antibiotics and growth hormones, chances are Pollan had something to do with it.

"Cooking is still largely a woman's responsibility," Pollan observes. "Men need to step up to the plate." (According to Pollan, just 13 percent of our meals eaten at home are cooked by men.) "With an increasing number of women in the workforce, if men don't cook more, our kids risk never knowing what a home-cooked meal is. Sure, we men grill, but we shouldn't be intimidated by pots and pans in the kitchen. We need to cook more—for our personal well-being and for the health of our marriages, our kids, and our planet." Amen.

What's the first dish you ever cooked?
Scrambled eggs—I'd make them as an after-school snack.

What's your go-to dish when you're by yourself?
Pantry pasta. I rifle through the pantry for ingredients that look interesting. Recently I've been making pasta with chickpeas, canned tuna, and sesame oil.

What's your go-to dish when you have company?
I go one of two ways: braised meat or grilled fish. The beauty of braising is that you start in the morning, so dinner is essentially done by the time guests arrive. Grilling you do at the last minute, so it becomes part of the evening's entertainment.

Name three techniques every guy should master.

Grilling (but I don't have to tell you that): You invest money in buying tender premium cuts of meat and seafood, but you save on time. The cooking time for direct grilling is measured in minutes, not hours.

Braising: This means cooking larger, tougher cuts of meat with liquid in a sealed pot at a low temperature for a long time. You invest time (three to four hours of cooking time, although your active participation is much less than that), but you save money, as braising is designed to make cheap cuts of meat tender. [For a guide to braising, see page 9.]

Cooking pasta: The secret is to use lots of water and plenty of salt and boil the pasta just long enough so it's tender. Basically, if you can boil water, you can cook pasta. One of my favorite side dishes is pasta tossed with extra virgin olive oil, fresh lemon juice, and sea salt.

What are three ingredients you can't live without?

Good salt: I like the crunchy crystals of Maldon salt from England.

Soy sauce: Asia's version of sea salt

Extra virgin olive oil

What three dishes should every guy know how to make?

Pork shoulder: Thanks to its generous marbling of fat there's no more forgiving cut of meat. It's virtually impossible to overcook a pork shoulder. Of course, if you're a devout Jew or Muslim you'd pick a lamb shoulder or another large cut of meat.

Grilled salmon: I like it Greek style, marinated with olive oil, lemon juice, garlic, and fresh herbs. To make a sauce, whirl olive oil, garlic, and fresh herbs from the garden in a blender.

Pasta with clam sauce: Steam and shell the clams. Make the sauce with the cooking liquid, adding wine, garlic, tomatoes, and oregano. Cook the pasta al dente and finish it in the sauce. It's as simple as that.

Name three kitchen tools you can't live without.

Again, Steven, I don't have to tell you: my grill. I use it year-round.

A cast-iron skillet: I use one daily.

Tongs: One of those great inventions that didn't seem to be available to home cooks when I was growing up.

What are the three things to keep in mind if you're just starting out in the kitchen?

Pay attention to where your food comes from. I won't buy meat unless it's grass-fed or pastured and ideally raised within a 150-mile radius of my home. Buy local first, then organic. If the ingredient list on the package has a lot of polysyllabic chemicals you're not familiar with or can't pronounce, don't buy it.

Make friends with your butcher, fishmonger, produce man, and cheese vendor. Ask what he's most excited about today and tailor your shopping list and menu accordingly.

Think quality, not quantity. It's better to eat 4 ounces of local grass-fed beef than a cheap 14-ounce industrially processed steak.

What are the three most common mistakes guys make in the kitchen?

Underseasoning. Salt foods, especially meats and pasta cooking water, generously.

Overcooking fish. I like my fish with a blush of pink or translucence in the center and will send it back when it comes overcooked at a restaurant. Remember, fish continues to cook after you take it off the heat.

Serving too much meat. Reverse the 8 ounce/4 ounce rule (8 ounces of meat to 4 ounces of vegetables for one serving). We have to give up this idea of a giant hunk of animal protein in the center of the plate. Great meals can be made with 4 ounces of meat per person, which in the long run, is the only sustainable way to eat meat.

What is something unexpected you've learned over the years that really helps you up your game in the kitchen?

Salt early. Salt steaks several hours prior to cooking and chicken as early as twenty-four hours ahead. This may seem counterintuitive—after all, doesn't the salt draw out the juices, drying out the meat? True, initially the salt extracts moisture, but after a while the salty meat juices are reabsorbed back into the meat, resulting in a deeper, richer flavor.

What else?

Remember, shopping well is as important as cooking well—maybe even more so.

A Summer Salad of Tomatoes, Green Beans, and Corn

FARM STAND SALAD

Maybe you like to shop at farm stands and farmers' markets. (You should.) Maybe your significant other likes to shop at farm stands and you go along for the ride. (Smart man.) However you get there, there's no question that you eat better, feel better, and do good for your community when you buy produce raised on local farms. Case in point, this colorful summer salad, made with sugar-sweet corn, crisp-tender green beans, and local tomatoes. **Serves 2 to 4; can be multiplied as desired**

2 ears sweet corn, husked, silk removed

1 pint local cherry tomatoes, cut in half, or 1 large ripe heirloom tomato, cut into 1-inch pieces

6 ounces haricots verts or slender green beans, rinsed, stem ends snapped off

1 bunch arugula, rinsed and patted dry with paper towels

2 tablespoons coarsely chopped fresh dill, basil, tarragon, chervil, or other summer herb or a combination of herbs

2 tablespoons hazelnut or walnut oil or extra virgin olive oil, or to taste

1 tablespoon rice vinegar or wine vinegar, or to taste

1 tablespoon pure maple syrup

Coarse salt (kosher or sea) and freshly ground black pepper

1 Cut the corn kernels off the cobs. To do this, place an ear of corn flat on a cutting board and remove the kernels by making broad lengthwise strokes with a chef's knife, rotating the ear as you go. Repeat with the second ear. Place the corn kernels in a large salad bowl. Add the tomato(es), green beans, arugula, and herb(s). Pour the oil, vinegar, and maple syrup over the salad, but don't toss it. The salad can be assembled a couple of hours before serving (keep the salad refrigerated if it will be more than 1 hour).

2 Just before serving, toss the salad and season it with more oil and/or vinegar, if needed, and salt and pepper to taste.

SHOP Sorry guys, but if you missed making this salad in summertime, save it for next season. The term *heirloom* refers to the traditional varieties of tomatoes (and other vegetables) developed at a time when physical appearance or the ability to be shipped in a boxcar cross-country mattered less than the texture and taste. If it smells like a tomato and has the zingy acidic flavor of a tomato when you bite into it, you're in business. Haricots verts are skinny French green beans, and the reason to buy the beans when they are small is that you can munch them whole without cooking them.

Nut oils, like those made from hazelnuts or walnuts, are available at natural food stores. Refrigerate these once opened and use them within a few months; they have a short shelf life.

GEAR Your basic kitchen gear plus a large salad bowl

WHAT ELSE If you happen to have a lit grill handy, give the salad a smoky flavor by grilling the corn before you add it (see page 503).

TIME about 15 minutes

A Winter Salad of Endive, Walnuts, and Cheese

BLACK AND WHITE SALAD

SHOP Walnut oil has a fantastic nutty flavor. It's sold in metal cans at natural foods stores and specialty food stores. It spoils quickly, so buy a small can and store it in the refrigerator. Or, you can use extra virgin olive. For the full effect of this salad, use cave-aged Gruyère, which has more bite than regular Gruyère, or opt for genuine French Roquefort.

GEAR Your basic kitchen gear including a large (10- to 12-inch) cast-iron skillet plus a large heatproof salad bowl

WHAT ELSE I call for toasting the walnuts in a skillet, but you can also do it in a toaster oven. Spread the walnuts out in a roasting pan and bake them at 400°F until fragrant, about 5 minutes.

TIME about 20 minutes

Salad in summertime is a no-brainer. But what do you serve in the dead of winter? Belgian endive—those tapered white cylinders with pale-green-tipped leaves that are crunchy, moist, and pleasantly bitter—is one of the few salad "greens" that are actually in season in January. Add black olives, crunchy walnuts, walnut oil, and tangy cheese and you get a big-flavored salad that's a visual knockout. You can go two routes with the cheese: the nutty sweetness of Gruyère (a cow's milk cheese from the Swiss or French Alps) or the salty tang of Roquefort (a sheep's milk blue cheese from southwest France). **Serves 2 to 4**

⅓ cup shelled walnut halves or pieces

2 heads Belgian endive

3 ounces Gruyère cheese, cut into 1-by-¼-by-¼-inch strips, or 3 ounces Roquefort, crumbled

¼ cup black olives, such as kalamata or oil-cured

2 tablespoons walnut oil or extra virgin olive oil, or more to taste

1 tablespoon sherry vinegar or red wine vinegar

Coarse salt (kosher or sea) and freshly ground black pepper

2 tablespoons finely chopped chives or scallion greens

1 To toast the walnuts, heat a dry cast-iron skillet over medium heat for about 20 seconds. Add the walnuts and cook until fragrant, about 2 minutes, shaking the skillet. Transfer the walnuts to a heatproof salad bowl and let cool.

2 Cut the endive crosswise into ½-inch-thick slices, discarding the stem ends. Place the endive in the salad bowl. Add the Gruyère or Roquefort and the olives. Pour the walnut oil

and vinegar over the salad but don't toss it. The salad can be assembled a couple of hours before serving (keep the salad refrigerated if it will be more than 1 hour).

3 Just before serving, toss the salad and season it with more oil, if needed, and salt (just a little—the cheese is salty) and pepper to taste; the salad should be highly seasoned. Sprinkle the chives over the salad and serve.

CREAMY HORSERADISH SLAW

Here's your basic creamy slaw invigorated with prepared horseradish. For an interesting variation, substitute thinly sliced kale or collard greens for the cabbage. **Makes about 4 cups; serves 4 to 6**

For the dressing

⅓ cup mayonnaise, preferably Hellmann's

2 tablespoons prepared white horseradish

2 tablespoons Dijon mustard

1 tablespoon distilled white vinegar

½ teaspoon celery seeds

1 tablespoon poppy seeds (optional)

For the slaw

1 small (about 1 pound) Savoy, green, or purple cabbage, cored and cut into thick wedges

1 carrot, trimmed, peeled, and cut into 2-inch pieces

Coarse salt (kosher or sea) and freshly ground black pepper

SHOP Poppy seeds are those little earthy-tasting seeds you find on kaiser rolls. They taste great and look even better.

GEAR Your basic kitchen gear plus a large salad bowl and a food processor (optional)

WHAT ELSE Want to take this slaw over the top? Buy a whole fresh horseradish root and grate it yourself.

TIME about 15 minutes

1 Make the dressing: Place the mayonnaise, horseradish, mustard, vinegar, celery seeds, and poppy seeds (if using) in a large salad bowl and whisk to mix.

2 Make the slaw: Shred the cabbage and carrot in a food processor fitted with a slicing disk. Work in several batches and run the machine in short bursts. Or, thinly slice the cabbage wedges and carrot by hand.

3 Stir the slaw mixture into the dressing. and season with salt and pepper (lots of pepper) to taste. The slaw should be highly seasoned. Refrigerate the slaw if not serving within an hour. The slaw will keep covered in the refrigerator for at least 3 days.

Slaw Five Ways

Slaw is so deeply rooted in American food culture that you may find it hard to believe cole slaw came from Holland (in Dutch it's called *koolsla*; *kool* means cabbage, *sla* means salad). Like many ethnic foods here in the U.S. we've made it our own, and any food-savvy guy should have a few big-flavored slaw recipes in his portfolio. The basic formula is simple: shredded cabbage (or another veggie) plus a dressing that can be creamy with mayonnaise, spicy with mustard, or sweet-sour with sugar and vinegar.

There are lots of options for cabbage: white, red, Savoy (which has crenellated leaves), or even an Asian cabbage, like napa. A pound of cabbage yields four to five cups of shredded or chopped cabbage.

I'm including five of my favorites in this chapter. Tweak the flavorings to make them yours.

SOUTHERN MUSTARD SLAW

SHOP Dry mustard is a sort of flour made from mustard seeds—when mixed with vinegar or water, it becomes prepared mustard. Colman's in the yellow can is the brand you want, and can be found in most supermarkets with the other spices. While there, pick up a jar of celery seeds, which have a nutty celery flavor.

GEAR Your basic kitchen gear plus a large salad bowl and a food processor (optional)

WHAT ELSE For an interesting variation on the slaw, substitute honey or maple syrup for the brown sugar.

TIME about 15 minutes

Fortified with both wet and dry mustard, this slaw pays homage to the mustard slaws served on barbecue pork sandwiches in Memphis and the Carolinas. **Makes about 4 cups; serves 4 to 6**

For the dressing
¼ cup Dijon mustard

2 tablespoons brown sugar, or to taste

1 tablespoon dry mustard, preferably Colman's

2 tablespoons vegetable oil

2 tablespoons distilled white vinegar

1 tablespoon hot sauce, or to taste (I like Texas Pete)

For the slaw
1 small (about 1 pound) green cabbage, cored and cut into thick wedges

1 carrot, trimmed, peeled, and cut into 2-inch pieces

About ½ teaspoon celery seeds

Coarse salt (kosher or sea) and freshly ground black pepper

1 Make the dressing: Place the Dijon mustard, brown sugar, and dry mustard in a large salad bowl and whisk to mix. Gradually whisk in the oil, vinegar, and hot sauce.

2 Make the slaw: Finely chop the cabbage and carrot in a food processor fitted with a metal chopping blade. Work in several batches so as not to overcrowd the processor bowl, and run the machine in short bursts. If you don't have a processor, thinly chop the cabbage and carrot by hand.

3 Stir the slaw mixture into the dressing. Add the celery seeds to the slaw and season it with salt and pepper (lots of pepper) to taste; the slaw should be highly seasoned. Refrigerate the slaw if not serving within an hour. The slaw will keep, covered, in the refrigerator for at least 3 days.

KOREAN KIMCHI SLAW

Y ou could describe kimchi as Korean sauerkraut. It's made with cabbage or other vegetables and fermented with garlic (lots), chile powder, and salt. It's one of those when-in-doubt-add-it ingredients—instantly electrifying the flavor of any dish. **Makes about 4 cups; serves 4 to 6**

For the dressing

1 clove garlic, peeled and minced

1 tablespoon finely chopped peeled fresh ginger

2 tablespoons sugar

2 tablespoons rice vinegar

2 tablespoons Asian (dark) sesame oil

Coarse salt (kosher or sea) and freshly ground black pepper

For the slaw

1 small (about 1 pound) Napa cabbage or green cabbage

1 small red bell pepper, stemmed and seeded

1 small Asian pear or ripe regular pear (optional), cored and seeded

$\frac{1}{3}$ cup prepared kimchi, thinly sliced

2 scallions, trimmed, white and green parts thinly sliced crosswise

1 tablespoon black sesame seeds (optional)

Coarse salt (kosher or sea) and freshly ground black pepper

SHOP It used to be you had to go to an Asian market to buy kimchi. Today, you'll find it at Whole Foods and many supermarkets. Asian pears are round, crunchy, and wet-fleshed, with a less pronounced pear flavor than western Boscs or Anjous.

Black sesame seeds taste pretty much like regular toasted sesame seeds, but look really cool—again, you'll find them at Whole Foods or an Asian market.

Napa is an Asian cabbage with flat white ribs and crinkly leaves.

GEAR Your basic kitchen gear plus a large salad bowl and a food processor (optional)

WHAT ELSE Want to try something weird but really good? Add a couple tablespoons chopped dried shrimp (available at Asian and Hispanic markets) to the slaw. They're briny *and* sweet.

TIME about 15 minutes

1 Make the dressing: Place the garlic, ginger, and sugar in the bottom of a large serving bowl and mash to a paste with the back of a wooden spoon. Whisk in the rice vinegar and sesame oil and season with salt and pepper to taste.

2 Make the slaw: Shred the napa cabbage, bell pepper, and pear, if using, in a food processor fitted with a shredding disk. Work in several batches so as not to overcrowd the processor bowl and run the machine in short bursts. If you don't have a processor, thinly shred the cabbage, bell pepper, and pear by hand.

3 Stir the slaw mixture into the dressing. Stir in the kimchi, scallions, and sesame seeds, if using. Taste for seasoning, adding more salt and/or pepper as necessary; the slaw should be highly seasoned. Refrigerate the slaw if not serving within an hour. The slaw will keep, covered, in the refrigerator for at least 3 days.

MANGO PEANUT SLAW

SHOP Thai and bird's-eye chiles are tiny red or green chiles whose fierce bite is indirectly proportional to their diminutive size. Any fresh hot chile—from serranos to jalapeños—will work. Fish sauce is sold at Asian markets and in the ethnic foods section of most upscale supermarkets. You can also buy it online through amazon.com. The best brands come in glass bottles.

GEAR Your basic kitchen gear plus a large salad bowl and a food processor (optional)

WHAT ELSE If you have sensitive skin, wear rubber gloves when handling mangoes. Some people get a poison ivylike reaction to the sap.

TIME about 15 minutes

Here's slaw that riffs on *som tam*, the legendary sweet, spicy, salty green papaya slaw of Thailand. This one gives you the piney sweetness of fresh mango, plus raw green beans and peanuts for crunch. You need to know about one unusual ingredient—fish sauce—a malodorous umami-rich condiment made with fermented anchovies (you can read more about fish sauce on page 27). Or, if you prefer, you can substitute soy sauce. Choose a mango that's ripe: It will be fragrant and gently yielding when pressed, but not soft or squishy. **Makes about 4 cups; serves 4 to 6**

For the dressing
2 to 4 Thai or bird's-eye chiles or serrano peppers, stemmed, seeded, and minced (for a hotter slaw, leave the seeds in)

1 clove garlic, peeled and minced

3 tablespoons sugar, or more to taste

½ teaspoon freshly ground black pepper

¼ cup fresh lime juice, or more to taste

¼ cup Asian fish sauce or soy sauce

For the slaw
1 small (about 1 pound) head green cabbage, or 1 green (unripe) papaya (about 1 pound), peeled

1 ripe mango

18 slender green beans, cut sharply on the diagonal into 1-inch pieces

½ cup coarsely chopped fresh cilantro

⅓ cup coarsely chopped dry-roasted peanuts, salted or unsalted

1 Make the dressing: Place the chiles, garlic, sugar, and black pepper in a large serving bowl and mash to a paste with the back of a wooden spoon. (In Thailand this would be done in a mortar with a pestle. Pounding seems to bring out more flavor than mashing or chopping in a food processor.) Whisk in the lime juice and fish sauce.

2 Make the slaw: If using a food processor, cut the cabbage into wedges that will fit through the feeding tube. Or pit and cut the papaya into chunks. Shred either in a food processor fitted with a shredding disk. Work in several batches so as not to crowd the machine, and run the machine in short bursts. If you don't have a processor, thinly slice or grate the cabbage or papaya by hand.

3 Peel the mango and cut the flesh off the seed. Cut the mango into thin slivers.

4 Add the cabbage or papaya, mango, green beans, and cilantro to the dressing. Toss and taste for seasoning, adding more sugar and/or lime juice as necessary; the slaw should be highly seasoned. Sprinkle the peanuts over the slaw and serve. Refrigerate the slaw if not serving within an hour. It tastes best if served within a few hours of making it.

Mortar and Pestle

I have in my kitchen an old mortar and pestle my pharmacist grandfather used in his drugstore. The bowl and pestle were carved from solid marble, and when it comes to mashing garlic, chiles, lemongrass, anchovies, and other flavorings into aromatic pastes, nothing, ahem, beats it. This truth is appreciated wherever cooks have a hunger for big flavors—from Latin America to Southeast Asia. (Mexico's *molcajete* is a lava stone mortar and pestle used for making guacamole.)

If you're really serious about flavor, you may want to consider investing in what you might call a pre-industrial food processor. Look for it at an ethnic market or cookware shop and buy the largest, heaviest one you can find.

FENNEL-ORANGE SLAW

Here's a slaw built on the bright Mediterranean flavors of olive, orange, and anise. Eat it as a salad or side dish or serve it as a condiment for simple grilled chicken or fish. Oil-cured olives are shriveled like raisins. If unavailable, substitute kalamata or nicoise. **Makes about 4 cups; serves 4 to 6**

1 large or 2 small fennel bulbs
(about 1 pound)

2 large oranges

½ cup pitted or oil-cured black olives

3 tablespoons extra virgin olive oil

2 tablespoons fresh lemon juice or lime juice

Coarse salt (kosher or sea) and freshly ground black pepper

SHOP Fresh fennel (not to be confused with fennel seeds) comes in greenish-white bulbs with slender celerylike stalks. (It's sometimes described as licorice-flavored celery.) Look for it in the produce section of good supermarkets.

GEAR Your basic kitchen gear including a food processor or sharp chef's knife plus a large salad bowl

WHAT ELSE I call for the fennel to be sliced by hand or in a food processor, but if you want to add a cool tool to your collection, invest in a mandoline. It looks like a flat metal or plastic board with a sharp blade in the center. That's how chefs slice spuds to make potato chips.

TIME about 15 minutes

1 Cut the fennel bulbs crosswise into paper-thin slices in a food processor fitted with a slicing disk or by hand with a chef's knife. Transfer the fennel to a large serving bowl. If the fennel bulbs came with their stalks and leaves, finely chop 1 tablespoon of the feathery fennel leaves. Discard the stalks.

2 Cut the rind and all of the white pith off 1 orange. Working over the bowl with the fennel to catch any juices, make V-shape cuts between the membranes to release neat segments of orange. Remove and discard any seeds and add the orange segments to the fennel. Repeat with the remaining orange. Add the olives (remove the pits, if any), olive oil, and lemon juice but don't mix the slaw. The slaw can be prepared several hours ahead to this stage. Keep refrigerated if not serving within an hour.

3 Toss the slaw just before serving, then season it with salt and pepper to taste; the slaw should be highly seasoned.

BALL JAR SALAD DRESSINGS

SHOP You'll want good oils and vinegars here: canola or extra virgin olive oil, for example, and a top-drawer wine vinegar or balsamic vinegar.

GEAR Your basic kitchen gear plus a 1-pint (16-ounce) jar with a tight-fitting lid

WHAT ELSE Most of these salad dressings will keep in the refrigerator for at least 3 days. But they're so quick and easy, the idea is to make them as often as you need them.

TIME about 5 minutes

You may wonder, "What's in Steven Raichlen's refrigerator?" Barbecue sauce, to be sure. Hot sauces and chili pastes. *Lots* of hot sauces and chili pastes. But one thing you'll never find in my fridge is commercial bottled salad dressings. The reason is simple: It's too easy, too satisfying, and too darned delicious to make your own salad dressing from scratch. Just add the ingredients to a clean jar, seal it, and shake. I like Ball-style canning jars, but you can use just about any large (1 pint) jar with a screw-on lid that you have on hand. Of course you can make salad dressing the traditional way, whisking the ingredients together in a bowl. Here are seven irresistible salad dressings. (Note: Figure on 1 to 2 tablespoons of dressing per serving of salad.)

MUSTARD SHALLOT VINAIGRETTE

You may be surprised to see that this dressing, a classic vinaigrette, uses canola oil instead of (or in addition to) extra virgin olive oil. In France, where I learned to cook, vinaigrette was more about the mustard and vinegar than the oil. **Makes ¾ cup**

MUSTARD SHALLOT
VINAIGRETTE

PARMESAN PEPPERCORN
DRESSING

SESAME SOY
SALAD DRESSING

FRESH HERB
RANCH DRESSING

HONEY POPPY
BALSAMIC VINAIGRETTE

½ cup canola oil, or ¼ cup each canola oil and extra virgin olive oil

2 to 3 tablespoons red wine vinegar

1 tablespoon Dijon mustard

1 tablespoon heavy (or whipping) cream or mayonnaise

1 small shallot, peeled and minced (about 2 tablespoons)

Coarse salt (kosher or sea) and freshly ground black pepper

Place the oil, wine vinegar, mustard, cream, and shallot in a jar. Add 2 tablespoons of water. Tightly cover the jar and shake it until the vinaigrette is emulsified (well combined). Season the dressing with salt (about ½ teaspoon should be sufficient) and pepper to taste. The vinaigrette will keep in the refrigerator for at least 3 days. Shake the jar again just before serving to recombine the ingredients.

HONEY POPPY BALSAMIC VINAIGRETTE

For people who like a salad dressing with texture in addition to sweetness. Poppy seeds possess an offbeat earthy flavor and crunch. **Makes about 1 cup**

½ cup extra virgin olive oil

3 tablespoons good-quality balsamic vinegar

1 to 2 tablespoons honey

1 tablespoon Dijon mustard

1 tablespoon poppy seeds

Coarse salt (kosher or sea) and freshly ground black pepper

Place the olive oil, balsamic vinegar, honey, mustard, and poppy seeds in a jar. Add 2 tablespoons of hot water. Tightly cover the jar and shake it until the vinaigrette is emulsified (well combined). Season the vinaigrette with salt and pepper to taste. The dressing will keep in the refrigerator for at least 3 days. Shake the jar again just before serving to recombine the ingredients.

FRESH HERB RANCH DRESSING

This ranch dressing brings us into the realm of creamy mayonnaise-based salad dressings. Buttermilk gives you a nice sour-ish tang, while the herbs and lemon zest (the outer yellow peel of the lemon) add fragrance and brightness. **Makes about 1 cup**

⅓ cup buttermilk

¼ cup mayonnaise, preferably Hellmann's

2 tablespoons canola oil

1 tablespoon cider vinegar, or more to taste

3 tablespoons minced fresh herbs, such as chives, tarragon, and/or slivered basil

1 clove garlic, peeled and minced

½ teaspoon freshly grated lemon zest

Coarse salt (kosher or sea) and freshly ground black pepper

Place the buttermilk, mayonnaise, oil, cider vinegar, herbs, garlic, and lemon zest in a jar. Tightly cover the jar and shake it until the dressing is emulsified (well combined). Taste for seasoning, adding more cider vinegar as necessary and salt and pepper to taste. The dressing will keep in the refrigerator for at least 3 days. Shake the jar again just before serving to recombine the dressing.

PARMESAN PEPPERCORN DRESSING

If you like Caesar salad but don't care for anchovies, this creamy peppery cheese dressing is for you. To get the full effect, you must use genuine Parmigiano Reggiano cheese (see page 97). **Makes about ¾ cup**

¼ cup buttermilk

¼ cup mayonnaise, preferably Hellmann's

½ cup (2 ounces) freshly and finely grated Parmigiano Reggiano cheese

2 tablespoons extra virgin olive oil

½ teaspoon finely freshly grated lemon zest

1 tablespoon fresh lemon juice

1 teaspoon cracked black peppercorns or freshly ground black pepper

Coarse salt (kosher or sea)

Place the buttermilk, mayonnaise, Parmigiano Reggiano, olive oil, lemon zest, lemon juice, and peppercorns in a jar. Tightly cover the jar and shake it until the dressing is emulsified (well combined). Season the dressing with salt to taste (about ¼ teaspoon should be sufficient). The dressing will keep in the refrigerator for at least 3 days. Shake the jar again just before serving to recombine the dressing.

SESAME SOY SALAD DRESSING

This dressing brings you squarely into the realm of Asian salads, and it's also pretty awesome spooned over grilled chicken and seafood. For information on buying soy sauce and sesame oil, see page 28. **Makes about 1 cup**

¼ cup soy sauce or tamari

3 tablespoons rice vinegar

3 tablespoons Asian (dark) sesame oil

1 tablespoon minced peeled fresh ginger

1 tablespoon minced fresh scallion greens

1 clove garlic, peeled and minced

Place the soy sauce, rice vinegar, sesame oil, ginger, scallion greens, and garlic in a jar. Add 2 tablespoons of water, tightly cover the jar, and shake it until the dressing is emulsified (well combined). The dressing will keep in the refrigerator for at least 3 days.

CREAMY MISO DRESSING

Miso is a highly nutritious, sweet-salty Japanese condiment made with specially cultured (fermented) soy beans. You've probably had it even if you've never heard of it: It's the main ingredient in the miso soup served at Japanese restaurants. Miso explodes with rich, salty umami flavors (see page 28)—it's definitely worth adding to your flavor arsenal. **Makes about ¾ cup**

¼ cup miso (preferably white, see page 27)

¼ cup mayonnaise, preferably Hellmann's

2 tablespoons vegetable oil

2 tablespoons sugar

½ teaspoon freshly grated lemon zest

2 tablespoons fresh lemon juice

Place the miso, mayonnaise, oil, sugar, lemon zest, and lemon juice in a jar. Stir the mixture a few times with a fork to break up the miso. Add 2 tablespoons of water, tightly cover the jar, and shake it until the dressing is emulsified (well combined). The dressing will keep in the refrigerator for at least 3 days. Shake the jar again just before serving to recombine the dressing.

Meyer Lemons

Meyer lemons are to citrus fruit what Michter's or Templeton is to a house whiskey. Believed to be a cross between a conventional lemon and a mandarin orange, Meyer lemons have a haunting perfumed aroma in addition to their tart juice. Try them just once and you'll buy them over conventional lemons whenever possible. I like them so much, I planted a Meyer lemon tree in my backyard. Look for Meyer lemons at upscale supermarkets and produce shops.

BLUE CHEESE DRESSING

Finally, you need a blue cheese dressing to go with that wedge salad (cut a head of iceberg lettuce through the stem end in quarters—voilà, the wedge). You have lots of choices for blue cheese, and each will give your dressing a different personality. I like the sharp mineral tang of Roquefort (aged in limestone caves), but pungent Gorgonzola (Italian), aromatic Stilton (English), tangy Cabrales (Spanish), and creamy Maytag Blue (American) all have their partisans. **Makes about 1 cup**

3 ounces blue cheese, at room
temperature

⅓ cup mayonnaise, preferably
Hellmann's

Freshly ground black pepper

⅓ cup buttermilk, or as needed

1 tablespoon rice or white vinegar or
lemon juice (optional)

Press the cheese through a strainer with the back of a spoon. (This gives you lump-free dressing.) Or mash it with a fork (OK, you'll get a few lumps). Place the cheese in a jar with the mayonnaise, pepper, and buttermilk. Tightly cover the jar and shake until creamy.

You may need to stir the mixture a few times with a fork if it clumps. Taste and, if you like your dressing tangier, add the vinegar or lemon juice. The dressing will keep in the refrigerator for at least 3 days. Shake the jar again just before serving to recombine the dressing.

STARTERS

Starters—the term doesn't begin to capture the importance of those salty, savory small dishes you serve at the start of a meal. The right assortment of appetizers makes an awesome meal in itself, which is why the Spanish invented tapas— that and to keep flies out of the sherry. (In Spanish, *tapar* means "to cover" and these small plates of bar food were served atop wine glasses—so the story goes—to keep them covered.)

So what makes a great appetizer? It should be small enough to snap up with your fingers and salty enough to drive you to drink. Many offer a contrast of textures (crisp exterior, gooey center), with crunch being most important. The short list of world-class starters includes dips and chips, nachos and poppers, chicken wings, and anchovy hot tubs. Salami chips? Check. How about grilled cheese flambéed with brandy? Think of them as small plates that deliver big flavors.

SPICED CHICKPEAS

Chickpeas spiced with cumin and coriander and roasted in a skillet over an open fire are a popular snack in the Middle East. (Try *that* at your next barbecue!) They're also a healthy snack, boasting 5 grams of protein and oversize doses of folate and manganese. Use the following recipe as a blueprint, spicing the chickpeas with barbecue rub (page 531), blackening spices (page 381), or other favorite spice mix. Beats bar nuts hollow. **Makes about 1½ cups**

1 can (15 ounces) chickpeas

1 tablespoon extra virgin olive oil

1 teaspoon hot or sweet paprika

½ teaspoon ground cumin

½ teaspoon ground coriander (optional)

Coarse salt (kosher or sea) and freshly ground black pepper

1 Preheat the oven to 400°F.

2 Drain the chickpeas in a colander, rinse them with cold water, drain them again, and blot them dry with paper towels. Transfer the chickpeas to a mixing bowl. Add the olive oil, paprika, cumin, and coriander, if using, and stir to mix. Season with salt and pepper to taste.

3 Line a rimmed baking sheet with aluminum foil for easy cleanup. Spread the chickpeas in a single layer on the baking sheet. Bake until browned and crisp, 10 to 15 minutes, stirring them once or twice with a spatula. Transfer the chickpeas to a plate and let cool. Serve them in a bowl and eat like peanuts.

SHOP For the best results, use organic low- or no-sodium chickpeas. One good brand is Eden Foods.

GEAR Your basic kitchen gear including a rimmed baking sheet

WHAT ELSE I've given you the Middle Eastern version of these chickpeas, but you could certainly spice them with a tablespoon or so of smoked paprika, Chinese five spice powder, Old Bay Seasoning—the possibilities are endless.

TIME about 20 minutes

BEN SHEWRY

Ben Shewry is on a roll. *Gourmet Traveller* magazine called him "Australia's Best New Talent." San Pellegrino added Attica, his fifty-five-seat restaurant in Melbourne, to its coveted list of the 100 Best Restaurants in the World. Emirates airline crowned him "Chef of the Year." Shewry represented Australia at Madrid Fusion (a prestigious international food conference), and at the Melbourne Food & Wine Festival he staged a four-act "Theater of Ideas" that featured beekeepers, ceramicists, and chefs.

Not bad for a guy who grew up on a sheep and cattle farm in the remote Taranaki region in northwest New Zealand. Remote? His district numbers fifty inhabitants with the nearest "town" (a road, a pub, and a service station) thirty minutes away. But the lack of supermarkets or restaurants had its advantages: Ben's father taught the boy how to hunt, fish, and forage. From nearby Maori neighbors, Ben learned the art of the *hangi*, a sort of New Zealand luau featuring pork, mutton bird, *kumara* (aboriginal sweet potato), and other native vegetables cooked in an underground pit lined with stones, flax, and fire. The *hangi* inspired one of Shewry's most famous dishes: Virginia rose potatoes roasted for six hours in the soil in which they were grown, then served with cold-smoked goat's milk curds.

"Being such a young country, we New Zealanders don't have much of a cuisine of our own," says Shewry. But he finds the lack of culinary tradition liberating. "We feel the freedom—and obligation—to invent our own."

First food memory?
My dad slaughtering and butchering one of the family cows for us to eat. He had great empathy for animals and did everything he could to minimize their suffering. I try to keep that sense of humanity in my restaurant today.

When did you realize you wanted to be a chef?
When I was five years old. It's the only thing I ever wanted to do. I wasn't interested in toys, but I loved to play with pots and pans—especially an old Polaris teapot with a Bakelite handle. I'm not sure how I knew what a chef was, as there were none in the backcountry where I grew up.

Why is it important for men to cook?
Knowing how to cook is an essential skill at any stage in a man's life. When you're a son, you want to learn how to cook so you can carry on family traditions. When you're a university student, being the guy in your dorm who knows how to cook makes you a prized commodity, especially with women. When

you're a husband and father, knowing how to cook is part of being able to provide for your family.

Do men and women cook differently?

Most men treat cooking as a job. It's like building a fence—you get in and get it done. We don't taste or nurture the food like a woman would. Women cook in a way that's more sensitive, delicate, and thoughtful.

The quintessential guy dish?

We take our cue from you Americans. Anything cooked on the grill.

What's your go-to dish when you're by yourself?

Odd as it sounds, lasagna. When I was growing up, it was our family's special occasion dish. It's meant to be shared, which is really what food is all about.

> ▶ Leave yourself twice as much time to get everything done as you think you need.

Favorite seduction dish?

Scones. I made scones the first time my wife-to-be came over. She fell in love with my scones, then she fell in love with me.

Three dishes every man should know how to make?

A great hamburger. Start with chuck and grind it yourself. (Don't have a meat grinder? Buy one.) Keep the seasonings simple—sea salt and freshly ground pepper. Top it with strong cheese (I'm partial to a Tasmanian Cheddar called Pyengana). Homemade pickles are nice, like pickled beets. You Americans make *really* good hamburgers.

An omelet. Keep it simple—farm eggs whisked with a fork and cooked in a cast-iron skillet with a little salt and maybe stuffed with chives and tomatoes. I like it the French way—with no visible browning.

Souvlaki—that is, grilled lamb on pita bread with cucumber, tomato, and garlicky yogurt. We have a large Greek community in Melbourne and this is our go-to party dish.

Three ingredients you can't live without?

Wallaby: The really lean meat from an animal that looks like a small kangaroo. I like to grill it like venison.

Wattleseed: The seeds of a native acacia tree used by the Aborigines. When roasted, they take on malty-coffee overtones. We use it like pepper in sourdough bread.

Lemon aspen: It's a wild berry that looks like a miniature pumpkin, with a powerful citrusy flavor.

Three tools you can't live without?

Microplane: It's the best grater in the world. We have fifteen different shapes and sizes at the restaurant and we use them for grating everything from citrus zest to spices to cheese.

Electric frying pan: It's simply the most versatile tool in the kitchen. You can use it for boiling, stewing, sautéing, and frying. When I was young, we often cooked the entire meal in it.

Rotary evaporator: It enables you to boil foods at low temperature in a vacuum, extracting the essence without denaturing the flavor. When we make raspberry jam in a rotary evaporator, we need only half as much sugar, so the emphasis stays on the fruit.

What are the three most important things to keep in mind if you're just starting out?

Read a recipe from start to finish *before* you start cooking.

Be organized. Make a shopping list before you go to the store. Write out a plan of attack complete with prep sequence before you start cooking. Leave yourself twice as much time to get everything done as you think you need.

Don't be afraid to make mistakes. That's how you learn and make other people's recipes your own.

What are the three most common mistakes guys make in the kitchen?

Too much salt.

Too much heat. There's a difference between cooking and burning.

Too much hurry. Train yourself to slow down and think before you start cooking.

Something unexpected you've learned over the years that really helps you up your game in the kitchen?

Spend time with people who know more than you do. Eat meals cooked by chefs who are far better than you are.

Parting words of advice?

Mallee wood charcoal. It's an Australian species of eucalyptus. It burns hot, clean, and aromatic.

THAI BAR SNACKS

SHOP You can approach this dish in two ways. Make a quick trip to the supermarket and buy fresh leaf spinach (the kind sold in bunches rather than in cellophane packages), jalapeños, and roasted peanuts. Or, make an expedition to an Asian market or to Chinatown to ferret out the ingredients they'd actually use in Thailand: Chinese spinach (earthier and a little more bitter than conventional spinach) or *bai cha plu* (Thai wild pepper leaves); fiery Thai bird's-eye chiles; and dried shrimp. (Alternative wrappers could include fresh basil leaves, Japanese shiso, or even Boston lettuce leaves.) Thai or other Asian sweet chili sauce is available at most supermarkets and natural foods stores. One good brand is Mae Ploy.

GEAR Your basic kitchen gear. For serving, it's cool to have matching small bowls, but you can arrange the various ingredients in piles on a platter or plate.

WHAT ELSE To be strictly authentic, you'd include dried shrimp, which look like oversize pink commas and explode in your mouth with a briny sweet flavor. I love them; my wife doesn't. Look for dried shrimp at Asian and Hispanic markets, but you can omit them without detracting from the overall spectacularness of this dish.

TIME about 15 minutes

Y ou've heard about some of the more infamous Thai bar snacks: chilied crickets, fried water beetles, and silk worms. (Yes, I've sampled them all.) Well, here's one that requires no arthropods, and each bite bombards you with the hot flavors of ginger and chile, the sweet taste of toasted coconut, the sour tang of diced lime, the earthy punch of peanuts and shallots, and if you like, the briny flavor of dried shrimp (more on that in the What Else section). *Miang kum* is infinitely customizable (don't worry if you run short or run out of a particular ingredient), and you can make it as fiery as magma or as mild-mannered as a vegan salad bar. Plus, I guarantee you'll be the first guy on the block to serve it. **Makes 24 pieces; serves 4 to 6**

24 large fresh spinach leaves, fresh Chinese spinach leaves, Thai wild pepper leaves, whole large basil leaves, or Boston lettuce leaves torn into 2-inch squares

½ cup dried unsweetened shredded coconut

2 jalapeño peppers, 4 serrano peppers, or 8 Thai bird's-eye chiles

1 piece (2 inches) fresh ginger, peeled

2 shallots, or ½ red onion, peeled

1 juicy whole lime

½ cup dry roasted peanuts—unsalted or salted—your choice

¼ cup small dried shrimp (optional)

1 cup Thai sweet chili sauce in a small bowl (or divided among several), for dipping

1 Thoroughly rinse the spinach leaves (they can be very gritty). Pat them dry with paper towels and arrange them in a serving bowl or on a plate.

2 Place the coconut in a dry skillet over medium heat and toast it until lightly browned, stirring with a wooden spoon, 2 to 4 minutes.

Or, spread the coconut out on a piece of aluminum foil and toast it in a toaster oven. Place the coconut in a small serving bowl.

3 Cut the chile peppers, ginger, shallots, and lime into ¼-inch pieces. The easiest way to do this is to cut them crosswise into ¼-inch-thick slices, then cut each slice into

¼-inch pieces. If you like your food hot, leave the seeds in the peppers; if not, cut the chiles in half lengthwise and scrape out the ribs and seeds before dicing into smaller pieces. Cutting a lime this way will seem weird, but you'll be amazed how intense each bite of rind and pulp tastes. Arrange the chile peppers, ginger, shallots, lime, peanuts, and shrimp, if using, in separate serving bowls.

4 To serve, place the bowls of the various ingredients on a platter or tray with small spoons for each ingredient. To eat the *miang kum,* take a spinach leaf, top it with some coconut, peppers, ginger, shallot, lime, peanuts, and dried shrimp, if using. Roll the whole shebang up into a bundle, dip it in chili sauce, and pop it into your mouth.

Cheese-Stuffed, Bacon-Roasted Jalapeño Peppers

POPPERS

Who first had the idea to stuff a jalapeño pepper with cheese and roast it wrapped in bacon? A guy, no doubt, and I bet it was a Texan. The popper (aka armadillo or rattlesnake egg) may be a fixture on the American barbecue circuit, but you can't keep an idea this good (fire plus cheese plus cured meat) secret for long. So here's the basic procedure. Invent your own version and email me photos (barbecuebible.com). **Makes 16 poppers; serves 4**

16 large jalapeño peppers

8 ounces cheese (cheddar, Jack, pepper Jack, cream cheese, or other favorite cheese), cut into matchstick slivers if using cheddar or either Jack

16 sprigs fresh cilantro

8 slices artisanal bacon, cut in half crosswise

1 Preheat the oven to 400°F. If you have a wire rack, place it on top of a baking sheet.

2 *To stuff a whole jalapeño:* Cut the top (stem end) off each pepper. Scrape out the seeds using a jalapeño coring tool or the blade of a vegetable peeler. Place the cheese and cilantro in the jalapeño. Replace the cap.

SHOP There are lots of possibilities for cheese here: pepper Jack, Manchego, cheddar, or smoked mozzarella.

GEAR Your basic kitchen gear including toothpicks, a baking sheet, and if you have a wire rack to put on top of it, so much the better. A grapefruit spoon, with its jagged edge, or the blade of a vegetable peeler works well for seeding the jalapeños.

WHAT ELSE The first poppers were cooked on a grill (which lets you add a blast of wood smoke), but you can cook excellent poppers in the oven, under the broiler, or even in a contact grill.

TIME 30 to 40 minutes

To stuff a jalapeño by cutting it in half: Cut each jalapeño pepper in half lengthwise through the stem, and using a spoon, scrape out the seeds. Stuff 16 of the jalapeño halves with the cheese (if using cream cheese, mound it in the jalapeño halves with a spoon) and cilantro and place the other jalapeño halves on top.

3 Wrap each reassembled jalapeño crosswise with a piece of bacon, securing the end with a toothpick. Arrange the jalapeños on the baking sheet.

4 Bake the jalapeños until the bacon is browned and crisp and the jalapeños feel soft when squeezed, 20 to 25 minutes. Drain the jalapeños on paper towels, then serve at once.

Variations

Poppers around the world and on the grill: Replace the jalapeños with canned Spanish piquillo (drained and patted dry) or fresh padron peppers or Japanese *shishitos*. Replace the cheddar with Manchego cheese, goat cheese, mascarpone, or crabmeat moistened with mayonnaise. Replace the bacon with pancetta, prosciutto, or serrano ham. Instead of baking the jalapeños, indirect grill them on a grill preheated to medium-high until the bacon is browned and crisp and the jalapeños feel soft when squeezed, 20 to 25 minutes. Drain the jalapeños on paper towels, then serve at once.

Other foods to cook wrapped in bacon:

Shrimp or scallops: Wrap peeled deveined large shrimp or sea scallops in bacon, placing a fresh jalapeño slice between the seafood and the bacon (secure with a toothpick). Panfry, broil, or grill over medium-high heat until the bacon is crisp and the shellfish is cooked through, 2 to 4 minutes per side.

Prunes or dates: Stuff tiny cubes of Gouda, Gruyère, or other cheese into pitted dried prunes or dates and wrap in bacon (secure with toothpicks). Panfry, broil, or grill over medium-high heat until the bacon is crisp and the fruit is hot enough to melt the cheese, 2 to 4 minutes per side.

GRILLED CHEESE THREE WAYS
(SANS SANDWICH)

Say "grilled cheese" and most guys think of a sandwich, and starting on page 72, you'll find the basic formula plus variations. But in many parts of the world, grilled, broiled, or fried cheese comes by itself—without bread—and it is no less delectable for this omission. Here are three classics—think of them as grilled cheese for a low-carb diet.

SAGANAKI

GREEK GRILLED CHEESE

Maybe you've seen it at a Greek restaurant: A sizzling skillet arrives at the table, followed by a Vesuvian whoosh of fire. You sip a milky anise-flavored spirit called ouzo to neutralize the salt and heat of the cheese. The Greeks call it *saganaki*. I call it one of the best excuses around to mix food with fire. **Serves 4**

SHOP You need a cheese with a high melting temperature so you can fry it without it collapsing into a puddle. Tradition calls for Haloumi, a semi-firm Cypriot cheese that derives its robust flavor from brining, and, sometimes, the addition of mint. Other options include Manouri, Kasseri, or Kefalograviera, all available at cheese stores, Greek markets, and many large supermarkets. Yes, these cheeses are salty—that's why they're served with ouzo (an anise-flavored liquor) or another aperitif.

GEAR Your basic kitchen gear including a large (10- to 12-inch) cast-iron skillet and a trivet

1 pound Haloumi, Manouri, Kasseri, or other semi-firm Greek cheese

1 cup unbleached all-purpose flour

2 tablespoons extra virgin olive oil, or as needed

⅓ cup ouzo, Metaxa, or Cognac

1 lemon, cut into wedges

Pita bread (fresh, grilled, or toasted; see page 220), for serving (optional)

1 Cut the cheese into flat slices ½ inch thick. Place the flour in a shallow bowl.

2 Heat the olive oil in a large cast-iron skillet over medium-high heat. Dip each piece of cheese in the flour on both sides, shaking off the excess. Arrange the cheese in the skillet in a single layer and cook until browned on both sides, 2 to 4 minutes per side, turning once with a spatula. Work in multiple batches as needed.

3 Take the hot skillet off the burner and place it on a trivet. Make sure there is nothing flammable close to the skillet. Pour the ouzo or brandy into the hot skillet and immediately touch a long lit kitchen match or lighter to the edge; it should flambé. (I hope you've invited everyone to watch. If so, make sure they aren't standing too close to the skillet. If you're new to flambéing, see page 566 for details.)

4 When the flames have burned out, transfer the cheese to small plates and serve with the lemon wedges (squeeze them over the cheese) and the pita, if desired.

WHAT ELSE Saganaki takes its name from the special frying pan with a handle on each side in which it's traditionally cooked and served. A cast-iron skillet works great, too.

TIME about 10 minutes

QUESO FUNDIDO

MEXICAN GRILLED CHEESE

This classic Mexican appetizer is so simple I'm embarrassed to include a recipe—except that it often slips off my radar. Like saganaki, you bring it sizzling to the table—but you bake it in the oven or broil it first. **Serves 4**

½ pound Monterey Jack or pepper Jack cheese, coarsely grated

½ pound sharp white cheddar cheese, coarsely grated

Rajas, chorizo, refried beans, and/or huitlacoche (see page 200; optional)

Corn tortillas or tortilla chips, for serving

1 Preheat the oven to 500°F. Or, preheat the broiler.

2 Place the Jack and cheddar cheeses in a mixing bowl and toss to mix. Arrange one or more of the fillings, if using, in a single layer on the bottom of an earthenware dish or a cast-iron skillet. Sprinkle a ½-inch-thick layer of the grated cheese mixture into the dish or the skillet.

3 *If you are baking* the *queso fundido,* place it in the oven and bake it until the cheese is melted, bubbling, and lightly browned on top, 8 to 12 minutes.

If you are broiling the *queso fundido,* place it on a broiler pan a couple of inches under the heat source and broil the cheese until it is melted, bubbling, and lightly browned on top, 4 to 6 minutes.

SHOP Lots of options for cheese. I like a mixture of Monterey Jack (or pepper Jack) and white cheddar— the Jack for its creamy consistency, the cheddar for its bite.

GEAR Your basic kitchen gear plus a trivet. Traditionally, *queso fundido* comes cooked and served in a shallow terracotta dish called a *cazuela*. You can find these at cookware shops or online at tienda.com. You can also use a small baking dish or cast-iron skillet.

WHAT ELSE One thing I like about *queso fundido* is its versatility. You can melt plain cheese or dress it up with *Rajas* (roasted poblano chiles), chorizo (Mexican sausage), refried beans, or even *huitlacoche* (an earthy-tasting black corn fungus— see page 200).

TIME about 15 minutes

Fillings for Mexican Grilled Cheese

This quartet of flavor-packed fillings turns up in many Mexican dishes in this book, from grilled cheese to quesadillas (page 78) to tacos (page 244) and fajitas. Make one or all.

Rajas (roasted poblano pepper strips): Char two poblano peppers on a hot grill (better still, directly on the glowing embers of a charcoal grill), over a stovetop burner, or in a cast-iron skillet. Turn the peppers so that the skin is blistered and blackened on all sides. Let the peppers cool, then scrape off the burnt skin. Cut the peppers into ¼-inch-thick strips, discarding the stem, ribs, and seeds.

Chorizo: A spicy sausage (flavored with paprika, garlic, and wine) enjoyed throughout the Spanish-speaking world. The Mexican version comes fresh in casings or in bulk, or cooked in links. If using fresh chorizo in casings, panfry in 1 tablespoon olive oil in a cast-iron skillet over medium heat until browned on all sides and cooked through, 4 to 6 minutes per side. Let cool, discarding the fat, then slice crosswise and arrange the slices under the cheese. If in bulk, add it to the hot oil in the pan and cook until browned, 5 to 8 minutes, breaking the sausage into pieces with a wooden spoon. Drain in a strainer, discarding the fat, and arrange the cooked sausage under the cheese. If you are using already cooked chorizo, thinly slice or finely dice 1 to 2 sausages and arrange under the cheese.

Frijoles refritos: You can add 1 cup of your favorite store-bought brand of refried beans.

Huitlacoche: An inky black fungus sometimes found in corn, *huitlacoche* has an earthy mushroomy flavor that makes it a delicacy in Mexico. It's rarely available fresh in the U.S., but if you live near a well-stocked Hispanic market you'll find it canned or frozen. (Or you can order it from mexgrocer.com.) To cook *huitlacoche*, dice a small onion and panfry it in 1 tablespoon of extra virgin olive oil or butter in a skillet over medium-high heat. Add 6 to 8 ounces of fresh, frozen, or canned *huitlacoche* and cook until most of the liquid has evaporated, 5 to 8 minutes.

4 Serve the *queso fundido* at once at the table on a trivet with fresh tortillas or tortilla chips, taking care not to burn yourself on the hot dish.

PLANKED CAMEMBERT WITH CHUTNEY

If you're like millions of American grilling fanatics, you might have made planked salmon (you can read all about it on page 379). What you may not realize is how handy a plank can be when it comes to making a ridiculously simple, over-the-top appetizer for your next tailgate party or Super Bowl bash. (Handy, yes, but also flavorful, as the cedar infuses the cheese with an aromatic wood taste all its own.) Vary the cheese; vary the toppings; use this recipe as a blueprint. **Serves 6 to 8**

1 Camembert (8 ounces), or 1 small Brie (13 ounces)

½ cup mango, pear, or other chutney

½ cup whole pecans

Grilled bread (page 571), toast points (page 63), or really good crackers, for serving

1 Preheat the oven to 400°F. Soak the cedar plank in water for about 30 minutes, then drain it.

2 Arrange the cheese in the center of the plank. Spoon the chutney evenly over the top of the cheese. Arrange the pecans on top.

3 Bake the cheese on the plank until the pecans brown, the chutney bubbles, and the cheese is soft to the touch on the side, 15 to 20 minutes. (Do not overcook or the cheese will breach the rind and leak onto the plank.)

4 Transfer the plank with the cheese to a heatproof platter for serving. Spread the cheese and toppings on the grilled bread, toast points, or crackers.

Variations

Pesto and pine nut planked cheese: Top the cheese with ½ cup of good store-bought pesto and ½ cup of pine nuts. Bake the cheese as described in the Planked Camembert with Chutney recipe on the facing page.

Tapenade planked cheese: Top the cheese with ½ cup of tapenade (olive paste), preferably homemade (page 313) or good store-bought tapenade, and ½ cup of walnut pieces. Bake the cheese as described in the Planked Camembert recipe on the facing page.

SHOP You'll want a soft-ripened cheese here, which means a Camembert or a small Brie from France or a similar disk-shaped cheese with a white mold rind from North America or elsewhere. FYI: It's called soft-ripened because they spray the cheese culture on the surface and let it ripen until soft from the outside in.

GEAR You'll need a cedar plank that is about 5 by 11 inches. Cedar planks are available at cookware shops and most supermarkets. Alternatively, you can cut one from a board procured at your local lumberyard; just make sure you use untreated lumber.

WHAT ELSE Yes, you can reuse the plank. Scrub it clean in hot water and let it dry.

TIME 30 minutes for soaking the plank, about 5 minutes preparation time, plus 15 to 20 minutes cooking time

ANCHOVY TOASTS

SHOP These toasts work best made with oil-cured anchovies sold in flat 2-ounce cans. For more info, see the facing page.

GEAR Your basic kitchen gear including a food processor (optional)

WHAT ELSE I like the simplicity of this version, but some guys add garlic, capers, and/or Worcestershire sauce.

TIME about 25 minutes

Here's a retro hors d'oeuvre (when's the last time you heard *that* term?) to serve with your favorite vintage cocktail. (You'll find cocktail formulas starting on page 575.) It takes its inspiration from the great gentlemen's cookbooks of the last century, but Anchovy Toasts have everything you could wish for in cutting-edge bar food: salt to make you thirsty; fat to neutralize the alcohol; audibly crisp bread to sink your teeth into. Of course, back in the 1960s few guys used French-style baguettes and genuine Parmigiano Reggiano cheese. So you're ahead of the game already. **Makes 24 toasts, enough to serve 6 to 8**

1 can (2 ounces) good-quality anchovy fillets, drained

¾ cup freshly grated Parmigiano Reggiano cheese (about 3 ounces)

1 cup mayonnaise, preferably Hellmann's

A few drops of fresh lemon juice

½ teaspoon freshly ground black pepper

1 loaf French bread

1 Preheat the oven to 400°F.

2 Place the anchovies and Parmigiano Reggiano cheese in a food processor and puree them (grind to a smooth paste). Add the mayonnaise, lemon juice, and pepper and process to a smooth paste. Don't have a food processor? Finely chop the anchovies by hand, place them in a bowl with the cheese, and mash them with a wooden spoon. Then whisk in the mayonnaise, lemon juice, and pepper.

3 Cut the French bread crosswise on the diagonal into ½-inch-thick slices. Arrange the slices of bread on a baking sheet and bake them until toasted on top, about 5 minutes. Remove the baking sheet from the oven and turn the toasts over (they'll be hot; it helps to use tongs).

4 Spread the anchovy mixture on the untoasted side of the bread slices. Return the toasts to the oven and bake them until the anchovy mixture is puffed and browned, about 5 minutes. Do not let the toasts burn. Serve the Anchovy Toasts hot out of the oven.

ANCHOVIES

Anchovies are like cats or Stravinsky. You either love them or hate them. Partisans praise their salty tang and bold in-your-face flavor. Detractors decry what they perceive as a strong fishy flavor. Yes, anchovies taste fishy. They're *supposed* to taste fishy. Caviar tastes fishy. Smoked salmon tastes fishy. Tuna fish tastes fishy. A fish flavor can be a good thing.

Anchovies possess at least three attributes that make them the perfect guy food. They're salty—exceedingly salty—and eating them demands the relief of a well-shaken cocktail, a craft beer, or a chilled, slightly effervescent wine like a Portuguese Vinho Verde. Anchovies are loaded with those pungent, earthy, mouth-filling, tongue-soothing flavors the Japanese call umami (read about umami on page 28). And, unlike caviar or smoked salmon, anchovies are cheap, delivering more flavor bang for the buck than almost any other ingredient. These virtues have endeared anchovies to foodies throughout history and around the world. The ancient Romans fermented them with salt in the sun to make a cooking and table sauce called *garum*. The Vietnamese use the same technique today to make their malodorous but oh-so-tasty fish sauce.

Sicilians panfry anchovies and bread crumbs in olive oil to make a sort of poor man's Parmesan cheese. (Try it—you'll be amazed.) For many guys, pizza would be miserly stuff without anchovies. And,

I'd be remiss not to acknowledge Caesar Cardini, the Italian owner of a restaurant in Tijuana, Mexico, who dressed romaine lettuce with anchovies, pecorino romano cheese, and egg to make the first Caesar salad (you'll find a recipe on page 163).

Anchovies may be ubiquitous, but they're not all created equal. Here are the major types.

OIL-CURED | Dark silvery-brown anchovy fillets packed in oil in flat metal tins are my personal favorite: tangy, meaty, full of forthright flavors. You can buy them flat or coiled around capers. Pick the flat ones—you can always add capers later.

SALT-CURED | From southern Italy, where the fish are preserved in a thick sludge of sea salt. A traditional ingredient in tapenade (page 313), these taste even fishier than oil-packed anchovies. Soak or rinse the salt off in cold water before using them.

VINEGAR-CURED | Best known by their Spanish name, *boquerones* (Italians have a version, too), these anchovies are lightly pickled in white vinegar. Think of them as Mediterranean pickled herring. They're tart and moderately fishy.

ANCHOVY PASTE | Cured anchovies pureed with butter, oil, or another emulsifying agent. You squeeze anchovy paste out of a tube like toothpaste—great for spreading on toast, grilled fish, lamb chops, and steaks.

ANCHOVY HOT TUB

SHOP You'll want good quality oil-cured anchovies here, the kind sold in flat cans—preferably without capers.

GEAR Your basic kitchen gear including an immersion blender or food processor, plus ramekins or small bowls and a platter for serving

WHAT ELSE Anchovy Hot Tub may be a dip, but it also makes a hell of a sauce for grilled fish (especially swordfish) and steak.

TIME about 30 minutes

Italians call it *bagna cauda* (warm bath). I call it Anchovy Hot Tub. And it's one of sneakiest ways to turn people on to the briny pleasure of anchovies. What, you don't like anchovies (or *think* you don't like anchovies)? The slow, gentle simmering with heavy cream and garlic removes any strong fishy taste, leaving you with a mild creamy dip brimming with salty umami flavors. Killer as a dip for bread sticks and raw vegetables and not half bad spread on toast or eaten straight off a spoon. **Serves 6**

For the hot tub

3 cups heavy (whipping) cream

2 cloves garlic, peeled

1 can (2 ounces) oil-packed anchovy fillets, drained

2 tablespoons (¼ stick) unsalted butter

Freshly ground black pepper

For dipping

12 slender Italian bread sticks (grissini)

2 carrots, trimmed, peeled, quartered lengthwise, and cut into sticks

2 cucumbers, quartered lengthwise and cut into sticks

1 bunch scallions, both white and green parts, trimmed and cut in half crosswise

1 Make the hot tub: Place the cream, garlic, and anchovies in a heavy saucepan over medium-high heat. Simmer until the mixture is thick, creamy, and reduced by about half (to 1½ cups), 15 to 20 minutes, stirring often. If the anchovy mixture starts to scorch or boil over, reduce the heat.

2 Place the anchovy mixture in a blender or food processor and puree it. Return the pureed mixture to the pan and whisk in the butter and a ton of black pepper. Keep the anchovy mixture warm over low heat but do not let it boil.

3 Meanwhile, arrange the bread sticks, carrots, cucumbers, and scallions on a platter or stand them up in cups or mugs. Pour the warm anchovy mixture into small bowls or ramekins. Dip in the bread sticks and vegetables.

A NEW SHRIMP COCKTAIL

I've never understood the popularity of the conventional shrimp cocktail. After all, boiling is the worst way to cook shrimp—it removes, not adds, flavor and produces a rubbery texture. And cocktail sauce made by mixing ketchup and bottled prepared horseradish is hardly what you'd call heroic. This shrimp cocktail starts with spice-crusted shrimp, which you sear in a skillet or under the broiler. The sauce gets a double blast of heat from grated horseradish and chipotle peppers. Now *that's* a shrimp cocktail. **Serves: 4; can be multiplied as desired**

SHOP Buy fresh shrimp that's still in the shell (fist bump if they're local with their heads on). To save time, ask your fishmonger to do the peeling and deveining.

GEAR Your basic kitchen gear including a grater or food processor for the horseradish (optional), a large (10- to 12-inch) skillet or broiler pan, and serving bowls for the shrimp and cocktail sauce

WHAT ELSE I've given two options for shrimp spices. For Maryland-style shrimp, use the commercial Old Bay seasoning, while for Kansas City–style shrimp, use Raichlen's Rub #2 on page 531.

TIME about 20 minutes cooking, plus 1 hour to chill the shrimp

For the shrimp
1½ pounds peeled, deveined raw jumbo shrimp

2 to 3 tablespoons Old Bay seasoning or Raichlen's Rub #2 (page 531)

1 tablespoon extra virgin olive oil or butter, plus 2 tablespoons olive oil or butter if panfrying (optional)

4 cilantro sprigs (optional)

For the chipotle cocktail sauce
¾ cup ketchup

¼ cup (drained) prepared horseradish

1 teaspoon grated fresh orange zest (see Note)

3 tablespoons fresh orange juice

1 tablespoon Worcestershire sauce

1 to 2 canned chipotle peppers in adobo sauce, minced, with 1 to 2 teaspoons of the juices

1 Prepare the shrimp: Place the shrimp in a bowl and sprinkle them with the spice mixture of your choice. Toss the shrimp well to coat, then add the 1 tablespoon of olive oil or butter and toss again.

2 *If you are panfrying the shrimp,* heat the oil or melt the butter in a large skillet over medium-high heat. Add the shrimp and cook until browned on both sides and cooked through, 2 to 3 minutes per side.

If you are broiling the shrimp, preheat the broiler to high. Place the shrimp on a broiler pan a couple of inches under the broiler and broil them until browned on the outside and cooked through, 2 to 3 minutes per side.

3 Transfer the cooked shrimp to a serving platter and let cool to room temperature, then cover and refrigerate them for at least 1 hour. The shrimp can be prepared up to 24 hours ahead to this stage.

4 Meanwhile, make the cocktail sauce: Place the ketchup, horseradish, orange zest, orange juice, Worcestershire sauce, and chipotles with their juices in a mixing bowl and whisk to mix. Refrigerate the cocktail sauce, covered, until you are ready to serve the shrimp.

5 To serve, divide the cocktail sauce among 4 small bowls, one for each diner. Serve the shrimp on the platter, with the cilantro sprigs, if using, arranged on top.

Note: The zest is the oil-rich outer rind of the orange. Remove it with a Microplane (see page 15), being careful to grate only the orange rind, not the bitter white pith underneath.

FIRE-EATER CHICKEN WINGS

Every man should be able to cook up a batch of kick-ass chicken wings. Extra points if they're spicy enough to sear your tongue to the roof of your mouth. You could go the Buffalo route—created by the owner of the Anchor Bar, who deep-fried wings dredged in cayenne-spiked flour, then doused them with melted butter and hot sauce. I prefer to get the smoke from *pimentón* (smoked paprika) and the fire from butter-fried jalapeños. **Serves 6 as an appetizer**

For the chicken wings and spice mixture

3 to 3½ pounds chicken wings

1 tablespoon pimentón or sweet paprika

1 teaspoon coarse salt (kosher or sea)

1 teaspoon freshly ground black pepper

1 teaspoon onion or garlic powder

½ to 1 teaspoon cayenne pepper

½ teaspoon celery seed (optional)

2 tablespoons extra virgin olive oil or vegetable oil, plus extra for oiling the wire rack

For the sauce

8 tablespoons (1 stick) unsalted butter

3 to 6 jalapeño peppers (preferably red) or other hot peppers—depends on your tolerance for heat, thinly sliced crosswise

½ cup fresh cilantro leaves

½ cup Louisiana-style hot sauce, such as Frank's RedHot, Crystal, or Tabasco (or to taste)

½ teaspoon liquid smoke (optional)

SHOP *Pimentón* (Spanish smoked paprika) can be found at Spanish markets and most supermarkets or online at tienda.com.

GEAR Your basic kitchen gear, including a wire rack, baking sheet, and a large (10- to 12-inch) skillet

WHAT ELSE The main method here calls for roasting the wings in the oven (crisp skin, less fat). For crisp skin, more fat, dredge the wings in flour, shaking off the excess, then deep-fry them in batches in 1 quart of vegetable oil in a heavy saucepan until golden brown and cooked through, 6 to 8 minutes. Transfer to a baking sheet lined with paper towels to drain. (Follow the procedure outlined for the Fried Chicken on page 340.) For crisp skin and more smoke, indirect grill the wings on a charcoal grill, tossing 1½ cups soaked drained wood chips on the coals.

TIME about 30 to 40 minutes

1 Prepare the chicken wings: Cut each chicken wing through the joints into 2 sections, the drumette (the part that looks like a little drumstick) and the flat, discarding the wing tips (or save them for stock). Place the wings in a large mixing bowl.

2 Combine the *pimentón*, salt, black pepper, onion or garlic powder, cayenne, and celery seed, if using, in a small bowl and mix them with your fingers. Sprinkle the spice mixture over the chicken wings and toss to mix. Add the olive oil and toss to mix.

3 Preheat the oven to 400°F. Place a wire rack over an aluminum foil–lined baking sheet. Oil the rack with a folded paper towel dipped in vegetable oil.

4 Arrange the chicken wings on the wire rack. Bake the wings until browned and cooked through, 30 to 40 minutes, turning them once or twice with tongs. To check for doneness, make a slit in the thickest part of the largest drumette; there should be no traces of pink.

5 Meanwhile, make the sauce: Melt the butter in a 10-inch skillet over medium-high heat. When the butter is hot, bubbles will dance when you dip a slice of jalapeño in it. Add the jalapeños and cilantro to the butter and cook until fragrant, about 2 minutes. Stir in the hot sauce and let the mixture come to a boil. Add a few drops of liquid smoke, if desired.

6 Transfer the baked chicken wings to a large shallow serving bowl. Pour the sauce over them and toss to mix. Dig in.

SALSA THREE WAYS

Never mind the political debates. If you really want to know where our country is heading, consider salsa. Sales of this south-of-the-border condiment now far surpass ketchup and have for more than a decade. You can buy bottled salsa, of course, but why bother? It's quick and easy to make salsa from scratch, with infinitely more vibrant results. Salsa seems to make everything better: tortilla chips, grilled fish or steak, eggs, sandwiches, even hot dogs. Here are three basic salsas every man should know how to make.

SHOP There's no cooking technique to speak of here, so a great salsa is all about the ingredients. That means farm stand or garden tomatoes, sweet onions, luscious ripe tropical fruits, and fresh cilantro or mint.

WHAT ELSE The virtue of salsa is its spontaneity. You can chop the ingredients ahead (a few hours, not a few days), but mix the salsa right before serving.

GEAR Your basic kitchen gear

TIME about 15 minutes

PICO DE GALLO

Think of this as the primordial salsa—a five-ingredient condiment found on virtually every table in Mexico; one you can mash up a hundred different ways. Use red, yellow, or green tomatoes; onions or scallions; mild, hot, or incendiary peppers. Grill or smoke the vegetables or roast them in the embers or on the stovetop. Acidulate the salsa with lime juice, orange juice, lemon, or *naranja agria* (sour orange juice). Spice it up with fresh cilantro or mint, dried oregano, or cumin. Just dive in using the following recipe as your springboard.

Makes 2 cups; serves 4

For the salsa

2 luscious red ripe tomatoes, cut into $\frac{1}{4}$-inch dice

2 jalapeño peppers, seeded and finely chopped (for a hotter salsa, leave the seeds in)

$\frac{1}{2}$ medium-size sweet white onion, finely diced

$\frac{1}{3}$ cup finely chopped fresh cilantro

3 tablespoon fresh lime juice, or more to taste

Additional ingredients (optional)

4 red radishes, trimmed and finely diced

1 clove garlic, peeled and minced

$\frac{1}{2}$ to 1 teaspoon chopped canned chipotle pepper in adobo

$\frac{1}{2}$ teaspoon ground cumin and/or dried oregano

Coarse salt (kosher or sea) and freshly ground black pepper

Place the tomatoes, jalapeños, onion, cilantro, and lime juice in a mixing bowl with any additional ingredients, if using, and toss to mix. Taste for seasoning, adding more lime juice if necessary. Serve the salsa within 1 hour of mixing.

Variation

For even more soulful-tasting salsa, grill, smoke, or char the vegetables on the embers or roast them in a hot dry skillet until the skins are blistered and dark. Let the vegetables cool to room temperature, then scrape off the blackened skins, chop the vegetables, and mix them into the salsa. Salsa just went from black and white to Technicolor.

SALSA CHIPOTLE

Here's a cooked tomatillo-based salsa smoky with chipotles (smoked jalapeños). Besides being an obvious dip for tortilla chips, Salsa Chipotle is terrific over chicken or fish. The name notwithstanding, tomatillos actually belong to the botanical family that includes cape gooseberries and ground cherries. They look like green tomatoes encased in a papery husk. The flavor is fruity with a suggestion of green tomato. Tomatillos are available fresh in the produce section of most supermarkets. **Makes 2 cups; serves 4**

GEAR Your basic kitchen gear including a large (10- to 12-inch) cast-iron skillet, plus a food processor

TIME about 20 minutes

4 tomatillos (8 to 10 ounces), husked and rinsed

4 plum tomatoes (8 to 10 ounces)

½ small white onion, peeled and cut in half

4 cloves garlic, peeled

1 to 2 canned chipotle peppers in adobo with 2 teaspoons of the juices

¼ cup chopped fresh cilantro leaves

½ teaspoon coarse salt (kosher or sea), or more to taste

½ teaspoon sugar, or more to taste

1 lime (optional)

1 Heat a dry large cast-iron skillet over medium-high heat for 1 to 2 minutes. (When hot enough, a drop of water shaken from your finger will evaporate in 2 to 3 seconds.) Add the tomatillos, tomatoes, onion, and garlic and cook, turning with tongs, until nicely browned on all sides, 4 minutes for the garlic, 6 to 10 minutes for the other vegetables (if your skillet is too crowded with all the vegetables, brown them in 2 batches, tomatillos and tomatoes first).

2 Place the vegetables in a food processor. Add the chipotles and their juice, the cilantro, salt, and sugar. Puree to a coarse paste, running the processor in short bursts. Taste for seasoning, adding more salt and/or sugar as necessary. (For a sharper salsa, add a squeeze of lime juice.) Salsa Chipotle will keep for several days, covered, in the refrigerator.

MANGO SALSA

SHOP Living in Miami, I'm partial to Florida mangoes, such as the luscious Glenn, Keitt, and Florigold. Look for them in the summer months.

GEAR Your basic kitchen gear

WHAT ELSE For an interesting variation on this salsa, substitute fresh pineapple or ripe cantaloupe or honeydew melon for the mango.

TIME about 15 minutes

Last up, a Caribbean-inspired salsa perfect as a dip for fried yucca and plantain chips. It's also pretty awesome spooned over grilled or fried fish, shrimp, chicken, or pork. A ripe mango will smell fragrant (the way peaches and coffee are fragrant) and will feel yielding, but not soft when pressed with your finger. If you have sensitive skin, wear rubber gloves when handling mangoes: The sap can make you break out with a poison ivy–like rash. Scotch bonnets and habaneros used to be the world's hottest chiles, but they've been left in the dust by the *bhut jolokia*, aka "ghost pepper," and Moruga Scorpion—each 10,000 times hotter than Tabasco sauce! **Makes 2 cups; serves 4**

1 large or 2 medium-size ripe mangoes, pitted and diced (1½ cups)

1 small cucumber, peeled, seeded (see Note), and diced

2 scallions, both white and green parts, trimmed and thinly sliced crosswise

1 tablespoon minced candied or peeled fresh ginger

½ to 1 Scotch bonnet or habanero pepper or a smaller amount of ghost pepper or Moruga Scorpion (or hot pepper of your choice), seeded and minced

¼ cup chopped fresh mint

3 tablespoons fresh lime juice

1 to 2 tablespoons light brown sugar

Place the mango, cucumber, scallions, ginger, Scotch bonnet, mint, and lime juice in a mixing bowl but don't mix them until a few minutes before serving. Add brown sugar to taste.

Note: To seed a cucumber, cut the cuke in half lengthwise and scrape the seeds out with a spoon.

Onion, Artichoke, Chickpea, Clam, and Guacamole

RETRO DIPS REINVENTED

Dips may lack the machismo of grilling a steak or smoking a pork shoulder. But no Super Bowl spread or weeknight poker game would be quite complete without them. The trick is to ditch the demeaning shortcuts while retaining the bold flavors we love. That means no onion soup mix or canned artichokes. But it doesn't mean no dips. Here are remakes of five classics.

MICHAEL SCHWARTZ'S ONION DIP

The soulful flavor of the caramelized onions comes as a revelation in this remake of an old standard—a hit since the day the Miami chef Michael Schwartz opened Michael's Genuine Food & Drink in the Design District. Homemade potato chips, pita chips, or any of your favorite crisps are perfect for dipping (you'll find recipes starting on page 220). **Makes 2 cups**

2 tablespoons (¼ stick) butter, or
    2 tablespoons extra virgin olive oil,
    or more as needed

1 large sweet onion, peeled, cut in half,
    and thinly sliced crosswise

4 ounces cream cheese (half an 8-ounce
    package), at room temperature

½ cup mayonnaise, preferably
    Hellmann's

½ cup sour cream

¼ cup freshly grated Parmigiano
    Reggiano cheese (optional—my twist
    on Michael's dip)

Coarse salt (kosher or sea) and freshly
    ground black pepper

Potato chips or pita chips, for serving

SHOP Nothing terribly exotic here, but if you can find sweet onions, like Vidalias, Walla Wallas, Maui onions, or Texas Sweets, your dip will be even better. Look for them at natural foods supermarkets.

GEAR Your basic kitchen gear including a large (10- to 12-inch) cast-iron or nonstick skillet

WHAT ELSE Yes, there is a difference between genuine Parmigiano Reggiano and lesser grating cheeses. For details, see page 76.

TIME about 20 minutes

1 Melt the butter or heat the oil in a heavy skillet over medium heat. Add the onion and cook until caramelized (dark golden brown) and very tender. You'll need to lower the heat as the onion browns, and stir often. The whole process will take 10 to 15 minutes. Do not let the onion burn. Add more butter or oil if needed. Let the onion cool to room temperature.

2 Meanwhile, place the cream cheese in a mixing bowl and whisk in the mayonnaise followed by the sour cream and Parmigiano Reggiano cheese, if using. Stir in the cooled onion and season with salt and pepper to taste. Serve with your favorite potato or pita chips (page 220) for dipping.

GRILLED ARTICHOKE DIP

I would never have contemplated including this hackneyed dip until I discovered the awesome grilled artichoke hearts called ArtiHearts from Monterey Farms in California (montereyfarmsartichokes.com)—real artichokes and tons of wood smoke flavor. **Makes 1 cup**

SHOP ArtiHearts grilled artichokes are available at many supermarkets and natural foods stores.

GEAR Your basic kitchen gear including a food processor (optional)

WHAT ELSE Can't find grilled artichokes? Grill your own. Or use canned, bottled, or frozen cooked artichokes and add a couple of drops of liquid smoke.

TIME 10 minutes

1 package (6 ounces) Monterey Farms grilled ArtiHearts (grilled artichoke hearts)

¼ cup sour cream or Greek-style yogurt

1 tablespoon fresh lemon juice

Coarse salt (kosher or sea) and freshly ground black pepper

Crackers, breadsticks, or pita chips (page 220), for serving

1 *For a coarse dip,* combine the artichoke hearts, sour cream, and lemon juice in a serving bowl and stir to mix. Season the dip with salt and pepper to taste; the dip should be highly seasoned. *For a finer dip,* place the artichoke hearts, sour cream, and lemon juice in a food processor, running the processor in short bursts to get the consistency you like. Season the dip with salt and pepper to taste; the dip should be highly seasoned.

2 Serve with your favorite crackers, bread sticks, or chips for dipping.

ASIAN HUMMUS

Here's a twist on commonplace hummus featuring the Asian flavors of ginger, soy sauce, and sesame oil in place of the traditional Middle Eastern seasonings. **Makes 1½ cups**

1 scallion, both white and green parts, trimmed and thinly sliced

1 can (15 ounces) chickpeas (garbanzo beans), preferably organic, drained

1 piece (1 inch) fresh ginger, peeled and coarsely chopped

1 clove garlic, peeled and coarsely chopped

1 tablespoon soy sauce, or more to taste

1 tablespoon rice vinegar, or more to taste

1 tablespoon Asian (dark) sesame oil, or to taste

Crackers, bread sticks, or toasts, for serving

1 Set aside 1 tablespoon of the scallion greens. Place the chickpeas, remaining scallion, ginger, and garlic in a food processor and puree to a smooth paste. Add the soy sauce, rice vinegar, and sesame oil, running the processor in short bursts and adding a few tablespoons of water if necessary to obtain a smooth dip. Taste for seasoning, adding more soy sauce, rice vinegar, and/or sesame oil as necessary. Transfer the hummus to a serving bowl and sprinkle the reserved scallion greens on top.

2 Serve with your favorite Asian-style rice crackers, bread sticks, or toasts for dipping.

SHOP As always, use organic low- or no-sodium chickpeas when possible.

GEAR Your basic kitchen gear including a food processor

WHAT ELSE To make traditional Middle Eastern hummus, puree the chickpeas with 1 clove garlic, 3 to 4 tablespoons extra virgin olive oil, 2 to 3 tablespoons freshly squeezed lemon juice, and an optional 3 tablespoons tahini (sesame seed paste).

TIME 10 minutes

SMOKED CLAM DIP

Clam dip is a favorite at our home on Martha's Vineyard—especially when I dig the clams in the morning and smoke them on our kettle grill. You can buy artisanal smoked clams at many fish markets (especially in the Northeast and Northwest). Canned smoked clams will work, too. **Makes 1½ cups**

AVOCADOS

Avocados taste good—a cross between a green vegetable and butter. Avocados are good for you, too, containing more than a dozen essential nutrients, including folate, vitamins B_6 and E, cholesterol-lowering sterols, and an abundance of vitamin C. Besides the obvious guacamole (see the Chipotle Guacamole on the facing page), avocados are great on salads, tacos, and nachos and diced over chili *verde* (page 151). Avocado halves make cool serving bowls for ceviche and crab salad.

Avocados come in two main varieties: Hass (small, dark green, with a pebbled skin and dense buttery flesh) and Florida (large, light green, with a smooth skin and moist sweet flesh). When buying avocados, look for unblemished fruit (yes, avocados are a fruit) free of bruises, mold, or soft spots.

Never cut into a hard avocado. Instead, let it ripen at room temperature until it yields gently when squeezed between your thumb and forefinger. To extend the shelf life of a ripe avocado, store it in the refrigerator.

To stuff avocados, use a paring knife to cut the fruit in half lengthwise to the pit. Cupping one half in each hand, twist the halves in opposite directions to separate them. Leave the peel on. To remove the pit, sink the knife blade into it with a flick of your wrist. Rotate the knife a quarter turn. The pit will pop out, and you will have two avocado bowls.

To obtain crescent-shaped slices of avocado, cut the avocado in half and remove the pit. Then carefully peel each half with a paring knife and slice the avocado lengthwise.

To dice an avocado, cut it in half and remove the pit but do not peel the avocado. Using the tip of a paring knife, cut a cross-hatch pattern into the flesh of each half, to—but not through—the thick skin. Using a large spoon, carefully scoop out the flesh; it will fall into neat cubes.

To keep an avocado from browning, dip, sprinkle, or toss it with an acid, like lemon juice, lime juice, pineapple juice, or orange juice.

Not immediately useful but curious fact: The word *avocado* comes from the Nahuatl (Mexican Indian) *ahuacatl*, which translates as testicle, on account of its shape.

7 to 8 ounces smoked clams, drained

1 package (8 ounces) cream cheese, at room temperature

1 tablespoon prepared or freshly grated horseradish, or as much of your preferred hot sauce as you desire

A few drops of Worcestershire sauce

Freshly ground black pepper

Crackers, bread sticks, or chips, for dipping

Place the clams in a food processor and puree to a thick paste. Add the cream cheese, running the processor in short bursts until smooth. Add the horseradish or hot sauce, Worcestershire sauce, and pepper, continuing to process in short bursts. Transfer the clam dip to a bowl for serving with your favorite crackers, bread sticks, or chips.

SHOP Two good widely available brands of smoked clams are Crown Prince or Roland. You'll need two tins. Look for them at fish shops, natural foods markets, or online at amazon.com.

GEAR Your basic kitchen gear including a food processor

WHAT ELSE Use this as your basic template for any smoked seafood dip. Smoked mussels, scallops, salmon, trout, bluefish—all are delectable.

TIME 10 minutes

CHIPOTLE GUACAMOLE

No dip repertory is complete without guacamole. The twist here is to supplement the fresh jalapeños with chipotle peppers (smoked jalapeños), which blast your guacamole with fire and smoke. I give a range of peppers here so you can mete out the punishment as you like. It may seem odd to add the jalapeños, onion, and cilantro in two separate stages. The reason is simple: You want some of the mixture in paste form to flavor the guacamole and some in chunks for crunch when you take a bite. **Makes 3 cups; serves 6**

½ to 1 canned chipotle pepper with the juices

1 teaspoon coarse salt (kosher or sea), or more to taste

½ teaspoon freshly ground black pepper, or more to taste

1 to 3 jalapeño peppers, seeded and diced (for a hotter guacamole, leave the seeds in)

¼ medium-size sweet onion, diced (3 to 4 tablespoons)

½ cup chopped fresh cilantro leaves

2 ripe avocados, peeled, pitted, and diced

1 luscious red ripe tomato, diced (reserve the juices)

2 tablespoons fresh lime juice, or to taste

Tortilla chips, for serving

SHOP Guacamole flourishes or flops by the quality of the avocados. They should be ripe, that is, squeezably soft when pressed between your thumb and forefinger. If they aren't, you'll need to let them ripen at room temperature until they are. No sense trying to rush the process.

GEAR Your basic kitchen gear

WHAT ELSE If you want to up the ante (and add an old twist to a new favorite), get yourself a *molcajete*, a Mexican lava stone mortar and a pestle. These are available from such kitchenware stores as Sur la Table. Then make the guacamole tableside before your admiring guests.

TIME 15 minutes

1 Place the chipotle, salt, and black pepper in a bowl. Add half of the jalapeño(s), onion, and cilantro and mash them to a paste with a pestle or wooden spoon. Add the avocados, tomato, lime juice, and the remaining jalapeño(s), onion, and cilantro. Stir just enough to mix but leave the guacamole chunky (this chunky consistency will mark you as a master). Taste for seasoning, adding more salt, black pepper, and/or lime juice as necessary.

2 Serve with your favorite tortilla chips.

TOASTS AND CHIPS

Toasts, tortilla chips, pita chips—you've used all of these at one point or another to scoop up your favorite dip. You can certainly buy commercial versions, but if you take the time to make your dips from scratch, go the extra mile and make the toasts and chips from scratch, too. Why? Better flavor, less fat, and you'll avoid the polysyllabic chemical preservatives found in packaged chips and toasts.

BUTTER-BAKED TOASTS

A slice of brioche or baguette baked noisily crisp with butter is a glory to sink your teeth into. **Makes 16 to 32 toasts (depending on the size of loaf you start with)**

1 loaf brioche, country-style white bread, thin-sliced whole wheat sandwich bread, rye bread, pumpernickel, or French-style baguette

8 tablespoons (1 stick) butter, melted

SHOP Feeling health-conscious? Use a whole grain bread and brush with extra virgin olive oil.

GEAR Your basic kitchen gear including a baking sheet, basting brush, and serrated knife

WHAT ELSE To make homemade melba toast, start with Pepperidge Farm thin-sliced white or whole wheat bread. Bake dry (without butter) in a 350°F oven. Beats the packaged stuff hollow.

TIME 20 minutes

1 Preheat the oven to 350°F.

2 If you are using a whole loaf of bread, using a serrated knife (aka bread knife), cut it into slices that are ¼ to ½ inch thick. Slice baguettes crosswise sharply on the diagonal. If you are using pre-sliced sandwich bread, cut each slice in half on the diagonal to make triangles. Arrange the bread slices on a baking sheet and lightly brush them on both sides with the melted butter (use a pastry brush or clean natural-bristle paintbrush).

3 Bake the bread until golden brown on both sides, turning it with tongs, 5 to 8 minutes per side. Do not let it burn. Serve the toasts warm if you like or at room temperature for maximum crispness. If serving at room temperature, let the toasts cool on the baking sheet. Cool any toasts you don't devour on the spot to room temperature, then store them in a sealed plastic bag for up to 2 days.

PARMESAN TOASTS

Add freshly grated real Parmigiano Reggiano and a little parsley to the preceding recipe and you get the ultimate cheese toasts. **A long baguette should make 32 toasts**

1 French-style baguette

8 tablespoons (1 stick) unsalted butter, melted

1 cup freshly grated Parmigiano Reggiano cheese

¼ cup finely chopped fresh flat-leaf parsley (optional)

Freshly ground black pepper

SHOP Go for a crusty French-style baguette from a good bakery.

GEAR Your basic kitchen gear including a baking sheet, and serrated knife, plus a basting brush

WHAT ELSE Parsley is optional here, but it adds color and extra flavor.

TIME about 15 minutes

1 Preheat the oven to 350°F.

2 Thinly slice the bread crosswise on the diagonal (a serrated knife works best for this). Arrange the slices in a single layer on a baking sheet. Lightly but thoroughly brush the slices of bread on both sides with the melted butter. Sprinkle the Parmigiano Reggiano on top of the slices of bread, topping it with the parsley, if using, and some pepper.

3 Bake the toasts until they are browned and the cheese is sizzling, 6 to 10 minutes.

SESAME PITA CHIPS

The flat hearth-baked bread we know as pita has been a staple in Middle Eastern, Mediterranean, and Balkan food cultures for millennia. Not only is it great for sandwiches, but when cut into wedges and re-baked, it's sturdy enough to carry payloads of hummus, tzatziki, or bean dip without breakage. **Makes 24 chips**

SHOP Pita breads are available at any supermarket; for healthier chips, buy whole wheat.

GEAR Your basic kitchen gear plus a baking sheet and basting brush

WHAT ELSE For an Asian twist, brush the pita with toasted sesame oil and sprinkle with black sesame seeds.

TIME 15 minutes

4 pita breads (each 6 inches)

Extra virgin olive oil

2 tablespoons sesame seeds

1 Preheat the oven to 350°F.

2 Lightly brush each pita on both sides with olive oil. Using a chef's knife, cut each pita into 6 wedges. Sprinkle the wedges with sesame seeds, tossing to coat both sides.

3 Arrange the pita wedges in a single layer on a rimmed baking sheet. Bake until crisp and lightly browned, 6 to 10 minutes. Let cool on the baking sheet to room temperature; the chips will crisp up. Store leftovers in a resealable plastic bag for up to 2 days.

TOTOPOS

BAKE-FRIED TORTILLA CHIPS

Back in my restaurant reviewing days (and before the advent of Lipitor), I developed a cholesterol problem, which I treated successfully with a reduced-fat diet. I took to bake-frying tortilla chips, which produced the requisite crunch without the collateral fat. I've come to prefer the clean flavor of these bake-fried chips to that of the deep-fried. **Makes 24 to 32 chips**

SHOP The dream scenario would be to start with fresh tortillas from a Mexican bakery. Otherwise, use the freshest you can find—usually in a refrigerated case in your supermarket.

2 tablespoons extra virgin olive oil (optional)

4 corn (or flour) tortillas

Coarse salt (kosher or sea; optional)

GEAR Your basic kitchen gear including a baking sheet and basting brush

WHAT ELSE Tortillas come both in corn and flour versions and so do the chips you make from them. If you're feeling ambitious, make a blend.

TIME 15 minutes

1 Preheat the oven to 350°F.

2 If using olive oil, lightly brush each tortilla on both sides. Using a chef's knife, cut each tortilla into 6 to 8 wedges. Arrange the wedges in a single layer on a rimmed baking sheet. Sprinkle the tortilla wedges lightly with salt, if desired.

3 Bake the tortilla chips until they are crisp and lightly browned, 6 to 10 minutes. Let cool on the baking sheet to room temperature; the chips will crisp up. Store leftovers in a resealable plastic bag for up to 2 days.

BAKE-FRIED POTATO CHIPS

Here's a homemade potato chip that eliminates the hassle and fat of deep-frying and is especially good with the onion dip on page 213. The basic procedure works with white, yellow, red, or blue potatoes and sweet potatoes. This is a good occasion to invest in a mandoline slicer which will enable you to cut the spuds into slices of a uniform thickness (ideally that of a silver dollar). **Serves 2; can be multiplied as desired**

SHOP I usually buy large organic baking potatoes for these chips—they're easier to slice and yield larger chips.

GEAR Your basic kitchen gear including a baking sheet and pastry brush

WHAT ELSE You don't need to peel the potato. Just scrub the skin well with a vegetable brush. Think of the skin as extra fiber. To speed up slicing the potato, you could use a mandoline (see page 181) or a good processor fitted with a slicing disk.

TIME 20 minutes

1 large or 2 medium-size potatoes or sweet potatoes, rinsed and scrubbed clean with a brush

About 2 tablespoons extra virgin olive oil

Coarse salt (kosher or sea) and freshly ground black pepper

1 Preheat the oven to 350°F.

2 Using a carefully wielded knife, cut the potatoes crosswise into 1/8-inch-thick slices. Blot the slices dry with paper towels. Place the potato slices in a large bowl, add the olive oil, and toss well to coat. Add as little olive oil as possible; you want each chip covered with a *light* film of oil. Season the potato slices with salt and pepper to taste; the chips should be highly seasoned.

3 Arrange the chips in a single layer on a nonstick baking sheet. Bake the chips until lightly browned on top, 5 to 8 minutes. Turn each chip over and bake them until both sides are browned and crisp, 5 to 8 minutes longer. Transfer the chips to a large bowl and serve warm or cooled on the baking sheet to room temperature.

SALAMI CHIPS, PEPPERONI CHIPS, AND PROSCIUTTO CHIPS

Sometimes less is more. Sometimes more is more. You could serve pita chips or *totopos* (freshly fried tortilla chips) at your next Super Bowl party. You should and you probably will. But what if you could combine the satisfying crunch of a chip with the foods we guys *really* want to eat: salami, pepperoni, and ham? Experimenting in the test kitchen one day, I discovered you can turn almost any dry-cured sausage or meat into outrageous chips with remarkably little time and effort. **Makes 16 to 20 chips, enough to serve 2 to 4 with a lot of other finger food**

SHOP You can certainly make chips from cheap supermarket cold cuts, but you get what you pay for. (In other words, the better the fabric, the better the suit.) Try this with imported Genoa or *finocchio* (fennel) salami or a really good prosciutto, like La Quercia from Iowa (yes, Iowa).

GEAR Your basic kitchen gear including a baking sheet and wire rack

WHAT ELSE You don't really need a dip for these rich meaty chips, but I wouldn't say no to Michael Schwartz's Onion Dip on page 213.

TIME about 15 minutes

4 ounces thinly sliced salami, pepperoni, or other dry-cured sausage or prosciutto or serrano ham

1 Preheat the oven to 350°F.

2 Spread a baking sheet with aluminum foil or parchment paper. (This facilitates cleanup.) Place a wire rack on top.

3 Arrange the sausage slices or ham on the rack in a single layer. Bake until dry and crisp, 5 to 8 minutes. Work in several batches if necessary; you want to cook the chips in a single layer without crowding. Pepperoni browns faster than salami or prosciutto.

4 Remove the rack and baking sheet from the oven. Blot the chips (especially salami or pepperoni) with a folded paper towel to remove any excess grease. Let the chips cool to room temperature (they'll crisp up) and serve.

STEER

And now we come to the ultimate guy food— beef. If you master only one technique and one recipe in this book, it should be how to cook a steak. Or more broadly speaking, several, because every man should know how to prepare a steak in a skillet, a pepper steak, and a London broil marinated with fresh lemon juice and soy sauce.

But I know you won't stop there. You'll want to tackle the most magisterial roast from a steer: a standing rib roast (aka prime rib). You'll want to share the luxury of roasted whole beef tenderloin. You'll want to master short ribs braised with lemongrass and chuck steak cooked in beer. You'll want to learn how to make a Korean beef taco worthy of a food truck. Read on, scholar. Your education is about to begin.

WHAT YOU NEED TO KNOW ABOUT BUYING BEEF

As a member of the male gender (assuming you're not a vegetarian), you will probably buy a lot of beef. So you probably have lots of questions: Should you buy Prime or Choice? Grass-fed or corn-fed? Here's how to speak with your butcher so you sound like you know what you're talking about.

PRIME VERSUS CHOICE

The USDA (United States Department of Agriculture) grades beef according to tenderness, texture, and "marbling"—the distribution of intramuscular fat. (Remember this equation: Fat equals flavor.) There are eight USDA grades, but two, Prime and Choice, are the most likely to turn up at your local market.

Prime designates beef of the highest quality with the best marbling. The USDA uses a complicated inspection system that evaluates the marbling in the rib eye muscle but factors in the age of the animal. (As with much in life, younger is considered better.) Only 2 percent of all American beef is graded Prime, and most of that goes to restaurants and specialty meat markets—or to high-end Internet purveyors like Allen Brothers (allenbrothers.com) or Lobel's (lobels.com). Do you need to buy Prime? No, but when it comes to steak, you'll definitely taste the difference. Splurge if you can for a special occasion.

Choice is the grade generally sold at supermarkets, and because meat classification guidelines are fairly subjective, it can be adequate, good, or very good. Choice beef is fine for braised or other slow-cooked dishes (it would be a waste to use Prime in these). I've also had many tasty Choice steaks over the years.

ORGANIC VERSUS CONVENTIONAL BEEF

If you believe that you are what you eat (the nineteenth-century French food philosopher Brillat-Savarin did), you'll probably join me in eating organic beef and other meats whenever possible. Not that organic automatically means more flavor (it generally does) or more tenderness (often it doesn't). But organic meats come free of the growth hormones, antibiotics, pesticide residues in the feed, or other chemicals associated with feedlot livestock. Organic cattle are generally raised more humanely than stockyard animals, and this enhances your eating experience. I believe it also enhances the taste.

GRASS-FED VERSUS CORN-FED

In their natural state, cows evolved to eat grass, not corn or other grains. But grass-fed beef is leaner than grain-fed, resulting in drier, tougher meat that may lack a rich mouthfeel. So most Americans have come to appreciate the flavor of grain-fed beef.

On the downside, grain-fed cows are treated with antibiotics and other chemicals to help them digest what's essentially an unnatural diet. One compromise used by many progressive cattle ranchers is to raise the steer on a grass diet for most of its life, then finish it on a grain diet six months prior to processing. Many South Americans prefer the texture and aromatic flavor of grass-fed beef. Decide for yourself.

WET-AGED VERSUS DRY-AGED

Unlike vegetables and shellfish, which taste best the moment they're harvested, beef needs to be aged to develop its tenderness and flavor. This can be done one of two ways: by wet or dry aging.

◄ Remember this equation: Fat equals flavor.

T-BONE

RIB EYE

NEW YORK
STRIPSTEAK

FLANK STEAK

HANGER
STEAK

SKIRT
STEAK

PORTERHOUSE

FILET MIGNON

Wet-aged meat is vacuum-sealed in plastic and stored under refrigeration for a few days or weeks to allow the natural enzymes to tenderize it from within and deepen its flavor. There is no shrinkage as there is in dry aging, so wet-aged meat costs less.

Dry-aged meat is hung or racked in a walk-in refrigerator with a controlled temperature, humidity level, and air circulation. Over the two to four weeks (or even longer) of dry-aging, enzymes in the meat tenderize it and deepen the flavor. Some of the water in the meat evaporates, further concentrating the taste. But because the meat ages unwrapped, the exterior dries out and must be trimmed off and discarded, so as much as 35 percent goes to waste. Time and shrinkage cost money, so dry-aged beef is considerably more expensive than wet-aged. It's definitely worth the splurge.

WAGYU VERSUS KOBE

"Kobe" and wagyu beef began turning up on American menus a decade ago—at prices ranging from lofty to exorbitant. Kobe refers to a super-premium richly marbled beef from the city of Kobe in Japan. Richly marbled? A slice of raw Kobe beef looks like white lace laid over a red tablecloth. You may have heard tales of special massage sessions for Kobe bovines. They're false. However, the traditional Kobe diet does include beer as an appetite stimulator in hot weather. Unfortunately, the Japanese don't export this premium beef, so any "Kobe" beef you see in the United States is a misnomer at best and a rip-off at worst. Kobe-style refers to wagyu beef raised and processed like Kobe beef, but to be honest with you, I've never had anything in North America that approaches the exquisite flavor of what you get in Japan.

Wagyu refers to the breed of cattle that produce Kobe-style beef. They are raised in the U.S. Wagyu beef can be exceptionally well-marbled, flavorful, and worth the price. It can also disappoint. Respected purveyors include Snake River Farms, Allen Brothers, and Lobel's, but know you will pay a premium—up to $100 per pound for rib eye. And that's before shipping!

How to Use Salt

I like to keep a bowl of sea salt by the stove or grill, so it's easy to take a pinch for seasoning. Salting by hand gives you more control than shaking it from a carton or shaker (not to mention the tactile pleasure). Gourmet shops sell salt grinders modeled on the commonplace peppercorn grinder. Don't bother with them: Freshly ground salt tastes the same as regular salt.

When salting, take a big pinch, raise your hand high above the food, and release the salt by rubbing your thumb and forefinger back and forth. You want the salt crystals to fall in an even layer. One of the most common mistakes made by culinary neophytes is underseasoning, so salt like you mean it. (The second most common mistake is overseasoning: Remember, you can always add more salt, but you can't take it away.)

Here are some other things you can do with salt:

Make a brine: Combine salt, sugar, and water in a ratio of roughly one part salt to one part sugar to sixteen parts water (for example 1 cup each salt and sugar to 1 gallon of water) and you wind up with a brine—a saline solution used for brining (marinating) seafood, poultry, pork chops, and other inherently dry meats before smoking, grilling, or roasting them. (The dry meat absorbs the brine, making it moist.) One great example of brining is the Bourbon-Brined Roast Turkey on page 349. The brine should cover the meat by 2 inches.

Make a cure: Combine coarse salt and brown sugar in a ratio of one part salt to two parts brown sugar to make a cure for smoked salmon and other fish, or gravlax (raw cured salmon).

Make a salt crust: Salt crusting is a dramatic and tasty way to cook fish and poultry. To make a salt crust, mix salt with enough water to obtain a slushlike slurry, like wet snow (see page 236).

Add it to dessert: A pinch of salt helps counterpoint the sweetness of a dessert—a trick familiar to bakers and confectioners. (Salted caramels actually taste sweeter than unsalted.) A pinch of salt has a terrific way of focusing the flavor of butterscotch—see the Butterscotch Pudding with Miso on page 567.

IS IT DONE YET?

Is it done yet? How many times have you wondered if that steak sizzling on the grill or pork shoulder roasting in the oven is cooked to the proper degree of doneness? Recognizing when food is cooked is one of the most important tasks in the kitchen. Fortunately, there are a number of visual, olfactory, and scientific indicators to let you know.

BY SIGHT AND SMELL | First, use your eyes and nose. Cooked roasts will look crusty and dark golden brown on the outside. Properly seared steaks and chops (of both the land and sea variety) will have a visibly dark crust. Cooked meats have a distinctive aroma, too—toasted, caramelized, and smoky.

THE POKE TEST | One of the best ways to judge doneness of steaks, chops, and other relatively thin cuts of meat is to poke them with

The Poke Test If the meat is soft and squishy, the steak is rare (or still raw). If yielding, it's medium-rare; gently yielding, it's medium; resistant, it's medium-well or well-done.

your forefinger. Depending on its squishiness or firmness, you can tell if the meat is rare, well-done, or somewhere in between (see the chart in this box).

THE PIERCE TEST | Piercing is a way to test the doneness of foods that are hard to poke or see (like baked potatoes or something being cooked wrapped up in foil). To do this, insert a slender metal skewer into the center of the food. If it meets no resistance, the food is cooked. You can also use the pierce test to check the doneness of whole or planked fish. Insert a skewer through one of the narrow ends to the center of the fish and leave it for fifteen to twenty seconds. If the skewer feels hot to the touch when you pull it out, the fish is cooked.

THE CUT TEST | While it's frowned upon by most food writers, everybody, from chefs on down, does it: Using the tip of a paring knife, make a small slit in a steak or chop (ideally in the side you will serve on the bottom) and look at the center to check for doneness. Note: This technique should be used sparingly, as it violates the integrity of the meat.

THE FLAKE TEST | This test is used for fish steaks, fish fillets, and whole fish. Press the surface with your forefinger. The flesh will break into clean flakes when the fish is cooked.

THE SHRINK TEST | For baby backs, spareribs, and short ribs: When the ribs are cooked, the meat shrinks back leaving the last ¼ to ½ inch of the bone exposed on baby backs and ½ inch bare on beef ribs and spareribs.

THE TEAR TEST | Also used for ribs, when the meat is tender enough to tear a rack of ribs apart with your fingers, they're done.

THE INSTANT-READ THERMOMETER TEST | This is the most accurate way to tell when meats are cooked to the proper temperature, and yes, even the pros do it. Insert the slender probe of an instant-read thermometer into the center of the meat. (Don't let the probe touch any bones or you will get a false reading.) If you are checking a thin piece of meat, like a hamburger, steak, or chicken breast, go in through the side. Digital thermometers will give you the most accurate reading. To verify the accuracy of an analog instant-read thermometer when you are at sea level, dip the probe in a pot of boiling water. It should read 212°F.

The Six Degrees of Doneness

Here are the six degrees of doneness with their corresponding temperatures. Meats continue to cook after they have been removed from a heat source, so you might want to set them aside to rest when they reach the first (lower) number.

DEGREE OF DONENESS	INTERNAL TEMPERATURE (use for roasts, whole birds, etc.)	POKE TEST (use for steaks, chops, and chicken breasts)	APPROPRIATE FOR
Rare	120° to 125°F	Soft and squishy	Beef and lamb steaks, tuna
Medium-rare	135° to 145°F	Gently yielding	Beef and lamb, duck breasts, tri-tip, pork (chops, loin, or tenderloin)
Medium	140° to 145°F	Flakes easily when pressed	Fish and lobster
Medium	155° to 160°F	Half yielding; half firm	Pork and duck
Medium	160° to 165°F	Half yielding; half firm	Ground beef and chicken
Medium-well	170° to 180°F	Firm	Turkey
Well-done	190° to 195°F	Hard and springy for meat, but barbecued foods, like brisket and pork shoulder, will feel soft to the touch	Brisket, pork shoulder, spareribs, and baby back ribs

New York Strip with Anchovy Butter

THE BASIC STEAK

SHOP **SHOP** You want strip steaks that are 1 to 1½ inches thick and generously marbled, with a nice strip of fat at the edge (the melting fat will flavor the meat). Extra points for organic or grass-fed beef.

GEAR Your basic kitchen gear including a medium-size saucepan, plus a grill. Don't have a grill? Follow the instructions on page 243 for cooking the steak in a cast-iron skillet.

WHAT ELSE Nothing beats steak grilled over a wood fire. Perhaps you're lucky enough to own a wood-burning grill, like an Argentinean-style front-loader from The Grillworks (grillery.com). Here's an option if you own a charcoal kettle grill: Buy hardwood chunks at your local grill shop or hardware store and light them in a chimney starter, as you would charcoal. Once the embers glow orange, spread them over the bottom of the grill and you're ready.

TIME about 5 minutes for the anchovy butter, plus about 10 minutes grilling time

You now know the secrets of buying beef and cooking the perfect steak. So, my friend, it's showtime. You'll start with one of the world's easiest, most satisfying steaks (not to mention my personal favorite), the New York strip. You'll cook it the way steak fanatics do the world over—on the grill, preferably over a wood fire. And to go with it, a simple condiment with a distinguished history in gentlemen's cookbooks: anchovy butter. Anchovy with steak isn't quite as strange as it sounds. The salty fish is a primary ingredient in such traditional steak sauces as Worcestershire sauce and A.1. Steak Sauce. Anchovies, especially the kind packed in oil and sold in flat cans or jars, possess salty umami flavors that go great with flame-seared beef. Serve the steaks with a bottle of malbec, shiraz, or Bordeaux. Just don't forget to call me. **Makes 2 steaks; can be multiplied as desired**

4 tablespoons (½ stick) unsalted butter

3 oil-cured anchovy fillets, drained and finely chopped

2 tablespoons finely chopped fresh flat-leaf parsley

1 clove garlic (optional), peeled and thinly sliced crosswise

2 New York strip steaks (each 8 to 12 ounces)

Smoked Salt Rub (page 534), or coarse salt (kosher or sea) and freshly ground black pepper

Vegetable oil, for oiling the grill grate

1 Melt the butter in a medium-size saucepan over medium-high heat. Add the anchovies, parsley, and garlic, if using, and cook until sizzling and the garlic is lightly browned, about 2 minutes. Remove the pan from the heat and set it aside.

2 Set up the grill for direct grilling and preheat it to high.

3 Generously season the steaks on both sides with the Smoked Salt Rub or salt and pepper.

4 When ready to cook, brush the grill grate with a stiff wire brush. Oil the grate using a tightly folded paper towel that has been dipped in vegetable oil. Holding the paper towel with grill tongs, draw it across the bars of the grate. (Oiling the grate helps prevent sticking and it also helps give you killer grill marks.)

5 Arrange the steaks on the grill at a 45-degree angle to the bars of the grate. Grill the steaks for about 2 minutes, then give each steak a quarter turn to create a crosshatch of grill marks. Continue grilling the steaks until the bottoms are sizzling and dark brown, 2 to

3 minutes longer. Turn the steaks over and grill the second sides the same way. The total cooking time will be 8 to 10 minutes for medium-rare. To test for doneness, use the poke method (page 228).

6 Transfer the steaks to a platter or plates and let them rest for about 2 minutes. (Resting makes the meat juicer. You never want to cut into a steak hot off the grill.) In the meantime, reheat the anchovy butter, pour it over the steaks, and dig in.

SKILLET RIB STEAK

In the best of all worlds (my world, at least), everyone would own a grill and use it for cooking steaks. But that excludes some of my apartment- and condo-dwelling friends. And some steaks—especially those from grass-fed cattle—are so lean they tend to dry out on the grill. Enter the skillet steak, which is seared in a cast-iron skillet on the stove, then roasted in the oven. The skillet holds the fat and meat juices, keeping the steak moist. You do virtually nothing once the steak goes in the oven and the result will leave the person lucky enough to share it with you awestruck. **Serves 2 or 3**

1½ tablespoons extra virgin olive oil

1 bone-in rib steak (1½ to 2 inches thick and 1½ to 2 pounds)

1 head garlic, cut in half crosswise

2 to 3 teaspoons Fennel Mustard Peppercorn Steak Rub (page 239) or Smoked Salt Rub (page 534), or 1 to 1½ teaspoons each coarse salt (kosher or sea) and cracked black peppercorns

2 large sprigs fresh rosemary, or 2 bay leaves

SHOP Rib steak (cut from a standing rib roast) isn't a standard supermarket meat case item. You'll want to order it ahead of time—preferably from your butcher. The downside of a rib steak? The meat will serve two to three, but only one person gets to gnaw on the bone. Who said that life is fair?

GEAR Your basic kitchen gear including a large (10- to 12-inch) cast-iron skillet

WHAT ELSE Other steaks I like for skillet roasting are porterhouses and T-bones. If the steak is done before the garlic cloves are soft, place the garlic on a piece of aluminum foil and return it to the oven for 5 to 10 minutes longer while the meat rests.

TIME about 5 minutes preparation time, plus about 20 minutes cooking time

1 Preheat the oven to 400°F.

2 Drizzle most of the olive oil over the steak on both sides, rubbing it over the meat with your fingertips. Drizzle the remaining oil over the cut sides of the garlic halves.

3 Very generously season the steak on both sides with one of the rubs (reserving a little for the garlic). Don't have the rub? Season the steak generously on both sides with salt and pepper. Rub or season the cut sides of the garlic halves, too.

4 Heat a cast-iron or other ovenproof skillet over medium-high heat for 1 to 2 minutes. To check the temperature, sprinkle a few drops of water in the skillet. They should dance and evaporate in about 3 seconds.

5 Add the steak and cook it until the bottom is darkly browned, 3 to 5 minutes. Turn the steak over and brown the second side the same way. Add the garlic halves to the skillet cut sides down and cook them until browned, 1 to 2 minutes.

6 Turn the garlic in the skillet so it is cut sides up. Place the rosemary sprigs or bay leaves on the steak. Place the skillet with the steak in the oven. Cook the steak until it is done to taste, about 20 minutes for medium-rare. To test for doneness use the poke test (see page 228) or insert an instant-read thermometer through the side of the steak into the center (do not let the thermometer probe touch the bone). The thermometer should read 135°F for medium-rare.

7 Transfer the skillet with the steak to the stovetop or a trivet and let the steak rest in the skillet for 3 to 5 minutes. Present the steak in the skillet—it's impressive—then transfer it to a cutting board. Remove and discard the rosemary sprigs or bay leaves. Cut the meat off the bone, cutting the meat into ½-inch-thick slices. Return the slices to the skillet with the bone. Serve the steak with the roasted garlic on the side. To eat the roasted garlic, squeeze the cloves out of their skins and onto the steak slices.

DIRTY STEAKS
WITH BELL PEPPER PANFRY

From the moment our first prehistoric ancestors put meat to fire (circa 1.8 million BCE) the caveman T-bone has rocked cookouts. To say it's one of the most popular dishes at Barbecue University would be putting it mildly. And at least one American president—Dwight D. Eisenhower—made it a signature

SHOP For information on buying steaks, see page 225. For the panfry you can use strips of bell pepper or mini bell peppers cut in half.

GEAR Your basic kitchen gear plus a charcoal grill and natural lump charcoal along with a basting brush and a large (10-inch) cast-iron skillet

WHAT ELSE Don't have a charcoal grill? Roast the steaks in a skillet as described on page 231.

TIME about 20 minutes

dish at the White House. (He called it "dirty steak.") There's something about cooking a steak right on the embers that mesmerizes, shocks, and delights. That something is the high drama of cooking meat on a bed of live embers, producing an incomparable crust and intense smoky flavor you just can't achieve on a conventional grill. To this add a Technicolor red and yellow bell pepper panfry that doubles as a sauce. Cooking doesn't get more primal than this. **Serves 2; can be multiplied as desired**

For the steaks
2 T-bone steaks (each 1¼ to 1½ inches thick and 12 to 14 ounces)

Coarse salt (kosher or sea) and coarsely cracked black peppercorns

For the bell pepper panfry
¼ cup extra virgin olive oil

1 red bell pepper, stemmed, seeded, and sliced into ¼-inch-by-2-inch strips

1 yellow bell pepper, stemmed, seeded, and sliced into ¼-inch-by-2-inch strips

4 cloves garlic, peeled and thinly sliced crosswise

¾ cup coarsely chopped fresh flat-leaf parsley leaves

1 **Cook the steaks:** Light charcoal in a grill and rake the coals in an even layer, leaving the front third of the grill bare. When the coals glow orange, fan them with a newspaper to blow off any loose ash.

2 Generously season the steaks on both sides with salt and cracked pepper. Place the steaks directly on the embers, arranging them about 2 inches apart. Grill the steaks until cooked to taste, about 4 minutes per side for medium-rare, turning with tongs. After about 2 minutes on each side transfer the steaks to a different section of the coals so they cook evenly.

3 Using tongs, lift the steaks off the coals, shaking each to dislodge any clinging embers. Using a basting brush, brush off any loose ash

and place the steaks on a platter or plates. Let the steaks rest for about 2 minutes, while you make the bell pepper panfry.

4 **Cook the bell peppers:** Heat the olive oil in a large cast-iron skillet directly on the pile of embers with the handle over the bare section of the gril or on the stove over high heat. When the olive oil is hot, add the bell peppers, garlic, and parsley and cook until the bell peppers and garlic are golden brown, about 2 minutes. Spoon the bell pepper mixture over the steaks and you're good to go.

STEAK ON A PITCHFORK

Medora, North Dakota, may not spring to mind as a dining destination, but there's at least one reason to put it on your culinary bucket list: pitchfork steak. Seven nights a week from June through September a crew of Stetson-hat-and-bandanna-clad chefs from the TR Medora Foundation impale rib eye steaks on clean pitchforks and plunge them into huge kettles of scalding oil to make a cowboy version of beef fondue. Try this yourself and, besides the wow power of the process, you now have another reason to justify the purchase of a turkey fryer. **Serves 4; can be multiplied as desired**

For the dipping sauces
(I'd go with at least three)
Dark and Stormy Barbecue Sauce
(page 537)

Lemon Pepper Mayonnaise (page 543)

Curry Sauce (page 544)

Horseradish Sauce (page 545)

Chipotle Mayonnaise (page 545)

For the steaks
2 gallons vegetable oil, such as canola or
peanut oil

4 rib eye steaks (each 1 to 1¼ inches
thick and 8 to 10 ounces)

Smoked Salt Rub (page 534) or another
steak seasoning, or coarse salt (kosher
or sea) and freshly ground black pepper

1 Place your choice of sauces in small serving bowls and set them aside.

2 Set up a turkey fryer on a ring burner outdoors. (See the Fried Turkey recipe on page 354 for guidelines.) Pour the vegetable oil into the fryer and heat it to 360°F. Use a deep-fry thermometer to check the temperature.

3 Generously season the steaks on both sides with steak seasoning or salt and pepper. Impale the steaks from top to bottom on a pitchfork, leaving about 2 inches between them.

4 Carefully plunge the steaks into the hot oil and fry them until crusty and brown on the outside and done to taste, about 3 minutes for medium-rare. Lift the steaks out of the hot oil and let them drain on the pitchfork for about 30 seconds, then transfer them to a platter or plates for serving. Use tongs to slide the steaks off the pitchfork, taking care not to touch the hot tines. Serve the steaks with the bowls of dipping sauce on the side.

SHOP My suggestion for the rib eye steaks is that they be organic and/or grass fed. As for the oil, the TR Medora Foundation folks use an institutional shortening made with soybeans. You'll be fine with canola oil or peanut oil in your fryer.

GEAR Your basic kitchen gear plus a turkey fryer with a ring burner (see page 354), a deep-fry thermometer, and a clean pitchfork

WHAT ELSE There's another version of pitchfork steak that's more in my arena. You season the beef with your favorite rub, impale it on the pitchfork, and roast it over a campfire (or a charcoal kettle grill fortified with a couple of small hardwood logs or wood chunks). There are two advantages here: You get added smoke flavor from the wood and a lot less fat without the oil.

TIME about 30 minutes, most of which is spent waiting for the oil to heat

STEAK

Steak is the one dish every self-respecting man—no matter how kitchen-phobic—should know how to cook. Cooking a great steak isn't gender specific, of course, and plenty of women excel in its preparation. But even if your mother/wife/girlfriend cooks like a pro or *is* a pro, there's a good chance she'll look to you to cook the steak. Will you shy away from a hunk of raw beef or raging fire, or will you calmly take tongs in hand and step up to the grill with confidence?

You can master the basics in thirty minutes (and spend a lifetime perfecting the fine points). There's a lot, um, at stake in this chapter, so listen up.

THE STEAK

Steaks come in a hunger-inducing array of cuts, shapes, and thicknesses (see photo on page 226). You can think of them in three categories.

TOP CUTS | The intrinsically tender steaks, which include New York strip, filet mignon, rib steak, rib eye, sirloin, porterhouse, and T-bone. (They come from the upper part of the steer, hence "top" cuts.)

BOTTOM CUTS | Fibrous, somewhat tough steaks that become tender when thinly sliced across the grain. These include skirt steak, flank steak, and hanger steak, which are cut from the steer's underbelly.

TOUGH LOVE CUTS | Steaks that require prolonged cooking with liquid at a low temperature (braising—see page 9), like chuck or blade.

THE SEASONINGS

Some of the world's greatest steaks, like Spain's *chuletón* (rib steak), are prepared using only one seasoning: salt. Italy's magnificent *bistecca alla fiorentina* requires only two seasonings: salt and extra virgin olive oil. No matter what the seasoning, it should remain subservient to the beef—in other words, enhance the flavor, not overpower it.

SALT | A great steak demands salt—preferably in coarse crystals, which stay intact during cooking. I prefer coarse sea salt or flat crunchy crystals of *fleur de sel* (naturally evaporated sea salt). Kosher salt also works. Table salt won't give you a great crust.

PEPPER | For me pepper is a mandatory seasoning. The pepper should be freshly and coarsely ground. (To get a coarse grind, loosen the top nut on the pepper mill.) If you cook a lot of steak, you may want to pregrind your pepper in a spice mill (more fresh pepper for less work). There's one exception to the freshly ground rule: Store-bought cracked black peppercorns. Why? The pieces are sufficiently large to taste like whole peppercorns.

RUBS | Rubs are combinations of salt, pepper, herbs, and/or spices that are literally rubbed onto the surface of the steak, flavoring it before the meat is cooked. On page 239 you'll find my Fennel Mustard Peppercorn Steak Rub.

MARINADES | These wet seasonings work well with popular tougher cuts such as flank steak and sirloin. One popular marinade for steak is Japanese teriyaki (soy sauce for salt, sugar or mirin—sweet rice wine—for sweetness, and dark Asian sesame oil for nuttiness).

FAT | When it comes to cooking and serving steak, fat is a good thing. Fat equals flavor. Fat keeps your meat moist. Enhancing with fat raises a great steak to the stratosphere. Among the ways to do this: Wrap a filet mignon in bacon, sauté a hanger steak in plenty of butter, drizzle a *bistecca alla fiorentina* (Tuscan steak) with olive oil, or crown a T-bone with a disk of truffle butter while it rests.

THE HEAT

As the author of eight grill books (and three grilling TV series), you'd expect me to say that there is only one way to cook a great steak: on the grill. True, it's hard to beat a T-bone charred over a wood or charcoal fire (or directly on the embers). But, in fact, there are many great ways to cook a steak.

GRILLING | My favorite way to cook tender steaks. Set up the grill for direct grilling and make sure it's screaming hot. (You want a three-Mississippi fire, see page 12.) The exception is when you're cooking a porterhouse that's more than 1½ inches thick; in that case, work with a two-zone fire: one hot zone and one medium zone. You sear the outside of the steak over the hot zone for a couple of minutes, then move the steak to the medium zone to cook it through.

CAVEMAN GRILLING | My favorite way to cook T-bones. You light natural lump charcoal in a chimney starter and rake out the coals in an even layer over the bottom of the grill. Fan off any loose ash with newspaper. Place the steaks on the glowing coals. No grill grate needed.

PANFRYING | Panfrying a steak may seem like an also-ran next to the live fire methods, but most chefs (and civilians) in France use a skillet. You heat it screaming hot, grease it with butter or vegetable oil, and sear the steaks in the hot fat. Sizzling crust? Check. Moist center? Check. And unlike grilling, which has a tendency to dry out lean steaks, panfrying adds fat to the meat. On page 238 you'll find a great recipe for a new take on steak au poivre (Filets Mignons with Peppercorn Cream).

SKILLET ROASTING | This is my favorite method for cooking thick, intrinsically lean steaks, like a grass-fed porterhouse. You sear the steak on both sides in an ovenproof skillet, such as a cast-iron one, then place the skillet in a hot oven to finish cooking. The pan holds in all the fat and helps keep the meat from drying out. On page 231 you'll find a great recipe for garlic and rosemary-roasted Skillet Rib Steak.

BROILING | When I was growing up, my grandmother served sirloin broiled to the color of gray flannel. Broiling remains my least favorite method for cooking a steak. If you do broil a steak, preheat the broiler screaming hot and get the steak as close to the heat source as possible (within ½ inch) to sear the meat. Trick: When you season steak for broiling, sprinkle on a *little* sugar (½ teaspoon): It will caramelize, giving you a better crust.

FILETS MIGNONS
WITH PEPPERCORN CREAM

SHOP I call here for a steak I don't often grill: filet mignon. It's a good steak to panfry because the butter keeps it moist and the meat is tender enough to cut with the side of a fork. But you can certainly make pepper steak with New York strip, which has more flavor.

GEAR Your basic kitchen gear including a large (10- to 12-inch) skillet, preferably cast iron

WHAT ELSE The sauce calls for green peppercorns. They're the fruit of the pepper plant, which when processed and dried, become white or black pepper. Look for green peppercorns bottled in brine at specialty food shops, or for even more flavor, find fresh or frozen green peppercorns at an Asian market. I've made the peppercorns optional. In the event you can't find them, season the sauce with an additional spoonful of the pepper steak rub.

TIME 25 to 30 minutes

I'm about to make a heretical statement: Steak doesn't *always* need to be grilled to be great. Consider French pepper steak. This bistro classic is traditionally cooked in a skillet, which helps keep the peppercorn crust on the meat and gives you pan juices for making the sauce. A Frenchman would use cracked black pepper: I up the ante with a rub made with peppercorns, mustard seeds, fennel, and other spices, all skillet-toasted to give them a smoky flavor, then freshly ground in a spice grinder or with a mortar and pestle. And in the Lone Star Pepper Steak recipe (page 240), you blast the meat with jalapeños. These steaks are meat with heat and you should definitely know how to make them. **Serves 2 really hungry guys or 4 people with normal appetites**

For the steaks

4 filets mignons, cut from the center of a beef tenderloin (each about 1¼ inches thick and 5 to 6 ounces)

2 to 3 tablespoons Fennel Mustard Peppercorn Steak Rub (recipe follows), or 4 teaspoons coarse salt (kosher or sea) and 4 teaspoons cracked black peppercorns

2 tablespoons extra virgin olive oil

2 tablespoons (¼ stick) salted butter

For the peppercorn cream sauce

2 large shallots, peeled and minced (about ½ cup)

3 tablespoons green peppercorns, drained, or an additional 2 teaspoons Fennel Mustard Peppercorn Steak Rub

About 3 tablespoons Cognac

1 cup heavy (whipping) cream

2 teaspoons Dijon mustard, or more to taste

Coarse salt (kosher or sea)

1 Cook the steaks: Thickly crust (rub) the steaks on all sides with the Fennel Mustard Peppercorn Steak Rub. Drizzle 1 tablespoon of the olive oil over the steaks and rub it onto the meat on all sides.

2 Melt the butter in the remaining oil in a large skillet over high heat, swirling the pan to coat the bottom evenly. Add the steaks and sear them on both sides until crusty and brown, about 2 minutes per side. Reduce the heat to medium and continue cooking the steaks until done to taste, 2 to 4 minutes more per side for medium-rare. (Check for doneness using the poke test on page 228.) Transfer the steaks to a warm platter and keep warm by loosely laying a sheet of aluminum foil over the steaks. Don't seal the foil to the platter or you'll wind up steaming the crusty exterior.

3 **Make the pepper sauce:** Add the shallots and green peppercorns or the additional steak rub to the skillet and cook over medium heat until the shallots begin to brown, about 2 minutes, stirring constantly with a wooden spoon.

4 Add the Cognac and let it come to a boil, scraping the bottom of the skillet with the spoon to dissolve any meat juices. Boil the Cognac until it is reduced to about 1 tablespoon. Add the cream and mustard and boil until thick, flavorful, and reduced by about half, about 3 minutes, whisking well. Season with salt or additional mustard to taste; the sauce should be highly seasoned. Pour the sauce over the steaks and serve at once.

FENNEL MUSTARD PEPPERCORN STEAK RUB

Spicy, sweet, and intensely aromatic, this rub was inspired by Florida Keys chef and caterer Mike Ledwith. Toasting the spices in a dry skillet gives them a smoky flavor. This makes a little more rub than you need for the Filets Mignons with Peppercorn Cream, but it's easier to roast and grind the spices in larger batches. Any excess makes a killer seasoning for all sorts of meats. Note: You'll also need a spice grinder or clean coffee grinder or mortar and pestle for grinding the spices. **Makes about ⅔ cup**

2 tablespoons black peppercorns

2 tablespoons mustard seeds

2 tablespoons fennel seeds

2 whole allspice berries, or ¼ teaspoon ground allspice (see Note)

3 tablespoons coarse salt (kosher or sea)

1 teaspoon hot red pepper flakes

1 Heat a dry cast-iron skillet over medium heat until hot. Add the peppercorns, mustard seeds, fennel seeds, and whole allspice berries, if using. Cook the spices until they are fragrant and lightly toasted, 1 to 3 minutes, stirring with a wooden spoon. Add the ground allspice in the last 10 seconds of roasting. Do not let the spices burn. Transfer the spices to a heatproof bowl to cool.

2 Place the toasted spices in a spice grinder and coarsely grind them, running the machine in short bursts. Add the salt and hot pepper flakes.

Note: If you can find it, use grains of paradise (*Aframomum melegueta*) in place of the allspice. This is a West African spice in the ginger family that looks and tastes like miniature black peppercorns but has a pungent sweet aftertaste reminiscent of allspice. Look for it online at thespicehouse.com or at specialty spice shops. You'll need 1 tablespoon here.

LONE STAR PEPPER STEAK

SHOP Another reason to buy filets mignons

GEAR Your basic gear including a large (10- to 12-inch) skillet

WHAT ELSE Most of the jalapeños sold in the U.S. are green and will look fine on this steak. If you can find red jalapeños, they'll look even better.

TIME 25 minutes

Here's a Texas riff on the classic French pepper steak. The pepper in question is jalapeño—panfried with cilantro, garlic, and olive oil and poured sizzling hot over the steak. **Serves 2 really hungry guys or 4 people with normal appetites**

For the steaks

4 filets mignons, cut from the center of a beef tenderloin (each about 1¼ inches thick and 5 to 6 ounces)

Coarse salt (kosher or sea) and cracked black peppercorns

1 tablespoon butter

1 tablespoon extra virgin olive oil

For the topping

3 tablespoons extra virgin olive oil

5 jalapeño peppers, thinly sliced crosswise

4 cloves garlic, peeled and thinly sliced

¾ cup finely chopped fresh cilantro

1 Cook the steaks: Generously season the steaks on all sides with salt and pepper.

2 Melt the butter in the oil in a large skillet over high heat, swirling the pan to coat the bottom evenly. When the mixture stops hissing, add the steaks and sear them on both sides until crusty and brown, about 2 minutes per side. Reduce the heat to medium and continue cooking the steaks until done to taste, 2 to 4 minutes more per side for medium-rare. (Check for doneness using the poke test on page 228.) Transfer the steaks to a warm platter and keep warm by loosely laying a sheet of aluminum foil over the steaks. Don't seal the foil to the platter or you'll wind up steaming the crusty outside.

3 Make the topping: Add the 3 tablespoons of olive oil to the skillet and heat over high heat almost to smoking (the oil will shimmer when hot enough), about 1 minute. Add the jalapeños, garlic, and cilantro to the skillet and cook over high heat until the mixture is sizzling and the jalapeños and garlic begin to brown, about 2 minutes. Pour this mixture over the steaks and dig in.

LEMON SOY LONDON BROIL

You won't find London broil on any beef anatomical charts. It exists midway between your imagination, stomach, and wallet. Which is to say, it's a cut dreamed up by a guy with more hunger than money—both of which drove him to buy a tough, cheap, but flavorful cut of beef, season it boldly, cook it over or under high heat, and then slice it paper-thin across the grain, shortening those stringy meat fibers, making the meat taste a lot more tender than it could have been. You have lots of options for London broil—flank steak, skirt steak, top round, bottom round—but all will benefit from a lemon and soy marinade that has plenty of acid to tenderize the meat fibers and add the soulful flavors of soy sauce, rosemary, and garlic. **Serves 4**

SHOP Buy a budget steak like flank steak, skirt steak, top round, bottom round, or even sirloin, but try to keep the steak between 1 and 1½ inches thick.

GEAR Your basic kitchen gear including a really sharp chef's knife or slicing knife, plus a glass baking dish for marinating the steak and a broiler or large (10- to 12-inch) skillet

Despite the name, you don't need to cook London broil under a broiler. If you do use your broiler, get it screaming hot and preheat the broiler pan before you add the steak for a better sear.

Diced lemon rind gives the marinade and sauce an astringent adult quality—the same as found in a cocktail that contains no sugar. For a mellower version, you could use 1 teaspoon of finely grated lemon zest (the oil-rich outer rind) in place of the diced whole rind.

TIME about 20 minutes preparation and cooking time, plus 2 to 4 hours for marinating the steak

2 lemons

1 cup soy sauce

½ cup red wine vinegar

½ cup extra virgin olive oil, plus 1 tablespoon olive oil if panfrying (optional)

1 medium-size onion, peeled and finely chopped

2 cloves garlic, peeled and minced

1 tablespoon chopped fresh rosemary

2 teaspoons ground coriander or coriander seed

1 teaspoon freshly ground or cracked black pepper

1½ to 2 pounds flank steak, skirt steak, top round, bottom round, or sirloin (if using round or sirloin, have the steaks cut 1 to 1½ inches thick)

1 Cut the lemons in half crosswise and squeeze the juice into a nonreactive (glass, stainless steel, ceramic, or plastic) mixing bowl, discarding the seeds. Finely chop 1 of the lemon rinds (discard the other) and add it to the bowl with the lemon juice; this aromatic rind is what will give your steak such an interesting flavor. Add the soy sauce, wine vinegar, ½ cup of olive oil, and the onion, garlic, rosemary, coriander, and pepper and whisk to mix.

2 Using a chef's knife, lightly score the steak in a crosshatch pattern on both sides by making a series of shallow (⅛-inch deep) cuts ¼ inch apart, first in one direction on the diagonal, then at a 90-degree angle to the first set of cuts. This helps the marinade flavor the meat and prevents the steaks from curling. Place the steak in a glass or ceramic baking dish or in a resealable plastic bag just large enough to hold it.

3 Whisk the marinade again and pour half of it over the steak, turning the meat a couple of times to coat both sides. Set aside the remaining marinade to serve as a sauce. Cover the baking dish with plastic wrap or seal the plastic bag, and let the steak marinate in the refrigerator for 2 to 4 hours, turning it over a couple of times.

4 Thoroughly drain the marinade from the steak, discarding the marinade (see Note).

5 *Broiler method:* Preheat the broiler as hot as it will go. Place a broiler pan or cast-iron skillet in the oven under the broiler and preheat it as well (about 3 minutes). Carefully remove the hot pan from the broiler and place the steak in it. Place the pan back under the broiler close to the heat source. Broil the steak until sizzling and browned on top, 3 minutes for flank or skirt steak, 4 to 5 minutes for round or sirloin. Turn the steak over and broil the second side the same way (you'll need less time as the hot pan will cook the bottom partially). This will give you a medium-rare steak; let the steak cook a little longer if you prefer it done to medium.

Skillet method: Heat 1 tablespoon oil in a cast-iron skillet over medium-high heat until shimmering. Blot the steak dry with paper towels and add it to the skillet. Cook the steak until it is browned on the bottom and beads of blood start to pearl up on the top, 3 to 4 minutes for flank and skirt steaks, a little longer for round or sirloin. Turn the steak over and cook the second side the same way. The steaks should be medium-rare.

6   Transfer the steak to a cutting board and let it rest for 2 to 3 minutes. Using a sharp chef's knife or slicing knife, cut the steak across the grain sharply on the diagonal, into paper-thin slices. Serve with the reserved marinade spooned on top.

How to Slice Flank Steak

1 Hold the steak flat on the cutting board with tongs. Holding the knife blade sharply on the diagonal, slice off an end piece.

2 Continue slicing the steak on the diagonal. The slices should be about ¼ inch thick.

3 When you get it right, the steak will be crusty on the outside and rare and moist inside.

◄ You won't find London broil on any beef anatomical charts. It exists midway between your imagination, stomach, and wallet.

KOREAN BEEF TACOS

SHOP To build your tacos you may want to visit an Asian market or well-stocked natural foods supermarket to find toasted sesame oil (one good brand is the Japanese Kadoya), kimchi (pickled cabbage), and a jar of *kochujang* (Korean chili paste) or *doenjang* (Korean bean paste, a salty, tangy condiment made from fermented soy beans).

GEAR Your basic kitchen gear, plus a glass or nonreactive baking dish or resealable plastic bag large enough to hold the skirt steaks, and a broiler or large (10- to 12-inch) skillet

WHAT ELSE Traditionally, the steak would be grilled over charcoal. Indoors you can cook the steak under the broiler or in a skillet.

TIME about 30 minutes preparation time, 1 to 2 hours marinating time, plus about 8 minutes cooking time

Do you have a favorite food truck? I like Kogi BBQ, parked during my last visit at the corner of Abbot Kinney Boulevard and Millwood Avenue in Venice Beach, California. I'm not alone. It was 4 p.m. and already the waiting line snaked around the parking lot. My quest? Korean beef tacos.

Inspired by Korean *bool kogi* (grilled rib eye steak), the beef taco starts with one of the world's most flavorful marinades, a sweet-salty-nutty mixture of soy sauce, sesame oil, and mirin (sweet rice wine), with ginger, garlic, and scallions to make sure you're paying attention. It also boasts one of the most stimulating arrays of condiments—fresh cucumber, kimchi (pickled cabbage), and *kochujang*, (a fiery chili paste—sometimes spelled *gochujang*) at a bare minimum, plus grilled scallions, garlic, and peppers for the more ambitious. Like so many great finger foods, you wrap everything up, in this case in lettuce leaves, and eat it with your hands. The resulting bundle is hot and cold and chewy-crisp and lights up your mouth like a Roman candle.

Korean beef tacos have the virtue of being infinitely customizable. Just you and a friend on a weeknight? Serve the steaks with lettuce leaves and hot sauce. Party time? Set out a full Monty spread of grilled vegetables, kimchis, salads, and dipping sauces. You can make these as simple or elaborate as the occasion calls for. **Serves 4 to 6**

For the steaks and the marinade and dipping sauce

2 pounds skirt steaks (trim off any silverskin (see page 251)

½ cup soy sauce

½ cup mirin (sweet rice wine), sake, or dry sherry

¼ cup sugar, or more to taste (a little more if you use sake or sherry)

¼ cup Asian (dark) sesame oil, plus 1 tablespoon for the skillet

1 tablespoon fresh lime juice

4 scallions, trimmed, both white and green parts minced

1 tablespoon minced peeled fresh ginger

1 teaspoon freshly ground black pepper

3 tablespoons toasted sesame seeds (optional, see Note)

1 kiwi fruit or small Asian pear (optional), peeled and cut into ¼-inch dice (core the pear before dicing)

3 cloves garlic, peeled and minced

Any or all of the following for serving

1 head romaine lettuce, separated into leaves, rinsed, and dried

1 cucumber, thinly sliced

Kimchi

¼ cup kochujang (Korean chili paste), doenjang (Korean bean paste), Chinese or Vietnamese chili paste, Sriracha (page 27), or another Asian hot sauce

1 bunch fresh cilantro, washed, patted dry with paper towels, and stemmed

2 cups cooked white rice (page 488)

Optional vegetables

8 cloves garlic, peeled and skewered on toothpicks

4 scallions, trimmed

4 jalapeño peppers, or 2 Anaheim peppers

1 Prepare the steaks: Using a chef's knife, lightly score the steaks in a crosshatch pattern on both sides by making a series of shallow (⅛-inch deep) cuts ¼ inch apart, first in one direction on the diagonal, then at a 90-degree angle to the first set of cuts. Place the steaks in a glass or nonreactive baking dish or in a resealable plastic bag just large enough to hold them.

2 Prepare the marinade: Place the soy sauce, mirin, and sugar in a mixing bowl and whisk until the sugar dissolves. Whisk in the ¼ cup sesame oil, lime juice, minced scallions, ginger, black pepper, and sesame seeds, and kiwi (if using). Pour half of the mixture into a serving bowl, or 4 small bowls, for the dipping sauce. If making the sauce more than 3 hours in advance of serving, cover and refrigerate it in the mixing bowl. Remove it ½ hour before serving, and whisk again.

3 Add the minced garlic to the remaining mixture. Pour it over the steaks, turning them a couple of times to coat both sides. Cover the steaks with plastic wrap and let marinate in the refrigerator for 1 to 2 hours.

4 When ready to serve, arrange the lettuce leaves on a plate or platter. Place the cucumber, kimchi, chili or bean paste (or hot sauce), cilantro, and rice in small bowls for serving.

5 *Broiler method:* Just before serving, preheat the broiler as hot as it will go. Place a broiler pan or cast-iron skillet under the broiler and preheat it as well (about 3 minutes). Drain the steaks well, discarding the marinade. Carefully remove the hot pan from the broiler and arrange the steaks on it. Broil the steaks until cooked to taste, 3 to 4 minutes per side for medium (Koreans like their meat cooked medium to medium-well), turning with tongs. If you are using the skewered garlic, scallions, and/or peppers, arrange them on the broiler pan and broil until browned on both sides, 3 to 4 minutes per side.

Skillet method: Just before serving, drain the steaks well, discarding the marinade. Heat the 1 tablespoon sesame oil in a large skillet over medium-high heat until shimmering. Add the steaks to the pan in a single layer without crowding, working in batches as needed, and cook until done to taste, 3 to 4 minutes per side for medium (Koreans like their meat cooked medium to medium-well), turning with tongs. Transfer the steaks to a cutting board. If you are using the skewered garlic, scallions, and/or peppers, add them to the hot pan and brown on both sides, 3 to 4 minutes per side, again, working in batches as needed so as not to crowd the pan.

Grill method: Set up your grill for direct grilling and brush and oil the grill grate. Drain the steaks well, discarding the marinade. Arrange the steaks on the hot grill and grill until cooked to taste, 3 to 4 minutes for medium. If you are using the skewered garlic, scallions, and/or peppers, arrange them on the grill and grill until browned on both sides, 3 to 4 minutes per side.

6 Transfer the steaks to a cutting board and let them rest for about 30 seconds. Slice the vegetables, if using. Stir the bowl(s) of dipping sauce again. Slice the steaks very thinly on the diagonal across the grain.

7 To eat, pile slices of steak on lettuce leaves. Top with your choice of cucumber slices, kimchi, chili paste (*kochujang*), bean paste (*doenjang*) or hot sauce, cilantro, rice, and grilled vegetables, and roll or fold up. Dip the taco in the dipping sauce and dig in.

Note: To toast sesame seeds, place them in a dry skillet and cook over medium-high heat until fragrant and lightly browned, 2 to 4 minutes, shaking the pan so they cook evenly. Watch carefully to prevent burning.

SKIRT STEAK

The Spanish name says it all—*fajita*, literally "girdle." This robust steak has everything a carnivore hungers for: a no-nonsense texture and bold taste at a price you can afford. Anyone can look like a genius cooking a tender filet mignon. It takes skill to turn out a good skirt steak.

The skirt steak belongs to a family of fibrous, big-flavored, moderately priced steaks cut from the steer's underbelly. Other examples include the flank steak, hanger steak, and brisket. All come from well-exercised muscles, ensuring a rich flavor.

But don't those muscle fibers make for tough meat and arduous chewing? Normally, they would, but cooks from Mexico to Thailand have contrived an ingenious technique for making them tender. Simply stated, you quickly sear the steak at a high heat on a grill or in a skillet or wok, then slice it thinly across the grain (perpendicular to the muscle fibers) before serving. The flash-searing cooks the meat without toughening the muscle fibers, while slicing the meat paper-thin (a variation on the old divide and conquer strategy) shortens the length of each fiber to a few millimeters, reducing its overall chewiness.

GO FOR THE WHOLE NINE YARDS | A whole skirt steak measures 18 to 20 inches in length. (Most of what you buy in the supermarket has been cut into sections.) For an eye-popping presentation, cook it whole.

TRY A LITTLE TENDERNESS | There are two ways to make skirt steak more tender. The chemical method involves marinating the skirt steak in some sort of acid, like lime juice or vinegar, for several hours or overnight. This helps break down some of the meat fibers and also imparts additional flavor.

The mechanical method involves scoring the top and bottom of the steak in a crosshatch pattern. To do this, see page 242, Step 2. Or you can perforate the meat with a meat tenderizer, which pierces it with dozens of tiny stainless steel needles that sever the meat fibers. Better yet, do both.

EXPAND YOUR OPTIONS | Here are some alternative cuts to skirt steak.

Flank steak A flat fibrous beef steak from the underbelly that measures $\frac{1}{2}$ to 1 inch thick, 5 to 6 inches wide, and 10 to 14 inches long. Often sold as "London broil."

Hanger steak A slender, flattish cylindrical, richly flavored steak that hangs from the diaphragm of the steer near the kidney (hence the name—it "hangs" rather than being attached to a bone). Quickly grill or panfry the steak over high heat (it tastes best rare), then thinly slice it on the diagonal across the grain.

Brisket A large, flat pectoral muscle cut from the chest of the steer. Incredibly flavorful and intrinsically tough, brisket requires long slow smoking or braising to make it tender (see page 9).

FRANCIS MALLMANN

Blame it on potatoes. The year was 1995. The International Academy of Gastronomy (an organization that normally hosted such culinary luminaries as Ferran Adrià and Alain Ducasse) had just invited its first South American chef to prepare a dinner. Ever the iconoclast, Francis Mallmann decided on a menu featuring the least likely food his august hosts expected—"the great gift of South America to the world's larder." He dispatched one of his chefs to purchase a half-ton of Andean potatoes—golden, red, purple, marbled. The meal blew the guests away.

Today, Mallmann presides over five internationally acclaimed restaurants—two in Argentina and three in Uruguay, including one at a boutique hotel in a nearly defunct railroad town called Garzón, which Mallmann has resurrected. "For inspiration, I turn to the methods of the frontier, of the gauchos, and the Indians before them," says Mallmann. "My cooking has returned to its mother tongue."

What do men cook in Argentina?
Every red-blooded Argentinean man knows how to cook *parrilla* and *asado* (grilled and campfire roasted meats).

Quintessential guy dish?
Matambre, literally hunger killer, a butterflied steak you stuff with cheese, sausage, and vegetables, then roll into a tight cylinder, which you cook, slice, and serve cold. No Argentinean barbecue would be complete without it.

What did you learn from your most important mentor?
I trained at a lot of famous French restaurants. But the chef who taught me the most was Raymond Olivier at Le Grand Véfour restaurant in Paris. He was the last great master of classical French cuisine—quite old when I went to work for him. Like all young chefs at the time, I wanted to plunge into nouvelle cuisine. He counseled me to master the classics first. Today, young chefs want to start with molecular cuisine. But without understanding the classics, it's a disaster.

Why is it important for men to cook?
It's a way of sharing our lives with other people, which is a beautiful thing.

What's your go-to dish when you're by yourself?
Steak and salad. Or pasta with olive oil and lemon juice.

Your favorite seduction meal?
Goulash and spaetzle. I'd cook them in the fireplace. Talk about romantic!

Three dishes every guy should know how to make?
Steak. Pasta. Salad.

I can't give you a recipe for salad. You have to learn to measure with your eyes. You need to know your olive oil—the farm it comes from. The strength of your vinegar. The right season and moment for each green. A salad needs to be nicely seasoned—salt, pepper, olive oil, vinegar, mustard. Sometimes I make the vinaigrette in the bowl ahead of time; other times, I'll simply pour the oil, vinegar, and seasonings over the leaves. It changes every day.

Three ingredients you can't live without?
Bread. It's a language all its own around the world.

Butter. It's the most elegant fatty thing I eat. We have ours custom-made by a farm in Patagonia.

Cheese. I love it in all its diversity. Hard cheeses like Parmigiano Reggiano. Soft, creamy cheeses like Camembert. With bread, butter, and cheese, you can eat well for the rest of your life.

Three tools you can't live without?
A good knife. A wooden spoon. And a *chapa*. The latter is a cast-iron griddle—Argentina's answer to the Spanish *plancha*. Sometimes we heat it over a wood fire; sometimes in a wood-burning oven. What I like about the *chapa* is that it offers so many different temperatures and cooking experiences: hot in the center for fast searing; warm at the edges for slow cooking.

What are the most important things to keep in mind if you're just starting out in the kitchen?
Patience. When guys start out in the kitchen, they're constantly flipping and flopping the food. It's bad for a steak. It's bad for fish and potatoes. You need to let food sit in the pan for a while so it sears properly on the bottom.

Space. If you crowd a sauté pan, food will stew, not sear. If you put a small piece of fish in a large pan, it will burn before it's cooked through. Choose a pan that has enough room so that there are two fingers of space between each piece of food.

> ▶ If you put a small piece of fish in a large pan, it will burn before it's cooked through.

Heat. Understand how it works. Where it comes from. How it moves through the pots, pans, and ingredients.

What are the three most common mistakes guys make in the kitchen?
Overcooking, and we men tend to do that to everything. Meat. Pasta. Vegetables. The best way—the only way—to avoid overcooking is to cut off a piece of the food and taste it.

Oversalting. This is typical guy behavior.

Being messy. It's a huge mistake to be untidy in a professional kitchen.

Something unexpected you've learned over the years that really helps you up your game in the kitchen?
Understanding the silent language of cooking that you can't get from a cookbook. Like how to season food and tell when beef, lamb, or chicken are cooked just by looking at them. This comes from repetition—cooking a dish thousands of times. The knowledge grows inside of you without even paying attention.

You're the most famous grill man in South America. So what's the secret to cooking a great steak?
The first secret is to pick a great steak. It should be thick—three fingers. Ideally, grass-fed. We have a cut in Argentina called *tapa de ojo*—it's the well-marbled top half of a rib steak. If you can get that, you're in for an unbelievable experience.

Then, there's the salt. It's the only seasoning I use. I put it on quite heavily, but only on one side of the steak, and I season just before grilling. This gives you a delicious salty crust on one side of the steak and you can taste the sweetness of the meat on the other side. I don't like marinades—they "invade" the meat.

You may be surprised to learn that you can make a great steak in a skillet. But as you know, Steven, it's hard to beat the taste of the wood and smoke on the grill.

Most people cook steak for the same amount of time on both sides. You get better results if you cook the first side longer than the second—eight minutes on one side, four minutes on the other for that three-finger-thick rib eye.

I don't go in for a lot of fancy steak sauces. We serve *chimichurri* on the side, so you can taste the contrast between the parsley-garlic-vinegar sauce and the sweetness of the meat.

Anything else you wish to add about cooking for and by men?
Learn to cook a meal from start to finish using only ingredients you find in your refrigerator. *That's* cooking for men.

THE TWENTY-MINUTE ROAST TENDERLOIN

SHOP Ask the butcher to trim the tenderloin (call ahead) or save some money and do it yourself.

GEAR Your basic kitchen gear including a heavy rimmed baking sheet and instant-read thermometer plus butcher's string

WHAT ELSE I call for an amazing Fennel Mustard Peppercorn Steak Rub here, but you could certainly use one of the other rubs in this book, like the Smoked Salt Rub on page 534 or the herb paste with Porchetta on page 277.

TIME about 30 minutes

Every man needs at least one showstopper in his culinary repertory that he can make at a moment's notice. A hunk of protein that's meaty enough to satisfy your inner carnivore, yet sufficiently upscale to wow your boss or girlfriend's parents. That shows you to be the magnanimous guy that you are (this *is* the most expensive cut from the steer) but economizes on time in the kitchen. Enter this eye-popping beef tenderloin crusted with cracked pepper and other spices and flash roasted in a screaming hot oven. Serve it just shy of charred on the outside and a few degrees warmer than still mooing inside, and you've got a regal centerpiece for a dinner party or a simple but elegant Sunday supper. **Serves 6**

For the tenderloin
1 beef tenderloin, trimmed (see below or ask your butcher to do it—about 3 pounds)

¼ cup Fennel Mustard Peppercorn Steak Rub (page 239), or plenty of coarse salt (kosher or sea) and cracked black peppercorns

2 tablespoons extra virgin olive oil

For serving (optional)
Peppercorn Cream (page 238)

Joe's-Style Mustard Sauce (page 412)

Chimichurri (page 539)

Horseradish Sauce (page 545)

1 Place a heavy rimmed baking sheet in the oven and preheat the oven to 450°F.

2 Prepare the tenderloin: About 4 inches up from the tail of the tenderloin (the narrow end) make a crosswise cut halfway through the meat.

Fold the tail under the roast at this cut and tie it in place with butcher's string. This gives the tenderloin a cylindrical shape so it will roast more evenly. Thickly crust the tenderloin on all sides with the Fennel Mustard Peppercorn Steak Rub or salt and cracked black pepper, patting the spices onto the meat. Drizzle the olive oil over the tenderloin and rub it into the meat on all sides.

3 Remove the hot baking sheet from the oven and place the tenderloin on it; you may need to place it on a diagonal so it fits. Immediately return the pan to the oven and roast the tenderloin until it is browned on all sides and done to taste, 4 minutes per side (16 minutes in all) for rare; 6 minutes per side (24 minutes in all) for medium-rare. Give the tenderloin a quarter turn every 4 minutes so all sides brown evenly. Use an instant-read thermometer to check for doneness; when the tenderloin is done to rare, the thermometer will register 120°F; when medium-rare, it will register 135°F. (Remember, the tenderloin will continue cooking after it leaves the oven.) Do not overcook the tenderloin.

4 Transfer the tenderloin to a cutting board and let it rest for about 3 minutes, then cut it crosswise into ½-inch-thick slices for serving. Serve any of the sauces, if desired, on the side.

How to Trim a Tenderloin (or Be Your Own Butcher)

A whole untrimmed beef tenderloin weighs five to six pounds. You can find whole tenderloins at most supermarkets. Once you've trimmed the tenderloin you will have about three pounds of pure beef.

Cut off most of the visible fat and all of the silverskin—the tough, silvery membrane covering the meat. To remove the silverskin, slide the point of a paring knife under it at the head of the tenderloin (the wider end), angle the knife away from the meat, and gently pull it toward the tail (the slender end). A fatty strip of muscle called the chain runs the length of one side of the tenderloin. I like to remove it; you can almost pull it off with your fingers. Clean it and cut into chunks for shish kebab.

THE BIG KAHUNA PRIME RIB

This is it. The big kahuna: a barrel-shaped roast served with the rib cage (at least part of it) still attached. The English call it roast beef; your butcher sells it as prime rib. I call it one of the best ways I know to create high drama (and not a little envy) when you bring this dark, crusty, sizzling, garlic- and rosemary-scented monster to the table. And that's before you carve it! Despite its "wow" power, prime rib is easy to cook; it takes only ten minutes of prep time and between one and two hours for roasting (during which you perfect your martini skills—see page 577). **Serves 8 to 10**

SHOP Choice beef from the supermarket makes a respectable dinner. Prime beef from a premium purveyor knocks it out of the park. Ask your butcher to "french" the roast, that is, scrape the meat off the last inch or so of bone.

GEAR Your basic kitchen gear including a roasting pan, instant-read thermometer, carving knife, and a cutting board, preferably with a deep well—a channel around the edge—to capture the juices when you carve the cooked roast

WHAT ELSE You can make a killer prime rib in the oven.

TIME 1¼ hours or more, depending on how rare you like your prime rib

1 prime rib roast (4 ribs; about 8 pounds—figure on 1 pound per person; you can always use leftovers)

1 bunch rosemary, rinsed, patted dry with paper towels, and torn or cut into 1-inch sprigs

6 cloves garlic, peeled and cut into matchstick slivers

Coarse salt (kosher or sea) and cracked black peppercorns

1 Preheat the oven to 450°F.

2 Using the tip of a paring knife, make a series of slits in the roast on all sides. Each slit should be about ½ inch wide, ½ inch deep, and about 1½ inches apart. Insert sprigs of rosemary in half of the slits; insert garlic slivers in the remaining slits. Generously season the roast on all sides with salt and pepper, patting them onto the meat.

3 Place the roast in a roasting pan with the ribs standing upright. Cook the roast at this high heat until the exterior starts to brown, 20 to 30 minutes. Reduce the oven temperature to 325°F and cook the roast until the exterior is crusty and darkly browned and the meat is cooked to taste. From time to time spoon the fat that collects in the bottom of the roasting pan back over the roast. For a roast this size, you'll need 1¼ to 1½ hours in all for rare and 1¾ to 2 hours for medium-rare. Do not overcook. To test for doneness insert an instant-read thermometer into the center of the roast, so that it does not touch a bone. When cooked to rare, the temperature will be 120°F; 135°F for medium-rare; 155°F for medium. We won't go any more well done than that. Remember, the prime rib will continue to cook after it leaves the oven.

4 Transfer the roast to a cutting board, preferably one with a grooved border to catch the meat juices when you carve the roast. Loosely tent the roast with aluminum foil (drape the foil over it; don't bunch the foil around the meat) and let it rest for about 15 minutes. (This is a good time to make Classic Yorkshire Pudding, see page 521.)

5 Show off the roast, then carve it at the table. Start by sliding a carving knife just behind the ribs down to the bottom. Remove the ribs and cut into individual bones. Let 8 guests fight over 4 bones. That will give you time to cut the meat crosswise into slices, thick or thin depending on your preference.

BEER-BRAISED CHUCK STEAK

A guy should know how to cook with beer. Peter De Clercq is going to show us how. Owner of the restaurant Elckerlijc in Belgium, Peter is one of the foremost grill masters of Europe. So what's he doing here with a dish you cook in the oven? Peter is Flemish, you see, and carbonnade, beef braised with onions and beer, is one of the national dishes—make that one of the national obsessions—of Belgium. You start with a tough, cheap cut of beef and braise it in rich, malty Belgian beer with sweet caramelized onions—lots of onions. After about twenty minutes prep time you can sit back for three or four hours and let the low, moist heat do the work of breaking down tough meat fibers to produce a roast so tender, you can cut it with the side of a fork. **Serves 6 to 8**

SHOP There are several options for the beef in addition to chuck steak: blade steak, pot roast, even brisket. Whatever cut you choose, the beef should be flavorful, tough, and relatively cheap.

GEAR Your basic kitchen gear including a large heavy pot or Dutch oven with a tight-fitting lid, plus a serving platter (optional; you can serve right from the pot)

WHAT ELSE For the best results (and the most authentic), use a Belgian-style red ale. Want to use *really* good canned plum tomatoes? Try the organic "Fire-Roasted" by Muir Glen.

TIME 3½ to 4 hours

---

1 chuck steak (3 to 4 pounds)

Coarse salt (kosher or sea) and freshly ground black pepper

About 3 tablespoons unbleached all-purpose white flour

2 tablespoons vegetable oil

2 tablespoons (¼ stick) butter

2 pounds onions (3 to 4 large onions), peeled and thinly sliced

1 tablespoon dark brown sugar, or to taste

1 tablespoon tomato paste

1 tablespoon Dijon mustard, plus mustard for serving

1 can (28 ounces) plum tomatoes, coarsely chopped with their juices

1½ cups red or dark Belgian beer

About 1½ cups beef or chicken stock, preferably homemade (page 549), or water

2 bay leaves

---

1 Preheat the oven to 275°F.

2 Generously season the meat on both sides with salt and pepper. Sprinkle the flour on both sides, shaking off any excess.

3 Heat the oil in a large heavy pot or Dutch oven over medium heat. Brown the beef on both sides, about 5 minutes per side, turning with tongs. Brown the sides, too. Transfer the beef to a platter. Pour off and discard all but about 2 tablespoons of fat from the pot.

4 Melt the butter in the fat in the pot over medium heat. Add the onions and cook them until they are a deep golden brown, 8 to 12 minutes, stirring often. Lower the heat as necessary to keep the onions from burning.

5 Stir the brown sugar, tomato paste, and mustard into the onions and cook for 1 minute. Add the tomatoes with their juice and the beer, 1½ cups of beef stock, and the bay leaves to the onions, stir to mix, and let come to a boil. Return the browned meat to the pot, spooning half of the onion mixture on top so it covers the beef. Cover the pot with a tight-fitting lid and place it in the oven.

6 Cook the beef until very tender (you'll be able to pull it apart with 2 forks), 3 to 4 hours, checking every half hour or so to make sure it doesn't dry out or burn. If the meat starts to dry out (the cooking liquid in the pan should be at least 1½ inches deep), add a little more stock or water.

7 Remove the pot from the oven, uncover, and let the beef cool for about 5 minutes. Taste the sauce for seasoning, adding salt and pepper (and a little additional brown sugar if needed) to taste. Remove and discard the bay leaves. When you serve the beef, make sure everyone gets plenty of onions and sauce. Serve with mustard and the same beer you used for cooking. Like most braises and stews, carbonnade tastes great the day it's made and even better the day after. Leftovers will keep for at least 3 days covered in the refrigerator. Reheat in a low (275°F) oven.

BEEF STEW
WITH SCOTCH WHISKY AND LEMON

SHOP There's nothing here you can't find at your local supermarket.

GEAR Your basic kitchen gear including a large heavy pot or Dutch oven with a tight-fitting lid, plus a Microplane

Beef stew eases your hunger the way a pair of old sneakers soothes your feet. It isn't complicated—you need no special culinary skills to prepare it. You can't wax rhapsodic about the juxtaposition of unexpected ingredients or the ingenuity of the technique. But you just can't beat it on a cold winter night or after a strenuous day of hiking, hunting, or football (played or watched). I'm not about to reinvent the wheel, but I will tell you that if your average beef stew tastes good made with water or stock, it becomes absolutely heroic fortified with red wine and smoky Scotch whisky. The freshly grated lemon zest gives the stew the brightness of high definition TV. **Serves 4**

2 pounds top round, bottom round, or other stew beef, cut into 2-inch pieces

Coarse salt (kosher or sea) and freshly ground black pepper

About ½ cup unbleached all-purpose white flour, plus 1 tablespoon for thickening the stew

2 tablespoons canola oil

1 large onion, peeled and diced

1 rib celery, diced

1 clove garlic, peeled and finely chopped

½ cup Scotch whisky or bourbon

1 cup red wine

About 3 cups beef or chicken stock, preferably homemade (page 549)

1 bay leaf

1 sprig fresh thyme or 1 teaspoon dried thyme

1 pound carrots, peeled, trimmed, and cut crosswise into 2-inch chunks

1 pound fingerling potatoes or new potatoes, scrubbed, large potatoes cut into 1½-inch pieces

6 ounces shiitake mushrooms, stems removed, mushrooms wiped clean with a damp paper towel, and quartered

½ pound green beans, ends snapped off, beans cut crosswise into 2-inch pieces

1 teaspoon Worcestershire sauce

2 teaspoons finely grated fresh lemon zest (see Note)

WHAT ELSE Don't be put off by the number of ingredients in the recipe. And if you don't have an ingredient (other than the beef), don't let that deter you. By its very nature, stew is a dish of improvisation.

TIME about 30 minutes preparation time, plus about 3 hours cooking time

1 Preheat the oven to 300°F.

2 Generously season the beef on all sides with salt and pepper. Place the ½ cup flour in a brown paper or large zip-top plastic bag. Add the beef, seal the bag, and shake till the beef is coated in the flour. Remove the beef and shake off any excess flour.

3 Heat the oil in a large heavy pot or Dutch oven over medium-high heat until shimmering. Working in several batches, add the beef in a single layer and cook it until darkly browned on all sides, 6 to 8 minutes. Don't overcrowd the pot; you should leave at least 1 inch between the pieces of meat (if you overcrowd the pot, the meat will stew rather than sear to a rich brown). Transfer the browned meat to a platter. Work in batches as needed.

4 Pour out and discard all but about 2 tablespoons of fat from the pot. Add the onion, celery, and garlic and cook over medium heat until golden brown, about 3 minutes, stirring with a wooden spoon.

5 Return the beef to the pot. Add the Scotch and boil over high heat until reduced by half, 3 to 5 minutes.

6 Add the wine and bring to a boil over high heat. Add enough beef or chicken stock to cover the beef by 1 inch and let come to a boil, scraping up the brown bits from the bottom of the pot with a wooden spoon. Add the bay leaf and thyme. Cover the pot with a tight-fitting lid and place it in the oven. Bake the stew for 1 hour. (You can certainly cook the stew on the stovetop, but I prefer the oven so you don't need to worry about the stew scorching on the bottom.)

7 Remove the pot from the oven and uncover. Using a ladle or soup spoon, skim off any fat (oily residue) from the surface of the stew. Stir in the carrots and potatoes. Add more stock or water as needed so all of the ingredients are covered. Re-cover the pot and continue baking the stew for 1 hour.

8 Stir in the shiitakes, green beans, and 1 teaspoon of pepper (or to taste; I'll leave it to you to dose your own punishment). Continue baking the stew, uncovered, until the beef and vegetables are tender and the sauce is concentrated and flavorful, another 30 minutes, about 2½ hours in all.

9 Remove and discard the bay leaf and thyme sprig. Place the Worcestershire sauce and 2 teaspoons water in a small bowl and stir in the 1 tablespoon of flour to make a smooth paste. Stir this paste into the stew and place the pot on a stovetop burner. Let come to a boil over medium-high heat; the sauce should thicken slightly. Stir in the lemon zest. Let the stew simmer to meld the flavors, about 5 minutes. Taste for seasoning, adding salt and pepper to taste; the stew should be highly seasoned. Serve the stew from the pot.

Note: The zest is the oil-rich outer rind of the lemon. Remove it with a Microplane (see page 15), being careful to grate only the yellow rind, not the bitter white pith underneath. Don't have a Microplane? Get one. You could use a box grater (small hole side), but a Microplane works easier and better.

How to Cube Beef

1 Lay the slab of beef on the cutting board and cut crosswise into wide (2-inch) strips.

2 Some of the end pieces may wind up a little wider than 2 inches—don't worry.

3 Using the flat part of the knife blade, turn the steak 90 degrees.

4 Cut the steak crosswise again to form wide (2-inch) cubes.

5 Make the cubes as even as possible.

6 Here's your cubed beef ready for searing and stewing.

PAC-RIM SHORT RIBS
BRAISED WITH GINGER AND LEMONGRASS

These ribs were inspired by iNG ("imagining New Gastronomy"), Homaro Cantu's visionary restaurant in Chicago's meatpacking district. If you're like me, you'll love the aromatic blast of ginger and lemongrass and soulful flavors of sake and soy sauce. Homaro Cantu takes the additional step of crisping the braised ribs on a hot grill. Such is our haste to eat them hot out of the oven, I rarely get to that step at my house, but you will find instructions below. **Serves 4**

4 pounds bone-in beef short ribs, cut into individual ribs

Coarse salt (kosher or sea) and freshly ground black pepper

2 tablespoons vegetable oil

1 bunch scallions, trimmed, both white and green parts finely chopped; set aside 2 tablespoons of the green parts, for serving

2 carrots, peeled, trimmed, and finely chopped

5 cloves garlic, peeled

5 stalks lemongrass, trimmed (cut off and discard the top two-thirds) and cut into 2-inch pieces

1 piece (2 inches) peeled fresh ginger, cut into ¼-inch slices

1 cup soy sauce

1 cup sake

¼ cup rice vinegar

½ packed cup dark brown sugar

SHOP Lemongrass is an Asian herb with an herbal, lemony flavor but no acidity. It looks a little like an overgrown scallion. You can find it in the produce section of most supermarkets (look for it with the packaged herbs), but you'll get bigger, better lemongrass for less money at an Asian market. Can't find lemongrass? Substitute four ½-by-1½-inch strips of lemon zest.

GEAR Your basic kitchen gear including a large heavy pot or Dutch oven with a tight-fitting lid and a platter

WHAT ELSE When selecting short ribs, look for ones with a high proportion of meat to bones and fat.

TIME about 30 minutes preparation time, plus about 3 hours cooking time

1 Preheat the oven to 300°F.

2 Very generously season the short ribs on all sides with salt and pepper. Heat the oil in a large heavy pot or Dutch oven over high heat until shimmering. Working in several batches, add the short ribs and cook until browned, 2 to 3 minutes per side, 8 to 12 minutes in all per batch. Don't overcrowd the pot; there should never be more than 1 layer of ribs and always 1 inch between ribs. Transfer the browned ribs to a platter. Pour off and discard all but about 2 tablespoons fat from the pot.

Short Ribs Two Ways

You could think of braised short ribs as barbecue you make indoors. As with traditional barbecue, you start with tough ornery meat on the bone. You cook the short ribs in an enclosed moist environment (here a large heavy pot with a tight-fitting lid) over low heat for a long time. Cooking "low and slow" this way turns the collagen (the tough connective tissue) into gelatin, resulting in incredibly flavorful meat with an intense, concentrated flavor. I've included versions—one with a Pac-Rim combination of ginger, lemongrass, and soy sauce and one braised with wine in the French style.

3 Add the scallions, carrots, garlic, lemongrass, and ginger to the pot and cook over high heat until lightly browned, about 3 minutes. Stir in the soy sauce, sake, rice vinegar, brown sugar, and 4 cups of water and bring to a boil.

4 Return the ribs to the pot, turning and immersing them in the braising mixture. Cover the pot with a tight-fitting lid and place it in the oven. Cook the ribs until very tender, 3 to 4 hours, turning them a couple of times so that they cook evenly. Check from time to time to make sure the liquid in the pot is at least 2 inches deep. Add water as needed. The meat will have shrunk back from the ends of the bone and be easy to pull apart with two forks.

5 Remove the pot from the oven. Let the ribs rest for about 5 minutes, then using a metal soupspoon, skim off as much fat as possible from the surface of the cooking liquid. A purist would transfer the ribs to a platter, then strain the sauce over them, but I like the chunky appearance of the lemongrass pieces and ginger. You can nibble on the pieces of lemongrass to extract the flavor, but you don't really eat them (too fibrous). Yes, you can eat the ginger. Taste for seasoning, adding salt and pepper to taste. Sprinkle the reserved scallion greens over the ribs and dig in.

WINE-BRAISED SHORT RIBS
WITH BACON AND MUSHROOMS

This is what beef Burgundy would taste like if the French used short ribs instead of cubes of stewing beef. Bacon and mushrooms give you rich umami flavors, while the potatoes and carrots make this a one-pot meal. I know this looks complicated because the recipe is lengthy. Don't let that mislead you—it's really just a series of simple steps. **Serves 4**

4 slices thick-sliced artisanal bacon, cut crosswise into $\frac{1}{4}$-inch slivers

4 pounds bone-in beef short ribs cut into individual ribs

Coarse salt (kosher or sea) and freshly ground black pepper

3 tablespoons unbleached all-purpose white flour

1 pound fingerling potatoes, scrubbed and dried

1 pound carrots, peeled, trimmed, and cut crosswise into 2-inch pieces

12 ounces cremini, shiitake, or button mushrooms, stems removed, mushrooms wiped clean with a damp paper towel

3 shallots, or 1 medium-size sweet onion, peeled and finely chopped

1 clove garlic, peeled and minced

1 bottle (750 milliliters) dry red wine

2 tablespoons tomato paste

1 bay leaf

2 tablespoons chopped fresh chives (optional)

1 Preheat the oven to 300°F.

2 Place the bacon in a large heavy pot or Dutch oven over medium heat. Cook until lightly browned, about 3 minutes, stirring often. Using a slotted spoon, transfer the cooked bacon to a platter lined with paper towels and set aside. Keep the bacon fat in the pot for browning the short ribs.

3 Very generously season the short ribs on all sides with salt and pepper. Sprinkle the flour over the short ribs, tossing them to coat evenly. Working in several batches, add the short ribs to the pot and cook over high heat until browned, 2 to 3 minutes per side, 8 to 12 minutes in all per batch. Don't overcrowd the pot; there should never be more than 1 layer of ribs and always 1 inch between the ribs. Transfer the ribs to the platter with the bacon.

4 Pour off and discard all but 3 tablespoons fat from the pot. It's best to brown the vegetables separately, so first add the potatoes and cook over high heat, stirring with a wooden spoon, until browned well, 3 to 4 minutes. Using a slotted spoon, transfer the potatoes to the platter with the ribs.

5 Next add the carrots to the pot and brown them well, 3 to 4 minutes, stirring as needed. Using a slotted spoon, transfer the carrots to the platter.

6 Add the mushrooms to the pot and brown well, 3 to 4 minutes, stirring as needed. Transfer the mushrooms to the platter. Lightly cover the bacon and vegetables with aluminum foil. They won't be added back to the pot until the short ribs have cooked for 2 hours. Leave the pot on the heat until any mushroom juices evaporate. You should be left with about 1½ tablespoons of fat.

SHOP Lots of options for wine here: Beaujolais, Cabernet Sauvignon, Pinot Noir, Shiraz, and Malbec, to name a few. The wine needn't be your most expensive ingredient, but don't use a wine so cheap for cooking that you wouldn't willingly drink it by itself. Fingerlings are elongated bite-size potatoes—harvested young and characterized by a rich, creamy texture and flavor. If they are unavailable, cut Yukon Golds into 1½-inch pieces.

GEAR Your basic kitchen gear including a large heavy pot or Dutch oven with a tight-fitting lid, plus a large platter

WHAT ELSE Once you understand the basic principle of braising, you can do it with just about anything. Substitute chicken for the short ribs and you get coq au vin (cooks in about 1½ hours). Use veal shanks instead of the ribs, white wine instead of red, and add tomatoes, and you get osso buco (cook it for about 3 to 4 hours). The point is to use this recipe as a broad guide rather than a specific formula.

TIME about 30 minutes preparation time, plus about 3 to 3½ hours cooking time

7 Once the liquid has evaporated, add the shallots and garlic and cook until lightly browned, about 3 minutes, stirring often.

8 Add the wine to the onions and garlic and let it come to a boil over high heat, about 3 minutes, scraping up the brown bits from the bottom of the pot with a wooden spoon (this is called deglazing, and it's one of the secrets to building a rich sauce layered with flavor). Stir in the tomato paste, then return the ribs to the pot. Add the bay leaf, cover the pot with a tight-fitting lid, and place it in the oven. Cook the ribs until partially cooked, about 2 hours, turning them a couple of times so that they cook evenly. Check from time to time to make sure the liquid in the pot is at least 2 inches deep. Add water as needed.

9 Remove the pot from the oven and uncover it. Using a metal soupspoon, skim any visible fat off the top of the cooking liquid. Stir in the bacon and the browned potatoes, carrots, mushrooms, shallots, and garlic to the pot, stirring to mix them with the ribs. Cover the pot again and return it to the oven. Cook the mixture until the rib meat is very tender (it will have shrunk back ½ to 1 inch from the ends of the bones) and the potatoes and carrots are cooked through (they're easily pierced with the tip of a knife), about 1 hour.

10 Remove the pot from the oven and uncover. Let the ribs rest for about 5 minutes, then using the soupspoon, skim off any additional fat from the surface of the cooking liquid. Discard the bay leaf. Taste for seasoning, adding salt and pepper to taste. Serve the ribs and vegetables right out of the pot with chives sprinkled on top.

Variation
Beer-Braised Short Ribs

Prepare the ribs as described above, substituting 1 cup beer and 2 cups beef or chicken stock for the wine. A tablespoon of curry powder stirred in once the onions and garlic are browned (Step 7) and right before you add the beer in Step 8 wouldn't hurt, and you may need a spoonful of brown sugar to offset the bitterness of the hops in the beer.

FRENCH BISTRO STYLE BRISKET
BRAISED WITH RED WINE AND COGNAC

The Paris bistro Benoit opened its doors in 1912. I've dined there off and on for the last forty years, and what I like best, besides the vintage bistro setting—tin ceiling, black and white tile floors, comfy banquettes with glass partitions—is a menu that's a veritable time capsule of classical French cuisine.

French mega-chef Alain Ducasse owns it now, but for decades a large, stern, mustachioed man named Monsieur Petit ran Benoit like his personal fiefdom. His job was to serve you his conception of the perfect French meal, and if he didn't approve of the way you ordered or your choice of wine, he set you straight without asking. The menu paid homage to classic French guy food—oysters, organ meats, snails, wild game—the sort of fare favored by the burly butchers who worked the old Les Halles food market nearby. One dish I ordered without fail was *boeuf à la mode*, a wine-braised pot roast. It came in a heavy pot, the aroma invading the room, the sauce a soulful amalgam of red wine and root vegetables, the meat tender enough to slice with your fork. When I make it at home, I like to use brisket. **Serves 6 to 8**

SHOP This is a good dish to prepare with a small piece of brisket—3½ to 4 pounds—a size that is difficult to cook on a grill. The wine needn't be vintage but it should be good enough to drink while you're cooking. Thanks to the braising liquid, you can use a leaner cut of brisket for this dish than you would for smoking.

GEAR Your basic kitchen gear including a large heavy pot or Dutch oven with a tight-fitting lid and a platter

WHAT ELSE Tradition calls for marinating the brisket overnight with red wine to cover and finely chopped vegetables. If you have the time, this will definitely deepen the flavor. The next day, drain the meat and vegetables and blot both dry with paper towels before cooking. You can re-use the wine to braise the meat (Step 7).

TIME about 45 minutes
preparation time, plus 4 to 5
hours cooking time

1 slab (about 3 pounds) center-cut beef
   brisket

4 slices thick-sliced artisanal bacon, cut
   crosswise into ¼-inch slivers

24 pearl onions, peeled (warning: this can
   be time-consuming), or 6 small onions,
   peeled and quartered

8 medium-size carrots, peeled, trimmed,
   and cut crosswise into 2-inch pieces,
   plus 2 carrots, peeled, trimmed, and
   finely chopped

1 pound small red or new potatoes,
   cut in half

Coarse salt (kosher or sea) and freshly
   ground black pepper

1 onion, peeled and finely chopped

2 ribs celery, finely chopped

2 cloves garlic, peeled and finely chopped

2 bay leaves

½ cup Cognac

1 bottle (750 milliliters) fruity red wine,
   like Beaujolais

2 tablespoons tomato paste

1 tablespoon chopped chives (optional)

1 Preheat the oven to 275°F.

2 Trim any excess fat (more than ¼ inch) off the brisket.

3 Place the bacon in a large heavy pot or Dutch oven over medium heat and cook until browned, about 3 minutes. Using a slotted spoon, transfer the bacon to a platter.

4 Add the pearl onions, carrot pieces, and potatoes to the pot, increase the heat to medium-high, and cook until browned, about 3 minutes, stirring often. Using the slotted spoon, transfer the browned onions, carrots, and potatoes to the platter with the bacon. Lightly cover the bacon and vegetables with aluminum foil. They won't be added back to the pot until the brisket has cooked for 3 hours. Pour off and discard all but about 2 tablespoons of the bacon fat from the pot.

5 Very generously season the brisket on all sides with salt and pepper. Place the brisket in the pot and sear it in the hot bacon fat over medium-high heat until darkly browned, about 5 minutes per side. Transfer the brisket to a plate. Pour off and discard all but 2 tablespoons of fat.

6 Add the chopped carrots, onion, celery, garlic, and bay leaves to the pot and cook until browned, about 4 minutes, stirring often.

7 Add the Cognac and let come to a boil, stirring up the brown bits from the bottom of the pot with the wooden spoon (this is called deglazing). Return the brisket to the pot. Add the wine and tomato paste and bring to a boil. Cover the pot with a tight-fitting lid and place it in the oven. Cook the brisket until semi-tender, about 3 hours, checking once or twice to make sure the meat doesn't stick to the pot or scorch on the bottom.

8 Remove the pot from the oven. Uncover the pot, and using a large spoon, spoon off and discard any fat floating on the surface. Stir in the bacon, browned pearl onions, carrot pieces, and potatoes. Cover the pot, return it to the oven, and continue cooking the brisket for 1 hour longer.

9 Remove the pot from the oven. Uncover the pot, spoon off the fat again, and return the uncovered pot to the oven. Cook the brisket until it is very tender, some of the pan juices have evaporated, and the sauce starts to thicken, 30 minutes to 1 hour more. Remove the pot from the oven and let the brisket rest for about 10 minutes.

10 Again, spoon off any fat that has risen to the surface. Remove and discard the bay leaves. Transfer the brisket to a cutting board and thinly slice it crosswise across the grain.

11 Place the pot with the sauce and vegetables on the stove over medium-high heat and bring to a boil. Boil the sauce until concentrated and flavorful, about 3 minutes. Taste for seasoning, adding salt and pepper to taste; the sauce should be highly seasoned.

12 Return the sliced brisket to the sauce and vegetables. Sprinkle the chopped chives, if using, on top. Serve the brisket French bistro style directly from the pot.

Rice Bowl with Fried Eggs, Mini-burgers, and Pac-Rim Gravy

LOCO MOCO

Hamburger, fried egg, white rice, and instant gravy may not sound like a formula for gustatory wonderment. But for many Hawaiians, loco moco (for that's what they call this rib-sticking combination) is the ultimate comfort food, equally welcome at breakfast, lunch, dinner, or as a midnight snack. In the last few years, I've watched loco moco move from the confines of the Aloha State to hip restaurants in Los Angeles, Portland, and Seattle, and along the way, it's gotten a makeover. My rendition features Pac-Rim seasonings, like ginger, sesame oil, and hoisin sauce, and homemade gravy in place of the traditional store-bought glop. Surf's up, guys. Loco moco will make sure you don't meet it on an empty stomach. **Serves 4**

SHOP Hoisin sauce is a sweet-salty Chinese condiment available in the ethnic food section of most supermarkets and at natural foods stores. Use an Asian-style sesame oil, pressed from roasted seeds; it will have a nuttier flavor than an oil made from raw sesame seeds.

GEAR Your basic kitchen gear including a large (10- to 12-inch) nonstick skillet

WHAT ELSE Loco moco isn't complicated, but it does require a bit of choreography to have all the elements come together at once. I generally start with rice left over from a previous dinner or Chinese carryout.

TIME about 1 hour

1 bunch scallions, trimmed, both white and green parts thinly sliced crosswise; set aside 2 tablespoons of the green parts for serving

1 piece (3 inches) ginger, peeled and minced

2 cloves garlic, peeled and minced

2 pounds ground beef

4 tablespoons soy sauce, or more to taste

4 tablespoons hoisin sauce

3 tablespoons Asian (dark) sesame oil

½ teaspoon freshly ground black pepper

4 cups warm cooked rice (page 488)

½ teaspoon hot red pepper flakes

½ cup mirin (sweet rice wine) or sake

1½ cups beef or chicken stock, preferably homemade (page 549)

1 tablespoon brown sugar or granulated sugar, or more to taste

1 teaspoon cornstarch dissolved in 1 tablespoon water (stir it to form a paste)

2 tablespoons (¼ stick) butter

4 large eggs

1 Place half of the scallions, ginger, and garlic in a mixing bowl. Add the beef, 2 tablespoons each of soy sauce, hoisin sauce, and sesame oil, and the black pepper, and stir to mix. Lightly wet your hands with cold water and divide the meat into 12 equal-size portions. Form each portion into a 1½-inch patty. Arrange the patties on a plate lined with plastic wrap and cover them with more plastic wrap. Refrigerate the patties until you are ready to cook them.

2 Divide the rice among 4 bowls.

3 Heat the remaining 1 tablespoon of sesame oil in a large nonstick skillet over medium heat. Working in batches if necessary, add the patties, spacing them about 1 inch apart. Cook the burgers until browned on the outside and cooked through, about 3 minutes per side for medium. Arrange 3 burgers on top of each bowl of rice and keep warm (loosely cover with aluminum foil).

4 Pour off and discard all but about 1 tablespoon of the burger fat from the skillet. Add the remaining scallions, ginger, and garlic and the hot pepper flakes to the skillet and cook over medium-high heat until aromatic and browned, 1 to 2 minutes. Add the mirin and boil for 1 minute. Stir in the remaining 2 tablespoons of soy sauce and hoisin sauce and the beef stock and sugar and boil for 2 minutes to merge the flavors. Whisk the cornstarch mixture into the gravy and boil until slightly thickened, about 30 seconds, whisking steadily. Taste for seasoning, adding more soy sauce and/or sugar as necessary. Pour the gravy over the burgers and rice.

5 Rinse out the skillet and wipe it clean. Melt the butter in the skillet over high heat. Crack the eggs into the skillet and fry them to taste: 2 minutes for sunny-side up, 3 minutes for over-easy. Slide 1 egg into each bowl over the burgers. Sprinkle the reserved scallion greens on top and dig in.

STEAK TARTARE

ext to steak, there's no dish more primal than the hand-chopped, assertively seasoned uncooked beef dish known as steak tartare. Like oysters or sashimi, it offers irrefutable proof that first-rate ingredients are often best appreciated raw. Steak tartare makes a refreshing lunch (especially welcome in warm weather), an invigorating supper, and you can serve it as a starter or main course. Salty with anchovies and capers and tangy with mustard and fresh lemon juice, it is infinitely customizable. (Koreans season it with chili paste and sesame oil; Turks make it with minced raw lamb and bulghur.) In short, steak tartare belongs in every guy's repertory: Here's your blueprint. **Serves 4 as an appetizer, 2 or 3 as a main course**

SHOP No cheaping out on this one: You want fresh beef tenderloin purchased from a butcher you trust. As when serving any raw meat or seafood, follow the food safety tips on page 104.

GEAR Your basic kitchen gear

WHAT ELSE Many are the uses for a food processor, but chopping steak for tartare is not one of them. (The blade tears and mashes the meat, rather than chops it.) Use a well-sharpened chef's knife and some elbow grease. Traditionally, steak tartare comes crowned with a raw egg yolk, which is mixed into the beef at the moment of serving for extra richness. To avoid the risk of any food-borne illnesses, use a pasteurized egg (see page 41).

TIME 15 minutes

1 pound best-quality beef tenderloin, preferably cut from the center

1 large shallot, peeled and minced (about 4 tablespoons)

2 tablespoons minced fresh flat leaf parsley

2 tablespoons drained capers

2 anchovy fillets, drained, blotted dry, and finely chopped, plus 3 whole fillets for serving

1 tablespoon Dijon mustard, or to taste

1 tablespoon extra virgin olive oil

1 tablespoon fresh lemon juice, or to taste

2 teaspoons Worcestershire sauce, or to taste

1 teaspoon coarse salt (kosher or sea), or to taste

½ teaspoon freshly ground black pepper, or to taste

2 or 3 Boston lettuce leaves for serving (optional)

1 raw egg yolk (optional)

Thin baguette slices, toasted, for serving

1 Trim and discard any fat, sinew, or silverskin from the beef. Cut the meat crosswise into ½-inch-thick slices, then cut the slices into ½-inch chunks. Chop the chunks as fine as possible. Place the chopped meat in a large mixing bowl. (You can chop the beef up to an hour ahead and store it wrapped in plastic in the refrigerator. You should mix in the flavorings right before serving.)

2 Add the shallot, parsley, capers, and chopped anchovies to the bowl and stir with a wooden spoon to mix. Stir in the mustard, olive oil, lemon juice, Worcestershire sauce, salt, and pepper. Taste for seasoning, adding any ingredient you want more of; the steak tartare should be highly seasoned.

3 Line a plate or shallow bowl with lettuce leaves, if using. Mound the steak tartare on top, making a 1-inch depression in the center. Arrange the 3 whole anchovies in a triangle around the depression and place the raw egg yolk, if using, in the center. Serve with large spoons, breaking the egg yolk and mixing it and the anchovies into the meat. Serve the toasts on the side.

Variation
Salmon Tartare

Prepare as described above, using 1 pound of wild salmon fillets for the steak and 2 ounces smoked salmon for the anchovies.

Run your fingers over the salmon, feeling for bones. Pull out and discard any you find with needle-nose pliers.

HAMMERED VEAL CHOPS

SHOP You need veal rib chops for this preparation—about 1 inch thick, preferably organic. For a really dramatic rendition, order long-bone veal chops from a specialty meat purveyor, like Allen Brothers or Lobel's.

Picture a crisp, golden, monster-size breaded veal chop that all but buries the plate at a really good Italian restaurant. Now picture that chop at home. The secret is to pound it with a meat mallet—an act that summons your inner Thor. Pounding tenderizes the meat, but it also helps flatten the chop enough so that it cooks through without burning the crust. And to take your veal chop over the top, you're going to add lemon zest and Parmigiano Reggiano cheese to the crust. Actually, this is *better* than what you order at an Italian restaurant. **Serves 2; can be multiplied as desired**

2 veal rib chops (each ¾ to 1 pound)

Coarse salt (kosher or sea) and freshly ground black pepper

2 teaspoons dried oregano

1 cup unbleached all-purpose white flour

2 large eggs

½ cup milk

2 cups bread crumbs, preferably homemade (page 459)

¾ cup (3 ounces) freshly and finely grated Parmigiano Reggiano cheese (optional)

1 teaspoon finely grated lemon zest (see Note)

1 tablespoon butter

1 tablespoon extra virgin olive oil, or more as needed

Lemon wedges, for serving

1 Preheat the oven to 400°F.

2 Place a veal chop in a large heavy-duty resealable plastic bag (the bone will probably stick out of the top). Starting at one edge and working to the other, pound the chop with the meat mallet or a heavy skillet or meat cleaver to flatten it to about ¼ inch thick. Repeat with the second chop. Generously season the chops with salt and pepper and the oregano.

3 Place the flour in a shallow bowl or on a piece of aluminum foil. Place the eggs and milk in a second shallow bowl and beat with a fork to mix. Place the bread crumbs in a third wide shallow bowl or a pie plate and stir in the Parmigiano Reggiano cheese, if using, and lemon zest.

4 Dip each chop in the flour on both sides, shaking off the excess, then in the egg mixture, then in the bread crumb mixture, coating it well. Place the chops on the baking sheet.

5 Melt the butter in the oil in a large cast-iron or nonstick skillet over medium-high heat, swirling the skillet to coat it. When the foaming subsides, add 1 chop and brown it on both sides, about 3 minutes per side, turning it over with a spatula. Transfer the browned chop back to the baking sheet. Add a little more oil to the skillet if it seems too dry. Brown the second chop the same way and place it on the baking sheet.

6 Bake the chops on the baking sheet until cooked through, about 15 minutes. To test for doneness, make a little cut in one side of the chops near the bone (ideally on the less attractive bottom side). Transfer the chops to a platter or plates and serve with lemon wedges.

Note: The zest is the oil-rich outer rind of the lemon. Remove it with a Microplane (see page 15) or box grater, being careful to grate only the yellow rind, not the bitter white pith underneath.

GEAR The first thing you need is a meat pounder. A butcher's mallet works well (buy the heaviest one you find), but so will the bottom of a heavy skillet or the side of a heavy cleaver. In addition to your basic kitchen gear including a large (10- to 12-inch) cast-iron or nonstick skillet and a baking sheet, you'll also need a large heavy-duty resealable plastic bag.

WHAT ELSE You can certainly cook the veal chops all the way through in a skillet. But I like to brown them on the stovetop and finish cooking them in the oven—there's less attention required and less risk of burning the crust.

TIME about 30 minutes

Variations

Veal chops with lemon and caper butter: To make a simple skillet sauce for the chops, just before serving add 4 tablespoons (½ stick) of butter to the skillet in which you browned the chops (there is no need to clean the skillet). Cook the butter over medium-high heat until browned, 1 to 2 minutes. Watch carefully: Don't let the butter burn (become black); reduce the heat if necessary. Add 3 tablespoons of chopped fresh parsley and 2 tablespoons of drained capers and cook until both are crisp, about 2 minutes. Stir in the juice from the lemon you grated earlier (2 to 3 tablespoons). Let the lemon and caper butter boil for 1 minute, then pour half over each chop right before serving.

Veal chops Parmesan: Cook the veal chops as described above. Once they are fully baked, leave the oven on. Top each chop with thinly sliced fresh mozzarella—the good stuff, sold packed in water (see page 76). Spoon some of your favorite tomato sauce (homemade if possible) over the mozzarella and sprinkle 1 cup of finely grated Parmigiano Reggiano cheese over the sauce. Return the veal chops to the oven and bake them until the sauce is bubbling and the cheese is melted and very lightly browned, 5 to 10 minutes.

Wiener schnitzel: Substitute 1 pound of veal cutlets for the veal chops and you get Wiener schnitzel. The cooking time for veal cutlets will be shorter, 3 to 4 minutes per side in the skillet. (There's no need to bake them in the oven.)

If you top the breaded veal cutlets with anchovies and fried eggs you get a belt-loosening German specialty called Wiener schnitzel à la Holstein (named for a province in northern Germany—the same region that gave us Holstein cattle).

Hammered pork chops: A more affordable version of the veal chops can be made with pork rib chops. You'll need two chops, each 1 inch thick and weighing 12 to 14 ounces. The cooking time will be the same as for the veal chops.

HOG

Think of your culinary bucket list—dishes you need to master before you consider your culinary education complete. I'll wager at least a half dozen come from a pig. There's bacon, which I'm pretty sure you eat and would probably like to know how to fry without spattering fat all over your stove. There are baby backs to barbecue in the best Kansas City tradition, and pork shoulders to smoke and "pull" like they do in the Carolinas. There's *porchetta*—Italy's rosemary-, sage-, and garlicky pork roast. You might even want to stir-fry pork belly in the style of Chairman Mao.

Well, in this chapter, we're going to eat high on the hog—an expression, incidentally, that dates from Colonial times, when the upper classes ate pork loin, tenderloin, and other tender cuts adjacent to the pig's backbone, while the poor had to content themselves with pork belly, ribs, ears, ham hocks, and pigs' feet. I'll tell you how to panfry the perfect pork chop (keeping it moist) and roast the best bargain in the meat department—pork tenderloin—here with a coffee crust and redeye gravy.

CAROLINA PULLED PORK SANDWICHES
WITH PIG PICKER PUCKER SAUCE

You can't get much more American than pulled pork, so patriotism alone requires you to learn how to make it. This spice-rubbed, hickory-smoked pork shoulder torn into meaty shreds, doused with vinegar sauce, and served on a sesame bun with sweet pickles epitomizes the barbecue of the Carolinas and Deep South. I'll leave it to local partisans to slug out the fine points: Should the meat be shredded, chopped, or sliced? Serve it with or without "brownies"—the burnt bits of pork skin? Should the sauce be flavored with mustard, ketchup, or hot pepper flakes? Well, you know how these debates go. All alternatives are here—the choice is yours. **Makes 12 pulled pork sandwiches**

For the pork
1 bone-in pork shoulder
   (aka Boston butt; 5 to 6 pounds)

½ cup Raichlen's Rub #1 (page 285) or
   your favorite barbecue rub

For the Pig Picker Pucker Sauce
1½ cups cider vinegar

2 tablespoons light or dark brown sugar,
   or more to taste

1 tablespoon Louisiana-style hot sauce,
   such as Crystal, or more to taste

2 teaspoons coarse salt (kosher or sea)

1 to 2 teaspoons hot red pepper flakes

1 teaspoon freshly ground black pepper

½ teaspoon liquid smoke (optional)

For serving
12 sesame seed hamburger buns

4 tablespoons (½ stick) butter, melted

1 jar (16 ounces) sweet pickle chips

4 cups Southern Mustard Slaw
   (page 178) or Creamy Horseradish
   Slaw (page 177)

SHOP See pork shoulder shopping information on page 275.

GEAR Your basic kitchen gear including an instant-read thermometer, plus insulated rubber gloves, and 2 large forks (optional); if grilling, your basic grilling gear including an aluminum foil pan and a charcoal grill

WHAT ELSE Tradition calls for the pork to be roasted for half a day in a smoky pit over a bed of glowing hickory embers. Thanks to a pork shoulder's high fat content, you can cook it at a higher temperature in about three hours. The best way to approximate a pit at home (unless you have a smoker) is with a charcoal-burning kettle grill and 3 cups hardwood chips soaked in water for 30 minutes and drained.

Apartment-bound pork lovers can produce a credible pulled pork in the oven, and you'll find instructions for doing that here. (If you do cook the pork indoors, I suggest you add a few drops of liquid smoke to the vinegar sauce.)

TIME about 15 minutes preparation time, plus 3 hours cooking time

1 **Prepare the pork:** Place the pork shoulder in a roasting pan and generously season it on all sides with the rub, massaging the spices onto the meat. You can cook the pork right away, but you'll get even more flavor if you let it cure in the refrigerator for a couple of hours or overnight.

2 *Roasting Method*: Preheat the oven to 325°F. Place the pork, fat side up, in the roasting pan in the oven. Roast until sizzling, crisp, and darkly browned on the outside and the internal temperature registers 190° to 195°F on an instant-read thermometer inserted into the thickest part of the meat, about 3 hours. From time to time, spoon any pan juices over the top of the pork shoulder.

Grilling method: Set up the grill for indirect grilling, place an aluminum foil drip pan in the center, and preheat the grill to medium (325°F). When ready to cook, brush and oil the grill grate. Place the pork shoulder, fat side up, over the drip pan. Toss 1½ cups wood chips on the coals of a charcoal grill (¾ cup on each mound of coals) or place the chips in the smoker box of a gas grill (charcoal works best). Cover the grill and cook the pork shoulder until sizzling, crisp, and darkly browned on the outside and the internal temperature registers 190° to 195°F on an instant-read thermometer inserted into the thickest part of the meat, about 3 hours. Add coals as needed (about every hour) to maintain this temperature (you'll need 8 to 10 coals per side), adding the remaining wood chips after 1 hour. (Don't oversmoke the meat or it will taste bitter.) In the unlikely event the pork browns too much, loosely tent it with aluminum foil.

3 **Meanwhile, make the Pig Picker Pucker Sauce:** Combine the vinegar, brown sugar, hot sauce, salt, hot red pepper flakes, black pepper, and ½ cup of water in a mixing bowl and stir until the salt and sugar dissolve. Taste for seasoning, adding more sugar and/or hot sauce as necessary. If you roasted the pork in the oven, add a few drops of liquid smoke to the sauce. The sauce will mellow when mixed with the pork.

4 Transfer the pork to a cutting board, loosely tent it with aluminum foil, and let it rest for 15 minutes. Then, wearing insulated food gloves, pull off the skin and crust. (If the skin is leathery, crisp it directly over the fire.) Finely chop these to add to the pulled pork at the end. Using your gloved fingers or 2 large forks, pull the pork into large chunks, discarding any bones or lumps of fat or gristle. Tear the pork into meaty shreds. Alternatively, you can coarsely or finely chop the pork with a meat cleaver. You can also cut it into slices across the grain with a knife.

5 Transfer the meat (and skin, if using) to a large mixing bowl or to the roasting pan once you have discarded the excess fat. Stir in Pig Picker Pucker Sauce to taste (start with ¾ cup and add more ¼ cup at a time); the pork should be tart and spicy. Transfer any remaining sauce to a bowl for serving.

6 Split the sesame buns and lightly brush the insides with the melted butter. Lightly toast the buns on the grill, under the broiler, or in a skillet over medium-high heat. Pile shredded pork onto the buns and top it with sliced pickles. Add one of the slaws. Serve additional Pig Picker Pucker Sauce on the side.

A GUY'S BEST FRIEND

PORK SHOULDER

The pork shoulder has everything a guy could wish for in a hunk of meat. Heft. Fat. Flavor. Affordability. And surprising ease of preparation. Although a whole pork shoulder tips the scale at fourteen to eighteen pounds and a Boston butt (the top half of the shoulder; the cut most commonly sold at the supermarket) weighs five to seven pounds, this large hunk of meat comes out remarkably tender. And that's true whether you roast, braise, grill, smoke, or spit-roast it—methods commonly used for pork shoulders by hog-o-holics around the world.

Easy? To cook a pork shoulder, you season the hell out of it and cook it at a low to moderate heat for several hours. What emerges from your oven, grill, or rotisserie gives you a paradisiacal counterpoint of crisp crust and moist, meltingly tender meat. But not all pork shoulders are equal, and to get the biggest bang for the buck, you need to know a little about anatomy and animal husbandry.

CHOOSE THE RIGHT BREEDS | Hogs used to be bred for flavor; today most supermarket pork is an industrial product raised for the maximum growth in minimal time so the meat can be sold quickly and cheaply.

You often hear the complaint that pork "just doesn't taste like it used to." Ironically, the culprit may have been one of the most effective marketing campaigns in recent history: the 1987 decision by the National Pork Board to combat slumping pork sales by adopting the slogan "Pork: The Other White Meat." It was the board's declaration of war on pork fat, and one of the first casualties was flavor (because, if you recall, fat equals flavor).

But you don't want your pork to taste like chicken breast. You want it to taste like pork. Furthermore, you want your hogs raised humanely and with respect. Family farmers have heard you. A growing number raise pork the old-fashioned way—mostly outdoors—focusing on heritage breeds, like the Berkshire pig.

Often referred to by its Japanese name, *kurobuta* (literally "black pig"), the Berkshire is the crown prince of hogs, with generously marbled, dark-pink, rich-tasting meat that makes supermarket pork seem downright bland. Other heritage breeds include Red Wattle, Mangalitsa, Tamworth, and Duroc— each with its own distinct texture and flavor. Look for them at specialty butcher shops and farmers' markets. One of the trailblazers in the campaign to save heritage breeds is the SlowFood offshoot Heritage Foods USA. On their website, they sell pork shoulder samplers so you can compare the different breeds (go to heritagefoodsusa.com).

(continued on the next page)

(continued from the previous page)

CHOOSE THE RIGHT CUT | A whole pork shoulder extends from the bottom of the front leg to the top of the shoulder, excluding the trotters (feet). Commercial smoke-houses buy and cook the whole shoulder, but at the retail level you're more likely to find the top or bottom section of the shoulder.

Pork shoulder butt (also known as *Boston butt*) refers to the top of the shoulder, a gorgeous hunk of protein with tender meat and generous marbling, with a blade bone running through part of it.

Shoulder ham (also known as a picnic ham) refers to the bottom of the shoulder, including the top of the foreleg. It is not quite as well-marbled as the pork shoulder butt, but responds well to low and slow cooking.

HOW MUCH TO SERVE | When serving pork shoulder, figure on eight ounces per person for straight meat or four to six ounces per person when making sandwiches. Because pork shoulder is so fatty, it's often paired with vinegar or mustard sauce, pickles, cucumbers, and/or slaw.

USE THE RIGHT COOKING METHOD | Thanks to its generous marbling, pork shoulder lends itself to a variety of cooking methods, including roasting, indirect grilling, smoking, and spit-roasting. The advantage of these methods is that you get both crisp crust and moist, tender meat.

You can also braise pork shoulder or cook it in a slow cooker, but these methods don't give you a crust.

PLEASE OVERCOOK | In recent years, it's been fashionable in the U.S. to serve pork medium or even medium-rare, and this is fine for lean tender cuts, like loin and tenderloin. Most of the world's cultures serve pork shoulder well-done, that is, cooked to about 195°F, and you should, too. Only at this internal temperature can the shoulder be "pulled" (torn) or chopped into the meaty shreds so prized for Carolina pulled pork.

SHOULDER GEAR

AN INSTANT-READ THERMOMETER | A vital piece of equipment when gauging the doneness of a thick cut of pork as collagen and tough connective tissue don't break down until they reach a critical internal temperature of 195°F.

INSULATED FOOD GLOVES | These aren't your mother's kitchen sink gloves—not with their thick-gauge rubber and fabric lining, which protect your hands when you manually pull the still-hot pork shoulder (cold pork won't pull) into meaty shreds for pulled pork sandwiches.

Italian Garlic and Herb Stuffed Pork Loin

PORCHETTA

To judge from the current *porchetta* mania (it's been featured widely in magazine articles and cookbooks, and there's even a *porchetta* restaurant in Manhattan), you might think that this garlic- and herb-blasted roast pork sprang to life in some Little Italy here in America. But *porchetta* (pronounced por-ketta) is Italian through and through. And long before we had food trucks in North America, *porchetta* trucks plied the Italian market circuit (Wednesday, Lucca; Thursday, San Gimignano; and so on), dishing up still warm slices of the fragrant pork on bread toasted with pork fat. What you may not realize is how utterly easy it is to make authentic-tasting *porchetta* in the oven. **Serves 6**

For the herb paste and pork roast

4 cloves garlic, peeled and coarsely chopped

¼ cup packed fresh sage leaves

¼ cup packed fresh rosemary leaves

2 teaspoons coarse salt (kosher or sea)

1½ tablespoons cracked black peppercorns

1 teaspoon fennel seeds

2 strips (each ½ by 2 inches) orange zest

1 tablespoon fresh lemon juice

⅓ cup extra virgin olive oil, or more as needed

1 pork loin (3 pounds)

4 slices pancetta, unrolled into long strips

For serving (optional)

Ciabatta rolls

Olive Relish (page 91)

Caramelized onions (see page 497)

SHOP Pancetta is Italian cured pork belly. It resembles bacon, but it's not smoked, and it comes rolled up, not in flat strips. Buy it sliced and simply unroll each slice to wrap the pork. (You can find it at upscale supermarkets and natural foods supermarkets, like Whole Foods, not to mention Italian delis.) Alternatively, use conventional bacon.

GEAR Your basic kitchen gear, including a food processor, roasting pan, an instant-read thermometer, and 4 pieces of butcher's string each about 15 inches long

WHAT ELSE Smoke isn't really part of the Italian flavor palette, so this is a great dish to cook in the oven or on a gas grill. The herb paste makes more than you need for a single pork loin, but you will need all of it if you make the pork shoulder variation. Any leftover herb paste keeps well in the refrigerator, covered, for at least 1 week. It's great smeared on whole chickens or chicken breasts and veal chops.

TIME about 20 minutes preparation time, plus 2 to 12 hours for marinating (optional) and 1 to 1½ hours cooking time

1 Place the garlic, sage, rosemary, salt, pepper, fennel seeds, and orange zest in a food processor and finely chop them. Add in the lemon juice and enough olive oil to obtain a thick paste.

2 Butterfly the pork loin: Place the pork loin on a cutting board. Using a long slender sharp knife, cut through from 1 side of the loin almost to the other side about ¾ inch from the bottom. Roll open the pork. Continue cutting and

unrolling the loin as shown on page 280 until you have a flat piece of pork that's evenly ¾ inch thick. Generously spread the inside of the pork with 2 to 3 tablespoons of the herb paste and roll the loin back together so it's once again cylindrical. Generously spread the outside of the loin with more herb paste. Don't forget to coat the ends. The loin should be coated with a ⅛-inch-thick layer of paste. Set any left over paste aside for another use.

3 Preheat the oven to 375°F.

4 Tie up the stuffed loin: Arrange the 4 pieces of butcher's string going east to west on a work surface parallel to one another, each 1 inch or so apart. (Both ends of the loin should extend about 1 inch beyond the strings when they're tied.) Place 1 strip of pancetta down the center of the strings so that it is perpendicular (lay it north to south) to them. Arrange 2 more strips of pancetta parallel to and on either side of the first strip. Arrange the loin lengthwise on top of the middle strip of pancetta. Arrange the remaining strip of pancetta lengthwise on top of the loin. Pull the ends of each string up over the loin and tie them tightly together to hold the pancetta and loin in place. Put the pork loin in a roasting pan.

5 Roast the pork until sizzling and brown on the outside and cooked to taste, 1 to 1½ hours for medium. To test for doneness, insert an instant-read thermometer into the side of the loin; when done to medium the internal temperature should be 160°F, medium-well 175°F. As the loin cooks, from time to time spoon any juices that gather in the bottom of the roasting pan over the meat.

6 Transfer the *porchetta* to a cutting board and let it rest for about 5 minutes. Remove and discard the strings. Cut the pork crosswise into ½-inch-wide slices. Serve the *porchetta* by itself (more formal) or pile it onto ciabatta rolls along with Olive Relish and caramelized onions.

Variation
Pork Shoulder *Porchetta*

Thanks to its high fat content, pork shoulder makes terrific *porchetta*. Start with a 5- to 6-pound bone-in Boston butt. Using the tip of a paring knife, make a series of holes in the meat all over, each ½ inch deep and 1½ inches apart. Using a spoon and your fingers, force some herb paste into the holes. Place the pork shoulder in a roasting pan and spread more herb paste over it on all sides. Cover the roasting pan tightly with plastic wrap. Let the pork cure in the refrigerator for at least 2 hours, preferably overnight. The longer it cures, the richer the flavor will be.

Preheat the oven to 300°F. Place the pork shoulder, fat side up, on a rack in a roasting pan in the oven. Roast the pork until it is sizzling, crisp, and darkly browned on the outside and the internal temperature registers 190° to 195°F on an instant-read thermometer inserted into the thickest part of the meat, about 3 hours. From time to time, spoon any juices in the roasting pan over the pork. Rest and serve as described above.

► The secret to butterflying? Use a well-sharpened knife.

How to Butterfly a Pork Loin

1 Using a long, slender, sharp knife, make a cut the length of the loin about 2 inches deep into the loin and about ¾ inch above the cutting board.

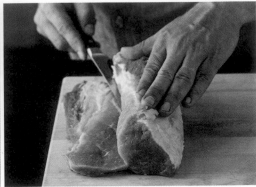

2 Unroll the loin and holding the knife parallel to the cutting board, make another 2-inch-deep lengthwise cut. Be careful not to cut through the layer.

3 As you cut, continue unrolling the pork, rather like unspooling a roll of paper towels.

4 To keep the loin from sliding, hold it down with the hand that's not doing the cutting.

5 If the layer is uneven, pound it with a meat mallet or the side of a cleaver to make it uniform.

6 When you get to the end, you'll have a flat rectangle of pork about ¾ inch thick.

COFFEE-CRUSTED PORK TENDERLOINS
WITH REDEYE GRAVY

Coffee may seem like an odd ingredient to pair with meat—well, maybe not if you're a cowboy. But there's something about coffee's earthy, bittersweet flavor that tastes awesome with roast pork. To push the coffee theme further, serve these coffee-crusted pork tenderloins with a ham-infused redeye gravy. The dish is quick enough to make on a weeknight but dramatic enough to serve at a party. **Serves 4**

1½ to 2 pounds pork tenderloin (2 to 3 tenderloins)

3 tablespoons ground coffee

1 tablespoon dark brown sugar

2 teaspoons sweet paprika

1½ teaspoons coarse salt (kosher or sea)

½ teaspoon freshly ground black pepper

½ teaspoon ground cumin

2 tablespoons extra virgin olive oil

1 tablespoon butter

Redeye Gravy (recipe follows), optional

SHOP Pork tenderloin gives you some of the biggest bang for the buck of any cut in the meat department. Like a beef tenderloin, it cooks quickly and tender with virtually no waste, but with twice the flavor of the former for a fraction of the price. Look for it in any supermarket meat case.

GEAR Your basic kitchen gear including a large (10- to 12-inch) ovenproof skillet

WHAT ELSE You can certainly cook the pork tenderloins entirely on the stove, but I find it easier to sear the meat in the skillet, then finish it in the oven.

TIME about 30 minutes

1 Preheat the oven to 400°F.

2 If the butcher hasn't done it, trim any silverskin (the shiny membrane covering the top) off the tenderloins. Arrange the tenderloins in a baking dish.

3 Place the coffee, brown sugar, paprika, salt, pepper, and cumin in a small bowl and mix with your fingers. Sprinkle the rub over the pork on all sides, rubbing it over the meat. Drizzle 1 tablespoon of the olive oil over the pork and rub it over the meat.

4 Melt the butter in the remaining 1 tablespoon of olive oil in a large ovenproof skillet over high heat. Add the pork tenderloins and sear until browned on all sides, about 2 minutes per side, 8 minutes in all. Work in two batches, if needed, so as not to crowd the pan.

5 Arrange all the seared tenderloins in the skillet and place in the oven. Continue cooking the tenderloins until they are cooked through, about 15 minutes. When done they'll feel gently yielding to the touch. The internal temperature on an instant-read thermometer inserted through the fat end will read 155° to 160°F for medium.

6 Transfer the tenderloins to a warm platter and lay a sheet of aluminum foil on top of them (do not wrap) to keep warm while you make the Redeye Gravy, if using, in the skillet.

7 To serve, transfer the pork to a cutting board and cut it on the diagonal into ½-inch slices. Serve the sliced pork on a platter or plates with Redeye Gravy spooned over it, if serving.

REDEYE GRAVY

Make the gravy right in the skillet in which you cooked the pork. (Warning: The pan's handle will be hot.) Smithfield ham is a deliciously salty, naturally cured, lightly smoked ham from Virginia. It's available at specialty markets (see Note below). **Makes about 1½ cups**

1 small onion, or 2 to 3 shallots, peeled and finely chopped (about ½ cup)

2 ounces Smithfield ham (see Note), cut into matchstick slivers

2 teaspoons unbleached all-purpose flour

1 cup brewed coffee

¼ cup heavy (whipping) cream

Coarse salt (kosher or sea) and freshly ground black pepper

Pour off all but 2 tablespoons fat from the skillet in which you cooked the pork tenderloins. Add the onion and ham and cook over medium-high heat until browned, about 3 minutes, stirring with a wooden spoon. Stir in the flour and cook, stirring steadily, until lightly browned, 30 seconds. Stir in the coffee, let it come to a boil, and boil until it is reduced to about ¾ cup, about 3 minutes, using the wooden spoon to scrape up the brown bits from the bottom of the skillet. Stir in the cream and let the gravy simmer until lightly thickened and richly flavored, about 3 minutes. Season the gravy with salt (you won't need much; the ham is salty already) and pepper to taste; the gravy should be highly seasoned.

Note: Smithfield ham can be found at most natural foods markets. If it is unavailable, you can substitute Canadian bacon or your favorite cooked smoked ham.

BABY BACK RIBS
WITH CIDER RUM BARBECUE SAUCE

These ribs sound an apple theme—you smoke them with apple wood chips and serve them with a made-from-scratch cider rum barbecue sauce. Once you master the process, you can infinitely vary the character of the ribs by changing the seasonings. Texas style? Use a rub based on cumin and chile powder and spray the ribs with beer. Jamaican style? Use jerk seasoning and spray the ribs with pineapple juice. You get the idea. **Makes 2 racks of ribs; serves 4 normal guys as part of a full meal or 2 big guys with corresponding appetites**

2 racks baby back pork ribs
(4 to 5 pounds total)

6 tablespoons Raichlen's Rub #1
(recipe follows) or your favorite
barbecue rub

1 cup apple cider in a spray bottle

Cider Rum Barbecue Sauce (page 286) or
your favorite barbecue sauce

You'll also need: 1½ cups hardwood
chips or chunks, preferably apple or
hickory, soaked in water to cover for
30 minutes, then drained

1 Set up the grill for indirect grilling (page 12), place a large aluminum foil drip pan in the center of the grill under the grate, and preheat the grill to medium (325°F).

2 Place a rack of ribs meat side down on a baking sheet. Remove the thin, papery membrane from the back of the rack by inserting a slender implement, such as the tip of an instant-read thermometer, under it; the best place to start is on one of the middle bones. Using a dishcloth, paper towel, or pliers to gain a secure grip, peel off the membrane. Repeat with the remaining rack (or ask your butcher to do it).

3 Season the ribs with barbecue rub (about 1½ tablespoons per side), rubbing the spices onto the meat with your fingertips.

4 When ready to cook, brush and oil the grill grate. Place the ribs, bone side down, in the center of the grate over the drip pan and away from the heat. (If your grill has limited space,

SHOP Baby backs are the easiest ribs to cook, thanks to their generous marbling and intrinsic tenderness. To up your game, try an heirloom breed, like Berkshire pork or Tamworth.

GEAR Your basic kitchen and grilling gear including an aluminum foil drip pan, a charcoal grill (sorry guys; you can cook the ribs on a gas grill, but you need charcoal to smoke them), a rib rack (optional), and a spray bottle

WHAT ELSE I like to smoke baby backs at a somewhat higher temperature than the low and slow guys on the barbecue circuit. Which is to say, I grill the ribs using the indirect method at 325°F rather than the 225°F of traditional barbecue. I like the way the heat melts the fat and crisps the meat fibers, giving you chewier, meatier ribs than with the lower-heat method. If you prefer your ribs to have a softer texture, cook them at 225°F for 4 to 5 hours.

TIME about 20 minutes preparation time, plus about 1½ hours cooking time

stand the racks of ribs upright in a rib rack.) Toss the wood chips on the coals. Cover the grill and cook the ribs for about 45 minutes.

5 Spray the ribs with some of the apple cider. This keeps them moist and adds an extra layer of flavor. Cover the grill again and continue cooking the ribs until they are darkly browned, cooked through, and tender enough to pull apart with your fingers, 45 minutes to 1 hour longer, 1¼ to 1½ hours in all, spraying the ribs with cider once or twice more. When the ribs are cooked, the meat will have shrunk back from the ends of the bones by ¼ to ½ inch. If you are using a charcoal grill, replenish the coals after 1 hour or as needed.

6 Just before serving, brush the ribs on both sides with about ½ cup of the Cider Rum Barbecue Sauce or the barbecue sauce of your choice. Move the ribs directly over the fire. Grill

the ribs until the barbecue sauce is browned and bubbling, 2 to 3 minutes per side.

7 Transfer the ribs to a large platter or cutting board. Let the ribs rest for a few minutes, then cut the racks in half or into individual ribs. Serve the ribs at once with the remaining barbecue sauce on the side.

The Only Rib Recipe You'll Ever Need—Outdoors and Indoors

Ribs may not be the *most* iconic guy food. That honor belongs to steak. But no man worthy of our gender should consider his culinary knowledge complete without knowing how to cook ribs. Fortunately, you can master the basics in a single recipe (OK, two: one outdoor, one indoor), adding the fine points with practice. For this master recipe, I've chosen baby backs spiced with homemade barbecue rub and misted with apple cider as they cook.

RAICHLEN'S RUB #1

Here's a barbecue rub—sweet with brown sugar, spicy with pepper and paprika—that would feel right at home in Kansas City, Memphis, or North Carolina. For a variation, see page 531. **Makes ½ cup**

2 tablespoons coarse salt (kosher or sea)

2 tablespoons dark brown sugar

2 tablespoons sweet paprika

1 tablespoon freshly ground black pepper

2 teaspoons dry mustard, preferably Colman's

1 teaspoon onion powder

½ teaspoon celery seeds

Place the salt, brown sugar, paprika, pepper, dry mustard, onion powder, and celery seeds in a small bowl and mix with your fingers, breaking up any lumps in the brown sugar or onion powder. Stored in an airtight jar away from heat and light, the rub will keep for several months.

CIDER RUM BARBECUE SAUCE

A sweet, mellow barbecue sauce invigorated with dark rum and apple cider. Good choices for rum include Myer's Rum from Jamaica, Gosling's Black Seal from Bermuda, or the new Ipswich rum from Massachusetts. The recipe makes more than you'll need. Refrigerate any excess in a sealed jar—it will keep for several weeks. **Makes about 2½ cups**

1 cup apple cider

About 1 teaspoon grated lemon zest (see page 610)

Juice of 1 lemon (about 3 tablespoons)

2 cups ketchup (I like Heinz)

½ packed cup brown sugar

½ cup dark rum, or more to taste

2 tablespoons molasses

1 tablespoon Worcestershire sauce

2 teaspoons Dijon mustard, or more to taste

1 teaspoon liquid smoke

1 teaspoon onion powder

½ teaspoon freshly ground black pepper

¼ teaspoon ground cinnamon

1 Place the cider, lemon zest, and lemon juice in a large heavy saucepan and let come to a boil over high heat. Let the cider mixture boil until reduced by about half, 4 to 6 minutes.

2 Add the ketchup, brown sugar, rum, molasses, Worcestershire sauce, mustard, liquid smoke, onion powder, pepper, and cinnamon and whisk to mix. Reduce the heat to medium and let the sauce simmer until thick and flavorful, 10 to 15 minutes, stirring occasionally. Taste for seasoning, adding more rum and/or mustard as necessary. Transfer the sauce to a bowl or clean jars and let it cool to room temperature. Refrigerate the sauce until serving. It will keep covered in the refrigerator for 3 weeks. Reheat it over low heat before using.

TEN THINGS YOU NEED TO KNOW ABOUT

RIBS

Ribs are perhaps the most perfect food known to man: rich in flavor; versatile enough to cook by almost any method; capable of culinary sophistication, yet primal enough to eat with your bare hands.

1 | Ribs come in full racks, individual bones, and crosscut into short ribs and steaks. See page 288 for a guide to the various types and cuts.

2 | When buying ribs, figure on 1 pound per person.

3 | "Shiners" are racks with so much meat cut off the ribs, the tops of the bones are exposed. Sometimes "cheap" ribs aren't worth the price.

4 | All ribs have a papery membrane on the inside (concave side). Do you absolutely need to remove it? No, but it's tougher than the rest of the meat and it blocks the absorption of the spice and smoke flavors. To remove the membrane, see Step 2, page 283. Note: The membrane is often removed by the time the ribs get to your supermarket meat case; if you can't find it, the butcher did the work for you.

5 | So how do you cook four racks of ribs (dinner for four to eight) on a common 22½-inch kettle grill? Use a rib rack, which enables you to cook the racks standing upright. There are many fine rib racks on the market.

6 | There are two ways to use a rub: as a seasoned salt applied just prior to cooking or rubbed onto the meat the night before. The latter both seasons and cures (chemically transforms) the meat.

7 | Ribs can be cooked by any of the following methods: grilling (using either the direct or the indirect method), smoking, braising, roasting, stewing, or spit-roasting. The one method I *don't* advocate is boiling: This transfers the flavor from the meat to the water. Ribs don't have to be boiled to be tender.

8 | To tell when pork ribs are cooked, examine the ends of the bones. When the meat has shrunk back ¼ to ½ inch, the ribs are cooked. Another way to recognize doneness: If you can pull the bones apart with your fingers, the ribs are cooked.

9 | If you are using a barbecue sauce, don't apply it too early: The sugars will burn before the meat is fully cooked. I brush the sauce on toward the end of cooking (about five minutes before you'd take it off) and move the ribs directly over the fire (or under the broiler). This sears the sauce into the meat.

10 | Braised ribs can be served fall-off-the-bone tender, but barbecue ribs should have a little chew to them: That's why God gave you teeth.

SPARERIBS

BABY BACK RIBS

RIB CHOP

LOIN CHOP

COUNTRY-STYLE RIB

PORK PORTERHOUSE

BONELESS LOIN CHOP

In the Oven

BABY BACK RIBS INDOORS

No, guys, I haven't gone over to the dark side. I recognize that many readers live in apartments without access to a grill. So these ribs possess the same digit-licking properties as ribs cooked on a grill. Just don't call them barbecue. **Makes 2 racks of ribs; serves 2 really hungry guys or 4 as part of a larger meal**

2 racks baby back pork ribs
(4 to 5 pounds total)

6 tablespoons Raichlen's Rub #1
(page 285) or your favorite barbecue
rub

3 tablespoons butter

½ teaspoon liquid smoke

Cider Rum Barbecue Sauce (page 286) or
your favorite barbecue sauce

1 Preheat the oven to 325°F.

2 Place a rack of ribs meat side down on a baking sheet. Remove the thin, papery membrane from the back of the rack by following the directions in Step 2 on page 283.

3 Place each rack of ribs on a baking sheet lined with heavy-duty aluminum foil on both sides. Season the ribs with barbecue rub (about 1½ tablespoons per side), rubbing the spices onto the meat.

4 Arrange each rack of ribs convex (rounded) side up on a baking sheet and bake for 1 hour.

5 Meanwhile, melt the butter over medium-low heat. Stir in the liquid smoke.

6 After the ribs have cooked for 1 hour, brush them with the smoky butter. Continue cooking the ribs until the meat has shrunk back from the ends of the bones by ¼ to ½ inch and they are tender enough to pull apart with your fingers, about 30 to 60 minutes more. Brush them with more smoky butter every 15 minutes. Remove the ribs from the oven and pour off and discard the excess fat. Leave the ribs on the baking sheet.

7 Preheat the broiler.

SHOP You may be surprised to find liquid smoke among the ingredients. (Isn't that cheating?) In fact, it's a natural flavoring made by burning hardwood logs and condensing the smoke into an extract. Use sparingly.

GEAR Your basic kitchen gear, plus heavy-duty aluminum foil and a basting brush

WHAT ELSE You can also use this baking technique for spareribs. Lower the heat to 275°F and increase the cooking time to 2½ to 3 hours.

TIME about 20 minutes preparation time, plus about 2 hours cooking time

8 Generously brush the ribs on both sides with some of the Cider Rum Barbecue Sauce or your favorite barbecue sauce. Broil the ribs until they are smoky and browned, applying additional barbecue sauce as needed, 2 to 4 minutes per side.

9 Transfer the ribs to a large platter or cutting board. Let the ribs rest for a few minutes, then cut the racks in half or into individual ribs. Serve the ribs at once with the remaining barbecue sauce on the side.

A GUY'S BEST FRIEND
PORK CHOPS

There are four major types of pork chops, each with unique characteristics, yet they're similar enough to be interchangeable for most pork chop recipes.

THE RIB CHOP | Cut from the front of the hog's rib cage, this chop includes a section of rib and a meaty medallion (round) of pork loin. Rib chops are available pencil-thin, two fingers thick, and everywhere in between.

THE LOIN CHOP | Cut from the back section of the hog, the loin chop includes a piece of loin and one of tenderloin connected by a T-shaped bone. When cut thick, the loin chop is sometimes called a pork porterhouse.

THE BONELESS LOIN CHOP | This is a lean round slice of pork loin with the rib removed. You could think of it as the pork version of a skinless, boneless chicken breast (in terms of the way it's used, not its anatomy).

THE COUNTRY-STYLE RIB | A long slender pork chop cut from the neck that may or may not contain a bone. (Technically speaking, the country-style rib is not a true rib.) So tender and quick-cooking, you can sauté, broil, or direct grill it like a pork chop.

SWEET SOY PORK CHOPS
DOUBLE-DIPPED IN WHITE SOY SAUCE

These sweet-salty pork chops come from Chicago food dude Paul Kahan. If you live in or have been to the Windy City, you know his restaurants—Blackbird, avec, The Publican, and the new Nico. If you don't, put them on your hit list. Kahan specializes in ingenious twists on familiar favorites, like these pork chops glazed with white soy sauce. Most guys ignore the very existence of white soy sauce (*shiro-shoyu* in Japanese)—a gold-colored condiment made mostly from wheat with just a small portion of soybeans. This gives the sauce a sweeter aroma and milder flavor than conventional soy sauce. A little advance planning (you have to marinate the chops for at least two hours) rewards you with the rich umami flavors of the soy sauce and garlic, along with brown sugar and ginger for sweetness. Another example of how upgrading one ingredient can deliver a huge dividend in overall taste. **Serves 4**

SHOP Look for white soy sauce at Japanese markets and natural foods stores. You can also buy it online from amazon.com. If you can't find it, you can use ¾ cup conventional soy sauce and ¼ cup mirin (sweet rice wine), sake, or sherry. This marinade works well for any lean cut of pork from chops to tenderloin.

GEAR Your basic kitchen gear including a nonreactive baking pan (that is, glass, ceramic, or stainless steel), strainer, small saucepan, broiler or large (10- or 12-inch) skillet, and tongs

WHAT ELSE The actual prep time is short, but you'll want to marinate the chops for at least two hours or as long as overnight, so plan accordingly. The double-dipping technique involves dipping the pork in the boiled marinade after they have cooked for about four minutes. This adds an extra layer of flavor and helps keep the chops moist.

TIME about 30 minutes preparation time, plus 2 to 8 hours for marinating

- 2 pounds (about eight ½-inch-thick) pork rib chops
- 1 cup white soy sauce (see Shop)
- ¼ cup Asian (dark) sesame oil or vegetable oil
- ¼ packed cup light brown sugar
- 1 piece (1 inch) fresh ginger, peeled and minced
- 3 scallions, trimmed, both white and green parts minced; set aside 2 tablespoons of the green parts for serving
- 2 cloves garlic, peeled and minced
- 2 tablespoons vegetable oil (optional; use only if you are cooking the chops in a skillet)

1 Arrange the pork chops in a nonreactive baking pan just large enough to hold them in a single layer. Combine the soy sauce, oil, brown sugar, ginger, scallions, and garlic in a mixing bowl and whisk to mix. Pour this mixture over the chops and let them marinate in the refrigerator for at least 2 hours and as long as 8 hours (the longer chops marinate, the richer the flavor will be), turning the chops from time to time so that they marinate evenly. Alternatively, you can marinate the chops in a resealable plastic bag.

2 Transfer the chops to a platter. Pour the marinade through a strainer set over a saucepan and let it come to a boil over high heat. Cook the marinade at a rolling boil for 3 minutes to sterilize it. Let the marinade cool in the saucepan.

3 *Broiler method:* If you are broiling the chops, preheat the broiler to high. Broil the chops until nicely browned on both sides, about 2 minutes per side.

Skillet method: If you are cooking the chops in a skillet, heat the 2 tablespoons of vegetable oil over medium-high heat. Add the chops and cook until nicely browned on both sides, about 2 minutes per side.

4 Dip the chops in the cooled marinade, turning to coat both sides. Let the chops marinate for about 3 minutes, then drain them well. (At this point you can either discard the marinade or boil it down and spoon a little over the chops by way of a sauce.)

5 Return the drained chops to the broiler or skillet and continue cooking them until they are darkly browned on both sides and cooked through, 2 to 4 minutes per side. Transfer the chops to a platter or plates. Sprinkle the reserved scallion greens on top and serve at once.

Stanley Tucci's

PAN-BRAISED PORK CHOPS
WITH SHIITAKES AND GREEN PEPPERCORNS

Stanley Tucci achieved foodie fame with *timpano*, the elaborate pastry "drum" filled with, among other things, sausage, meatballs, and cheese, that served as the centerpiece of his cult movie *Big Night*. Since then, he's played Julia Child's husband, Paul, in the movie *Julie & Julia*. (You can read more about Stanley on page 294.) But not only does the actor make movies about food, he's a damn good cook, and these skillet pork chops are the sort of dish he prepares for his family on a weeknight. The flavor comes at you from all directions: shiitake mushrooms, green peppercorns, white balsamic vinegar. I know it sounds complicated, but you can prepare the chops from start to finish in thirty minutes. **Serves 4**

4 boneless pork loin chops
  (each about 8 ounces and 1 inch thick)

Coarse salt (kosher or sea) and freshly
  ground black pepper

1 tablespoon butter

1 tablespoon extra virgin olive oil

1 medium-size onion, peeled and
  finely chopped

1 clove garlic, peeled and minced

6 ounces shiitake mushrooms, trimmed
  (see Note)

¾ cup dry white wine

2 tablespoons white or red balsamic
  vinegar

1 tablespoon Dijon mustard

1 tablespoon green peppercorns in brine,
  drained

¾ cup heavy (whipping) cream

1 Generously season the pork chops on both sides with salt and black pepper. Melt the butter in the olive oil in a large skillet over high heat. Add the pork chops and brown well on both sides, about 2 minutes per side. Transfer the chops to a large platter.

2 Reduce the heat to medium, add the onion and garlic, and cook until lightly browned, about 4 minutes, stirring with a wooden spoon. Add the shiitakes and saute until cooked, about 3 minutes.

3 Increase the heat to high and stir in the white wine. Bring to a boil and boil until reduced by half, 2 minutes, scraping up any brown bits from the bottom of the skillet with the wooden spoon. Add the balsamic vinegar, mustard, and peppercorns and bring to a boil. Boil, stirring,

for 1 minute. Add the cream and boil, stirring often, until the mixture is reduced by about half (you should have a little less than a cup), 3 to 5 minutes; the sauce should be creamy and flavorful.

4 Reduce the heat to medium. Return the pork chops to the skillet, spooning the sauce over them. Let the chops simmer until just cooked through, 5 to 8 minutes, turning with tongs after 3 minutes. Do not overcook. Taste for seasoning, adding salt and pepper to taste; the chops and sauce should be highly seasoned. Serve at once.

Note: To trim shiitakes, cut off the stem flush with the cap. Leave the caps whole. Discard the stems.

SHOP You'll have to ferret out a few special ingredients to make this dish the way Stanley does. White balsamic vinegar has a lighter color and flavor than the conventional red, but red will work in a pinch. Green peppercorns give you the heat of black pepper plus the aromatic fruitiness of the tiny berry from which pepper is made. Look for both the vinegar and the peppercorns at specialty food shops and natural foods stores. For pork chops, try to use a heritage breed like Berkshire.

GEAR Your basic kitchen gear including a large (10- or 12-inch) skillet and tongs

WHAT ELSE For an interesting variation, substitute bone-in veal chops for the pork chops and sliced apples for the mushrooms.

TIME about 30 minutes

STANLEY TUCCI

It's Tuesday night and Stanley Tucci is cooking pork chops. He's not the Emmy award–winning, Oscar-nominated actor tonight, not the man who played Nigel in *The Devil Wears Prada* or Flickerman in *The Hunger Games*. He's just Dad making his daughters' favorite dinner. He sears the pork chops, browns the onion and shiitake mushrooms, and deglazes the pan with wine and balsamic vinegar (the recipe is on page 292). And he and his kids sit down to what may be the most important thing in the actor's life: family dinner.

a magisterial *timpano*—immortalized in the cult food film *Big Night*, which marked Stanley's debut as a screenwriter and director.

In 2011 Tucci turned his passion for wine into a smart, celebrity-studded wine tasting show for PBS. More recently, he published *The Tucci Cookbook*. The actor wooed the new love of his life (now his wife) by spit-roasting a twenty-six pound suckling pig for her. "Unlike most guys, I like making really complicated dishes," Tucci says. "You have a few glasses of wine. You really get into the process. You have so much fun, you just don't want it to stop."

But it was Primo—the perfectionist chef (played by Tony Shalhoub) and in some sense Stanley's alter ego in *Big Night*—who summed up the Tucci philosophy: "To eat good food is to be close to God."

Do men and women cook differently?
Men make more of a show of it.

What's your go-to dish when you're by yourself?
Cannellini beans. Sometimes I'll make a simple salad with beans and tomatoes or warm beans with cold tuna and red onions. Sometimes I'll cook a can of beans with garlic and onion sautéed in olive oil. Add chicken stock and hit the mixture with an immersion blender and you've got a terrific soup.

"I'm completely food-obsessed," says Tucci, who attributes his passion for cooking and eating to his parents and his grandparents, who were born in Calabria, Italy. "We didn't eat out much because we never had any money. We always sat down to a home-cooked dinner." It was only when friends came over that Stanley realized that not everyone in 1960s America sat down to made-from-scratch meatballs with homemade ragu. Come Christmas, his was certainly the only family on the block (and very likely in Westchester County, New York, where he grew up) to cut into

What's your favorite seduction dish?
Risotto. It takes a long time, so you can talk while you're making it. It takes care and attention to detail, and you can show the lady you have good hands.

Three dishes every guy should know how to make?
Uova fra diavolo—eggs poached in marinara sauce. My father used to make it every Friday night for dinner. It's one of those grand simple dishes you can enjoy equally as breakfast, lunch, or dinner. [You'll find the recipe on page 56.]

Paella. I learned to make it in the mountains in Majorca, Spain, where we were shooting a movie. We cooked it outside over a wood fire. It's a lot of work, but I like a dish that's a lot of work. The harder it is to make it, the more satisfying it is when you succeed.

Rabbit. Underutilized, but it's delicious.

One dish really worthy of attention and connoisseurship?
Timpano. It's this incredibly complicated pasta dish from my grandparents' village, Serra San Bruno, in Calabria, Italy. It takes a whole day to make, and there are, perhaps, three men in all of North America who know how to make it—my dad, my cousin, and me. You start by making a dough that's a cross between pasta and pizza dough. You use it to line a drum-shaped basin and fill it with homemade ziti, hard-boiled eggs, Romano and provolone cheese, ham, Genoa salami, marinara sauce, and these tiny homemade meatballs. You bake it, let it sit, and invert it, and if all stars are aligned, when you cut into it you see all these beautiful striations and layers of genius.

Three ingredients you can't live without?
Eggs, rice, and wine. Eggs are the protein; rice the starch; and wine you can mix with both.

Three tools you can't live without?
A cast-iron skillet. You can cook with it on the stove *and* in the oven.

My grill. I've been through four. My fiancée gave me a grill when we got engaged. Talk about the way to a man's heart.

My wood-burning pizza oven. I fire it up at noon so it's ready for dinner. You have to tear me away from it.

> ► You have a few glasses of wine. You really get into the process.

What are the three most important things to keep in mind if you're just starting out in the kitchen?
Spend money on your ingredients. If you skimp on the quality, you'll never get great results.

Learn how to sauté—you know, flick the pan with your wrist to send the food sailing up in the air, then have all the ingredients land back in the pan. You use the same motion for flipping a frittata. It's controlled recklessness and women find it very sexy. Hell, *I* find it sexy.

Cook for the woman you love. It's the best way to get to know someone.

What are some common mistakes guys make in the kitchen?
Rushing when you should take time and lollygagging when you should work quickly. A typical guy will take a half hour to chop vegetables, when he should be able to do it in ten seconds. Then he'll rush the sautéing or panfrying, without taking the time to preheat the pan (this is *very* important—it should be really hot) to brown the meat properly.

Forgetting to taste. The only way you know if a dish is properly seasoned is if you taste it. Often.

Not cleaning up as you go along. You can't make fine food in a messy kitchen.

Something unexpected you've learned over the years that really helps you up your game in the kitchen?
The guy syndrome: If some is good, more must automatically be better. More salt. More wine. More hot sauce. Sometimes some really is enough.

Parting words of advice?
I rarely buy expensive wines. I typically spend $12 to $25 a bottle. You can get some really great wines for that price. The best wine values these days are coming out of Spain, Portugal, Argentina, and Chile. The Portuguese make a fantastic crisp summer wine called Vinho Verde. These countries give you a lot more wine for the money than France or Italy.

PORK CHOPS PAPRIKAS

SHOP To be strictly authentic, use a Hungarian paprika, like Szeged. For a contempo twist, try *pimentón* (Spanish smoked paprika—see page 28).

GEAR Your basic kitchen gear including a large (10- to 12-inch) cast-iron skillet

WHAT ELSE Chicken and veal are equally good prepared this way. For chicken, you could use boneless breasts or skin-on thighs. For veal, you could use loin chops or scaloppini.

TIME about 20 minutes

Paprikás refers to a family of Hungarian meat dishes flavored with paprika, red peppers, and sour cream. If you think chicken—the traditional protein—is good prepared this way, wait until you try it with pork. **Serves 4**

2 tablespoons extra virgin olive oil, bacon fat, or butter

4 large center-cut boneless loin pork chops (1½ to 2 pounds total)

Coarse salt (kosher or sea) and freshly ground black pepper

¾ cup plus 2 teaspoons unbleached all-purpose flour

1 large onion, peeled and thinly sliced

1 red bell pepper, stemmed, seeded, and cut into thin (¼-inch) strips

1 tablespoon sweet, hot, or smoked paprika, or to taste, plus more for serving

1 cup chicken stock, preferably homemade (page 549)

1 cup sour cream (not low- or no-fat or the sauce may curdle)

1 Heat the oil in a large skillet over medium-high heat.

2 Meanwhile, season the pork chops on both sides with salt and black pepper. Place the ¾ cup of flour in a shallow bowl. Dredge each pork chop in the flour on both sides, shaking off the excess. Add the pork chops to the skillet and cook them until nicely browned on both sides, about 2 minutes per side. Transfer the pork chops to a platter.

3 Add the onion and bell pepper to the skillet and cook over medium heat until just beginning to brown, about 3 minutes, stirring often. Add the paprika and the remaining 2 teaspoons of flour, stir to blend, and cook until fragrant, about 1 minute, stirring well.

4 Add the chicken stock and stir to mix. Return the pork chops to the pan and simmer gently until cooked through, 5 to 8 minutes, turning once or twice. Don't overcook the chops; they should still have a faint blush of pink in the center. Transfer the chops with tongs to a platter or plates.

5 Stir ¾ cup of the sour cream into the pan juices and let simmer over medium heat until the sauce thickens, 2 to 3 minutes, stirring with a wooden spoon. Taste for seasoning, adding salt or additional smoked paprika to taste; the sauce should be highly seasoned. Spoon the sauce over the pork chops. Dollop the remaining sour cream on top and sprinkle on a little more smoked paprika. Dig in.

CHAIRMAN MAO'S GINGER-SOY BRAISED PORK BELLY

Meat means manliness. Meat projects power. These notions are as old as warfare and the generals who conduct it. And according to Chinese author and dissident Sasha Gong, this sweet, salty, gingery pork stew—carpeted with pungent cilantro—was a favorite of Mao Tse-tung. The Chairman believed the fat in the dish possessed the power to boost his brainpower and the meat itself made fighting men tougher. I'm not about to vouch for either claim, but I will tell you that it is an astonishingly flavorful and exceedingly simple way to enjoy pork belly. The recipe was inspired by Gong's book (written with Scott Seligman), *The Cultural Revolution Cookbook*. **Serves 4**

1½ pounds pork belly, skin removed, or boneless pork shoulder

1 piece (4 inches) fresh ginger, cut on the diagonal into ½-inch-thick slices (you don't need to peel the ginger)

2 tablespoons vegetable oil

⅓ cup sugar

⅔ cup rice wine or sherry

⅓ cup soy sauce

1 cinnamon stick (3 to 4 inches), or 1 teaspoon ground cinnamon

1 bunch fresh cilantro, rinsed, shaken dry, stemmed, and coarsely chopped

Boiled white or brown rice (page 488), for serving

1 Cut the pork into 1-inch cubes. Gently crush the ginger slices with the side of a heavy cleaver or skillet to release the juices.

2 Place the oil in a large heavy pot, Dutch oven, or a wok over medium-high heat and heat. Add the ginger, then the sugar. Stir-fry (stir continually while cooking) until the sugar dissolves, about 1 minute. Add the cubed pork and stir-fry until browned and most of the liquid has evaporated but do not let it dry completely, about 3 minutes. Stir in the rice wine and soy sauce. Add the cinnamon stick.

SHOP Pork belly comes from the hog's undercarriage. Cured and smoked, it becomes bacon. You'll probably need to buy it at a butcher shop. Look for Chinese rice wine (Shaoxing) in Asian markets, or substitute sake, dry white wine, or dry sherry.

GEAR Your basic kitchen gear plus a heavy cleaver or skillet. Tradition calls for the pork to be braised in a wok with a tight-fitting lid. A large heavy pot or Dutch oven with a tightly-fitting lid will work equally well.

WHAT ELSE In Mao's native Hunan province, the dish would be made with pork belly—a rich fatty cut that, while wildly popular in American restaurants, is still difficult to find in American supermarkets. Pork shoulder makes a tasty, leaner, and healthier substitute, but buy all pork belly if you can find it.

TIME about 10 minutes preparation time, plus 40 to 60 minutes cooking time

3 Tightly cover the pot or wok. Reduce the heat to medium-low and let the pork simmer gently until very tender, 40 to 60 minutes, stirring occasionally. If the pork starts to dry out, add a little water or chicken stock.

4 Sprinkle the pork with the cilantro and serve it at once with boiled white or brown rice.

OAXACAN PORK FAJITAS

SHOP In Oaxaca, they use thinly sliced pork shoulder, which is loaded with fat, so it stays moist on the grill. If you have the patience, thinly slice boneless pork shoulder (we're talking poker chip thin here), or bribe your butcher to do it. Otherwise, use pork loin or tenderloin thinly sliced across the grain. It helps if you partially freeze it first. *Crema* is Mexican sour cream. (It's a little more sour and pungent than American sour cream.) Look for it in Hispanic markets. Pure powdered ancho or pasilla chiles are available in some supermarkets, but if you can't find them, substitute regular pure chile powder.

GEAR Your basic kitchen gear including a blender and a nonreactive (that is, glass, ceramic, or stainless steel) baking pan for marinating the pork, plus a grill, a cloth-lined basket for keeping the tortillas warm, a large (10- or 12-inch) cast-iron skillet and a trivet (both optional), and a pair of tongs for serving

It's hard to remember American cuisine without fajitas, but there was a time when you had to travel to Texas (specifically to Ninfa's restaurant in Houston) to try them. Who knew that a cheap cut of beef—the skirt steak—would become a popular party food? (*Fajita* means "little girdle" in Spanish.) Here's a pork version, fragrant with cinnamon, orange, and ancho chiles. **Serves 4 to 6**

For the pork and marinade

2 pounds boneless pork shoulder, loin, or tenderloin, sliced as thinly as possible

⅓ cup pure ancho or pasilla chile powder

¼ cup distilled white vinegar

¼ cup fresh orange juice

4 cloves garlic, peeled and minced

1 teaspoon coarse salt (kosher or sea)

1 teaspoon freshly ground black pepper

1 teaspoon dried oregano

½ teaspoon ground cumin

½ teaspoon ground cinnamon

For the vegetables

2 poblano peppers, or 1 green bell pepper

1 red bell pepper

1 yellow bell pepper

1 large sweet onion, peeled, but root intact, cut into 6 wedges

1 bunch scallions, trimmed

For serving

12 small (7-inch) flour tortillas if serving 4 people; 18 if serving 6 people

2 cups Pico de Gallo (page 210) or Salsa Chipotle (page 211), or your favorite store-bought salsa

1 cup sour cream or Mexican crema

1 bunch fresh cilantro, rinsed, stemmed, and coarsely chopped

2 limes, cut into wedges

WHAT ELSE Fajitas
aren't complicated, but
they do require a certain
choreography to have all the
components ready at once.
Grill the vegetables first.
Then warm the tortillas and
place them in a cloth-lined
basket to keep warm. Finally,
grill the meat.

TIME about 30 minutes
preparation time, plus 1 to 4
hours for marinating the pork

1 **Prepare the pork and marinade:** Place the pork in a nonreactive baking pan. Place the chile powder, vinegar, orange juice, garlic, salt, black pepper, oregano, cumin, and cinnamon in a blender and blend until smooth. Pour the marinade over the pork, turning the pieces to coat well. Let the pork marinate, covered, in the refrigerator for 1 to 4 hours.

2 **Grill the vegetables:** Set up the grill for direct grilling and preheat it to high.

3 When ready to grill, brush and oil the grill grate. Place the poblano peppers and bell peppers on the grate and grill until darkly browned on all sides, turning with tongs, about 15 minutes. Transfer the grilled peppers to a cutting board and let them cool. Meanwhile, grill the onion wedges and scallions until browned, 2 to 4 minutes per side, turning with tongs. When the peppers are cool, stem and seed them. Cut the peppers and onions into thin (½-inch) strips. Cut the scallions into 2-inch pieces. The vegetables can be grilled up to 30

minutes ahead. If grilling ahead on a charcoal grill, you may need to add fresh coals.

4 Just before serving, heat the skillet in a 400°F oven for 10 minutes. (Or preheat the skillet on the grill.) Warm the tortillas (10 to 15 seconds per side), and place in the cloth-lined basket. Place the salsa, sour cream, and cilantro in separate small bowls with serving spoons.

5 Just before serving, drain the pork slices well. Arrange on the hot grate and grill them until browned and cooked through, 2 minutes per side. Transfer the grilled pork to a cutting board and cut it into thin strips. You can serve the fajita ingredients hot off the grill. Or, for the sizzling platter effect, arrange the slivered pork and the vegetables in the preheated skillet and place the skillet on a trivet. Use tongs to load up the tortillas with sliced pork and grilled veggies. Top the fajitas with salsa, sour cream, and cilantro, and serve with lime wedges for squeezing.

Variation
Fajitas in a Skillet

Don't have access to a grill? Follow the above directions through Step 1. While the pork is marinating, roast the peppers, onion wedges, and scallions on a baking sheet in a preheated 450°F oven until deeply browned on all sides, 5 to 10 minutes per side. You'll have to turn the peppers from time to time. Once browned, cut the vegetables as described in Step 3. Warm the tortillas as described in Step 4. Drain and cook the pork in a large cast-iron skillet over medium-high heat, 2 minutes per side. Cut into thin strips and serve as described in Step 5.

LAMB AND
A GOAT

On average, Americans eat less than two pounds of lamb per person per year. That's all. The appeal of this robust red meat sure isn't lost on guys in other cultures. Lamb is the default meat in Morocco and Mauritania, Greece and India, Australia and New Zealand, and pretty much everywhere in between. So if you like meat that's big-flavored and you want to step out of the predictable beef/pork/chicken box, you need to know your way around lamb and its increasingly popular cousin, goat.

In this chapter, you'll learn how to prepare some of the world's best lamb dishes: garlic- and herb-roasted leg of lamb, frenched rack of lamb, lamb shanks braised with soy sauce and honey, lamb ribs spiced with cocoa and chile, and killer shish kebab. You'll burn your fingers on Italian *scottadito* ("finger-burner" lamb chops) and scorch your gullet on Indian vindaloo (fiery lamb curry). And you'll experience a soulful curried goat from the West Indies. Lamb—it's the other red meat. Dig in.

LEG OF LAMB THREE WAYS

Imagine a leg of lamb pulled fragrant and sizzling from the oven, the exterior crusty and dark, rare or pink in the center (depending on your preference). It's one of those dishes that simultaneously showcase your generosity, sophistication, and culinary competence. What you may not realize is that you're looking at maybe ten minutes actual preparation time for a main course that knocks it out of the park. The only thing for you to decide is which of the following three big-flavored spice pastes to use: Italian, North African, or Greek.

#1: THE ITALIAN
(WITH GARLIC AND ROSEMARY)

This leg of lamb roars with the elemental Mediterranean flavors of garlic and rosemary—both inserted deep into the meat for extra flavor. **Serves 6 to 8**

1 boned leg of lamb (3 to 4 pounds), tied into a cylinder

3 cloves garlic, peeled and cut lengthwise into matchstick slivers

1 bunch rosemary, torn into small sprigs

2 tablespoons extra virgin olive oil

Coarse salt (kosher or sea) and cracked black peppercorns

1 Preheat the oven to 400°F.

2 Using the tip of a paring knife, make a series of slits in the lamb, each ½ inch long and deep and spaced 2 inches apart. Twist the knife point to open the slit. Insert slivers of garlic in half of the slits and sprigs of rosemary in the other half. Brush the leg of lamb with the olive oil. Very generously season the lamb on all sides with salt and peppercorns, using about 2 teaspoons of each.

3 Place the leg of lamb fat side up in a roasting pan. Bake until seared and partially browned, about 30 minutes.

SHOP Ask for a whole leg of lamb, but with the aitchbone removed. That's a section of the rump bone and your butcher will be mightily impressed that you know to ask him to remove it.

When buying boneless leg of lamb (which is killer on the rotisserie), ask your butcher to tie it into a compact cylinder so it roasts evenly. Boneless leg of lamb cooks faster than bone-in.

GEAR Your basic kitchen gear including a roasting pan, a food processor (optional), and an instant-read thermometer

WHAT ELSE Thanks to the conical shape of a leg of lamb everyone gets a piece of meat with the degree of doneness he or she prefers: rare at the loin end, well-done at the shank end. So when you check the temperature, insert the probe of the instant-read thermometer in the thickest part. This will be the rarest section of the meat.

TIME about 10 minutes preparation time and 1 to 1½ hours roasting time

4 Reduce the heat to 375°F and continue cooking the lamb until it is darkly browned on the outside and done to taste, about 1 hour in all for medium-rare, about 1¼ hours in all for medium. Use an instant-read thermometer to check for doneness; when done to very rare the thermometer will register about 120°F; for medium-rare, 135°F; and for medium, about 150°F. Remember, the lamb will continue cooking as it rests and that if you roasted the whole leg, the meat at the shank (skinny) end will be more well-done.

5 Transfer the lamb to a cutting board and lay a sheet of aluminum foil loosely over it. Let the lamb rest for 5 to 10 minutes before slicing.

#2: THE NORTH AFRICAN
(WITH GINGER AND CUMIN)

Here's a Moroccan-inspired leg of lamb seasoned with North African spices such as ginger, cumin, coriander, paprika, and, for a sweet touch, cinnamon and cardamom. The latter has a haunting perfumed flavor that may remind you of Swedish cookies or Turkish coffee: It's an ingredient in both. **Serves 6 to 8**

1 boned leg of lamb (3 to 4 pounds), tied into a cylinder

3 slices (each ¼ inch thick) fresh ginger, peeled and cut into matchstick slivers

1 small onion, peeled and cut in quarters, each quarter cut into ¼-inch-wide slivers

1 teaspoon ground cumin

1 teaspoon ground coriander

1 teaspoon ground turmeric

1 teaspoon sweet or hot paprika

½ teaspoon ground cardamom

½ teaspoon ground cinnamon

Coarse salt (kosher or sea) and cracked black peppercorns

2 tablespoons extra virgin olive oil

1 Preheat the oven to 400°F.

2 Using the tip of a paring knife, make a series of slits in the lamb, each ½ inch long and deep and spaced 2 inches apart. Insert the slivers of ginger in half of the slits and the slivers of onion in the other half.

3 Place the cumin, coriander, turmeric, paprika, cardamom, cinnamon, and salt and pepper (using about 2 teaspoons of each) in a bowl and stir to mix. Brush the leg of lamb with the olive oil, then sprinkle the spice rub over it.

4 Place the leg of lamb fat side up in a roasting pan. Bake until seared and partially browned, about 30 minutes.

5 Reduce the heat to 375°F and continue cooking the lamb until it is darkly browned on the outside and done to taste, about 1 hour in all for medium-rare, 1¼ hours in all for medium. Use an instant-read thermometer to check for doneness; when done to very rare the thermometer will register about 120°F; for medium-rare, 135°F; and for medium, about 150°F. Remember that the lamb will continue cooking as it rests and that if you roasted the whole leg the meat at the shank (skinny) end will be more well-done.

6 Transfer the lamb to a cutting board and lay a sheet of aluminum foil loosely over it. Let the lamb rest for 5 to 10 minutes before slicing.

How to Stud a Leg of Lamb with Onion and Ginger

▶ This method of studding works for garlic, shallots, ginger, and whatever else you prefer using to flavor a roast.

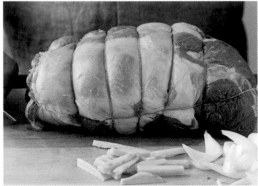

1 Start with a boned leg of lamb tied into a tight cylinder.

2 Using the tip of a paring knife, make a series of slits in the lamb, each ½ inch wide and deep, spaced 2 inches apart.

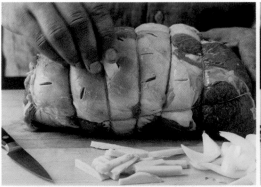

3 Insert slivers of onion in half the holes.

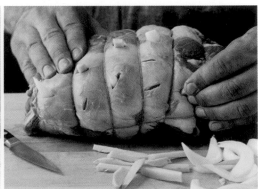

4 Insert slivers of ginger in the remaining holes.

#3: THE GREEK

(WITH LEMON, SCALLIONS, AND DILL)

Finally, the Greek version—a leg of lamb fragrant with lemon, scallions, and dill. Serve with grilled bread and a simple Greek salad comprised of lettuce, tomatoes, cucumber, olives, bell peppers, and sliced feta cheese dressed with olive oil and red wine vinegar. **Serves 6 to 8**

1 bunch scallions, both white and green parts, trimmed and rough chopped

1 bunch fresh dill, rinsed, shaken dry, and chopped

1½ teaspoons finely grated fresh lemon zest

2 tablespoons extra virgin olive oil

Coarse salt (kosher or sea) and cracked black peppercorns

1 boned leg of lamb (3 to 4 pounds), tied into a cylinder

1 Preheat the oven to 400°F.

2 Place the scallions, dill, and lemon zest in a food processor and finely chop them. Add the olive oil, running the processor in short bursts to obtain a thick paste. Season the herb paste with salt and peppercorns to taste, using about 1½ teaspoons of each. Alternatively, mash the scallions, dill, lemon zest, salt, and pepper together in a mortar with a pestle, then work in the olive oil to make a thick paste.

3 Using the tip of a paring knife, make a series of slits in the lamb, each ½ inch long and deep and spaced 2 inches apart. Twist the knife tip a quarter turn to widen the holes. Using a spatula, spread the herb paste over the lamb on all sides, using your fingers to force some of it into the slits.

4 Place the leg of lamb fat side up in a roasting pan. Bake until seared and partially browned, about 30 minutes.

5 Reduce the heat to 375°F and continue cooking the lamb until it is darkly browned on the outside and done to taste, about 1 hour in all for medium-rare, 1¼ hours in all for medium. Use an instant-read thermometer to check for doneness; when done to very rare the thermometer will register about 120°F; for medium-rare, 135°F; and for medium, about 150°F. Remember that the lamb will continue cooking as it rests and that if you roasted the whole leg the meat at the shank (skinny) end will be more well-done.

6 Transfer the lamb to a cutting board and lay a sheet of aluminum foil loosely over it. Let the lamb rest for 5 to 10 minutes before slicing.

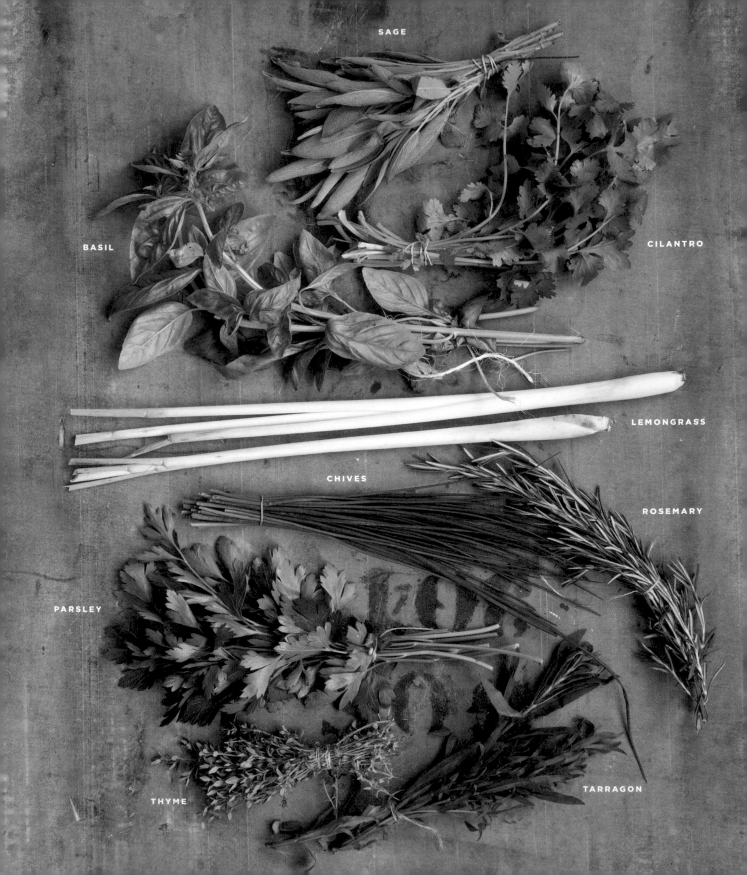

SAGE

BASIL

CILANTRO

LEMONGRASS

CHIVES

ROSEMARY

PARSLEY

THYME

TARRAGON

HERBS 101

Fresh herbs make a vivid link between the garden and your table. Without them you wouldn't have pesto (essential herb: basil), salsa (essential herb: cilantro), or mojitos (essential herb: mint). I'm not going to go all potpourri on you, but there are a dozen herbs every guy should be familiar with and know how to use.

Is there a big difference between fresh and dried herbs?

It depends on the herb. Rosemary, thyme, oregano, and sage dry well, although the dried herbs have a flavor that's different from the fresh. Cilantro, tarragon, and parsley lose virtually all of their flavor when dried. For these, you must use fresh.

What's the best way to buy fresh herbs?

Ideally in a pot of dirt with the roots still attached—this is the most economical way, and it's comforting to have something alive and green in your house or apartment. Otherwise, buy bunches of fresh herbs at your local supermarket.

How do I clean fresh herbs?

Easy: Fill a mixing bowl with cold water. Grab the bunch of herbs by the stem ends and plunge it up and down like a plumber's helper. Lift the herbs out of the bowl and shake the leaves dry over the sink or on the porch. If they need to be super-dry, gently pat off the excess water with paper towels.

How should I store fresh herbs?

After the herbs are rinsed and dried, loosely wrap them in a paper towel moistened with cold water. The paper towel should be damp, not soaking wet. Then *loosely fold* the herbs into plastic wrap. Remoisten the towel every few days—the fresh herbs will keep for at least a week. Don't seal the plastic tightly or the herbs will turn musty.

What are the twelve herbs every guy should know about?

BASIL | The king of herbs, literally. (*Basilikon* means "kingly" in Greek.) Basil is the primary flavoring in pesto. *Caprese salad* (slices of tomato, mozzarella, and whole basil leaves alternating in a row or stacked; a drizzle of olive oil and splash of balsamic vinegar and you're set) and pizza margherita (see page 523) would be poor stuff without it.

CHIVES | "He who has chives on his breath / needn't worry about being kissed to death," quipped the Roman satirist Martial. Actually, chives are the mildest member of the onion family. I often use chives instead of parsley (the former far more flavorful than the latter) when a burst of green is called for to dress up a dish.

CILANTRO | The leaves of the plant that gives us coriander seed (the round tan seeds used to flavor pickles and pastrami). Pungent and aromatic, cilantro is one of the defining

(continued on the next page)

(continued from the previous page)

flavors of Mexican, Caribbean, and Southeast Asian cooking. You must use it fresh, as the flavor all but disappears when cilantro is dried.

DILL | One of the signature flavors in Scandinavian cooking—used in everything from gravlax (cured salmon) to Swedish meatballs. The feathery-leafed herb goes particularly well with salmon.

LEMONGRASS | One of the essential seasonings of Southeast Asia, where its herbaceous lemony tang invigorates everything from Vietnamese stir-fried squid (page 441) to Thai beef salad. Use lemongrass when you want an aromatic lemon flavor but no acidity. For instructions on trimming lemongrass, see page 608.

MINT | Available in a dozen different varieties (peppermint—the hottest; spearmint—the mildest; chocolate mint—the weirdest; and so on), mint is essential for making mojitos (mint muddled with sugar, plus rum and club soda). And, of course, mint pairs up superbly with lamb. Mint is one fresh herb that dries well.

OREGANO | The aromatic herb you find sprinkled on pizza and infused in marinara sauce. Oregano is equally at home in Italian, Greek, and Mexican food. All three cultures have distinctive varieties, so if you're used to the supermarket spice rack stuff, try imported Greek oregano (more minty) or Mexican (more earthy) from an ethnic market. Oregano is another herb that dries well.

PARSLEY | Its indiscriminate use as a garnish has tarnished parsley's street cred, but flat-leaf parsley possesses an interesting flavor that's halfway between herb and salad green. It also has breath-freshening properties, which is why parsley is often combined with garlic (for example, in the *chimichurri* sauce you'll find on page 539). Always use parsley fresh.

ROSEMARY | One of the sturdiest fresh herbs—able to survive New England winters, Miami summers, and my general horticultural ineptitude. Intensely aromatic, rosemary is indispensable for roast chicken (page 327), roast lamb (page 303), and prime rib (page 251). Strip the leaves off the bottom half of branches of rosemary to make aromatic skewers for shish kebab. Rosemary dries well, but loses some of its aromatic oils in the process.

SAGE | No, I'm not going to tell you to burn dried bunches of this aromatic flat-leaf herb to increase your spirituality and drive away evil spirits. I *will* tell you to combine sage with rosemary and garlic to make a fragrant seasoning for *porchetta* (Tuscan pork roast—page 277). The combination is awesome with grilled meats of all sorts. It dries well.

TARRAGON | This slender-leafed herb has an elegant anise flavor (think of a plant that channels Pernod). The French use it in salads, on roast chicken, and in béarnaise sauce. The flavor dissipates when dried: if you can't use tarragon fresh, don't bother.

THYME | The tiny pungent leaves of this hardy herb (another plant that's tough to kill) round out the flavor of everything from clam chowder (page 143) to beef stew (page 254). Thyme dries well.

RED-COOKED LAMB SHANKS

Gone are the days when osso buco (veal shanks braised Italian style) was a dish you prepared on a student budget. But lamb shanks remain affordable, offering rich-flavored, moist, tender meat for a reasonable price. Like all lower leg cuts, lamb shanks require prolonged, moist, gentle heat to make them tender. The Chinese use a technique called "red cooking"—braising the lamb in an aromatic sweet-salty mixture of soy sauce, rice wine, and honey. The actual prep time takes maybe twenty minutes. Basically, you throw everything in a pot in the oven and forget about it for about three hours. The flavor will leave you gobsmacked. **Serves 4**

5 tablespoons Asian (dark) sesame oil

4 lamb shanks (each 1 to 1¼ pounds)

1½ cups soy sauce

1½ cups rice wine or sake

¼ cup honey or sugar

4 cloves garlic, peeled and flattened with the side of a cleaver

1 piece (3 inches) fresh ginger, cut lengthwise into ¼-inch slices, flattened lightly with the side of a cleaver

4 scallions, trimmed, white parts flattened with the side of a cleaver, green parts finely chopped; set aside 2 tablespoons of the green parts for serving

2 strips (each ½ by 1½ inches) orange zest

2 pieces of star anise, or 1 teaspoon Chinese five-spice powder (optional)

SHOP Lamb shanks are available at a growing number of supermarkets. If you can't find them there, order them at a butcher shop. For soy sauce, I like Kikkoman or Eden. Chinese rice wine (Shaoxing) may require a trip to an Asian market, but Japanese sake works great as well and can be found pretty much everywhere. Star anise comes in star-shaped pods and has a smoky licorice-like flavor. You'll find it, or Chinese five-spice powder (of which it's a prominent ingredient), in a supermarket or natural foods store spice rack.

GEAR Your basic kitchen gear including a large heavy pot or Dutch oven with a tight-fitting lid

WHAT ELSE Once you get the hang of red cooking, you can use it for just about everything: chicken, short ribs, pork shoulder. It's a great technique to have in your toolkit.

TIME about 20 minutes preparation time, plus 2½ to 3 hours cooking time

1 Preheat the oven to 300°F.

2 Heat the 2 tablespoons of sesame oil in a large heavy pot or Dutch oven over medium-high heat. Brown the lamb shanks on all sides, turning with tongs, 6 to 8 minutes total. Don't crowd the pot; leave at least 1 inch between the shanks. Work in 2 batches if necessary. Transfer the browned shanks to a platter and pour off the lamb fat.

3 Add the soy sauce, rice wine, the remaining 3 tablespoons of sesame oil, the honey, garlic, ginger, scallion whites and all but 2 tablespoons of the greens, orange zest, and star anise or Chinese five-spice powder, if using. Let come to a boil over medium-high heat and scrape up all the browned bits from the bottom of the pot with a wooden spoon. Return the lamb shanks to the pot.

4 Tightly cover the pot and place the lamb shanks in the oven. Braise the lamb until very tender, 2½ to 3 hours. Turn the lamb shanks from time to time so they absorb the sauce evenly. Make sure the lamb shanks don't stick to the bottom of the pot or dry out. If they do start to dry out, stir in ½ cup of water or as needed. The water should be at a depth of 1 inch.

5 Uncover the pot for the last half hour or so of cooking to let the braising liquid concentrate. Once you have removed the lamb shanks from the oven, using a soupspoon, spoon off and discard any visible lamb fat that pools on the top of the braising liquid. If it still seems too liquid, place the pot on the stove and let the liquid boil until concentrated and richly flavored.

6 Serve the red-cooked lamb shanks out of the pot with the remaining scallion greens sprinkled on top.

RACK OF LAMB
WITH GARLIC AND MINT

SHOP If you have a choice in selecting your meat, the best lamb for the money is imported from New Zealand (population: three million human beings and sixty million sheep). When it comes to American lamb, farms in Colorado, Pennsylvania, and California produce some of the best. Ask your butcher to french the rack for you—that is, cut and scrape the meat off the last couple of inches of the bones. (This gives you a clean handle to grab when you gnaw each chop.)

Rack of lamb offers everything you could ask of a guy food: sufficient style to impress, with a gnaw-it-off-the-bone directness that calls to your inner caveman. This is the mildest, most tender cut of the lamb, but it still has plenty of flavor. I like to think of it as prime rib built for two. All this, and it requires little more in the way of cooking skills than knowing how to turn on your oven. **Serves 2**

1 rack of lamb (1 to 1¼ pounds)

¼ cup packed fresh mint leaves or stemmed rosemary, or 2 tablespoons dried mint or rosemary

1 to 2 cloves garlic, peeled and roughly chopped

1 teaspoon coarse salt (kosher or sea)

1 teaspoon cracked black peppercorns

1 teaspoon finely grated fresh lemon zest (see Note)

About 2 tablespoons extra virgin olive oil

1 Preheat the oven to 450°F.

2 If your butcher hasn't already done so, french the lamb: Using a paring knife, scrape the meat off the last 2 to 3 inches of each of the rib bones.

3 Place the mint or rosemary, garlic, salt, peppercorns, and lemon zest in a food processor or mini chopper and finely chop them. Add enough olive oil to make a thick paste, running the processor in short bursts. Don't have a food processor? Using a chef's knife, mince the fresh mint or rosemary and garlic and place in a bowl. Add the salt, cracked peppercorns, lemon zest, and dried mint or rosemary, if using. Stir in enough olive oil to make a paste.

4 Using a spatula, spread the herb paste all over the meat of the rack of lamb. Place the lamb, frenched bones pointed up, in a roasting pan and place it in the oven. Reduce the heat to 400°F. Cook the lamb until it is sizzling and browned on the outside and done to taste, 18 to 20 minutes for medium-rare. To check for doneness, insert an instant-read thermometer through the thickest end of the rack but not touching a bone. When done to very rare it will register 120°F; medium-rare will register 135°F; and medium will register 150°F.

5 Transfer the rack to a platter and let it rest, loosely covered with aluminum foil, for about 3 minutes. (This "relaxes" the meat and makes it juicy. Do not bunch the foil around the lamb or it will become soggy.) If you have not already done so, cut the rack in half and serve.

Note: The zest is the oil-rich outer rind of the lemon. Remove it with a Microplane (see page 15) or the fine grating side of a box grater, being careful to grate only the yellow rind, not the bitter white pith underneath.

GEAR Your basic kitchen gear including a food processor (optional), a roasting pan, and an instant-read thermometer

WHAT ELSE You can also cook the rack of lamb on the grill. Set up your grill for indirect grilling (see page 12) and preheat to medium-high (400°F). Place the rack of lamb on the grate away from the flames over the drip pan. Indirect grill until cooked to taste, about 20 minutes for rare, about 30 minutes for medium.

Variation

Rack of Lamb with a Tapenade Crust

Tapenade is a Provençale olive paste. If you don't have time to make your own (instructions follow), use a good store-bought brand. Preheat the oven to 450°F. Place 1 cup pitted oil-cured black olives, 2 tablespoons drained capers, 1 clove garlic peeled and coarsely chopped, 2 to 4 coarsely chopped anchovy fillets (optional), and ½ teaspoon freshly ground black pepper in a food processor and finely chop (you can also do this in a mortar with a pestle). Work in enough olive oil (1 to 2 tablespoons) to obtain a thick but spreadable paste. Using a spatula, spread the olive paste over a 1 to 1¼ pound rack of lamb on all sides (but not on the bones). You may not need all of the olive paste. Any that is left over is great spread on grilled bread or toasts. Place ½ cup bread crumbs in a shallow bowl. Dredge the lamb in the bread crumbs, spooning them over to coat all sides. Lightly drizzle 1 tablespoon of olive oil over the crust. Place the lamb in a roasting pan and roast as described in Step 4 on page 305.

FINGER-BURNER LAMB CHOPS

The name says it all—*scottadito*. That's Italian for "finger burner"—an apt description of lamb chops served so hot they scorch your fingers when you dig in. As with all great meat cooked on the bone, these chops taste best eaten with your bare hands, so ask the butcher to "french" the bones (scrape the meat clean off the last 2 or 3 inches of bone). In keeping with the dish's Italian origins, the seasonings are pretty simple: rosemary, garlic, and extra virgin olive oil. I like to pump up the burn factor with hot pepper flakes. **Serves 4**

2½ pounds small lamb rib chops, cut ½ inch thick

Coarse salt (kosher or sea) and cracked or freshly ground black peppercorns

1 tablespoon hot red pepper flakes, or to taste

3 cloves garlic, peeled and minced

3 tablespoons finely chopped fresh rosemary

1 to 4 tablespoons extra virgin olive oil, depending on the cooking method

Lemon wedges, for serving

1 Arrange the lamb chops in a single layer on a baking sheet. Generously season the chops on one side with salt and pepper and half of the hot pepper flakes, minced garlic, and rosemary. Drizzle 2 tablespoons of olive oil over the chops and pat the ingredients onto the meat with your fingertips. Turn the chops and repeat on the second side. Let the chops marinate in the refrigerator for about 20 minutes.

2 Heat 1 tablespoon extra virgin olive oil in a large cast-iron skillet or on a *plancha* over high heat until shimmering. Add the lamb chops in a single layer (work in batches as needed) and cook until well-browned on the bottom, about 3 minutes. Turn the chops over and cook until well-browned and the meat is cooked through or to taste, about 3 minutes for medium.

3 Place the chops on a platter and encourage everyone to pick them up and eat the meat straight from the bone. Serve with lemon wedges for squeezing and plenty of napkins.

SHOP You need lamb rib chops for this dish, the smaller the better. (Some people call them lamb lollipops.)

GEAR Your basic kitchen gear including a baking sheet and a 12-by-18-inch piece of heavy-duty aluminum foil

WHAT ELSE Tradition calls for grilling the *scottadito* over live wood or charcoal fire, but you can also cook the chops in a large (10- to 12-inch) cast-iron skillet or a *plancha* or under a broiler. Incidentally, these simple flavorful seasonings go great with virtually any grilled meat, poultry, or seafood. For heightened drama, make a basting brush with a bunch of fresh rosemary and use it for basting the lamb.

TIME about 20 minutes for marinating the lamb, plus 6 to 8 minutes cooking time

JAKE'S LAMB RIBS
WITH A COFFEE-COCOA–BROWN-SUGAR CRUST

SHOP You'll probably need to preorder lamb ribs from your supermarket meat department or local butcher shop. Or look for them at a Greek, Middle Eastern, or halal meat market. *Pimentón* is Spanish smoked paprika. Look for it at your local well-stocked supermarket.

GEAR Your basic kitchen gear including a baking sheet and wire rack

WHAT ELSE The recipe calls for roasting the lamb in the oven, but you could certainly cook them on the grill (see the Variation on the facing page).

TIME about 15 minutes preparation time, plus about 1½ to 2 hours cooking time

Have you ever tried lamb ribs? If not, what are you waiting for? More tender than beef and more flavorful than pork, lamb ribs can stand up to any spice or seasoning you throw at them. My stepson, Jake, a Brooklyn chef, crusts them with coffee, cocoa powder, and brown sugar producing sit-up-and-take-notice ribs with a sweet, spicy, subtly chocolaty crust. Normally, I'm a grill guy, but Jake's method of slow roasting the ribs has given me a newfound respect for the oven. **Serves 4**

4 racks of "Denver cut" lamb ribs, each about 1 pound

6 tablespoons (¾ cup; packed) dark brown sugar

3 tablespoons mild pimentón

3 tablespoons ground coffee

2 tablespoons coarse salt (kosher or sea)

1 tablespoon freshly ground black pepper

1½ teaspoons unsweetened cocoa powder

1 cup Dark and Stormy Barbecue Sauce (page 537) or other favorite sauce

To Skin Lamb Ribs

Place a rack of ribs meat side down on a baking sheet. Remove the thin, papery membrane from the back of the rack by inserting a slender implement, such as the tip of an instant-read thermometer, under it. The best place to start is on one of the middle bones. Lift the thermometer to pry up the skin. Using a dishcloth or paper towel to gain a secure grip, peel off the membrane. Repeat with the other rack of ribs.

1 Preheat the oven to 275°F.

2 Place a rack of ribs meat side down on a baking sheet. Remove the thin, papery membrane from the back of the rack. Turn the ribs over and, using a knife, score a crosshatch pattern on the meat side, making cuts about ½ inch apart and ¼ inch deep. Repeat with the second rack of ribs. (Scoring helps render the fat and crisp the meat.)

3 Place the brown sugar, pimentón, ground coffee, salt, black pepper, and, cocoa powder in a small bowl and stir to mix, breaking up any lumps in the sugar with your fingers. Sprinkle the rub on both sides of the ribs, rubbing it onto the meat. You won't need all the rub—just enough to crust the meat. Refrigerate any extra.

4 Line a second baking sheet with aluminum foil to facilitate cleanup. Place a wire rack on top of the foil and arrange the ribs, meat side up, on top. Bake the ribs until sizzling, browned, and very tender, 1½ to 2 hours.

5 Transfer the racks of ribs to a cutting board and let rest for 5 minutes, then cut into individual ribs. Serve with Dark and Stormy Barbecue Sauce or other favorite sauce on the side.

Variation
Smoke-Roasted Lamb Ribs on the Grill

Prepare and rub the ribs as described above. Set up the grill for indirect grilling and preheat to medium-low (275°F). Place a large drip pan in the center of the grill under the grate. Brush and oil the grate.

Place the lamb ribs, bone side down, in the center of the grate over the drip pan and away from the heat. Toss 1½ cups soaked, drained hickory or cherry chips on the coals. Cover the grill and indirect-grill the ribs until tender (the meat will shrink back from the ends of the bones by ¼ to ½ inch), 1½ to 2 hours. Serve as described above.

YOUR BASIC SHISH KEBAB

The first leap forward in culinary "technology" was roasting chunks of meat on a stick. Today, we call it shish kebab (from the Turkish words for "sword" and "meat"), and it remains one of the world's most popular guy foods. Popular? Variations include Peruvian *anticuchos,* French brochettes, Greek souvlaki, and Indonesian saté. It sounds simple, but a lot of mediocre shish kebab gets served. One common mistake is to place ingredients with different cooking times on the same skewer. If you've ever had kebabs with overcooked meat, still raw onions, and tomatoes so soft they fell off the skewer, you know what I mean. The solution?

SHOP Nothing too esoteric here: I prefer lamb shoulder to leg—it has more fat, which makes for more succulent kebabs.

GEAR Your basic kitchen gear plus a grill or broiler. For small kebabs, flat or round bamboo skewers. For larger kebabs, use flat metal skewers. They keep the ingredients aligned when you turn the kebabs and the heat-conducting metal helps cook the meat more quickly. You'll also need a large baking pan.

WHAT ELSE The marinade is limited only by your imagination. For Greek-style kebabs, substitute fresh mint for the tarragon, basil, or rosemary. For Spanish kebabs, substitute ¼ cup of sherry or sherry vinegar for the lemon juice and 1 tablespoon of smoked paprika for the herb.

TIME about 30 minutes preparation and cooking time, plus 30 minutes to 4 hours for marinating the kebabs

Grill the lamb, peppers, and thinly sliced onions on the same skewer. If you wish to cook tomatoes and mushrooms, they should go on separate skewers because they cook faster. **Serves 4**

For the kebabs

1½ pounds boneless lamb shoulder or leg

1 large onion

1 red bell pepper

1 yellow or green bell pepper or poblano pepper

16 fresh or dried bay leaves or fresh basil leaves (optional)

For the marinade

2 cloves garlic, peeled and minced

1 teaspoon coarse salt (kosher or sea)

1 teaspoon freshly ground black pepper

1 bunch fresh tarragon, basil, or rosemary, (3 tablespoons finely chopped, plus a couple of whole branches for basting)

1 teaspoon finely grated fresh lemon zest

¼ cup fresh lemon juice or dry white wine

½ cup extra virgin olive oil

1 Prepare the kebabs: Cut the lamb into 1-inch chunks. Be sure to include the fatty parts; these will baste the meat as they melt, keeping the kebabs moist. Peel the onion and cut it in half crosswise. Cut each half into 6 wedges. Separate the onion chunks into individual layers. Stem and seed the peppers and cut them into 1-inch squares.

2 Thread the lamb onto skewers, alternating the meat with the larger onion pieces, pepper squares, and bay leaves or basil leaves, if using. Arrange the kebabs in a large baking pan.

3 Make the marinade: Place the garlic, salt, and pepper in the bottom of a mixing bowl and, using a wooden spoon, mash them together. Mash in the chopped tarragon and lemon zest. Whisk in the lemon juice or wine

followed by the ½ cup of olive oil and any small pieces of onion left over from cutting the onions.

4 Pour two-thirds of the marinade over the kebabs, turning them so they marinate evenly. Set aside the remaining marinade for basting. Let the kebabs marinate, covered, in the refrigerator for as little as 30 minutes or as long as 4 hours; the longer the kebabs marinate, the richer the flavor will be. Turn the kebabs a few times so they marinate evenly.

5 *To grill the kebabs:* Set up the grill for direct grilling and preheat it to high. When ready to cook, brush and oil the grill grate. Drain the kebabs and arrange them on the hot grate. Grill the kebabs until browned on all sides and cooked to taste, about 2 minutes per side (about 8 minutes in all) for medium-rare, about 3 minutes per side (about 12 minutes in all) for medium. After about 4 minutes, start basting the kebabs with the reserved marinade, using the rosemary sprigs as a basting brush.

To broil the kebabs: Preheat the broiler to high and have the top oven rack on the highest level. Line a broiler pan with aluminum foil and arrange the kebabs in the pan. Broil the kebabs about 2 inches from the heat source until the lamb is browned on all sides and cooked to taste, 2 minutes per side (8 minutes in all) for medium-rare, 3 minutes per side (12 minutes in all) for medium. Start basting the kebabs with the reserved marinade after 4 minutes, using the tarragon sprigs as a basting brush.

6 Transfer the kebabs to a platter or plates and baste them one final time. If you serve the kebabs on metal skewers, remind everyone to slide the meat off the skewers with a fork before eating. *Never* eat shish kebab directly off a hot metal skewer.

Variations

Persian lamb kebabs: Among the world's greatest kebabs: Make a yogurt marinade by mashing the garlic, salt, and pepper in a mixing bowl as described in the shish kebab recipe. Whisk in 1 cup of plain Greek yogurt and 3 tablespoons each of extra virgin olive oil and fresh lemon juice. Add ½ teaspoon of saffron threads that have been soaked in 1 tablespoon of hot water for about 5 minutes. Use this mixture to marinate the kebabs as directed in Step 4 above. Baste them with 3 tablespoons of melted butter as they grill or broil, following the instructions in Step 5.

Yankee teriyaki kebabs: Combine ¼ cup each of soy sauce, Asian (dark) sesame oil, sake or sherry, and maple syrup in a mixing bowl and whisk to mix. For even more flavor, add 1 tablespoon each of minced scallion and peeled minced fresh ginger and 1 peeled minced clove of garlic. Marinate the kebabs in this mixture as directed in Step 4 above. Cook as described in Step 5. To make a sauce, strain the marinade into a saucepan and cook it at a rolling boil for about 4 minutes. Use this sauce for basting the kebabs during the last 2 minutes of cooking, and spoon the remaining sauce over the kebabs at the end.

JON SHOOK AND VINNY DOTOLO

If Americans now eat pigs' ears and lambs' feet with an enthusiasm once reserved for nachos or Buffalo wings, we have Jon Shook and Vinny Dotolo to thank. When the self-styled duo opened Animal, their unrepentantly carnivorous restaurant in Los Angeles's Fairfax district, they loaded the menu with brains, testicles, kidneys, bone marrow, and pigs' ears and tails (the latter done Buffalo wing-style). One reason was economic—they had a shoestring budget, and offal was a lot more affordable than porterhouse. Another was the shock value, and Animal certainly made headlines—and lots of new customers—with its organ-centric menu. But ultimately, the chefs use these traditionally maligned, underutilized meat cuts because they like the taste. "Who would have ever thought veal balls would be cool?" Shook says, marveling at Animal's success.

They've since opened a seafood joint called Son of a Gun and partnered with French pop-up chef Ludo LeFebvre to open Trois Mec. But the dudes weren't always the darlings of the Los Angeles food scene, and their restaurants didn't always play to capacity crowds. Long before the James Beard and *Food & Wine* awards, Vinny and Jon earned their living catering parties out of the back of their car, shopping at local supermarkets, cooking in cramped home kitchens—in short, preparing food like most guys who aren't professional chefs do.

"Why blow your budget on veal loins and exotic produce when the most crowd-pleasing dishes are riffs on taco night and pancake breakfasts?" says Vinny. He and Jon hardly ever use chicken or veal stock, preferring to build flavor with, for example, mustard, beer, ketchup, tomato sauce, and Tabasco sauce. "The idea is to keep things simple—feed the most people for the least money while still creating excellent and exciting food," adds Jon. If these two can do it, you can do it, too.

What's your go-to dish when you're by yourself?
Jon: Bloody Mary with a shrimp cocktail on the top. I like my Bloody Mary

looking like a mixed salad, with cornichons, olives, celery, and shrimp spilling over the rim of the glass.

What's your go-to dish when you have company?
Jon: Roast chicken. It's so easy, but when you do it right, everyone will be salivating.

> ▶ The idea is to keep things simple—feed the most people for the least money while still creating excellent and exciting food.

Do you have a seduction dish?
Vinny: My wife was a vegan when we met, so what impressed her wasn't so much the food as how efficient I was in the kitchen.

Name three dishes every guy should know how to make.
Mac and cheese.
A great hamburger.
A really good salad. It can be as simple as arugula with olive oil, lemon juice, and shaved Parmesan cheese. Hey, this is California.

Name three types of offal every guy should know how to prepare.
Calf's brains: Soak them in cold water overnight, then poach for 1 minute in court bouillon (water flavored with onion, carrot, celery, herbs, wine, and peppercorns).
Chicken feet: Poach them in chicken fat for 4 hours or cook them in a pressure cooker for 45 minutes, then deep-fry as you would chicken wings. We like chicken feet because, from a flavor point of view, they're like a blank canvas.
Pigs' ears: Cook them in water to cover with onions, carrots, and celery for 30 hours (keep the water just below a boil). Drain, cool, thinly sliver, and deep-fry until crisp. We like to serve pigs' ears with chiles, lime, garlic, scallions, and a fried egg on top. [Take it from me, they're delicious.]

Three ingredients you can't live without?
Grapeseed oil. It has a neutral flavor, which makes it great for sauces and vinaigrettes and it has a high burning point, which makes it ideal for sautéing.
Vinegar. Red wine vinegar, white wine vinegar, balsamic vinegar, champagne vinegar—you name it, we use it. We love the way it cuts the fat, focuses the flavor, and makes sauces shine.
Foie gras. The mild buttery liver of an overfed duck or goose—simply the richest tasting food on the planet.

Three tools you can't live without?
A mortar and pestle. Pounding spices and aromatics in a mortar with a pestle gives you a very different flavor than pureeing them in a food processor.
A 10-inch frying pan. There's almost nothing you *can't* cook in it.
A tasting spoon. None of that finger dipping-licking for us.

What are the three most important things to keep in mind if you're just starting out in the kitchen?
Work clean, as in "clean up as you go along." Cooking is a lot easier if you don't have to wade through a mess.
Choose a knife that feels comfortable in your hand and have it sharpened professionally every few months.
Enjoy yourself when you cook. Your food feels your emotions. If you feel stressed, your food will taste like it.

What are the three most common mistakes guys make in the kitchen?
Underseasoning. Don't be afraid to use salt. We like the texture and taste of kosher salt.
Being impatient. Wait for your pan to reach the right temperature—hot—before you add the food. Otherwise, you'll never get the proper browning, which is essential to flavor.
Risking cross-contamination. Use different cutting boards for raw meats and raw vegetables and never cut cooked food on a board that's held raw.

Name something unexpected you've learned over the years that really helps you up your game in the kitchen.
Bacon. It's not just for breakfast or BLTs anymore. We use it in everything from bacon chocolate crunch bars to iced tea.

LAMB VINDALOO

SHOP For chiles, Raghavan Iyer (see headnote) suggests dried red cayenne or Thai chile peppers—available at most supermarkets and natural foods stores. If they are unavailable, you can use 1 to 2 tablespoons of hot red pepper flakes. If you're making this in the U.K., it may be easier for you to find malt vinegar than cider vinegar.

GEAR Your basic kitchen gear including a blender and a large heavy pot or Dutch oven with a tight-fitting lid

WHAT ELSE You can make a similar vindaloo with goat, chicken, pork, or seafood.

TIME about 50 minutes preparation and cooking time, plus 30 minutes to 8 hours for marinating the lamb

There are curries and there are curries, but none tortures your tongue like a fiery Goan stew known as vindaloo. The name tells an old story—it's a corruption of the Portuguese *vinha-d'alho* ("garlic wine") and a reminder of a Portuguese presence in Goa on India's southwest coast that stretches back five centuries. In fact, it was the Portuguese who introduced the chile pepper to India in the form of a fierce tiny red chile known in its land of origin, Brazil, as *piri-piri*. If some curries are famous for their complex spicing, vindaloo is defined by its searing heat and vinegary bite. But don't take my word for it. The final word on any curry (and the inspiration for this one) comes from award-winning cooking teacher Raghavan Iyer, who wrote the bible on curry: *660 Curries*—the inspiration for the lamb vindaloo that follows. **Serves 4**

For the spice paste
$\frac{2}{3}$ cup cider vinegar

1 piece (3 inches) fresh ginger, peeled and coarsely chopped

10 cloves garlic, peeled and coarsely chopped

10 small dried cayenne or Thai red chiles

1 cinnamon stick (3 inches), broken into $\frac{1}{2}$-inch pieces, or 1 teaspoon ground cinnamon

1 tablespoon cumin seeds

$1\frac{1}{2}$ teaspoons coarse salt (kosher or sea), or more to taste

1 teaspoon freshly ground black pepper

1 teaspoon ground turmeric

For the lamb
$1\frac{1}{2}$ pounds boneless lamb leg or shoulder, cut into 1-inch pieces

2 tablespoons canola oil

$\frac{1}{4}$ cup chopped fresh cilantro

For serving
Boiled rice (page 488), preferably basmati

1 Make the spice paste: Place the cider vinegar, ginger, garlic, chiles, cinnamon stick, cumin seeds, salt, black pepper, and turmeric in a blender and puree to form a gritty paste. You'll need to scrape down the inside of the blender jar several times with a spatula to obtain a smooth spice paste.

2 Prepare the lamb: Place the lamb in a nonreactive (glass, ceramic, or stainless steel) mixing bowl, pour in the spice paste, and stir to coat the meat. Let the lamb marinate in the refrigerator for at least 30 minutes or as long as overnight; the longer the lamb marinates, the richer the flavor will be.

3 Heat the oil in a large heavy pot or Dutch oven over medium-high heat. Add the lamb with its marinade and cook, uncovered, until all the liquid evaporates and the lamb browns, 10 to 15 minutes, stirring from time to time.

4 Stir in 1 cup of water, scraping up the brown bits from the bottom of the pot with a wooden spoon. Reduce the heat to medium-low so that the vindaloo simmers gently. Cover the pot and let the lamb simmer until it is very tender and the sauce is thick, 45 to 60 minutes, stirring occasionally, and adding more water if the sauce level is too low.

5 Stir half of the cilantro into the vindaloo and simmer for 2 minutes to blend the cilantro flavor into the sauce. Taste for seasoning, adding more salt if necessary; the vindaloo should be highly seasoned. Sprinkle the remaining cilantro over the vindaloo just before serving. Boiled rice (especially basmati) makes a good accompaniment.

CURRIED GOAT

Goat is the new lamb. This lean, rich-flavored meat is turning up at hipster restaurants and cutting-edge cookouts from Brooklyn to Berkeley. Sure, part of its appeal is a certain one-upmanship. Beef cheeks? Been there. Pigs' ears? Done that. But goat remains exotic. Part of the mystique is taste, for young goat can be as mild as veal while mature goat tastes as gamy as mutton. This comes as no surprise to French West Indians, for whom this intensely flavorful curried goat is comfort food and party dish combined. **Serves 4**

SHOP Look for goat at West Indian and halal markets or preorder it from your butcher. Calabaza is a West Indian squash. Find it at West Indian or Hispanic markets or use another orange squash, like butternut.

GEAR Your basic kitchen gear including a large heavy pot or Dutch oven with a tight-fitting lid

1½ pounds boneless goat meat (from the leg or shoulder), cut into 1-inch cubes

Coarse salt (kosher or sea) and freshly ground black pepper

1 to 2 tablespoons canola oil

1 medium-size onion, peeled and finely chopped

3 cloves garlic, peeled and minced

2 bunches chives, or 1 bunch trimmed scallions, both white and green parts, finely chopped (about 1 cup)

1 tablespoon curry powder, or to taste

2 tablespoons tomato paste

1 quart (4 cups) chicken stock (preferably homemade, page 549) or water, or more as needed

1 pound potatoes, scrubbed and cut into 1-inch pieces

1 pound calabaza (West Indian squash) or butternut squash, peeled, seeded, and cut into 1-inch pieces

Boiled rice (page 488), for serving

1 Generously season the goat on all sides with salt and pepper. Heat 1 tablespoon of oil in a large heavy pot or Dutch oven over high heat. Working in several batches so as not to crowd the pan, add the goat and cook it until browned on all sides, about 2 minutes per side, 6 to 8 minutes in all, adding more oil as needed. Transfer the browned goat to a platter.

2 Pour off all but 2 tablespoons of fat from the pot. Add the onion, garlic, and chives or scallions (reserving 2 tablespoons chives or scallion greens for serving) and cook over medium-high heat until lightly browned, 3 to 5 minutes, stirring often with a wooden spoon.

3 Stir in 1 tablespoon of curry powder and cook until fragrant, about 2 minutes. Stir in the tomato paste and cook until fragrant, about 1 minute.

4 Return the goat and any of its juices to the pot. Stir in the stock, scraping up any brown bits from the bottom of the pot with a wooden spoon. Let the mixture come to a boil, then reduce the heat and let it simmer gently, covered, about 1 hour, stirring from time to time.

5 Stir in the potatoes and calabaza. If necessary, add more stock or water to cover the ingredients. Let the curry simmer until the goat and vegetables are tender, 30 to 40 minutes more. Uncover the pot for the last 15 minutes of cooking to let some of the liquid evaporate and thicken the sauce. It should be a loose gravy when finished cooking.

6 Taste for seasoning, adding more salt, pepper, and/or curry powder to taste; the stew should be highly seasoned. If you add a little more curry powder, simmer the stew, covered, for another 5 to 10 minutes to incorporate the flavor. Sprinkle the reserved chives or scallion greens on top, and serve the curried goat right out of the pot with boiled rice.

BIRDS AND
A RABBIT

Poultry may lack the sanguine glory of steak or the machismo awesomeness of a roasted pork shoulder, but a well-executed roast chicken—skin crackling, meat moist—is equally essential to a man's happiness. So are deep-fried turkey and Brandy-Brined Pheasants. Your growing roster of skills should include how to cook America's favorite birds.

In this chapter, you'll learn how to roast the perfect chicken and how to turn that convenient but boring parcel of protein, the skinless, boneless chicken breast, into a comforting cutlet and ingenious low-carb "calzone." Fried chicken? I'll show you how they prepare it at the popular Yardbird restaurant on Miami Beach. Spatchcocking? I'll tell you what it is and how it can help you serve an incredible mustard-and-curry-crusted whole chicken in a hurry. Big bird? You bet.

ROAST CHICKEN
WITH LEMON AND GARLIC

Asked to name one dish every guy should know how to make, the überchef Thomas Keller (page 92) cited a great roast chicken. So did modernist cuisine visionary Nathan Myhrvold (page 52). So a perfectly roasted chicken belongs in any man's repertory. This one veers toward the Mediterranean with lemon, garlic, and rosemary. **Serves 2 to 4**

1 chicken (3½ to 4 pounds), preferably organic

Coarse salt (kosher or sea) and freshly ground black pepper

1 head garlic, cut in half crosswise

1 lemon, rinsed, dried, and cut in half crosswise

3 sprigs fresh rosemary (optional)

1 tablespoon butter, at room temperature, or 1 tablespoon extra virgin olive oil

1 Preheat the oven to 400°F.

2 If there is a package of giblets, remove it from the cavity of the chicken (freeze the heart, gizzard, and neck for making stock, page 549). Rinse the chicken inside and out under cold water and blot it dry with paper towels. Put the chicken in a roasting pan. Generously season the neck and main cavities of the chicken with salt and pepper (the neck cavity is under the flap of skin where the neck used to be). Break off 3 garlic cloves from one half of the garlic head and place 2 of them in the main cavity along with 1 of the lemon halves and a sprig of rosemary, if using. Place the third garlic clove in the neck cavity.

3 Rub the outside of the chicken with the cut side of the garlic and the remaining lemon half. Rub the outside of the bird with the butter or olive oil, concentrating it on the breast. Generously season the bird on all sides (including the bottom) with salt and pepper. Truss the chicken (see page 330), then place it, breast side up, in a roasting pan. Arrange the garlic halves and the remaining lemon half and rosemary sprigs, if using, around the bird with the cut side of the garlic and lemon facing the bird.

4 Place the chicken in the oven and roast it

TIME about 1½ hours

SHOP You get what you pay for. Factory-raised supermarket chicken may be cheap, but it will never have the satisfying texture and intense taste of a pastured farm-raised or organic bird. Don't overlook local varieties, either. If you live in southern California, try a Japanese-style bird called Jidori. Other marquee varieties include Belle Rouge and Plymouth Rock.

GEAR Your basic kitchen gear including a roasting pan, plus a 12-inch bamboo skewer or butcher's string and an instant-read thermometer

WHAT ELSE For an Asian roast chicken, substitute a 2-inch piece of fresh ginger and 2 scallions for the lemon and rosemary. (Rub the chicken with the cut side of the ginger, then place it and the scallions in the cavity of the chicken.) Use 1 tablespoon of Asian (dark) sesame oil in place of the butter or olive oil. A splash of soy sauce wouldn't hurt either.

To Carve a Chicken

When carving a chicken I take a less-is-more approach. I carve the bird into basic pieces (wings, breast halves, thighs, drumsticks) and let each eater do the slicing.

1. Using a sharpening steel, theatrically sharpen a carving knife or chef's knife (actually, you're whetting the edge). Don't work directly over the chicken—you don't want to dust it with metal filings. You'll also need a carving fork or spring-loaded tongs.

2. Place the chicken on a cutting board breast side up. Cut off the wings. Starting at the front of the bird, slide the knife in a downward motion to, then through the joint to remove a wing. Position the knife so that you include an inch or so of breast meat attached to the wing—this gives the wingman more to eat. Repeat with the second wing.

3. Remove one of the breast halves. Make a lengthwise cut down one side of the breastbone (sometimes called the keel bone), following the rib cage down the side of the bird. Cut around the wishbone in the front to release the breast half. Remove the second half breast the same way.

4. Remove a leg. Using a carving fork, pull the leg away from the carcass and cut through the joint at the hip. Place the leg flat on the cutting board skin side down. Cut through the joint between the thigh and the drumstick. Repeat with the remaining leg.

5. Go over the carcass, cutting or pulling off any meat left behind. Don't forget to save the carcass for making chicken stock (page 549).

until the skin is crisp and golden brown and the meat is cooked through, 1 to 1¼ hours. After about 30 minutes, start basting the bird with the fat and juices that accumulate in the bottom of the roasting pan. (Collect them with a soupspoon and pour them over the breast; this is why I recommend roasting the chicken in the bottom of the roasting pan, not on a rack—so you have easy access to the pan juices.)

5 To test the chicken for doneness insert an instant-read thermometer into the thickest part of a thigh but not so that it touches a bone (touching the bone will give you a false reading). When done the internal temperature should be 165°F. If the chicken breast starts to brown too much before the bird is fully cooked, loosely lay a piece of aluminum foil over the breast.

6 Transfer the chicken to a cutting board and let it rest for about 5 minutes. Remove the trussing string before carving the bird.

Variation

To make a simple sauce for the chicken, while the chicken rests, spoon off most of the fat in the roasting pan. Add ¾ cup of chicken or beef stock (preferably homemade, see page 549) to the roasting pan and place it on the stove. Let the liquid come to a boil, scraping up the brown bits from the bottom of the pan with a wooden spoon. Let the sauce boil until slightly reduced and richly flavored, about 5 minutes.

Add 2 tablespoons butter and stir until it melts and is incorporated. Then, serve.

▶ *Roast Chicken with Lemon and Garlic*

▶ A lot of roast chicken and other poultry recipes begin with trussing the bird. So what's the big deal about this act of kitchen bondage? Trussing serves two purposes. It gives your bird a compact cylindrical shape, which helps it cook more evenly. And it makes the bird look more appetizing and you—the preparer—more professional.

Here are two methods. Use cotton butcher's string, not nylon, which might melt in the oven.

How to Truss a Chicken or Other Bird

QUICK METHOD

1 Stuff the cavity with lemon, garlic, and rosemary, or herbs of choice. Note how the wing tips are tucked under the body.

2 Cross the ends of the drumsticks.

3 Tie the drumsticks together and cut the string.

ELABORATE METHOD

1 Once the legs are tied, loop the ends of the string around the front of the bird at the neck end.

2 Pull the string back around the cavity end of the bird and tie again at the legs.

3 The fully trussed bird ready for roasting.

THE WHOLE BIRD

Here's what you need to know about buying and cooking your chicken whole.

BUY ORGANIC | It costs more, but the chicken is raised in a certified facility on a natural grain diet, with space to run around, and without being subjected to growth hormones or antibiotics. This is the only certification backed up with legal minimum standards of quality and safety.

BUY LOCAL | Chances are the chicken at your local farmers' market has been raised according to organic principles, even if it doesn't carry organic certification.

KNOW THE NOMENCLATURE | In theory *free range* means the birds spend part of their day outdoors on the grass, not just in cramped factory cages. *Grain fed* means chickens have been fed a cereal diet, not raised on fishmeal or other animal by-products commonly used in factory farming. *Natural* may mean all or some of these attributes, or the term may simply be used for marketing.

CHECK THE DATE | To make sure you buy the freshest possible chicken, check the "sell by" and "use by" dates on the label.

HOW MUCH IS ENOUGH? | A frying chicken (3½ to 4 pounds) will feed two hungry guys or four people.

SIZE MATTERS | Whole chickens come in a variety of sizes. Here's how to decode the lingo.

Fryer or frying chicken The most common bird, weighing 3½ to 4 pounds. Unless otherwise stated, the recipes in this book—including roasting—call for fryers.

Roasting chicken A larger, more mature bird, weighing 4 to 6 pounds, it's used for roasting.

Stewing chicken A tough, mature, big-flavored bird—often a retired laying hen—traditionally cooked in soups and stews (it's too tough for roasting).

Poussin French for a young chicken. A poussin typically weighs 1 to 2 pounds. Exceptionally sweet and tender.

Game hen aka Cornish game hen or Rock Cornish game hen. A small chicken weighing less than 2 pounds. The "hens" can be male or female and are a cross between the Cornish game hen and the Plymouth or White Rock chicken breeds.

Capon A castrated mature male chicken with rich-flavored meat, typically weighing 6 to 8 pounds, which will serve six to eight.

COOK IT SAFE | Up to 75 percent of the raw chicken sold in America today carries the salmonella bacteria. Sad but true. When preparing chicken, always use a dedicated knife and cutting board for raw chicken and never place any other food (raw or cooked) on that cutting board until you wash it thoroughly with hot water and soap. Ditto for platters or baking dishes that have held raw chicken.

FOOD DUDE
FRANCIS REDDY

Imagine a TV show like *The View* hosted by men and shot live at Montreal's fabulous open-air Jean-Talon food market. That summed up *Des Kiwis et des Hommes* (*Of Kiwis and Men*), a popular French-Canadian show featuring some of Quebec's top actors, musicians, writers, artists, and occasionally a French-speaking American—yours truly—whom our northern neighbors call *Le Maître du Grill*. Presiding over the show: Francis Reddy, a forty-something host with a perennially boyish demeanor and a deep love of food. French-Canadians know him as the star of the hit movie *Mario* and as Pete Béliveau in the cult Québécois TV series *Chambres en Ville* (*Rooms in Town*). I know him as a guy who makes a mean braised rabbit with olives (page 359) and shares a lot of my philosophies about food.

Like many food dudes, Reddy learned to cook from his father. "He was a salesman, so he got home from work late. At eight p.m., he'd open the refrigerator and start cooking with whatever he found. He called it a *repas de rien* (a meal made from nothing), and it taught me the importance of improvising in the kitchen." Another lesson Reddy learned from dad was the sanctity of the family meal—a lesson he tries to teach his own kids. "Mealtimes are a privileged moment," he says. "It's important to stop what you're doing once a day and make time to eat with your family. A proper home-cooked sit-down meal, not dinner grabbed on the fly—and especially no smart phones or TV."

Like many of the food dudes in this book, Reddy overreached the first time he cooked for a dinner party. "I tried to make classic French *cailles aux raisins* (quail with grapes). It was an absolute disaster." The moral of the story? Never attempt a dish for company you haven't cooked at least once before.

Why should a man know how to cook?
First and foremost, autonomy. So you can take care of yourself.

Do men and women cook differently?
Men cook like they're always hungry (which we are) and we do it in a spirit of excess. To serve four people we cook for eight. If a recipe calls for a tablespoon of Cognac, we add half a bottle. We gravitate to fast-cooking methods,

like grilling, but we also need to learn how to cook slowly, like long-simmered stews and braised dishes that take a half day.

What's your go-to dish when you're by yourself?

Calf's liver. I caramelize a ton of onions with red wine and butter. Then I fry the calf's liver in the same pan with a spoonful of capers.

▸ Never attempt a dish for company you haven't cooked at least once before.

What's your favorite seduction dish?

Fruits de mer (shellfish). Oysters and clams on the half shell, plus cold poached lobster and shrimp—the simpler, the better. It worked for Casanova.

What's your secret vice?

I adore cheese and I eat a lot of it. A well-assembled cheese platter can make you look like a genius even if you don't know how to boil water. Find a cheese merchant you trust and load up on some great local artisanal cheeses, quince jelly, fig jam, dried fruits, almonds, and walnuts. Arrange them on a platter and you've got an instant feast. Incidentally, and this probably sounds like heresy, the best way to store cheese is not in plastic wrap, but tightly bundled in aluminum foil.

Three dishes every guy should know how to make?

Chicken. There must be a thousand ways to prepare it.

An omelet. You'll never go hungry if you know how to cook an omelet.

A big T-bone steak. You'd never call *that* girl food.

Three ingredients you can't live without?

Garlic. Tomatoes. Eggs.

Three tools you can't live without?

A whisk. A good knife. An espresso machine. The espresso machine provides the fuel for all my activities in the kitchen.

What are the three most important things to keep in mind if you're just starting out in the kitchen?

Learn to sear. Heat your pan first, then add the fat and heat that. Finally, add the meat. You need a hot pan to produce a flavorful crust and sear in the juices.

Learn to roast. Start with a hot oven (450°F) and cook the meat for twenty minutes to caramelize (deeply brown) the exterior of the meat. Then lower the heat to 350°F to finish the cooking. Use this method whether roasting large hunks of beef, pork, or lamb or whole ducks or chickens.

Learn how to make crepes. You've got breakfast, lunch, dinner, a midnight snack, and everything in between. My formula is simple: 1½ cups milk, 1 cup flour, 2 eggs, 4 tablespoons (½ stick) melted butter, a splash of vanilla, and salt to taste. Put in a bowl, whisk until smooth, and panfry in thin circles over medium heat to make crepes.

What are the three most common mistakes guys make in the kitchen?

Cooking everything too fast. It takes three to four hours to braise a good rabbit. Slow down, guys.

Burning food, which comes from wanting to cook everything too fast. There's a difference between cooked and burnt.

Overcooking vegetables. Boil them in salted water until barely tender, then shock chill them in ice water to stop the cooking.

What do guys in the kitchen need to do more of?

Taste. Taste. Taste. A lot of guys think they're done once they put the ingredients in the pot. Food changes as it cooks, and you need to taste it often so you can adjust the seasonings accordingly.

Parting words of advice?

This is an extraordinary time for a man to learn how to cook. It seems that fewer women are cooking these days. The women I know find it incredibly sexy when a man knows how to cook.

Gordon Hamersley's

LEMON AND MUSTARD ROAST CHICKEN

SHOP Herbes de Provence is a French dried herb blend (think oregano, rosemary, and, for a sweet note, lavender) available at most specialty food shops and markets.

GEAR Your basic kitchen gear including a grater, a food processor, a roasting pan, and an instant-read thermometer, plus a 12-inch bamboo skewer or butcher's string and a fat separator

TIME 20 minutes preparation time, at least 4 hours marinating time, and 1 to 1¼ hours roasting time

Starting on page 327, you learned what it takes to roast a proper chicken. Here, courtesy of my chef friend Gordon Hamersley of Hamersley's Bistro in Boston, comes what may be the best roast chicken I've eaten on six continents. Lemon gives it bite, mustard kicks up the heat, and extra virgin olive oil keeps it fragrant and juicy. **Serves 2 to 4**

1 lemon, rinsed and dried

3 shallots, peeled and coarsely chopped

3 cloves garlic, peeled and coarsely chopped, plus 3 cloves garlic, peeled

½ cup coarsely chopped fresh flat-leaf parsley leaves

1 tablespoon chopped fresh rosemary

1 tablespoon herbes de Provence (optional)

1½ teaspoons coarse salt (kosher or sea)

1 teaspoon freshly ground black pepper

¼ cup Dijon mustard

⅓ cup extra virgin olive oil

1 chicken (3½ to 4 pounds), preferably organic

Garlic Lemon Jus (recipe follows)

1 Grate 1 teaspoon zest (the oil-rich outer rind) from the lemon and place it in a food processor. Cut the lemon in half crosswise and cut off an ⅛-inch-thick slice from the cut side of each half. Juice the lemon halves, discarding the seeds. Set the slices and juice aside.

2 Add the shallots, chopped garlic, parsley, rosemary, herbes de Provence, if using, and

the salt and pepper to the food processor. Run the processor in short bursts to finely chop and then puree the herb mix. Mix in the lemon juice and mustard. Add the olive oil in a thin stream, processing the herb mixture to obtain a smooth paste. Set the marinade aside.

3 If there is a package of giblets, remove it from the cavity of the chicken (freeze the heart, gizzard, and neck, for making stock, page 549). Rinse the chicken inside and out under cold water and blot it dry with paper towels. Place 1 slice of lemon and 1 garlic clove in the neck cavity of the chicken and the remaining lemon slice and 2 garlic cloves in the main cavity. Spoon a little of the marinade in the neck and main cavities of the chicken. Place the chicken in a large heavy-duty resealable plastic bag and add the remaining marinade. Squeeze the bag to coat the chicken all over with marinade. Let the chicken marinate in the refrigerator for at least 4 hours, or as long as overnight.

4   Preheat the oven to 400°F.

5   Remove the chicken from the bag with the marinade and truss it using one of the methods on page 330. Place the chicken in a roasting pan breast side up, place the roasting pan in the oven, and roast the chicken until the skin is crisp and golden brown and the meat is cooked through, 1 to 1¼ hours. After about 30 minutes, start basting the bird with the fat and juices that accumulate in the bottom of the roasting pan.

6   To test the chicken for doneness insert an instant-read thermometer into the thickest part of a thigh but not so that it touches a bone (touching the bone will give you a false reading). When done, the internal temperature should be 165°F. If the chicken breast starts to brown too much before the bird is fully cooked, lay a piece of aluminum foil over the breast.

7   Transfer the roasted chicken to a cutting board, setting aside the roasting pan. Let the chicken rest while you make the Garlic Lemon Jus with the juices from the roasting pan. Remove the trussing string and carve the chicken. Pour the Garlic Lemon Jus over it, and dig in.

GARLIC LEMON JUS

A *jus* ("juice" in French) is a natural gravy—pan drippings free of starchy thickeners or cream. In this case the *jus* is enriched with garlic, lemon, and chicken stock. It's helpful to use a fat separator—a measuring cup or gravy boat that has a spout attached to the bottom. You pour the pan drippings into the separator; the fat floats to the top, leaving the drippings from the chicken to settle at the bottom. Because the spout is attached at the bottom, the drippings pour out clear. You need to add enough chicken stock so that, when combined with the drippings, you get about one cup of liquid. **Makes about 1 cup**

Drippings from the roasted chicken

1 tablespoon unsalted butter

2 cloves garlic, peeled and thinly sliced crosswise

1 tablespoon diced lemon, seeds, rind, and pith removed

1 teaspoon fresh lemon juice

1 cup chicken stock (preferably homemade, page 549)

Coarse salt (kosher or sea) and freshly ground black pepper

1 Pour the drippings from the roasting pan into a fat separator and let them settle until you can pour the meat juices out from under the fat that has risen to the top. If you do not have a fat separator, pour the drippings into a small bowl and let them stand for about 3 minutes. Spoon off and discard the fat that rises to the surface.

2 Melt the butter in a small saucepan over medium heat. Add the garlic and diced lemon and cook until the garlic is lightly browned, 1 to 2 minutes. Add the lemon juice, chicken juices, and chicken stock. Increase the heat to high and let the sauce boil until it is reduced to about 1 cup, 5 minutes, or as needed. Whisk in salt and pepper to taste. Pour the *jus* over the chicken.

SPATCHCOCK CHICKEN
WITH A CURRY MUSTARD CRUST

Some dishes you make because they're both easy and drop-dead delicious. Others because they feature a killer technique. This mustard-crusted chicken has it all—showmanship, complex layers of curry mustard flavor, moist tender meat, and a sizzling crisp crust. It also gives you the opportunity to use one of the coolest words in the culinary lexicon: *spatchcocking* ("dispatch the cock"—the chicken, that is)—the process of removing a chicken's backbone and opening it up like a book, so it lays flat and cooks quickly and evenly, maximizing the ratio of skin and crust to the meat. **Serves 2 to 4**

SHOP See page 331 for a guide to buying chicken. There are several options for mustard: grainy mustard from Meaux; a sharp, tangy mustard in the style of Dijon; a honey or maple syrup mustard from New England; or even a green peppercorn or tarragon mustard from France. Ditto for the bread crumbs. I'm lucky enough to have a wife who makes homemade bread crumbs from brioche (see How to Make Your Own Bread Crumbs on page 459), but you could also use rye or pumpernickel crumbs or Japanese *panko* (see page 344).

GEAR Your basic kitchen gear including a roasting pan, and an instant-read thermometer, plus poultry shears or kitchen shears

WHAT ELSE Spatchcocking was originally done to enable you to cook a whole chicken on a grill without a cover. This recipe tells you how to make it in the oven, but if you'd like to grill it, set up your grill for indirect grilling and preheat to medium-high (400°F). Place the bird away from the heat over the drip pan and indirect grill for about 30 minutes.

TIME about 15 minutes preparation time, plus 30 to 40 minutes cooking time

1 chicken (3½ to 4 pounds), preferably organic

2 teaspoons curry powder

1 teaspoon coarse salt (kosher or sea)

1 teaspoon freshly ground black pepper

¾ cup prepared mustard

1 cup bread crumbs

1 tablespoon extra virgin olive oil, or 1 tablespoon butter, melted

1 Preheat the oven to 400°F.

2 If there is a package of giblets, remove it from the cavity of the chicken (freeze the heart, gizzard, and neck for making stock, page 549). Rinse the chicken inside and out under cold water and blot it dry with paper towels. Place the bird, breast side down, on a cutting board. Using poultry or kitchen shears or a sharp knife, cut through the flesh and bone along both sides of the backbone so that you can completely remove the backbone.

3 Open the bird like a book by gently pulling the halves apart. Using a sharp paring knife, cut along and under both sides of the breastbone and cartilage attached to it. Discard the breastbone. Cut off the tips of the wings. Spread the bird out flat.

4 Using the tip of the knife, make a slit in the loose skin between the lower end of the breast and the leg, on each side, approximately ½ inch long. Stick the end of each drumstick through the slit on that side. This step is optional, but it makes the bird look cool.

5 Place the curry powder, salt, and pepper in a small bowl and stir to combine. Sprinkle the curry seasoning over the chicken on both sides, rubbing it onto the meat.

6 Place the bird skin side down and, using a spatula, spread about a third of the mustard over the flesh side of the chicken. Sprinkle ⅓ cup of the bread crumbs on top. Arrange the chicken skin side up in a roasting pan. Spread the remaining mustard on the skin side of the bird and crust it with the remaining ⅔ cup of bread crumbs. Drizzle the olive oil or melted butter over the bread crumbs.

7 Place the bird in the oven and roast it until the crust of crumbs is browned and sizzling and the chicken is cooked through, 30 to 40 minutes. Use an instant-read thermometer to test for doneness, inserting it sideways through a thigh but not so that it touches a bone. When done the internal temperature should be 165°F. If the crust browns too much before the bird is cooked through, loosely cover it with a piece of aluminum foil.

8 Transfer the chicken to a platter. Let it rest for about 3 minutes, then cut it into pieces, 2 legs, 2 thighs, 2 wing sections (with a little breast meat attached), and 2 breasts, for serving.

How to Spatchcock a Chicken

1 Using poultry shears or a sharp paring knife and starting at the neck, cut through the flesh and ribs on both sides of the backbone. Discard the backbone.

2 Open up the bird like a book by gently pushing the halves apart.

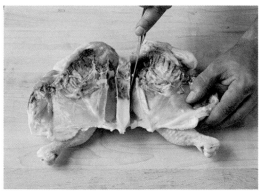

3 Using a sharp paring knife, make a lengthwise cut along and under both sides of the breastbone and cartilage attached to it. Discard the breastbone.

4 Using a sharp paring knife, make a ½-inch-long slit in the skin between the lower end of the breast and a leg.

5 Stick the end of the drumstick through the slit. Repeat on the other side.

6 The spatchcocked chicken ready for roasting or grilling. Note how it now lies flat.

FRIED CHICKEN

SHOP Jeff uses farm-raised chickens from central Florida. When possible, you should use a local and/or organic bird—you'll have better flavor and a cleaner conscience.

GEAR Your basic kitchen gear including a rimmed baking sheet, a rectangular wire rack, a large (10- to 12-inch) deep cast-iron skillet, tongs, and an instant-read thermometer, plus a deep-fry thermometer

WHAT ELSE Just so you know, lard is the traditional fat for frying chicken, but vegetable oil gives you excellent results.

Don't have a deep-fry thermometer? Dip the edge of a piece of battered chicken in the oil. If bubbles dance around it after a few seconds, the oil is hot enough. If it starts to burn after a few seconds, the oil is too hot.

TIME I won't tell you this fried chicken is fast food, but once you brine the chicken for 6 hours to overnight, you can dredge and fry the chicken in about 30 minutes.

Picture the perfect fried chicken: a shatteringly crisp crust over moist meat so assertively seasoned you don't need salt or pepper shakers on the table. In short, just the sort of fried chicken chef Jeff McInnis created for Yardbird Southern Table & Bar in what may be the least southern city in the South: Miami Beach. "We spent four months and more than one hundred batches developing our fried chicken," recalls McInnis, who settled on brining the bird, then dredging and frying it in cayenne-fired flour. Try it with tupelo honey spiked with Crystal hot sauce. **Serves 2 really hungry people or 4 with moderate appetites**

1 cup hot water

⅓ cup coarse salt (kosher or sea)

⅓ cup sugar

3 teaspoons freshly ground black pepper

3 teaspoons granulated garlic

3 teaspoons granulated onion

2 teaspoons cayenne pepper

5 cups cold water

1 chicken (3½ to 4 pounds), preferably organic, cut into 8 equal pieces

2 cups unbleached all-purpose white flour

¼ cup cornstarch

2 teaspoons sweet or hot paprika

2 cups buttermilk

3 cups lard, solid vegetable shortening, like Crisco, or canola oil for frying

Hellfire Honey Dipping Sauce (recipe follows)

1 Combine the hot water, salt, and sugar and 1 teaspoon each of the black pepper, granulated garlic, granulated onion, and cayenne in a large deep bowl. Whisk until the salt and sugar dissolve, then stir in the cold water. Let the brine cool completely.

2 Rinse the chicken pieces under cold running water and add them to the brine. Let the chicken brine in the refrigerator, covered, 6 to 8 hours or even overnight.

3 Place the flour, cornstarch, and paprika and the remaining 2 teaspoons each of black pepper, granulated garlic, granulated onion, and 1 teaspoon of cayenne in a large shallow bowl and whisk or stir with a fork to mix.

4 Pour the buttermilk into a shallow bowl. Line a rimmed baking sheet with paper towels and set a wire rack on top of them. Place the bowls of seasoned flour and buttermilk close to the stove.

5 Drain the chicken pieces well, discarding the brine. Using tongs, dip each piece of chicken in the buttermilk, coating it on all sides. Drain off the excess liquid. Then dip each piece of chicken in the seasoned flour to coat it on all sides, shaking off the excess, and lay each on a platter.

6 Meanwhile, heat the lard, shortening, or oil in a large deep skillet, preferably cast-iron, over medium heat to 350°F. Use a deep-fry thermometer to check the temperature or, after you have floured the chicken, dip the edge of a piece into the fat; when the fat is sufficiently hot, bubbles should dance around it.

7 Gently lower the chicken pieces into the hot fat, skin side down. Don't overcrowd the skillet; work in batches if necessary. Fry the chicken until it is golden brown on all sides and cooked through, 5 to 8 minutes per side, turning with tongs (the leg pieces will take longer than the breast pieces). Raise or lower the heat to keep the oil temperature around 350°F. To test the chicken for doneness, use an instant-read thermometer; the internal temperature in the thickest part of a piece of chicken should be about 165°F.

8 As each piece of chicken is cooked, transfer it to the wire cooling rack to drain. Serve with the Hellfire Honey Dipping Sauce.

HELLFIRE HONEY DIPPING SAUCE

Simple? This sauce contains only two ingredients, but the double blast of heat and sweet takes fried chicken to another level. It's also pretty terrific on smoked chicken wings (page 207) and ribs. For hot sauce, I like Crystal or Frank's RedHot. **Makes 1 cup**

½ cup tupelo or other honey

½ cup of your favorite hot sauce, or more to taste

Place the honey and hot sauce in a bowl and whisk to mix. Taste for seasoning, adding more hot sauce as necessary. Pour the sauce into individual small bowls or ramekins and serve with the fried chicken. Any leftover sauce can be stored, covered, at room temperature.

CHICKEN BREASTS

I have an unfashionable confession to make: I *like* chicken breasts—not always, but often, and not just on the grill. When I hunger for comfort food, I'll pound and bread chicken breasts to make chicken cutlets (page 344). When I want a fast stir-fry, I appreciate the lightning quick cooking time and the breast's ability to absorb flavors. I like the chicken breast's neutrality; the way you can cook it with eastern or western seasonings, serve it by itself simply grilled or simmered in a complex stew. You can even stuff a chicken breast to make a low-carb "calzone" (page 347). So here's what you need to know when selecting chicken breasts so you can extract the maximum flavor from this convenient, if bland, cut of meat.

ANATOMY LESSON | To most guys *chicken breast* means a skinless, boneless half breast. Generally, these come 2 to 3 to a pound; figure on 6 to 8 ounces per serving. Occasionally, you find whole skinless, boneless chicken breasts (two half breasts), which tip the scale at ¾ to 1 pound and are well suited to cooking as a substitute for the spatchcocked chicken on page 336; shorten the cooking time to twenty minutes.

The "airline cut" or "supreme": Both refer to otherwise boneless chicken breast halves with the first section of the wing attached. Ask your butcher for them. They look cool and everyone loves chicken wings.

COOK IT RIGHT | Cook chicken breasts to a minimum temperature of 165°F. To test for doneness, insert the probe of an instant-read thermometer through the narrow end of the breast into the center (do not insert it through the top). Or you can use the poke test: The chicken breast should feel firm to the touch when you poke it with your finger.

SKIN AND BONES | The skin is the tastiest part of the chicken, and the bones add extra flavor. Even if you prefer your chicken breasts skinless, you can dice and panfry or bake the skin to make cracklings and chicken fat. Cook the skin until brown and crispy, five to ten minutes in a skillet over medium heat or twenty to thirty minutes in a 350°F oven. Crumble the cracklings over mashed potatoes or steamed cauliflower.

I also like bone-in chicken breasts: The bones add extra flavor. Bone-in chicken breasts are great for grilling.

TENDER CARE | Remove the chicken tenders (see the photos on the facing page) and cook them separately.

BREAST MAN NO MORE | Once you've mastered the chicken breast, consider adding legs, thighs, or whole birds to your repertory. They're cheaper, richer, better marbled, and more flavorful than chicken breasts. When cooking whole chickens or chicken parts, cook them to at least 165°F.

How to Remove a Chicken Tender

1 Lift the loose end of the tender and use a sharp paring knife to cut it off where it attaches to the breast.

2 Find the end of the sinew that runs the length of the tender. Slide a knife tip under it.

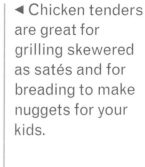

◀ Chicken tenders are great for grilling skewered as satés and for breading to make nuggets for your kids.

3 Hold the end of the sinew in one hand and slide the knife between the sinew and the tender.

4 Continue sliding the knife under the sinew. When you get to the end, cut it off.

5 A boneless chicken breast with the trimmed tender beside it.

PANKO-CRUSTED CHICKEN CUTLETS

SHOP *Panko* is made from an airy crustless white bread that produces exceptionally flaky, crunchy crumbs. Look for it at Asian markets and most natural foods stores and supermarkets. You can certainly use conventional bread crumbs (ideally homemade—a great way to recycle stale bread, see page 459), or even brioche, pumpernickel, or pretzel crumbs.

GEAR Your basic kitchen gear including a large resealable plastic bag or plastic wrap, a large (10- to 12-inch) skillet, a baking sheet, and a plate lined with paper towels or paper bags, plus a meat pounder or a heavy cleaver (optional)

WHAT ELSE The chicken cutlets make a great dish by themselves. Dress them up with Parmigiano Reggiano and mozzarella cheese and tomato sauce to make chicken Parmesan, or you can top them with capers and anchovies along with fried eggs. You'll find recipes for these variations on the facing page.

TIME about 30 minutes

When you hunger for comfort food what you *really* crave is a dish like your mama used to make. Enter the chicken cutlet. Crusty on the outside, succulent and tender inside, the chicken cutlet does for a boneless chicken breast what Austrian Wiener schnitzel does for veal (you'll find that recipe on page 270). Closer to home, this was our son Jake's favorite dish growing up. The following version ups the ante with the hypercrisp Japanese bread crumbs called *panko*. **Serves 2 to 4**

---

4 skinless, boneless half chicken breasts (each 6 to 8 ounces), preferably organic

Coarse salt (kosher or sea) and freshly ground black pepper

1 cup unbleached all-purpose white flour

2 large eggs

2 cups panko or bread crumbs

2 tablespoons (¼ stick) butter

1 tablespoon extra virgin olive oil, or more as needed

1 lemon, cut into wedges for serving

---

1 Using a paring knife, remove the chicken tenders, if any, from the underside of the breasts (you'll find instructions for doing this on page 343). You can cook the tenders with the cutlets or set them aside to make chicken nuggets (see page 345). Place a chicken breast in a large resealable plastic bag or between 2 pieces of plastic wrap and, using a meat pounder, the side of a heavy cleaver, or the bottom of a cast-iron skillet, pound it until it is about ¼ inch thick. Repeat with the remaining chicken breasts. Pound the tenders, if using, the same way. Do you absolutely need to pound the breasts? No, but pounding increases the ratio of crust to meat (and the tenderness). Do you absolutely need to remove the tenders? No, but it's easier to flatten the breasts without them. Generously season the pounded chicken on both sides with salt and pepper.

2 Place the flour in a shallow bowl. Crack the eggs into a second bowl and beat them with a fork. Place the *panko* in a third bowl. Bread the chicken cutlets by first dipping them in the flour to coat both sides, shaking off the excess. Then dip them in the beaten eggs, and finally in the *panko*, again shaking off the excess. Bread the chicken cutlets right before you're ready to cook them, placing them on a clean, dry baking sheet to transfer them to the skillet.

3 Melt the butter in the oil in a large skillet over medium-high heat until the butter sizzles, swirling the pan so the oil and butter mix.

4 Using tongs, gently lower the breaded chicken cutlets into the hot fat and cook them until they are crusty and browned on the bottom, 3 to 4 minutes. You may need to cook the chicken cutlets in batches so as not to overcrowd the skillet. Add more olive oil as needed so the chicken doesn't stick. Turn the chicken cutlets over and cook them until the second side is crusty and browned, 3 to 4 minutes. Use the poke test (see page 342) to check for doneness; the center of a chicken cutlet should feel firm to the touch when cooked through. Alternatively, make a cut in the thickest part of one of the breasts with a paring knife. The chicken should be white with no trace of pink. Transfer the cutlets to a plate lined with paper towels or paper bags to drain. Serve the chicken cutlets with the lemon wedges.

Variations

Chicken nuggets: These are for that special kid in your life or maybe just that inner child in you: Remember those tenders you trimmed off the chicken breasts? (Find instructions on page 343.) Cut each tender into 1-inch pieces. Bread them and cook them like the Panko-Crusted Chicken Cutlets on page 344; the cooking time will be 2 to 3 minutes per side. Serve the chicken nuggets with the "Secret Sauce" for Burgers on page 542.

Quick chicken Parmesan: Preheat the oven to 400°F. Pound, bread, and fry the chicken cutlets as described on page 344. Make a spicy tomato sauce like the one in the Spaghetti with Turbocharged Red Sauce recipe on page 446 or use your favorite store-bought sauce; you'll need 2 cups. Spoon 1 cup of the sauce into a baking dish. Arrange the cutlets in a single layer on top. Top each cutlet with 1 or 2 thin slices of fresh mozzarella—the good stuff sold packed in water. Spoon the remaining 1 cup of sauce on top and sprinkle 1 cup of finely freshly grated Parmigiano Reggiano cheese on top. Bake the chicken cutlets until the sauce bubbles and the cheese is bubbling and lightly browned, about 10 minutes.

Chicken cutlets with smoked ham and cheese: Preheat the oven to 400°F. Prepare and cook the chicken cutlets as directed on page 344 then arrange them in a single layer in a baking dish. Top each cutlet with thinly sliced smoked ham and thinly sliced Gruyère cheese. Bake the chicken cutlets until the cheese is melted, bubbling, and browned, 8 to 12 minutes. We're talking killer good.

Chicken Breasts Stuffed with Provolone, Salami, and Ham

LOW-CARB "CALZONES"

Cross a chicken breast with a pizza joint standby and you get this singular low-carb "calzone." (Curious factoid: The word *calzone* means trousers in Italian.) The salami, *coppa* (wine-and-garlic-seasoned shoulder ham, also known as *capicola*), and provolone cheese flavor the chicken breast from the inside out. They also keep it moist. Fillings are limited only by your imagination. You could make awesome chicken calzones with chorizo, Jack cheese, and jalapeño peppers, for example, or with thinly sliced feta cheese and fresh mint. **Serves 2 to 4**

2 tablespoons extra virgin olive oil, or more as needed, plus olive oil for oiling the toothpicks

4 plump skinless, boneless half chicken breasts (each 6 to 8 ounces)

2 ounces coppa, prosciutto, or other thinly sliced ham (you'll need at least 4 slices)

2 ounces soppressata or other Italian dry-cured salami or pepperoni, thinly sliced (you'll need at least 4 slices)

2 ounces thinly sliced provolone cheese (you'll need at least 4 slices)

Coarse salt (kosher or sea) and freshly ground black pepper

About ½ cup unbleached all-purpose white flour, whole wheat flour, or white cornmeal (optional)

8 fresh sage or basil leaves

SHOP See page 342 for a guide to buying chicken breasts. I'd go with imported Italian cold cuts, like *coppa* and *soppressata* (a flat salami spiked with hot pepper) for stuffing the chicken breasts.

GEAR Your basic kitchen gear including a large (10- to 12-inch) skillet and 8 wooden toothpicks

WHAT ELSE This recipe suggests flouring the chicken breasts before panfrying. (Flour plus hot fat equals crust.) If you're off flour, simply omit this step before panfrying.

You can also cook the calzones outdoors on the grill. In this case, omit the flour or cornmeal and brush the olive oil on the breasts before seasoning them with salt and pepper and adding the sage or basil leaves. Preheat the grill to high, then grill the stuffed chicken breasts using the direct-grilling method. They will be done after cooking 3 to 5 minutes per side.

TIME about 20 minutes

1 Lightly oil the toothpicks with olive oil. Using a paring knife, remove the chicken tenders, if any, from the underside of the breasts (you'll find instructions for doing this on page 343). Set the tenders aside for another use. Cut a deep pocket in the side of a chicken breast (see page 348). Stuff it with a quarter of the *coppa*, *soppressata*, and provolone slices. Pin the pocket shut with 2 oiled toothpicks. Prepare and stuff the remaining chicken breasts the same way. Generously season both sides of the breasts with salt and pepper.

2 Place the flour or cornmeal, if using, in a large shallow bowl. Place a sage or basil leaf on the center of each side of a stuffed chicken breast. Dip each breast on both sides in the flour, shaking off the excess. Place the floured breasts on a dry plate.

3 Heat the olive oil in a large skillet over medium-high heat until shimmering. Using tongs, gently lower the stuffed breasts into the hot olive oil. Cook the breasts until they are nicely browned on the bottom, 3 to 5 minutes. Using tongs, turn the chicken breasts over and cook the second side until browned, 3 to 5 minutes. You may need to cook the breasts in batches so as not to overcrowd the skillet. Add more olive oil as needed so the chicken doesn't stick. Use the poke test (see page 342) to check for doneness; the chicken breasts should feel firm to the touch when cooked through. When serving the chicken breasts, remind everyone to remove the toothpicks.

How to Cut and Stuff a Chicken Breast Pocket

1 Cut a deep pocket in the breast through the thickest side. Keep an equal thickness above and below the cut and don't cut through the far side.

2 Stuff the pocket with the filling.

3 Pin the pocket closed with oiled toothpicks.

4 The stuffed chicken calzone ready for panfrying.

BOURBON-BRINED ROAST TURKEY

The biggest challenge of roasting a turkey is cooking the dark meat through without drying out the breast. The best solution is precisely that: a mixture of water, salt, and sugar known as brine. By the miracle of osmosis (remember your high school chemistry?—sans bourbon, of course), the turkey meat absorbs some of the brine, plumping, tenderizing, and flavoring the meat. **Serves 8 with leftovers**

1 turkey (about 12 pounds)

1 cup coarse salt (kosher or sea)

¾ cup packed light brown sugar, or ¾ cup honey

4 cups hot water

3 quarts cold water

½ cup bourbon

4 tablespoons (½ stick) unsalted butter, melted

1 Remove the packet of giblets and neck, if any, from the cavities of the turkey (freeze the heart, gizzard, and neck for making stock, page 549). Rinse the turkey inside and out with cold water and drain it well. Place the salt, brown sugar, and hot water in a large stockpot. Whisk until the salt and brown sugar are completely dissolved. Whisk in the cold water and bourbon. Refrigerate the brine until thoroughly cooled, about 1 hour.

2 Immerse the turkey in the brine, neck end down. Weight it with a heavy saucepan or tightly sealed plastic bags filled with ice to keep the bird submerged. Brine the bird for 24 hours in the refrigerator, covered, turning it a couple of times so it brines evenly. Don't have space in your refrigerator? Place the stockpot in a large cooler and arrange bags of ice around the stockpot to keep it cold (add more ice as needed).

3 Preheat the oven to 350°F.

SHOP For this and the Fried Turkey recipe that follows, I call for a twelve-pound bird, which will feed eight people comfortably with leftovers. For advice on buying turkey, see page 352.

GEAR Your basic kitchen gear including a stockpot or other container large enough to hold the turkey for brining, a roasting pan, a roasting rack (optional), a basting brush, and an instant-read thermometer

WHAT ELSE Once you master brining, it's a useful technique for all sorts of meats that tend to dry out, from chicken breasts to pork chops to pheasant (page 357). You'll need to adjust the brining time depending on the weight of the meat you are brining. Some guys brine turkeys in clean plastic garbage bags. Resourceful, but potentially dangerous, as some garbage bags are treated with antibacterial chemicals that could leach into the bird.

If you don't own a roasting rack, you can improvise one by placing whole carrots, onion wedges, and celery ribs in the bottom of the roasting pan.

TIME 24 hours for brining the turkey, plus 2½ to 3 hours roasting time

4 Drain the turkey well and blot the outside dry with paper towels. Truss the turkey as described for a chicken on page 330. Place the turkey, breast side up, in a shallow roasting pan, preferably on a roasting rack. Brush the turkey with a little of the melted butter and place it in the oven.

5 Roast the turkey until the skin is crisp and well-browned and the meat is cooked through, 2½ to 3 hours. Baste the turkey with melted butter every half hour. After the first 1½ hours start basting the turkey with the juices that accumulate in the bottom of the roasting pan. To test for doneness, insert an instant-read thermometer deep in a thigh but not touching a bone; when done the internal temperature should be 165°F.

6 Transfer the turkey to a platter and loosely drape it with aluminum foil. Let the turkey rest for at least 20 minutes before carving and serving. Remove the trussing string and carve the turkey as described on page 353.

Six Things You Might Not Know About Turkey

► Turkey is native to the New World—North and Central America—where it has strutted, gobbled, and graced tables for thousands of years.

► So how did turkey come to be named for a country halfway around the planet? In the sixteenth century, Turkey (the country) was associated with luxury goods, including foods (much the way Italy and France are today). By calling it "turkie bird," merchants gave this New World import Asian cachet.

► Many cultures named turkey for a faraway land that had little to do with its place of origin. In France, it's called *dinde* (from the French words *d'Inde*, from India). The Dutch call it *kalkoen*; Norwegians, *kalkun*; Finns, *kalkkuna*—all after the Indian city of Calcutta.

► Today, the country with the highest per capita turkey consumption is . . . Israel. (The bird is often roasted on a vertical rotisserie to make *shawarma*.)

► Benjamin Franklin thought so highly of turkey he proposed it, not the eagle, be named our national bird.

► In the week prior to Thanksgiving, over forty-five million turkeys will meet their maker. On this holiday, turkey will be eaten in 90 percent of American homes.

SEVEN THINGS YOU NEED TO KNOW ABOUT

COOKING TURKEY

There's a first time for every guy and it may be accompanied by a certain amount of anxiety. Forgive me if the following sounds rudimentary:

1 There's a big difference in texture and taste between ice-hard factory-frozen turkeys and fresh organic birds. The organic bird may seem a little tougher, but you can't beat the flavor—or the knowledge that it's free of hormones and chemical additives.

2 How big a turkey should you buy? Figure on 1½ pounds per person. This will make you feel properly overfed (as you should at Thanksgiving) and leave you with welcome leftovers. For me, a 12- to 14-pound turkey is ideal. For large gatherings, I'd rather cook two 12 pounders than one 24-pound monster. (It's easier to control the cooking.)

3 A lot of industrially raised birds come preinjected with stock, water, and/or butter or vegetable oil—comprising up to 15 percent of their weight. Try to buy your turkey uninjected. Avoid birds with "added liquid" on the label.

4 The best and safest way to thaw a turkey is in the refrigerator. Depending on the size of the bird, you'll need to start thawing it up to five days ahead of when you plan to cook it: Figure on one day for every four pounds of turkey. Alternatively, you can thaw the turkey in a deep sink or cooler filled with cold water. It's important for food safety reasons to keep the water at 40°F or colder. You can add resealable bags of ice to the water to keep it cold. Never thaw the turkey in hot water as the outside will thaw long before the inside, risking dangerous bacterial growth.

5 Most turkeys come with some of the innards (liver, heart, gizzard) and neck in a plastic bag secreted inside. These are called giblets. There are two places to look for them: in the main cavity and in the front cavity (under the neck skin). Be sure to remove them. This may sound obvious, but once I was served a roast turkey that still had the innards in their plastic bag inside.

6 One thing that makes a turkey challenging to cook is that the legs (the dark meat) take longer to cook than the breast (the white meat). This explains why so much turkey tastes dried out. One way to keep the breast moist even while cooking the legs to a safe temperature is to brine the turkey (see page 349). Another way is to deep-fry it.

7 Despite the name, stuffing is best cooked separately, not in the turkey cavity. For one thing, you can brown and crisp the top of the stuffing. You also greatly reduce the risk of bacterial contamination by cooking the stuffing separately.

How to Carve a Turkey

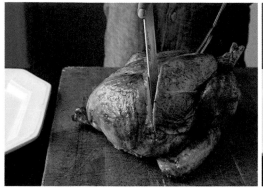

1 To remove one of the breast halves, use a sharp carving knife to make a lengthwise cut down one side of the breastbone.

2 Remove the half breast and set it aside.

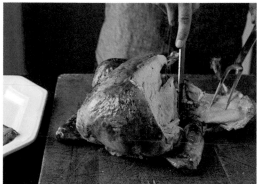

3 Pull the leg away from the body with a carving fork. Slide the knife down the carcass through the leg joint and remove the leg. Set it aside.

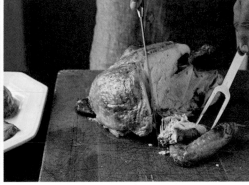

4 Pull the wing away from the body with the carving fork. Slide the knife down the ribcage through the wing joint and remove the wing. Set the wing aside.

5 Cut the breast crosswise into ½-inch-thick slices, or as thick as you desire.

6 Separate the thigh from the drumstick by cutting through the joint. Place both pieces on the serving platter and repeat on the other side of the turkey.

▶ Funny thing about turkey—you may never have to cook one, but as a guy, you're sure expected to know how to carve and serve it. So step up to the cutting board with confidence (after making sure that everyone has had ample opportunity to admire that gorgeous bird whole) and take knife (a long, slender carver) in hand. You'll also need a carving fork or spring-loaded tongs.

Never carve or serve a turkey hot out of the oven. Let it rest, loosely draped with aluminum foil, for at least fifteen minutes—it will be moister.

FRIED TURKEY

SHOP Be sure you get a natural bird, one not previously brined or injected with liquid by the manufacturer. Hot oil plus water or chicken stock do not happy bedfellows make.

GEAR Turkey fryer kits are available at hardware stores and online. The brand I use is Bayou Classic. You'll also need a deep-fry thermometer, a propane cylinder (the kind used for gas grills), heatproof gloves, and a baking sheet with a wire rack set on top.

WHAT ELSE While you have your fryer set up and you've invested in all that cooking oil, you might want to try the Steak on a Pitchfork on page 235.

TIME 45 minutes

History fails to tell who first fried a turkey. I bet it was a man and more than likely there was alcohol on the premises. So here's what can result when you fry a turkey: supernaturally moist meat and mahogany-hued skin so crisp, it crackles when you take a bite. Less happily, you could burn your feet (especially if you're wearing flip-flops—don't laugh—I've seen it). You could oil-slick your patio or, heaven forbid, set fire to your garage or house. (Yes, it's happened.) So while frying remains the most thrilling way to cook a turkey, you do need to take reasonable care. The following tips should help make the process safer.

▶ Always work outdoors, away from your house, garage, carport, or shrubbery.

▶ Set up your fryer on level ground where nothing will be ruined if the oil bubbles over and where nothing can catch fire.

▶ Don't try to improvise: Invest in a turkey fryer. In addition to a ring burner and a sufficiently large pot, you'll need a rack, lifter, and long-probed deep-fry thermometer.

▶ Do not attempt to fry a turkey when you've been drinking or are surrounded by curious young children or pets.

▶ Never submerge a turkey that is partially frozen or that has not been thoroughly patted dry, inside and out, with paper towels. Water of any kind will cause the hot oil to bubble up dangerously, perhaps over the side of the fryer.

▶ Dispose of the cooking oil responsibly—this does not mean pouring it on your neighbor's property.

1 turkey (about 12 pounds)

Coarse salt (kosher or sea) and freshly ground black pepper

Approximately 5 gallons canola or peanut oil

1 Remove the neck and packet of giblets, if any, from the turkey (freeze the heart, gizzard, and neck for making stock, page 549). Rinse the turkey inside and out with cold water and drain it well. Fill the frying pot with water. Thread the turkey on the rack, legs up, and lower it into the pot. Add enough water to cover the bird by 4 inches. Remove the turkey and measure the water: That's how much oil you'll need. Blot the bird dry really well, inside and out, with paper towels. Very generously season the turkey inside (both the neck and main cavities) and out with salt and pepper, using 1 to 2 tablespoons of each. Dry off the rack and put the turkey back on it.

2 Pour out the water from the pot, thoroughly dry it, and pour in the measured amount of oil. Attach the ring burner to the propane cylinder. Open the cylinder and light the gas ring with a match or lighter. Place the pot over the ring burner and heat the oil to 350°F. Using the turkey lifter, *gently* lower the bird into the hot fat, wearing heatproof gloves and keeping your feet and body as far away from the fryer as possible. Figure on 3 minutes per pound cooking time, so you're looking at about 36 minutes. Adjust the heat to maintain a constant frying temperature.

3 Gently lift the turkey out of the fryer, holding it over the pot to drain off the oil. Check the doneness by inserting an instant-read thermometer deep in the thigh but not touching a bone; when done the internal temperature should be 165°F. Transfer the turkey to a baking sheet with a wire rack to drain some more. Loosely drape the turkey with aluminum foil and let it rest for at least 20 minutes. Carve the turkey as described on page 353.

TURKEY MUSHROOM MEAT LOAF
WITH MAPLE GLAZE

Meat loaf is one of those classic comfort foods that belongs in every guy's repertory. Most versions fall into the ground beef-ketchup glaze school—satisfying, but hardly memorable. I wanted to create a meat loaf worthy of your ambition. So I took a cue from Montreal chef/TV host Danny St. Pierre, lightening up the loaf with ground turkey and veal, glazing it with maple syrup and Canadian whisky. I added a hash of the morels, chanterelles, and other wild mushrooms so prized by my French Canadian pals. What results is a surprisingly sophisticated twist on a blue-plate staple. **Serves 4**

SHOP Ground turkey can be bought anywhere, but be sure to check the fat content—you want it to contain 5 to 8 percent. There's some really fatty ground turkey out there, so read the label. Ground veal is sold at butcher shops and high-end supermarkets and natural foods stores. For more on mushrooms, see page 477.

GEAR Your basic kitchen gear including a large (10- to 12-inch) skillet, plus a 9-by-5-inch loaf pan, preferably nonstick, and kitchen matches

WHAT ELSE Some guys like to enrich their meat loaf with chorizo or Italian sausage. If you're one of those guys, fill the loaf pan halfway with meat loaf mixture, then lay the sausage end to end down the center. Spoon the remaining meat mixture on top and bake as described below.

TIME 15 minutes prep, plus 1 hour for cooking

For the meat loaf

8 ounces fresh morels, chanterelles, cèpes, shiitakes, and/or other wild or exotic mushrooms

1 tablespoon extra virgin olive oil, plus extra oil for oiling the loaf pan

2 shallots or 1 small onion, peeled and finely chopped

1 rib celery, finely chopped

2 tablespoons Canadian whisky or Scotch

12 ounces chilled lean ground turkey

12 ounces chilled lean ground veal or more ground turkey

¾ cup bread crumbs, preferably homemade (page 459)

2 large eggs, lightly beaten with a fork

1 teaspoon freshly grated lemon zest

About 1 teaspoon coarse salt (kosher or sea)

About ½ teaspoon freshly ground black pepper

For the glaze

¼ cup maple syrup

2 tablespoons Canadian whisky or Scotch

2 tablespoons tomato paste

2 tablespoons soy sauce

1 tablespoon dry mustard or prepared mustard

1 **Make the meat loaf:** Trim the mushrooms, cutting off and discarding any sandy stem ends. Wipe the mushrooms clean with a damp paper towel and coarsely chop them.

2 Heat the olive oil in a nonstick skillet. Add the shallots and celery and cook over medium heat until just lightly browned, 3 minutes, stirring often. Stir in the chopped mushrooms. Increase the heat to high and cook until the mushrooms are cooked down and the juices have evaporated, about 3 minutes.

3 Add the whisky, remove the pan from the heat, and flambé the liquor by touching the mixture with a lit kitchen match (for tips on flambéing, see page 566). Or keep the skillet on the heat and boil the whisky for 1 minute without actually flambéing it. Let the mixture cool to room temperature.

4 Preheat the oven to 350°F. Lightly oil a 9-by-5-inch loaf pan.

5 Place the turkey and veal in a large mixing bowl. Add the cooled mushroom mixture, bread crumbs, eggs, lemon zest, and salt and pepper. Stir to mix well. To test the meat loaf for seasoning, fry a little meatball of the mixture in the skillet (no need to clean it first). If needed, add salt and pepper to taste; the mixture should be highly seasoned. Spoon the meat mixture into the prepared loaf pan and smooth the top with a spatula.

6 **Make the glaze:** Place the maple syrup, whisky, tomato paste, soy sauce, and mustard in the skillet. Bring to a boil over medium-low heat and cook, whisking constantly, until the mixture forms a thick glaze, 2 minutes. Pour half of this mixture over the meat loaf.

7 Place the meat loaf in the oven and bake for 45 minutes. Pour the remaining glaze over the meat loaf and continue baking until the loaf is browned on top and cooked through, 15 minutes more. To test for doneness, insert an instant-read thermometer into the top middle of the loaf; it should read 165°F. Transfer the pan to a wire rack and let the meat loaf rest for 10 minutes. Then, tip the pan and pour off and discard any excess grease.

8 Place a large plate over the pan and invert the meat loaf onto it. Turn the meat loaf right side up and cut it crosswise into ¾-inch-thick slices. It's excellent hot out of the oven and the leftovers taste pretty darn great on a sandwich.

BRANDY-BRINED PHEASANTS

My first serious writing job was as restaurant critic for *Boston* magazine. Once a year we'd do a roundup of country inns, which is how I discovered a rambling white clapboard farmhouse called The Hermitage in West Dover, Vermont. At the time The Hermitage was run by an avid hunter, duck decoy aficionado, inveterate wine collector, and irrepressible teller of tall tales named Jim McGovern. Among Jim's many obsessions were game birds, and he raised pheasant, partridge, and wild turkeys in netted enclosures around the property. It was at The Hermitage that I first ate pheasant, and from the first taste of the lean, clean-tasting meat—stronger than chicken, but not as gamy as squab— I was hooked. But leanness is a double-edged sword, and like all game, pheasant has a frustrating tendency to dry out. The solution comes from the roast turkey playbook: Soak the bird in a brandy-flavored brine, then roast it wrapped in bacon. If you've never tried a game bird, mild but rich-tasting pheasant is a fine place to start. **Serves 4**

SHOP Once available only to hunters, pheasant can now be found at specialty food shops, specialty butchers, and markets like Whole Foods. Virtually all of the pheasant sold in the United States is farm raised so you never have to worry about an overly gamy flavor—or buckshot. (If you hunt your own, let the eater beware.) Can't find pheasant? Try making the dish with Cornish game hens. Pheasant deserves the best bacon, so look for an artisanal brand, like Nueske's.

GEAR Your basic kitchen gear including a stockpot or large container for brining the pheasants plus butcher's string, a roasting pan and rack, and an instant-read thermometer

WHAT ELSE This cranberry relish would make a great condiment for the pheasant: Brown 2 strips diced bacon in a large skillet over medium heat. Add ½ cup each dried cranberries, chopped walnuts, and minced shallots, plus 1 teaspoon finely grated lemon zest and brown them as well. Add 1 cup port wine and boil over high heat to reduce by half. Let cool to room temperature and serve with the pheasant.

TIME 6 to 8 hours for brining the pheasants, plus about 1 hour roasting time

2 pheasants (each 2 to 2½ pounds)

1 cup coarse salt (kosher or sea)

¾ cup honey

4 cups hot water

12 cups cold water

½ cup Cognac

2 strips lemon zest
(each ½ by 1½ inches)

2 cinnamon sticks (each 3 inches)

2 bay leaves

6 slices artisanal bacon

1 Remove the giblets from the pheasants (freeze the heart, gizzard, and neck for making stock, page 549). Rinse the pheasants inside and out with cold water and drain them well.

2 Place the salt, honey, and hot water in a large stockpot or other large container and whisk until the salt is completely dissolved. Whisk in the cold water and Cognac, add the lemon zest, cinnamon sticks, and bay leaves, and let the brine cool to room temperature.

3 Add the pheasants to the brine and place a heavy saucepan on top to keep the birds submerged. Brine the pheasants for 6 to 8 hours in the refrigerator.

4 Preheat the oven to 450°F.

5 Drain the pheasants well and blot them dry with paper towels. Place 3 slices of bacon on each pheasant so that they cover the breast. Truss the birds with butcher's string using the traditional method (see page 530) and looping

extra string over the bacon to hold it in place. Position the pheasants on a rack in a roasting pan and place them in the oven.

6 Roast the pheasants for about 20 minutes. Reduce the heat to 350°F and continue roasting the pheasants until they are golden brown and cooked through, 30 to 40 minutes longer; do not overcook. To test the pheasants for doneness, insert an instant-read thermometer into the thickest part of a thigh but not so that it touches a bone. When done the internal temperature should be 165°F. Baste the pheasants from time to time with any juices that accumulate in the bottom of the roasting pan.

7 Transfer the pheasants to a platter and let them rest for about 5 minutes, loosely tented with aluminum foil (lay a piece of foil over the pheasants; don't wrap them tightly or the crisp skin will soften). Remove and discard the trussing string. Using a chef's knife or poultry shears, cut each bird in half and dig in. Don't forget to divvy up the bacon.

BRAISED RABBIT
WITH KALAMATA OLIVES

Rabbit has been slow to turn up on American tables—and even now you find it primarily at restaurants. Europeans and French Canadians have enjoyed this lean mild meat for centuries. (Italians eat some 300,000 tons a year!) Richer tasting than chicken, but delicate like veal, rabbit stands up to bold seasonings—mustard, wine, olives, prunes—without surrendering its unique flavor. And, it's low in fat and cholesterol. Even if most rabbit is farm raised today, it takes you back to an age when men hunted the meat they ate. Rabbit is still considered weird enough to make eating it an adventure. Otherwise put, it's not all that hard to be the first guy on your block to cook rabbit, and doing so earns you certain bragging rights. (You'll also eat *very* well.) This meltingly tender braised rabbit—tangy with wine and kalamata olives—comes from my French Canadian actor friend Francis Reddy (read about him on page 332). **Serves 2 or 3**

SHOP Your main challenge will be to find rabbit—look for it at a specialty butcher or Italian market. Sometimes you'll find it at Fresh Market. Cipollini are small sweet flat Italian onions. You'll find them at most natural foods stores and many supermarkets, or you can substitute pearl onions.

GEAR Your basic kitchen gear including a large heavy pot or Dutch oven with a tight-fitting lid

WHAT ELSE The key to this dish is slow braising at a low heat. This keeps the meat moist.

TIME about 30 minutes preparation time, 3 to 4 hours cooking time

2 thick slices bacon, cut crosswise into ¼-inch pieces

8 to 12 cipollini onions, peeled

3 carrots, peeled and cut crosswise into 2-inch pieces

1 rabbit (about 3 pounds)

Coarse salt (kosher or sea) and freshly ground black pepper

½ cup unbleached all-purpose white flour

2 tablespoons (¼ stick) butter, or more as needed

1 clove garlic, peeled and finely chopped

1 cup dry red or white wine, such as shiraz or cabernet sauvignon for a red wine or sauvignon blanc or chardonnay for a white

2 cups chicken or veal stock

2 sprigs fresh thyme, plus 2 sprigs for serving

1 cup pitted kalamata or other olives

1 cup pitted prunes

1 Preheat the oven to 275°F.

2 Place the bacon in a large heavy pot or Dutch oven and cook it over medium heat until browned, about 3 minutes. Using a slotted spoon transfer the bacon to a plate.

3 Add the onions and carrots to the pot with the bacon fat and cook over high heat until browned, about 3 minutes. Using a slotted spoon, transfer the onions and carrots to the plate with the bacon and set them aside in the refrigerator, covered with aluminum foil. Pour off all but 1 tablespoon of the bacon fat from the pot.

4 Using a paring knife, trim any papery skin off the rabbit. Using a chef's knife, cut the rabbit into 6 pieces (or ask your butcher to do it): 2 foreleg pieces, 2 hind leg pieces, and 2 loin (back) pieces. Generously season the rabbit on all sides with salt and pepper. Sprinkle the rabbit pieces with the flour, tossing them to coat on all sides and shaking off the excess flour.

5 Add the butter to the pot and melt it over medium heat. Add the rabbit pieces and brown them on all sides, about 3 minutes per side. The pieces should cook in a single layer with about 1 inch between pieces—work in batches if needed, transferring the pieces to a plate once browned. During the last 2 minutes of cooking of the last batch, stir in the garlic and brown it with the rabbit. Add a little more butter if the pot seems too dry. If you worked in batches, return all the rabbit pieces with juices to the pan.

6 Stir in the red wine and let come to a boil, scraping up the brown bits from the bottom of the pot. Add the stock and 2 sprigs of thyme and let come to a boil. Cover the pot with a tight-fitting lid and place it in the oven. Braise the rabbit for about 2 hours.

7 Remove the pot from the oven. Stir in the bacon, onions, carrots, olives, and prunes recover the pot, and continue braising the rabbit until the meat and vegetables are very tender and the sauce is thick and richly flavored, about 1 hour longer, 3 hours in all cooking time for the rabbit. If the sauce is too watery, uncover the rabbit for the last 30 minutes or so to evaporate some of the excess liquid.

8 Taste for seasoning, adding more salt and/or pepper as necessary; the rabbit should be highly seasoned. Serve the rabbit, garnished with the remaining sprigs of thyme, right from the pot.

FISH

You know the old saying: Give a man a fish and you feed him for one day; teach him how to fish and you feed him for a lifetime. That sums up the philosophy of this book. Sure, I try to give you the *what*—great recipes—but even more important, I try to teach you the *how*—the principles and techniques you need to cook anything. And nowhere do we guys need more guidance than when it comes to preparing fish.

So what can go wrong when you cook fish? It can stick to the skillet or break apart when you try to turn it. A minute too short and you serve it still raw in the center. (Which is just fine for tuna, but not so fine for swordfish or trout.) A minute too long and you overcook it and it dries out. Then there are the moral questions you may face before you even turn on the stove: wild fish versus farmed, endangered versus sustainable.

In this chapter you'll learn how to tell when fish is fresh. And then how to cook salmon, tuna, swordfish, trout, and other fish we love, using methods as varied as blackening, panfrying, and deep-frying. I'll also teach you how to know when fish is done and how to skin and bone a whole fish. And you'll also learn when *not* to cook fish, starting with ceviche, sashimi, and poke.

PERUVIAN CEVICHE

I 've started this chapter with one of the easiest fish dishes of all—ceviche. Easy? You don't even need to cook it. Simply cut raw fish into chunks and mix it with onion, peppers, tomato, cilantro, and lime juice. Presto: You've got a Peruvian-style ceviche (for more about ceviche, see page 364). **Serves 4 as a starter, 2 as a warm-weather light main course**

1 pound delicate, impeccably fresh white fish, such as fluke, flounder, snapper, halibut, or hamachi

½ medium-size sweet or red onion, peeled and diced

½ red or green bell pepper, stemmed, seeded, and diced

1 small tomato, diced with its juice

1 jalapeño, serrano, or other fresh hot pepper, seeded and finely chopped (for a hotter ceviche, leave the seeds in)

1 clove garlic, peeled and minced

½ cup chopped fresh cilantro or flat-leaf parsley

⅓ cup fresh lime juice, to taste

About 1 teaspoon coarse salt (kosher or sea)

About ½ teaspoon freshly ground black pepper

1 Cut the fish into ½-inch dice.

2 Not more than 20 minutes before serving, place the fish, onion, bell pepper, tomato, jalapeño, garlic, cilantro, lime juice, salt, and black pepper in a nonreactive (glass, stainless steel, or ceramic) mixing bowl. Mix well and serve the ceviche in martini glasses, bowls, or hollowed coconut shells (see page 366).

SHOP As with all raw fish dishes, the particular species matters less than the freshness. Buy the freshest fish you can find.

GEAR Your basic kitchen gear

WHAT ELSE Most ceviche starts with uncooked seafood, but that doesn't mean what you eat is completely raw. The acids in the citrus juice or vinegar whiten and tenderize the fish in a manner similar to cooking. It may sound strange, but for an interesting contrast of textures and flavors, top the ceviche with popcorn or roasted corn nuts. That's what they do in Peru.

TIME 15 minutes

WHAT YOU NEED TO KNOW ABOUT
CEVICHE

Seafood soaked in a tongue-blasting bath of citrus juice, chiles, and aromatics—that pretty much sums up one of the most popular appetizers in South America, which is now enjoyed everywhere: ceviche (sometimes written *cebiche* or *seviche*). Yet no two ceviches are alike, even in their country of origin (likely Peru—a claim disputed by Ecuador). And if you don't like raw seafood, you can find ceviches made with cooked shrimp, crab, squid, and even mushrooms. Hawaii's poke (page 367) and Polynesia's *oka popo* (page 365) belong to a ceviche family that spans the globe.

Ceviche is easy to make and always thrilling to eat. Here's how to make it like a pro.

TALKING FRESH You must start with impeccably fresh seafood—especially when serving it raw. If you live in a community where there is commercial or sport fishing, buy the seafood off the boats. Or go to a reliable fishmonger specializing in local fish. Ask what seafood arrived that morning—even if it's a different variety from what your recipe calls for. Unless you know the fish guy, the supermarket should be your supplier of last resort.

THE POWER OF SOUR Acid is a key component of ceviche, playing the role of both flavoring and "cooking" agent. Of course, you'll start with fresh citrus fruit: lime (or tiny key lime), lemon (for an aromatic twist, try Meyer lemon), or orange. Shake things up with exotic citrus fruits, like *naranja agria* (sour orange, which tastes like a cross between lime and orange and is available in most urban supermarkets), blood oranges, *calamansi* (a tart Filipino fruit), or yuzu (an aromatic citrus fruit from Japan). Avoid bottled or reconstituted citrus juice—with the exception of yuzu, which bottles well and is hard to find fresh in the U.S.

CRANK UP THE HEAT No ceviche is complete without some sort of chile pepper. Fresh jalapeños and serranos are at the milder end of the scale, while Scotch bonnets and ghost peppers have firepower to blow your head off.

ADD AROMATICS Onion, garlic, scallions, chives, parsley, cilantro, grated ginger, even toasted coconut—these are the aromatics that give ceviche its character. It goes without saying that all should be freshly chopped and dosed with a generous hand.

PUTTING IT ALL TOGETHER The essence of ceviche is freshness. Some ceviches are made and marinated several hours ahead of time. But most owe their brio to their spontaneity—the ingredients aren't mixed until a few minutes before they will be eaten.

SERVE WITH STYLE Ceviche is traditionally served in martini glasses. Scallop shells, avocado halves, and hollowed coconuts also make great vessels for serving ceviche.

POLYNESIAN FISH SALAD

Samoans call it *oka popo*; for Hawaiians it's *lomi-lomi*. For me it's one of the world's best ways to enjoy fresh fish. The basic elements are uncooked fish (tuna in Polynesia, salmon in Hawaii); fresh tomatoes, scallions or sweet Maui onions; bell peppers or chiles; salt or soy sauce; and coconut milk, vinegar, and/ or sesame oil. The embellishments range from ginger to cucumber to shredded coconut. You can cut the fish into cubes or shred it, season it to order or salt it overnight. You can eat it with a fork—or with your fingers as a dip on crisp fried wonton skins. And if you're feeling really creative, you can serve it in a cracked fresh coconut (see box, page 366). Because it's so quick and easy to make and infinitely variable, it belongs in your repertory for a pool party or midsummer luau. **Serves 4 as an appetizer, 2 as a light main course**

SHOP For fish, use wild salmon or sushi-quality tuna. Coconut milk is the heavy cream of the tropics—it's available canned (two good brands are Chaokoh from Thailand and Goya). Be sure to buy unsweetened coconut milk, not the sweet coconut cream used for bartending.

GEAR Your basic kitchen gear plus a small (6-inch) skillet

WHAT ELSE Hawaiians have a singular technique for making *lomi-lomi*. They knead the fish with salt (*lomi* also refers to a Hawaiian massage technique) and let it cure for several hours or overnight. This gives you a texture reminiscent of gravlax. I opt for the speed method you'll find here, but try the traditional Hawaiian version if you're so inclined.

TIME about 30 minutes

1 pound skinless salmon fillet, preferably wild, or 1 pound sushi-quality tuna

1 luscious red ripe tomato

1 small cucumber

½ green bell pepper or Anaheim pepper

2 scallions, trimmed and finely chopped; set aside 1 tablespoon of the green parts for serving

2 teaspoons minced or grated peeled fresh ginger, to taste

1 serrano or jalapeño pepper (optional), seeded and minced

¾ cup unsweetened coconut milk

1 tablespoon soy sauce, or more to taste

Coarse salt (kosher or sea; optional)

Wonton Crisps (optional; recipe follows), for serving

1 If you are using salmon, run your fingers over the fillet feeling for pin bones. Remove any you find with needle-nose pliers or kitchen tweezers (or your fingers). Cut the salmon or tuna into ½-inch dice and place it in a mixing bowl.

How to Crack a Coconut

Start with a ripe (hard brown) coconut. Holding it in one hand over a large bowl, tap it around the circumference (if the coconut were a globe, this would be the equator) with the back of a cleaver. Make a series of firm taps, rotating the coconut as you do. After a dozen or so taps, it will crack in half. Drink the juice that drains into the bowl. Use the hollow halves as serving bowls. After you've eaten the *lomi-lomi,* scrape out and eat the sweet white meat with a spoon.

and seed the cucumber (cut it in half lengthwise and scrape out the seeds with a spoon) and cut it into ½-inch dice. Seed and cut the bell pepper into ½-inch dice. Add the cucumber and bell pepper to the fish. Add the scallions, ginger, and serrano pepper, if using. Stir in the coconut milk and soy sauce. Let the fish marinate in this mixture until richly flavored, 15 to 30 minutes.

3 Just before serving, taste for seasoning, adding more soy sauce or salt to taste; the fish should be highly seasoned. One cool way to serve *lomi-lomi* is in half coconuts (see above). Or use martini glasses. Serve Wonton Crisps, if desired, alongside for dipping.

2 Cut the tomato in half crosswise and squeeze out the seeds. Cut each half into ½-inch dice and add them to the salmon. Peel

WONTON CRISPS

Think of these crispy fried wonton skins as Pac-Rim tortilla chips. Wonton skins (aka wrappers) are available at Asian markets, of course, and in the produce or refrigerated section of most supermarkets. Nasoya is a good brand. Serve the chips with any of the fish tartares in this chapter. **Makes 24 crisps**

1 to 2 cups canola or other vegetable oil

24 wonton skins (2 packages)

1 Pour oil to a depth of ¾ inch into a small skillet and heat it over medium heat. Dip a corner of a wonton skin into the oil; when bubbles dance around it, the oil is hot enough for frying (about 350°F).

2 Fry the wonton skins a few at a time until golden brown, blistered, and crisp, 1 to 2 minutes. Don't crowd the skillet. Transfer the fried crisps to a plate lined with paper towels to drain.

Hawaiian Tuna Tartare

POKE

Say poke (rhymes with OK) to a Hawaiian and his eyes will blaze with pleasure. With good reason: This sesame-flavored fish tartare—made with Hawaii's amazingly fresh ahi tuna—strikes the perfect balance of sweet, salty, nutty, and spicy. Once available only in Hawaii, poke is turning up at edgy restaurants across the U.S. My version has a little more firepower than what I ate in Hawaii. One cool Hawaiian way to serve poke is on fresh banana leaves. **Serves 4 as an appetizer, 2 as a light main course**

1 pound superfresh ahi tuna

2 scallions, trimmed, both white and green parts finely chopped; set aside 1 tablespoon of the green parts for serving

1 to 2 Hawaiian, Thai, or serrano chiles, seeded and minced (for a spicier poke, leave the seeds in)

1 tablespoon toasted white sesame seeds (see Note), or black sesame seeds

½ teaspoon freshly ground black pepper

1½ tablespoons Asian (dark) sesame oil, or more to taste

1 tablespoon soy sauce, or more to taste

Cut the tuna into ½-inch dice by hand; a food processor chops it too finely. Place the tuna in a mixing bowl and stir in the scallions, chile(s), sesame seeds, pepper, sesame oil, and soy sauce. Taste for seasoning, adding more soy sauce and/or sesame oil to taste. Serve within 1 hour of mixing.

Note: To toast sesame seeds, place them in a hot dry skillet over medium heat till lightly browned and fragrant, about 2 minutes, shaking the skillet. Immediately pour them into a heatproof bowl so they don't burn. Better yet, use the black sesame seeds, available at Japanese markets and natural foods stores.

SHOP As with all raw fish dishes, you need to get sushi-quality ahi tuna. If you can't find it, use another impeccably fresh fish, like albacore, bonito, or salmon. Be sure to buy toasted sesame oil—one good brand is Kodoya.

GEAR Your basic kitchen gear

WHAT ELSE Hawaiians enrich their poke with a local seaweed called *lipoa*. I don't bother with it on the mainland, but if you're so inclined you could add a half cup of chopped *wakame* salad (*wakame*, also called sea mustard, is an edible seaweed), available ready-made at fishmongers and natural foods stores. Or toast a sheet of nori seaweed over an open fire (like on your grill or a lit stove burner) for a few seconds, then crumble it over the poke.

TIME about 15 minutes

ANDREW ZIMMERN

He's the guy who eats weird stuff—very weird stuff, like rotten shark in Reykjavik and giant fruit bats in Samoa. You may have watched him on *Bizarre Foods* or *Bizarre Worlds* on the Travel Channel, read his column in *Delta Sky* magazine, or know his singular travelogue: *The Bizarre Truth: How I Walked Out the Door Mouth First . . . and Came Back Shaking My Head*. What you may not know about journalist, author, teacher, chef, and TV host Andrew Zimmern is that he graduated from Vassar with a joint degree in history and art history (he wrote his thesis on daguerreotypes). And he may be the only major food celebrity to have a motto in Latin: *Semper exploro, mysterium expecto* ("I always explore, I always expect mystery").

An inveterate traveler, Zimmern has visited more than one hundred countries in his relentless quest for new tastes (he's currently a million mile flyer with two separate airlines). This self-described "bald white Jew from Minnesota" has eaten raw liver with the Himba tribe of northern Namibia and camel kidneys dipped in *berbere* (a pepper and spice paste) in Ethiopia. "When you visit a new tribe, they test your mettle by thrusting a rifle in your hands," says Zimmern. "They want to see if you have the John Wayne skill set—can you hunt and put food on the table?"

What are the three strangest foods you've ever eaten?

Giant fruit bat from Samoa. It has a six-foot wingspan and tastes extremely gamy. Eat it grilled with ginger juice—an Asian flavor and disinfectant.

Giant porcupine from Botswana. It weighs eighty pounds and takes painstaking hours to pluck off the quills. There's an inch-thick layer of fat just below the skin, which the tribesmen grill over a wood fire with a layer of ash on top. What results tastes like the nugget of fat at the narrow end of a New York strip. Totally amazing.

Palolo. It's a tiny worm that lives in coral beds fifty miles off the coast of Samoa. You scoop it off the water by the hundreds and eat it smeared on bread. Think foie gras crossed with iodine with an exquisitely creamy texture.

Why should a man know how to cook?

As a guy, I'm lousy at expressing my feelings. Cooking is as touchy-feely as I get. There's nothing more honest than cooking, and when I do it, I can show people what's in my heart. It's also my time to Zen out.

What's your go-to dish when you're by yourself?

Shrimp and grits or fish and grits. It's leftovers raised to the level of high art.

Or after I've been hunting, I like deer liver *alla veneziana* (with caramelized onions). It's quick and easy, and deer liver has a cleaner taste than calf's.

What's your favorite seduction dish?

Braised duck legs. You brown them in fat and cook for an hour and a half with vegetables, tarragon, and red wine. You serve them with spaetzle or pasta with wild mushrooms. I made it when I was courting my wife and let's just say that that evening worked out *really* well.

Three things every guy should know how to do in the kitchen?

Make bread. There's nothing more spiritual or elemental. It's a rite of passage with my seven-year-old. The first time we made bread together, my son realized that not everything you eat has to come from a supermarket. Note to dads: Bread takes several hours to rise and young boys have short attention spans. You may want to have some dough that's already risen as a swap-out to keep the process moving.

Cook fish. For some reason, every guy who's been to a sushi bar thinks all fish should be served undercooked. The fact is that most fish does not taste best raw or even rare. This is particularly true in my part of the country (Minnesota), where we eat a lot of wall-eye. Learn to cook fish and learn to cook it through.

Learn how to light and use your grill. You need to know how to drag meat back to your cave and cook it. If you don't know how to grill, you're doing a great disservice to mankind.

Three ingredients you can't live without?

Chile peppers. I'm a hot freak and I need to have that big explosion of flavor. At any given time, we have thirty different chile condiments—most of them homemade—in the refrigerator.

Miso (a tangy paste of cultured soy beans and grains from Japan). It's sweet, salty, and loaded with umami flavors. I use it for everything from curing salmon to grilling chicken. I prefer imported Japanese miso—it has a fermented quality that smells like a cross between the best mushrooms you've ever tasted and the dirtiest gym socks. [For more information on miso, see page 27.]

Pickles. Kimchi. Pickled cabbage. Sauerkraut. I love fermented flavors. With chiles, pickles, and miso, you can take over the world.

> ▶ There's nothing more honest than cooking, and when I do it, I can show people what's in my heart.

Three kitchen tools you can't live without?

My Popsicle maker. We buy a ton of fruit, and now that we have a Popsicle maker, none of it goes to waste. We're always trying unexpected combinations. The latest? Fresh pineapple and basil from our garden.

My *caja china*. It looks like a metal-clad steamer trunk. You put a fifty-pound pig inside and pile hot charcoal on top. Three hours later, you serve the most succulent roast pig ever.

My Zojirushi rice cooker. We often have to delay a meal because of my work. It keeps rice hot and moist for hours.

What are the three most important things to keep in mind if you're just starting out in the kitchen?

Work hot. A lot of guys fear heat, but unless your pan or grill is screaming hot, you won't get a good sear.

Taste often. I hate wimpy food. You can't achieve the proper balance of salt, acid, and heat unless you taste your food throughout the cooking process.

Work big. Most guys start with too small a cutting board, then too small a bowl for mixing, then too small a frying pan for cooking. You know what I'm talking about: The guy who tries to sear four burgers in an eight-inch frying pan. Make sure you have plenty of room when you cook.

What are the three most common mistakes guys make in the kitchen?

Overcooking. Guys overcook everything. A dry pot roast drives me crazy.

Food fatigue. Most guys cook and eat the same half dozen dishes over and over. At our house, we almost never cook the same thing twice. Often, we'll devote a whole week to cooking a new cuisine. Our son picks the country and we all get to learn about new ingredients, cooking techniques, and cultures.

American breakfasts. Most of the world does *not* start its day with bacon, eggs, and potatoes. It's a very unhealthy way to eat.

What should men be cooking in the future?

Alternative proteins. Goat. Whole small oily fish, like fresh sardines. Offal. The best way to start is to eat meats that *don't* come from factory feedlots. Even once a month will make a huge difference.

BLOWTORCH SALMON

A few years ago I started seeing blowtorches at sushi bars where they were used to shoot fire at icy-cold sliced raw fish. The intense heat did something extraordinary—it brought the flavorful oils to the surface of the fish and singed the edges, imparting a smoky, almost baconlike flavor. And of course, any dish that encourages you to use a welder's tool is a winner in my book. This dish was inspired by a boldly innovative Boston restaurant called o ya, but you'll find blowtorched sashimi everywhere from Sushi Roku in Santa Monica to Kushi in Washington, D.C. *Crudo* (raw fish) turns up in many cutting-edge restaurants. Think of this as *crudo* with a live-fire twist. **Serves 4 as an appetizer, 2 or 3 as a light main course**

SHOP For the best results, you want really fatty salmon—the cut that comes from the belly. Ask your fishmonger for this, or buy the center cut of the fillet. Like all raw fish, the salmon should be impeccably fresh and purchased from a first-rate fish store.

GEAR Your basic kitchen gear plus a kitchen or hardware store blowtorch (see page 22) and 4 small bowls

WHAT ELSE Yuzu is a Japanese citrus fruit with an intensely aromatic flavor. Look for the bottled or frozen juice at Japanese markets or natural foods stores—see page 29. If unavailable, use rice vinegar or equal parts fresh lemon and lime juice.

TIME about 10 minutes

- 1 pound skinless salmon fillet, preferably wild, well-chilled
- 1 heaping tablespoon wasabi powder (see below)
- 1 tablespoon hot water, or as needed
- ½ cup good soy sauce, such as Kikkoman
- ¼ cup yuzu juice or rice vinegar (or 2 tablespoons each fresh lemon and lime juice)

1 Run your fingers over the salmon fillet, feeling for bones. Pull out any you find with needle-nose pliers or tweezers (or your fingers). Holding a knife on a 45-degree angle to the cutting board, cut the salmon fillet crosswise on the diagonal into thin (not more than ¼-inch) slices. Arrange the salmon slices in a single layer on a heatproof platter or plates. Slice the salmon not more than 1 hour before serving and keep the platter or plates of salmon slices on ice or in the refrigerator.

What's with Wasabi?

You think you know wasabi? The green stuff at most sushi bars isn't real wasabi. It's a spicy powder made from powdered horseradish, mustard seed, and green food coloring. Perfectly pleasant, but fresh wasabi is simultaneously more flavorful and more refined. If you really want an extraordinary dipping sauce, order fresh wasabi rhizomes from realwasabi.com and grate them just before serving. To be strictly authentic you'd grate the root on a traditional shark-skin grater called an *oroshi*. A Microplane works well, too.

2 Meanwhile, make the dipping sauce: Place the wasabi in a small bowl and add 1 tablespoon of hot water or as needed—enough to form a thick paste when stirred. Let this paste stand for 5 minutes to let the heat and flavor develop. Place a marble-size blob on each plate.

3 Divide the soy sauce and yuzu juice or rice vinegar evenly among 4 small bowls.

4 Just before serving, light the blowtorch and run the flame over the salmon just long enough to lightly singe the edges and to bring the oils to the surface, about 15 seconds. The leading edge of the flame should be about 1 inch above the fish.

5 Serve at room temperature. Have each eater add wasabi paste to taste to the soy sauce mixture, stirring it in with chopsticks. Dip the salmon into the wasabi sauce and get ready to experience *crudo* at its electrifying best.

How to Blowtorch Salmon

1 Place the salmon slices on a heatproof platter or plates. Singe the top of the fish with a blowtorch. The leading edge of the flame should be about 1 inch above the fish.

2 Continue torching the salmon until all the edges are singed and the fish oils pearl on the surface.

MAPLE TERIYAKI SALMON

I was born in Japan and spent much of my life in New England. Maybe that's why I've always been a sucker for food that spans East and West. Case in point: this maple teriyaki salmon, which offsets the Asian tang of sesame oil and soy sauce with the sweetness of maple syrup. The Japanese call it teriyaki (from the words *teri*, meaning "shine" or "luster" and *yaki*, meaning "grilled"). I call it one of the best ways there is to cook rich oily fish like salmon. **Serves 4**

2 pounds skin-on salmon fillet, preferably wild, cut into 4 equal pieces, bones removed

½ cup tamari or soy sauce

½ cup mirin (sweet rice wine), sake, or white wine

½ cup pure maple syrup (add 2 tablespoons more if using sake or white wine)

⅓ cup Asian (dark) sesame oil

1 piece (1 inch) fresh ginger (optional), peeled, cut into ¼-inch slices, and flattened with the side of a cleaver or chef's knife

1 scallion, trimmed, white part cut into 2-inch pieces and flattened with the side of a cleaver or chef's knife, green parts thinly sliced on the diagonal

1 tablespoon butter or more sesame oil, if panfrying

1 Run your fingers over the pieces of salmon, feeling for pin bones. Remove any you find with needle-nose pliers or kitchen tweezers. Arrange the salmon in a single layer in a baking pan.

2 Combine the tamari, mirin, maple syrup, the ⅓ cup of sesame oil, and the ginger and scallion white in a saucepan and whisk to mix. Pour this marinade over the salmon, turning the fish a few times to coat it. Set the saucepan aside. Let the fish marinate, covered, in the refrigerator for 1 to 2 hours, turning once or twice.

3 Drain the salmon well, pouring the marinade back into the saucepan. Gently bring the marinade to a boil over medium-high heat and let boil until syrupy and reduced by about one third, 4 to 8 minutes, whisking often. You should have about 1¼ cups. Set this teriyaki glaze aside for serving.

SHOP If you're not conversant with Asian cuisine, you'll need to know about a couple of special ingredients. Asian (dark) sesame oil—pressed from toasted sesame seeds—has a distinctive nutty flavor. Look for an Asian brand, like Kadoya. Tamari is a high-quality soy sauce brewed exclusively from soybeans (most "soy" sauce contains wheat as well). If unavailable, use a good regular soy sauce, like Kikkoman. Mirin is Japanese sweet rice wine. If unavailable, substitute sake or white wine and add a couple of extra tablespoons of maple syrup. Look for all three at your local natural foods market.

GEAR Your basic kitchen gear including a broiler (baking) pan or aluminum foil pan, a saucepan, a basting brush, and a small strainer

WHAT ELSE In Japan teriyaki would be cooked on a grill (see page 12), but a skillet or broiler also turns out excellent salmon. Incidentally, the teriyaki marinade works great with other fish and shellfish, not to mention with grilled, broiled, or panfried chicken breasts and pork chops.

TIME 1 to 2 hours for marinating the fish, plus 10 to 12 minutes cooking time

4 *If you are panfrying the salmon:* Place the butter or 1 tablespoon sesame oil in a skillet and heat over medium-high heat. Add the salmon (dark or skin side up) to the skillet. Cook the fish until it is browned on the bottom, 3 to 4 minutes. Turn the fish over and cook the second side until browned and the fish is cooked through, 3 to 4 minutes longer. Start basting the fish with the teriyaki glaze after 3 minutes. See page 378 on how to check for doneness.

If you are broiling the salmon: Preheat the broiler to high. Place the salmon in the broiler pan, arranging the pieces dark or skin side up.

Broil the salmon until the tops are browned, 3 to 4 minutes. Baste the fish with the teriyaki sauce. Turn the pieces over and baste them with additional teriyaki sauce. Continue broiling the fish until it is browned and glossy and cooked through, 3 to 4 minutes longer, 6 to 8 minutes in all. See page 378 on how to check for doneness.

5 To serve, transfer the salmon to a platter or plates. Re-boil the remaining glaze, whisk it well, then strain it over the fish. Sprinkle the chopped scallion greens on top and dig in.

A GUY'S BEST FRIEND

SALMON

When I was growing up, fresh salmon was something of a novelty and a luxury—not to mention a seasonal food you waited to enjoy in the late spring and early summer. No one knew from omega-3 fatty acids or worried if the fish was wild or farmed. These days, salmon has become a commodity—cheap, ubiquitous, and available year-round thanks to factory farms from Canada to Chile. But there's no free lunch and we actually pay a high price for our supposedly low-cost fish in the form of environmental degradation and compromised texture and flavor. So what sort of salmon should you buy, and what's the best way to cook it? The advice holds for pretty much any saltwater or freshwater fish.

GO WILD In the best of all worlds, you'd eat wild salmon all the time. Wild because it swam in a real ocean so it has a firmer texture and richer flavor than farmed salmon. Wild because it comes from the pristine waters of Alaska and the Pacific Northwest, so you know it grew up in clean waters. Wild because there are several species to choose from, each with its own distinct texture and taste.

PACIFIC VERSUS ATLANTIC If you want to eat wild salmon, source it from the Pacific. All, I repeat all, Atlantic salmon is farmed.

TALK FRESH How do you recognize truly fresh salmon or, for that matter, any really fresh fish? If you are buying a whole fish, look for clear eyes, red gills, and bright, glossy flesh. If you are buying fillets or fish steaks, ask to smell them. Really. A good fishmonger will let you. Bring your nose to within two inches of the fish: It should smell fresh and briny, like the seashore, not fishy. You may feel awkward the first time you ask to smell fish, but that's what professional chefs do, and there's no other way to tell for sure.

WHEN FROZEN IS CHOSEN Sometimes good frozen wild salmon is better than factory-farmed fresh. The texture may not be quite as firm, but the flavor will be better.

KEEP SKIN IN THE GAME Look for salmon fillets with the skin attached. The skin has a rich flavor and becomes crackling crisp when browned. If you feel compelled to remove the skin (perhaps your spouse doesn't like it), place the fillet, skin side down, flat on a cutting board. Starting at the narrow end, slide the blade of a chef's knife or filleting knife just above the skin under the flesh. Saw the knife back and forth toward the opposite end of the fillet, pinching the skin between the knife blade and the cutting board. Tip: To make salmon skin cracklings, brush the skin with sesame oil and season with salt and pepper, then bake it in a 350°F oven until crisp, about 20 minutes.

BONES BE GONE Salmon fillets come with a row of slender bones, called pin bones, running the length of the fillet. Often the fishmonger removes them, but if not, use a cool tool—needle-nose pliers—to take them out. Run your fingers the length of the fillet, feeling for the bone ends. It helps to put your other hand under the fillet, which will cause the bones to stick up. Pull out any bones you find with the pliers. Note to self: Wash pliers well with soap and dry thoroughly before returning them to your toolbox.

HOW TO COOK SALMON By pretty much any method you can think of: broiling, baking, panfrying, stir-frying, grilling, or smoking. The French like to poach salmon (gently simmer it in water or flavored liquid), but for me, any of the dry-cooking methods give you a better texture and flavor.

GRILL SESSION Naturally, my favorite way to cook salmon—indeed, most fish—is on the grill. This gives you crisp skin and burnt edges, and the abundant fat keeps the fish moist even when exposed to the high dry heat of the grill. Salmon fillets tend to stick to the grate, so grill them in an oiled fish basket. Thanks to the bones and skin, salmon steaks have enough internal structure to hold together grilled directly on the grate.

PLANKED SALMON
WITH LEMON MUSTARD GLAZE

Long before cedar planks started turning up on American grills, nineteenth-century chefs cooked fish on oak planks in the oven. Even earlier, the Indians of coastal Connecticut nailed shad fillets to boards that they stood in front of a campfire. All of which is to say that the "new" technique of planked fish dates back centuries, and that you don't need a grill to enjoy it. So why plank? It looks cool and fish tastes even better cooked this way. The plank itself adds an interesting flavor—somewhere between the oak in a bottle of chardonnay and the smoke from smoldering hardwood. Add a rich, tangy three-ingredient glaze (lemon zest, mustard, mayonnaise) and you've got salmon that's simple enough to make on a weeknight and dramatic enough to headline a party. **Serves 4**

2 pounds boneless salmon fillet, preferably wild

Coarse salt (kosher or sea) and freshly ground black pepper

⅔ cup mayonnaise, preferably Hellmann's

⅓ cup Dijon or Meaux mustard

1 teaspoon finely grated lemon zest, or to taste

1 Soak the plank in cold water in a large pot, the sink, or on a rimmed baking sheet for 30 minutes (keep it submerged by placing a pot on top). Drain and wipe the plank dry.

2 Preheat the oven to 400°F or set up the grill for indirect grilling and preheat it to medium-high.

3 Run your fingers over the salmon fillet feeling for pin bones. Remove any you find with needle-nose pliers or kitchen tweezers.

4 Generously season the salmon on both sides with salt and pepper. Arrange it, skin side down, on the damp plank.

5 Place the mayonnaise, mustard, and lemon zest in a mixing bowl and whisk to mix. Using

SHOP Cedar is the most common wood for planking, but you'll also get a great (and distinctly different) flavor from other hardwoods, such as maple, oak, and cherry. Look for planks near the seafood section of your supermarket or natural foods store or at a barbecue shop. Two good online sources are barbecuebible.com and fireandflavor.com. Yes, you can buy your planks at a lumberyard, but sand off any stray splinters and never, ever use pressure-treated lumber.

There are lots of options for mustard: tart Dijon, grainy Meaux, spicy deli mustard, or even sweet honey mustard. There is only one choice for mayonnaise: Hellmann's. See page 374 for my advice on buying salmon.

GEAR Your basic kitchen gear, plus a cedar or other hardwood plank at least 7 by 12 inches and a heatproof platter large enough to hold it

WHAT ELSE There are two ways to cook planked salmon: on the grill or in the oven. With a grill, you set it up for indirect grilling (explained in full on page 12).

a rubber spatula, spread the glaze over the top and sides of the salmon.

6 *If you are baking the salmon*, place the fish on its plank on a baking sheet or a piece of aluminum foil in the oven. Bake the salmon until the glaze is puffed, bubbling, and browned and the fish is cooked through, 20 to 30 minutes.

To check for doneness, insert an instant-read thermometer in the wide end of the fish for 15 seconds. When the salmon is done the thermometer will register 145°F. Or insert a thin metal skewer into the fish and leave it there about 15 seconds; when the salmon is done the skewer will come out hot to the touch.

If you are grilling the salmon, place the fish on its plank in the center of the grill away from the heat. Close the lid and grill the salmon until cooked through, 20 to 30 minutes. To check for doneness, insert an instant-read thermometer in the wide end of the fish for 15 seconds. When the salmon is done the thermometer will register 145°F. Or insert a thin metal skewer into the fish; when the salmon is done the skewer will come out hot to the touch.

7 Transfer the fish on its plank to a heat-proof platter and serve it right off the plank.

Testing Fish for Doneness

THE FLAKE TEST

Press the fish with your fingertips. If it breaks into clean flakes, it's cooked.

THE CUT TEST

Cut into the fish with a fork or knife tip. If the flesh at the center is hot and opaque, not translucent, it's cooked.

Preparing Planked Salmon

1 Run your fingers over the fillet feeling for pin bones. Pull out any you find with needle-nose pliers.

2 Using a palette knife or slender spatula, spread the lemon mustard glaze over the fish.

3 The partially glazed salmon on its soaked cedar plank ready for a second coating.

Salmon Varieties

Salmon may be America's best-selling fish, but the texture and flavor vary widely with the type. Here are the major varieties and what to expect with each.

WEST COAST SALMON

At this time, the vast majority of West Coast salmon is wild. It's more expensive than Atlantic salmon but worth the price.

King salmon (sometimes called Chinook): This is the largest variety of salmon, with a bright orange color, satiny texture, and rich fatty flavor. White salmon is a rare (occurring once in every hundred or so fish) ivory-colored king with an especially fine appearance and flavor.

Sockeye (aka red salmon): A deep red, full-flavored fish somewhat smaller and leaner than king.

Coho (aka silver salmon): Has a milder flavor than king or sockeye, but it still beats farmed salmon. Widely available in autumn.

Pink salmon: Milder still—most of it winds up canned.

Chum: Abundant but lean and bland. On the plus side, chum roe (eggs) are used to make salmon caviar, known by sushi lovers as *ikura*.

Copper River king salmon: Every May, announcements of the arrival of Copper River king salmon flood the blogosphere. So why all the fuss, and especially, why the high prices? The Copper River flows three hundred miles from south central Alaska to Prince William Sound, and every year salmon swim up its cold rushing waters to spawn. Only powerful swimmers rich in omega-3 fatty acids and other fats are fit for the journey, which makes these fish especially rich-tasting. The season runs from mid-May to mid-June. Look for Copper River salmon at a good fishmonger or specialty food market or order it by mail. Two sources: alaskaseafooddirect .com and farm-2-market.com.

ATLANTIC SALMON

Long gone are the days when wild salmon swam the Connecticut and Thames Rivers. Today, virtually all Atlantic salmon are farmed. Those that do swim wild have been given endangered species status.

BLACKENED SALMON

SHOP For fish, choose the tail section of the salmon fillet—it shouldn't be more than ¾ inch thick. I like the skin so I leave it on. You can buy commercial blackening spice, including Paul Prudhomme's own brand, but it's easy to make from scratch (you'll find a recipe on page 381).

GEAR Your basic kitchen gear including 2 large (10- to 12-inch) heavy (at least 1 cast-iron) skillets

WHAT ELSE Authentic blackening generates fearsome clouds of eye-stinging smoke, so although you cook it in a skillet, you may want to do so on your grill. Indoors, you'll need to run the exhaust fan on high, and you may wind up setting off your smoke detector.

TIME about 10 minutes

Blackened seafood has become such a fixture on America's food landscape, it's hard to remember the commotion New Orleans chef Paul Prudhomme caused when he first demonstrated it on national television. At the time, the technique, charring—make that damn near incinerating—spice-crusted fish in a screaming hot ungreased skillet—sent TV producers lunging for their fire extinguishers. As often happens in America, once a new dish is widely embraced, it becomes bastardized to the point where its creator would disavow it, if he even recognized it. Perhaps you're too young to remember blackened fish in its glory days, or perhaps you're nostalgic for the real McCoy before it became a cliché. I say it's time to resurrect this extreme cuisine technique for a fish like salmon that demands spice and smoke. **Serves 4**

2 pounds salmon fillet, preferably wild, no more than ¾ inch thick

½ cup Blackening Spice (recipe follows) or a good store-bought brand

4 tablespoons (½ stick) unsalted butter, plus 2 tablespoons (¼ stick) for serving

Lemon wedges (optional), for serving

1 Run your fingers over the salmon fillet feeling for pin bones. Remove any you find with needle-nose pliers or kitchen tweezers. Cut the fillet crosswise into 4 equal pieces.

2 Spread the Blackening Spice out in an even layer on a plate.

3 Heat a cast-iron skillet smoking hot over high heat.

4 Meanwhile, melt the 4 tablespoons of butter in a second skillet over medium heat. Dip the salmon fillets in the butter, turning to coat both sides.

5 Dip each piece of buttered salmon in the Blackening Spice, turning it to coat both sides, which should be thickly crusted with spice. Immediately place the spice-crusted salmon, skin side down, in the hot cast-iron skillet.

Continue coating the other salmon pieces, adding them to the skillet as you go. Do not crowd the pan; work in batches if necessary. Cook the salmon until very darkly browned on the bottom, 2 to 4 minutes. Turn the pieces over and cook the second side until it is darkly browned and the fish is cooked through, 2 to 4 minutes, 4 to 8 minutes in all. The fish should be darkly browned—almost black—and will break into clean flakes when pressed. Yes, you'll generate a lot of eye-stinging smoke. You're supposed to. It might be best to turn on the exhaust fan, turn off the smoke alarm, and watch carefully. Don't forget to turn the smoke alarm back on when you're done.

6 Transfer the blackened salmon to a platter or plates. Add the remaining 2 tablespoons of butter to the pan used to melt the first batch of butter and cook it over high heat until it is sizzling and melted, about 2 minutes. Pour this butter over the salmon and serve it with lemon wedges for squeezing, if desired.

BLACKENING SPICE

Commercial blackening seasonings are widely available, but many contain MSG and cheap spices. Here's a homemade version for the purist inspired by *Chef Paul Prudhomme's Louisiana Kitchen*. **Makes about ½ cup**

1½ tablespoons paprika

1½ tablespoons dried oregano

1½ tablespoons coarse salt (kosher or sea)

1 tablespoon garlic powder

1 tablespoon onion powder

1 tablespoon dried thyme

1½ teaspoons freshly ground black pepper

1½ teaspoons ground white pepper

1 teaspoon ground cayenne pepper

Place the paprika, oregano, salt, garlic powder, onion powder, thyme, black pepper, white pepper, and cayenne in a small bowl and mix them with your fingers, breaking up any lumps in the garlic or onion powder.

BLACK AND WHITE TUNA
SEARED WITH SESAME SEEDS AND SERVED SUSHI-RARE IN THE CENTER

SHOP Because you're eating it rare, you need sushi-quality tuna. Two popular varieties come to mind—bluefin and yellowfin—and you'll find them at your local fishmonger. Because most sushi-grade tuna comes frozen, this is one fish you can buy with confidence at a supermarket with a quality fish department.

Look for black sesame seeds at Asian markets, natural foods stores, and in the international section of many supermarkets. If they are unavailable, substitute more white sesame seeds. The tuna won't look quite as cool, but the taste will still be stunning. For sesame oil, use a roasted brand like the Japanese Kadoya.

GEAR Your basic kitchen gear including a pastry brush and a large (10- to 12-inch) skillet

WHAT ELSE With Black and White Tuna I recommend two possible sauces: the wasabi-spiked soy sauce traditionally served with sushi, or the Wasabi Cream Sauce on page 546.

TIME about 15 minutes

Tuna is the easiest fish in the world to cook. It has no bones (at least not the part of the tuna you eat) and it won't fall apart when you turn it. You don't need to worry about split-second timing or cooking it through. In fact, the less you do to tuna, the better. Which brings us to a dish pioneered by Wolfgang Puck: black and white tuna. You crust the tuna with black and white sesame seeds, which look as awesome as they taste. You sear it just long enough to char the outside while leaving the center as blood-rare as sashimi. Think of this mercifully minimalist fish dish as sushi you cook. Or carpaccio gone nutty with sesame. **Serves 4**

1 heaping tablespoon wasabi powder plus ½ cup soy sauce or tamari, or Wasabi Cream Sauce (page 546)

4 tuna steaks (6 to 8 ounces each and at least 1 inch thick)

3 tablespoons Asian (dark) sesame oil or canola oil

Coarse salt (kosher or sea) and freshly ground black pepper

¼ cup white sesame seeds

¼ cup black sesame seeds (or more white sesame seeds)

1 to 2 teaspoons hot red pepper flakes (optional)

1 Make the wasabi paste for the dipping sauce, if desired. Place the wasabi powder in a small bowl. Add 1 tablespoon of warm water and stir to make a paste. Let the wasabi paste stand for about 5 minutes for the flavor to develop. Form the wasabi paste into 4 balls. Pour 2 tablespoons of soy sauce in each of 4 small bowls. If you are using the Wasabi Cream Sauce, prepare it as described on page 546.

2 Lightly brush the tuna steaks on both sides with 1½ tablespoons of the sesame oil and season them generously on both sides with salt and pepper. Place the white and black sesame seeds and hot pepper flakes, if using, in a shallow bowl and stir to mix. Dip each tuna steak in the sesame seed mixture to coat both sides, pressing with your fingertips to pat the seeds onto the fish.

3 Heat the remaining 1½ tablespoons of oil in a large skillet over high heat until shimmering. Add the tuna steaks to the skillet and cook them until the sesame seeds are browned and crusty and the fish is cooked to taste, 1 minute per side for very rare tuna, 30 to 60 seconds more per side for medium-rare. I wouldn't cook the tuna much beyond that. Very rare tuna will feel soft and squishy when poked; medium-rare tuna will be yielding.

4 Serve the tuna steaks whole or cut them into thin slices. To eat the tuna steaks with the dipping sauce, stir wasabi paste to taste into a bowl of soy sauce. Dip pieces of the tuna into the wasabi soy sauce mixture. If you are using the Wasabi Cream Sauce, squirt or spoon squiggles over the tuna. One virtue of this dish is that you can serve the tuna hot or at room temperature.

SWORDFISH
WITH FRIED CAPERS

Here's a dish I prepare with the punctuality of a Swiss watch, starting in early spring when fresh swordfish first appears at my local fish market. I cook it at least once a week through the fall until the season is over. When fish is this fresh, I keep the seasonings—salt, pepper, lemon juice, and extra virgin olive oil—as simple as the cooking method: panfrying or grilling over a wood-enhanced fire. The "sauce" consists of capers flash-fried in butter. It takes maybe twenty minutes to make (plus a little more if you are lighting a grill). Simplicity at its primal best. **Serves 4**

4 swordfish steaks (6 to 8 ounces each and at least 1 inch thick)

Coarse salt (kosher or sea) and freshly ground or cracked black peppercorns

2 tablespoons extra virgin olive oil

1 lemon, cut in half

5 tablespoons unsalted butter

3 to 4 tablespoons drained capers

SHOP Swordfish is widely available, with the season varying depending on where you live. On Martha's Vineyard we find it from May through October. In Miami it's a winter fish, and we're sometimes lucky enough to score pink swordfish, which owes its amazing color and flavor to a diet of pink-shelled shrimp. Capers are described in full on page 26.

GEAR Your basic kitchen gear including a baking pan and a large (10- to 12-inch) skillet

1 Arrange the swordfish steaks in a single layer in a nonreactive (glass, stainless steel, or ceramic) baking pan dish and season them generously on both sides with salt and pepper. Drizzle 1 tablespoon olive oil over the fish and squeeze the lemon juice over it, turning the steaks to coat both sides. Let the swordfish marinate at room temperature for 10 minutes.

2 Melt 1 tablespoon of the butter in the remaining 1 tablespoon olive oil in a large skillet over high heat. Add the swordfish and panfry until the fish is browned on both sides and cooked through, about 4 minutes per side, turning with a spatula. There should be a 1-inch space between the pieces of fish (you won't get a proper sear if the pan is crowded)—so work in batches if necessary. Transfer the cooked swordfish to a platter and loosely cover with aluminum foil to keep warm.

3 Make the caper sauce: Melt the remaining butter in the skillet over high heat. Add the capers and cook over high heat until crisp and brown, about 2 minutes, shaking the pan so they cook evenly. Don't let the butter burn.

4 Pour the caper sauce over the fish and dig in.

Variation
Swordfish on the Grill

Set up the grill for direct grilling and preheat it to high. (For a smoky flavor, toss 1 cup of unsoaked oak or other hardwood chunks or chips on the coals or place them in the smoker box of a gas grill.) When ready to cook, arrange the marinated swordfish steaks on the grate (all should face the same way). Grill the swordfish until cooked through, about 4 minutes per side, giving each steak a quarter turn after about 2 minutes on each side to create a crosshatch of grill marks. Halfway through, pour any marinade left in the baking dish over the fish. Fry the capers in the butter in a saucepan on the stove as described above. Plate the swordfish and pour the sauce over the fish.

CRISPY SNAPPER

Every guy needs a fast, foolproof way to cook fish in his bag of tricks. This one requires nothing more exotic than salt, pepper, flour, and butter (or olive oil) and takes all of twenty minutes from start to finish. The French (no slouches when it comes to seafood) call it *cuisson à l'unilatérale*—unilateral cooking—which is a fancy way of saying that you panfry the fish on the skin side only, then finish it in the oven. The result: skin so crisp it crackles when you take a bite. The technique works especially well with soft-textured, mild-tasting fish fillets, like snapper, red fish, or arctic char. Ease coupled with taste coupled with the drama of a sizzling pan: It's quintessential great guy food. **Serves 4**

2 pounds skin-on snapper fillets

Coarse salt (kosher or sea) and freshly ground black pepper

About ¾ cup unbleached all-purpose white flour

1 tablespoon butter

1 tablespoon extra virgin olive oil

1 lemon, cut into wedges

Your choice of sauce (see What Else)

1 Preheat the oven to 450°F.

2 Run your fingers over the snapper fillets, feeling for pin bones. Remove any you find with needle-nose pliers or kitchen tweezers. Cut a shallow 1-inch X in the center of each fillet on the skin side (the idea is to cut through the skin but not through the fillet beneath it). Very generously season the fish on both sides with salt and pepper.

3 Spread out the flour on a paper plate or paper towel.

4 Melt the butter in the oil in a large cast-iron skillet over high heat until the butter is melted and the sizzling subsides.

5 Meanwhile, dip the snapper fillets in flour on both sides, shaking off the excess. Place the snapper in the skillet skin side down and cook over medium-high heat until the skin is browned and crisp, 2 to 3 minutes.

6 Using a spatula and tongs, carefully turn the fillets over. Place the skillet with the fish in the oven and continue cooking until the skin side is browned and the fish is cooked through, 6 to 10 minutes. For doneness tests, see page 378.

7 Serve the fish right out of the skillet (remember the handle will be hot). Serve the lemon wedges and sauce or slaw on the side.

SHOP This method is good for any fish fillet that's too delicate to cook on the grill. In Miami, I'd use red snapper, hog snapper, yellowtail, or pompano. On the Atlantic seaboard, I'd use black bass, porgie, or drum, while in the Midwest, I'd opt for pike, trout, walleye, or arctic char. Just be sure to buy fillets with the skin still on. A Southerner might use cornmeal in place of flour.

GEAR Your basic kitchen gear including a large (10- to 12-inch) cast-iron skillet

WHAT ELSE Lots of sauce possibilities here: for a Caribbean touch, serve the Mango Salsa on page 212. A Miamian might serve Joe's-Style Mustard Sauce (page 412), while a New Englander might use Made-from-Scratch Tartar Sauce (page 548). You could also serve the fish over one of the slaws on pages 177 to 181.

TIME about 20 minutes

BEER-BATTERED FISH

As a guy who spends most of his time at the grill, I sometimes forget the lure of the fish fry. But for many fish—the short list includes cod, haddock, flounder, walleye, pike, snapper, redfish, and catfish—frying is the best way to keep the soft delicate flesh in one piece, sealing in flavor and moistness while giving you a crisp crust to bite into. Especially when you flavor the batter with beer and *pimentón* (smoked paprika). **Serves 4**

3 cups unbleached all-purpose white flour

1 tablespoon smoked or sweet paprika

2 teaspoons baking powder

1 teaspoon coarse salt (kosher or sea)

1 teaspoon freshly ground black pepper

2 cups cold beer (light or dark, ale or stout—it's your choice)

1½ to 2 pounds cod, haddock, catfish, or other soft mild white fish fillets, cut into 2- to 3-inch pieces

3 cups canola, safflower, or other vegetable oil, or as needed

1 Place 2 cups of the flour, the paprika, baking powder, salt, and pepper in a large mixing bowl and whisk to mix. Gradually whisk in the beer; the batter should be the consistency of loose pancake batter (or cream soup).

2 Place the remaining cup of flour in a paper bag. Add the pieces of fish to the bag and shake them in the flour. Remove the fish, shaking off any excess flour and lay the pieces in a single layer on a platter or large piece of waxed paper or aluminum foil.

3 Pour oil to a depth of 1½ inches in a cast-iron skillet or other heavy deep pot and heat to 350°F over a medium-high heat. So how do you know when it's ready? Check the temperature with a deep-fry or candy thermometer if you have one. If not, drop a tiny spoonful of batter into the oil. When bubbles dance around it and it browns in 10 seconds, it's ready. Hint: If the oil smokes, it's too hot.

4 Using tongs, dip each piece of fish in the batter, turning it to coat all sides. Gently lower the battered fish into the hot oil. Do not drop it in from 6 inches over the skillet or it will send a hot spray of oil over your forearms and stove. Fry the fish until the batter is puffed and golden brown, 2 to 3 minutes per side, turning with tongs. Do not overcrowd the skillet—there should be at least 1 inch between the pieces

SHOP The best fish for frying are mild, soft-fleshed white fish. Check the endangered species roster to make sure the variety you use is sustainable. You can download a handy pocket guide from the Seafood Watch at montereybayaquarium.org.

GEAR Your basic kitchen gear, plus a deep cast-iron skillet or other heavy deep pot, a baking sheet lined with paper towels or a clean paper bag (for draining the fish), and a deep-fry or candy thermometer. OK, the latter is a little esoteric. If you bought a turkey fryer for the Fried Turkey on page 354, use the thermometer that comes with it. Or see instructions in Step 2 on how to check the temperature of the oil without a thermometer.

WHAT ELSE You might recognize what follows as English fish and chips. I try to limit my frying to one dish per meal, but if you hunger for chips, you'll find how to do it following this recipe.

TIME about 20 minutes

of fish; overcrowding lowers the temperature of the oil, resulting in soggy oily fish. Work in batches as needed and reheat the oil before adding more fish. Transfer the fish to a baking sheet lined with paper towels or a clean paper bag to drain, and serve.

Variation
Beer-Battered Fish Sandwiches

A buttered bun, crisp lettuce, tart pickle, and mustard mayonnaise make this your textbook fish sandwich. Make a batch of the beer battered fish. Lightly butter and toast 4 hamburger or brioche buns. Slather the buns with ½ cup of mustard or wasabi sauce (or one of the other mayonnaise-based sauces on pages 542 to 548). Line the bottom of each bun with a leaf of Boston lettuce or some arugula. Add the fish, a slice of ripe tomato, and some sweet or kosher pickle slices. And to drink? Cold beer, of course.

CHIPS FOR FISH

If you're so inclined, here's how to fry chips (potatoes) to serve with the batter-fried fish. If using only one fry pot: 1. Do the first round of frying the potatoes. 2. Then fry the fish. 3. Do the final potato fry right before serving. Or you can use two pots of oil.

2 pounds potatoes, such as russets

4 cups vegetable oil, such as canola or safflower

Coarse salt (kosher or sea) and freshly ground black pepper

1 Scrub the potatoes well and blot them dry. (I don't bother peeling the potatoes.) Cut each potato into ½-inch-wide strips or chunks and blot them dry again.

2 Heat the vegetable oil to 350°F in a large pot. Working in batches, if needed, fry the potatoes until they are soft but without color, 3 to 4 minutes. Drain the potatoes well in a wire basket or on plenty of paper towels.

3 Just before serving, heat the oil to 400°F. Fry the chips again until they are golden brown, 3 to 4 minutes. Drain them again. Sprinkle the potatoes with salt and pepper and serve immediately.

BURNED BUTTER TROUT

This big-flavored fish riffs on the way they cook trout in Grenoble—pumped up with lemon, capers, and nuts. The preparation harnesses your pyromaniacal tendencies, requiring the controlled burning of the butter—enough to darken it to the color of hazelnuts (which also gives it a nutty flavor), but not so much that it downright burns. **Serves 4**

1 lemon

4 tablespoons (½ stick) salted butter

1 tablespoon extra virgin olive oil

4 whole dressed trout
(12 to 16 ounces each)

Coarse salt (kosher or sea) and freshly ground black pepper

About 1 cup unbleached all-purpose white flour, spread out on a plate

3 tablespoons slivered almonds or pine nuts

3 tablespoons drained capers

3 tablespoons finely chopped chives or scallion greens

SHOP You can make this dish with whole trout (with head intact) or with headless boneless fish. I like to leave the heads intact.

GEAR Your basic kitchen gear including a large (10- to 12-inch) skillet

WHAT ELSE For a simple variation of this dish, make trout almondine. Triple the amount of slivered almonds and omit the capers. Replace the chives with the same amount of chopped flat-leaf parsley. Add a squeeze of fresh lemon juice instead of the sliced lemon. Delectable.

TIME about 20 minutes

1 Cut the rind and white pith completely off the lemon. Thinly slice the flesh crosswise into thin rounds. Remove any seeds with a fork. Reserve any juices by scraping them into a bowl with a knife.

2 Melt 1 tablespoon of the butter in the olive oil in a large skillet over medium-high heat.

3 Generously season each trout inside and out with salt and pepper. Holding each trout by the tail, dip it in the flour, thoroughly coating both sides and shaking off the excess.

4 Gently lower the trout into the skillet. Panfry the fish until golden brown on the outside and cooked through, 5 to 8 minutes per side. Start working over a medium-high heat and reduce the heat if the outside of the trout starts to burn before the fish is cooked through. To test for doneness, make a little cut in the back of the fish. The flesh next to the backbone should be white and should pull away from the bone easily. Transfer the trout to a platter or plates.

5 Increase the heat to high and add the remaining 3 tablespoons of butter and the almonds to the skillet. Cook the butter and nuts until they turn brown, about 2 minutes. Immediately add the capers, chives, and lemon slices and juices. Let the lemon mixture come to a boil, then pour it over the trout and serve.

EISENHOWER'S TROUT
CRUSTED WITH CORNMEAL AND FRIED IN BACON FAT

Little-known fact about Dwight D. Eisenhower: The five-star general and thirty-fourth president of the United States was a commander and chef in the kitchen. The Eisenhower steak (sirloin rolled in salt, pepper, and garlic powder) was cooked directly on the embers. When it came to trout, Eisenhower took an equally no-nonsense approach: Brown bacon in a skillet, crust the fish with cornmeal, and fry it in the bacon fat. **Serves 4**

4 slices thick-cut artisanal bacon

4 whole trout (12 to 16 ounces each), trimmed and gutted

Coarse salt (kosher or sea) and freshly ground black pepper

About 1 cup white or yellow cornmeal, spread out on a plate

1 lemon, cut into wedges for serving

SHOP I like to cook whole trout (with the head intact). But you may win more fans among women and children if you buy trout fillets.

GEAR Your basic kitchen gear including a large (10- to 12-inch) cast-iron skillet and a plate lined with paper towels

WHAT ELSE In the best of all worlds, you cook the trout you have just caught over a campfire by the side of the stream. To replicate some of the smoke flavor, you could cook the trout in the skillet over a charcoal grill fortified with wood chips.

TIME about 20 minutes

1 Place the bacon in a cold cast-iron skillet. Place it over medium heat or a campfire and cook the bacon until it is browned and crisp on both sides, 3 to 4 minutes per side, turning with tongs or a fork. Transfer the bacon to a plate lined with paper towels to drain. Reserve the fat in the skillet.

2 Generously season each trout inside and out with salt and pepper. Holding each trout by the tail, dip it in the cornmeal, thoroughly coating both sides and shaking off the excess.

3 Gently lower each trout into the skillet with the bacon fat. (It should be hot.) Panfry

the fish until golden brown on the outside and cooked through, 5 to 8 minutes per side. Start working over a medium-high heat and reduce the heat if the outside of the trout starts to burn before the fish are cooked through. To test for doneness, make a little cut in the back of the fish. The flesh next to the backbone should be white and should pull away from the bone easily.

4 Drain the trout on the paper towels and transfer it to a platter or plates. Crumble the bacon over the trout (or just halve the slices) and serve it with lemon wedges for squeezing.

How to Fillet a Cooked Whole Fish

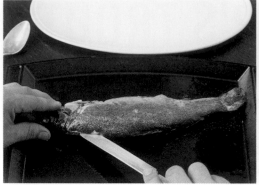

1 Using a fish knife or butter knife, make a cut along the back of the fish just above the backbone.

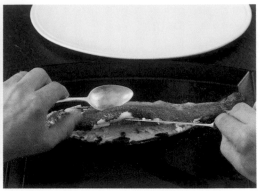

2 Insert the knife in the cut. Gently lift the blade to loosen the fillet from the backbone.

3 Pin the fillet between the knife blade and a large spoon. Pry the fillet away from the fish.

4 Transfer the fillet to a plate or platter.

5 Grab the tail end of the backbone with tongs and lift it off the bottom fillet. Pull out any stray bones.

6 Transfer the bottom fillet to the plate or platter and dig in.

SHAD ROE
WITH BACON AND CAPERS

Shad roe may look like an organ oozing out of a zombie, but it tastes like a cross between caviar and foie gras. Like caviar, it gives you crunchy, salty microbursts of flavor; like foie gras it fills your mouth with buttery richness. It's a seasonal delicacy prized up and down the East Coast, where enthusiasts impatiently await its arrival in February only to mourn its departure in mid-May. Shad roe is the banana-shaped orange egg sac of a silvery fish in the herring family that spawns in early spring. If you've ever tasted it, you know why it belongs in every man's seafood repertory, and if you haven't, what are you waiting for? **Serves 2 as an appetizer, 1 as a rich main course**

1 shad roe (2 lobes, 8 to 12 ounces in all)

4 slices artisanal bacon

Coarse salt (kosher or sea) and freshly ground black pepper

Approximately 1 cup unbleached all-purpose white flour, in a shallow bowl or on a paper towel

2 tablespoons (¼ stick) butter

1 tablespoon drained capers

1 lemon, cut into wedges

SHOP Look for shad roe at your fishmonger's in the springtime. The roe should smell briny, never fishy. It's normal for the thin membrane surrounding the eggs to be a little bloody; rinse it off under cold running water.

GEAR Your basic kitchen gear including a large (10- to 12-inch) skillet, a plate lined with paper towels, plus a spatter shield, a mesh cover placed over a skillet (and other low-sided pans used for frying) to keep hot fat from splattering on you, the stove, and anything else nearby.

WHAT ELSE You can panfry the shad roe from start to finish in a skillet, but you may find it less messy to use a common restaurant trick: Brown it on the stovetop and finish cooking it in the oven.

TIME about 20 minutes

1 Rinse the roe under cold running water, gently scraping off any bloody spots with your fingertips. Gently separate the roe into 2 lobes. Don't remove the membrane, or the roe will crumble.

2 Cook the bacon in a skillet over medium heat until lightly browned, 3 to 4 minutes. Transfer the bacon to a plate lined with paper towels to drain. Reserve the fat in the skillet.

3 Season the roe with salt and pepper to taste. Dredge the roe in the flour, shaking off the excess.

4 *If you are panfrying the shad roe:* Cook the roe in the bacon fat over medium heat until crusty and brown on the outside and cooked through, 6 to 8 minutes per side. Press the roe to check for doneness; it should feel firm to the touch. Reduce the heat as necessary so the outside doesn't burn. Some of the roe may burst and spatter. If it does, cover the skillet with a spatter shield, if you have one.

If you are frying and baking the roe: Preheat the oven to 400°F before you start. Brown the shad roe in the bacon fat in a skillet over medium heat, 3 to 4 minutes per side. Place the skillet in the oven and continue cooking the roe until it is cooked through, 10 to 15 minutes.

5 Transfer the shad roe to a plate. Pour off all but 1 tablespoon of the bacon fat from the skillet. Add the butter and melt it over medium heat. Crumble the bacon into the skillet. Add the capers and cook until sizzling, about 2 minutes. Spoon the caper mixture over the shad roe and serve with lemon wedges for squeezing.

SHELLFISH

Here are some of the foods guys like best: Lobsters. Oyster roasts. Littlenecks on the half shell. All feature sea creatures with shells. Not that men have a monopoly on shellfish, but they seem to bring us particular pleasure. It's not just the reputed aphrodisiacal properties of oysters (I've always believed that aphrodisiac is in the mind of the partaker). Neither is it the pragmatic efficiency of shrimp—pure protein you can cook in a matter of minutes. Nor is it the fact that when it comes to cooking a live crab or lobster, the task almost always devolves to a male.

In the following chapter you'll learn how to prepare all the major types of shellfish: shrimp, crab, lobster, oysters, clams, scallops, mussels, and squid. You'll learn how to cook them in a wok, in a frying pan, in the oven, and, naturally, on the grill. You'll also experience some of the most iconic feasts in the guy food world: from Maryland steamed crabs to a Lowcountry oyster roast.

Crabcakes? Check. Ceviche? Check. Creole shrimp? I've got you covered.

OYSTERS AND CLAMS ON THE HALF SHELL
WITH BIG-FLAVORED SAUCES

Most people expect a grill session when they come to my house, and I usually oblige them. But you should also know when *not* to cook, which brings us to oysters and clams on the half shell. Being lucky enough to spend time on Martha's Vineyard, I have access to some of the best bivalves on the planet. (Sorry for the chauvinism, but I dig my own clams; see page 408.) When the shellfish is this fresh, even a grilling fanatic like me keeps it simple. The fireworks come from the sauces, like French Mignonette Sauce, East-West Mignonette, Volcanic Cocktail Sauce, or Wasabi Whipped Cream. **Makes 2 dozen, serves 2 to 4**

24 fresh oysters or littleneck or cherrystone clams in the shells, or a mix of both

Crushed ice, for the serving platter

2 lemons, cut into wedges

A bottle of your favorite hot sauce

½ cup prepared or freshly grated horseradish

French Mignonette Sauce (optional, recipe follows)

East-West Mignonette Sauce (optional, page 399)

Volcanic Cocktail Sauce (optional, page 401)

Wasabi Whipped Cream (optional, page 401)

1 Rinse the oysters and/or clams with cold water and scrub off any grit or mud with a stiff-bristled brush. If you are serving oysters, shuck them following the method outlined on page 404. If you are serving clams, shuck them following the method outlined on page 409.

2 Pile crushed ice on a large platter. Arrange the oysters and/or clams on top of the ice and with plenty of the lemon wedges. Serve the hot sauce and horseradish and the sauce(s) of your choice, if desired, on the side.

SHOP Buy your oysters and clams from a fishmonger with a high turnover. The shells should be tightly shut and the shellfish should smell briny, not fishy. If one or two shells are slightly gapping, tap them: A fresh live bivalve will close in a few seconds.

GEAR Your basic kitchen gear, plus a shucking knife, a stiff-bristled brush, and a large platter

WHAT ELSE Oysters vary widely in taste and texture depending on where they come from. On page 405, you'll find some of my favorites. I always try to serve two or three kinds; sampling a variety is educational.

TIME about 20 minutes for shucking the oysters; 10 minutes to make each of the optional sauces

▶ In September, the Grand Central Oyster Bar in New York City holds an oyster shucking contest. One recent winner, Luis Iglesias, from Mexico, opened a mind-boggling fifteen shellfish in a single minute. His secret? Using a short, straight, slender knife honed to dagger sharpness and inserted into the side of the oyster. Great for the pros, but I've seen guys plunge oyster knives straight through their palms using this technique. So here, in six simple steps, is a tried-and-true method that will enable you to shuck your oysters while leaving your hands intact.

How to Shuck Oysters

1 Hold the oyster in your hand, lip facing your thumb; protect your palm with a folded dish towel.

2 Insert the tip of your oyster knife in the "hinge" (the narrow part where the two shells meet).

3 Wriggle the knife tip between the shells at the hinge.

4 Twist the blade to pry the shells apart.

5 Slide the blade under the top shell above the oyster to cut the adductor muscle. Discard the top shell.

6 Slide the blade under the oyster to loosen it from the bottom shell.

FRENCH MIGNONETTE SAUCE

Mignonette is a French oyster condiment comprised of red wine vinegar, finely chopped shallots, and cracked black peppercorns. **Makes about 1 cup**

½ cup good-quality red wine vinegar

2 to 3 large shallots, peeled and minced (about ½ cup)

1 tablespoon cracked black peppercorns

1 teaspoon coarse salt (kosher or sea)

Place the wine vinegar, shallots, peppercorns, and salt in a bowl. Add 2 tablespoons of water and whisk until the salt dissolves. Taste for seasoning, adding additional water if needed to blunt the edge of the vinegar. Serve the sauce in a small bowl for spooning over the shellfish. The sauce can be made up to 2 hours ahead and refrigerated.

EAST-WEST MIGNONETTE

This version of mignonette sauce takes an Asian approach, playing the sweetness of mirin (Japanese rice wine) off the salty tang of soy sauce and the bite of rice vinegar and ginger. **Makes about 1 cup**

1 scallion, both white and green parts, trimmed and thinly sliced crosswise

3 tablespoons chopped fresh cilantro

1 tablespoon minced peeled fresh ginger

½ cup rice vinegar

2 tablespoons soy sauce or fish sauce

2 tablespoons mirin (sweet rice wine), sake, or white wine

Place the scallion, cilantro, ginger, rice vinegar, soy sauce, mirin, and 2 tablespoons of water in a mixing bowl and whisk to mix. Serve the sauce in a small bowl for spooning over the shellfish. The sauce can be made up to 2 hours ahead and refrigerated.

VOLCANIC COCKTAIL SAUCE

Freshly grated horseradish and Caribbean hot sauce turn up the heat on traditional American cocktail sauce. Fresh horseradish comes in femurlike roots. Peel it with a paring knife and grate it with a box grater or finely chop it in a food processor. Store-bought cocktail sauce (one good brand is Heinz) isn't quite as sweet as ketchup, but you can certainly use ketchup instead. **Makes about 1 cup**

1 piece (3 inches) fresh horseradish, peeled

1 cup store-bought cocktail sauce or ketchup

1 tablespoon fresh lemon juice

1 teaspoon Scotch bonnet-based hot sauce, such as Matouk's from Trinidad, or 1 teaspoon minced canned chipotle peppers, or more of either to taste

1 If you are using a box grater, stand it in a mixing bowl and grate the whole horseradish root on the side of the grater with the smallest holes. If you are using a food processor, cut the horseradish into ¼-inch slices, then finely chop them, running the machine in short bursts. Place the chopped horseradish in a mixing bowl. Warning: Horseradish vapors will sting your sinuses—don't inhale too deeply.

2 Stir in the cocktail sauce, lemon juice, and as much hot sauce or as many chipotle peppers as you can bear. Serve in a small bowl for spooning over the shellfish. The sauce can be refrigerated, covered, for several days.

WASABI WHIPPED CREAM

This isn't your traditional whipped cream—not with the addition of spicy wasabi and soy sauce. But you'll love the way it counterpoints the briny tang of oysters and clams. Whip the cream with a hand or stand mixer if you have one. Whipping the cream by hand in a chilled metal bowl with a whisk works, too, but it requires more elbow grease. **Makes about 1 cup**

1 tablespoon wasabi powder

1 tablespoon soy sauce

¾ cup heavy (whipping) cream

How to Serve Oysters

Raw oysters are traditionally served on the half shell on a bed of crushed ice or seaweed—an obliging fishmonger can provide the seaweed. This keeps the oysters from tipping and spilling their juices. The seaweed adds nautical local color.

As you ascend the ladder of oyster enlightenment, you'll find yourself using fewer and fewer condiments. You might start with cocktail sauce or hot sauce and horseradish. As you come to appreciate the pristine marine flavor of the shellfish, you'll find yourself cutting back to mignonette (a French vinegar, shallot, and pepper sauce; find it on page 399) or a simple squeeze of lemon.

But perhaps the ultimate way to appreciate an oyster's flavor is to eat it "naked" (the oyster, not you), with its fresh juices as the only condiment.

For a beverage to serve with oysters you can't go wrong with Champagne, a crisp dry white wine like Chablis, Sancerre, Muscadet, Vinho Verde, Txakolí, or sauvignon blanc, or a dark bitter, like Guinness.

1 Place the wasabi powder and 2 tablespoons of water in a mixing bowl and stir to form a paste. Let the wasabi paste stand for about 5 minutes. Stir in the soy sauce.

2 Place the cream in a chilled metal bowl and using an electric mixer, or whisk, beat it until soft peaks form (it should have the consistency of soft ice cream). Do not overbeat.

3 Using a rubber spatula, gently fold the whipped cream into the wasabi paste and transfer it to a serving bowl. Add spoonfuls of wasabi cream to the oysters and/or clams. The sauce can be refrigerated, covered, for 1 to 2 days.

LOWCOUNTRY OYSTER ROAST

GEAR Your basic kitchen gear plus a grill, a metal sheet large enough to fit over the grill grate or a cast-iron *plancha* (optional), a burlap sack or cotton towel, and an oyster knife

TIME about 1 hour

Born on tidewaters of South Carolina, the oyster roast is the Lowcountry version of a New England clambake or Gulf Coast shrimp boil. But unlike the former, there's only one main ingredient—oysters, or more precisely, great clusters of oysters pried from the banks of tidal estuaries at low tide and roasted on a piece of sheet metal over a wood fire. **Serves 4 as a starter, 2 as a light main course**

2 quarts seawater, or 2 quarts water plus
    4 teaspoons salt

4 dozen fresh oysters in the shell

8 tablespoons (1 stick) salted butter,
    melted

Your choice of hot sauce

1 Soak the burlap sack or towel in the seawater for about 20 minutes. Don't have seawater? Dissolve the salt in the water and use it to soak the sack or towel.

2 Set up the grill for direct grilling and preheat it to high. If you are using a metal sheet, place it on top of the grill grate to preheat.

3 Arrange the oysters in a single layer directly on the grill grate or on the metal sheet. Cover the oysters with the soaked burlap or towel. Grill the oysters until the shells open, 6 to 10 minutes. As the shells open, transfer the oysters to plates, taking care not to spill the juices or burn yourself on the steam from the wet cloth.

4 Use an oyster knife to persuade any recalcitrant bivalves that haven't fully opened. Sometimes failure to open indicates a dead or bad oyster. Smell the oyster carefully and if the aroma seems off, throw the oyster out. Slide a knife under the top shell to cut the adductor muscle, then discard the top shell. Slide the knife under the oyster to loosen it from the shell.

5 Dip the oysters in the melted butter and/or sprinkle them with hot sauce. Eat the oysters with your bare hands. Or use a fork to dip them in the melted butter.

Oyster Roast 101

So how easy is it to stage your own Lowcountry oyster roast? Real easy. Here's what you need to know:

▸ Oyster roasts take place in late fall, when the oysters are fat and briny.

▸ South Carolina oysters generally come in clusters—ten to twelve shells fused together in a calcareous clump. No problem. You roast them until most of the shells open and pry any laggards open with an oyster knife. If you live somewhere other than South Carolina, buy your oysters freestanding. Two to three dozen make a proper meal for one.

▸ For a traditional oyster roast you build a blazing log fire in a three-sided box constructed with cinderblocks and capped with a sheet of metal. You stoke the fire with oak, hickory, apple, or another hardwood (no pine or softwood, or you'll get a sooty resinous smoke). But you can make an excellent oyster roast on the grill and it works equally well whether your grill burns gas or charcoal (see page 10).

▸ The cooking process involves both roasting and steaming. The oysters roast on the grill and steam in the vapor released from a seawater-soaked burlap sack or towel. The cooking time is brief—six to ten minutes—long enough to steam open the shells, but short enough to keep the oysters themselves moist and briny.

▸ This brings us to condiments. Melted butter and hot sauce, to be sure. (Why not some local fire, like Texas Pete hot sauce—surprisingly, made in Winston-Salem, North Carolina.) Cocktail sauce? If you insist, although I personally think it overpowers the oysters. Beer? Of course. Side dishes? Not that you need them, but mustard or vinegar slaw (page 178), potato salad (page 170), and garlic bread (page 513) couldn't hurt— as long as you keep the focus on the oysters.

OYSTERS

Oysters—few foods are more closely linked to a guy's notion of masculinity. Knowing how to savor them raw is a rite of passage and a mark of manhood. First, there's the challenge of shucking the oysters, unlocking the tightly closed shells with nothing more than a knife and your bare hands, preferably without shedding blood. Then there's the primal thrill of slurping a live oyster off the half shell.

Finally, there are the bivalve's infamous alleged aphrodisiacal properties. Oysters contain high levels of zinc, D-aspartic acid, and N-methyl-D-aspartate—compounds some scientists claim increase male testosterone levels. Even if there are no definitive studies on the oyster's efficacy in the bedroom, there's the psychological factor: If you believe it works, it likely will. Case in point? Casanova, who consumed four dozen oysters for breakfast each morning—and he certainly didn't want for action.

Maybe you're a newcomer to the world of oysters and you've always wondered how to ready yourself for the first slurp. Or you love oysters, but you want to up your game in shucking and serving. Here's what you need to know.

LOCATION, LOCATION An oyster is basically a filter that absorbs the flavors from the water around it. That's why the same oyster species can taste dramatically different depending on where it's raised and harvested. Buying oysters is a little like picking a hotel room: It's all about location. I've included a list of seven of the best oysters in North America in this box.

DOCUMENT CHECK The Grand Central Oyster Bar in New York City serves only oysters that are FDA certified. This means that each bag of oysters comes with a tag specifying the producer's name, the lot number, and the date they were harvested. Your fishmonger should also have such a certificate. Don't feel awkward about asking him or her to show it to you.

YOUR NOSE KNOWS Smell the oysters and the shop that sells them. The scents should be fresh and briny—like the seashore. If an oyster smells funky, it probably tastes funky (or worse). Don't buy it.

FORGET THE "R" MONTH MYTH Popular wisdom holds that you should eat oysters only in months with an "r" (September through April) on the theory that oysters spawn (breed) in the summer months and taste flabby or unpleasantly milky. According to Grand Central Oyster Bar chef Sandy Ingber, the real reason for this tradition was to avoid the perishable shellfish in the summer before the age of refrigeration. Today there are more than one thousand oyster varieties to choose from in North America, so even in the summer you can find great-tasting, nonspawning bivalves.

MAKE SURE THE OYSTER IS TIGHTLY CLOSED If the shells gap a little, tap the oyster. If it snaps shut within twenty seconds, it's still alive and safe to eat. If it doesn't, discard it. As with all shellfish, when in doubt, throw it out.

MIX AND MATCH When trying oysters in a restaurant or serving them to friends, select a variety. This makes for interesting tasting, and you'll educate your palate for the future.

HOW MUCH IS ENOUGH? "We'll get guys who will eat one hundred oysters at a sitting," says Ingber. For the normal guy, figure on six to twelve for an appetizer, twenty-four to thirty-six as a main course.

COLD STORAGE Oysters are usually sold on ice at the fishmonger, but once you get them home, Ingber recommends transferring the oysters to a perforated or solid metal pan lined with a dish towel and set over a pan of ice. In other words, the shellfish should rest on, but not be buried in, the ice. Oysters are saltwater creatures, so you don't want to drown them in the freshwater released as the ice melts.

THE FRESHER THE BETTER The ancient Romans used to ship oysters in ice-filled carts from Great Britain over the Alps to Rome. But don't keep them that long. As with all shellfish, very fresh is best—keep oysters refrigerated and try to serve them the same day you buy them.

SEVEN OYSTERS YOU SHOULD TRY NOW

BELON A flat-shell oyster originally from France and today raised in Maine. A true oyster lover's oyster with an intense brine, sophisticated flavor, and a strong mineral-iodine bite.

BLUEPOINT A plump, meaty, light-brined, mild-flavored oyster from Blue Point, Connecticut, on the Long Island Sound. The best seller at the Grand Central Oyster Bar—more than one thousand are served each day.

KATAMA BAY An oyster from my stomping grounds, Katama Bay in Martha's Vineyard. Moist and tender, with a perfect balance of salt and sweetness.

KUMAMOTO A small, deep-shelled oyster with a creamy texture and sweet briny flavor. Originally from Japan, they are now found in California, Oregon, Washington State, and British Columbia.

PECONIC PEARLS Medium-brine oysters with plump meat. Best of all, part of the sales of these Long Island oysters goes toward preserving Peconic Bay.

PEMAQUID A tangy, full-brine, full-flavored oyster from the Damariscotta River in Maine.

PENN COVE SELECT A luscious, clean, briny oyster from Whidbey Island in the Puget Sound. The Oyster Guide (oysterguide.com) likens its flavor to the "freshness of a salted cucumber."

JIM DENEVAN

A full moon rises over a not-your-everyday dinner party. A table long enough to seat 150 people snakes through a grove of California redwoods—or amid rows of vines in a Napa Valley vineyard or on a wave-lapped beach or in the mouth of a sea cave in the Pacific Northwest. Freshly gathered shellfish, local farm vegetables, and naturally leavened bread bake in an improvised wood-burning oven; an enormous hog roasts in a stone-lined, wood-fire-heated underground pit. Presiding over these activities is a tall, fashionably bald, former fashion model-turned-surfer dude, chef, artist, and farm foods advocate and impresario: Jim Denevan.

If Denevan seems somewhat jet-lagged, forgive him. Weeks earlier, the Californian natural foods activist flew to Australia to make a commercial for Hyundai. On returning home to Santa Cruz, California, he hosted a New Year's Eve dinner celebration on the beach. Then he staged one of his Outstanding in the Field dinners on a farm in Redland, Florida—one of more than seventy such events celebrating local farmers and fishermen he'll put on this year. Next stop: Brazil, then Hawaii, bringing his unique blend of performance art and culinary show-manship to foodies around the world.

"There are lots of advocates for sustainable agriculture—journalists, filmmakers, policy makers," says Denevan. "Our mission is to help people speak directly with the people who produce their food."

You'll find Denevan's recipe for Orecchiette with Italian Sausage and Bitter Greens on page 456.

When did you become an evangelist for organic farming?
My brother was one of the first certified organic farmers in California. I used to help out at the farm, so I've always been committed to organic farming.

How did Outstanding in the Field get started?
Thanks to Alice Waters, chefs were just starting to mention farmers and farms on their menus, but no one had actually brought the public to the farm. We figured if we could set up tables in the fields and have chefs come to cook at the farm—and later to the ranch, vineyard, and fishing grounds—people could see where their food actually comes from and develop a deeper, more intimate relationship with cooking and eating.

Why is it important for men to cook?
Well, first of all, there's the sheer physicality of cooking. I love the masculine aspect of pushing the food out at a jamming restaurant. Cooking on a busy

night is like throwing long pass after long pass. Saturday night is like the Super Bowl.

Besides, according to my girlfriend and her girlfriends, a guy who can cook is pretty darned attractive to women.

The quintessential guy dish?
Barbecue. Hunks of meat and fire. Shellfish you pry off the rocks with a crowbar is pretty manly, too.

What's your go-to dish when you're by yourself?
Pasta. I might start with garlic, anchovies, some chorizo sausage, and barely cooked tomatoes. Or some freshly harvested mussels or local rockfish.

What's your go-to seduction dish?
Pasta again. It's easy to cook at home, which means she's already in your house or apartment. It goes well with alcohol, which is another plus. It's not complicated, but she'll notice if you do it right, and that's the third plus. Should be a good night.

Three dishes every guy should know how to make?
Shellfish. I do a lot of surfing, and I'll often paddle my board to rocky coves to harvest wild oysters and mussels. Place them in a dry pan over high heat. The minute they begin to open, add the wine and aromatics.

A roast chicken. The trick is to buy a good bird (a grain-fed, free-range farm chicken) and cook it through without drying out the breast. [For a great roast chicken, see page 327.]

Braised meat. You put the meat in a sealed pan with aromatic vegetables and a flavorful liquid, like beer or wine. You put it in the oven at low heat and basically forget about it. A few hours later, you have lamb shanks or osso buco that are so tender, you can cut the meat with the side of your fork.

Three ingredients you can't live without?
Salt. For its flavor, of course, and simply for the tactile pleasure of the way it feels between your fingers and in your hand.

Bitter greens. I love the astringent flavor of escarole, radicchio, chicory, and rapini (broccoli rabe). In our sugar-saturated American culture, most people overlook the bitter flavors and how satisfying they can be.

Wild food, such as thistles, sea buckthorn, and wild mushrooms. I'm a huge fan of any food you forage instead of pick up at your local supermarket.

> ▶ The best way to learn how to cook is to cook. Just jump in and do it.

Three tools you can't live without?
A crowbar. When it comes to dislodging mollusks from rocks, nothing beats a crowbar.

A shovel. We do a lot of underground pig roasts.

A hotel pan (a rectangular metal pan with raised sides). Put some hardwood chips in the bottom and a raised wire rack with food over them. Tightly tent the top with aluminum foil, and you have an instant stovetop smoker.

What are the three most important things to keep in mind if you're just starting out in the kitchen?
The best way to learn how to cook is to cook. Just jump in and do it. Don't be afraid to make mistakes. You'll never learn if you don't fail occasionally.

Think texture as well as flavor. When I make a seafood stew (a staple since I live so close to the beach), I'll add firm fish that you can sink your teeth into, soft fish that falls apart and thickens the broth, and jellyfish just to give you an interesting texture.

Taste, taste, and taste again. That's the only way you'll get the flavors right.

What are the three most common mistakes guys make in the kitchen?
Mindless shopping. Buying any old thing at the supermarket. If you're in a place that has amazing tomatoes in July, why settle for mediocre tomatoes in May?

The "guy syndrome," which means if some of a flavoring or ingredient is good, more must be even better. A lot of guys are way too aggressive with flavor.

Ignoring the "who" of cooking—the farmers, fishermen, ranchers, butchers, cheese makers who stand behind the chef.

Something unexpected you've learned that really helps you up your game in the kitchen?
It may seem counterintuitive, but limiting yourself to cooking only with local foods that are in season can actually focus and increase your creativity.

Final words of wisdom?
What I like best about cooking is that it's easy to grasp the basics, but you can spend a lifetime mastering the fine points. For me, the most interesting, fulfilling activities in life are those of which you can never claim to possess complete knowledge.

CLAMS

I have in my basement a rake that looks like a lethal weapon. Armed with long, inwardly curving claws, it's called a "bear paw." When it comes to digging littlenecks and other clams in Cape Poge Bay in Chappaquiddick (Martha's Vineyard), nothing beats it—except possibly raking the sandy bottom with your toes.

Clams. However you serve them—steamed, stuffed, stir-fried, deep-fried, roasted, or just shucked and served raw on the half shell—the bivalves will reward you with a rich array of textures (crispy, meaty, chewy, gooey) and a sweet-briny flavor unique among sea creatures.

The premier clam of the East Coast is *Venus mercenaria* (the hard-shell clam), the size of which ranges from littlenecks, the smallest, best eaten raw; to cherrystones, a little larger, good raw and steamed; to quahogs, large, tough clams best for mincing and stuffing or chowder.

Another popular East Coast clam is the steamer, also known as the softshell, long-neck, Ipswich, or Essex clam. Its shell is softer than that of a hard-shell clam—it will crack if you pinch it hard. Enjoy these clams steamed, then dipped in clam broth and melted butter.

On the West Coast look for colorful, tender Manila clams and mild-flavored geoducks (pronounced "gooey duck"), giant phalliclike clams from the Pacific Northwest.

Razor clams have shells shaped like old-fashioned straight razors and delectable mild sweet meat. I buy them whenever I can.

When buying clams, make sure the shells are tightly closed. If a clam is open, tap it: The clam should close at once. Fresh clams will smell like the seashore. Avoid clams with cracked shells. Scrub any grit off the clam shells with a stiff-bristled brush under cold running water.

Steamers can be sandy—this often happens during stormy weather—so before preparing them, try purging them in a bucket of seawater or salt water mixed with a handful of cornmeal. The clams eat the cornmeal, the theory goes, and spit out the sand. Does this really work? Old-timers on Martha's Vineyard swear by it.

How to Shuck Clams

1 Place the clam in the palm of your hand, hinge toward the base of your thumb, your palm protected by a dish towel. Position the knife where the two shells meet.

2 Gently slide the blade between the shells toward the hinge.

3 Cut through the adductor muscle, which holds the shells together: The clam will open.

4 Slide the blade under the clam to loosen it from the shell. Take care not to spill the flavorful clam juices.

◄ To shuck hard-shell clams, such as littlenecks and cherrystones, you need a flat-bladed knife, like a butter knife. If you are going to shuck a lot of clams, invest in a clam knife, available at kitchenware stores such as Sur La Table or Williams-Sonoma or online through amazon.com.

STOVETOP CLAMBAKE

In the best of worlds, you'd have access to your own private beach where you could dig a pit, line it with stones, and build a raging bonfire, which you'd let burn down to embers. You'd top the coals with seaweed, then pile on lobsters, steamers, *linguiça* (Portuguese sausage), sweet corn, new potatoes, and more seaweed. You'd cover these ingredients with a tarp and bury the whole shebang

SHOP Your chief challenge will be finding seaweed: Make friends with your local fishmonger. *Linguiça*, a cooked, paprika-flavored Portuguese sausage, is available at ethnic markets and many supermarkets. Precooked chorizo or kielbasa make good substitutes.

GEAR Your basic kitchen gear plus a large stockpot (at least 4 gallons) with a tight-fitting lid (tradition calls for one of the inexpensive black-and-white speckled enamelware pots sold at hardware stores) and four small bowls or ramekins for serving the melted butter

WHAT ELSE Can't find seaweed? Don't worry. Start with the lobsters on the bottom and layer the remaining ingredients over them. You'll still get plenty of flavor.

Can't find lobsters? Use 3 pounds of shrimp (preferably with heads and shells intact). They cook quicker than lobsters, so add them with the clams and mussels, once the wine comes to a boil.

TIME about 45 minutes

---

1 gallon of fresh seaweed

4 live and wriggling lobsters, 1¼ pounds each

5 tablespoons Old Bay seasoning

1½ pounds new potatoes, scrubbed and cut in half

4 ears sweet corn, shucked and cut crosswise into 2-inch rounds

1 fennel bulb, trimmed and cut in quarters from the top to the root

1 pound linguiça or kielbasa, cut crosswise into 1-inch pieces

1 bottle (750 milliliters) dry white wine, like sauvignon blanc

36 steamers or littleneck clams, scrubbed

24 mussels, washed and bearded (see page 437)

16 tablespoons (2 sticks) salted butter

2 tablespoons chopped fresh chives or tarragon (optional)

---

1 Place one-fourth of the seaweed in the bottom of a large stockpot. Place the lobsters on top. Sprinkle 2 tablespoons of the Old Bay seasoning over the lobsters.

2 Spread a 1-inch-thick layer of seaweed over the lobsters. Arrange the potatoes, corn, fennel, and *linguiça* on top and sprinkle 2 more tablespoons of Old Bay seasoning over them. Spread another 1-inch-thick layer of seaweed on top. Add the wine. Tightly cover the pot and place it on a burner over high heat. Let the wine come to a boil and boil for 10 minutes. Remove the pot from the heat.

3 Add the clams and mussels (arrange them so they lie flat on the seaweed). Sprinkle the remaining 1 tablespoon of Old Bay seasoning over the shellfish and top them with the remaining seaweed.

4 Return the pot to the heat and cook until the lobsters turn bright orange and are cooked through (see page 432 for tips on checking for doneness), the clams and mussels are open, and the potatoes and fennel are easy to pierce with a skewer, 10 to 15 minutes longer, 20 to 25 minutes in all.

5 Meanwhile, melt the butter in a saucepan over medium heat. Add the chives or tarragon, if using, to the butter and cook until fragrant, 2 to 4 minutes. Don't let the butter brown. Divide the butter among 4 small bowls.

6 To serve, remove the seaweed in layers with tongs, transferring the clambake ingredients to a platter or plates. For instructions on how to eat a lobster, see page 430. Pull the clams and mussels from the shells with your fingers or a fork. Dip each ingredient in butter with your fingers prior to popping it in your mouth. Have a large bowl on hand for the empty shells.

CHILLED CRABS
WITH HOT SAUCES

Joe Weiss didn't set out to make seafood history. He simply wanted to escape New York winters, which aggravated his asthma. So he moved his family to Miami Beach—then accessible only by ferry—and set up a little seafood eatery in the front room of his one-story cottage. The house specialty? The chilled claws of a crustacean native to Florida. You know it today as Weiss's namesake and the most famous restaurant in Miami: Joe's Stone Crab.

Stone crab claws with mustard sauce are what we Miamians eat at Super Bowl parties, on New Year's Eve, for seduction dinners, and pretty much any occasion in between. Take the party to Maryland and you'd serve crab "fingers" (cracked blue crab claws). On the West Coast you'd dish up Dungeness crab from Washington State or king or snow crab from Alaska. The point being that if you serve a large platter of icy cold crab claws with a couple of spicy dipping sauces, the spread becomes as magnanimous as the guy serving it. **Serves 4; can be multiplied as desired**

SHOP Stone crab season runs from October through April, and if you live in Florida, you can find the claws at fishmongers and many food markets. If not, order them directly from Joe's: joesstonecrab.com. King crab claws can be ordered from vitalchoice .com, snow crab claws from marxfoods.com, and blue crab fingers from mdcrabbers.com. Either way, they will have been cooked when you buy them.

GEAR Your basic gear plus a wide-headed mallet, a large platter for serving, and small bowls for the sauces

WHAT ELSE Sure, you could serve the crab claws cold from the fridge, but for maximum drama, arrange them on a platter piled with crushed ice. Your freezer doesn't make crushed ice? Put ice cubes in a pillowcase and pound them with a hammer.

TIME about 15 minutes

One or more of the following cooked crab claws or fingers (figure on 1 to 1½ pounds per person):

Stone crab claws

King crab or snow crab claws

Blue crab fingers

Crushed ice, for the serving platter

1 lemon, cut into wedges

Joe's-Style Mustard Sauce (recipe follows)

Volcanic Cocktail Sauce (page 401)

1 Keep the crabs refrigerated until ready to serve. Crack the crab claws if necessary (some companies sell them already cracked). To crack the claws, place them on a cutting board and cover them with a dish towel (the towel keeps bits of shell and meat from spattering). Using a mallet, gently pound the claws. Most king and snow crab claws come split already, but if not, cut them in half lengthwise using kitchen shears or tin snips (clean the tin snips well before using if they came off your workbench).

2 To serve the crab, pile crushed ice on a large platter. Arrange the crab on top and strew it with lemon wedges. Place the sauces in small bowls and wedge them in the ice.

JOE'S-STYLE MUSTARD SAUCE

This is modeled on the creamy, tangy, mildly mustardy sauce served at Joe's Stone Crab. Look for Colman's dry mustard in yellow and red rectangular cans in your supermarket's spice aisle. Or substitute an equal amount of prepared Dijon mustard. **Makes about 1 cup**

1 cup mayonnaise, preferably Hellmann's

4 teaspoons Colman's dry mustard

2 tablespoons heavy (whipping) cream or half-and-half

2 teaspoons Worcestershire sauce

1 teaspoon A.1. Steak Sauce

Coarse salt (kosher or sea) and freshly ground white pepper

Combine the mayonnaise, dry mustard, cream, Worcestershire sauce, and steak sauce in a small bowl and whisk to mix. Season with salt and white pepper to taste. The sauce can be refrigerated, covered, for at least 3 days.

MARYLAND STEAMED CRABS

SHOP Buy crabs that are alive and kicking. You'll also need Old Bay seasoning, a traditional Baltimore blend of ginger, mace, bay leaf, and other spices.

Call it the last meal question: If you could choose your last meal on earth, what would you select? Porterhouse steak? Caviar? I know my choice and I'd eat it with bare hands: a mess of Maryland steamed crabs. I use the word *mess* deliberately. In Baltimore, where I grew up, crab is a no-nonsense dish slathered with spice paste and steamed with vinegar and beer. The finished crabs look like they were dredged from a swamp and burn your mouth like napalm. In the process of teasing the delicate crabmeat from the shells, you will cut your fingers and burn your lips. You're supposed to. But come my last meal, I wouldn't trade a single bite of Maryland steamed crab for all the lobster in Maine. **Serves 2 to 4**

GEAR Your basic kitchen gear plus a large stockpot (at least 4 gallons) with a tight-fitting lid and a rack to keep the crabs above the steaming liquid, a brick or cast-iron skillet, and a wooden mallet

WHAT ELSE Eighty years ago my grandfather set about steaming several dozen live crabs, but he forgot to place a brick on the pot lid. A few minutes later, my grandmother's shrieks summoned him to a kitchen crawling with angry live crabs. So remember always to secure the lid of the pot with a brick or other heavy object, like a cast-iron skillet.

TIME 30 minutes

1 bottle (12 ounces) beer (leave the bottle open for a few hours to allow it to go flat)

1 cup distilled white vinegar

½ cup Old Bay seasoning

2 tablespoons coarse salt (kosher or sea)

2 tablespoons Colman's dry mustard

1 tablespoon freshly ground black pepper

1 teaspoon cayenne pepper, or as much as you can bear

12 jumbo blue crabs, alive and kicking

1 Combine the beer and vinegar in a large stockpot. Combine the Old Bay seasoning, salt, dry mustard, black pepper, and cayenne in a bowl and mix with your fingers.

2 Arrange the crabs on the rack in the stockpot in 3 layers, sprinkling a third of the spice mixture over each layer. Tightly cover the pot and weight the lid with a brick or cast-iron skillet.

3 Place the pot over high heat and steam the crabs until they are fire-engine red, about 20 minutes, or as needed. Pile the cooked crabs in the center of the table, crack them with a mallet, and eat them with your hands.

How to Eat Steamed Crabs

Preferably outdoors on a table spread with butcher paper—the only implements you'll need are a wooden mallet (for cracking the claw shells), a paring knife (for prying open the carapaces), and a bowl for those empty shells. And rolls of paper towels—you eat steamed crabs with your hands. Here's how we do it in Baltimore.

1. Twist off the claws and crack them with a mallet to expose the sweet meat—my favorite part of the crab to eat.

2. Break off the swimmerets (the tiny claws), crack them in half, and suck out the tender flesh.

3. To get to the meat in the body, turn the crab on its back and pull off the "apron" (the V-shape tab on the belly). Pry off the carapace.

4. Before discarding the carapace, use a paring knife to scrape out and eat the "mustard," the creamy yellow fat in the pointy corners. (Yeah, I know it looks gross, but for Marylanders it's a delicacy.)

5. Scrape off the featherlike gills and spaghetti-like entrails and discard.

6. Break the body in two and, using the paring knife and your fingers, pry the sweet meat from the shell.

PANFRIED SOFT-SHELL CRABS

SHOP Soft-shell crab season traditionally starts with the first full moon in May (when the crabs come out of hibernation) and lasts through September. Look for soft-shell crabs at fishmongers and natural foods supermarkets.

GEAR Your basic kitchen gear including a large (10- to 12-inch) skillet

WHAT ELSE To trim and clean the crabs, cut off the eyes and mouth using kitchen shears. Lift up the pointy ends of the shells and pull out the gills—the feathery-looking stuff under the shell. Better yet, ask your fishmonger to do this.

There are several options for breading. Straight flour is the simplest; flour mixed with cornmeal has a bit more flavor and crunch. Cracker crumbs give you the richest crust of all. Look for packages of cracker crumbs in your local supermarket, or make your own by placing crackers in a heavy-duty resealable plastic bag and pounding them with a cast-iron skillet or rolling pin.

TIME about 15 minutes

Not a separate species, soft shell is a stage in a blue crab's life when the crustacean molts (sheds its shell) to make way for a larger carapace. This leaves the crab highly vulnerable to predators—foremost among them, you and me. For the beauty of a freshly molted crab is that you get to eat it whole—crunchy exterior (it tastes like a briny potato chip) and sweet meat. **Serves 4**

1 large egg

½ cup milk

¾ cup unbleached all-purpose white flour

¾ cup cracker crumbs, white cornmeal, or more flour

1 tablespoon Old Bay seasoning

1½ tablespoons unsalted butter, or more as needed

1 tablespoon extra virgin olive oil, or more as needed

8 large or 12 medium-size soft-shell crabs, cleaned

Lemon wedges, for serving

1 Place the egg in a wide shallow bowl and beat it with a fork. Beat in the milk.

2 Place the flour, cracker crumbs, and Old Bay seasoning in a wide shallow bowl and mix with a fork.

3 Melt the butter in the olive oil in a large skillet over medium-high heat.

4 Using tongs or two forks, dip a crab first in the egg mixture, holding it over the bowl to drain off the excess. Next dip the crab in the flour mixture to coat both sides, shaking the crab over the bowl to remove the excess flour. Flour the remianing crabs as you fry them.

5 Working in batches so as not to overcrowd the skillet, gently lower the crabs into the skillet. There should be about 1 inch between the crabs. Fry the crabs, turning with tongs, until they are browned on both sides and cooked through, 2 to 4 minutes per side, depending on their size. When the crabs are cooked through, the shells will turn red. Make a little cut in the bottom of the thickest part of the crab; the flesh will be white and firm. Add more butter or olive oil as needed.

6 Transfer the crabs to a platter or plates and serve with lemon wedges.

THE REAL DEAL BALTIMORE CRAB CAKES

I grew up in Baltimore, so I hold strong opinions about crab cakes—especially about what you should put in a crab cake and what you shouldn't. Onions, for example, do not belong in crab cakes. Nor do garlic, bell peppers, or celery. Crab cakes should not be spiced with Cajun seasoning or tarted up with rosemary or cilantro. Because, as anyone who grew up in Charm City knows, a crab cake should contain one primary ingredient: crab. Big, sweet, meaty lumps of crab with mayonnaise for richness and just enough binder (bread and egg) to hold the crab cake together. Seasonings? Tradition calls for a whisper of mustard powder and Old Bay seasoning. But not so much that you'd overpower the crab.

Makes 4 crab cakes; serves 4 as a starter, 2 as a main course

1 slice white bread, preferably country-style, crusts removed, bread cut into ¼-inch dice

¼ cup half-and-half

1 pound jumbo lump crabmeat

1 large egg

2 teaspoons Old Bay seasoning

¼ cup mayonnaise, preferably Hellmann's, or as needed

1 teaspoon dry mustard, preferably Colman's

1 tablespoon unsalted butter, or more as needed, plus 1 tablespoon olive oil, for frying

Made-from-Scratch Tartar Sauce (page 548)

1 Place the bread in a bowl with the half-and-half and let soak for about 5 minutes. Drain off the half-and-half (you can save it for cereal), squeezing liquid from the bread through your fingers.

2 Gently pick through the crabmeat, removing any pieces of shell. Place the egg in a large mixing bowl and beat it with a fork until smooth. Stir in the Old Bay seasoning, mayonnaise, and mustard. Add the crab and soaked

SHOP For the ultimate Maryland crab cake, use fresh jumbo lump crabmeat. It doesn't come cheap (expect to pay upward of $25 per pound). Check with your local fishmonger or order it online from farm-2-market.com. If you live on the West Coast, you can make awesome crab cakes with Dungeness crab.

GEAR Your basic kitchen gear including a large (10- to 12-inch) skillet

WHAT ELSE There are three ways to cook a crab cake: panfrying, deep-frying, and broiling. Panfrying gives you the perfect ratio of crustiness to fat.

TIME 20 minutes actual work, plus 1 hour for chilling the crab cakes

bread and gently stir just to mix. If the mixture looks dry, add a little more mayonnaise. Refrigerate the crab mixture, covered, for at least 30 minutes.

3 Wet your hands with cold water and divide the crab mixture into 4 equal portions. Form each portion into a patty about 1½ inches thick (good crab cakes are supposed to be thick). Place the patties on a plate lined with plastic wrap and cover them with more plastic wrap. Refrigerate the patties for at least 30 minutes, or as long as 3 hours.

4 Just before serving, melt 1 tablespoon butter in the olive oil in a large skillet over medium-high heat. Gently lower the crab cakes into the hot fat and panfry them until golden brown on both sides and cooked through, 4 to 6 minutes per side. Reduce the heat as needed to keep the crab cakes from burning and add more butter as needed to keep the crab cakes from sticking.

5 Serve the crab cakes with homemade tartar sauce and make this Maryland boy proud.

CRAB CEVICHE
WITH AVOCADO AND PEANUTS

SHOP As with most simple dishes, your success or failure will lie in the quality of the raw materials: sweet crabmeat—fresh, not canned or frozen (one good mail-order source is The J. M. Clayton Co., jmclayton.com); ripe avocados; ripe heirloom tomatoes; and if you can find them, fragrant Meyer lemons.

GEAR Your basic kitchen gear including a Microplane or box grater

Here's an offbeat ceviche for people who don't like raw seafood. Crab and avocado have long been served together in sushi. This ceviche gives them the chile-lime treatment with an unexpected touch: the sweet, nutty crunch of peanuts. Save the avocado shells for serving the ceviche. **Serves 4 as a starter, 2 as a light main course**

1 pound precooked jumbo lump crabmeat

2 ripe avocados

1 or 2 Meyer lemons or regular lemons

1 large luscious red ripe tomato

½ cup chopped fresh cilantro, plus 4 sprigs for serving

3 scallions, both white and green parts, trimmed and thinly sliced crosswise

1 to 2 jalapeño peppers, seeded and minced (for a hotter ceviche leave the seeds in)

2 tablespoons extra virgin olive oil

½ cup dry-roasted peanuts, salted or unsalted, your choice

Coarse salt (kosher or sea) and freshly ground black pepper

1 Pick through the crabmeat, removing any pieces of shell, and place the crabmeat in a mixing bowl.

2 Cut each avocado in half lengthwise to the pit. Twist the halves in opposite directions to separate them. Remove the pit as described on page 216. Using the tip of a paring knife, cut through the flesh (but not the skin) of each avocado half in a ½-inch crosshatch pattern. Using a soupspoon, scoop out the avocado (it will come out in a neat dice) and add the avocado pieces to the crab. Save the avocado shells for serving, if desired.

3 Finely grate the zest of 1 lemon (a Microplane works well for this) into the avocado and crab. Then squeeze the juice from this lemon into the avocado and crab. Pick out any seeds if they've fallen into the mixture.

4 Cut the tomato in half crosswise and squeeze out and discard the juices and seeds (see page 133). Cut the tomato into ½-inch dice and add it to the crab mixture. Add the cilantro, scallions, jalapeño(s), and olive oil, but don't mix. The ceviche can be prepared to this stage up to 2 hours ahead. Refrigerate it covered.

5 Just before serving, add the peanuts and toss the ceviche to mix. Season the ceviche with salt and pepper to taste; it should be highly seasoned. If a tangier ceviche is desired add juice from the second lemon. Spoon the ceviche into the avocado shells, bowls, or large martini glasses and dig in.

WHAT ELSE The avocados we use in Miami (some call them gator pears) are larger, sweeter, and wetter than the Hass avocados from California. Either one works fine. A ripe avocado will be gently yielding when squeezed between your thumb and forefinger.

TIME about 20 minutes

Meyer Lemons

Meyer lemons are to citrus fruit what Michter's or Templeton are to a house whiskey. Believed to be a cross between a conventional lemon and a mandarin orange, Meyer lemons have, in addition to their tart juice, a haunting perfumed aroma. Try them once and whenever you can find them, you'll want to use them in place of conventional lemons.

CHIPOTLE ORANGE SHRIMP AND SCALLOP CEVICHE

C eviche may have originated in Peru, but Mexicans have made it their own. Or perhaps the concept of marinating seafood in lime juice and chiles is so elemental it simply sprang up spontaneously in fishing villages throughout the Americas as a way to preserve perishable fresh seafood before refrigeration. This Yucatán-inspired ceviche owes its smoke and heat to the chipotle pepper (smoked jalapeño). **Serves 4 as an appetizer**

½ pound peeled, deveined, cooked small shrimp

½ pound uncooked bay or sea scallops

2 large oranges

½ to 1 canned chipotle chile, minced, with 1 to 2 teaspoons can juices

1 luscious red ripe tomato, cut into ½-inch dice, with its juice and seeds

1 small red onion, peeled and cut in half lengthwise, then thinly sliced crosswise

½ cup coarsely chopped fresh cilantro

1 clove garlic, peeled and minced

¼ cup fresh lime juice, or more as needed

Coarse salt (kosher or sea) and freshly ground black pepper

4 romaine lettuce leaves from the heart of the lettuce (optional)

1 If the shrimp are large, cut them crosswise into ½-inch pieces. Remove and discard the small crescent-shaped muscle on the side of the scallops (it's tough). If you are using sea scallops, cut them into quarters. Place the shrimp and scallops in a nonreactive (glass, stainless steel, or ceramic) mixing bowl.

2 Using a Microplane or a box grater, finely grate 1 teaspoon of orange zest into the shellfish. Cut the rinds off the oranges, trimming away all of the white pith. Make V-shape cuts between the membranes to release segments of orange, then cut each orange segment in half crosswise. Discard any seeds. Add the orange pieces to the shellfish. Squeeze the juice out of the orange membranes over the shrimp and scallops.

3 Add the chipotle, tomato, onion, cilantro, garlic, and lime juice to the bowl with the shrimp and scallops and toss to mix. Season with salt and black pepper to taste. Serve at once or refrigerate the ceviche, covered, until serving time, within 2 hours of mixing. Just before serving, taste again for seasoning, adding more salt and/or lime juice as necessary; the ceviche should be explosively flavorful. If desired, serve the ceviche on the romaine lettuce leaves, dividing it equally among them.

HOW TO PEEL SHRIMP

1 Grab the front legs with one hand, holding the body of the shrimp with the other.

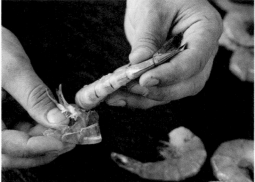

2 Lift a piece of shell; tear up and over to remove it (the gesture is rather like peeling a tangerine).

◄ The vein is the slender black tube running the length of the shrimp down the back. Without getting graphic, let's just say that it's part of a shrimp's alimentary tract and while it won't harm you, the shrimp tastes better without it.

TO DEVEIN PEELED SHRIMP USING A PARING KNIFE

1 Using a paring knife, make a deep cut down the back of the shrimp.

2 Using the knife tip or the tine of a fork, pull out and discard the black vein.

HOW TO DEVEIN SHRIMP WITH THE SHELL INTACT

1 Using small kitchen scissors, make a lengthwise cut through the shell along the back of the shrimp.

2 Use the tip of a bamboo skewer to lift and pull out the vein.

SHRIMP

Five things you may not know about shrimp:

1 Shrimp are an incredibly healthy food, containing 18 grams of protein per 3-ounce serving but only 83 calories.

2 The world's smallest shrimp, Holland's gray *garnaal*, is so tiny that it takes three hundred to make one pound. The Dutch munch them—heads, shells, and all—like popcorn. Tiger shrimp are so large a single crustacean can weigh up to ¾ pound.

3 The world's fiercest shrimp is the Filipino tiger. Fishmongers lodge them in empty soda bottles, one to a bottle, to prevent them from cannibalizing their neighbors.

4 The shrimp gave its name to a country in West Africa, Cameroon, named for a river once so teaming with shrimp that the Portuguese explorers called it Rio dos Camarões—"Shrimp River."

5 The most macho way to eat shrimp? Japanese *odori ebi* (dancing shrimp). You dunk live *Pandalus borealis* in sake just long enough to intoxicate them, then munch them, wriggling legs, antennae, and all, as sashimi.

Shrimp is the world's most popular shellfish, ubiquitous, affordable, and enjoyed in homes, at food stalls, and in restaurants in virtually every corner of the world. When shrimp is good (read sweet and fresh), few crustaceans can rival it, but there's a lot of not-so-good shrimp out there—raised in crowded farms or reeking of disinfectants or otherwise processed to enable producers to ship the shellfish halfway around the world. Like the skinless, boneless chicken breast, shrimp has become a commodity protein—prized more for its affordability than its flavor. On the plus side, more and more fish markets and even natural foods supermarkets now carry fresh local shrimp—often with the shells and heads intact.

Here's what you need to know to buy and cook shrimp at its peak.

BUY IT FRESH The vast majority of the shrimp sold in the U.S. comes frozen. Fortunately, shrimp freezes well, without too much deterioration of texture or flavor. But you can find fresh shrimp at select fishmongers.

SEEK OUT LOCAL VARIETIES For most Americans, shrimp is, well, shrimp. If you look harder, you can find regional varieties, like

Maine shrimp (small but incredibly sweet), Key West pinks (briny and tender), rock shrimp from Florida (with lobster-hard shells and mild meat), spot prawns from the West Coast (buttery and succulent), and so on. Local varieties of shrimp offer the same nuances of texture and flavor that, say, heirloom tomatoes do, and the more we ask for them, the more merchants will see value in carrying them.

BUY AND COOK SHRIMP WITH THE HEADS ON Although you'd never guess it to look at the seafood section of a typical American supermarket, most of the world's shrimp enthusiasts insist on buying their shellfish with the heads intact. There are good reasons to do so: Whole shrimp look really cool. The juices in the heads are incredibly tasty. ("Eat the tails and suck the heads," says a friend of mine from New Orleans.) And shrimp heads add loads of flavor to soups, stews, and shrimp boils.

BUY AND COOK SHRIMP IN THE SHELLS Even if you can't get shrimp with the heads on, you can probably buy them with the shells intact. When grilling shrimp, the shells add flavor and keep the meat from drying out. Plus, you get to eat the shrimp with your fingers, which always makes everything taste better.

SIZE MATTERS Shrimp are sized by the number it takes to make a pound. Thus, it takes fewer than ten U-10s (colossal) to make a pound; fewer than thirty U-30s (large) for a pound; and so on (the U stands for under). But bigger doesn't always mean better. Maine shrimp may be small, but few shellfish match them in sweetness.

SHRIMP VERSUS PRAWNS In North America, people say shrimp. In the U.K. (and elsewhere in the English-speaking world), people say prawns, except in the Pacific Northwest and Hawaii, where aficionados seek out spot prawns. So what's the difference?

Scientifically speaking, both shrimp and prawns are decapods (ten-legged shellfish), but due to subtle anatomical differences, shrimp belong to the *Pleocyemata* suborder, while prawns are classed as *Dendrobranchiata*. In popular parlance, people tend to use the word *prawn* to refer to large shellfish with heads and shells intact, while *shrimp* refers to smaller peeled, deveined shellfish without their heads. The flavor varies subtly with the variety and water of origin.

HOW TO COOK SHRIMP Shrimp are enjoyed raw by the Japanese and Peruvians and are cooked everywhere by every imaginable method: boiling, stewing, griddling, panfrying, and of course, grilling—to mention a few. Most North Americans like shrimp cooked through; in Spain, chefs cook them just long enough so that the outside meat is firm but the centers are translucent and the juices in the heads are still runny.

TAPAS BAR SHRIMP
(WITH GARLIC AND CHILES)

SHOP For information on buying shrimp, see A Guy's Best Friend: Shrimp on page 420. The parsley should be fresh flat-leaf. The olive oil, Spanish.

GEAR Your basic kitchen gear including a large (10- to 12-inch) cast-iron skillet

WHAT ELSE I'm going to tell you how to make tapas bar shrimp with the shellfish you're probably used to, that is headless, peeled, and deveined. However, as you ascend the ladder of culinary enlightenment, I hope you'll get to the point where you use shrimp with their heads and shells. The shrimp heads reward you with incredibly flavorful juices, while the shells add flavor, keep the shrimp moist, and give you the primal pleasure of eating them with your bare hands.

TIME about 20 minutes

A staple in tapas bars throughout Spain, this is one of the easiest ways I know to cook shrimp. You sizzle the shellfish in olive oil with garlic, parsley, and hot pepper flakes—a combination that is as popular in Italy as in Spain. These seasonings have the virtue of intensifying the briny shrimp flavor without drowning it out. **Serves 4**

2 pounds jumbo shrimp, peeled and deveined, or 2½ pounds shrimp with the heads on

Coarse salt (kosher or sea) and freshly ground black pepper

3 tablespoons extra virgin olive oil, preferably Spanish

2 cloves garlic, peeled and gently flattened with the side of a knife, or for a more intense garlic flavor, minced

1 generous handful fresh flat-leaf parsley leaves, rinsed, shaken dry, and finely chopped (about ¼ cup)

1 teaspoon hot red pepper flakes

1 lemon, cut into wedges, for serving

1 Blot the shrimp dry with a paper towel. Season them generously on all sides with salt and pepper.

2 Heat the olive oil in a large cast-iron skillet over medium-high heat. Add the whole garlic cloves and cook until fragrant and beginning to brown, about 30 seconds. If you are using minced garlic, cook it until sizzling, about 10 seconds.

3 Increase the heat to high and add the shrimp, parsley, and hot pepper flakes. Cook the shrimp until they are pinkish-white, firm, and cooked through, 2 to 4 minutes, stirring with a wooden spoon (or flicking the pan with your wrist). Serve the shrimp with lemon wedges for squeezing.

Variation

For Mexican shrimp, substitute cilantro for the parsley and a sliced jalapeño pepper or two for the hot pepper flakes. Add them in Step 3 and continue with the recipe.

TUSCAN SHRIMP AND BEANS

Here's a dish from Tuscany (a word that imbues any conversation with gustatory gravitas) that reflects the high value Italians put on simplicity and big flavors. Simple because you can prepare it in fifteen minutes and intensely flavorful thanks to the addition of garlic, hot pepper flakes, fresh herbs, and fresh tomato. **Serves 4**

2 tablespoons extra virgin olive oil, preferably Tuscan

1 clove garlic, peeled and gently flattened with the side of a knife

1½ pounds shrimp, peeled and deveined

1 teaspoon hot red pepper flakes, or more to taste

Coarse salt (kosher or sea) and freshly ground black pepper

¼ cup chopped fresh basil, rosemary, sage, and/or flat-leaf parsley

1 luscious red ripe tomato, stem end removed, tomato cut into ½-inch dice, with seeds and juices

1 can (15 ounces) cannellini beans, drained, rinsed in a colander, and drained again

SHOP When shopping for shellfish, see A Guy's Best Friend: Shrimp on page 420. For beans, you want small white beans, like cannellinis, preferably organic and low-sodium.

GEAR Your basic kitchen gear including a large (10- to 12-inch) skillet

WHAT ELSE For herbs, base your selection on what you can get fresh: basil, rosemary, sage, or flat-leaf parsley are all part of the Tuscan palette. Better still—use a blend.

TIME about 15 minutes

1 Heat the oil in a large skillet over medium-high heat. Add the garlic and cook until sizzling and starting to brown, about 30 seconds. Do not let the garlic burn.

2 Meanwhile, season the shrimp with the hot pepper flakes and salt and black pepper to taste. Add the shrimp and all but 1 tablespoon of the chopped herbs to the skillet. Cook the shrimp until they turn firm and pink and begin to brown, about 2 minutes.

3 Add the tomato and cannellini beans and cook until bubbling and hot, about 2 minutes. Taste for seasoning, adding more hot pepper flakes, salt, and/or black pepper as necessary; the shrimp should be highly seasoned. Serve the shrimp and beans in the skillet or on plates with the remaining 1 tablespoon herbs sprinkled on top.

COCONUT SHRIMP
WITH THAI CHILI ORANGE SAUCE

SHOP See page 420 for a guide to buying shrimp. For coconut, be sure to buy *unsweetened* shredded coconut.

GEAR Your basic kitchen gear including 3 wide shallow bowls, a large (10- to 12-inch) skillet, tongs, and a plate lined with paper towels

WHAT ELSE Want to raise the bar? Buy yourself a whole coconut and use the freshly grated flesh for crusting the shrimp (you'll find instructions for cracking a coconut on page 366). Once you get the hang of crusting shrimp with coconut, try other flavorful coatings, like chopped macadamia nuts or slivered almonds.

TIME about 20 minutes

It's a favorite at tiki bars throughout the Caribbean and the Florida Keys: sizzling shrimp crusted with sweet, crunchy coconut. Dipped in a chili marmalade sauce, it may be the single best finger food ever created to eat with a Rum Runner or other tropical cocktail. Most bars and restaurants deep-fry their coconut shrimp, but you, dude, will achieve a lot more finesse by panfrying it in butter and olive oil. **Serves 6 to 8 as a starter, 4 as a main course**

2 pounds jumbo shrimp, peeled and deveined

Coarse salt (kosher or sea) and freshly ground black pepper

1 cup unbleached all-purpose flour

2 large eggs

2 cups shredded unsweetened coconut

2 teaspoons finely grated orange or lemon zest

2 tablespoons (¼ stick) unsalted butter

2 tablespoons extra virgin olive oil

Thai Chili Orange Sauce (recipe follows)

1 Generously season the shrimp on all sides with salt and pepper. Place the flour, eggs, and coconut in 3 separate wide shallow bowls. Lightly beat the eggs. Using a fork, stir the orange zest into the coconut.

2 Melt 1 tablespoon of the butter in 1 tablespoon of the oil in a large skillet over medium-high heat and cook until the mixture is sizzling, 30 seconds to 1 minute. Kitchen science: The olive oil raises the temperature at which the butter will burn.

3 Using tongs and holding a few shrimp by their tails, dip the shrimp in the flour, shaking off the excess. Next, dip the shrimp in the beaten egg, shaking off the excess. Finally, dip the shrimp in the shredded coconut mixture.

4 Working in batches, add enough shrimp to the skillet to cover the bottom of the skillet in a single layer without crowding. Panfry the shrimp until the bottoms are crisp and golden, about 2 minutes. Using tongs, turn the shrimp over and cook the second side until it is crisp and golden and the shrimp are cooked through, about 2 minutes. The total cooking time will be 4 to 5 minutes. Transfer the shrimp to a plate lined with paper towels to drain. Add the remaining 1 tablespoon each of butter and oil to the skillet as needed and continue frying the shrimp until all are cooked.

5 Serve the coconut shrimp with the Thai Chili Orange Sauce for dipping.

THAI CHILI ORANGE SAUCE

Sweet and fruity with a hint of fire, this orange sauce riffs on the chili jams of Thailand. One good widely available brand of sweet Thai chili sauce is Mae Ploy. **Makes about 1 cup**

⅔ cup sweet Thai chili sauce

⅓ cup orange marmalade

1 tablespoon fresh lime juice or rice vinegar

1 tablespoon Cointreau or Grand Marnier

Place the chili sauce, orange marmalade, lime juice or rice vinegar, and orange liqueur in a small serving bowl and whisk to mix. The sauce will keep, covered, in the refrigerator for several days.

SKILLET CREOLE SHRIMP

SHOP Buy fresh local shrimp (see page 420) with the heads on when possible.

GEAR Your basic kitchen gear including a large (10- to 12-inch) skillet

WHAT ELSE My version of shrimp creole is inspired by that of Alchemy chef Craig Decker. You can cook it from start to finish in a single pan in fifteen minutes or less. Round out your meal with a green salad (page 161) and crusty bread for mopping up the sauce. Decker likes the mild malty flavor of Pabst Blue Ribbon beer, but any mild lager will do.

TIME about 15 minutes

This spicy shrimp Creole is a standby at the Alchemy restaurant in Edgartown, Martha's Vineyard, where we order it at the bar, sipping gimlets and watching the Red Sox (the only permissible excuse for having a TV on in a proper restaurant). The shrimp has at least three things going for it: its spontaneity, its in-your-face flavors, and a sauce that plays the richness of cream against the heat of Tabasco sauce and with Pabst Blue Ribbon beer serving as backstop. **Serves 2 as a main course**

---

3 tablespoons unsalted butter

2 shallots, peeled and finely chopped

1 clove garlic, peeled and gently flattened with the side of a knife

1 pound jumbo shrimp, peeled and deveined

Coarse salt (kosher or sea) and freshly ground black pepper

½ cup mild beer, like Pabst Blue Ribbon

3 tablespoons prepared chili sauce, such as Heinz

1 tablespoon Worcestershire sauce

1 teaspoon Tabasco sauce, or more to taste

¼ cup heavy (whipping) cream

1 tablespoon finely chopped chives or scallion greens

---

1 Melt half of the butter (1½ tablespoons) in a large skillet over medium heat. Add the shallots and garlic and cook until just beginning to brown, about 3 minutes.

2 Meanwhile, season the shrimp with salt and pepper. Increase the heat to high and add the shrimp to the skillet with the shallots. Cook the shrimp, adding more butter as needed, until seared on the outside, 1 to 2 minutes. Add the beer and let come to a boil and boil until the beer is reduced to about ¼ cup, 2 to 3 minutes.

3 Stir in the chili sauce, Worcestershire sauce, Tabasco sauce, and cream and let boil until the sauce is thick and creamy and the shrimp are cooked through, about 2 minutes longer, 6 to 7 minutes in all. Taste for seasoning, adding more salt and/or Tabasco sauce as necessary. Sprinkle the shrimp with chives and enjoy.

THE LOWDOWN ON
LOBSTER

Allen Daggett lives lobster. A third-generation lobsterman, Daggett runs the Cape Porpoise Lobster Company in Kennebunkport, Maine, which processes more than 600,000 pounds a year. He also runs a lobster bait company and the Cape Pier Chowder House, so when he speaks of crustacean, I listen.

Want to sound like a pro the next time you buy lobster or eat one in Maine? Daggett explains the lingo.

BULL A lobster that has no claws.

CHICKEN A lobster that weighs less than 1¼ pounds.

CULL A lobster that has only one claw—lobsters will "throw" a claw to deter predators.

HARD SHELL A molted lobster with a shell that is fully hardened. (Lobsters molt—shed their shells—periodically to make room for new growth.) The meat of a hard shell will be a little denser and tougher than that of a soft shell.

JELLY ROLL A lobster that has just molted. The flesh will be soft and watery.

JUMBO Any lobster weighing more than 3 pounds.

POUND An open-air eatery in Maine where you eat lobster "in the rough"—steamed or boiled in seawater over a wood fire—usually at picnic tables overlooking the water.

QUARTER A lobster that weighs 1¼ to just shy of 1½ pounds.

SELECT A lobster that weighs 1½ to just shy of 2 pounds. For Daggett, this is the best eating lobster.

SOFT SHELL A molted lobster whose new shell is still hardening. These are much prized by lobstermen, as the meat is exceptionally tender and succulent.

Lobster is available year-round and is cheapest in August and September, but according to Daggett, the best time of year to eat it is June and July. That's when jelly rolls have finished molting and become soft shells, so the meat is succulent but has not yet filled out the shell. Later in the year, when they become hard shells, the meat inside the rigid carapace becomes denser and tougher. I know this sounds complicated, but in Maine guys make these distinctions.

LOBSTER LIKE THEY COOK IT IN MAINE

Lobster is one food you must cook when it's alive and kicking. Being a guy (assuming you're in mixed company), the task of wrangling and cooking the lobsters will almost always fall to you. Fortunately, this is no more challenging than boiling a pot of water. The lobster scene in the movie *Annie Hall* set our gender back decades. Be a man and step up to the pot. **Makes 2 lobsters; can be multiplied as desired**

Coarse salt (kosher or sea)

2 live and wriggling lobsters, 1¼ to 1½ pounds each

6 tablespoons (¾ stick) salted butter, melted, for serving

1 Pour water to a depth of 6 inches in a large stockpot, measuring it as you pour, and add 1 teaspoon of salt for every quart of water. Let the salted water come to a rolling boil over high heat.

2 Add the lobsters and cover the pot with a tight-fitting lid. Let the lobsters boil until they are bright red and cooked through. The chart on page 432 gives approximate cooking times for 1 lobster of different weights and tests for doneness. Add a few more minutes when you are cooking additional lobsters. Remember: Every lobster cooks differently.

3 Transfer the lobsters to a deep platter and pour the melted butter into 2 small bowls for dipping. Provide a large bowl for the lobster shells. And the best way to eat lobster? Everyone has a preferred method for removing the meat from the shell; you'll find mine on page 430. Dip the lobster meat in the melted butter.

SHOP Rule number one about buying lobsters: the feistier, the better. If the claws hang limp, pick another lobster or switch to shrimp. Your local fishmonger is a good source as is a food market with a high turnover. Alternatively, order your lobsters via overnight mail from a reputable supplier in Maine. I'm not a big partisan of the lobster tanks in supermarkets: I always wonder how often they're cleaned.

GEAR Your basic kitchen gear plus a large stockpot (at least 3 gallons) with a tight-fitting lid, tongs, lobster crackers, and slender forks

WHAT ELSE To determine the sex of a lobster, look at the first set of swimmerets on the underside (where the tail meets the body). A male's swimmerets will be hard; a female's, soft and feathery. This is important, because for guys like me, the female's briny, waxy red lobster roe (eggs) is the next best thing to caviar.

TIME 14 to 30 minutes, depending on the size of the lobsters

How to Eat a Lobster

1 Grab the lobster body with one hand and the claw with the other.

2 Twist the claw to snap it off the body. Remove the other claw the same way.

3 Break the knuckles off the claw.

4 Crack the knuckle shells and pull out the meat.

5 Using the back of a chef's knife or a mallet, crack the claw shell.

6 Pull out the claw meat.

◀ Dip the meat in melted butter as you crack and eat the lobster.

7 Grab the tail and body with opposite hands and twist to separate them.

8 Separate the tail from the body.

9 Break the flipper off the end of the tail section.

10 Push the tail meat from the flipper end through the shell.

11 Remove the tail meat.

12 Snap the legs off the body. Break them in half and suck out the meat.

Lobster Cooking Times

LOBSTER SIZE	COOKING TIME
Chicken (less than 1¼ pounds)	7 to 9 minutes
Quarter (1¼ up to 1½ pounds)	10 to 12 minutes
Select (1½ to 2 pounds)	13 to 15 minutes
Two pounder	16 to 18 minutes
Three pounder	20 to 24 minutes

There are four ways to tell when a lobster is done:

▶ Pull on one of the antennae. If it comes off easily, the lobster is done.

▶ Starting in the middle of the lobster's back, lift up the carapace (shell). If the tomalley (the green liver) is set like custard and the roe (eggs) are waxy and firm, the lobster is done.

▶ Make a small cut in the belly (the underside of the lobster) where the lobster tail meets the body. If the flesh is firm, the lobster is done.

▶ Insert the probe of an instant-read thermometer in a cut made where the lobster tail meets the body. When done, the internal temperature of the lobster will be about 145°F.

SPINY LOBSTER
WITH GARLIC, CUMIN, AND LIME

You eat only the tails, which are firm-textured and meaty, of the clawless spiny lobster. The flavor is more robust and less sweet than that of Maine lobster, so you can use assertive seasonings, like garlic, lime, cilantro, and cumin. Here's how we prepare them in Miami, inspired by a Spanish Caribbean sauce called *mojo*. **Serves 4**

¾ cup (12 tablespoons) extra virgin olive oil plus 1 tablespoon more if pan frying, or 12 tablespoons (1½ sticks) unsalted butter

4 cloves garlic, peeled and thinly sliced crosswise

1 teaspoon ground cumin

½ cup coarsely chopped fresh cilantro leaves

1 teaspoon finely grated lime zest

¼ cup fresh lime juice

Coarse salt (kosher or sea) and freshly ground black pepper

4 large or 8 small spiny lobster tails (2½ to 3 pounds in all)

Lime wedges, for serving

SHOP The commercial season for Florida lobster runs from August through March. The rest of the year, you can find it (or its South African cousin, rock lobster) frozen. Most spiny lobster is sold as tails, as the body contains little meat. But a whole spiny lobster looks mighty impressive: If you can find it, have your fishmonger split it for you.

GEAR Your basic kitchen gear including a medium-size saucepan, broiler pan or baking sheet, grill, or large (10- to 12-inch) heavy skillet, and basting brush

WHAT ELSE Cook spiny lobster any way you would shrimp, especially broiled, grilled, or panfried.

TIME about 20 minutes

1 Heat the olive oil or melt the butter in a saucepan over medium-high heat. Add the garlic and cumin and cook until the garlic is golden brown, about 30 seconds, stirring often. Add the cilantro and lime zest after the garlic mixture has cooked for 15 seconds. Add the lime juice (it may sputter a bit) and let come to a boil. Season the mixture with salt and pepper to taste. Pour half of the sauce into a small bowl for basting and set the remaining sauce aside in a bowl for serving.

2 If they have not already been cut, using a heavy knife, cut the lobster tails almost in half lengthwise through the back. Cut to but not through the soft shell on the belly. Open the lobster tails up, pressing on them so they lie flat. If you can find it, remove the "vein" that runs the length of each tail. Brush the cut side of each lobster tail with some of the sauce.

3 *If you are broiling the lobster tails,* preheat the broiler to high. Arrange the lobster tails cut side up on the broiler pan or on a baking sheet and place them about 2 inches from the heat source. Broil the lobster tails without turning until they are nicely browned and cooked through, 5 to 8 minutes, basting them with the basting sauce a couple of times.

If you are grilling the lobster tails, set up the grill for direct grilling and preheat it to high. When ready to cook, brush and oil the grill grate. Baste the lobster tails well with the basting sauce, then place them cut side down on the hot grate. Grill the lobster tails until the meat is browned, about 4 minutes, giving each tail a quarter turn after 2 minutes. Turn the lobster tails over and grill them shell side down until the lobster is cooked through, 2 to 4 minutes, basting them well as they cook.

If you are panfrying the lobster tails, melt the butter in the olive oil over medium heat in a large heavy skillet. Working in batches, baste the lobster tails and arrange them cut side down in the skillet. Cook the tails until they are well browned, about 4 minutes. Turn the lobster tails over and continue panfrying them until the lobster meat is cooked through, basting them well with the basting sauce.

4 Transfer the lobster tails to a platter or plates and arrange the lime wedges alongside. Spoon the remaining sauce on top or serve on the side.

BACON-WRAPPED SCALLOPS
WITH SCOTCH WHISKY GLAZE

SHOP The bivalve of choice is the "diver scallop," a huge (usually 1½ to 2 inches across) sea scallop traditionally harvested from rocky nooks by divers in scuba gear. Look for diver scallops at good fish markets or online through purveyors like Farm 2 Market (farm-2-market.com). Alternatively, you can use conventional sea scallops. Avoid scallops sitting in a bath of milky liquid; they were likely previously frozen and thawed.

GEAR Your basic kitchen gear including a glass baking pan, toothpicks or bamboo skewers, a small saucepan, and a large skillet (10- to 12-inches) or a broiler pan or rimmed baking sheet

WHAT ELSE A note of personal partisanship here. To make a killer finger food, use the sweetest of all shellfish: bay scallops from Martha's Vineyard. (Nantucket bays get all the press, but ours are sweeter by far.) Cut each slice of bacon crosswise in quarters to wrap the scallops. Cook the scallops on short bamboo skewers and serve the whisky glaze as a dip.

TIME about 30 minutes

Think of this as the original surf and turf: sweet, meaty sea scallops seared in smoky salty bacon. It's hardly a new idea, but few combinations deliver more satisfaction or flavor bang for the buck. To reinforce the smoke flavor, baste the bivalves with a simple Scotch whisky glaze. **Serves 6 to 8 as an appetizer, 4 as a main course**

For the scallops

16 fresh diver scallops, or 2 pounds regular sea scallops

2 tablespoons extra virgin olive oil, plus olive oil for cooking the scallops

1 tablespoon fresh lemon juice

Coarse salt (kosher or sea) and coarsely ground black pepper

About 1 pound thinly sliced bacon, preferably artisanal

For the whisky glaze (optional)

½ cup Scotch whisky, preferably a smoky scotch, like Laphroaig

½ cup chicken stock (preferably homemade, page 549) or bottled clam broth

2 tablespoons pure maple syrup

1 teaspoon fresh lemon juice

3 tablespoons unsalted butter, cut into ½-inch cubes

Coarse salt (kosher or sea) and coarsely ground black pepper

1 Prepare the scallops: Trim or pull off and discard the small crescent-shaped muscle from the side of the scallops. (It's tougher than the rest of the scallop. This may have been done by the fishmonger.) Place the scallops in a baking pan and drizzle the olive oil and the 1 tablespoon of lemon juice over them. Season the scallops with salt and pepper and gently toss to mix.

2 Place a scallop flat on a work surface. Wrap a slice of bacon around the scallop, using a piece just large enough to encircle the scallop with the ends overlapping slightly. Insert a toothpick or skewer through the overlapped ends to hold the bacon tight to the scallop. Repeat with the remaining scallops. Return the scallops to the baking dish and refrigerate while you make the glaze, if using.

3 **Make the whisky glaze:** Combine the whisky, chicken stock, maple syrup, and the 1 teaspoon of lemon juice in a saucepan. Bring to a boil over high heat and let boil until reduced by half, about 5 minutes. Reduce the heat to low and whisk in the butter piece by piece; the glaze will thicken. Do not let it boil. Season the glaze with salt and pepper to taste and remove from the heat.

4 *If you are panfrying the scallops,* preheat a cast-iron skillet or other large skillet over medium-high heat for about 10 seconds. Film the bottom of the pan with olive oil. Working in batches if necessary, arrange the scallops in the skillet in a single layer and cook them until the bacon is browned and the scallops are cooked through, 5 to 8 minutes in all, turning with tongs. Be sure to turn the scallops on their sides to brown the bacon. Baste the scallops with some of the whisky glaze, if using.

If you are broiling the scallops, preheat the broiler. Arrange the scallops on a lightly oiled broiler pan or sturdy rimmed baking sheet and broil the scallops about 3 inches from the heat until the bacon is browned and the scallops are cooked through, 5 to 8 minutes in all, turning with tongs. Baste the scallops with some of the whisky glaze, if using.

5 Transfer the scallops to a platter or plates and pour the remaining whisky glaze over them, if using. Don't forget to remove the toothpicks before eating.

STEAMED MUSSELS THREE WAYS

Black gold. That's one way to describe a shellfish with the virtues of being intensely flavorful, eminently affordable, and quick and easy to prepare. Below you'll find the basic formula for steaming mussels, plus a cream and Pernod version from the south of France, and a smoked paprika and chorizo rendition from Spain. Added benefit: Like a lot of great guy food, you get to eat mussels with your fingers. **Serves 4**

#1: BASIC STEAMED MUSSELS

Don't have dry white vermouth on hand? (What do you use in your martinis?) Any dry white wine will do. Add a green salad (like the Crazy Salad on page 157) and you've got dinner.

4 pounds really fresh mussels

1 cup dry white vermouth (I'm partial to Noilly Prat) or dry white wine

3 shallots, or 1 medium-size onion, peeled and finely chopped

1 rib celery, thinly sliced

1 carrot, peeled and thinly sliced

2 cloves garlic, peeled and gently flattened with the side of a knife

¼ cup coarsely chopped fresh flat-leaf parsley or other fresh herbs, such as tarragon or basil

2 teaspoons black peppercorns

Crusty bread, for serving

1 Scrub the mussels well with a stiff-bristled brush under cold running water, discarding any with cracked shells or shells that fail to close when tapped. Pull out and discard any "beards" (clumps of black strings) on the side of the mussels.

2 Place the vermouth, shallots, celery, carrot, garlic, parsley, and peppercorns in a large heavy pot or Dutch oven. Bring to a boil, uncovered, over high heat and let boil for 5 minutes.

3 Stir the mussels into the pot, cover the pot with a tight-fitting lid, and cook the mussels over high heat until the shells open wide, 5 to 8 minutes. Using a long-handled spoon, stir the mussels once or twice so they cook evenly.

4 To serve, ladle the mussels, broth, and vegetables into bowls, providing an empty bowl for the shells. Serve the mussels with crusty bread for dunking.

#2: MUSSELS IN THE STYLE OF MARSEILLE
(WITH SAFFRON, PERNOD, AND CREAM)

Mussels head to the south of France and uptown (thanks to the addition of saffron and cream) in this version brimming with Mediterranean flavors. Pernod is an anise-flavored aperitif from the south of France. If unavailable, substitute anisette, ouzo, or absinthe. Saffron—the world's costliest spice—comes from the fragrant orange stigmas of an edible crocus. Buy saffron in threads, not powdered.

4 pounds really fresh mussels

½ teaspoon saffron threads

¾ cup dry white wine

¼ cup Pernod or other anise-flavored liqueur

1 medium-size onion, peeled and finely chopped

1 rib celery, thinly sliced crosswise

½ cup heavy (whipping) cream

Crusty bread, for serving

1 Pick through, clean, and "debeard" the mussels as described in Step 1 below.

2 Meanwhile, place the saffron in a small bowl with 1 tablespoon of hot water. Stir to mix and let sit for about 5 minutes. This releases the saffron flavor.

3 Place the wine, Pernod, onion, celery, and cream in a large heavy pot or Dutch oven. Add the saffron with its soaking liquid, bring to a boil over high heat, uncovered, and let boil for about 5 minutes.

4 Stir the mussels into the pot, cover the pot with a tight-fitting lid, and cook the mussels over high heat until the shells open wide, 5 to 8 minutes. Using a long-handled spoon, stir the mussels once or twice so they cook evenly.

5 Using a slotted spoon, transfer the mussels to a serving bowl. Boil the cream and vegetable mixture until it is richly flavored, 2 minutes more, then strain it through a fine strainer over the mussels. Serve the mussels with crusty bread for dunking, providing a bowl for the shells.

How to "Debeard" Mussels

1 Pinch the "beard" (black threads) on the side of the mussel between the back of a paring knife and your thumb.

2 Twist the knife blade to pull the threads away from the shell.

#3: SPANISH-STYLE MUSSELS

(WITH SMOKED PAPRIKA AND CHORIZO)

Here's how mussels would be steamed in Spain—with *pimentón* (smoked paprika) and chorizo (Spanish sausage). Littleneck clams are terrific steamed the same way.

4 pounds really fresh mussels

2 tablespoons extra virgin olive oil

1 medium-size onion, peeled and finely chopped

1 cooked chorizo sausage (3 to 4 ounces), thinly sliced crosswise

2 teaspoons pimentón (smoked paprika, see page 28)

1 cup dry white wine

¼ cup chopped fresh flat-leaf parsley

Crusty bread, for serving

1 Pick through, clean, and "debeard" the mussels as described in Step 1 on page 437.

2 Heat the olive oil in a large heavy pot or Dutch oven over medium heat. Add the onion and chorizo and cook until the onion is lightly browned, 3 to 4 minutes, stirring with a long wooden spoon. Stir in the *pimentón* and cook until fragrant, about 30 seconds. Add the wine and parsley and let boil until the mixture is richly flavored, about 5 minutes.

3 Stir the mussels into the pot, cover the pot with a tight-fitting lid, and cook the mussels over high heat until the shells open wide, 5 to 8 minutes. Using a long-handled spoon, stir the mussels once or twice so they cook evenly.

4 To serve, ladle the mussels, chorizo, and broth into bowls, providing an empty bowl for the shells. Serve the mussels with crusty bread for dunking.

WHAT YOU NEED TO KNOW ABOUT
STIR-FRYING

What's the world's most popular way to cook? On a grill? In the oven? I'd say stir-frying. On any given day, from Beijing to Bali, lunch, dinner, and even breakfast spills screaming hot from a wok. Stir-frying offers the advantages of one-pot cooking at flavor-intensifying high heat, with a cooking time measured in minutes. All you need is a single burner, so it's great for apartment dwellers with small kitchens.

Stir-frying is easy if you follow the proper sequence. To remind us how, I checked in with Simpson Wong, chef/owner of Wong and Café Asean in Greenwich Village (you may know him as the man who serves roasted duck ice cream).

First, the wok. It's a wide bowl-shaped metal pot with U-shape handles at opposite sides. (Some models have a single handle.) The pros use carbon steel woks, which spread the heat quickly and evenly but require frequent use to prevent rusting and sticking.

Next, the heat. Professionals do stir-frying over a powerful propane ring burner. At home, if you have a gas burner, you'll want to get a wok ring, which raises the bottom of the wok above the burner slightly to boost and spread the heat. If you have electric burners, buy a wok with a flat bottom.

The secret to successful stir-frying is organization. Because of the speed of the actual cooking, you need to have every ingredient precut and measured out. Arrange them on a baking sheet in the order in which you'll add them: aromatics first, then protein, vegetables, herbs, sauce, and thickener, if you are using one. When you do all this right, your food will acquire an intense, caramelized, almost smoky flavor the Chinese call *wok hay*, the "breath of the wok."

There are seven steps, which, when choreographed properly, produce intensely flavorful seared meats, vegetables that retain crunch and moistness, and satisfying rich-tasting sauces. Watch closely: It's so quick, you might miss a step if you blink.

1 Heat the wok over a medium-high to high flame. Then add the oil, swirling it to coat the side of the wok. This takes about fifteen seconds. Wong uses equal parts olive oil (for richness) and canola or grapeseed oil (for its high burn-point—the temperature at which the oil burns).

2 Add the aromatics. Typically, these include minced garlic, ginger, scallion whites, and chiles. Fry these until fragrant but not brown (and certainly not burned), about ten seconds.

3 Add the protein, which can range from chicken, beef, or pork to shrimp, squid, or tofu.

(continued on the next page)

(continued from the previous page)

All should be cut into even, quick-cooking, bite-size pieces—ideally about 1½ inches long by ½ inch wide and ¼ inch thick (this shape maximizes the surface area exposed to the hot wok and seasonings). Spread the protein over the bottom of the wok and let it cook for about thirty seconds without moving it. This sears the protein, which will stick at first, then come away from the bottom of the wok. Then start stir-frying—stirring and tossing the food in the wok with the wok spatula (and even by flicking the wok itself with your wrist)—to sear the exterior of the protein, two to three minutes.

4 Add the vegetables. Good candidates include onions, mushrooms, green beans, snow pea pods, napa (Chinese) cabbage, and the like. Again, cut the pieces small so they cook quickly and evenly. Parboil any hard vegetables, like broccoli and carrots, by partially cooking them in boiling water for one to two minutes before adding them to the wok. Stir-fry the vegetables until crisp-tender, two to three minutes.

5 Add the herbs, like lemongrass, cilantro, scallion, and/or Thai basil. Stir-fry the mixture briefly, until aromatic, about twenty seconds.

6 Add the sauce. For Chinese stir-fries, this would include soy sauce, rice wine, and sugar. For Thai stir-fries, you'd use coconut milk and curry paste. For a Vietnamese-style stir-fry, add fish sauce, sugar, and chile paste. Let the sauce boil for about one minute.

7 Add the thickener, typically cornstarch dissolved in a little water, to make a loose paste (called a slurry). Adding a slurry, rather than dry cornstarch, prevents lumps. Boil the stir-fry until the sauce thickens, about twenty seconds. Thickening the sauce is optional. Not all chefs or Asian cuisines do it.

Added up, the actual stir-fry process takes about 7 minutes from start to finish.

MORE ABOUT WOKS

Like a cast-iron skillet, the best way to season a wok is to use it often. Scrub a new wok with soap and water to remove any factory grease. Heat it over high heat until hot, thirty seconds to one minute. To test whether the wok is hot enough, add a drop of water: It should evaporate in two seconds. Next, oil the wok by adding one tablespoon of canola or other vegetable oil. Swirl the wok to coat the inside, then wipe out the excess oil with a paper towel. Repeat as needed

To clean your wok after using, heat it over high heat. Add water and scrub it with a straw brush (buy it when you purchase your wok). Dry the wok out over the heat, then oil it with an oil-soaked paper towel. The more you use a wok, the less likely food is to stick to it.

HELLFIRE SQUID STIR-FRY

After I graduated from college, I spent a year backpacking through Europe. I brought with me a single cooking utensil: a wok I hung from my backpack. I used it to boil soups, simmer stews, sauté seafood, even as an improvised charcoal grill, and above all, for stir-frying. If cooking were a smartphone, stir-frying would be the killer app—versatile enough to cook any protein or vegetable on a single burner. Which brings me to this Vietnamese-inspired squid stir-fry, modeled on a Simpson Wong signature dish at Café Asean in Greenwich Village (more on Wong and stir-frying on page 439). The protein here is squid, but you could make a similar stir-fry with chicken, pork, shrimp, or tofu. With its twisty tentacles and tubular body, squid (aka calamari) looks cool and provides an excellent source of cheap, mild, tasty protein. Every guy should have at least one squid dish under his belt, and this one is a knockout. **Serves 2**

1 tablespoon soy sauce or fish sauce

1 tablespoon sugar

1 teaspoon Vietnamese garlic chili paste

1 tablespoon canola oil

1 tablespoon olive oil, or more canola oil

1 garlic clove, peeled and minced

12 ounces cleaned fresh squid, cut crosswise into ½-inch pieces (enough to make 1 cup)

1 to 2 jalapeño peppers, seeded and thinly sliced crosswise (for a hotter stir-fry, leave the seeds in)

16 fresh Thai basil or basil leaves, stems removed

1 stalk lemongrass (optional), trimmed (cut off and discard the top two thirds) and minced

2 cups thinly sliced vegetables, including sweet onion, carrot, zucchini, napa or savoy cabbage, and/or bok choy

½ teaspoon cornstarch dissolved in 1 tablespoon water

Cooked noodles or boiled rice (page 488), for serving

SHOP Most fish stores and seafood departments sell squid already cleaned (tentacles and body separated; head and entrails discarded). Otherwise, ask the fishmonger to do it for you. To be strictly authentic, you'll need a few Asian ingredients. Thai basil tastes less sweet and has a stronger anise flavor than regular basil, but the latter will work just fine. Lemongrass has an herbal lemony flavor but none of the acidity associated with the fruit (or substitute 1 teaspoon finely grated lemon zest). Vietnamese garlic chili paste is available at most supermarkets and at natural foods stores. One good brand is made by Huy Fong Foods, or use another Asian chili paste or Sriracha (Thai hot sauce, see page 27).

GEAR Your basic kitchen gear plus a wok and a wok spatula

WHAT ELSE Consider this recipe the blueprint for any Vietnamese-style stir-fry. Vary the protein or vegetables according to what you have in your fridge. Ditto for the peppers or chiles (jalapeño, serrano, Thai, and so on). Organization is key: Have everything ready before you start stir-frying.

TIME about 20 minutes

1 Place the soy sauce, sugar, chili paste, and 1 tablespoon of water in a small bowl and stir to mix. Set the soy sauce mixture aside.

2 Heat a wok over medium-high heat. Add the canola and olive oils and swirl the wok to coat the inside.

3 Add the garlic and stir-fry until fragrant but not brown, about 10 seconds. Use the wok spatula to keep it moving.

4 Add the squid and cook for about 30 seconds without moving it. Then, stir it with the spatula and stir-fry until the squid turns white, about 1 minute.

5 Add the jalapeño(s), basil leaves, and lemongrass, if using. Stir-fry until aromatic, about 20 seconds.

6 Add the vegetables and stir-fry until crisp-tender, about 2 minutes.

7 Stir in the soy sauce mixture and stir-fry for about 20 seconds. Stir the cornstarch and water mixture to form a loose paste the consistency of heavy cream and add it to the wok. Stir-fry until the sauce thickens slightly, 20 to 30 seconds. Serve the squid at once over noodles or boiled rice.

NOODLE

There's a lot more to preparing great noodles than throwing a box of pasta in a pot of water. For starters, you need to select the right noodle. Egg pastas (made with flour and eggs), like fresh linguine, cook faster than durum-wheat-and-water-based pastas, like spaghetti. Asian noodles come in a thrilling array of shapes, sizes, and starches, including Japanese ramen (wheat noodles), Thai rice sticks, and Korean *dang myun* (sweet potato vermicelli).

In this chapter you'll learn how to cook pasta in its major incarnations from spaghetti with the ultimate red sauce, to linguine with a fresh clam sauce, to soba (buckwheat) noodles with a spicy peanut sauce, and a gorgeous bubbling browned pepper Jack macaroni and cheese. Noodles: Think of them as high-carb nirvana for runners and other athletes—because man can't live by protein alone.

SPAGHETTI
WITH NO-COOK VEGETABLE SAUCE

This may be the simplest noodle dish on the planet—hot spaghetti tossed with chopped summer vegetables (tomatoes, sweet corn) and fresh basil. It's so quick and spontaneous, you don't even cook it. Just coarsely chop the ingredients in a food processor or with a sharp chef's knife. The heat of the spaghetti does the cooking; it's enough to remove the rawness of the vegetables, but not so hot that you lose their freshness and crunch. **Serves 2 or 3; can be multiplied as desired**

2 or 3 luscious red ripe tomatoes (about 1½ pounds)

1 ear sweet summer corn, shucked

2 scallions, trimmed

12 fresh basil leaves

1 clove garlic (optional), peeled

2 to 3 tablespoons plus 1 teaspoon extra virgin olive oil

Coarse sea salt and freshly ground black pepper

8 ounces spaghetti (one half of the standard 16-ounce package)

1 chunk (3 ounces) ricotta salata, Parmesan, or other hard cheese, for grating

1 Core the tomatoes and cut them into 1-inch pieces. Cut the kernels off the corn cob by placing the ear flat on a cutting board and slicing off the kernels with lengthwise strokes of a chef's knife. Thinly slice the scallions crosswise. Coarsely chop 8 of the basil leaves. For a strong garlic flavor mince the garlic; for a milder garlic flavor lightly crush the clove with the side of a knife (or omit the garlic altogether).

2 Place the tomatoes, corn, scallions, chopped basil, and minced garlic, if using, in a food processor and process to a coarse sauce, running the machine in short bursts. Work in 2 to 3 tablespoons of the olive oil. Don't have a food processor? Finely chop the tomatoes, corn, scallions, chopped basil, and minced garlic, if using, and place in a mixing bowl. Stir in 2 to 3 tablespoons of olive oil; the mixture will be a little coarser in texture but the flavor

SHOP A dish this simple soars or sinks by the quality of the ingredients, starting with ripe tomatoes, which should come from a garden or farm stand. Heirlooms come to mind—those oddly shaped, multicolored tomatoes that hark back to the pre-agribusiness age when vegetables were grown for flavor, not solely for appearance and shelf life. And while we're on the subject of flavor, whenever possible, buy tomatoes that have never seen the inside of a refrigerator—and keep them that way. Refrigerating mutes a tomato's flavor. Ditto for summer corn.

Want to up the ante? For a grating cheese, buy some *ricotta salata*—harder and saltier that its soft white cousin ricotta—and an interesting switch from the usual Parmesan.

GEAR Your basic kitchen gear including a stockpot, a food processor (optional), a large heatproof serving bowl, a colander, and a box grater

WHAT ELSE Consider this recipe as a rough guide rather than a detailed itinerary. Take it in a Mexican direction if you like, substituting cilantro for the basil and adding a sliced jalapeño or two. Go Asian by adding ginger, scallions, and dark sesame oil along with the garlic. To make it quicker, use capellini (angel-hair pasta) in place of the spaghetti, which shortens the cooking time by a couple of minutes.

TIME about 20 minutes, plus 20 minutes if you are using a whole garlic clove to flavor the sauce

will still be great. Season the tomato mixture with salt and pepper to taste; it should be highly seasoned. Transfer the tomato mixture to a large heatproof bowl. If you are using a whole crushed garlic clove, stir it in now and let it flavor the tomato mixture for about 20 minutes, then remove and discard it.

3 Bring 4 quarts of water, 1 tablespoon of salt, and the remaining 1 teaspoon of olive oil to a rapid boil in a stockpot. Stir in the spaghetti and cook until done to taste, about 8 minutes for al dente. Stir the spaghetti a couple of times as it cooks. Drain the spaghetti in a colander, setting aside about

3 tablespoons of the hot pasta cooking water from the stockpot.

4 Immediately add the hot spaghetti and the pasta cooking water to the bowl with the tomato mixture and toss well to mix. Serve at once topped with the whole basil leaves. Using the coarse side of a box grater, grate the *ricotta salata* over the spaghetti and dig in.

SPAGHETTI
WITH TURBOCHARGED RED SAUCE
(HOOKER'S SPAGHETTI)

SHOP For notes on which spaghetti to buy, see page 450. For tomatoes, pick up a can of San Marzano (imported from Italy) or organic tomatoes from California (one good brand is Muir Glen).

GEAR Your basic kitchen gear including a stockpot, a saucepan, a colander, and a box grater

Born in a Roman red-light district (so the tale goes), *spaghetti alla puttanesca*—pasta with a spicy red sauce—is fiery in temperament like the *puttane* (hookers) for which it was named. Or perhaps the name refers to the slam-bam speed with which the whole dish comes together. We're talking bold, in-your-face flavors here: garlic, capers, olives, anchovies, hot peppers, and basil. Stimulating, to say the least. Have all the ingredients for the sauce measured out and ready. This dish is quick and simple to make, but you need to do some chopping and measuring before you start cooking. **Serves 2 or 3; can be multiplied as desired**

For the sauce

1 can (28 ounces) whole peeled tomatoes with their juices

2 tablespoons extra virgin olive oil

2 cloves garlic, peeled and thinly sliced crosswise

1 shallot, minced

1 teaspoon dried oregano

½ to 1 teaspoon hot red pepper flakes, or 1 to 2 jalapeño peppers, thinly sliced crosswise, seeded or not depending on your tolerance for heat

2 tablespoons tomato paste

2 tablespoons capers, drained

¼ cup pitted black olives, such as kalamata

4 anchovy fillets, drained and cut crosswise into ½-inch pieces

6 fresh basil leaves, cut into slivers

Freshly ground black pepper

For the spaghetti

1 tablespoon coarse sea salt

1 teaspoon extra virgin olive oil

8 ounces spaghetti (one half of the standard 16-ounce package)

1 chunk (3 ounces) pecorino romano or Parmigiano Reggiano cheese, for grating

1 Make the sauce: Open the can of tomatoes and, using 2 knives in a scissorlike motion or the edge of a wooden spoon, cut the tomatoes into bite-size pieces right in the can.

2 Heat the 2 tablespoons of olive oil in a saucepan over medium-high heat. Add the garlic, shallot, oregano, and hot pepper flakes or jalapeño(s) and cook until fragrant, about 1 minute, stirring with a wooden spoon. Stir in the tomato paste, capers, olives, and anchovies and cook until fragrant, about 1 minute. Stir in the tomatoes with their juices and let simmer until the flavors combine, about 5 minutes. Stir in half of the basil and season with black pepper to taste. You may have a little more sauce than you need for 2 servings; any leftover sauce can be refrigerated, covered, at least 3 days or frozen for several weeks (it's always good to have some tomato sauce on hand).

3 Cook the spaghetti: Bring 4 quarts of water and the salt, and 1 teaspoon of olive oil to a rapid boil in a stockpot. Add the spaghetti to the boiling water and cook until done to taste, about 8 minutes for al dente. Stir the spaghetti a couple of times as it cooks. Drain the spaghetti in a colander.

4 Using tongs, transfer the spaghetti to plates or shallow bowls and ladle sauce on top. Serve at once topped with the remaining basil slivers. Using a box grater, grate the cheese over the spaghetti and sauce.

BACON AND EGG SPAGHETTI

Combine Italy's most popular noodle with America's favorite breakfast and you get spaghetti carbonara. This classic originated in Italy in the months following World War II when Rome was awash with American GIs and their inevitable bacon and eggs. Fast. Easy. Big-flavored and stick-to-your-ribs filling. That's what I call guy food. **Serves 2; can be multiplied as desired**

1 tablespoon coarse sea salt

1 teaspoon extra virgin olive oil

8 ounces spaghetti (one half of the standard 16-ounce package)

4 slices bacon, 2 left whole, 2 cut crosswise into ¼-inch pieces

½ cup heavy (whipping) cream

¾ cup (3 ounces) freshly and finely grated Parmigiano Reggiano cheese

¼ cup chopped fresh flat-leaf parsley

Freshly ground black pepper

2 large eggs

1 Bring 4 quarts of water and the salt and olive oil to a rapid boil in a stockpot. Stir in the spaghetti and cook until done to taste, about 8 minutes for al dente. Stir the spaghetti a couple of times as it cooks. Drain the spaghetti in a colander, leaving about 3 tablespoons of the hot pasta cooking water in the stockpot. Return the spaghetti to the stockpot.

2 Place the bacon slices and pieces in a large skillet over medium heat and cook until browned and crisp, 3 to 5 minutes, stirring and turning as needed. Transfer the bacon slices to a plate lined with paper towels to drain, leaving the pieces of bacon in the skillet. Pour off all but 1 tablespoon of the bacon fat into a small heatproof bowl and set aside.

3 Add the cream, cheese, and parsley to the skillet with the bacon pieces and season with pepper to taste. Let come to a boil over high heat and let the sauce boil until it is thick and creamy, about 2 minutes, stirring with a wooden spoon. Stir the sauce into the stockpot with the spaghetti. Wipe the skillet clean.

4 Pour the reserved bacon fat back into the skillet and heat over high heat. Crack the eggs into the skillet and cook them until done, about 2 minutes for sunny-side up, or flip using a spatula and cook them 1 minute longer for over easy.

5 Divide the spaghetti between 2 shallow bowls or plates. Slide a fried egg on top of each mound of pasta and top with a slice of bacon.

SHOP In Italy you'd use pancetta—pork belly cured like prosciutto, but without the blessing of wood smoke. Don't get me wrong; it's pleasant enough. But the Italians must have gone crazy when they got their first taste of smoky American bacon. For the best results, use thick-sliced smokehouse bacon, like Nueske's. And freshly grated genuine Parmigiano Reggiano cheese. For notes on which spaghetti to buy, see page 450.

GEAR Your basic kitchen gear including a stockpot, a colander, a large (10- to 12-inch) skillet, and a plate lined with paper towels

WHAT ELSE Tradition calls for the eggs to be mixed into the sauce, but I like to serve them fried on top. Why? It looks cool, tastes even better, and it gives you the sensual pleasure of watching the egg yolk ooze into the noodles. For a variation, replace the spaghetti with a thick tubular pasta like *perciatelli* or *bucatini*.

TIME about 20 minutes

SPAGHETTI

You should always have spaghetti on hand for an emergency dinner. This is a truth just about every guy knows. What you may not know is that not all spaghettis are created equal. Some go from hard to mushy without ever reaching the perfect firm-tender texture Italians call *al dente* (literally "to the tooth"). There's also a right way to cook spaghetti, involving a proper ratio of pasta to water to salt to oil, and how to tell when it's done.

Here are ten things you need to know to cook perfect spaghetti every time. And in this chapter you'll find four of my spaghetti favorites.

1 BUY THE RIGHT BRAND. Good spaghetti will cook to perfect al dente; inferior noodles go from undercooked to overcooked without ever quite hitting the sweet spot. So how do you find a good brand? Try imported spaghetti, like De Cecco, Latini, or Delverde. (Hey, sixty million Italians can't be wrong.)

2 WHOLE GRAIN REIGNS. For health reasons—not to mention flavor—I prefer spaghetti with at least some whole wheat flour in it. One good brand is the Italian Bionaturæ.

3 ENOUGH IS HOW MUCH? A normal serving size of spaghetti is two and a half to three ounces. Don't have a scale? A one-pound box will serve four really hungry guys and six people with normal appetites.

4 USE A *BIG* POT. The secret to great spaghetti is to cook it in a lot of boiling water. At least one gallon per pound of pasta. That's four quarts or sixteen cups. Why so much? You should use enough boiling water so that when you add the pasta, the water keeps boiling. And of course, add the pasta all at once so it cooks evenly. (Did you ever have pasta that tasted starchy and gummy? Chances are it was cooked in too little water.) Remember that stockpot I suggested you buy on page 19? This is a perfect time to use it. While you're at it, set up a large colander in the sink for draining the pasta.

5 SEASON IT RIGHT. You're not done yet, because before you bring the water to a boil you should season it with sea salt. Why salt? It adds flavor. Why sea salt? It adds more flavor. You also want to add one teaspoon of extra virgin olive oil or butter to the water. It will help to keep the individual strands of pasta from sticking together as they cook.

6 MASTER THE ART OF BOILING WATER. The other secret to great pasta is to cook it in rapidly boiling water. This doesn't mean hot or simmering. It means large, vigorous bubbles breaking the surface all over, like a hot tub gone berserk. Why rapidly boiling? When the pasta hits the boiling water, the starch granules on its surface swell up and pop, then wash away, making the pasta less starchy.

7 CHECK FOR DONENESS. Italians eat their paste al dente, meaning with a little chew to it and just shy of being fully cooked. So how do you check for doneness? Grab a strand of spaghetti with tongs (or on the blade of a serrated knife), run it under cold water to cool it, then bite into it. If it's still hard in the center, it's not ready. If it's gently yielding, you're in business. If it's soft and mushy, you've gone too far. It generally takes seven to eight minutes to cook spaghetti at sea level, three to four minutes longer in high-altitude locations like Denver.

8 DON'T DRAIN *TOO* WELL. Pour the pasta with its cooking water into a colander to drain, but leave about three tablespoons of the cooking water in the pot. Italians use this water to emulsify and mellow the sauce for the pasta.

9 OIL IT UP. Return the pasta to the pot and toss it with a spoonful of extra virgin olive oil. This coats the individual strands to keep them from sticking together. And it also gives you a richer mouthfeel.

10 GET FRESH. Most spaghetti is dried pasta—made with flour from a hard wheat called durum and water. Fresh pasta is made by mixing flour and eggs (and sometimes oil and flavorings). All of the recipes in this chapter can be made with fresh pasta. Figure on four to five ounces per serving, and remember, fresh pasta cooks more quickly than dried. Follow the instructions on the package. Some fresh pastas cook in a couple of minutes, so do not desert your post.

For extra credit, learn the lingo:

SPAGHETTI (round strands): "little strings"

LINGUINE (flat strands): "little tongues"

VERMICELLI (thin strands): "little worms"

BUCATINI (large hollow strands): "little holes"

THOMAS JEFFERSON

ost Americans remember Thomas Jefferson as the author of the Declaration of Independence, third President, and a statesman savvy enough to make the Louisiana Purchase (to list just a few of his oversize accomplishments). What you may not know is that the plantation owner turned revolutionary, and Founding Father, was America's first foodie. In 1784 Congress tapped Jefferson to travel to Paris as a Minister Plenipotentiary charged with expanding trade between the fledgling United States and Europe. Paris was the epicenter of the civilized world, where Europe's top chefs prepared sumptuous meals paired with extraordinary wines for some of the most brilliant minds of the era. Some Americans, like John Adams, deplored the pretension. Jefferson couldn't pack his bags fast enough.

Eighteenth-century Americans knew virtually nothing about French cuisine. We ate well, but ours was an uncomplicated meat-centric English diet bolstered by Native American foods, like maple syrup and corn, and slave imports from Africa, such as okra and peanuts. So curious was Jefferson about French food, he brought along one of his slaves, James Hemings, with the express purpose of apprenticing him to some of the top chefs in Paris. When the men returned home five years later, they brought eighty-six crates filled with fine wine, cookware, and foods, such as olive oil and Dijon mustard, that were then unavailable in the U.S. More important, they brought the knowledge of a new style of cooking and dining that transformed America's food sensibility forever. It was Thomas Jefferson—not Julia Child—who introduced us to french fries and pasta, to Champagne and crème brûlée.

Writer Thomas Craughwell chronicles Jefferson's obsession with wine and food in a fascinating little book called *Thomas Jefferson's Crème Brûlée*. I asked Craughwell to channel Jefferson as a Food Dude for this book.

You are well known as an epicure and wine expert. Have you yourself ever tried to cook?
No American gentleman of my acquaintance cooks his own meals. I visit the Monticello kitchen, but rarely. That is to say, only to wind the kitchen clock.

But you chose to bring one of your slaves, James Hemings, with you to Paris to train in the art of French cuisine. Why?
I had learned through my reading and from French friends, like the Marquis de Lafayette, that France had the finest cuisine in Europe. For my own enjoyment and that of my family and guests, I decided to have James Hemings trained as a French chef.

What most surprised you about French cuisine?

Until Congress sent me to France, I had known only women cooks. In France, the great houses employed men as chefs.

So which do you like better? French cuisine or Virginia plantation food?

My enthusiasm for "plantation fare," as we call it in the South, remains undiminished. In Paris I planted American corn in the garden of my house on the Champs-Elysées. Once we had returned to America, James performed a kind of culinary marriage between plantation fare and French cuisine, introducing my guests to the great dishes of France, while preserving the hearty dishes that have nourished us here in the New World.

What is a typical meal at Monticello?

If I dine alone, I have eight dishes. If I have guests, then as many as thirty-two dishes might be served, which imitates the French fashion of offering guests an abundance of choices.

> ▶ Until Congress sent me to France, I had known only women cooks.

What are your favorite foods?

Virginia ham. I often had Virginia hams shipped to me in Paris.

Capon (castrated rooster). In Paris James learned to stuff it with truffles, artichoke bottoms, chestnut puree, and chopped Virginia ham and serve it with a Calvados sauce based on apple brandy. Now that was capon!

But above all, I'm a vegetable eater—especially cabbage, asparagus, and English peas, which I eat daily when in season. Nothing charms me like a well-dressed salad.

So what's the secret to a great salad?

My salads are dressed with olive oil, "the richest gift of heaven," vinegar, the yolks of hard-boiled eggs, mustard, salt, and a bit of sugar. When we can't get olive oil (the War of 1812 closed sea trade with Europe), we use sesame oil.

What's your favorite seduction dish?

I'm not sure I could name a single seduction dish (remember, I am a widower), but I quickly learned the power of a fine meal served with French wines to seduce your political opponents. In July 1790 I invited James Madison and Alexander Hamilton to dinner. The two—implacable enemies—were involved in a bitter dispute over whether or not the federal government should assume the state debts from the Revolutionary War. The wines flowed (Hermitage as the aperitif, montepulciano with the main course, and Champagne for dessert), and by the end of the evening we forged a compromise on the debt problem and resolved to move the nation's capital to Washington, D.C.

Your secret indulgence?

Ice cream. My slaves churn it by hand in an ice cream machine chilled by ice and rock salt.

Three dishes every guy should know how to make?

It was my good fortune to introduce to my fellow Americans such culinary delights as potatoes cut into long, thin slices and fried; a casserole of macaroni, butter, cream, and cheese; and burned cream—custard sprinkled with sugar and caramelized with a fire-heated shovel. In other words, french fries, macaroni and cheese, and crème brûlée.

Three ingredients you can't live without?

Parmigiano Reggiano cheese. Olive oil. Mustard. I also brought home boxes of truffles and 680 bottles of wine.

Three tools your kitchen staff can't live without?

Copper pots. Before my trip to France all the pots and pans in the Monticello kitchen were made of cast iron. They were heavy and cumbersome and had a tendency to crack. Copper is much more durable.

A pasta machine: When I was in Italy, I bought a macaroni-making machine—the first ever seen in America.

My brick cook stove: Prior to my trip to Paris, Monticello, like all American kitchens, had an open hearth for cooking. It was dirty, smoky, and dangerous. Once we returned from France, I redesigned the Monticello kitchen along the French model, complete with a charcoal-burning stove with eight "burners" (open grates), a ventilation window, and a heated copper cauldron so my chefs would always have hot water.

Advice for future generations of men and Americans?

Don't eat so much meat. As I often explained to my children, "I have lived temperately, eating little animal food, and that . . . as a condiment for the vegetables, which constitute my principal diet."

SPAGHETTI
WITH BROWNED BUTTER AND CHEESE

SHOP The preferred cheese is a firm white *mizithra* from the island of Crete. Made from sheep's or goat's milk, it has a sharp, salty tang—if it were a fish and not a cheese, it would be an anchovy. Look for it at cheese shops, Greek markets, and a growing number of natural foods stores. Or you can substitute another sharp grating cheese, like Italian pecorino romano or even Parmigiano Reggiano.

GEAR Your basic kitchen gear including a stockpot, a colander, and a heavy saucepan

WHAT ELSE You want the cheese to be finely grated. There are several ways to do this. One way is in a food processor, using the fine grating disk (you can also cut the cheese into one-inch pieces and finely chop these with the chopping blade, running the processor in short bursts). Or you can use a box grater, grating the cheese on the small-hole side. If you have one, you can use a rotary-style cheese grater. You can even use a Microplane grater (see page 15), but that takes a lot of elbow grease.

TIME about 10 minutes

Here's a noodle dish I've been making since my college days. It possesses several attributes of great guy food. It's ridiculously simple, containing just three main ingredients, including the spaghetti. It involves an element of danger: You brown the butter a few degrees shy of actually turning it black. It's cheap, always welcome on a student budget, and it's quick, requiring not much more cooking time than it takes to boil the pasta. Best of all, it brims with salty, buttery flavor.

Wine note: If you've never tasted retsina—a Greek resin-flavored wine—this would be a good occasion. (The process dates from Homer's day, when wine skins were sealed with resin to keep them from leaking.) **Serves 2 or 3; can be multiplied as desired**

For the spaghetti

1 tablespoon coarse sea salt

1 teaspoon butter or extra virgin olive oil

8 ounces spaghetti (one half of the standard 16-ounce package)

For the browned butter and cheese

6 tablespoons (¾ stick) unsalted butter, cut into ½-inch pieces

8 ounces mizithra cheese, finely grated (about 2 cups)

Coarse salt (kosher or sea) and freshly ground black pepper (optional)

1 Cook the spaghetti: Bring 4 quarts of water and the 1 tablespoon of salt, and the 1 teaspoon of butter or olive oil to a rapid boil in a stockpot. Stir in the spaghetti and cook until done to taste, about 8 minutes for al dente. Stir the spaghetti a couple of times as it cooks. Drain the spaghetti in a colander, leaving about 3 tablespoons of the hot pasta cooking water in the stockpot. Return the spaghetti to the stockpot with the pasta cooking water to keep it warm.

2 Prepare the browned butter and cheese: Place a large bowl of cold water near the stove so you can plunge the bottom of the saucepan in it if the butter starts to burn. Melt the 6 tablespoons of butter in a heavy saucepan over high heat. Cook the butter until it browns, about 2 minutes, swirling the saucepan so the butter cooks evenly. First the butter will sputter as the water in it evaporates, then the butter will start to brown. At this point watch it very carefully; you want it to turn dark brown but not black. If the butter starts to burn, set the saucepan in the cold water to stop it.

3 Pour the browned butter over the spaghetti and, using a wooden spoon, stir to mix. Stir in 1½ cups of the cheese. Transfer the spaghetti to plates and sprinkle the remaining cheese on top. Pass the salt and pepper, and let diners add it to taste (the cheese can be pretty salty).

LINGUINE
WITH CREAMY CLAM SAUCE

I'm not much of a fisherman, but I do wield a mean clam rake in Cape Poge Bay off Chappaquiddick Island (see page 408). If you find the right spot, you can fill your wire basket in a couple of hours. That's enough for two dozen littlenecks on the half shell (page 397) and two dozen cherrystones for the grill and leaves you with big, tough quahogs (chowder clams), perfect for dicing to make linguine with clam sauce. You'll find two twists on the traditional preparation here: shallots instead of garlic, for a subtler, more complex flavor, and heavy cream in addition to butter, to make a sauce you can slurp with a spoon. Definitely not your usual red-checkered-tablecloth restaurant linguine with clams. **Serves 2 or 3; can be multiplied as desired**

Coarse salt (kosher or sea)

1 teaspoon olive oil or vegetable oil

1 cup shucked fresh clams with their juices (20 to 24 littlenecks or 6 to 10 quahogs)

3 tablespoons butter

2 to 3 shallots, peeled and finely chopped (about ½ cup)

½ cup heavy (whipping) cream

Freshly ground black pepper

¼ cup chopped fresh flat-leaf parsley

8 ounces fresh or dried linguine (one half of the standard 16-ounce package)

SHOP If you have an obliging fishmonger, ask him (or her) to shuck the clams for you.

GEAR Your basic kitchen gear including a stockpot, a large (10- to 12-inch) nonstick or cast-iron skillet, and a colander

WHAT ELSE If fresh clams aren't available, make linguine with shrimp. You'll need 12 ounces diced peeled deveined shrimp.

I call for fresh linguine here, available at pasta shops and Italian markets and at most supermarkets and natural foods stores. Figure on 3 to 4 ounces per person. Or use an equal amount of dried linguine.

TIME about 30 minutes

1 Bring 4 quarts of water, 1 tablespoon of salt, and the oil to a rapid boil in a stockpot.

2 Shuck the clams. Drain the clam juices into a bowl and set them aside. Using a chef's knife, finely chop the clams.

3 Melt the butter in a large skillet over medium heat. Add the shallots and cook until lightly browned, about 3 minutes. Increase the heat to high and add the clam juices. Let boil until reduced to about ¼ cup, 3 to 5 minutes. Add the cream and boil until the mixture reduces to about ½ cup, 3 to 5 minutes. Reduce the heat to medium and stir in the chopped clams. Let the clams simmer until they are cooked through and the sauce is thick and richly flavored, about 2 minutes. Stir in the parsley in the last 10 seconds. Taste the clam sauce for seasoning, adding salt if necessary (the clams will already be quite salty) and plenty of pepper. Keep the sauce warm over a low heat.

4 Stir the linguine into the stockpot of boiling water and cook until done to taste, 4 to 6 minutes for fresh linguine, about 8 minutes for dried, when cooked to al dente. Stir the linguine a couple of times as it cooks. Drain the linguine in a colander, then transfer it to a platter or plates. Spoon the clam sauce over the linguine and serve.

Jim Denevan's
ORECCHIETTE
WITH ITALIAN SAUSAGE AND BITTER GREENS

SHOP Orecchiette (little ears, literally) are a concave, disk-shaped pasta from the heel of the Italian boot—Puglia—often made with whole wheat flour. Other pasta options include penne or rigatoni. For bitter greens, use any or a combination of the following: broccoli rabe, mustard greens, escarole, chicory, or radicchio.

Jim Denevan founded Outstanding in the Field, which brings together growers and consumers (read about him on page 406). When it comes to greens, he's a no-nonsense guy, preferring the assertive taste of bitter greens like rapini (broccoli rabe), radicchio, and escarole to the milder, more socially acceptable spinach. This simple pasta delivers the manly flavors of anchovies, garlic, hot pepper flakes, and Italian sausage. Best of all, it's a two-pot dish you can assemble in thirty minutes. **Serves 2 or 3; can be multiplied as desired**

Your basic kitchen gear including a stockpot, a large (10- to 12-inch) cast-iron or nonstick skillet, a colander, and a box grater

WHAT ELSE Popular in southern Italy, broccoli rabe (also called rapini) has dark green jagged-edged leaves and flowering buds with a pleasantly bitter flavor that may remind you of broccoli crossed with turnip greens. A member of the turnip family, it's rich in calcium and vitamin D.

TIME about 30 minutes

Coarse sea salt

2 tablespoons plus 1 teaspoon extra virgin olive oil

1 clove garlic, peeled and minced

2 anchovy fillets, drained and finely chopped

½ teaspoon hot red pepper flakes

1 fresh (uncooked) sweet or hot Italian sausage (about 4 ounces)

2 cups finely chopped, well rinsed bitter greens, such as broccoli rabe, escarole, chicory, mustard greens, and/or radicchio

1 cup dry white wine

1 pint cherry tomatoes (preferably organic), rinsed and cut in half

Freshly ground black pepper

8 ounces orecchiette or other pasta (preferably whole wheat)

1 chunk (3 ounces) pecorino romano or Parmigiano Reggiano cheese (optional), for grating

---

1 Bring 4 quarts of water, 1 tablespoon of salt, and 1 teaspoon of the olive oil to a rapid boil in a stockpot.

2 Heat the remaining 2 tablespoons of olive oil in a large skillet over medium heat. Add the garlic, anchovies, and hot pepper flakes and cook until the garlic is lightly browned, about 3 minutes.

3 Slit the sausage casing lengthwise and crumble the sausage meat into the skillet. Discard the casing. Increase the heat to high and cook the sausage until it is cooked through, about 5 minutes, chopping and stirring it with a wooden spoon. Pour off all but 2 tablespoons of the fat. Add the bitter greens and white wine and let boil until the greens are tender and the wine is reduced by half, about 5 minutes. Stir

in the cherry tomatoes and cook until they soften, about 1 minute. Season with salt and pepper to taste.

4 Stir the orecchiette into the stockpot of boiling water and cook until done to taste, about 8 minutes for al dente. Stir the orecchiette a couple of times as it cooks. Drain the orecchiette in a colander, leaving about 3 tablespoons of the hot pasta cooking water in the stockpot. Stir this pasta cooking water into the skillet with the sausage and greens and let boil for about 1 minute to blend the flavors.

5 Stir the orecchiette into the sausage and greens or, if the skillet is too small, mound it on plates or a platter and spoon the sausage and greens on top. Using a box grater, grate the cheese, if using, over the orecchiette and serve.

HOW TO MAKE YOUR OWN
BREAD CRUMBS

There are at least five reasons to make your own bread crumbs from scratch.

- Food doesn't go to waste.
- You can vary the flavor and texture of the crumbs, from brioche to pumpernickel to whole wheat.
- Look at the ingredient list on a store-bought package of bread crumbs—you might find such inviting compounds as stearoyl lactylate, ammonium sulfate, and monocalcium phosphate. When you make your own crumbs, you can use unadulterated bread.
- Macaroni and cheese (page 460) and breaded veal chops (page 268) depend on them. Homemade bread crumbs make the difference between average and exceptional.
- Finally, homemade bread crumbs just taste better. Period.

So here's your game plan.

Store stale bread scraps in resealable plastic bags in the freezer until you have three or four cups. Let the bread thaw on a baking sheet at room temperature.

To make fresh bread crumbs, cut or tear the stale bread into two-inch chunks. Place the bread in a food processor fitted with a metal blade and pulse the machine in short bursts to make coarse or fine crumbs, depending on your intended use. Don't have a food processor? You could grate chunks of stale bread on the coarse side of a box grater. On second thought, buy a food processor.

To make toasted bread crumbs, which are more flavorful than untoasted, spread the crumbs in a thin layer on a rimmed baking sheet and brown them in an oven preheated to 350°F, stirring them from time to time so the crumbs brown evenly. Five to ten minutes will do it.

To store toasted or untoasted bread crumbs, let them cool to room temperature, then transfer the crumbs to a plastic container or freezer-weight resealable plastic bag and freeze them until ready to use. The crumbs will keep for at least six months. Thaw the bread crumbs 10 to 15 minutes.

Use untoasted bread crumbs for crusting chicken breasts, fish fillets, and other dishes that will be browned in oil or butter.

Use toasted bread crumbs for sprinkling over pasta, gratins, and other moist dishes you wish to top with a crust. They'll become even toastier in the oven.

PEPPER JACK MAC AND CHEESE
WITH CARAMELIZED ONIONS AND HAM

SHOP Nothing superexotic here, but if you're going to take the time to make mac and cheese from scratch, you should start with good cheese and grate it yourself. I call for pepper Jack here, but you might just as easily grate a sharp cheddar from Vermont, Wisconsin, Oregon, or New York State, or a Cheshire or Leicester from Great Britain. For a barbecue-inflected mac and cheese you can make indoors, use a smoked cheese. For the macaroni itself, use a tubular pasta, like elbow macaroni or ziti. For a more healthful version, use whole wheat noodles.

GEAR Your basic kitchen gear plus a 9-inch square baking pan, a stockpot, a colander, and a large heavy saucepan

WHAT ELSE Mac and cheese with freshly grated cheddar cheese is good. Mac and cheese with caramelized onions is better. Mac and cheese with ham or bacon knocks it out of the ballpark.

TIME about 1 hour

If you want *real* comfort food, make macaroni and cheese. Comforting? Name another dish that's simultaneously soft and crisp; rib-sticking and flavorful; kid-friendly (both for your kids and your inner child), yet capable of gastronomic sophistication. But don't take my word for it. Jean-Georges Vongerichten and Wolfgang Puck are two of the legions of high-profile chefs who serve it at their restaurants. The bad news is that for some guys, the closest they get to real mac and cheese is a freeze-dried mix sold in rectangular cardboard boxes. (No multinational food corporations mentioned by name here, but you know who I'm talking about.) Well, here's a mac and cheese with personality to spare, complete with smoked ham for protein, pepper Jack cheese and poblano pepper for kick, and caramelized onions and mustard for extra flavor. It's rich, gooey, creamy, cheesy, and unapologetic in its excess. **Serves 4 to 6 as a side dish; 2 to 3 as a main course**

4 tablespoons (½ stick) butter, plus butter for greasing the baking pan

Coarse salt (kosher or sea)

2 cups elbow macaroni (about 8 ounces)

1 teaspoon olive or vegetable oil

½ cup bread crumbs (preferably homemade, page 459) or crushed tortilla chips

1 medium-size onion, peeled and finely chopped

1 poblano pepper, seeded and cut into ¼-inch dice

3 ounces smoked ham, prosciutto, or serrano ham (optional), thinly sliced and cut into matchstick slivers

3 tablespoons unbleached all-purpose white flour

2 cups milk (whole, low-fat, or skim, your choice) or half-and-half

1 tablespoon Dijon mustard

2 cups (about 8 ounces) coarsely grated pepper Jack cheese

Freshly ground black pepper

1 Preheat the oven to 350°F. Lightly grease a 9-inch square baking pan with butter.

2 Bring 4 quarts of water and 1 tablespoon of salt to a rapid boil in a stockpot. Stir in the macaroni and cook until just al dente, about 8 minutes, stirring once or twice to prevent sticking. Drain the macaroni in a colander, rinse it with cold water until cool, and drain it again. Toss the macaroni with the oil to prevent clumping.

3 Melt 1 tablespoon of the butter in a large heavy saucepan over medium heat. Add the bread crumbs or crushed tortilla chips and cook until toasted, about 1 minute, stirring with a wooden spoon. Transfer the toasted bread crumbs or chips to a bowl.

4 Melt the remaining 3 tablespoons of butter in the saucepan over medium heat. Add the onion, poblano pepper, and ham, if using, and cook until lightly browned, about 4 minutes. Stir in the flour and cook until it loses its raw taste, about 1 minute. Gradually whisk in the milk. Increase the heat to high and cook the sauce until bubbling and thickened, about 3 minutes, whisking often.

5 Remove the pan from the heat and whisk in the mustard. Using a rubber spatula, stir

in the cooked macaroni, then the pepper Jack cheese. Season with salt and pepper to taste; the mixture should be highly seasoned.

6 Spoon the macaroni and cheese into the prepared baking dish. Sprinkle the toasted bread crumbs or crushed tortilla chips on top. Bake the macaroni and cheese until bubbling, 30 to 40 minutes. Serve at once.

Variations

Other Stuff You Can Add to Make Great Mac and Cheese Even Better

▸ **Shiitakes or other mushrooms:** You'll need about 6 ounces. Wipe the mushrooms clean, remove and discard the stems, thinly slice the mushroom caps, and cook them with the onion.

▸ **Red or yellow bell pepper:** Use 1 stemmed, seeded, and diced bell pepper (or half a red bell pepper and half a yellow bell pepper) in place of or in addition to the poblano pepper. Colorful.

- **Lobster or crab:** Stir in 2 cups of diced cooked lobster or crab meat when you add the macaroni.

- **Truffled mac and cheese:** Replace the conventional butter with black or white truffle butter (sold by my friends Amy and Thierry Farges under the Transatlantic Foods brand and available at natural foods stores).

SOBA
WITH SPICY PEANUT SAUCE

SHOP You'll need to know about a few Asian ingredients here. All are available at a good natural foods store or supermarket. The first is Asian sesame oil, pressed from toasted sesame seeds. Choose a Chinese or Japanese brand. The second is rice vinegar, which is milder than wine vinegar or distilled white vinegar (you can substitute distilled vinegar in a pinch). The third is Asian chili paste, which gives you a triple blast of garlic, salt, and chili hellfire. Options here include Chinese Lee Kum Kee chili garlic sauce, Vietnamese-style Huy Fong chili garlic sauce, or the Korean Wang brand *kochujang*. In a pinch you could even use Thai Sriracha or a domestic hot sauce, like Tabasco or Crystal.

GEAR Your basic kitchen gear including a large (10- to 12-inch) cast-iron skillet, a food processor, and a stockpot

This cold noodle dish, made with Japanese buckwheat soba noodles, takes a page from China's playbook, inspired by two classic Szechuan dishes: *dan dan* noodles and *bon bon* chicken. Both feature a spicy sesame and peanut sauce electrified with ginger and Chinese chili paste. It's the sort of sauce I happily eat by itself straight off a spoon. Don't be intimidated by the long list of ingredients: The sauce takes all of five minutes to make in a food processor. Cold noodles. Fiery sauce. A winning play in my book. **Serves 2 or 3; can be multiplied as desired**

½ cup sesame seeds

2 scallions, trimmed, white parts coarsely chopped, green parts thinly sliced crosswise

1 clove garlic, peeled and coarsely chopped

2 teaspoons minced peeled fresh ginger

⅓ cup smooth peanut butter

⅓ cup warm chicken stock, preferably homemade (page 549), or water

1 tablespoon soy sauce, or more to taste

1 tablespoon plus 2 teaspoons Asian (dark) sesame oil

1 tablespoon rice vinegar

1 tablespoon sugar, or more to taste

1 teaspoon Asian chili paste or hot sauce, or more to taste

½ teaspoon freshly ground black pepper

1 tablespoon coarse sea salt

8 ounces soba noodles

1 cucumber (optional)

1 Place the sesame seeds in a dry skillet over medium heat and toast them until golden brown, 2 to 4 minutes. Shake the skillet so the sesame seeds cook evenly. Don't overcook the sesame seeds or they will become bitter. Immediately transfer the toasted sesame seeds to a heatproof bowl.

2 Place 5 tablespoons of the sesame seeds in a food processor. Add the scallion whites, garlic, and ginger. Pulse the processor a few times to chop them finely. Add the peanut butter, chicken stock or water, soy sauce, 1 tablespoon of the sesame oil, and the rice vinegar, sugar, chili paste, and pepper and run the machine until a thick smooth sauce forms. Taste for seasoning, adding more soy sauce and/or sugar as necessary; the sauce should be nutty, sweet, salty, and as spicy as you can bear. Refrigerate the sauce, covered, until serving time; it can be made several hours ahead.

3 Bring 4 quarts of water, the salt, and 1 teaspoon of the sesame oil to a rapid boil in a stockpot. Stir in the soba noodles and cook them until done to taste, about 8 minutes for al dente. Stir the soba noodles a couple of times as they cook. Drain the noodles in a colander, rinse them with cold water until they are completely cool, then rinse and drain them again. Toss the noodles with the remaining 1 teaspoon of sesame oil.

4 If you are using the cucumber, peel it, cut it in half lengthwise, scrape out the seeds with a spoon, and thinly slice each half crosswise.

5 To serve, place the soba noodles on a platter or plates. Spoon the sauce over them, top them with the cucumber, if using, and sprinkle the scallion greens and the reserved 3 tablespoons of sesame seeds over all.

WHAT ELSE You could use fresh or dried ramen noodles in place of the soba. If you are using fresh ramen you'll need about 4 ounces per person. If you are using dried, you'll need about 8 ounces. Cook the ramen noodles according to the instructions on the package. To make a more substantial summer dish, slice cooked shrimp or chicken—about ¼ pound per person—on top.

TIME about 20 minutes

MEATBALLS
WITH PARMESAN AND HERBS

As a final bow to the noodle, here's a recipe for its best-loved companion—the meatball. For a lot of guys, spaghetti with red sauce (page 446) just wouldn't taste right without them. So what makes a great meatball? Well, first there's the meat, or more accurately, the meats, because most great meatballs feature a combination of beef, pork, and veal. Then, there's the binder—often bread or bread crumbs soaked in milk or cream—enough to hold the mixture together, but not weigh it down. You'll need seasonings—onions or other alliums, herbs (preferably fresh), hot peppers, grated cheese, and plenty of salt and pepper.

Out of spaghetti? Pile the meatballs onto hoagie rolls and spoon on the red sauce. They're pretty awesome by themselves. **Makes 24 meatballs**

SHOP The basic ingredients are available at any supermarket. You may need to go to a butcher to find ground veal. Can't find veal? Use ground chicken, turkey, or lamb. Or substitute more beef and pork.

GEAR Your basic kitchen gear including a large (10- to 12-inch) cast-iron skillet, slotted spoon, and a baking sheet

WHAT ELSE I like my meatballs panfried (better crust), but some guys prefer the convenience of baking. Better yet, do both (see below).

You can cook the meatballs entirely in the oven, in which case the cooking time will be 30 to 40 minutes.

TIME 1 hour (30 minutes of which is chilling the meat and cooking)

1½ cups cubed white bread

½ cup half-and-half

2 tablespoons extra virgin olive oil

2 slices bacon, finely chopped

1 medium onion, finely chopped (about ¾ cup)

1 to 2 cloves garlic, finely chopped

1 pound ground beef

½ pound ground pork

½ pound ground veal (or more pork or veal)

1 teaspoon coarse salt (kosher or sea)

½ teaspoon freshly ground black pepper

1 cup finely grated imported Parmigiano Reggiano cheese

2 tablespoons minced fresh herbs, including basil, sage leaves, and flat-leaf parsley,

1 Preheat the oven to 400°F.

2 Place the bread in a large mixing bowl and stir in the half-and-half. Let soak for 3 minutes, then thoroughly wring out and drain off the half-and-half.

3 Meanwhile, heat 1 tablespoon olive oil in a large cast-iron skillet over medium heat. Add the bacon, onion, and garlic and cook until golden brown, 3 minutes, stirring with a slotted spoon. Using a slotted spoon, transfer the bacon mixture to the soaked bread, leaving the fat in the pan. Let this mixture cool completely.

4 Add the beef, pork, veal, salt, and pepper to the bread mixture. Add the cheese and herbs and knead the mixture together until just mixed, working with a light touch. To test the meatballs for seasoning, fry a little ball of the mixture in the skillet until cooked through, 3 minutes. Taste and add flavorings as needed. Chill the mixture for 30 minutes first.

5 Lightly wet your hands with cold water. Pinch off 1½-inch pieces of the mixture and roll them into balls between your palms. Place the meatballs on a baking sheet.

6 Add enough olive oil to the fat in the skillet to obtain 2 tablespoons and heat over medium heat. Add the meatballs and cook until golden brown on all sides, 2 minutes per side (6 to 8 minutes in all). Don't crowd the pan—leave a couple of inches between the meatballs. Transfer the meatballs to the baking sheet as they are browned. Continue until all the meatballs are browned.

7 Bake the meatballs on the baking sheet until cooked through, 15 to 20 minutes. To test for doneness, cut 1 meatball in half: there should be no pink in the center. Or use an instant read thermometer: the internal temperature should be 165°F.

VEGETABLES

Eat your vegetables. Three simple words uttered by legions of mothers. Who would have guessed that carrots would become the new designer food? That Mondays would become meatless? That marquee chefs would serve $150 vegetable tasting menus? (And that we'd have to make reservations a month ahead to try them?) The truth is that thanks to the heirloom vegetable movement and the boom in farmers' markets, there has never been a better time to eat your vegetables, and that's true whether you're a lifelong vegetarian (like cartoonist Scott Adams of *Dilbert* fame or actor Tobey Maguire) or a diehard meat and potatoes man. (Remember, potatoes are veggies.)

So why should you learn to cook vegetables? Let me count the ways: Bake-Fried Chiles Rellenos and Chile Bean Burgers; mashers (mashed potatoes) and baked potatoes loaded with scallions and cheese; wild Mushroom Hash; Crispy Kale; Cauliflower "Steaks" Sicilian Style; Brazilian Steak House Collard Greens; and what may just be the most awesome baked beans on the planet—you'll find them all here.

MEATLESS MONDAY TACOS
(BLACK BEANS, POBLANO, AND CORN)

Son-in-law does not look happy. Son-in-law is dreaming of skirt steak—edges charred, meat sizzling hot off the grill. Instead, he reaches for the black beans spiced with cumin, cilantro, and poblano pepper. It's a Meatless Monday—an institution at son-in-law's home—and he's trying to be a good sport and a role model for his kids. So he grabs a tortilla and piles it high with beans, avocado, grated cheese, salsa, and sour cream. He takes a bite. Hmmmm, not so bad. He takes another bite. This is actually good. Son-in-law belongs to a growing number of American families who are forgoing meat once a week for their own health and the health of the planet. Which brings us to these intensely flavorful poblano, bean, and corn tacos, which could make you look forward to Meatless Monday. **Serves 4**

SHOP Tacos are only as good as the tortillas you use to assemble them. If you live in an area with a large Mexican community, you should be able to buy them fresh. Otherwise, pick the most artisanal-looking brand you can find at your supermarket. For the corn and beans choose an organic, low-sodium brand if possible. For cheese, I like the kick of pepper Jack, but you can certainly use regular Jack or cheddar.

GEAR Your basic kitchen gear including two large (10- to 12-inch) skillets (one cast iron), and a cloth napkin or cloth-lined basket for the tortillas

WHAT ELSE There are two ways to approach these tacos. Use canned beans and corn and your favorite commercial salsa or hot sauce and make them in fifteen minutes. Or take the time to grill or roast fresh corn and the poblano pepper and make your salsa from scratch. The first rewards you with a quick, surprisingly full-flavored meatless dinner; the second with something bordering on the sublime.

TIME about 30 minutes

For the taco filling
2 tablespoons extra virgin olive oil

1 medium-size onion, peeled and finely chopped

1 poblano pepper, or 1 to 2 jalapeño peppers, seeded and finely chopped

½ teaspoon ground cumin

1 bunch fresh cilantro, rinsed, shaken dry, and stemmed

1 can (about 15 ounces) black beans, drained in a colander, rinsed, and drained again

1 can (about 15 ounces) corn kernels, drained, or 1 package (8 ounces) frozen corn, thawed

Coarse salt (kosher or sea; optional)

Any or all of the following toppings for serving
1 large ripe avocado

2 limes, cut into wedges

1 large luscious red ripe tomato, diced

¼ head green cabbage or iceberg lettuce (optional), thinly sliced or shredded

8 ounces (2 cups) coarsely grated pepper Jack, Jack, or white cheddar cheese

1 cup sour cream

2 cups Pico de Gallo (page 210), Salsa Chipotle (page 211), or another favorite salsa

12 corn or flour tortillas

1 **Make the taco filling:** Heat the olive oil in a large skillet over medium heat. Add the onion, poblano or jalapeño pepper(s), and cumin and cook until golden brown, about 4 minutes, stirring often. Meanwhile, finely chop half of the cilantro and add it to the onion mixture. Tear the remaining cilantro into sprigs, place them in a serving bowl, and set aside. Stir the black beans and corn into the onion mixture and cook until richly flavored, about 3 minutes, stirring often. You probably won't need salt, as the beans and corn will be salted already, but taste for seasoning, adding salt if necessary. The taco filling can be prepared and refrigerated, covered, up to 24 hours ahead. If you make the filling in advance, reheat it in a skillet just before serving.

2 **Prepare the toppings:** Dice the avocado (see page 216) and place it in a serving bowl. Squeeze 1 lime wedge over the avocado to keep it from browning. Place the remaining lime wedges and the tomato, cabbage or lettuce, if using, grated cheese, sour cream, and salsa in separate serving bowls with spoons alongside.

3 Heat a second large skillet over medium-high heat—this one should be cast-iron. Heat the tortillas in the skillet, 1 or 2 at a time until warm and pliable, about 20 seconds per side, turning with tongs. Wrap the tortillas in a cloth napkin or cloth-lined basket to keep warm.

4 To eat the tacos, take a tortilla in one hand and fill it with the bean mixture, followed by your choice of toppings and a squeeze of lime juice. You'll never miss the meat.

Variation

Up the ante by using a couple of grilled ears of fresh sweet corn in place of the canned. Shuck the corn, brush the ears lightly with olive oil, season them with salt and pepper, and grill them over a hot fire until darkly browned, 8 minutes or so, turning with tongs. Cut the kernels off the cob.

While you have the grill fired up, roast the poblano or jalapeño pepper(s) until the skin is charred. Scrape off the burnt skin and seed and dice the peppers. To spread out the work, you can grill the corn and peppers ahead at a previous grill session.

If the grill is still fired up you can use it for warming the tortillas.

MEATLESS MONDAY

My stepdaughter, Betsy Berthin, is a dietician with an A-list clientele that includes Grammy Award–winning musicians and the Miami Heat basketball team. So when Betsy talks nutrition (follow her at betsyberthin.com), I listen. And one thing she talks about a lot these days is Meatless Monday.

The concept is simple: Skip meat on Mondays. This simple sacrifice can have big benefits for your personal health and the health of the planet. A six-ounce serving of beef contains about 150 milligrams of cholesterol and more than 7 milligrams of saturated fat; the same amount of tofu contains *zero* cholesterol and less than 2 milligrams of saturated fat. (Cooked beans contain *no* cholesterol or saturated fat.) Not that I recommend a steady diet of beans and tofu, but once a week I can live with.

The savings are equally dramatic from an ecological perspective. According to meatlessmonday.com, it takes 2,000 gallons of water to produce a pound of beef and only 220 gallons of water to produce a pound of tofu. A single calorie of protein from beef requires fifty-four calories of fossil fuels, while one whole calorie of protein from soy requires only two calories of fossil fuel.

Despite its New Age-sounding trappings, Meatless Monday actually originated during World War I, when Herbert Hoover ran the U.S. Food Administration (precursor of the USDA). By 1917, more than 10 million American families, 7,000 hotels, and 425,000 food distributors had pledged to observe weekly meatless days to help the war effort.

The modern Meatless Monday campaign was revived in 2003 by Madison Avenue hotshot Sid "Squeeze the Charmin" Lerner in partnership with the Johns Hopkins University Bloomberg School of Public Health. Today, it's practiced in more than twenty-one countries and endorsed by numerous celebrities and trendsetters, from musician Paul McCartney to food activist Michael Pollan (see page 172) and *The New York Times* columnist Mark Bittman (page 482). In 2011, Aspen, Colorado, became the first city in the U.S. to adopt a Meatless Monday program; in 2012, Los Angeles became the largest American city to do so. And Baltimore, where I grew up, has made it part of the school lunch program.

One thing is for sure, if you give up meat every Monday, you won't be alone.

CHILE BEAN BURGERS

The New York Times food columnist Mark Bittman is a strong advocate of a largely plant-based diet. For reasons regarding both personal health and the health of the planet, he rarely eats meat before 6 p.m. (you can read more about Mark's food philosophies on page 482). Here's a blueprint for Mark's meatless burgers, made with beans and invigorated with pure chile powder, onion, and cilantro. Think of them as a vegetarian chili you can eat on a bun. Like most of Mark's recipes, this one should be viewed as a broad guide rather than a formula to be slavishly followed to the tablespoon. Customize it as you like by adding grated cheese and whatever other fillings and toppings you like. **Serves 4**

1 can (about 15 ounces) white beans, preferably organic and low-sodium, drained in a colander, rinsed, and drained again

1 medium-size onion, peeled and coarsely chopped

½ cup old-fashioned rolled oats, or more as needed

3 tablespoons chopped fresh cilantro

2 to 3 teaspoons pure chile powder

½ teaspoon ground cumin (optional)

Coarse salt (kosher or sea) and freshly ground black pepper

2 tablespoons extra virgin olive oil

2 tablespoons (¼ stick) butter

4 hamburger buns, preferably whole wheat

Boston or romaine lettuce leaves, for serving

Sliced red ripe tomato, for serving

Sliced red onion, for serving

Chipotle Mayonnaise (optional, page 545), for serving

SHOP Mark suggests making these with white beans, like cannellinis. Garbanzo beans (chickpeas), pinto beans, and black beans also give you interesting burgers. And you want to use a pure chile powder, like one made from ancho chiles, rather than a blended one.

GEAR Your basic kitchen gear including a food processor and a large (10- to 12-inch) nonstick skillet

WHAT ELSE Much as I like to grill all burgers, veggie burgers in general and bean burgers in particular have a tendency to fall apart on the grill. So cook them in a skillet.

TIME about 20 minutes, plus 30 minutes for chilling the bean burgers

1 Place the white beans, onion, oats, cilantro, chile powder, and cumin, if using, in a food processor and coarsely chop them, running the machine in short bursts. You want to mix the ingredients, not reduce them to a puree. If the mixture looks too loose (soft and wet), add a little more oatmeal. Season the bean mixture with salt and pepper to taste; it should be highly seasoned.

2 Lightly wet your hands with water and form the bean mixture into 4 burgerlike patties, each ½ inch thick and about 3 inches across. Place the patties on a plate lined with plastic wrap and refrigerate them for about 30 minutes or until you're ready to cook them (chilling helps firm up the bean mixture). The bean burgers can be made several hours ahead to this stage.

3 When ready to cook, heat the olive oil in a large nonstick skillet over medium-high heat until shimmering, 30 seconds to 1 minute. Add the bean burgers and cook them until they are crusty and brown on both sides, 3 to 4 minutes per side, carefully turning them with a spatula.

4 Meanwhile if desired, lightly butter the cut-side tops and bottoms of the hamburger buns. Place the buns cut side down in the skillet over medium heat and toast them until golden, about 2 minutes.

5 Serve the bean burgers on the buns with lettuce, tomato, onion, and Chipotle Mayonnaise, if desired.

BAKE-FRIED CHILES RELLENOS

SHOP The traditional chile for stuffing is a poblano pepper, an aromatic dark green capsicum with more bite than a conventional bell pepper. You can also use the elongated Anaheim peppers or Hatch or New Mexican chiles. Poblanos are available at most supermarkets; Anaheim peppers and seasonal Hatch chiles can be found at supermarkets in the West or online at melissas.com.

GEAR Your basic kitchen gear including a large (10- to 12-inch) skillet, a colander, and a 9-by-13-inch baking dish

Before me a plate of chiles rellenos beckons, the egg batter crisp, the cheese filling gooey—the luscious deep-fried concoction, tipping the scales at 450 calories and a whopping 37 grams of fat—and that's for each chile pepper. Which is to say, this is the sort of dish you indulge in from time to time but not the stuff of a sustainable diet. Now, I like fried foods as much as the next guy, but on a daily basis I try to eliminate excess fat from my diet. One of my favorite strategies to achieve this is to "bake fry" chiles rellenos in the oven. Another is to replace part of the cheese with beans, which has the added advantage of boosting fiber and reducing fat. There's a third benefit: Bake-fried Chiles Rellenos taste cleaner than the traditional version—the bright flavors of cumin and cilantro, of walnuts and raisins are not obscured by a film of fat. **Makes 8 chiles rellenos; serves 4**

Tradition calls for roasting and peeling the peppers, a process that adds an interesting smoke flavor but also doubles the prep time. I've made this optional. If you're so inclined, here's how to do it.

Char the peppers over a hot fire on your grill, directly on the burner of your stove, or under the broiler (see Burn This on page 485). The skins should be blistered and black. Place the peppers on a cutting board and let them cool completely, then scrape off the burned skins with a knife. Charring gives the peppers a smoky flavor, which I like, and eliminates the skin, which some people find offensive (I don't).

TIME about 30 minutes preparation time, plus about 30 minutes cooking time

4 large poblano peppers, or 8 Anaheim peppers or Hatch chiles

2½ tablespoons extra virgin olive oil

1 medium-size onion, peeled and finely chopped

½ cup coarsely chopped walnuts or whole pine nuts

¼ cup raisins or currants

1 teaspoon ground cumin

½ teaspoon freshly ground black pepper, or more to taste

¼ cup chopped fresh cilantro

1 can (about 15 ounces) pinto, black, or kidney beans, drained in a colander, rinsed, and drained again

12 ounces (3 cups) coarsely grated cheddar or Jack cheese or crumbled goat cheese or Cotija cheese

Coarse salt (kosher or sea; optional)

1 cup crumbled tortilla chips or bread crumbs (optional)

1 If you are using poblano peppers, cut each in half lengthwise and scrape out the seeds and ribs. If you are using Anaheim peppers or Hatch chiles, make a lengthwise slit in each. Using a spoon, scrape out the seeds and ribs.

2 Heat 1½ tablespoons of the olive oil in a skillet over medium heat. Add the onion, walnuts, raisins, cumin, and black pepper and cook until the onion is browned, stirring with a wooden spoon, 3 to 4 minutes. Stir in the cilantro after about 2 minutes.

3 Stir the beans into the onion mixture and cook them until fragrant, about 3 minutes. Remove the skillet from the heat and let the bean mixture cool to room temperature, then stir in 2 cups of the cheese. Taste for seasoning, adding more black pepper and/or salt, if necessary, to taste; the bean filling should be highly seasoned.

4 Spoon the bean filling into the peppers or chiles and arrange them in a 9-by-13-inch baking dish. Sprinkle the remaining 1 cup of cheese on top. If you are using tortilla chips or bread crumbs, sprinkle them on top. Drizzle the remaining 1 tablespoon of olive oil over everything. The stuffed peppers can be prepared to this stage up to a day ahead and refrigerated, covered.

5 When ready to cook, preheat the oven to 400°F.

6 Bake the stuffed peppers or chiles until they are browned on top, the sides have softened, and the cheese is melted and bubbling, about 20 minutes.

TOFU STIR-FRY
WITH GINGER AND CHILES

A tofu recipe in a cookbook for men? From the author of eight books celebrating meats from around Planet Barbecue? Well, as it turns out, most of the men in my family and many of my male friends eat tofu—and like it. Not every day, but from time to time, especially on a Meatless Monday (read about these on page 470). We're in good company: Prominent guy vegetarians include Ben Stiller, Mike Tyson, and the Red Hot Chili Peppers vocalist Anthony Kiedis. I can understand if you want to skip over this recipe. But if you're willing to try it, you will be richly rewarded with skull-rattling doses of ginger and jalapeño peppers. For more about stir-frying, see page 9. **Serves 2 or 3**

12 to 14 ounces extra firm tofu or prebaked tofu (see Shop)

2 teaspoons cornstarch

3 tablespoons rice wine, sake, or dry sherry

2 tablespoons soy sauce, or to taste

2 tablespoons oyster sauce (optional)

1 tablespoon sugar

1 teaspoon freshly ground black pepper

2 tablespoons canola oil or another vegetable oil

1 piece (2 inches) fresh ginger, peeled and cut on the diagonal into ¼-inch-thick slices

2 cloves garlic, peeled and minced

4 scallions, both white and green parts, trimmed and cut crosswise into 1-inch pieces

1 to 2 jalapeño peppers, thinly sliced crosswise

¼ cup chopped fresh cilantro (optional)

Boiled white or brown rice (see page 488), for serving

1 Cut the tofu into pieces that are 1 by 1 by ½ inches. Set the tofu aside.

2 Place the cornstarch in a small bowl and stir in 1 tablespoon of the rice wine to make a paste. Stir in the remaining 2 tablespoons

SHOP One-stop shopping here: All the ingredients can be found at your local natural foods store or supermarket. Look for extra firm tofu: Good brands include Nasoya and Trader Joe's. Oyster sauce is a thick, dark brown condiment with a briny, oystery tang. Good brands include Lee Kum Kee and Wok Mei. If you omit the oyster sauce, you may want to add more soy sauce.

GEAR Your basic kitchen gear and a wok if you have one (see page 439). This is a good occasion to buy a wok if you don't; a large (10- to 12-inch) skillet will work in a pinch.

WHAT ELSE For even firmer tofu, buy a prebaked brand like Wildwood, Small Planet, or WestSoy. They're so substantial, you can actually sink your teeth into them.

TIME about 20 minutes preparation time, plus about 10 minutes cooking time

of rice wine and the soy sauce, and oyster sauce, if using, sugar, and black pepper. Set the sauce aside.

3 Just before serving, heat a wok or large skillet over high heat. Swirl in the oil and heat until shimmering, 30 seconds to 1 minute. Add the ginger, garlic, scallions, and jalapeño(s) and stir-fry until fragrant but not brown, about 15 seconds. Add the tofu and stir-fry until lightly browned, about 2 minutes.

4 Stir the sauce again with a fork to recombine and add it to the wok. Continue stir-frying the tofu until the sauce has boiled and thickened, about 1 minute. During the last 30 seconds of cooking, stir in the cilantro, if using. Serve with white or brown rice.

MUSHROOM HASH

SHOP The days when you had to wander the woods to get exotic mushrooms are long gone. Natural foods stores and conventional supermarkets sell a wide variety of mushrooms in the produce section. Select whatever looks freshest.

GEAR Your basic kitchen gear including a large (10- to 12-inch) skillet

Maybe you're one of those fearless dudes who forages for wild mushrooms, confident in the knowledge that you can tell your *Volvarviella volvacea* (straw mushroom, deliciously edible) from your *Amanita phalloides* (death cap, decidedly toxic). Maybe you're drawn to the exotic mushrooms in the produce section because they look so darned cool: honeycombed morels; curvaceous cèpes; feathery hen of the woods; dark and smoky black trumpets. Maybe you just like the way exotic mushrooms taste—always earthy and musky, with wine, pepper, herbaceous, even cheesy overtones, depending on the variety. Whatever your reasons, here's an infinitely customizable, foolproof way to cook any fungi: mushroom hash.

I give you a lot of leeway here. Depending on the mushroom or your taste, you can leave it whole, thinly slice it, or chop it. Cook it in butter, olive oil, or bacon or duck fat (but not on Meatless Monday!). Flavor it with parsley, basil, rosemary, or other fresh herbs. Flambé it with brandy or whiskey. You could even sauté it Mexican style with chiles and cilantro. **Serves 2 as a light main course (top it with fried or poached eggs), or 4 as a side dish**

1 pound mushrooms, wild, exotic, or conventional (see below)

2 tablespoons butter, extra virgin olive oil, or bacon fat

3 to 4 shallots, peeled and finely chopped, or 6 scallions, trimmed, both white and green parts finely chopped, or 1 medium-size onion, peeled and finely chopped (¾ to 1 cup)

1 clove garlic (optional), peeled and minced

¼ cup chopped fresh flat-leaf parsley, or 2 tablespoons chopped fresh basil, sage, and/or rosemary

2 tablespoons Cognac, Armagnac, whiskey, dry sherry, or Madeira

Coarse salt (kosher or sea) and freshly ground black pepper

1 Trim the mushrooms, cutting off and discarding any sandy stem ends. Wipe the mushrooms clean with a damp paper towel. Depending on the mushrooms and your mood, leave them whole, cut them into bite-size pieces, thinly slice them, or coarsely chop them; just be sure the mushrooms or pieces are all approximately the same size.

2 Melt the butter or heat the olive oil in a large skillet over medium heat. Add the shallots, scallions, or onion and garlic and cook until just lightly browned, about 3 minutes, stirring often.

3 Stir in the mushrooms and herbs and increase the heat to high. Cook, stirring, until the mushrooms are cooked down and the juices have evaporated, about 3 minutes.

4 Add the Cognac and let the mixture boil until most of the Cognac has evaporated, about 2 minutes.

5 Season the mushrooms with salt and pepper to taste; the mushroom hash should be highly seasoned.

WHAT ELSE Mushrooms are essentially giant sponges, so the worst way to clean them is to immerse them in a bowl of cold water, as you would do with other vegetables. Instead, trim off the sandy end of the stem and wipe the outside of the mushroom clean with a damp paper towel. (Speaking of mushroom stems, most are edible, but shiitake stems are tough; save them for stock.) The one exception is morels, which are firm, dense, and hollow. Soak morels in lightly salted water to dislodge any bugs, then shake them dry and slice them.

TIME about 20 minutes

Mushroom Quick Take

Mushrooms come in three categories. Each variety has a unique flavor and texture, but mushrooms also taste excellent mixed. Here are your options.

Truly wild mushrooms: Found only growing wild in the woods, this category includes cèpes, chanterelles, morels, hen of the woods, and black trumpets.

Cultivated exotic mushrooms: Shiitakes, oyster mushrooms, and enotakis (also called enokis) are cultivated but have some of the bold musky flavor of wild mushrooms.

Cultivated common mushrooms: Think of the mild-tasting farmed white button mushroom most of us grew up with; its cousins now include the brown cremini and large-capped portobello.

CHOP, MINCE & SLICE

Throughout these pages—and those of any cookbook—you'll be asked to chop, dice, cube, mince, slice, and puree ingredients. Here's what the terms mean and how to do it.

CHOP To cut ingredients into small pieces. To chop onions and other round vegetables, follow the step-by-steps on the facing page.

For carrots, leeks, and other long vegetables, make a series of lengthwise cuts, followed by a series of crosswise cuts. Chop the vegetable as finely as you like using a forward cutting motion with a chef's knife.

To chop vegetables in a food processor, place 1-inch chunks in the processor bowl fitted with a steel chopping blade. Run the machine in short bursts until the pieces are the desired size. Don't overprocess or you'll turn wet vegetables, like onions, into mush.

FINELY CHOP Chop as described above, cutting the ingredients into smaller pieces.

MINCE To chop into the finest imaginable particles. Using a chef's knife, coarsely chop the ingredient, then cut it into the smallest possible pieces, rocking the knife blade up and down in one direction, then at a right angle to the first set of cuts.

DICE Similar to chopping, but cut the pieces into ¼-inch cubes. The pieces should have square sides like miniature dice.

CUBE Similar to dicing, but you cut the pieces ½ inch square.

For long vegetables like carrots, peel, trim, and slice lengthwise into strips.

Gather the strips together and cut them crosswise into the right size pieces called for in the recipe.

SLICE To cut an ingredient into rounds or strips that are ⅛ to ¼ inch thick.

PUREE To reduce ingredients to a smooth paste or liquid in a blender or food processor fitted with the metal blade (cut the ingredients into 1-inch pieces first).

How to Chop Onions and Other Round Vegetables

1 Cut the onion in half lengthwise (from tip to furry root end).

2 Peel off the onion skin. Place a half onion cut side down on the cutting board.

3 Holding the knife blade upright, make a series of downward parallel lengthwise cuts ¼ inch apart from the tip of the onion to the root end.

4 Holding the blade parallel to the cutting board, make a second series of horizontal parallel cuts from the tip to the root end.

5 Holding the blade vertically again, make a series of crosswise parallel cuts from the tip to the root end.

6 Once chopped, the onion will break into ¼-inch pieces. Save the root end for stock (page 549).

◄ No surprise: Chopping onions can cause your eyes to water. Hold a piece of bread between your teeth to absorb the fumes. Or man up: no pain, no gain.

SWEET AND SMOKY BAKED BEANS

SHOP In the interest of speed, I call for canned beans here—ideally an organic low-sodium brand, like Eden. Smoked sausage options include andouille (Cajun sausage) or kielbasa (Polish sausage). For a homemade barbecue sauce, try the Dark and Stormy Barbecue Sauce on page 537. For a store-bought barbecue sauce, I'm partial to my Best of Barbecue Lemon Brown Sugar or Chipotle Molasses Barbecue Sauce (available at barbecuebible.com) or a classic like KC Masterpiece.

GEAR Your basic kitchen gear including a colander and a large heavy pot or Dutch oven with a tight-fitting lid

WHAT ELSE This book isn't written for barbecue fanatics, but if you happen to be one, cook the beans in a smoker or grill fueled with charcoal and wood chips. Likewise, your beans will be greatly improved by the addition of smoked brisket, ribs, or pork shoulder trimmings if you have them.

TIME about ½ hour preparation time, plus about 2 hours cooking time

I have in my archives a photo snapped in a Maine logging camp at the turn of the last century. It shows a man with a shovel and a large cast-iron kettle standing next to what looks like the entrance to a mineshaft. The objective of his labors? Baked beans. If baked beans are a fixture at any barbecue or cookout today, in nineteenth-century New England, they were a culinary fetish. Blacksmiths forged massive bean pots that lumberjacks would fill with salt pork, beans, and molasses to be cooked, clambake style, in a wood-fire-heated underground pit for durations of up to seventy-two hours. Now *those* were baked beans—guy food at its rib-sticking best, designed to fuel the high-calorie hunger of men who felled forests in Maine, New Hampshire, and Quebec. Fortunately, you don't need to go to such extremes to produce awesome baked beans today. Just follow these four simple steps:

- Use a variety of beans: navy, pinto, red, black. Each brings its own unique flavor—together they add up to more than the sum of their parts.
- It's not just about molasses and mustard. Smoke is the animus of world-class baked beans. Add it in the form of bacon, smoked sausage, and/or brisket or rib trimmings, not to mention barbecue sauce and liquid smoke. Vegetarians can flavor a batch of meatless baked beans with Soyrizo (a chorizo substitute) or a smoked tofu sausage such as Smart Sausages.
- Make the beans sweet, but not *too* sweet, using mustard to offset the sugar.
- Don't sweat the cooking time. However good baked beans may taste the first day, they'll taste equally awesome rewarmed the next.

Serves 8 to 10

5 cans (about 15 ounces each) beans, ideally including navy beans, kidney beans, and black beans

8 ounces bacon, cut into $\frac{1}{4}$-inch slivers

8 ounces andouille, kielbasa, or other smoked sausage, cut crosswise into $\frac{1}{4}$-inch slices

1 large onion, peeled and finely chopped

1 red or yellow bell pepper, stemmed, seeded, and finely chopped

1 poblano pepper or green bell pepper, stemmed, seeded, and finely chopped

2 cloves garlic, peeled and minced

1 cup of your favorite sweet barbecue sauce, or more to taste (see Shop)

1 cup packed dark brown sugar, or more to taste

$\frac{1}{3}$ cup Dijon mustard, or more to taste

1 teaspoon liquid smoke (optional)

1 teaspoon freshly ground black pepper

2 cups cooked chopped brisket, smoked pork, or rib trimmings (optional)

1 Preheat the oven to 300°F.

2 Place the beans in a colander and drain them under cold running water.

3 Heat a large heavy pot over medium heat. Add the bacon and sausage and cook, stirring with a wooden spoon, until some of the bacon fat renders, about 3 minutes. Stir in the onion, bell pepper, poblano, and garlic and brown well, 5 to 8 minutes, stirring often. Pour off all but 3 tablespoons of the fat.

4 Stir in the drained beans, barbecue sauce, brown sugar, mustard, liquid smoke, if using, black pepper, and brisket or meat trimmings, if using. Let come to a gentle simmer.

5 Tightly cover the pot and transfer it to the oven. Bake the beans until they are thick, brown, and richly flavored, $1\frac{1}{2}$ to 2 hours. If the beans seem too liquid, uncover the pot for the last half hour of cooking to evaporate some of the excess liquid. Taste for seasoning, adding more brown sugar and/or mustard as necessary. You shouldn't need any salt.

MARK BITTMAN

He's author of the bestselling *How to Cook Everything* series and a columnist for *The New York Times* op-ed pages and Sunday magazine. His column "The Minimalist" ran in the *Times* food section for thirteen years, shaping the cooking habits of a generation and nation. He faced down such chefs as Jean-Georges Vongerichten and Daniel Boulud in his PBS series *Bittman Takes on America's Chefs*. His name is Mark Bittman, and as he's the first one to tell you, he is *definitely* not a chef.

Bitty, as he's known to friends, started cooking in 1968; his first culinary success was a chocolate nut meringue pie. ("It took me forever to beat the whites," he recalls.) He taught himself how to cook largely by working through cookbooks. Throughout his thirty-year career as a food writer, his mission has been simple: "to get people cooking simply, comfortably, and well."

In 2007, Bittman had a diet and life-changing epiphany: "I turned fifty-seven years old and all my numbers—weight, cholesterol, blood sugar—tipped on the wrong side of normal." At the same time he was deeply impressed by a United Nations report (*Livestock's Long Shadow—Environmental Issues and Options*) about the harmful effects of industrial livestock production (it accounts for one sixth of the greenhouse gases that cause global warming). He embraced a diet that consisted of eating only nonprocessed fruits and vegetables for breakfast and lunch and pretty much anything for dinner. His lifestyle change led to a thirty-five-pound weight loss—and to his most socially conscious book, *Food Matters: A Guide to Conscious Eating*. "The diet that most Americans grew up on is unsustainable and it's getting worse," Mark says. "It's bad for you and bad for the planet." You'll find his recipe for Chile Bean Burgers on page 471.

Why should men learn how to cook?
Everyone, regardless of gender, should know how to cook—for self-sufficiency, for health, and for pleasure.

Do men and women cook differently?
I think women are a little more spontaneous.

What's your go-to dish when you're by yourself?
I open the fridge and see what I have. Cooked beans or rice. Maybe some pasta. Today, I lunched on boiled new potatoes with olive oil and sea salt.

What's your favorite seduction dish?
For some odd reason, women tend to be intimidated when I get in the kitchen.

Three dishes every guy should know how to make?

Pasta. Add some broccoli or cauliflower. If you have sausage or anchovies on hand, so much the better. Or make a simple sauce with aromatic vegetables, like diced onion, garlic, carrot, and celery, sautéed in butter or olive oil and simmered with broth or water.

Beans. They're a staple around the world. Add beef and spices, and you get chili. Dress them up with sausage, duck, and bread crumbs, and you have French cassoulet. Add broth and puree the beans with an immersion blender, and you get an amazing soup.

Every man should know how to cook food on the grill without burning it. Master a couple dishes and you can grill pretty much everything.

What are the ingredients you can't live without?

Olive oil. Garlic. Tomatoes. They're a combination made in heaven to drive you crazy.

Salt. Most guys don't add enough.

Pimentón—Spanish smoked paprika. I've been using it a lot lately.

Three tools you can't live without?

A food processor. Chopping, pureeing, mixing—there's almost nothing it can't do.

A coffee grinder. Actually, two. One for grinding coffee beans. The second for grinding spices.

My immersion blender. Nothing beats it for making vinaigrette. Combine three quarters of a cup of extra virgin olive oil, one quarter cup of vinegar, a minced shallot, a spoonful of Dijon mustard, salt and pepper, and maybe some chopped fresh tarragon in a deep bowl. Puree them with the immersion blender and your vinaigrette will never break [separate].

What are the three most important things to keep in mind if you're just starting out in the kitchen?

Eat less but eat better. I eat 65 percent less meat than I did five years ago, for example, but I pay more to eat organic meat raised on local farms. It tastes better and it's better for you.

Season with your senses and do it aggressively. Most guys undersalt. "Season to taste" means just that—until the food tastes good to you.

Learn to cook. Once you become good at it, you're really going to like it. The better you cook, the more you'll enjoy it.

What are the three most common mistakes guys make in the kitchen?

Well, first and foremost, not cooking in the first place. Knowing how to cook brings you immense personal satisfaction and assures you a much healthier diet. Every time you cook, you get a payback.

Getting stuck in a rut. Men tend to cook the same foods over and over. We tend to avoid foods we haven't previously tried, like fresh sardines (which are great grilled) or broccoli rabe. Get yourself an Indian cookbook or a Chinese cookbook. Experiment and broaden your horizons. It's very rare that a dish comes out completely inedible.

Fear of fat. Fats like olive oil, butter, and even lard are important for their lubricating qualities (oiling a pan, dressing a salad) and also for their flavor. A healthy human body needs fat.

Something unexpected you've learned that really helps you up your game in the kitchen?

Dare to use high heat. Preheat skillets. Don't be afraid to set your oven to 550°F for roasting. You need high heat for browning, which is where the flavor resides. Of course, you need to watch it.

What one food would you pick to focus on?

My first book was on fish, and I've written about it a lot. Farmed salmon has proved to be a disaster—it's become the factory-raised chicken of the sea. Wild fish goes in and out of sustainability. For many years, I avoided cod, which was overfished; it seems to be making a comeback. You're pretty safe with dark, oily fish, like sardines, mackerel, king mackerel, and bluefish. And squid, of course. Squid represents one of the world's largest biomasses.

> ▶ It's very rare that a dish comes out completely inedible.

Some parting words?

We Americans have it all backward. We eat too many animal products and hyperprocessed snack foods and junk foods. And what's worse, as the developing world prospers, more and more people will want to eat the way we do.

You don't need to go on an extreme diet, but we all should eat more unprocessed and minimally processed plant foods and fewer animal foods. I try to eat vegan during the day and anything I want after 6 p.m. Three quarters of my meals are meatless. You wind up eating healthier, feeling better, and doing good for the planet.

How to Char Eggplant

▶ There are some dishes that you're supposed to burn, foods that just don't taste right unless they're charred beyond recognition.

1 Turn the burner on to high and place the eggplant directly over the flames.

2 Char the eggplants on all sides, turning with tongs.

3 Use a metal skewer to check for doneness. It should pierce the skin and flesh easily.

4 Cut the eggplant in half lengthwise.

5 Scrape the charred eggplant flesh out of the skin with a large spoon.

6 Transfer the smoky eggplant to a bowl to make baba ghanoush or other charred eggplant dips.

BURN THIS

You probably know someone who burns everything he attempts to cook: toast the color of charcoal briquettes, burgers black and hard as hockey pucks . . . Perhaps you *are* that person. Well, if you have a heavy hand at the stove and an unhappy tendency to burn your food on the grill, take heart: There are some dishes that you're *supposed* to burn, foods that just don't taste right unless they're charred beyond recognition. Here are ten foods you can burn with impunity—and pride.

1 EGGPLANT. Burn eggplant directly over a gas or electric burner on your stove and you imbue the flesh with a haunting smoky aroma (see facing page). You can also char eggplant under the broiler, on the grill grate, or best of all, directly on the embers of a charcoal grill. The eggplant is done when the skin is coal black and smoking and the flesh is as soft as wet bread. To test for doneness insert a metal skewer into the center of the eggplant—it should penetrate easily. Puree charred eggplant with garlic, lemon juice, olive oil, and tahini (sesame paste) and you've got first-rate baba ghanoush (Middle Eastern eggplant dip). Chop the eggplant with charred tomatoes, peppers, onions, parsley, cumin, and lemon to make an awesome North African eggplant salad.

2 PEPPERS. Another food you not only can, but should, burn—again on your stovetop burner, under the broiler, on your grill, or in the embers. Burning simultaneously removes the papery skin, heightens the peppers' natural sweetness, and infuses the flesh with smoke flavor. Char peppers until they are black on all sides, then place them on a cutting board to cool. Once the peppers are cool, use a paring knife to scrape off the black skin. Cut the peppers in half and scrape out the seeds and pith and you're ready for business. To make an amazing salad, arrange the charred peppers on a platter and season them with sea salt and a drizzle of balsamic vinegar and extra virgin olive oil.

3 CORN ON THE COB. I have a fondness for grilling corn on the cob *without* the husk (see page 503). For an even smokier flavor, place the ears of corn, husk, silk, and all, directly on the hot coals. When the stars align, the corn stays on the coals just long enough to burn off the husk and silk and—and this is key—brown the kernels. It will take about eight minutes and you need to turn the ears so they brown evenly. When done, you brush off the ash and baste the corn with melted butter. You'll never taste better corn.

4 TOMATOES. South American chef and grilling high priest Francis Mallmann (read about him on page 248) invented a revolutionary technique for burn-cooking everything from animal proteins to vegetables to fruit for dessert. He heats a *chapa*, a cast-iron plate similar to a Spanish *plancha*, over a wood fire (a cast-iron skillet works just fine). He then dips cut tomatoes or other fruits in sugar and chars them on the hot metal way beyond browned but just shy of completely

(continued on the next page)

(continued from the previous page)

burnt ("the uncertain edge of burnt" is what he calls it in his visionary cookbook *Seven Fires: Grilling the Argentine Way*). Try the Burnt Tomatoes on page 507.

5 ONIONS. Think caramelized onions are sweet? Wait until you try whole onions roasted in the embers. Build a fire in your charcoal grill or fireplace. Once it has burned down to embers, nestle the onions in their skins in the coals. Shovel a few more coals on top. Roast the onions until they are charred on the outside and soft inside, about thirty minutes (insert a metal skewer to test for doneness). Transfer the onions to heatproof plates. Pry open the tops and drizzle in balsamic vinegar and butter. Wow!

6 POTATOES. For millennia, people have roasted tubers, like potatoes and yams, in the ashes of their campfires or fireplaces. You bury them in the ashes, covering them with glowing cinders above and below. As the skin chars, it smokes the flesh from the outside in. The slow roasting (about one hour) imparts a soft, almost creamy texture thanks to the radiant heat of the coals.

7 SWEET POTATOES. Place sweet potatoes on top of the embers in a lit charcoal grill, grill them using the direct method, or broil them until the skins are black all over and the sweet potatoes are soft. Turn the sweet potatoes with tongs as needed as they cook. (If you are broiling the sweet potatoes, place the broiler pan 2 to 3 inches below the heat source.) Use a slender skewer to test for doneness. It will take 3 to 6 minutes per side, 12 to 24 minutes in all. Cut the sweet potatoes in half lengthwise and top them with butter and honey or maple syrup.

8 FISH. The first time chef Paul Prudhomme superheated a cast-iron skillet to cook spice-crusted redfish on national television, the eye-stinging smoke damn near got him banned from the airwaves. Today pan-blackening is old hat—used for everything from shrimp to lobster to chicken breasts. But few people take the time to do it properly, which means coating the fish with melted butter, crusting it with blackening spices, and cooking it in a screaming hot ungreased skillet. This may be best done outside on the grill on account of the smoke. You'll find my recipe for Blackened Salmon on page 380.

9 STEAK. Burning your food to redeem it? It sounds something like fifteenth-century Spain's zealous grand inquisitor Torquemada, and it isn't strictly limited to vegetables. One of the most popular dishes on *Primal Grill* (my TV show) and at Barbecue University is my "caveman T-bone," roasted directly on the embers of a lump charcoal fire—no grill grate needed. The coals char the surface of the steak producing a smoky crust you just can't achieve by conventional grilling. See the Dirty Steaks on page 233.

10 MARSHMALLOWS. Everyone has a favorite technique for roasting marshmallows over a campfire. Mine is to set them on fire, rotating the stick to blacken all sides. Blow out the fire and slap the immolated marshmallows on slabs of bittersweet chocolate and then between chocolate chip cookies. Now *that's* a s'more you'll want some more of.

RICE PILAF

Whether you're a guy struggling to eat on a student budget or an accomplished cook with a large 401(k), you'll probably eat lots of rice. It's a satisfying starch, with a world of varieties to choose from: The short list includes nutty basmati from India (or Texmati from Texas—an American hybrid), fragrant jasmine rice from Thailand, starchy Arborio from Italy (used for making risotto), and cool-looking Asian black rice (also called "forbidden rice"). Each has its own unique texture and flavor. I'm a big partisan of brown rice, which has a rich, malty flavor in addition to considerable health benefits. Whichever rice you choose, there's a simple preparation guaranteed to maximize the flavor while minimizing your time at the stove—pilaf. Basic operating procedure in a nutshell: You panfry the rice with aromatic vegetables, then bake it with stock in the oven. The flavor beats boiled rice hollow. **Serves 4**

SHOP Pilaf works best made with a long-grain rice, like basmati, Texmati, or jasmine, but you can certainly use short-grain rice—just rinse it well in cold water and drain it well before cooking. Short-grain rice may require you to add more liquid as it cooks.

GEAR Your basic kitchen gear including a large (10- to 12-inch) heavy or cast-iron skillet with a tight-fitting lid and an ovenproof handle

WHAT ELSE What follows is a blueprint for rice pilaf that you can customize by adding or varying the vegetables, dried fruits, or nuts. Mushrooms and walnuts make for a great pilaf. So do dried apricots, prunes, and pistachios.

You can also cook the pilaf on the stove. Once you have added the stock and it has come to a boil, turn the heat down as low as possible and let the rice simmer gently until all of the liquid has been absorbed, about 20 minutes.

TIME about 10 minutes preparation time, plus about 20 minutes cooking time

3 tablespoons butter, extra virgin olive oil, or a mixture of the two

1 medium-size onion, peeled and finely chopped

1 rib celery, finely chopped

1 red or green bell pepper or poblano pepper (optional), stemmed, seeded, and cut into ¼-inch dice

½ cup whole or coarsely chopped walnuts, pecans, pine nuts, almonds, or pistachios (optional)

1 cup thinly sliced cleaned, trimmed mushrooms (optional)

½ cup raisins, currants, dried cranberries, diced dried apricots, and/or prunes (optional)

1½ cups long-grain rice

3 to 4 cups chicken or vegetable stock (preferably homemade, page 549)

Coarse salt (kosher or sea) and freshly ground black pepper

1 Preheat the oven to 400°F.

2 Melt 2 tablespoons of the butter or heat 2 tablespoons of the olive oil in a large skillet over medium-high heat. Add the onion, celery, and bell pepper, nuts, mushrooms, and/or dried fruit, if using, and cook until the onion is lightly browned, 3 to 5 minutes.

3 Add the rice and cook until the grains are shiny, about 1 minute. Stir in 3 cups of the stock, 1 teaspoon of salt, and ½ teaspoon of black pepper and let come to a rolling boil. Do not stir the rice once the liquid has been added or it will become starchy.

4 Cover the skillet with a tight-fitting lid. Bake the pilaf until the rice is just tender, about 20 minutes. Check it after 10 minutes: If the rice starts to dry out too much, stir in up to 1 more cup of stock. If it is too soupy, uncover the skillet for the remainder of the cooking time.

5 Just before serving, fluff the rice by gently mixing it with a fork, adding the remaining 1 tablespoon of butter or olive oil and taste for seasoning, adding more salt and/or pepper as necessary; the pilaf should be highly seasoned. Serve the pilaf directly from the skillet.

Variations

Lamb pilaf: Uzbeks call this *plov* and prepare it outdoors on ingenious wood-burning field stoves. Cut 1 pound of lamb shoulder or leg into ½-inch dice and season it with salt, freshly ground black pepper, and about ½ teaspoon each of ground cumin, coriander, and cinnamon. Brown the lamb in 2 tablespoons of butter or olive oil in a large cast-iron skillet over high heat. Transfer the lamb to a platter, then follow the Rice Pilaf recipe, browning the onion and celery along with 1 clove of peeled minced garlic and ½ cup of walnuts. Add the rice and cook it until it is shiny, about 1 minute, then stir in 3 cups of stock, browned lamb, and dried fruits, if using. Bake and serve the pilaf as described in Steps 4 and 5 above.

Seafood pilaf: You could think of this seafood pilaf as a deconstructed jambalaya. Brown the onion, celery, and bell pepper, plus 1 clove of peeled minced garlic in 2 tablespoons of butter over medium-high heat. Add the rice and cook it until it is shiny, about 1 minute, then stir in 3 cups of stock, 1 diced ripe large tomato, and 1 pound of peeled deveined shrimp. (To make real jambalaya, also add ½ cup each of sautéed diced andouille sausage and Cajun tasso ham.) Bake and serve the pilaf as described in Steps 4 and 5 above.

Boiled Rice

Here's the simplest of all rice dishes: To boil rice, bring 3 cups of water, ½ teaspoon of salt, and 1 tablespoon of butter or olive oil to a rolling boil in a medium-size saucepan over high heat. Add 1½ cups of white rice and let the water return to a boil. Immediately reduce the heat to low and tightly cover the pan. Cook the rice until tender, 18 to 20 minutes. Uncover the pot and fluff the rice with a fork. Let the rice stand for about 2 minutes, uncovered, then serve. You can cook brown rice the same way, allowing 45 minutes cooking time and adding more boiling water as needed to keep the rice moist. Cook wild rice the same way; it will take 50 minutes to 1 hour, and you may need to add more boiling water to keep the rice moist. Makes enough to serve 4.

QUINOA PILAF

T alk about a modern success story. Twenty years ago, only foodistas knew about quinoa. Today this ancient Andean grain turns up in everything from breakfast cereal to salads to dessert. It's about time: Quinoa (pronounced keen-wah) contains more calcium than milk, twice as much protein as a cup of rice, and three times the phosphorus found in a banana. It also has a fine, earthy, nutty flavor reminiscent of wild rice and a softly crunchy, gooey texture that inspires some to call it vegetarian caviar. It grows in poor soil at high altitudes and has a natural coating that reduces the need for pesticides. It may be a part of your diet already, but if it isn't, it should be. **Makes about 3 cups; serves 4 as a side dish, 2 as a light main course**

SHOP Quinoa is widely available in natural foods stores and supermarkets—one good brand is Ancient Harvest. There are also red and black quinoas, which are even more aromatic than the regular.

GEAR Your basic kitchen gear including a large (10- to 12-inch) skillet

WHAT ELSE The basic pilaf preparation here works for many grains, including rice, millet, kamut, and farro, and grainlike pastas like couscous. Adjust the cooking time according to the size of the grain, allowing 30 to 40 minutes for larger grains such as kamut and farro.

TIME about 10 minutes preparation time, plus about 20 minutes cooking time

---

1 tablespoon extra virgin olive oil or butter

1 small onion or 2 shallots, peeled and finely chopped

3 tablespoons pine nuts or chopped walnuts or pecans

1 cup quinoa

2 cups chicken or vegetable stock (preferably homemade, page 549) or water, or more as needed

3 tablespoons currants or raisins

Coarse salt (kosher or sea) and freshly ground black pepper

---

1 Heat the olive oil in a large skillet over medium heat. Add the onion and pine nuts and cook until lightly browned, about 3 minutes. Add the quinoa and cook until shiny, about 1 minute.

2 Increase the heat to high, stir in the stock and currants, and let the mixture come to a rapid boil. Season the quinoa with salt and pepper (start with ½ teaspoon of salt and ¼ teaspoon of pepper). Reduce the heat to

What Else Can You Do with Cooked Quinoa?

▸ Stuff it in chiles or peppers (as in the meatless Baked-Fried Chiles Rellenos on page 472).

▸ Use the quinoa to fill portobello or other mushroom caps. This works especially well with cheese-enriched quinoa. Bake the stuffed mushrooms in a 350°F oven until tender, about 20 minutes.

▸ Wrap it in drained, rinsed, bottled grape leaves for an Andean twist on dolmas (stuffed grape leaves).

low, cover the skillet, and let the quinoa simmer gently until the grains are soft and all of the liquid is absorbed, about 20 minutes. Don't let the quinoa scorch (burn) on the bottom. If the liquid evaporates before the quinoa is fully cooked, add more stock or water.

3 Taste for seasoning, adding more salt and/or pepper as necessary, and stir the quinoa with a wooden spoon to fluff it up before serving.

Variations
Other Stuff You Can Add to Quinoa Pilaf

▸ Thinly sliced wild or cultivated mushrooms—cook 6 ounces of mushrooms with the onion and pine nuts as described in Step 1 on page 477.

▸ Dried cherries or cranberries—add ½ cup in addition to or in place of the currants in the pilaf.

▸ Freshly grated cheese like aged Gouda or Parmesan—stir in ¾ cup after fluffing the quinoa.

TENPENNY NAIL BAKED POTATO

SHOP Start with a proper baking potato, like an organic russet or Idaho. True bakers are large and elongated with a rough brown skin.

GEAR Your basic kitchen gear plus a vegetable brush and a stainless steel tenpenny nail (about 3 inches long)

What's the best way to bake a potato? You could just swaddle it in aluminum foil and throw it in the oven. You'd end up with an edible cooked potato, but you won't get crusty skin, the airy interior; or the hot puff of steam that rises so invitingly when you cut into a proper baked potato. No, for that you need the oven and a piece of equipment you will find at a hardware store: a tenpenny nail. The oven crisps the potato skin; the nail conducts the heat to the center of the spud, accelerating the cooking time. So here's the basic version, with a glorious bacony, cheesy loaded potato version to follow. **Serves 1; can be multiplied as desired**

For the potato

1 large baking potato (12 to 14 ounces)

1 teaspoon melted bacon fat or butter, or
   1 teaspoon extra virgin olive oil

Coarse salt (kosher or sea) and freshly
   ground black pepper

Any or all of the following for serving

Butter

Sour cream

Thinly sliced chives or scallions

Grated cheddar cheese

Crisped slivered bacon
   (no Fako-Bits, please)

WHAT ELSE I call for using the oven here, but you won't be surprised to learn that I often "bake" my potatoes on the grill. To do this, set up the grill for indirect grilling and preheat it to medium-high (about 400°F). Tossing a handful of soaked oak or hickory wood chips on the coals before you put on the potatoes adds an awesome smoke flavor. The cooking time is the same as for baking the potatoes in an oven.

TIME 40 minutes to 1 hour baking time

1 Preheat the oven to 400°F.

2 Scrub the potato all over with a vegetable brush. Rinse the potato well and blot it dry with a paper towel. Prick the potato skin 3 or 4 times with a fork. Drive a clean tenpenny nail through the potato into the center. Brush or rub the potato on all sides with the bacon fat, butter, or olive oil and season it generously with salt and pepper. Place the potato on a baking sheet or piece of aluminum foil.

3 Bake the potato until the skin is browned and crisp and the potato is cooked through, 40 minutes to 1 hour. When done the potato should feel soft when you squeeze it between your thumb and forefinger. Or use a skewer or fork to test for doneness; it should pierce the potato easily.

4 To serve, squeeze the sides of the potato between your thumb and forefinger in a few places to soften the flesh. Remove the nail (careful, it will be very hot) and, using a paring knife, make a 1-inch-deep slit along the top of the potato. Squeeze the ends of the potato to open it up. Spoon in some butter, sour cream, chives or scallions, cheddar cheese, and/or bacon slivers as desired.

The Original Mr. Potato Head

Antoine-Augustin Parmentier may not be a household name these days, but if the potato is the third most important food crop (after rice and corn), we have this eighteenth-century French pharmacist-scientist to thank. "If one tenth of the land in France were planted with potatoes," he explained to Louis XVI, "there would never be a shortage of food." To promote his claim, he posted armed guards around his potato field, which turned the previously spurned spud into a tuber deemed worthy of committing larceny for. (And people did.) He spent half a century and wrote ninety-five books and pamphlets promoting the potato—efforts which prompted Voltaire to observe that his efforts "merit the ovation of all who love mankind."

LOADED POTATOES

Bacon, cheddar cheese, scallions, and other flavorings turn a simple baked potato (aka stuffer or loaded potato) into a meal. **Makes 8 half potatoes**

4 large baking potatoes
(12 to 14 ounces each)

4 slices artisanal bacon, cut crosswise
into ¼-inch slivers

5 tablespoons butter, at room
temperature

4 tablespoons finely chopped scallions

2 cups (about 8 ounces) coarsely grated
white cheddar cheese

½ cup sour cream

Coarse salt (kosher or sea) and freshly
ground black pepper

Pimentón (smoked paprika) or sweet
paprika, for sprinkling

1 Bake the potatoes as described in Tenpenny Nail Baked Potato on page 490. Cut each potato in half lengthwise. Using a spoon, scrape out most of the potato flesh, leaving a ¼-inch-thick layer next to the potato skin; it's easier to scoop the flesh out of the potatoes when they're warm. Coarsely chop the potato flesh and place it in a mixing bowl.

2 Place the bacon slivers in a cold skillet and cook over medium heat until browned and crisp, 3 to 4 minutes. Using a fork, transfer the bacon to the bowl with the chopped potatoes, setting aside the bacon fat in the skillet for future use. Add 4 tablespoons of the butter, the scallions, and 1½ cups of the cheddar cheese to the chopped potatoes and gently stir to mix. Add the sour cream, stirring the mixture as little as possible so you keep some potato pieces to bite into. Season

the potato mixture with salt and pepper to taste; it should be highly seasoned.

3 Stuff the potato mixture back into the potato skins, dividing it evenly among them and mounding it in the center of each potato skin. Sprinkle each potato with some of the remaining cheddar cheese and top each with a thin slice of butter from the remaining 1 tablespoon and a sprinkling of *pimentón*. The stuffed potatoes can be prepared up to 24 hours ahead to this stage and refrigerated, covered.

4 When ready to serve, preheat the oven to 400°F.

5 Place the stuffed potatoes on a baking sheet. Bake the potatoes until they are browned and bubbling, about 15 minutes.

POTATO VARIETIES

Nearly five thousand different potato varieties are cultivated worldwide, but generally speaking, they fall into two broad categories—baking potatoes and boiling potatoes—each with distinct flavors and cooking properties.

BAKING POTATOES are prized for their high starch content (20 to 22 percent), which gives you the light, fluffy texture of a great baked potato. Common baking varieties include the russet and Idaho potato.

BOILING POTATOES contain less starch than baking potatoes (16 to 18 percent), which gives them a pleasantly waxy texture that's ideal for boiling and for potato salad. Common boiling potatoes include the Red Bliss and Yellow Finn.

Within these two broad families, you'll find:

RED POTATOES These have thin red to pink skins and mild-tasting white flesh; they're good for boiling, roasting, and mashing.

WHITE POTATOES Sometimes called Irish potatoes, these have thin, often speckled tan skins and white or yellow flesh and are good for boiling, mashing, sautéing, and in salads.

YUKON GOLD POTATOES Oval and with a light brown skin, yellow flesh, creamy texture, and elegant flavor, Yukon Golds manage to taste buttery even before you add butter. They're excellent cooked just about any way.

BLUE AND PURPLE POTATOES Native to the Andes mountains of Peru and today grown the world over, these striking spuds have a clean, rich flavor to match their purplish hue. Mash them, roast them, and use them in salads.

NEW POTATOES Because they are harvested before they are fully grown, these spuds have thin skins and a mild flavor. Delicately textured, new potatoes are good for boiling and in salads.

FINGERLINGS Small, thin-skinned, and elongated, fingerlings are often heritage varieties like Russian Bananas or the exquisitely creamy French *rattes*. They're awesome roasted and in salads.

BAKING POTATOES (RUSSETS)

NEW POTATOES

YUKON GOLD POTATOES

FINGERLING POTATOES

YELLOW FINN POTATOES

RED BLISS POTATOES

PURPLE POTATOES

RED-SKINNED NEW POTATOES

POTATOES

There was a time when potatoes were, well, potatoes. Today spuds come in a staggering variety: white, red, purple, yellow, blue; bakers, boilers, roasting potatoes; fingerlings, baby potatoes, new potatoes. And that's just what I can find at my neighborhood supermarket. Add in the local farmers' market, and you find the sort of connoisseurship of potatoes and other root vegetables once typical of wine. You'll find a guide to potato varieties on page 494.

WHAT POTATOES TO BUY Choose organic potatoes when possible (remember, potatoes being tubers absorb whatever farmers add to the soil). Preferably buy them in bulk from a bin where you can select the potatoes one by one. The spuds should be smooth-skinned and without sprouts, soft or wet spots, blemishes, or greenish skins (the greenish potatoes are underripe or were improperly stored).

HOW TO STORE POTATOES Keep potatoes in a cool, dark place, but not in the refrigerator. Don't store potatoes near onions, which can cause the potatoes to mold.

TO PEEL OR NOT TO PEEL I like the look, texture, and taste of potato skins (more fiber, too), so whenever possible I leave the skins on. Obviously, if you prefer your spuds peeled, do so.

HOW TO COOK POTATOES As the name suggests, baking potatoes should be roasted in a hot (400°F) oven or grilled using the indirect method. It will take forty minutes to one hour. Both methods give the starches in the potatoes a fluffy, airy consistency.

Boiling potatoes should be placed in *cold* salted water to cover by at least five inches and gradually brought to a rolling boil; the gradual heating keeps the potatoes from becoming mealy. Boil the potatoes until they are tender, that is, easy to pierce with a skewer or paring knife. Depending on the number and size of the potatoes, this will take fifteen to twenty-five minutes.

All potatoes are great roasted in a pan in a hot oven with olive oil or butter (see page 498).

MASHED POTATOES
WITH CARAMELIZED ONION

This age of high-protein diets has not been kind to rib-sticking, plate-licking starches. But when it comes to comfort food—not to mention the spot-on side dish for roast chicken or turkey, meat loaf, or steak—nothing can beat a steaming mound of buttery, creamy mashed potatoes made from scratch, especially when they're enriched with sweet caramelized onion. Follow three simple rules and you will make first-rate mashers every time: Use low-starch potatoes; start them in cold water, gradually bringing it to a boil; then mash the spuds with a potato masher, not in a food processor, which will make them gummy. **Serves 4 to 6**

SHOP You need a thin-skinned, waxy, relatively low-starch potato, like a Yukon Gold or Red Bliss, to make great mashed potatoes. Save thick-skinned, high-starch baking potatoes for the Tenpenny Nail Baked Potato on page 490.

GEAR Your basic kitchen gear including a large (10- to 12-inch) heavy skillet, a large saucepan, a colander, and a potato masher

WHAT ELSE Potato skins on or off? I like the texture of mashers with potato skins, so I don't bother with peeling.

TIME about 20 minutes

For the caramelized onion

2 tablespoons (¼ stick) butter or olive oil

1 medium-size sweet onion, like a Vidalia or Walla Walla, peeled and finely chopped

For the potatoes

2 pounds thin-skinned waxy potatoes, peeled (optional) and cut into 1-inch pieces

Coarse salt (kosher or sea)

3 tablespoons butter

½ cup milk (whole or skim, whatever you have in the refrigerator) or half-and-half

5 to 8 tablespoons heavy (whipping) cream, half-and-half, or more milk

Freshly ground black or white pepper

1 Caramelize the onion: Melt the 2 tablespoons of butter in a large skillet over medium heat. Add the onion and cook it until it is dark golden brown, stirring it often with a wooden spoon, lowering the heat as the onion browns. The total cooking time will be 8 to 15 minutes, but you have to take it slow or the onion will burn. Set the caramelized onion aside.

2 Prepare the potatoes: Place the potatoes and 2 teaspoons of salt in a large saucepan. Add cold water to cover by 5 inches. Let the potatoes come to a boil over medium-high heat and boil until soft, 15 to 20 minutes. Use a skewer or a paring knife to test for doneness; it should pierce the potatoes easily. Drain the potatoes well in a colander. Return the potatoes to the saucepan and cook them for 1 to 2 minutes over medium heat to evaporate any excess liquid, stirring often to ensure that the potatoes don't scorch (burn).

3 Using a potato masher, mash the potatoes. Gradually mash in the butter. Mash in the milk or half-and-half and the cream, starting with 5 tablespoons. I've given you a range for the cream here but obviously, the more you add, the richer your mashers will taste. Stir in the caramelized onion and season the potatoes with salt and pepper to taste. Low-carb diet be damned.

Variation
Horseradish and Prosciutto Mashed Potatoes

Prepare the Mashed Potatoes with Caramelized Onion as described on page 497, substituting 3 ounces of thinly slivered prosciutto or speck (smoked prosciutto) for the onion. Brown the prosciutto in a skillet over medium heat in 2 tablespoons (¼ stick) of butter until crisp, 2 to 4 minutes. Stir the crisped prosciutto into the mashed potatoes along with 2 tablespoons of freshly grated horseradish or prepared horseradish or to taste.

GARLIC ROASTED POTATOES

A perennial hit at Barbecue University, where we smoke-roast the spuds on the grill. A staple at my home, where we make some variation of these crusty, buttery, garlicky roasted potatoes once a week. Once you grasp the principle, no roasted vegetable is beyond your reach, indoors or out. Starting on the facing page, you'll find suggestions for more roasted vegetable combinations. **Serves 4**

1½ pounds fingerling potatoes, full-size potatoes, like Yukon Golds, or baby sweet potatoes, or a combination of the two

1 head garlic (2 heads if you really like garlic)

2 tablespoons extra virgin olive oil, or 2 tablespoons melted butter, duck fat, or bacon fat, or a mixture of any or all of these

Coarse salt (kosher or sea) and freshly ground black pepper

1 Preheat the oven to 400°F. Or, set up the grill for indirect grilling and preheat it to medium-high.

2 Scrub the potatoes well and blot them dry (they must be dry so they roast, not steam). There's no need to peel the potatoes. If you are using fingerlings or baby sweet potatoes, place them whole in a single layer in a roasting pan. If you are using larger potatoes, cut them into 1-inch chunks first. Break the garlic head into individual cloves, taking care not to split the skins, add them to the roasting pan, and stir to mix. Drizzle the olive oil or other fat over the potatoes and garlic and season them generously with salt and pepper.

3 *If you are baking the potatoes,* place the roasting pan in the oven and roast the potatoes until they are browned and tender and the garlic is soft, 40 minutes to 1 hour, stirring from time to time so they roast evenly. When done the potatoes will be easily pierced by a skewer or fork. Serve with the garlic cloves (nibble the soft, creamy roasted garlic out of the skins).

If you are grilling the potatoes, place the roasting pan in the center of the grill grate, away from the heat, and cover the grill. For a smoke flavor, toss the soaked wood chips on the coals or, if using a gas grill, place them in the smoker box. Grill the potatoes until they are browned and tender and the garlic is soft, 40 minutes to 1 hour, stirring from time to time so they roast evenly. When done the potatoes will be easily pierced by a skewer or fork. Serve as above.

SHOP Fingerling potatoes are miniature but mature spuds about the size of your thumb. Popular varieties include the Russian Banana, purple Peruvian, and the amazingly creamy French *ratte*. Buy organic potatoes when possible, ideally from a local farm or farmers' market.

GEAR Your basic kitchen gear including a roasting pan, or if you are grilling, a disposable foil pan, large enough to hold the potatoes in a single layer; if grilling, 1½ cups hardwood chips (optional), soaked in water to cover for 30 minutes, then drained

WHAT ELSE For great garlic-roasted potatoes, cook them in a hot oven. For unforgettable roasted spuds, smoke-roast them on the grill.

TIME about 15 minutes preparation time, plus 40 minutes to 1 hour cooking time

Three Variations on Roasted Vegetables

Roasted beets with shallots and walnuts: Any kind of beet is delectable prepared this way—especially baby beets or a colorful variety, like yellow, red, and candy-stripe beets (save the beet greens for boiling with ham hocks). Arrange 1½ pounds of fresh beets (if you are using large beets, cut them in half or quarters) and 2 unpeeled shallots cut in half in a single layer in a roasting pan. Drizzle 2 tablespoons of olive oil or other fat over the beets and season them with salt and pepper to taste. Bake or grill the beets as described in the Garlic Roasted Potatoes above, adding ½ cup shelled walnuts halfway through the cooking (after about 20 minutes). Serves 4.

Roasted carrots with ginger and scallions: I like to roast carrots and scallions whole; this looks cool but requires carrots that are more or less the same size. But, you can certainly cut the carrots into 2-inch pieces if you prefer. Arrange 1½ pounds trimmed carrots side by side in a roasting pan just large enough to hold them in a single layer, placing a whole scallion between the carrots.

Top the carrots and scallions with ¼-inch-thick slices of ginger, cut from a peeled 2-inch piece. Drizzle 2 tablespoons of Asian (dark) sesame oil or melted butter over all and season with salt and pepper to taste. Bake or grill the carrots and scallions as described in the

Garlic Roasted Potatoes on page 498, periodically turning the carrots and scallions in the pan so they cook evenly. Serves 4.

Roasted brussels sprouts with bacon: You don't think you like brussels sprouts? You haven't tried them roasted with bacon. Extra points if you use baby brussels sprouts from Holland (available between Thanksgiving and New Year's).

Trim the stem ends off 1½ pounds of brussels sprouts and remove any yellowed or blemished leaves. Place the brussels sprouts, 2 slices of bacon cut crosswise into ½-inch pieces, and 1 tablespoon of butter cut into small pieces or 1 tablespoon of extra virgin olive oil in a roasting pan. Season the brussels sprouts with salt and pepper to taste and toss to mix. Bake or grill them as described in the Garlic Roasted Potatoes on page 498 until they are tender and the bacon is crisp, about 40 minutes, stirring occasionally. Serves 4.

CAULIFLOWER "STEAKS" SICILIAN STYLE
(WITH CAPERS, CURRANTS, AND PINE NUTS)

SHOP If you're feeling adventurous, try one of the new colored cauliflower varieties. Currants are tiny raisins but commonplace raisins will work. Capers are the pickled buds of a Mediterranean shrub; think of them as tart, salty mini flavor bombs.

GEAR Your basic kitchen gear including a roasting pan

For decades cauliflower played pale wallflower to the more colorful members of the *Brassicaceae* family (broccoli, brussels sprouts, and collard greens). Suddenly it's turning up in fifty shades of orange, purple, and green, and chefs can't serve enough of it. The following "steaks" harness cauliflower's moistly firm texture and ability to absorb complementary flavors—in this case, a sweet-salty mix of currants, pine nuts, and capers popular in Sicily—without sacrificing the cauliflower's flavor, which is somewhere between the musty tang of a cabbage and the earthiness of a potato. **Serves 4 as a side dish**

1 large head cauliflower (1½ to 2 pounds)

3 tablespoons extra virgin olive oil, or
   3 tablespoons butter, melted

Coarse salt (kosher or sea) and freshly
   ground black pepper

3 tablespoons drained capers

3 tablespoons currants or raisins

3 tablespoons pine nuts

1 Preheat the oven to 400°F.

2 Trim the stem and any lower green leaves off the cauliflower. Using a chef's knife and cutting from top to bottom, cut the cauliflower into slices that are ½ inch thick. You'll have a few broken pieces; roast these with the cauliflower steaks. Brush the cauliflower slices on both sides with 1½ tablespoons of the olive oil or butter and season them generously with salt and pepper. Arrange the slices so they are slightly overlapping, like shingles, in a roasting pan just large enough to hold them. Sprinkle the capers, currants, pine nuts, and remaining 1½ tablespoons of olive oil or butter on top.

3 Bake the cauliflower until browned and tender (easily pierced with a skewer), 30 to 40 minutes. Serve the cauliflower steaks topped with the capers, currants, and pine nuts.

WHAT ELSE Cauliflower "steaks" can also be cooked on the grill. Set it up for indirect grilling and place the roasting pan in the center of the grill grate away from the heat. To add a smoke flavor, toss a handful of soaked hardwood chips on the coals or place them in the smoker box of a gas grill. Cover the grill and cook the cauliflower until browned and tender, 30 to 40 minutes.

TIME about 10 minutes preparation time, plus 30 to 40 minutes cooking time

Brazilian Steak House

COLLARD GREENS

Americans aren't the only people who like cooked greens with their steak. At Brazilian *churrascos* (barbecues) and *churrascarias* (steak houses) you'll find *couve a mineira*, collard greens sliced paper-thin and panfried with onion, garlic, and fragrant Portuguese olive oil. These quickly cooked collard greens make a nice change of pace from both the usual steak house creamed spinach and the tasty but boiled to death collard greens served at barbecue joints. **Serves 4**

SHOP Buy organic collards when possible.

GEAR Your basic kitchen gear including a large (10- to 12-inch) heavy skillet

WHAT ELSE The secret to slicing collards paper-thin is to stack and roll them into a tight cigarlike tube, then shave it crosswise using a chef's knife.

TIME about 15 minutes

1 pound collard greens (1 large bunch)

3 tablespoons extra virgin olive oil, preferably Portuguese

2 cloves garlic, peeled and gently flattened with the side of a knife

3 tablespoons minced peeled onion

Coarse salt (kosher or sea) and freshly ground black pepper

1 Rinse the collard greens and shake them dry. Place a leaf on a cutting board and, starting at the bottom of the leaf, make a V-shape cut to remove the stem. Repeat with the remaining collard green leaves. Place the collard leaves one on top of the other. Starting at one side of a leaf, roll them into a tight tube about the size of a cigar. Cut the tube crosswise into paper-thin slices and place them in a large mixing bowl. When all of the collard greens are sliced, fluff them with your fingers to separate them into individual strands. Sprinkle the collards with 3 tablespoons of cold water.

2 Heat the olive oil in a large heavy skillet over medium-high heat. Add the garlic and onion and cook until fragrant and golden, about 1 minute. Add the collard greens and season them with salt and pepper to taste. Cook the collard greens until they start to wilt, 3 to 5 minutes, turning them with tongs so they cook evenly. Do not overcook; the collards should remain bright green. If the greens start to scorch (burn) before they're tender add a few more tablespoons of water. Before serving, taste for seasoning, adding more salt and/or pepper as necessary.

CRISPY KALE

SHOP Kale comes in many varieties you can cook this way, but I prefer the dark green, intensely flavorful Tuscan kale, also known as lacinato kale, black kale, or dinosaur kale. Its leaves are rounder and smoother than commonplace curly kale.

When asked to pick an ingredient he absolutely can't live without, Chicago mega chef Paul Kahan (he of Blackbird, avec, and The Publican fame) named Tuscan kale. He grows it in his garden and hails it as nothing less than a "super food"—packed with some of the highest levels in the vegetable kingdom of carotenes (good for your eyes), calcium, B vitamins, and cancer-fighting antioxidants—more of all those good compounds than in broccoli. And that's *before* you consider its rich, earthy, minerally taste. Kale possesses one other genial property: It crisps like a potato chip when you bake or grill it. **Serves 4 as a snack, 2 as a side dish**

1 bunch Tuscan kale (12 to 16 ounces)

2 tablespoons Asian (dark) sesame oil or extra virgin olive oil

2 tablespoons tamari or soy sauce

2 tablespoons sesame seeds (optional)

GEAR Your basic kitchen gear including a baking sheet, plus a salad spinner (optional)

WHAT ELSE Not surprisingly, I like to cook kale on the grill, but it also crisps well in the oven.

TIME about 30 minutes

1 Preheat the oven to 350°F.

2 Rinse the kale and shake it dry or spin it dry in a salad spinner. Place a leaf on a cutting board and, starting at the bottom, make an elongated V-shape cut to remove the thick part of the stem (you can leave the thin stem at the top intact). Repeat with the remaining kale leaves. Spin the leaves dry in a salad spinner or blot dry with paper towels, then tear them into 2-inch pieces and place them in a large mixing bowl.

3 Pour the sesame oil and tamari over the kale and toss to coat well. Toss in the sesame seeds, if using. Arrange the kale in a single layer on a baking sheet. Bake the kale until browned and crisp, about 20 minutes.

4 Transfer the baked kale to a platter and serve. Eat the kale with your fingers. It's messy—it's supposed to be, so provide napkins.

GRILLED OR BROILED CORN

When I was growing up, everyone cooked corn by boiling. When you grill or broil corn, the high dry heat caramelizes the plant sugars, adding rich overtones of toffee and wood smoke. But this alchemy works only with the husk off, when the kernels face the fire directly. **Makes 4 ears of corn, serves 2 to 4**

4 ears sweet corn

4 tablespoons (½ stick) salted butter, melted, or 4 tablespoons extra virgin olive oil

Coarse salt (kosher or sea) and freshly ground black pepper

SHOP Corn used to be the most evanescent of summer pleasures—great only the day it was harvested—preferably from a farm within an hour's drive. Thanks to new super sweet varieties, like "Precocious" and "Sugar Buns," you can now find good corn all summer long. But nothing trumps same-day corn from your local farmers' market or farm stand, or if you're lucky enough to have one, your garden.

GEAR Your basic kitchen gear plus butcher's string, a basting brush, and a grill or broiler pan

WHAT ELSE Don't have a grill? Broil the corn. Or try the Boiled Corn with Smoked Paprika below.

TIME about 20 minutes

1 Cut the end opposite the stem off each ear of corn about ½ inch below the tip. Carefully strip back the husk, rotating the corn in a gesture similar to peeling a banana. Pull the husk down below the stem of the ear and tie it together with butcher's string to make a handle. Pull the corn silk off the kernels. Lightly brush the ears with some of the melted butter (too much butter and your corn will burn, imparting a sooty flavor). Season the corn with salt and pepper to taste.

2 *If you are grilling the corn,* set up the grill for direct grilling and preheat it to high. When you are ready to cook, brush and oil the grill grate. Arrange the corn on the hot grate with a piece of folded aluminum foil under the husks to keep them from burning. Grill the corn until handsomely browned on all sides, 2 to 3 minutes per side, 8 to 12 minutes in all, lightly basting the ears with a little more butter.

If you are broiling the corn, preheat the broiler to high. Arrange the corn in a broiler pan 3 inches from the broiler. Broil the corn until darkly browned on all sides, 2 to 3 minutes per side, 8 to 12 minutes in all, lightly basting the ears with a little more butter.

3 Transfer the corn to a platter, baste it with the remaining butter, and season it with salt and pepper to taste once more before serving.

Variation
Mexican Grilled Corn

Mexicans have a singular way to serve grilled corn: slathered with mayonnaise and sprinkled with grated cheese, such as *cotija* (a sharp, sourish cheese similar in taste to feta—look for it at Mexican markets or substitute Pecorino Romano or Parmigiano Reggiano). Once you have cooked the corn as described above, spread mayonnaise over it, using 1 to 2 tablespoons for each ear. Then sprinkle each ear with 3 tablespoons of freshly grated cheese and cayenne pepper or chile powder to taste. Serve the corn with lime wedges for squeezing.

BOILED CORN
WITH SMOKED PAPRIKA

Apartment-bound with no access to a grill or broiler? You can still have your corn and smoke it, too. The secret is a generous sprinkle of *pimentón* (Spanish smoked paprika). **Makes 4 ears of corn, serves 2 to 4**

Coarse salt (kosher or sea)

2 tablespoons sugar

4 ears sweet corn

4 tablespoons (½ stick) salted butter, melted, or 4 tablespoons extra virgin olive oil

1 to 2 tablespoons pimentón (smoked paprika, see page 28)

Freshly ground black pepper

SHOP Look for *pimentón* at Spanish markets and a growing number of supermarkets. Two good brands are Santo Domingo and Safinter.

GEAR Your basic kitchen gear including a large pot.

WHAT ELSE In the unlikely event you have corn left over from this or the preceding recipe, cut the kernels off the cob by placing it flat on a cutting board and making lengthwise slices with a chef's knife. Use the kernels for the corn chowder on page 144 or the corn bread on page 514.

TIME about 20 minutes

1 Bring 1 gallon of water, 1 tablespoon of salt, and 2 tablespoons sugar to a rapid boil in a large pot.

2 Meanwhile, shuck the ears of corn, pulling off the silk. Boil the corn until just tender,

4 to 6 minutes. Drain the corn and transfer it to a platter.

3 Brush the ears of corn with melted butter and sprinkle them on all sides with *pimentón*. Season the corn with salt and pepper to taste.

ROASTED TOMATOES

Roasting tomatoes works on a principle similar to dry-aging steaks (see page 227). You concentrate the flavor by evaporating some of the water. In addition, with tomatoes the gentle heat caramelizes some of the plant sugars, giving you rich umami flavors. You can serve roasted tomatoes as a side dish, on pizza or bruschetta, in pasta, or with cheese—the options are endless. **Makes 16 tomato halves**

SHOP Any tomato can be roasted this way, but I'm partial to the egg-shape plum tomatoes, sometimes called Roma tomatoes. As always when buying produce, organic, locally grown is best.

GEAR Your basic kitchen gear including a baking sheet and parchment paper or aluminum foil

8 ripe tomatoes, preferably plum tomatoes, rinsed and cut in half lengthwise

Coarse salt (kosher or sea) and freshly ground black pepper

⅓ cup extra virgin olive oil, or more as necessary

4 basil leaves, slivered, or 1 teaspoon fresh thyme leaves

ROASTING VEGETABLES

I t all started with garlic. Lots of garlic. A whole head, in fact, that you broke into cloves and placed, in their skins, in a roasting pan with whole baby potatoes. You drizzled olive oil (or melted butter or duck or bacon fat) on top and roasted the combination in a hot oven long enough to brown the spuds and transform the garlic from strong-smelling raw cloves to crusty skins filled with a mild, sweet, creamy, garlicky paste.

From there it was a short leap to roasting carrots, turnips, and/or brussels sprouts and, instead of garlic, adding other aromatics such as shallots, cipollini onions, or ginger. And, some lardoons (slivers of smokehouse bacon or pancetta).

So what began as a single killer recipe became an unbeatable method for cooking a wide range of vegetables. And, as it turns out, roasting has logistical, health, and taste benefits. You're looking at perhaps ten minutes of prep time, although the actual roasting takes longer. Unlike boiling, which washes away flavor and nutrients, roasting evaporates the water in the vegetables, thereby concentrating their flavor.

Here's what you need to know.

▸ Roasting works best for root vegetables, such as potatoes, carrots, turnips, beets, and rutabagas. It also works well for dense green vegetables, like brussels sprouts, artichokes, cauliflower, fennel bulbs, whole onions, broccolini, broccoli rabe, and broccoli pieces. Be sure the vegetables or pieces are roughly equal in size.

▸ If you are adding garlic, leave the skins on the cloves as they roast. The skins will keep the garlic from burning and becoming bitter. (To eat the roasted garlic, bite one end of a clove and squeeze the garlic paste into your mouth between your teeth.)

▸ The only way you can screw up roasting vegetables (short of burning the vegetables or forgetting to turn on the oven) is overcrowding the roasting pan. All of the vegetables should fit loosely in a single layer. If they don't, use two roasting pans.

▸ Add a fat (olive oil, butter, bacon or duck fat, whatever you like) and season them with salt, pepper, and the herbs of your choice.

▸ Roast the vegetables at a high heat (400°F) long enough to brown them well and cook them through (forty minutes to one hour). Stir the vegetables often with a wooden spoon or metal spatula so they cook and brown evenly.

Roasted vegetables taste great with meats, poultry, and seafood. Any leftovers make a terrific base for hash (you'll find the recipe on page 66).

1 Preheat the oven to 250°F. Line a baking sheet with parchment paper or aluminum foil to facilitate cleanup.

2 Arrange the tomato halves cut side up on the prepared baking sheet. Season each tomato half with salt and pepper to taste and drizzle about 1 teaspoon of olive oil over each. Place a pinch of basil slivers or thyme leaves on each tomato half.

3 Bake the tomatoes until they are lightly browned and shriveled but still pliant and moist, 3 to 4 hours. Serve the tomatoes right away or store them topped with a little olive oil in a covered container in the refrigerator; they'll keep for at least a week.

WHAT ELSE For a more extravagant way to roast tomatoes, arrange tomato halves cut side up in a baking dish just large enough to hold them. Top the tomatoes with slivered basil or thyme leaves and season them with salt and pepper, then add enough extra virgin olive oil to cover them completely. Roast for 3 to 4 hours. Let cool, and store with the oil in jars in the refrigerator. They will keep for several weeks.

TIME about 10 minutes preparation time, plus 3 to 4 hours roasting time

BURNT TOMATOES

Here's a vegetable dish for the guy who has a tendency to burn everything. It comes from South American superstar chef Francis Mallmann. Owner of several acclaimed restaurants in Argentina and Uruguay and author of one of the best books ever written on live-fire cooking, *Seven Fires: Grilling the Argentine Way*, Mallmann is a great advocate of cooking foods to within a whisper of being burned beyond recognition. This controlled charring develops rich, smoky, sophisticated, sweet-bitter caramel flavors—and it works equally well for both the proteins in meats and the natural sugars in fruits and vegetables. Consider these "burnt" tomatoes, which you char in a superheated cast-iron skillet. **Makes 8 tomato halves**

4 large ripe plum tomatoes

Extra virgin olive oil

Coarse salt (kosher or sea) and freshly ground black pepper

Slivered fresh basil or chopped oregano

You want ripe plum tomatoes—preferably when they are in season at your local farmers' market.

GEAR Your basic kitchen gear including a large (10- to 12-inch) cast-iron skillet

WHAT ELSE Once you get the hang of "burning" tomatoes, you can use the technique for a wide range of fruits and vegetables, from endive to carrots (you'll find instructions on page 485). Or try the "burnt" peaches on page 561.

TIME about 15 minutes

1 Heat a cast-iron skillet well over medium heat. This will take a good 10 minutes. To test the temperature, drip a drop of water on it; it should sizzle and evaporate in about 2 seconds.

2 Meanwhile, cut the tomatoes in half lengthwise. Brush the cut side of each tomato half with extra virgin olive oil and sprinkle it with salt.

3 Place the tomatoes cut side down in the hot skillet and cook them until charred on the cut side, 5 to 8 minutes; you'll see a thin black line of char around the edge of the tomato halves when they are done. Don't move the tomatoes before then or they'll lose their shape.

4 Using a thin-edged spatula, pry the tomato halves off the bottom of the skillet and place them cut side up on a plate. Using a paring knife, cut shallow crosshatch slits in the surface of each tomato half. Sprinkle the tomatoes with some pepper, basil or oregano, and more olive oil before serving.

Variations

Mallmann also "burns" endives and carrots. For endives, cut them in half lengthwise. Sprinkle the cut side of the endives with red wine vinegar, then dip them in sugar. Cook the endives, cut side down, in a hot skillet until darkly caramelized, 5 to 8 minutes.

For burnt carrots, peel them and cut them in half lengthwise. Brush the carrots with olive oil and season them with sea salt and fresh thyme leaves. Cook the carrots in a hot skillet, starting cut side down, until darkly caramelized, 6 to 10 minutes, turning as needed.

BREADS, BISCUITS, AND PIZZA

Man may not live by bread alone, but it's hard to imagine a fulfilling life without it. French toast and biscuits for breakfast. Sandwiches for lunch. Garlic bread and pizza for dinner. The low-carb movement has done plenty of bread bashing in recent years, yet bread will always occupy an honored place in a man's diet.

Every man should know how to make a few basic breads from scratch and turn store-bought loaves into triumphs. Happily, you don't need to spend hours in the kitchen. In the following pages you'll find biscuits that require no rolling and cutting and a beer bread that requires no kneading. You'll learn how to make a corn bread that's always moist and flavorful, thanks to the addition of bacon, jalapeño peppers, and cheddar cheese, and bruschetta the way they prepared it centuries ago in Italy. Hint—you toast the bread over a live fire and you *don't* bury it under a tomato salad. Plus there's a pizza you can make in about half an hour.

Bread alone won't make the man, but a well-made loaf sure boosts his standing.

The Original Garlic Bread
BRUSCHETTA

Long before garlic bread came in oven-baked loaves, Italians grilled bread slices over a wood fire, rubbed them with cut garlic, and topped them with olive oil and salt. They called the result bruschetta (from the verb *bruscare*, "to burn"), and no, it didn't come topped with tomato salsa like it does nowadays in so many restaurants in the U.S. Although I include an optional salsa here, I often serve the *real* bruschetta: It's a great way to get people gathered around the grill and involved in preparing the meal. **Makes 12 to 16 bruschetta slices**

1 loaf Italian bread

4 cloves garlic, cut in half lengthwise (leave the skins on; they'll keep your fingers clean)

½ cup of the most gorgeous fragrant, fresh Tuscan extra virgin olive oil money can buy, placed in a small pitcher

Coarse salt (kosher or sea) or better yet fiore di sale (fleur de sel) and freshly ground black pepper

Basil Tomato Salsa (optional; recipe follows), for serving

SHOP Tradition calls for using *pane toscano*, saltless Tuscan bread. (According to bread master Peter Reinhart, this odd bread may have originated as a way for bakers to dodge the high tax on salt.) If you live near an Italian bakery, you may be able to find it. Saltless bread is not to everyone's taste (especially not my editor's), but a good Italian or French loaf will be.

GEAR Your basic kitchen gear including a serrated knife, plus a grill

WHAT ELSE Don't have access to a grill? Toast the bread in a toaster oven or under the broiler. And if you do like your bruschetta topped with tomato salsa, follow the simple recipe on page 512.

TIME about 10 minutes

1 Build a wood fire and let it die down to embers. Or set up a charcoal or gas grill for direct grilling and heat it to medium-high. Naturally, a wood fire will give you the most fragrant results.

2 Cut the bread crosswise into slices that are ½ inch thick.

3 When ready to cook, arrange a few slices of bread on the grill grate and toast them until golden brown on both sides, 1 to 2 minutes per side. Repeat with the remaining slices of bread.

4 Hand a slice of bread on a napkin to one of your guests. Instruct him or her to rub the top with cut garlic, then drizzle olive oil over it and sprinkle it with salt and pepper. (If you use saltless Tuscan bread, dose the salt with a heavy hand.) It's important to rub the garlic on the bread when it's hot so the garlic cooks a little. Eat the bread while it's hot, too. If desired, serve the tomato salsa on top or on the side.

Variation

In Catalonia they make a similar preparation called *pa amb tomàquet* (tomato bread). Prepare the bruschetta as described, then rub the grilled bread with the cut side of a ripe tomato after the garlic.

BASIL TOMATO SALSA

OK, if you can't fight 'em, join 'em. In Italy, traditional bruschetta comes with garlic, olive oil, and salt only. In the spirit of more is more, we North Americans like to top the bread with a basil-scented fresh tomato salsa. **Makes about 1½ cups, enough for 6 to 8 slices of bruschetta**

2 luscious red ripe tomatoes

3 fresh basil leaves

2 scallions, both white and green parts, trimmed and thinly sliced crosswise

¼ cup pitted black olives (optional), diced

1 tablespoon drained capers (optional)

3 tablespoons extra virgin olive oil

1 tablespoon red wine or balsamic vinegar or fresh lemon juice

Coarse salt (kosher or sea) and freshly ground black pepper

1 Core the tomatoes then cut them into ¼-inch dice and place them in a mixing bowl with their juices.

2 Stack the basil leaves on top of each other and roll them lengthwise into a tube. Thinly slice the roll of basil leaves crosswise. Fluff the resulting threads with your fingers and add them to the tomatoes along with the scallions, olives, and capers, if using, and the olive oil and wine vinegar.

3 Just before serving, toss the salsa to mix. Season the salsa with salt and pepper to taste; it should be highly seasoned. (You can prepare the salsa several hours ahead, but don't mix it until the last minute.)

GARLIC BREAD IN THE OVEN

Here's how *not* to make garlic bread: Slather the bread with garlic butter, wrap it in aluminum foil, and bake it in the oven. Sure it comes out soft and puffy—a garlicky version of Wonder Bread. You deserve better. Like a loaf that's bubbling and browned on top—even with a smoky char at the edges—that makes a noisy crunch when you take a bite. That's why God gave you teeth. If this sounds like your vision of garlic bread paradise, here's your prayer book. **Makes 1 loaf**

8 tablespoons (1 stick) salted butter, at room temperature

2 cloves garlic, peeled and minced

2 tablespoons minced fresh flat-leaf parsley (optional)

½ cup finely freshly grated Parmigiano Reggiano cheese (optional)

1 loaf Italian bread or baguette

SHOP Tradition calls for "Italian" bread—a sort of soft-crusted oversize baguette sold in a plastic bag. Tradition sucks. Buy a loaf of real Italian bread (football-shaped and crisp-crusted) or a crusty baguette at an Italian, French, or artisanal bakery.

GEAR Your basic kitchen gear including a baking sheet, mixing bowl, and serrated knife

WHAT ELSE Not that you'd do this, but some people are tempted to use the oil-packed prechopped garlic sold in jars. The stuff is abominable and so are the results. Enough said.

TIME about 15 minutes

1 Preheat the oven to 400°F. Line a baking sheet with a piece of aluminum foil to facilitate cleanup.

2 Place the butter, garlic, and parsley and Parmigiano Reggiano, if using, in a mixing bowl and whisk to mix.

3 Using a serrated knife, cut the bread in half through the side lengthwise. Using a spatula, spread 1 tablespoon of the garlic butter on the crust of each half loaf. Spread the remaining 6 tablespoons of butter on the cut sides. Place the bread cut side up on the prepared baking sheet.

4 Bake the garlic bread until it is crusty on the outside and bubbling and browned on the cut sides, 5 to 8 minutes. Transfer the garlic bread to a cutting board, cut it crosswise into 2-inch slices, and serve.

Variation
Garlic Bread on the Grill

Want to cook your garlic bread on the grill? Hey, look who's talking—of course you do. Preheat a grill to medium. Cut the loaf of bread sharply on the diagonal into finger-thick slices. Lightly but evenly spread each slice on both sides with the garlic butter. Grill the slices of bread directly over the fire on a well-brushed, well-oiled grill grate until sizzling and browned on both sides, about 2 minutes per side. Warning: Garlic bread burns quickly. Don't leave the grill for a second.

Pepper Jack, Bacon, and Jalapeño
PB&J CORN BREAD

SHOP To up your corn bread game, buy the cornmeal at a natural foods supermarket. There you'll find stone-ground yellow and white cornmeal—often made from organic corn.

GEAR Your basic kitchen gear, including a large (10- to 12-inch) cast-iron skillet, and a mixing bowl

WHAT ELSE When fresh corn is in season, grill a few extra ears (see page 503), cut the kernels off, and add them to the batter. Respectable corn bread just got a lot better.

Buttermilk gives you a moister, tangier corn bread; milk a sweeter, more cakelike corn bread.

TIME about 15 minutes of preparation time, plus about 25 minutes baking time

I grew up in a bagel and challah sort of household, so I came relatively late to corn bread. It was not, I confess, love at first bite. I found this Southern staple gritty and dry, and I understood why the Pilgrims adopted it with such reluctance. It didn't help that corn bread—like so much American food—has gotten progressively sweeter over the years, to the point where you're not quite sure whether commercial versions are meant to be eaten for breakfast or dessert. But corn bread accompanies a great many traditional guy foods—chili, split pea soup, gumbo—so I figured I should give it another chance.

There are three secrets to great corn bread: the cornmeal itself, the milk or buttermilk, and the flavorings. The cornmeal most guys reach for is the coarse gritty yellow stuff sold in cardboard containers at the supermarket. Pleasant enough, but you'll get far superior results with small batch, stone-ground, pale yellow or white cornmeal from an artisanal gristmill in New England or the South. (My favorites include Haldeman Mills, Gray's Grist Mill, and Kenyon's Grist Mill.) Most recipes call for milk, but you'll get a more complex flavor if you use part milk

and part buttermilk, or even half-and-half and buttermilk. As for the flavorings, I went with the ingredients I use to remedy *any* dry or bland food: P (pepper Jack cheese), B (bacon), and J (jalapeños). Lesson for neophytes: When in doubt, add bacon, chiles, and cheese. I give you Raichlen's PB&J corn bread. No jelly needed. **Makes 8 wedges**

2 slices bacon, cut crosswise into ¼-inch slivers

1½ cups buttermilk or regular milk, or more as needed

2 large eggs

3 tablespoons unsalted butter, melted, or 3 tablespoons vegetable oil

1 cup yellow or white cornmeal, preferably stone-ground

1 cup unbleached all-purpose white flour

3 tablespoons brown sugar or honey

1½ teaspoons baking powder

½ teaspoon baking soda, or an additional ½ teaspoon baking powder

1 scant teaspoon table salt

2 to 4 jalapeño peppers, seeded and finely chopped

1 cup coarsely grated pepper Jack cheese (4 ounces)

1 Preheat the oven to 400°F.

2 Brown the bacon in a large cast-iron skillet over medium heat, about 3 minutes. Using a slotted spoon, transfer the bacon to a mixing bowl, leaving the bacon fat in the skillet.

3 Add the buttermilk, egg, and butter to the mixing bowl with the bacon and whisk to mix. Whisk in the cornmeal, flour, brown sugar or honey, baking powder, baking soda, salt, and jalapeños. Stir in the pepper Jack cheese. You want a pourable batter: If the mixture looks dry, add ¼ cup more buttermilk or milk. Spoon

the corn bread batter into the skillet and place it in the oven.

4 Bake the corn bread until it is puffed and browned and starts to pull away from the side of the skillet, 25 to 30 minutes. Another test for doneness is to insert a bamboo skewer or toothpick in the center of the corn bread; when done, the toothpick should come out clean.

5 Let the corn bread cool in the skillet for about 5 minutes, then cut it into 8 wedges for serving.

DROP BISCUITS

If you're lucky enough to live in the American South, breakfast without biscuits is as pitiful as a morning without coffee. And even for non-Southerners, a basket of these biscuits—crusty on the outside, buttery-soft and steamy inside—will wow your pals on a men's weekend, or endear you to your girlfriend or wife. Best of all, unlike traditional biscuit recipes, these require no rolling, folding, or cutting. **Makes 8 biscuits; serves 2 very hungry guys or 4 if served with eggs**

4 tablespoons (½ stick) unsalted butter, melted, or ¼ cup vegetable oil, plus butter or oil for greasing the baking sheet

2 large eggs

⅓ cup heavy (whipping) cream, or more as needed

Scant 1 teaspoon table salt

2 cups unbleached self-rising flour, or 2 cups unbleached all-purpose white flour plus 2 teaspoons baking powder

Honey, jam, and/or butter, for serving

1 Preheat the oven to 400°F. Lightly butter or oil a baking sheet.

2 Crack the eggs into a large mixing bowl and beat them with a fork. Beat in the cream, butter or oil, and salt. Add the flour and stir with a wooden spoon just enough to mix. Depending on the flour, you may need 1 to 3 tablespoons more cream. The dough should be moist, not dry. It's OK if it looks lumpy. Don't overmix the batter or the biscuits will be tough.

3 Using 2 large metal spoons, drop 2-inch blobs of dough onto the prepared baking sheet, spacing them about 2 inches apart.

4 Bake the biscuits until they are puffed and golden brown, 15 to 20 minutes.

5 Serve the biscuits hot out of the oven with honey, jam, and/or butter.

SHOP A staple of the South, self-rising flour can be found at most supermarkets. If it's unavailable, you can substitute two cups of unbleached all-purpose white flour plus two teaspoons of baking powder.

GEAR Your basic kitchen gear including a baking sheet and a mixing bowl

WHAT ELSE For richer biscuits use melted butter instead of vegetable oil. For truly outrageous biscuits, substitute bacon fat (you may want to pop an extra Lipitor). For healthier biscuits, replace a quarter to one-third cup of the self-rising flour with whole wheat flour. For extra flavor, fold in a cup of grated cheddar cheese and a couple of finely chopped scallions.

TIME about 10 minutes preparation time, plus about 20 minutes baking time

KEN FORKISH

To enter Ken Forkish's world you have to wake up early. Real early. By the time I arrived at Ken's Artisan Bakery in Portland, Oregon, at 2 a.m., the head baker had been working for hours. Moving at breakneck speed (he literally runs from workbench to oven), he transforms huge tubs of slow-fermented dough into hand-formed loaves one by one, letting each bread "proof" (rise) just so before slashing the top with a razor blade he grasps in his teeth when not in use. He bakes the loaves in a state-of-the-art oven from Italy to produce a crust dark and shaggy as tree bark with a soulful, fragrant, incredibly flavorful "crumb" inside. That's before the early morning shift arrives to roll out croissants and pipe pastry cream into éclairs and tart shells.

Forkish didn't always deal in *Flour Water Salt Yeast*, the title of his 2012 James Beard Award–winning cookbook. "For years I had a corporate career—suit and tie, overseas travel," he says. "But I wanted to work with my hands." So when Forkish read an article in *Smithsonian magazine* about Lionel Poilâne, France's famous artisanal baker in the 1990s, he decided to go into baking. Today, Forkish presides over a mini empire that includes Ken's Artisan Bakery, Ken's Artisan Pizza, and the Trifecta Tavern & Bakery.

Did either of your parents bake?
My mom made cakes for birthdays—that was about it.

What's the first bread you ever baked? Lessons learned?
Back in the 1980s I made an herb bread from the *Cafe Beaujolais* cookbook. That was before I saw the light. Lessons learned?
    1. Sugar does *not* belong in bread dough.
    2: It's amazing how good bread can taste *before* you put a bunch of stuff in it.

What's the most challenging bread to master?
Rye bread. By that I mean *real* rye bread, not American-style light "ryes," which typically contain only 10 to 15 percent rye flour. European-style rye breads need practiced hands and years of experience and knowledge to master. Then, even when they come out perfect, you need a clientele that knows how to appreciate them.

Who was your most important mentor and what did you learn from him?
Michel Suas of the San Francisco Baking Institute. He taught me that there are really very few secrets. The core set

of baking metrics, variables, and how to achieve desired tastes and textures in bread are thoroughly documented in books like Suas's *Advanced Bread and Pastry: A Professional Approach*, Raymond Calvel's *Le Goût du Pain* ["the taste of bread"], and hopefully, my book. A lot of guys think baking is full of secrets. Hooey.

What's the quintessential guy dish?

How about an Elvis sandwich (peanut butter, bacon, and bananas) made with toasted slices of my bacon bread?

> ▶ Learn how to bake killer bread or pizza in your home oven. It's not hard, and it's incredibly sexy.

What's your go-to bread dish when you're by yourself?

Cheese toast.

What's your favorite seduction dish?

Cheese toast with Champagne.

Three dishes every guy should know how to make or bake?

Besides cheese toast?! Steak on the grill. Burgers on the grill. Fish on the grill.

What's your proudest creation?

The 3-kilo *boule* [6-pound "round"] of *pain de compagne* [country bread] we make at Ken's Artisan Bakery. It starts with the same dough as our smaller loaves, but somehow it tastes better. This big guy—baked to a deep, dark, chestnut-colored crust—is not something I learned how to make elsewhere, so it feels like my own creation.

What's one pastry really worthy of attention and connoisseurship?

The croissant. You have to get twenty-eight things right to make a standout croissant. Screw up any one of those twenty-eight things and you wind up with an also-ran.

Three ingredients you can't live without?

Flour. Water. Salt. Yeast. Sorry, that's four, but I can't live without them.

Three tools you can't live without?

An oven. A proofing basket. And most important, the human hand.

What should you keep in mind if you're just starting out?

Learn the details and be patient enough to digest them and master them.

What are three essential techniques every guy should know how to do in the kitchen?

Learn how to handle a chef's knife: how to hold it and how to use it to slice and chop onions, fennel, carrots, and garlic. So many great dishes begin with *soffrito* [Latino chopped onions, garlic, and peppers] or *mirepoix* [French chopped onion, carrot, and celery].

Learn how to hand toss salad greens: First, get a big salad bowl—the metal ones that cost about $10 at a restaurant supply store. Then add the minimum amount of salad dressing, just what you need barely to coat the greens. Then gently toss all with your hands (metal utensils bruise the leaves). When you are done, wipe your hands on a kitchen towel, not your jeans.

Learn how to bake killer bread or pizza in your home oven. It's not hard, and it's incredibly sexy.

What are the three most common mistakes guys make when baking and cooking?

1. Forgetting that time is an ingredient, too. Don't rush it—good baking takes time.

2. Just own it and get into it. You can't half-ass good food. But you can have the ballgame on the TV while you're cooking.

3. See the last sentence in # 2.

Something unexpected you've learned over the years that really helps you up your game in the kitchen?

A lot of days, you'll work a long, hard day. Sometimes, you'll work eight really long, hard days in a row, but when you get it all done really well—and you *will* get it all done really well—you get this incredible "I'm a badass" feeling, and that makes it all worthwhile.

Parting words of advice?

If you are going to cook for yourself, for friends, or for a love partner wannabe, there's no self-respect in it unless you give it your best shot. No shortcuts. You can't dial it in. A really nice meal is the point and it's worth making the effort for.

NO-KNEAD HONEY WHOLE WHEAT BEER BREAD

SHOP Bread flour has a higher gluten content than regular all-purpose flour; either will produce a superior loaf of bread. (Gluten is the stretchy stringlike strands of protein that hold in air bubbles and give bread body.) For the beer, I like a dark full-bodied porter or stout.

GEAR Your basic kitchen gear including a large heavy cast-iron or enamel pot or Dutch oven with a tight-fitting lid

WHAT ELSE This recipe uses considerably more yeast than Lahey would, but you can make it in an afternoon. To try the Lahey version, use ¼ teaspoon of yeast and let the bread rise in a cool place for 24 to 36 hours.

TIME about 15 minutes preparation time and about 3 hours for rising, plus about 1 hour baking time

I first met Jim Lahey—freshly arrived from a karate class—at Co., his pizzeria in Manhattan, which draws standing-room-only crowds for its remarkably crisp-crusted pizzas served sizzling from his wood-burning oven. The next time was at his Sullivan St Bakery, where Jim's dark, aromatic breads so made my mouth water—I bought a suitcaseful to take back to Miami. Lahey has done something that has bedeviled amateur bread bakers for centuries: He has figured out how to bake a loaf with the sort of crust that shatters like glass when you cut into it, with the rich yeasty and malty flavor of the best European country bread. Not only that, but he's figured out how to make it without the one activity that intimidates most neophytes: kneading. His dough is considerably wetter than conventional bread dough, so you don't so much shape the loaf as dump it into a preheated pot with a tight-fitting lid. This simulates the steam-injected ovens used by professional bakers, producing a crisper crust than you ever thought possible with whole grain bread. What follows is a Lahey-inspired honey whole wheat bread enriched with beer. No kneading, er, needed. It's great for sandwiches, toast, or simply slathered with butter or olive oil. **Makes one 9- to 10-inch loaf**

2 cups bread flour or unbleached all-purpose white flour, plus flour for shaping the dough and for dusting your hands

1 cup whole wheat flour or rye flour, or a combination of the two

1½ teaspoons coarse salt (kosher or sea)

1 packet (¼ ounce) active dry yeast

½ cup beer

3 tablespoons honey or molasses

Vegetable oil, for oiling the bowl

1 Place the flours, salt, and yeast in a large mixing bowl and stir to mix.

2 Stir the beer and honey into 1 cup of cool water until well combined. Stir the beer mixture into the flour mixture until a loose, sticky dough forms. Cover the bowl with plastic wrap and let the dough rise at room temperature until it is dotted with bubbles and doubled in bulk, 1½ to 2 hours.

3 Lightly flour a work surface and turn the dough out of the bowl onto it. Lightly flour the top of the dough and your hands. Fold the dough over on itself twice. Loosely cover the dough with plastic wrap and let it rest for about 15 minutes.

4 Meanwhile, clean out the bowl. Use a paper towel to oil the inside of the bowl. Return the dough to the bowl and cover it with plastic wrap. Let the dough rise until doubled in bulk, about 1 hour. When ready, the dough will not spring back when poked with your finger.

5 Meanwhile, preheat the oven to 450°F. Place a heavy 6- to 8-quart cast-iron or enamel pot in the oven and preheat it for 30 minutes.

6 When the dough has doubled in bulk, carefully remove the hot pot from the oven and dump the dough into it. Don't worry if it looks lopsided—it will even out as it bakes. Cover the pot with its lid and bake the bread for about 30 minutes.

7 Uncover the pot and continue baking the loaf until it is darkly browned and sounds hollow when tapped with your knuckles, 15 to 30 minutes longer, 45 minutes to 1 hour in all. You want to tap the loaf on the bottom; carefully lift it from the pot using insulated gloves or tongs.

8 Turn the loaf out onto a wire rack and let it cool for at least 15 minutes before serving. Slice the loaf with a serrated knife.

CLASSIC YORKSHIRE PUDDING

Start with the most elemental ingredients—milk, eggs, flour, and salt. Combine them with a technique no more complicated than a few strokes of a sauce whisk. Bake the resulting batter in a hot pan in the oven, and zoom, it rises up like the Second Coming. I trust at some point you're going to try the prime rib on page 251; Yorkshire pudding is the requisite accompaniment. **Serves 8**

SHOP The traditional fat for Yorkshire pudding is suet, melted beef fat—the stuff that collects in the bottom of the roasting pan. Pour it into a heatproof container and use it now or store it in the freezer for later use (let it warm to room temperature first). Or you can use melted butter or olive oil.

GEAR Your basic kitchen gear including a blender (optional) and a 9-by-13-inch baking pan or a large (10- to 12-inch) cast-iron skillet

WHAT ELSE If you decide to serve Yorkshire pudding with a prime rib, mix the batter while the meat cooks and keep it in the refrigerator. Bake the Yorkshire pudding while the meat rests.

TIME about 15 minutes preparation time, plus about 30 minutes baking time

6 large eggs

2¼ cups milk

1 teaspoon coarse salt (kosher or sea)

½ teaspoon freshly ground black pepper

2 cups all-purpose unbleached white flour

3 to 4 tablespoons beef drippings, melted butter, or vegetable oil, or a combination of the three

1 Preheat the oven to 450°F.

2 Place the eggs, milk, salt, and pepper in a large mixing bowl or blender. Whisk or blend to mix. Whisk or blend in the flour and 2 tablespoons of the beef drippings, butter, or oil. Chill the batter in the freezer until it feels cold to the touch, about 10 minutes; chilling helps the batter puff more dramatically.

3 Use the remaining beef drippings, butter, or oil to grease the bottom and sides of a 9-by-13-inch baking pan or a cast-iron skillet (tilt the baking pan or skillet to coat both bottom and sides). Place the baking pan or skillet in the oven and heat it for about 5 minutes.

4 Carefully remove the hot baking pan or skillet from the oven and pour in the cold batter, then return it to the oven. Bake the Yorkshire pudding for about 10 minutes, then reduce the heat to 400°F. Continue baking the Yorkshire pudding until it is dramatically puffed and handsomely browned, about 20 minutes longer, about 30 minutes in all. Don't peek, at least not for the first 20 minutes, or the cool air will deflate the pudding. Cut the Yorkshire pudding into squares for serving.

CONVENIENCE PIZZA

I debated whether to include pizza in this book. After all, most guys have their favorite neighborhood local pizzeria. And the proliferation of wood oven pizzerias has brought the artisanal crusty, chewy, fire and smoke singed pies once found only in Italy (and in gourmet ghettos in California) to neighborhoods across the U.S. So no longer do you need to know how to make pizza from scratch. But that doesn't mean you won't want to, because a homemade pizza is a great way to show off to your poker buddies and look like a hero with your kids. A purist might make the dough from scratch. We'll take the pragmatic route and use a prebaked pizza crust or store-bought pizza dough, which leaves you plenty of time for the fun part: expressing your culinary creativity in the toppings. What follows are five of my favorites. **Makes 1 pizza; serves 1 or 2 and can be multiplied as desired**

NOT-SO-CLASSIC MARGHERITA

First up, a remake of the Neapolitan classic: margherita, which you're going to jazz up by using smoked mozzarella and freshly grated Parmigiano Reggiano cheese.

1 prebaked pizza crust

1 cup tomato sauce (I'm partial to the Turbocharged Red Sauce in the spaghetti recipe on page 446 or use your favorite store-bought sauce)

5 ounces smoked mozzarella, fresh mozzarella, or buffalo mozzarella, thinly sliced crosswise

⅓ cup freshly grated Parmigiano Reggiano cheese

Extra virgin olive oil, for drizzling

6 to 8 fresh basil leaves

Hot red pepper flakes (optional), for serving

1 Preheat the oven to 450°F.

2 Place the pizza crust on a baking sheet. Ladle the tomato sauce on top of the crust, spreading it out in a thin layer to within ½ inch of the edge of the crust. Arrange the mozzarella slices over the sauce and sprinkle on the Parmigiano Reggiano. Drizzle some olive oil over the pizza. Bake the pizza until the cheeses are bubbling and browned, 6 to 10 minutes, or according to the directions on the package.

3 Arrange the basil leaves on the hot pizza, then cut it into wedges or squares. Serve at once with hot pepper flakes sprinkled on top, if desired.

SHOP Your best option for pizza dough is to buy some from your favorite local pizzeria. A good commercial brand is organic Lamonica's, available frozen at most supermarkets, including Whole Foods. For the ultimate convenience use a prebaked pizza crust.

The cheese has to be first rate. If you're used to the rubbery preshredded mozzarella sold in vacuum-sealed packs at the supermarket, fresh mozzarella, still dripping with whey, will come as a revelation.

GEAR Your basic kitchen gear including a baking sheet

WHAT ELSE If you really get into pizza making you may want to invest in a pizza stone for your oven. This is a round or square ceramic slab that gives the crust a strong blast of heat from the bottom, resulting in that unique combination of crustiness and soft chewiness that defines a first-rate pizza. While you're at it, pick up a peel (a baker's paddle) to help you maneuver the pizza in and out of the oven. You'll find both of these at cookware shops.

TIME about 30 minutes

THE SICILIAN

Traditionally, the Sicilian is a cheeseless pizza, salty with anchovies, capers, and olives. But I wouldn't say no to a sprinkling of the sheep's milk pecorino romano cheese.

1 prebaked pizza crust

1 cup tomato sauce, like the Turbocharged Red Sauce in the spaghetti recipe on page 446, or your favorite store-bought sauce

⅓ cup black olives, like oil-cured olives or pitted kalamatas

8 oil-cured anchovies, drained

2 tablespoons drained capers

⅓ cup freshly grated pecorino romano cheese (optional)

Extra virgin olive oil, for drizzling

Hot red pepper flakes (optional), for serving

1 Preheat the oven to 450°F.

2 Place the pizza crust on a baking sheet. Ladle the tomato sauce on top of the crust, spreading it out in a thin layer to within ½ inch of the edge of the crust. Arrange the olives, anchovies, and capers over the sauce. Sprinkle the pecorino romano, if using, on top. Drizzle some olive oil over the pizza. Bake the pizza until the toppings are bubbling and browned, 6 to 10 minutes, or according to the directions on the package.

3 Cut the hot pizza into wedges or squares and serve at once, with hot pepper flakes sprinkled on top, if desired.

THE SPANIARD

If pizza came from Spain, you'd top it with *jamón serrano*, Manchego cheese, and, for an unexpected sweet touch, yellow raisins. (In Spain, raisins are often added to savory dishes, like meat empanadas.)

1 prebaked pizza crust

1 cup tomato sauce, like the Turbocharged Red Sauce in the spaghetti recipe on page 446, or your favorite store-bought sauce

2 ounces thinly sliced jamón serrano or other Spanish ham, sliced paper-thin and cut into 1-inch wide strips

¼ cup yellow raisins (optional)

4 ounces Manchego cheese, rind removed, cheese thinly sliced or coarsely grated

Extra virgin olive oil, for drizzling

1 Preheat the oven to 450°F.

2 Place the pizza crust on a baking sheet. Ladle the tomato sauce on top of the crust, spreading it out in a thin layer to within ½ inch of the edge of the crust. Arrange the ham and raisins, if using, over the sauce. Sprinkle the Manchego cheese on top. Drizzle some olive oil over the pizza. Bake the pizza until the toppings are bubbling and browned, 6 to 10 minutes, or according to the directions on the package.

3 Cut the hot pizza into wedges or squares and serve at once.

THE ALSATIAN

This pizza takes its inspiration from Alsatian *flammekueche*, a tomato-less flatbread from eastern France topped with bacon, potato, and onion.

3 slices bacon, cut crosswise into ¼-inch slivers

1 medium-size onion, peeled and finely chopped

1 medium-size potato, cooked, peeled, and cut into ¼-inch dice (about 1 cup)

Coarse salt (kosher or sea) and freshly ground black pepper

1 prebaked pizza crust

¾ cup sour cream (not reduced-fat)

PIZZA ON THE GRILL

Now you're on my turf, for if pizza tastes great baked in the oven, it's totally over the top hot off the grill. There are three ways to do it.

TRUE GRILLED PIZZA For pizzas made with unbaked dough, set up the grill for direct grilling, with one section of the grill heated to medium-hot, one section heated to medium-low, and one section of the grill fire free for a cool zone. Stretch out the pizza dough on a baking sheet that has been well oiled with olive oil. Oil the top of the pizza dough as well. Have all the toppings ready on a tray at grill side; grilled pizza cooks *really* quickly.

When ready to cook, brush and oil the grill grate. Slide the pizza dough over the medium-hot zone of the grill and cook it until the bottom is browned and the top starts to puff and blister, 2 to 3 minutes. Using 2 spatulas, turn the pizza dough over and move it to the medium-low zone. Add the toppings for the pizza, starting with the ones that take the longest to cook: The cheese goes on first, then the meats, and last, the sauce.

Move the pizza back over the medium-hot zone and continue grilling the pizza until the bottom is browned and the toppings are sizzling, 2 to 3 minutes. If the bottom browns too quickly, move the pizza over the cool zone. Drizzle a little more olive oil over the pizza, and serve at once.

GRILLED PIZZA WITH A PREBAKED CRUST Set up the grill as described for the true grilled pizza. Lightly brush the prebaked crust on both sides with extra virgin olive oil. Grill the crust over the medium-hot zone until browned on the bottom, 2 to 3 minutes. Turn the crust over and move it to the medium-low zone. Add the toppings as described. Return the pizza to the medium-hot zone and grill it until the bottom is browned and the toppings sizzle, 2 to 3 minutes longer. If the bottom browns too quickly, move the pizza over the cool zone. Drizzle a little olive oil over the pizza, and serve at once.

PIZZA GRILLED ON A PIZZA STONE For pizzas made with unbaked dough, set up the grill for indirect grilling and place a pizza stone in the center. Preheat the grill and pizza stone to medium-high. It will take about 20 minutes for the stone to heat. Stretch out the dough and add the toppings as described for true grilled pizza. When you are ready to cook, using a peel or a rimless baking sheet, slide the pizza onto the hot pizza stone. Cover the grill and cook the pizza until the bottom of the crust is browned, the sides are puffed and crisp, and the toppings are bubbling, 6 to 10 minutes, or as needed.

1 Preheat the oven to 450°F.

2 Place the bacon in a cast-iron skillet and cook over medium heat until the fat starts to render, about 2 minutes. Add the onion and cook until well browned, 5 to 8 minutes, stirring often with a spatula. You'll need to reduce the heat as the onion browns so it doesn't burn. Stir in the potato during the last 3 minutes of cooking so it browns, too. Season the onion and potato mixture with salt and pepper to taste; it should be highly seasoned.

3 Place the pizza crust on a baking sheet. Spoon the sour cream on top of the crust, spreading it out in a thin layer to within ½ inch of the edge of the crust. Spoon the onion and potato mixture over the sour cream. Bake the pizza until the toppings are sizzling and browned, 6 to 10 minutes, or according to the directions on the package.

4 Cut the hot pizza into wedges or squares and serve at once.

PROSCIUTTO AND FIG PIZZA

Another pizza for people who like pizza without tomato sauce, this one is topped with caramelized onions, fresh figs, prosciutto, and Gruyère cheese. When buying Gruyère, look for the words *cave aged*—indicative of the richest flavor.

2 tablespoons (¼ stick) butter, or 2 tablespoons extra virgin olive oil, plus olive oil for drizzling over the pizza

1 large onion, thinly sliced

1 prebaked pizza crust

2 ounces prosciutto, sliced paper-thin

6 fresh figs, stemmed and cut in half lengthwise or sliced ¼ inch thick

4 ounces (1 cup) coarsely grated Gruyère cheese

1 Melt the butter in a skillet over medium heat. Add the onion and cook until it is a dark golden brown, stirring often, 10 to 15 minutes. Reduce the heat as needed so the onion browns without burning. Remove from the heat, and let the onion cool to room temperature.

2 Preheat the oven to 450°F.

3 Spread the browned onion on top of the pizza crust. Top the onion with the prosciutto and figs. Sprinkle the Gruyère cheese on top. Drizzle some olive oil over the pizza. Bake the pizza until the toppings are browned and bubbling, 6 to 10 minutes, or according to the directions on the package.

4 Cut the hot pizza into wedges or squares and serve at once.

Variation
Pizza Made with Store-Bought Pizza Dough

To make pizza with premade dough, place a pizza stone or metal baking sheet on a rack in the center of the oven and preheat the oven to 500°F. Roll or stretch the pizza dough, thawed if previously frozen, into a 12-inch circle or a rectangle that is a little less than ¼ inch thick. Dust the back of a second baking sheet or peel with ¼ cup of yellow cornmeal and slide the pizza crust onto it. Top the pizza with your choice of toppings. Then, slide the pizza onto the pizza stone or hot baking sheet. Bake the pizza until the crust is browned on the bottom (lift one edge up to peek) and puffed and crisp at the edges and the topping is hot and bubbling, 6 to 10 minutes, or as needed.

RUBS, SAUCES, AND STOCK

"Hunger is the best sauce," a wise man once remarked. **I guess he never tasted Dark and Stormy Barbecue Sauce or Wasabi Cream Sauce.** If meals were cars, sauces would be the culinary equivalent of pimping your ride. And they don't need to be complicated to take any dish over the top.

But I put the cart before the horse. If sauces add flavor to cooked food, rubs pump up the flavor *before* cooking. The best-known is one of the myriad variations on the theme of salt, pepper, paprika, and brown sugar known as the barbecue rub. But don't stop there. How about a rub made with smoked salt that gives food a fire-blasted flavor—even if you cook indoors?

And finally there's stock, aka broth, aka the building block and indispensable flavoring for dishes as varied as soups, stews, chili, and pot roast. Think of stock as a sort of tea in which you brew bones, meat trimmings, herbs, and aromatic vegetables to extract their flavor. Why bother? For starters, homemade stock tastes vastly superior to salty bouillon cubes and synthetic-tasting store-bought stock. And a simmering pot of stock makes your home smell good—think aromatherapy for foodie guys.

Sauces. Rubs. Stocks. Master them and you'll rock the kitchen.

Made-from-Scratch Barbecue Rub
RAICHLEN'S RUB #2

What gives some guys the edge? What makes their ribs taste a little spicier, their briskets a little more soulful, their food in general a little brighter? Often the secret is as simple as a barbecue rub and sauce made from scratch. Making a rub is easier than you think, and thanks to the wide variations in paprikas, sugars, and other spices, you can follow my formula to the teaspoon and still give it your own personal touch. I've been using this rub in one variation or another (see page 285) for more than twenty years, and it works equally well with beef, pork, lamb, poultry, seafood, tofu, and vegetables. You'll find recipes for barbecue sauces starting on page 536. **Makes about 1 cup; figure on about 1 tablespoon per pound of meat**

- ¼ cup coarse salt (kosher or sea)
- ¼ cup packed brown sugar, light or dark—doesn't matter
- ¼ cup paprika, sweet, hot, smoked, or a combination of the three
- 2 tablespoons freshly ground black pepper
- 2 teaspoons granulated garlic powder
- 2 teaspoons granulated onion powder
- 1 teaspoon celery seed

Combine the salt, brown sugar, paprika, pepper, garlic and onion powders, and celery seed in a bowl and mix, breaking up any lumps in the brown sugar with your fingers (your fingers work better than a whisk or wooden spoon).

If you are not using the rub right away, store it in a sealed jar away from heat and light; it will keep for several months, but try to use it sooner than that. (I keep it in the refrigerator.)

SHOP For the best results, use an imported paprika from Hungary or Spain. For a mild rub, use sweet paprika. For a spicy rub, use some or all hot paprika, a specialty of Hungary. One good brand is Szeged. For a smoky rub, use some or all *pimentón* (smoked paprika) from Spain. For a Texas-style rub, replace the paprika with ancho or another pure chile powder and add one teaspoon each of dried oregano, ground cumin, and cayenne pepper. Like I said, this rub is versatile.

GEAR Your basic kitchen gear and a jar with a lid for storing the rub

WHAT ELSE You don't need to mix the seasonings on the spot every time you need a barbecue rub, but I'd try to use up each batch and make a fresh one every few weeks.

There are two ways to use a barbecue rub. The first is to apply it right before grilling or smoking, in which case it acts as a sort of seasoned salt. The second is to rub it onto the meat a few hours or even a day before you plan to cook it, in which case the seasonings partially cure the meat, resulting in a richer, more complex flavor.

TIME about 5 minutes

JOSH RUXIN

The year was 2006 and Josh Ruxin, a development expert and a Fulbright and Marshall fellow, arrived in Rwanda, one of the poorest countries in Africa, armed with a Ph.D. in the history of science and medicine from University College. With him, by way of a honeymoon, was his new bride, Alissa. The couple fell in love with Rwanda, and the people of this tragedy-scarred nation loved them back.

For the target of his relief efforts, Josh chose a cluster of villages called Mayange, where 80 percent of the population perished in the genocide and the survivors were malnourished to the point of starvation. The first mission was to arrange for a convoy of United Nations trucks loaded with corn-soy flour, sugar, and cooking oil. The second was to put locals in charge of the food distribution and health centers, running the aid effort like a business. The third and hardest task was to abandon the maize crop provided by well-intentioned international agricultural experts (ignorant of local drought conditions), planting a disease-resistant strain of cassava instead. Today, Mayange is a net *exporter* of food and—Congress take note—*everyone* has health care.

Meanwhile, Alissa Ruxin (with Josh's help) opened Heaven, a restaurant near their home in Kigali. Marrying local ingredients with Western culinary techniques (one house specialty is cassava *chimichurri* filet mignons), the couple succeeded in creating in a country with no native fine dining tradition one of the top rated restaurants in Africa. Between his development work, a professorship at Columbia University, and writing an inspiring memoir called *A Thousand Hills to Heaven*, Josh still finds time to run Heaven's kitchen when the executive chef is absent. Lesson learned: "The gap between professional chef and amateur cook is far greater than you could ever imagine."

Why should a man know how to cook?
Until you cook yourself, you'll never fully appreciate how much work goes into the meals prepared by your mother or spouse.

Do men and women cook differently?
I don't think the sexes cook differently, but I do believe that *people* cook differently. On the one side: those who follow recipes to the letter and, on the other, people for whom a recipe is an opportunity to innovate. Another dichotomy is cooks who clean up as they go along versus cooks who don't. If you're one of the latter, hopefully your partner appreciates your cooking and doesn't mind dish duty in return.

What's your quintessential guy dish?

As long as you indemnify me against charges of sexism, I'll go with pork belly. It's rich and crispy and most guys love it, while most women seem to avoid it.

In many traditional African cultures, the meat goes first to the men, and the women subsist on tubers, starches, and meat scraps. This is an unfortunate custom, as pregnant and breastfeeding women and young children need protein for physical and intellectual development.

What's your go-to dish when you're by yourself?
For me the pleasure of cooking has always involved feeding others.

What's your favorite seduction dish?
When I want to put the moves on Alissa, I go for her sweet spot: seafood stew. I sauté shrimp and mild white fish in plenty of butter and Pernod. I make the sauce with fresh fennel and tomatoes, tomato paste, capers, and cream.

What's your proudest creation?
That would be the dirty hot martini we serve at the Heaven bar. Vodka, olive juice, and just a hint of white vermouth. Shake it with a sliced habanero chile, then serve it straight up.

What are the three ingredients you can't live without?
Cardamom. Rice vinegar. Fish sauce.

What are three tools you can't live without?
Kitchen scissors. A shredder. A spice grinder (great for grinding coffee and spices, of course, and in an emergency, for blending a salad dressing).

What are the most important things to keep in mind if you're just starting out?
Pay attention to your ingredients and don't go overboard with the salt. You can always add more later.

Err on the side of undercooking. You can always throw the meat back on the grill or in the oven. If you overcook it, you're screwed.

Relax: You can only go so wrong in the kitchen. Few dishes come out complete unmitigated disasters.

What are the three most common mistakes guys make in the kitchen?
Guys tend to think about the cooking process chronologically. First I'll make the salad, then I'll work on the main dish, then I'll do dessert. Great cooks think about sequencing—how to prep and what to do first so everything is ready at once.

Related to the above: Guys always get a late start and underestimate how much time they need to cook the entire meal.

Guys forget to balance meals. We think in terms of the steak and potatoes. What about the salad, veggies, and a killer dessert?

Something you've learned over the years that really helps you up your game in the kitchen?
Always have decent bottles of red and white wine on hand. Nearly any dish can benefit from a splash of wine, and if the dish can't, the cook certainly can. Likewise, don't underestimate the power of a good beer to improve a stew.

What's the most important lesson about food you've taught your kids?

Wasting food will not be tolerated. After living in Africa amid such scarcity, I have learned that with abundance comes responsibility and the need for self-control.

What should men think about food in the future?
What we put in our mouths and feed our kids has a huge impact on life expectancy, not only in the developing world, but in the West.

> ▸ Wasting food will not be tolerated.

What can the average guy do to help alleviate world hunger?
Recognize that helping farmers and creating jobs through the private sector is the path forward. Donate to or invest in any organization or company that focuses on these areas. Here at Heaven restaurant in Kigali, we welcome help in all forms—from English language teachers to front of house managers to performers and of course chefs.

Some parting words?
Cooking is a focused task and a form of meditation (whether you meditate or not). You can't really cook while texting, surfing the Internet, or dealing with the distractions of daily life. Think of your time in the kitchen as a chance to unplug, unwind, and relax and you'll want to do it more. If you're single, you may also find that it will reduce your time spent as a bachelor.

SMOKED SALT RUB

SHOP There are many options for smoked salt. I like the intensely smoky, ebony-colored Danish Viking Smoked Sea Salt sold by Salt Traders (salttraders.com). Whatever salt you opt for, just be sure it's real wood-smoked salt, not smoke-flavored salt.

GEAR Your basic kitchen gear and a jar with a lid for storing the rub

WHAT ELSE If you like a rub with a kick, add 1 to 2 teaspoons of hot red pepper flakes.

TIME about 5 minutes

I have in my backyard a half dozen or so smokers, so when I want to smoke meats or seafood, I don't have far to go. Apartment dwellers are not so lucky. So I created the following rub for them. Combine coarse, crunchy crystals of wood-smoked salt and peppery cracked black peppercorns and it's easy to imagine yourself cooking over a smoky campfire. **Makes ½ cup; figure about 1 tablespoon per pound of meat**

5 tablespoons smoked salt

3 to 5 tablespoons cracked black peppercorns or freshly ground black pepper

Place the smoked salt and the pepper (add as much heat as you can take) in a bowl and mix with your fingers. If you are not using the rub right away, store it in a sealed jar away from heat and light. The rub is best used within 2 months.

Garlic, Rosemary, and Sage
MEDITERRANEAN RUB

SHOP If you use fresh rosemary and sage as often as I do, invest in plants instead of packaged herbs. They grow well without a lot of human intervention—especially rosemary.

GEAR Your basic kitchen gear including a food processor plus a jar with a lid for storing the rub

I've written literally hundreds of rub recipes, but the seasoning I use most on a daily basis is a variation on this Tuscan herb mix. Time and ingredients permitting, I make it fresh, which means finely chopping fresh herbs and garlic in a food processor. When I'm in a hurry, I use dried herbs, which give you a different, but equally flavorful, rub. Any extra will keep for at least a week in the refrigerator. **Makes about ¾ cup; figure about 1 to 2 teaspoons per pound of meat**

▶ *Left to right: Mediterranean Rub, Smoked Salt Rub, Raichlen's Rub #2*

WHAT ELSE So how do I use this Mediterranean rub? Let me count the ways. On shellfish, on chicken cooked on the rotisserie, on pork roasted in the oven, on steak or fish on the grill. No, I haven't yet used it for dessert. This seasoned salt is intense so a little goes a long way.

TIME about 5 minutes

3 cloves garlic, peeled and coarsely chopped

¼ cup stemmed fresh rosemary leaves

¼ cup stemmed fresh sage leaves

½ cup coarse salt (kosher or sea)

2 tablespoons cracked or freshly ground black pepper

Place the garlic, rosemary, and sage in a food processor fitted with a metal chopping blade. Run the machine in short bursts to finely chop the ingredients. Add the salt and pepper and process just to mix. Transfer the rub to a jar with a tight-fitting lid. Store any unused rub in the sealed jar in the refrigerator, where it will keep for at least 3 days.

Variation
Dried-Herb Mediterranean Rub

Prepare the rub using 3 tablespoons each of dried rosemary and sage in place of the fresh herbs and 2 tablespoons dried garlic flakes in place of the fresh garlic. Crumble the rosemary leaves into a bowl. Add the remaining ingredients and mix them with your fingers. Stored in a sealed jar, the rub will keep for several weeks in the pantry.

THREE-INGREDIENT BARBECUE SAUCE
(CAROLINA MUSTARD SAUCE)

Every guy should have his own signature barbecue sauce. Why? In two words: bragging rights. Having mastered the pork chapter, you know how to turn out competition-quality ribs and pork shoulder. You need a barbecue sauce you can call your own to serve with them. Enter this sweet tangy South Carolina-style mustard sauce—spiked with just enough vinegar to grab your attention. Easy? It requires only three ingredients, which you probably have in your kitchen already. **Makes 1½ cups**

½ cup Dijon mustard

½ cup (packed) dark or light brown sugar

½ cup cider vinegar or rice vinegar

Coarse salt (kosher or sea) and freshly ground black pepper (optional)

Place the mustard, brown sugar, and vinegar in a heavy saucepan and gradually bring the mixture to a boil over medium heat. Let the sauce simmer until richly flavored, about 5 minutes, whisking often. Add salt and pepper to taste (if using). Cool the sauce, then transfer it to a bowl for serving or a clean jar, where it will keep in the refrigerator for several weeks. Let the sauce return to room temperature before serving.

SHOP Tradition calls for using cheap ballpark mustard, but you're going to give your sauce pedigree by using a Dijon mustard, like Maille.

GEAR Your basic kitchen gear including a saucepan plus a jar with a lid for storing

WHAT ELSE To take this simple sauce over the top, add ½ teaspoon grated lemon zest and a little liquid smoke. To reinforce the smoke flavor, you can add a crumbled strip of fried bacon.

TIME 10 minutes

DARK AND STORMY BARBECUE SAUCE

Now that you've mastered the Three-Ingredient Barbecue Sauce, you're ready to tackle a more complex smoky red barbecue sauce. I've got a killer—inspired by the official cocktail of my *Barbecue University* TV series, the rum and ginger beer cocktail known as a Dark and Stormy. The gingery bite and sweet rum finish go well with a wide variety of grilled and smoked meats. (You'll find the recipe for the cocktail on page 588.) **Makes about 2½ cups**

SHOP To get the full effect of fire and spice, use genuine ginger beer. It's spicier and less sweet than commonplace ginger ale (the latter will work in a pinch). Good brands of ginger beer include Barritt's Bermuda Stone ginger beer and Maine Root Ginger Brew. For the alcohol, you want a dark rum, like Gosling's Black Seal from Bermuda.

GEAR Your basic kitchen gear including a saucepan plus jars with lids for storing

WHAT ELSE History lesson—rum looms so large in our image of the Caribbean, we forget that New England was a major producer. Newport, Rhode Island, alone once had twenty-two distilleries, and a cocktail confected from dark rum and ginger beer became the quasiofficial drink of the yacht crowd.

TIME about 20 minutes

1 cup ginger beer (see Shop)

2 cups ketchup

¼ cup light or dark brown sugar, or more to taste

¼ cup dark rum

2 tablespoons molasses

1 tablespoon Worcestershire sauce

1 teaspoon finely grated lemon zest

1 tablespoon fresh lemon juice, or more to taste

1 teaspoon liquid smoke

1 teaspoon onion powder

½ teaspoon ground cinnamon

½ teaspoon freshly ground black pepper

1 Place the ginger beer in a heavy saucepan, let come to a boil over high heat, and let boil until reduced by half, about 10 minutes.

2 Add the ketchup, brown sugar, rum, molasses, Worcestershire sauce, lemon zest and juice, liquid smoke, onion powder, cinnamon, and pepper and whisk to mix. Gradually let the sauce come to a simmer over medium heat and let simmer until thick and flavorful, 5 to 10 minutes, whisking occasionally. Taste for seasoning, adding more brown sugar and/or lemon juice to taste; the sauce should be very flavorful.

3 Transfer the sauce to a bowl for serving or to clean jars with lids for storing and let cool to room temperature. Refrigerate the sauce until serving. Refrigerated, it will keep for several weeks. Let the sauce return to room temperature before serving.

Caribbean Garlic Citrus Sauce

MOJO

Get your mojo rising? This garlicky sauce is the lifeblood of the Spanish Caribbean. The formula varies from island to island, but you can always count on fried garlic, fragrant cumin, and acidic *naranja agria* (sour orange) or lime juice. Roast pork, rotisserie chicken, and fried yucca and plantains pale without it. Use it as a table sauce, but it also makes an awesome marinade. Just pronounce it correctly: "mo-ho" not "mo-joe." **Makes about 1 cup**

½ cup extra virgin olive oil, preferably Spanish

8 cloves garlic, peeled and thinly sliced crosswise

¼ cup finely chopped fresh cilantro

1 teaspoon ground cumin

1 teaspoon dried oregano

½ teaspoon coarse salt (kosher or sea), or more to taste

½ teaspoon freshly ground black pepper, or more to taste

½ cup sour orange juice, fresh lime juice, or a mixture of the two

1 Heat the olive oil in a deep saucepan over medium heat. Add the garlic and cook until light golden brown, 1 to 2 minutes.

2 Stir in the cilantro, cumin, oregano, salt, and pepper and cook until sizzling and fragrant, about 20 seconds.

3 Stand back and stir in the sour orange juice; the sauce will hiss and bubble. Increase the heat to high and let the sauce boil until blended and mellow, about 3 minutes, stirring well. Taste for seasoning, adding more salt and/or pepper as necessary.

4 Serve the sauce warm or at room temperature. Stir it again before serving. The sauce can be refrigerated in a jar with a lid for at least 3 days. Let the sauce warm to room temperature, and shake it well before serving.

SHOP *Naranja agria*, sour orange, looks like a lumpy orange, but with a juice that tastes more like lime. Look for it at Hispanic markets and at cosmopolitan supermarkets, or substitute equal parts fresh lime juice and orange juice.

GEAR Your basic kitchen gear including a saucepan plus a jar with a lid for storing

WHAT ELSE For an interesting twist, substitute fresh grapefruit juice for the sour orange juice and fresh mint for the cilantro.

TIME about 10 minutes

FRESH HERB CHIMICHURRI

This pungent puree of garlic, herbs, olive oil, and vinegar is the steak sauce of Argentina and Uruguay. It may remind you of pesto but without the cheese and pine nuts. It does what any good condiment should—counterpoints and moistens the meat—but without the sugar found in many North American steak sauces. I use the traditional formula as a launchpad, adding whatever fresh

SHOP The traditional herb for *chimichurri* is flat-leaf parsley, but fresh mint or cilantro or even all three makes an awesome sauce.

herbs I can get my hands on. Roasted garlic in place of fresh? Sherry vinegar in place of red wine vinegar? These are variations you can use to make this classic South American condiment your own. **Makes about 1 cup**

GEAR Your basic kitchen gear including a food processor or blender

WHAT ELSE To rinse the herbs, hold them by the stem and agitate them in a bowl of cold water. Shake them dry, then cut off the stems.

TIME about 10 minutes

2 cups packed stemmed flat-leaf parsley or a blend of fresh herbs, such as parsley, fresh mint, oregano, and/or cilantro

3 cloves garlic, peeled and coarsely chopped

1 teaspoon dried oregano, if not using fresh

About 1 teaspoon hot red pepper flakes (more or less depending on your tolerance for heat)

½ teaspoon coarse salt (kosher or sea), or more to taste

¼ teaspoon freshly ground black pepper, or more to taste

¼ cup red wine vinegar

¾ cup extra virgin olive oil or vegetable oil

1 *If you are using a food processor,* place the herbs, garlic, dried oregano, if using, hot pepper flakes, salt, and black pepper in the processor bowl and process until finely chopped. Gradually add the wine vinegar, olive oil, and ¼ cup of cold water. You're looking for a loose paste the consistency of bottled salsa.

If you are using a blender, place the wine vinegar, olive oil, and ¼ cup of cold water in the blender first. Then add the herbs, garlic, dried oregano, if using, hot pepper flakes, salt, and black pepper. Blend until smooth.

2 Taste the *chimichurri* for seasoning just before serving, adding more salt and/or black pepper to balance the vinegar, or water, if the sauce is too intense. You bite the steak and the *chimichurri* should bite you back. *Chimichurri* looks and tastes best within 3 hours of being made. Try to serve it the day it's made although it can be refrigerated, covered, for about 3 days. Let it come to room temperature and taste for seasoning, adding more salt and/or pepper as necessary before serving.

◄ *Top to bottom: Dark and Stormy Barbecue Sauce, Fresh Herb Chimichurri, Lemon Pepper Mayonnaise*

"SECRET SAUCE" FOR BURGERS

SHOP Nothing esoteric here—all the ingredients will be found in your supermarket's condiment aisle, if not already in your pantry.

GEAR Your basic kitchen gear

WHAT ELSE The whole point of this sauce is that it's concocted with ready-made condiments. To kick up the heat, you could grate fresh horseradish from scratch following the instructions on page 401.

TIME about 5 minutes

Y ou've probably realized by now I'm a made-from-scratch kind of guy—even for a simple sauce for burgers. Here's my version of the "secret sauce" you find on chain restaurant burgers. It's considerably less sweet and more flavorful. **Makes about 1 cup**

½ cup mayonnaise, preferably Hellmann's

2 tablespoons Dijon mustard

2 tablespoons prepared horseradish

2 tablespoons steak sauce, such as A.1.

2 tablespoons ketchup or cocktail sauce

2 cornichons, minced, or 2 tablespoons minced dill pickles

Place the mayonnaise, mustard, horseradish, steak sauce, ketchup, and pickles in a bowl and whisk to mix. The sauce can be refrigerated, covered, for at least 3 days.

TEN MAYONNAISE SAUCES

SHOP My go-to mayonnaise for these and other sauces is Hellmann's. Do *not* use Miracle Whip—it's too sweet.

GEAR Your basic kitchen gear including a Microplane (optional)

"A well made sauce will make even an elephant or a grandfather palatable," observed Grimod de la Reynière, a nineteenth-century food writer who'd have been a blogger had he lived today. (Strange dude, Grimod: He had webbed fingers, like a duck, and he once staged his own funeral just to see who would come.) On sauces, Grimod was dead on the money because no great cuisine exists without them. A sauce has the power to dress up boiled shrimp or a grilled chicken breast. Fortunately, you don't need a degree from a culinary academy to stir up a great condiment. Here are ten big-flavored sauces quickly made by doctoring commonplace store-bought mayonnaise. Rounding out the group is a Made-from-Scratch Tartar Sauce in the true French tradition.

MUSTARD SAUCE

Great with stone crab, shrimp cocktail, and all manner of fish sandwiches. For a sharper sauce, add 1 to 2 teaspoons fresh lemon juice. **Makes about 1 cup**

⅔ cup mayonnaise, preferably Hellmann's

⅓ cup Dijon mustard or grainy Meaux mustard

½ teaspoon grated fresh lemon zest (see Note)

Combine the mayonnaise, mustard, and lemon zest in a mixing bowl and whisk to mix. The Mustard Sauce can be refrigerated, covered, for at least 3 days.

Note: Remove the lemon zest with a Microplane (see page 15), being careful to grate only the yellow rind, not the bitter white pith underneath.

LEMON PEPPER MAYONNAISE

Perfect for chicken and steak sandwiches and all manner of seafood, this sauce is even better if you use a fragrant Meyer lemon (see page 187). For pepper, I like whole Tellicherries from India that I grind in a spice mill. **Makes about 1 cup**

WHAT ELSE Want to make your own mayonnaise from scratch? It's easy if you have a food processor. After you have inserted a metal chopping blade, crack an egg, preferably pasteurized (see page 41) into the processor bowl. Add one tablespoon each of Dijon mustard and fresh lemon juice. With the machine running, add one cup of canola oil or another mild vegetable oil in a thin stream: The mayonnaise will thicken. Season the mayonnaise with salt and freshly ground white pepper to taste. The whole process takes maybe three minutes. Store homemade mayonnaise, covered, in the refrigerator; it will keep for at least three days.

TIME about 10 minutes

¾ cup plus 2 tablespoons mayonnaise, preferably Hellmann's

1 teaspoon finely grated lemon zest (see Note)

2 tablespoons fresh lemon juice

1 teaspoon freshly ground or cracked black pepper, or more to taste

Combine the mayonnaise, lemon zest and juice, and pepper in a mixing bowl and whisk to mix. Taste for seasoning, adding as much more pepper as you dare. The sauce can be refrigerated, covered, for at least 3 days.

Note: Remove the lemon zest with a Microplane (see page 15), being careful to grate only the yellow rind, not the bitter white pith underneath.

CURRY SAUCE

For a great curry sauce, stir the curry powder straight from the jar or tin into the mayonnaise. For even more flavor, sauté the curry with minced onion for a few minutes, then add it to the mayo. (You'll need a small skillet if you're sautéing the curry powder first.) This sauce is a killer with fried fish, grilled chicken, and lamb. **Makes about 1 cup**

1 tablespoon vegetable oil (optional)

3 tablespoons minced peeled onion (optional)

1 tablespoon curry powder

1 cup mayonnaise, preferably Hellmann's

3 tablespoons minced cilantro

1 If you are sautéing the curry powder, heat the oil in a small skillet over medium heat. Add the onion and curry powder and cook until fragrant and lightly browned, about 2 minutes, stirring with a wooden spoon. Let the curry mixture cool to room temperature.

2 Place the mayonnaise in a mixing bowl and whisk in the curry and onion mixture, if using, or just the curry powder and the cilantro. The sauce can be refrigerated, covered, for at least 3 days.

HORSERADISH SAUCE

Serve Horseradish Sauce with prime rib, roast beef, tri-tip, or oysters (fried or on the half shell), or any dish in need of fire and spice. **Makes about 1 cup**

½ cup mayonnaise, preferably Hellmann's

¼ cup sour cream

¼ cup finely grated fresh horseradish, or ¼ cup prepared horseradish (or as much as you can bear)

A few drops of fresh lemon juice (optional)

Coarse salt (kosher or sea) and freshly ground black pepper

Combine the mayonnaise, sour cream, horseradish, and lemon juice, if using, in a mixing bowl and whisk to mix. Taste for seasoning, adding more horseradish as necessary and salt and pepper to taste. The sauce can be refrigerated, covered, for at least 3 days.

CHIPOTLE MAYONNAISE

An awesome condiment for tacos and burgers, not to mention grilled beef, chicken, and shrimp. Use canned chipotles, which come packed in a spicy sauce called *adobo*. **Makes about 1 cup**

1 cup mayonnaise, preferably Hellmann's

1 to 2 canned chipotle peppers, minced, plus 2 teaspoons can juices

1 tablespoon fresh lime juice

Combine the mayonnaise, chipotle pepper(s) and their can juices, and the lime juice in a mixing bowl and whisk to mix. The sauce can be refrigerated, covered, for at least 3 days.

WASABI CREAM SAUCE

Serve this wasabi sauce with seared or raw tuna or grilled shrimp. If you have a squeeze bottle, use it to squirt flavorful zigzags of sauce onto your favorite grilled fish or chicken. Or just spoon it on. **Makes about 1 cup**

1 tablespoon wasabi powder

1 tablespoon soy sauce

1 cup mayonnaise, preferably Hellmann's

Place the wasabi powder and 1 tablespoon of warm water in a mixing bowl and whisk until a smooth paste forms. Let the wasabi paste stand for about 5 minutes. Add the soy sauce and mayonnaise and whisk to mix. The sauce can be refrigerated, covered, for 3 days.

Note: If you want to squirt decorative zigzags from a squeeze bottle, thin the sauce to a more liquid consistency by stirring in water or chicken stock, 1 tablespoon at a time, before adding the sauce to the squeeze bottle.

TOBIKO MAYONNAISE

WHAT ELSE *Tobiko* is sometimes referred to as *masago*. Start with 3 tablespoons and add more to the mayo, if desired. For a tangier sauce, add a few drops of lemon juice.

Similar to the Wasabi Cream Sauce, this mayonnaise is studded with crunchy briny bursts of *tobiko* (flying fish roe). Look for it at Asian markets or buy some from your local sushi parlor. This sauce makes a great dip for sushi, sashimi, and tempura. **Makes about 1 cup**

¾ cup mayonnaise, preferably Hellmann's

3 to 5 tablespoons tobiko (flying fish roe)

1 tablespoon sesame oil (see page 28)

A few drops of fresh lemon juice (optional)

Place the mayonnaise, *tobiko,* sesame oil, and lemon juice, if using, in a mixing bowl and whisk to mix. The sauce can be refrigerated, covered, for at least 3 days.

MOROCCAN FIRE

arissa is a Moroccan hot sauce made with chile peppers, garlic, and coriander.

H *arissa* is a Moroccan hot sauce made with chile peppers, garlic, and coriander. Look for it in jars or cans at specialty food markets. For preserved lemon you'll need to visit a North African grocery store or specialty foods shop. Or use grated lemon zest and lemon juice. **Makes about 1 cup**

¾ cup plus 2 tablespoons mayonnaise, preferably Hellmann's

2 tablespoons harissa

1 tablespoon minced preserved lemon, or 1 teaspoon finely grated lemon zest (see Note) plus 1 tablespoon freshly squeezed lemon juice

Combine the mayonnaise, *harissa*, and lemon in a mixing bowl and whisk to mix. The sauce can be refrigerated, covered, for at least 3 days.

Note: Remove the lemon zest with a Microplane (see page 15), being careful to grate only the yellow rind, not the bitter white pith underneath.

THAI CHILI MAYONNAISE

T his electrifying sauce owes its garlicky heat to a Thai chili sauce called Sriracha. It comes in a plastic squeeze bottle and can be found in the ethnic food section of your local supermarket. **Makes about 1 cup**

¾ cup mayonnaise, preferably Hellmann's

3 tablespoons Sriracha

1 tablespoon fresh lime juice

Place the mayonnaise, Sriracha, and lime juice in a mixing bowl and whisk to mix. The sauce

can be refrigerated, covered, for at least 3 days.

WHAT ELSE Preserved lemon is a hyper-intense Moroccan flavoring made by pickling lemons with fresh lemon juice and salt.

MADE-FROM-SCRATCH TARTAR SAUCE

I f you're like most North Americans, your notion of tartar sauce involves a sickly sweet condiment squeezed from a plastic packet. So you may be surprised to learn that tartar is a classic French sauce capable of great finesse. The secret is to leave out the sugar and use fresh tarragon. Serve this tartar sauce with any of the fried or grilled fish or shellfish recipes in this book. Hell, eat it right off a spoon. **Makes about 1 cup**

¾ cup plus 2 tablespoons mayonnaise, preferably Hellmann's

2 tablespoons Dijon mustard

1 shallot, peeled and minced (about 2 tablespoons)

1 tablespoon capers, drained and minced

1 tablespoon minced cornichons or dill pickles

1 tablespoon chopped fresh tarragon or another herb, like chervil or basil

1 tablespoon tarragon vinegar or distilled white vinegar, or to taste

Freshly ground black pepper

Place the mayonnaise, mustard, shallot, capers, cornichons, tarragon, and vinegar in a mixing bowl and whisk to mix. Season with pepper to taste. The tartar sauce can be refrigerated, covered, for at least 3 days.

STOCK

Want to cook like a pro? Learn how to make stock. This liquid essence of meat, bones, vegetables, and herbs is an essential building block in the world's great cuisines, both East and West. It reflects two of a chef's guiding principles—think flavor and don't waste food. To understand stock, consider tea and compost. Like tea, you steep the ingredients in hot water to extract their essence. Like compost, you turn kitchen scraps into something sustaining and useful. Homemade stock makes your kitchen smell good and measurably improves soups, sauces, stews, and braises. (To me, store-bought stock has a slighty artificial taste, but used sparingly, it's better than nothing.) The one thing stock is not is time sensitive: Keep chicken carcasses and necks, hearts, and gizzards, beef bones, steak and vegetable trimmings, and herb stems in a bag in your freezer. When you have enough, pull out your stockpot and simmer a batch. Store stock in cup and pint containers in your freezer so you always have premeasured amounts on hand. **Makes 4 to 6 cups**

SHOP There's no need to shop to make stock. Use your trimmings and leftovers.

GEAR Your basic kitchen gear including a roasting pan (optional), a stockpot or large saucepan, a ladle or large metal spoon, and a strainer

WHAT ELSE When I was in cooking school in Paris we learned to make both light and dark stock—the light with raw chicken, bones, and vegetables, the dark with these ingredients darkly roasted. Over the years, I've come to prefer brown to white and roasted to raw, so I always use roasted ingredients for stock, which is what you'll find in the extra-rich stock variation on the next page. For more stock tips see Taking Stock on the next page.

TIME about 10 minutes preparation time, plus 1 to 2 hours cooking time

For the meat

1 chicken carcass (use one left over from one of the roast chicken recipes starting on page 327)

Chicken neck, heart, and/or gizzard (optional)

Beef or veal bones and/or steak or roast trimmings (½ to 1 pound, optional)

For the vegetables

1 medium-size onion, skin on (it adds color), quartered

2 carrots, cut into 1-inch pieces

1 rib celery, cut into 1-inch pieces

1 clove garlic, peeled

**For the herbs and spices,
any or all of the following**

1 bay leaf

1 sprig fresh thyme

1 sprig or some stems fresh parsley, basil, or rosemary

6 to 8 whole black peppercorns

1 whole clove stuck in one of the onion quarters

1 Place the meat, vegetables, herbs, and spices in a large stockpot and add water to cover by 2 inches. Let come to a boil over medium-high heat (this is important for bringing any impurities to the surface). Immediately reduce the heat to medium-low to maintain a gentle simmer; bubbles should barely break the surface. Using a ladle or large metal spoon, carefully skim off any foam or fat that rises to the surface of the stock and discard it.

2 Let the stock continue to simmer until the liquid is level with the top of the bones and is richly flavored, about 1 hour. Skim the stock often and let it simmer gently over medium-low to low heat; do not let it boil. This is the secret to a clean, appetizing stock.

3 Strain the stock into plastic containers and let it cool to room temperature, then refrigerate it, covered. The stock will keep for 3 to 4 days in the refrigerator or can be frozen for up to 6 months.

Variations

Extra-rich stock: Preheat the oven to 400°F. Place the meat and vegetables in a flameproof roasting pan and roast them until well browned, 40 minutes to 1 hour. Transfer the meats and vegetables to a stockpot, then deglaze the roasting pan. Place the roasting pan on a burner over high heat, add ¼ cup of dry white wine, and let it come to a boil, scraping up the brown bits from the bottom of the pan with a wooden spoon. Add the wine mixture to the stockpot and proceed with the stock recipe.

Seafood stock: For the chicken carcass substitute 1½ to 2 pounds of fish heads and bones from such mild, nonoily fish as snapper, striped bass, or sole and/or lobster or shrimp shells or heads. Let the stock simmer until full flavored, 30 to 45 minutes.

Vegetable stock: Substitute 2 pounds of vegetables for the chicken carcass; see Taking Stock for suggestions as to what to use. Let the stock simmer until full flavored, about 1 hour. For extra flavor, roast the vegetables in the oven (see above) before simmering them.

Taking Stock

I'm ecumenical about my stock ingredients. Roast chicken, duck, or turkey carcasses all make a great starting point. Add the neck, heart, and gizzard that came with the bird. You can enhance this with beef or veal bones, steak trimmings, the odd piece of pork, aromatic vegetables, and herbs. But don't add poultry livers; they are too strong in flavor.

For vegetables, start with onion, carrot, celery, and garlic. Add squash, zucchini, mushrooms, and/or tomatoes in moderation. Avoid assertively flavored members of the brassica family, like cabbage, broccoli, or brussels sprouts. And don't add starchy vegetables, like potatoes, which will make the stock cloudy, or beets, which will turn it red.

SWEET

When you think of guy food, baking—pies, cakes, and cupcakes—does not leap to mind. But to cook well implies entertaining well. To entertain well is to choreograph a meal from start to finish. And in order to finish a meal with a flourish, you should have a small carefully curated cache of desserts to draw from.

So what makes a great guy dessert? Simplicity helps, and in the following pages you'll find a Rum and Coke Float, a Bourbon Brown Cow, Italian *Affogato* (espresso-doused ice cream), and other big-flavored ice cream desserts. Fire never fails to impress, and I've got you covered with a Deconstructed Bananas Foster you set ablaze at tableside.

Chocolate works wonders with women, so every man should have one or two killer chocolate desserts under his belt—in this case, Mexican Chocolate Pudding and brownies fortified with Belgian-style beer. A happy ending is all but guaranteed.

CANDIED BACON SUNDAES

Here's a dessert based on the assumption that everything tastes better with bacon—even dessert. It pays homage to my friends in Quebec (where I've taped my *Maître du Grill* TV show), offering a triple blast of maple flavor in the form of maple-glazed bacon, maple ice cream, and maple whipped cream. **Serves 4**

For the candied bacon and walnuts

4 thick slices bacon (4 ounces), cut crosswise into ¼-inch slivers

½ cup coarsely chopped walnuts

½ cup pure maple syrup

2 tablespoons sherry vinegar or rice vinegar

For the sundaes

¾ cup heavy (whipping) cream

2 tablespoons pure maple syrup

1 pint (2 cups) maple-walnut ice cream, or more to taste

Ground cinnamon, for sprinkling

SHOP You need real maple syrup for this sundae: I like the more flavorful Dark Amber grade; my wife prefers the delicate flavor of Light Amber. Use an artisanal smokehouse bacon, like Nueske's, or a local bacon.

GEAR Your basic kitchen gear including a large (10- to 12-inch) skillet and a strainer plus an electric handheld or stand mixer, a whisk, or a CO_2 charger

WHAT ELSE The candied bacon topping goes well on other desserts, from puddings (see Butterscotch Pudding with Miso on page 567) to Deconstructed Bananas Foster (page 564). It's not half bad on fried chicken (page 340) either.

TIME about 30 minutes

1 Make the candied bacon and walnuts: Place the bacon in a cold skillet over medium heat. Cook until the fat renders and the bacon begins to brown and crisp, 6 to 8 minutes, stirring with a wooden spoon. Add the walnuts and continue cooking until the bacon and walnuts are golden brown, about 2 minutes. Do not let them burn. Drain the bacon mixture by placing it in a strainer over a heatproof bowl. Save the bacon fat for a future use, like frying potatoes.

2 Return the bacon and walnuts to the skillet and add the ½ cup of maple syrup and the vinegar. Cook the bacon mixture over medium

heat until it is thick and syrupy, about 3 minutes, stirring with a wooden spoon. The mixture should have a pourable consistency. Set the skillet aside and keep warm. The candied bacon can be made earlier in the day; cover the skillet and set it aside. Rewarm the candied bacon over low heat when you are ready to serve the sundaes.

3 Make the sundaes: Place the cream and 2 tablespoons of maple syrup in a chilled metal bowl and, using a mixer or whisk, beat the cream until soft peaks form. Alternatively, pour the cream and maple syrup into a CO_2 charger and shake well to mix, 7 or 8 times.

Invert the charger and squeeze the handle to release the whipped cream. Refrigerate the maple whipped cream, covered, until serving.

4 To assemble the sundaes, scoop the ice cream into balls and place 1 scoop in each of 4 sundae glasses or bowls. Spoon the warm candied bacon and walnuts on top. Top with the maple whipped cream and a sprinkling of cinnamon.

How to Save Bacon Fat

Strain the bacon fat from the skillet into a heatproof jar with a tight-fitting lid. Stored in the refrigerator, bacon fat will keep for several weeks. Yes, you can add fresh bacon fat to the jar as you cook more bacon, in which case try to use the fat on the bottom first.

ICE CREAM FLOATS
FOR GROWN-UPS

"Too much of anything is bad," observed Mark Twain (a guy's writer if ever there was one). "But too much good whiskey is barely enough." I suspect Twain wasn't thinking of ice cream floats, but the right booze can turn this soda fountain classic into a dessert suitable for a grown man. **Serves 1; can be multiplied as desired**

RUM AND COKE FLOAT

The Cuba libre (rum and Coke) is a classic summer thirst quencher. It just got a lot more refreshing served as an ice cream float.

SHOP You can't make a silk purse from a sow's ear, nor can you make a great float with mediocre ice cream. Grab a pint from your local ice cream parlor or use an artisanal brand of gelato, like Ciao Bella or Talenti.

GEAR Your basic kitchen gear plus a soda fountain glass or highball glass and a long straw

WHAT ELSE Despite its simplicity, the sequence for assembling an ice cream float makes a difference. For more foam, add the ice cream first, then the soda. For less foam, add the soda first, then drop in a scoop of ice cream.

TIME about 5 minutes

1 scoop vanilla ice cream

1 ounce (2 tablespoons) light rum

8 ounces (1 cup) Coca-Cola

Place the ice cream in a tall glass. Pour the rum over it, followed by the Coca-Cola. Insert a long straw and stir a couple of times. Bottoms up.

DARK AND STORMY FLOAT

Fired up on ginger? Try this dessert twist on a cocktail popular with the Newport, Rhode Island, yacht set. You'll find the cocktail itself on page 588.

1 scoop ginger or vanilla ice cream

1 ounce (2 tablespoons) dark rum

8 ounces (1 cup) ginger beer (see Note)

Place the ice cream in a tall glass. Pour the rum over it, followed by the ginger beer. Insert a long straw and stir a couple of times.

Note: Ginger beer is spicier and not as sweet as regular ginger ale. Good brands include Barritt's Bermuda Stone and Maine Root Ginger Brew.

CHERRY LAMBIC FLOAT

You beer aficionados out there surely know Belgium's *kriek lambic* (cherry beer) or one of its North American counterparts. But I'd be willing to bet you've never added any of them to a cherry float.

1 scoop Ben & Jerry's Cherry Garcia ice cream or vanilla ice cream

½ ounce (1 tablespoon) maraschino liqueur (optional)

8 ounces (1 cup) kriek lambic

1 maraschino cherry (optional)

Place the ice cream in a tall glass. Pour the maraschino liqueur over it, if using, followed by the *kriek lambic*. Top the float with the cherry, if desired. Insert a long straw and stir a couple of times.

BOURBON BROWN COW

If whiskey is your booze of choice, try this brown cow made with root beer, vanilla ice cream, and bourbon. Or make it with a rye whiskey, like Old Overholt.

1 scoop vanilla ice cream

1 ounce (2 tablespoons) bourbon

8 ounces (1 cup) root beer

Place the ice cream in a tall glass. Pour the bourbon over it, followed by the root beer. Insert a long straw and stir a couple of times.

PAUL KITA

When Paul Kita started menshealth.com/guy-gourmet/ in 2009 he never imagined his biweekly musings on cooking would become one of the nation's most popular men's food blogs. Today, the Pennsylvania journalist and his staff of ten share the wisdom of such culinary heavyweights as Grant Achatz and David Chang—not to mention the suggestions of thousands of regular guys—on a daily blog visited by a half million men each month. What Paul has learned about the cooking habits of the twenty-first-century twenty-something male may surprise you. For example, 58 percent of women say their husbands cook better than they do. And guys actually enjoy their time in the kitchen more than women do (82 compared to 72 percent).

Like many men, Paul taught himself how to cook. "I couldn't afford the Culinary Institute of America, so I cooked my way recipe by recipe through their textbook." The first dish he attempted? A "severely ambitious" French onion soup. He tied up the dorm oven all day to roast beef bones, which did little to endear him to his roommates. Today, he sautés, grills, fries, and bakes with the best of them, but still sees value in kitchen disasters. "Every recipe is a teachable experience. Don't worry about screwing it up."

Why should a man know how to cook?

To take command of your diet and ownership of what you eat. In the old days, we might do woodworking or welding. Today, when men want to express themselves with their hands, we cook.

Do men and women cook differently?

Men still have a gather-round-the-fire-shoulder-to-shoulder, sharing-the-wildebeest mentality. Guys want to talk to the butcher, know what's in the burger blend, where the food comes from.

What's the quintessential guy dish?

An amazing grilled cheese sandwich.

What's your go-to dish when you're by yourself?

A rice bowl, like Japanese *chirashi* or Korean *bibimbap*. It's basically a mountain of rice with animal protein and veggies all around it.

What's your favorite seduction dish?

A dish that you cook *with* a woman rather than *for* a woman. Something you can both touch, like homemade pasta.

Three dishes every guy should know how to make?

A great weeknight meal, like pizza. Make your own pizza dough or buy some from your local pizza shop. Homemade pizza is worlds better than a delivery pie.

A dish that can feed a lot of people, like a smoked brisket.

A really good breakfast. So many guys screw up bacon and eggs.

Three ingredients you can't live without?

Smoked paprika [*pimentón*]. It adds depth and complexity to everything from roast chicken to pumpkin seeds to egg salad.

Old Bay seasoning. Its great salty, sweet, spicy flavors work with a lot more than just seafood.

Tabasco sauce. It gives you such a great lip burn. I like Sriracha [Thai hot sauce] as much as the next guy, but there's no way I'm putting it in my gumbo.

Three tools you can't live without?

An instant-read thermometer. It's indispensable, like the oil gauge in your car, and it can save you from serving a *lot* of burnt or undercooked meat.

A cast-iron skillet. Yeah, I know it requires a lot of maintenance. That's the point. If you take care of it, it will take care of you.

A Bob Kramer carbon steel chef's knife. The edge on the thing is unbelievable—this is how a chef's knife should cut.

What are the three most important things to keep in mind if you're just starting out in the kitchen?

It takes more than one recipe to learn how to cook. Mistakes may break your heart, but you won't repeat them.

Remember the salt and pepper. Nothing tastes good if you don't add enough salt and pepper. For salt I like kosher and for pepper, twist the grinder until your arm hurts.

The sauce makes the dish. It can be as simple as store-bought mayonnaise or mustard doctored with chopped shallots and tarragon. Don't let sauces intimidate you.

> ▶ Men still have a gather-round-the-fire-shoulder-to-shoulder, sharing-the-wildebeest mentality.

What are three techniques every guy should know how to do in the kitchen?

Execute a pan flip (when sautéing vegetables or making omelets). The trick is to tip the pan away from you and slightly downward (don't hold the pan horizontally). Then jerk the pan toward you while bringing the far edge up. Practice with a pan of dried beans until you can flip them without spilling. Stirring takes you only so far.

Learn to make a basil chiffonade, that is, fresh basil sliced into thread-thin slivers. Roll up the basil leaves lengthwise, then using a chef's knife, cut them crosswise into the thinnest imaginable slices. Toss the basil with your fingers to unfold the slices. It never fails to impress women and it's *way* cooler than chopping.

Learn to make scrambled eggs with chopsticks. You have to stir a lot faster and you'll be amazed how much this improves the texture.

What are the three most common mistakes guys make in the kitchen?

Surrendering your authority at the grocery store. Grill the butcher or fishmonger: If they don't have what you want, ask for a substitute. They have the info. You have the money. Use it to get what you want.

Performing without a rehearsal. Always run through a recipe once before you make it for other people.

Forgetting about dessert. A lot of guys don't like to bake, so dessert becomes an afterthought. Women love dessert and want a sense of closure. Learn to make a couple great desserts—even if they're as simple as *affogato* [vanilla ice cream doused with espresso; see page 560].

Something unexpected you've learned over the years that really helps you up your game in the kitchen?

Microwave fresh herbs until crisp, then freeze them in extra virgin olive oil in plastic ice cube trays. It's like putting the flavor of summer away for a dreary winter day.

Anything else you wish to add about cooking for and by men?

The best way to learn to cook well is to learn to eat well. My father taught me that.

Affogato
"DROWNED" GELATO

SHOP Tradition calls for vanilla gelato, but you can make *affogato* with any flavor: coffee, chocolate, mocha, even lemon gelato or ice cream. There are many fine espresso roast coffees on the market. In terms of packaged preground espresso, I'm partial to Cuban-style Pilon or Café Bustelo.

GEAR Your basic kitchen gear plus a coffeemaker or espresso machine

WHAT ELSE Some people like to put whipped cream atop *affogato*; others prefer a dusting of cinnamon or cocoa.

TIME about 5 minutes

While we're on the subject of ice cream floats, Italians take a high-octane approach with *affogato*, "drowned" gelato—ice cream doused with a scalding shot of espresso. **Serves 1; can be multiplied as desired**

1 scoop vanilla or other flavor gelato, frozen hard

¼ cup brewed hot espresso

Whipped cream (optional; below)

Ground cinnamon (optional)

Scoop the gelato into a low sturdy glass or bowl. Pour the hot espresso over it. Top the *affogato* with a dollop of whipped cream and/or dust it with cinnamon, if desired, and serve.

WHIPPED CREAM

SHOP Look for heavy cream or whipping cream—preferably organic.

GEAR Your basic kitchen gear including a chilled metal bowl plus an electric handheld or stand mixer, a whisk, or a CO_2 charger, such as the iSi brand of cream chargers, available through amazon.com

Everybody loves whipped cream. Not the sugary stuff squirted from aerosol cans, but real honest-to-goodness whipped cream high in butterfat and flavored with vanilla or your favorite spirit. What you may not realize is how easy it is to make whipped cream from scratch. Especially if you have an electric mixer or a CO_2 charger. **Makes 1½ cups**

1 cup heavy (whipping) cream, chilled

2 tablespoons confectioners' sugar

1 teaspoon pure vanilla extract, or
1 tablespoon of your favorite spirit or liqueur (rum, tequila, brandy, bourbon, Calvados, or Grand Marnier come to mind)

If you are beating the whipped cream, pour the cream into a chilled bowl. Using an electric mixer or a whisk, beat the cream until soft peaks form, 3 to 5 minutes. Whisk or beat in the confectioners' sugar and flavoring. Continue beating the cream until thick and fluffy, about 2 minutes longer. Do not overbeat or the whipped cream will separate. Cover and chill the whipped cream until serving; it can be refrigerated for several hours.

If you are using a CO_2 charger to whip the cream, unscrew the nozzle and place the cream, confectioners' sugar, and flavoring in the charger bottle. Add a fresh CO_2 cartridge. Invert the charger and shake it 7 or 8 times. Pull the handle to squirt the whipped cream over your dessert.

WHAT ELSE There are two basic ways to make whipped cream. The first is by beating the cream in a chilled bowl. An electric mixer (either stand or handheld) helps, but you can also beat the cream with a whisk and a little elbow grease. Alternatively, place the cream, sugar, and flavoring in a CO_2 charger and whip it as described in the recipe.

TIME 10 minutes

"BURNT" PEACHES AND ICE CREAM

Sometimes, the distance between cooked and burnt is a razor's width or a matter of a few seconds of cooking. But this is the zone where chefs like to hang out (think blackened fish) and it's where you get the most flavor. Sugar is sweet. Burnt sugar is bitter. But *almost* burnt sugar (aka caramel) has all sorts of interesting flavors: honey, smoke, butterscotch, to name a few. Which brings me to these peaches—inspired by South American grill master Francis Mallmann (read about him on page 248). If you think fresh peaches and cream are good, wait until you try these darkly caramelized peaches with ice cream. **Serves 4**

SHOP Like most simple recipes, this one is only as good as the raw materials: You need the sort of ripe peach that you can smell when you walk into the room and that dimples when you squeeze it. (The sort of fruit you find at peak peach season in summer.) Let unripe peaches ripen to this stage in a paper bag at room temperature. When possible, use freestone peaches, which have loose stones (pits). This makes them easy to cut in half.

GEAR Your basic kitchen gear including a large (10- to 12-inch) cast-iron skillet

WHAT ELSE This singular method works well with any moist, juicy fruit, from figs to plums to oranges (peeled and cut in half).

TIME about 15 minutes

4 ripe peaches

1 cup sugar

1 pint (2 cups) vanilla ice cream, for serving

8 fresh mint leaves, slivered, for garnish

1 Cut each peach in half lengthwise along the crease to the pit. Twist the halves in opposite directions to separate them. Pry out the pit and discard it. Place the sugar in a shallow bowl.

2 Heat a large cast-iron skillet over medium heat for about 5 minutes. To test the temperature, drip a drop of water in it; when the skillet is sufficiently hot, the water will sizzle and evaporate in about 2 seconds.

3 Dip the cut side of a peach half in the sugar, shaking off the excess. Place the peach half on a plate so the sugar-coated side is up. Repeat with the remaining peach halves.

4 Sprinkle the remaining sugar in the hot skillet and cook it until it begins to melt, 2 to 3 minutes.

5 Arrange the peaches cut side down on the melted sugar. Cook the halves without moving them until the cut sides are darkly browned, 3 to 5 minutes. Adjust the heat as needed so that the cut sides brown, not burn.

6 Using a spatula, transfer 2 peach halves to each of 4 bowls, browned side up. Place a scoop of ice cream between the peach halves in each bowl. Sprinkle the slivered mint on top and serve.

Variation

"Burnt" Oranges with Rosemary

This is a vintage Francis Mallmann (see page 248) dessert described in full in his book, *Seven Fires: Grilling the Argentine Way*. Cut the rinds off 4 navel oranges. Cut away any white pith remaining on the oranges and cut each orange in half crosswise. In a shallow bowl, mix 1 cup of sugar with 2 tablespoons of chopped fresh rosemary. Crust the cut side of each orange half with some of the sugar mixture. Melt the remaining sugar in a large cast-iron skillet and cook the orange halves as described for the peach halves above. Mallmann serves the oranges with unsweetened yogurt by way of a sauce.

FRUIT "SALSA"
WITH CINNAMON CHIPS

Want to turn pedestrian fruit salad into an electrifying dessert? Add chopped jalapeños and cilantro as though you were making salsa. Think sweet with heat, and to complete the metaphor, serve the fruit salsa with cinnamon sugar *totopos* (tortilla chips). **Makes about 4 cups; serves 4**

SHOP Fresh local fruit that's in season always takes precedence over what's listed in the recipe ingredient list.

GEAR Your basic kitchen gear

WHAT ELSE If cilantro sounds too weird for dessert (or you're allergic to it), substitute fresh mint. Sometimes I add chopped candied ginger, too.

TIME about 20 minutes

Whole fresh strawberries, blueberries, raspberries, or ripe melon, peaches, and/or nectarines (see Step 1)

2 to 4 jalapeño peppers, seeded and finely chopped (for a hotter fruit salad, leave the seeds in)

1 small bunch fresh cilantro or mint, rinsed, shaken dry, stemmed, and coarsely chopped (about ½ cup)

2 tablespoons brown sugar, or more to taste

2 tablespoons fresh lime juice, or more to taste

Cinnamon Chips (recipe follows)

1 If using strawberries or blueberries, remove the stems. Cut any large strawberries in half or quarters. If you are using melon, cut it in half and remove the seeds and rind. Halve the peaches or nectarines and remove the pit. Cut melon, peaches, and/or nectarines into ½-inch dice. You'll need about 4 cups of fruit. Place the fruit in a mixing bowl. Add the jalapeños, cilantro, brown sugar, and lime juice, but don't mix.

2 Not more than 10 minutes before serving, toss the fruit mixture, adding more brown sugar and/or lime juice to taste; the salsa should be sweet, tart, and spicy. Serve the salsa with Cinnamon Chips.

CINNAMON CHIPS

A twist on the usual tortilla chips—bake-fried with a light dusting of cinnamon sugar. **Makes 16 chips**

2 (10-inch) flour tortillas, each cut into 8 wedges

2 tablespoons (¼ stick) butter, melted

4 tablespoons cinnamon sugar (see Note)

1 Preheat the oven to 400°F.

2 Line a baking sheet with aluminum foil to facilitate cleanup, then place the tortilla wedges on the foil. Lightly brush the wedges with the butter and sprinkle the cinnamon sugar over them. Bake the chips until crisp and lightly browned, about 5 minutes. Let the chips cool slightly on a wire rack or the baking sheet, then serve them with the fruit salsa.

Note: To make cinnamon sugar, place ¼ cup of sugar and 1 teaspoon of ground cinnamon in a small bowl and stir to mix.

Deconstructed

BANANAS FOSTER

SHOP Buy bananas that are ripe but still firm; the skins should be yellow with a light speckling of sugar spots (tiny brown dots).

GEAR Your basic kitchen gear including a large (10- to 12-inch) cast-iron skillet or a heatproof platter and a blowtorch plus a skillet for the rum-pecan panfry (optional)

Invented at Brennan's restaurant in New Orleans in 1951, bananas Foster quickly became a de facto guy dessert. Why? Well, the booze (151 rum) helped and so did the fire—the former to fuel the latter. So did the theatrics of flambéing the dessert tableside. Here's an updated bananas Foster, using one of the handiest tools for tableside drama: a blowtorch. This gives the bananas a hard candy crust, augmented with an optional rum-pecan panfry and ice cream. **Serves 4**

For the simple version

4 bananas, ripe but not soft

½ cup granulated sugar

For the more elaborate version, with rum-pecan panfry

8 tablespoons (1 stick) unsalted butter

¾ cup pecan halves

½ cup dark brown sugar

¾ cup dark rum

For the full monty

1 pint (2 cups) vanilla ice cream, or more to taste

⅓ cup 151 proof rum, or more dark rum, for flambéing

WHAT ELSE There are three ways to approach these bananas Foster—from simple to elaborate—all awesome. On the simple end, you cut the bananas in half, sprinkle them with sugar, and caramelize them with the flame from a blowtorch. If you're feeling more ambitious, make the rum-pecan panfry to serve over the bananas. To go the full monty, serve the bananas and rum-pecan panfry over ice cream, flambéing the whole shebang with more rum at the table.

TIME about 10 minutes for the simple version; 30 minutes for the full monty

If you are making the simple version, just before serving, cut the bananas in their skins in half lengthwise. Gently remove the skins and arrange the banana halves cut side up in a large cast-iron skillet or on a heatproof platter. Sprinkle the tops of the bananas with a light, even layer of granulated sugar. Fire up the blowtorch and point it at the bananas to melt and brown the sugar. Let the bananas cool for about 1 minute; the sugar will turn into caramel. Dig in.

If you are making the more elaborate version, with rum-pecan panfry, before preparing the bananas, make the rum-pecan panfry. Melt the butter in a skillet over high heat. Add the pecans and brown sugar and cook until bubbling and the sugar is melted, about 3 minutes. Stir in the ¾ cup of rum and let it boil until thick and syrupy, about 3 minutes.

Cut and caramelize the bananas as described for the simple version. Spoon the warm rum-pecan panfry down the center of the bananas and serve.

If you are making the full monty, after you have made the rum-pecan panfry and caramelized the bananas, scoop the ice cream into 4 shallow heatproof serving bowls. Dim the lights and flambé the bananas again with the ⅓ cup of 151 rum. Top each serving of ice cream with a caramelized banana and some rum-pecan panfry. (See How to Flambé on this page and How to Make Bananas Foster on page 566).

How to Flambé

Flambéing is easy—and dramatic—but you need to follow some commonsense safety precautions. (The bananas should be the only thing going up in smoke.) So, clear the area of anything that can possibly catch fire. Roll up your sleeves and make sure your guests aren't sitting too close to the action. Have an optional spray bottle of water close at hand (no one need know what it's for). And it's not a bad idea to rehearse a few times in private before flambéing in front of an audience.

To flambé with dark rum (or bourbon, brandy, or another spirit), place ⅓ cup of rum in a saucepan and warm it to body temperature; test it with your finger. Do not let it boil, or you'll boil off the flammable alcohol. Light the rum with a butane match or long safety match and carefully pour it over the bananas.

To flambé bananas Foster with 151 rum, simply pour it over the bananas and light it with a butane match or safety match. You don't need to heat the rum first.

▶ The point of the blowtorch's flame should be about 1 inch above the bananas.

How to Make Bananas Foster

1. Simple version: Point a blowtorch at the halved and sugared bananas to caramelize them.

2 More elaborate: Sauté the pecans with the butter and brown sugar, then stir in the rum.

3 Pour the rum-pecan panfry over the caramelized bananas.

4 The full monty: Pour the 151 proof rum over the bananas and flambé again.

BUTTERSCOTCH PUDDING
WITH MISO

Butterscotch pudding derives its flavor from vanilla, brown sugar, and of course butter. It's about to get a lot more interesting thanks to the addition of the rich umami flavor of miso—a sweet, salty Japanese condiment made from cultured soybeans. The recipe comes from my stepson, Jake, a chef who worked for several years in Asia. **Serves 4 to 6**

8 tablespoons (1 stick) unsalted butter

1 cup packed dark brown sugar

2 tablespoons white miso, or
    1 tablespoon soy sauce

1⅔ cups whole milk

¾ cup heavy (whipping) cream

3 tablespoons cornstarch

1 teaspoon pure vanilla extract

2 gingersnap cookies, crumbled

1 cup Whipped Cream
    (optional; page 560)

SHOP You'll need one ingredient that may be a little out of your comfort zone. Miso is a Japanese condiment made from cultured (fermented) soy beans and/or grains. I call for white miso (the mildest and sweetest) here, but any color or flavor of miso will work. You don't need to buy imported Japanese miso, as many fine brands (South River Miso and Eden Foods, for example) are made right here in the U.S.

GEAR Your basic kitchen gear including a heavy saucepan and a strainer

WHAT ELSE If you can't find or don't have miso on hand, substitute 1 tablespoon soy sauce. You'll still get the salty counterpoint to the sweet butterscotch.

TIME about 20 minutes preparation time, plus about 2 hours chilling time

1 Place the butter, brown sugar, and miso or soy sauce in a heavy saucepan and gradually bring to a boil over medium-high heat, whisking to mix. Cook whisking constantly until the mixture caramelizes, that is, it becomes thick and bubbling and turns a deep golden brown, 6 to 8 minutes. Do not let it scorch or burn.

2 Remove the pan from the heat and add the milk and ¼ cup of the cream. The mixture will hiss and sputter; it's supposed to. Continue whisking until the sugar mixture is completely incorporated.

3 Place the cornstarch and vanilla in a small bowl. Add 1 tablespoon of the cream and stir to make a thick paste. Gradually whisk in the remaining cream to make a loose paste. Whisk this paste into the hot brown sugar and milk mixture. Return the pan to the heat, bring to a boil over medium-high heat, and boil,

Two Puddings for Grown-Ups

Pudding may not seem like the manliest of desserts. Just don't tell Travis Lett, the Californian who parleyed his *Top Chef* win into the red-hot restaurant Gjelina in Venice, California. Or Iron Chef Masaharu Morimoto, who made butterscotch pudding with miso one of his signature desserts. The truth is that pudding meets a lot of needs. It's comfort food at its best and quick and simple to make. On the next page you'll find a spicy Mexican Chocolate Pudding.

whisking steadily, until the pudding thickens, about 3 minutes.

4 Strain the pudding into a bowl. Do you need to strain it? No, but you'll get a smoother consistency. Press a piece of plastic wrap over the surface of the pudding. This will prevent a skin from forming. Let the pudding cool to room temperature, then refrigerate it until cold, about 2 hours.

5 To serve, spoon the pudding into bowls. Top with gingersnap cookie crumbs and whipped cream, if desired. Dig in.

MEXICAN CHOCOLATE PUDDING

SHOP You want to use unsweetened cocoa powder for this pudding. I'm partial to Dutch brands, like bitter, chocolaty Van Houten or Droste, but Hershey's unsweetened makes fine pudding too.

GEAR Your basic kitchen gear including a heavy saucepan and a strainer

WHAT ELSE Like the complex flavors of chocolate paired with cinnamon, cloves, vanilla, and chiles? Check out Montezuma's favorite drink: the Mexican Hot Chocolate on page 574.

TIME about 15 minutes preparation time, plus 2 hours chilling time

Chocolate pudding brings out the inner child in all of us. You'll score big time with this one if you have kids or a chocoholic girlfriend. The ancient Aztecs flavored their chocolate with cinnamon, cloves, vanilla, and yes, chiles. I've made the chile powder optional—it definitely adds an interesting dimension. But if you're making this with kids in mind, you probably ought to omit it. **Serves 4 to 6**

$\frac{1}{3}$ cup unsweetened cocoa, preferably Dutch process cocoa

$\frac{1}{3}$ cup sugar

2 tablespoons cornstarch

1 teaspoon ground cinnamon

1 teaspoon ancho chile powder (optional)

$\frac{1}{4}$ teaspoon ground cloves

$1\frac{1}{2}$ cups milk

$\frac{1}{2}$ cup heavy (whipping) cream or half-and-half or more milk

2 teaspoons pure vanilla extract

Whipped Cream (optional; see page 560), for serving

1 Place the cocoa, sugar, cornstarch, cinnamon, chile powder, if using, and cloves in a heatproof mixing bowl and whisk to mix.

2 Place the milk, cream, and vanilla in a heavy saucepan and bring to a gentle simmer over medium heat, about 5 minutes.

3 Whisk the hot milk into the cocoa mixture in a thin stream. Pour the cocoa mixture into the saucepan, bring to a boil over medium-high heat, and boil, whisking steadily, until the pudding thickens, 2 to 3 minutes.

4 Strain the pudding into a bowl. Do you need to strain it? No, but you'll get a smoother consistency. Press a piece of plastic wrap over the surface of the pudding. This will prevent a skin from forming. Let the pudding cool to room temperature, then refrigerate it until cold, about 2 hours.

5 To serve, spoon the pudding into bowls and top with whipped cream, if desired.

BELGIAN BEER BROWNIES

Brownies pass three acid tests for world-class guy food: great taste; they're easy to prepare; and women find them irresistible. The twist here comes with the addition of beer—more precisely, a haunting cherry-flavored ale called Three Philosophers from the Belgian-style Ommegang brewery in Cooperstown, New York. The ale adds a subtle malty, fruity flavor and virtually guarantees moist brownies. Don't know Ommegang? You should. They make some of the best beer in North America. Can't find Three Philosophers? You can make equally awesome brownies with *kriek lambic* (a Belgian cherry beer), chocolate stout, or Guinness stout. Shout out to Christine Alexander, who inspired this recipe. **Makes 12 brownies**

SHOP Ommegang ales can be found at premium liquor stores or online at ultimatewineshop.com. I've also made the brownies with oatmeal ale and Guinness stout (when using stout, there's no need to boil it down by half—just use ½ cup).

GEAR Your basic kitchen gear including a heavy medium-size saucepan and a 9-by-13-inch baking pan

WHAT ELSE In the interest
of excess, you're going to use
two types of chocolate for
these brownies: unsweetened
cooking chocolate for the
batter and a good bittersweet
eating chocolate to make
chocolate chunks. Sometimes
more is more.

TIME about 15 minutes
preparation time, plus 20 to
30 minutes baking time

1 cup Three Philosophers ale, or
   ½ cup stout, such as Guinness

2 ounces really good bittersweet eating
   chocolate (see page 572)

1 cup unbleached all-purpose white flour

1 cup (2 sticks) unsalted butter

5 ounces unsweetened chocolate

4 large eggs

2 cups granulated sugar

1 teaspoon pure vanilla extract

Pinch of salt

Confectioners' sugar (optional),
   for dusting the brownies

1 Preheat the oven to 350°F.

2 If you are using ale, pour it into a heavy saucepan and bring to a boil over high heat. Boil the ale until it is reduced by half (to ½ cup), about 5 minutes. Place the reduced ale in a heatproof bowl and let it cool. If you are using stout, there's no need to boil it down.

3 Coarsely chop the bittersweet chocolate into ½-inch pieces and place them in a separate bowl. Add 1 tablespoon of the flour and toss to coat the chocolate (this keeps the chocolate from sinking to the bottom of the batter).

4 Wipe out the saucepan, then add the butter and melt it over low heat. Brush or smear a little of the butter all over the inside of a 9-by-13-inch baking pan. Refrigerate the pan to chill it for about 5 minutes, then sprinkle 1 tablespoon of flour inside the baking pan, shaking and tilting the pan to coat the bottom and sides.

5 Add the unsweetened chocolate to the melted butter in the saucepan and melt it over low heat, about 4 minutes, stirring with a rubber spatula.

6 Place the eggs and granulated sugar in a mixing bowl and whisk to mix. Whisk in the reduced ale or the stout and the vanilla, salt, and the melted butter and chocolate mixture. Stir in the remaining flour and the bittersweet chocolate chunks. Spoon the batter into the prepared baking pan and place it in the oven.

7 Bake the brownies until the top is puffed and firm to the touch, 20 to 30 minutes. A skewer or toothpick inserted in the center will come out mostly dry—a little stickiness is OK.

8 Remove the brownies from the oven and let cool in the pan to room temperature. Cut the brownies into 12 rectangles for serving and dust them with the confectioners' sugar if desired.

CHOCOLATE

If the way to a man's heart is through his stomach, the way to a woman's affection is surely through chocolate. As a son and potential boyfriend, husband, and father, you probably know this already. If not, learn it fast.

This used to be easy: Chocolate was, well, chocolate. Today it comes in hundreds of categories, styles, and grades. All chocolate derives from the seedpod of a tropical fruit conveniently named *Theobroma cacao* (Greek for "food of the gods"). Ferment, roast, and shell the beans, and you get the building block of all chocolate: cocoa nibs. Perhaps you've had cocoa nibs in candy bars or sprinkled on ice cream—they're crunchy, chocolaty, and pleasantly bitter. (If you want to sample them on their own, one good brand is Scharffen Berger.) But it's not until the nibs are crushed between granite rollers to make a thick slurry called chocolate liquor (no, you can't buy or drink it) that they can be transformed into what most of us would recognize as chocolate. Depending on where the cocoa plants are grown and how the beans are processed, the result is chocolate for eating or for baking or cocoa powder.

EATING CHOCOLATES

Chocolate bars are made from all parts of the cocoa beans—the nibs, chocolate liquor, and cocoa butter, a pale fat extracted from the cocoa beans. The chocolate falls into several categories.

DARK CHOCOLATE starts with at least 35 percent cocoa products (often more) to which sweeteners and fats are added. Think intense flavor—somewhat bitter and very chocolaty—with only minimal sweetness. Premium chocolate bars often come marked with a percentage number on the label. The Lindt Excellence 90% bar, for example, consists of 90 percent pure cocoa products, which leaves room for only 10 percent sweeteners, flavorings, and other additives. The higher the cocoa percentage, the darker, richer, and more concentrated the chocolate. Scharffen Berger, Callebaut, and Valrhona all produce excellent premium chocolates.

MILK CHOCOLATE is made by adding milk, milk powder, or condensed milk to the chocolate. It has a much less intense chocolate flavor than dark chocolate (by law, milk chocolate is required to contain only a 10 percent concentration of chocolate liquor). Obviously, milk chocolate has its partisans, but I've never understood its appeal.

WHITE CHOCOLATE consists of sugar, milk, and cocoa butter, but has no cocoa nibs or liquor. To me, it is "chocolate" in name only.

SINGLE ORIGIN CHOCOLATES (also called **single estate chocolates**) contain beans from a single plantation, the location, soil, and climate of which produce chocolate of such distinction, it's sold on its own without blending (in much the same way that wine from a particularly choice vineyard becomes Château Lafite-Rothschild or Vosne-Romanée). Single origin chocolates can sell for as much as $25 per bar. Michel Cluizel from France, Chocolates El Rey from Venezuela, and Amano Artisan Chocolate from Utah all produce single origin chocolates.

FLAVORED CHOCOLATE BARS are studded with ingredients like almonds, peanuts, and raisins (remember the Chunky?). Today you can buy chocolate flavored with chiles, saffron, stout, smoke, and of course, the ubiquitous sea salt.

BAKING AND COOKING CHOCOLATE

UNSWEETENED CHOCOLATE, sometimes called **bitter chocolate**, **cooking chocolate**, or **baking chocolate**, consists of pure chocolate liquor mixed with cocoa butter or another fat to solidify it. It's too bitter to eat straight.

BITTERSWEET CHOCOLATE OR SEMISWEET CHOCOLATE is baking chocolate to which some sugar has been added. Used for cooking, it lacks the finesse of an eating chocolate.

CHOCOLATE CHIPS are chocolate morsels made with less cocoa butter so they retain their shape even when heated, like being baked in cookies.

MEXICAN CHOCOLATE is the descendant of *xocolatl*, the chocolate drunk by the Aztecs. Flavored with cinnamon, cloves, vanilla, and sometimes chiles, this chocolate is often processed in such a way that the sugar remains granulated. Mexicans beat it with hot milk to make hot chocolate; I like to munch the stuff raw.

COCOA POWDER is made by drying chocolate liquor and removing most of the cocoa butter. Dutch process refers to cocoa that has been treated with alkali to neutralize its acidity. Please note that I am describing *unsweetened* cocoa powder—the only sort you should use for making hot chocolate. Sweetened cocoa mixes (often made with powdered milk) produce wretched hot chocolate.

MEXICAN HOT CHOCOLATE

SHOP You'll want unsweetened cocoa powder for this hot chocolate like the Dutch brands Droste or Van Houten. Do not use presweetened cocoa mix.

GEAR Your basic kitchen gear including a large heavy saucepan

WHAT ELSE If you live in an area with a large Mexican community, you may be able to find Mexican cooking chocolate, which is gritty with granulated sugar and fragrant with cinnamon and cloves. (One good brand is Ibarra.) Whisk an ounce or two (rough chopped) into the following hot chocolate. Outstanding just got better.

TIME 10 minutes

Hot chocolate has long been a guy food. Remember Montezuma. The Aztec ruler reputedly drank 50 cups a day. Of course, pre-Colombian *xocolatl* was somewhat different from modern hot chocolate, starting with the flavorings, which included chile peppers and cornmeal. When I make hot chocolate, I still look south of the border, to the soulful colonial city of Oaxaca, where shops specialize in grinding the ingredients—freshly roasted cocoa beans, whole almonds, cinnamon sticks, cloves, and sugar—to order fresh each day. If you're used to the pale sugary stuff that passes for hot chocolate in much of the U.S., this dark, thick, spicy, intensely chocolaty, dessertlike brew will shock and awe your taste buds. **Serves 2**

3 tablespoons unsweetened cocoa powder

3 tablespoons sugar

1 teaspoon cornstarch

½ teaspoon ground cinnamon, plus 2 cinnamon sticks for serving (optional)

⅛ teaspoon ground cloves

1 cup milk

1 cup half-and-half (or more milk)

1 teaspoon pure vanilla extract

Pinch of fine salt

Whipped Cream (optional; page 560)

1 Place the cocoa powder, sugar, cornstarch, ground cinnamon, and cloves in a large heavy saucepan and whisk to mix. Gradually whisk in the milk, half-and-half or additional milk, vanilla, and salt.

2 Bring the mixture to a boil over medium-high heat, whisking steadily. Reduce the heat and let simmer until slightly thickened and richly flavored, 2 minutes. Serve in mugs, and I wouldn't say no to a spoonful of whipped cream.

DRINK

Something happened on the way to becoming a wine aficionado. The American male discovered the cocktail. More precisely, rediscovered the cocktail, because with the exception of that dark period between 1919 and 1933 (Prohibition), guys have always been more than a little obsessed with mixed drinks. By now you're up to speed on breakfast, lunch, and dinner, but your knowledge isn't complete until you master the fundamentals (at least) of bartending.

In the following pages, you'll learn when to shake and when to stir and how to make the classics, from the martinis to Manhattans, from margaritas to Bloody Marys. I'll show you how to warm up a party with what may be the world's best sangria and how to take the chill off a cold night with a French Canadian caribou (Cognac-fortified hot mulled wine). Vodka anyone? Trust me, it tastes better poured from a block of ice. And when you've had one too many, I'll show you how to make a classic prairie oyster and a power shake that will keep you at peak performance.

Unleash your inner bartender. Step up to the bar like a man.

THE BERTHIN MARTINI

Y ou know the adage: Give a man a fish and he eats for one day; teach him how to fish and you feed him for a lifetime. The best gift we ever gave our son-in-law, Gabriel Berthin, was a book called *Vintage Cocktails*. He quickly became a bartending force of nature. Gabriel's martini is everything this iconic cocktail should be: clean, refreshing, aromatic, and intensely flavorful. Ritualistic in its preparation and sophisticated in its serving. And not too dry—remember, a martini without vermouth is just cold gin. **Serves 1; can be multiplied as desired**

Ice cubes	1 dash of Angostura orange bitters
2 ounces (4 tablespoons) gin	1 dash of Regans' orange bitters
1 ounce (2 tablespoons) dry white vermouth	1 strip lemon zest (1 by 2 inches)

1 Fill a martini glass with ice cubes and add some water to chill it.

2 Place about 1 cup of ice cubes in a cocktail shaker. Add the gin, vermouth, and bitters and stir vigorously with a bar spoon until the shaker becomes painfully cold in your hand, about 30 seconds (20 to 30 revolutions).

3 Dump and discard the ice and water from the martini glass. Strain the martini into the glass. Holding the piece of lemon zest skin side down, twist it over the martini to spray its oils on top. Rub the rim of the glass with the lemon zest, drop it into the drink, and serve at once.

Variations

For extra flavor, flambé the lemon zest as described on page 587. If you prefer, add a skewer of pimento-stuffed olives or pickled onions to the martini.

SHOP For gin, Gabriel likes No. 3 (a dry gin from England) or one of the elegant complex gins from the St. George Spirits distillery in California. For the dry vermouth he insists on lemony Noilly Prat or aromatic Dolin, both from France. You'll need two types of orange bitters: Angostura and Regans'—both available at a good liquor store or from amazon.com.

GEAR Your basic bar gear including a martini glass, of course, and a cocktail shaker, a bar spoon, and a bar strainer

WHAT ELSE There's only one way to mix a great martini, Gabriel insists: by stirring. You want your martini to be crystal clear, and shaking adds tiny air bubbles, making it cloudy. "When stirring, hold the shaker so you can feel when the drink has the right chill." Father-in-law says, "Amen."

TIME about 5 minutes

HOW TO SET UP A HOME BAR

Setting up your bar is a lot easier than equipping your kitchen. A few essential tools, a selection of glasses, and the basic liquors, and you're in business.

Here's what you need:

EQUIPMENT

A jigger Used for measuring liquids in ounces. The standard double jigger looks like two metal cones attached point to point (some models have a handle attached). One good brand is Cocktail Kingdom; a good starter size is 1 ounce/2 ounce.

Metal measuring spoons Spoons for measuring tablespoons and teaspoons are probably part of your kitchen gear. If not, buy a nested set.

A paring knife and a cutting board Essential for cutting up lemons, limes, and other fruits. You've already got a paring knife and cutting board in your kitchen. If you're thinking of buying another one, I like a lightweight bamboo cutting board (8 by 12 inches is a good size), but many bartenders prefer plastic boards, which are dishwasher safe.

A zester Sometimes called a channel knife, this flat-bladed tool with a metal loop or sharp-edged hole is used for removing long, slender strips of lemon peel or other citrus zest for drinks like martinis and old-fashioneds. A vegetable peeler with a swiveling blade is equally, if not more, effective, and you probably already have one.

A Microplane A long, flat metal grater used for shaving fine particles of citrus zest or nutmeg (read more about it on page 15).

A muddler A wooden pestle used for mashing an orange to make an old-fashioned, crushing mint leaves for a whiskey smash or mojito, and more. You can also use the back of a wooden spoon.

A cocktail shaker The standard cocktail mixing device comes in two basic models. The **Boston shaker** has a 12- or 14-ounce metal base and a clear glass that serves as a cover. The **cobbler shaker** looks like a flask, usually metal, with a strainer and cap at the neck end.

A beaker This looks like the cylindrical glass cup with a pouring spout you used in your high school chemistry class. Use it for making stirred drinks, like martinis and Manhattans.

A bar spoon A spoon with a long, slender stem used for stirring cocktails—essential for martinis.

A bar strainer There are three types. At the very least you should own a Hawthorne strainer, which looks like a flat metal Ping-Pong paddle with a coiled wire Slinky along the outside edge to do the actual straining. Place it on top of your cocktail shaker and pour the drink through it into a glass when you are serving cocktails straight up—without ice.

A "julep" strainer is a round metal plate with small holes in it. Use it for straining mint juleps and other drinks with small particles in them.

Mesh strainers, which are rounded, and China cap strainers, which are conical, are used for straining out fine pieces of fruit pulp or seeds.

A hand juicer A hand juicer extracts citrus juice more efficiently than simply squeezing lemon or lime halves between your fingers. One popular model consists of a shallow bowl with a raised ribbed cone in the center. You press a half of a citrus fruit cut side down on top of the cone, twisting it to extract the juice. Another popular model looks like a pair of oversize scissors with a perforated metal or plastic cup where the blades would be at the end. Place a half lemon or lime in the cup and squeeze the handles to extract the juice. A third model, called a reamer, looks

◄ Your knowledge isn't complete until you master the fundamentals (at least) of bartending.

▶ Invest in a set of tall, slender Champagne flutes, which are designed to concentrate the bubbles.

like a fluted wooden, metal, or plastic cone with a stubby handle. Insert the cone into the flesh of the citrus, and the raised ribs help extract the juice from the rind as you twist the handle.

A whipped cream (CO₂) charger Just screw in the nitrous oxide cartridge, pull the trigger, and breathe in deeply. Seriously, use it for whipping cream (see page 561) and frothing milk.

And don't forget A corkscrew and a bottle opener.

GLASSES

Cocktail glasses come in dozens of shapes and sizes. For the basic bar, you need only the first five described here. Space and budget permitting, buy eight to twelve of each glass. If you're hosting a large party, consider renting; you won't even have to wash the glasses.

Martini glasses The classic cone-shaped, long-stemmed glasses. Everything looks elegant served in martini glasses, from martinis, of course, to shrimp cocktails to ceviche—even ice cream.

Old-fashioned glasses Aka rocks glasses or tumblers. Short, sturdy glasses for Manhattans, old-fashioneds, and other classic cocktails. Some

have vertical sides, others are rounded or flare outward.

Highball glasses Tall and straight-sided, holding ten to twelve ounces. Use these when serving highballs (carbonated mixed drinks like a collins) and long drinks (like gin and tonics and Bloody Marys).

Wine glasses You need two versions, both with stems: white wine glasses, which are tall and tulip shaped; and red wine glasses, which are round and balloon shaped. While you're at it, invest in a set of tall, slender Champagne flutes, which are designed to concentrate the bubbles.

Beer glasses Sure you can serve beer in tall glasses or out of the bottle, but an outwardly flaring beer glass makes the brew look and taste better.

Shot glasses Small heavy glasses that hold about one and a half ounces. Use these for serving the frozen vodka or aquavit on page 597.

Coupe glasses As your bar grows, consider adding coupes, stemmed glasses with a shallow rounded bowl. Use them for serving sweet mixed drinks like Cadillacs and sidecars.

THE BASIC LIQUOR SHELF

Depending on your taste and budget, your basic spirits should include a bourbon (and/or rye), Scotch, gin, rum, tequila, and vodka.

Here are some brands I particularly like:

Bourbon Maker's Mark. Woodford Reserve. Elijah Craig.

Rye Old Overholt. Rittenhouse. Redemption. Jim Beam.

Scotch The Famous Grouse, for a blended Scotch. Lagavulin or Laphroaig, for a single malt Scotch.

Gin Hendrick's. Plymouth. Old Tom Gin.

Rum Mount Gay. Myer's. Gosling's Black Seal. Barbancourt.

Tequila Don Julio. Sauza. Herradura.

Vodka A brand that costs less than $30 a bottle, such as Tito's or Grey Goose. Any more than that and you're paying too much for packaging and advertising.

VERMOUTHS

Vermouth is an aromatic fortified wine that once contained a medicinal herb called wormwood (*Wermut* in German—hence the name). You need both dry white and sweet red vermouth—the white for clear drinks, like martinis and vespers; the red for colored drinks, like Manhattans and Negronis. Preferred brands are Dolin and Noilly Prat, which come both white and red. Italian red vermouths include Carpano Antica and Punt e Mes.

CITRUS AND BITTERS

Citrus and bitters are like salt and pepper. Use citrus to bring out brightness; add bitters for spice and depth. For citrus use fresh lemons, limes, oranges, and grapefruit. Remember, a citrus fruit has two flavor components: the aromatic zest, used to flavor a martini, for example, and the acidic juice, an essential ingredient in a drink like a pisco sour or whiskey sour.

A basic assortment of bitters would include:

Angostura bitters flavored with allspice, cinnamon, cloves, and other spices.

Peychaud's bitters flavored with gentian and other aromatics.

Orange bitters flavored with citrus fruit (two good brands are Fee Brothers and Regans').

Pimento bitters flavored with allspice (one good brand is Dale DeGroff's Pimento Aromatic Bitters).

MIXERS

Mixers include soft drinks, used in everything from a gin and tonic to a Cuba libre. I'd also include eggs, which enrich cream-based drinks like eggnog, and egg whites, which make shaken drinks like a pisco sour frothy.

Here are some you'll want to have on hand:

Tonic water Schweppes or Fever-Tree. Mix these with gin or rum to make popular summer tall drinks.

Coca-Cola When possible, use Mexican cola, which is made with cane sugar not corn syrup (it has a richer taste). Look for Mexican cola in Hispanic markets.

Ginger beer Essential for Dark and Stormys (page 588) and Moscow Mules.

SWEETENERS

A wide range of cocktails, from mint juleps to old-fashioneds, call for sweetening. Use Simple Syrup, made by boiling equal parts of granulated sugar and water (see page 589 for a recipe). Alternatively, you can use superfine sugar, which dissolves more quickly than granulated sugar. Don't have any on hand? Pulverize granulated sugar in a blender or clean coffee grinder.

ICE

For clear ice cubes, boil spring water or purified (distilled) water and let it cool before freezing. Use large cubes, ideally two inches square, for strong drinks—you want large ice cubes so they chill the drink without diluting it. (You'll find ice cube trays that make these large cubes at high-end liquor stores, cookware shops, and on amazon.com. One good brand is Tovolo.) Use smaller ice cubes or crushed ice for long drinks and fruit-based cocktails. To crush ice, place it in a "Lewis bag" (a heavy cotton bag) or in a clean dishcloth and smash the ice with a mallet or rolling pin.

◄ You'll want to use large ice cubes so they chill the drink without diluting it.

BROADMOOR MANHATTAN

SHOP Drambuie is a Scotch whisky-based, herb- and honey-flavored liqueur from Scotland. For bourbon, The Broadmoor uses Maker's Mark.

GEAR Your basic bar gear including a martini glass, a cocktail shaker, a bar spoon, and a bar strainer

WHAT ELSE If you live in Colorado, try making this with a local spirit called Stranahan's Colorado whiskey. Awesome just got better. If you like Manhattans as much as I do, you may wish to drain the syrup out of a jar of maraschino cherries and replace it with Drambuie.

TIME about 5 minutes

From the moment I tasted this drink—clean-tasting and potent, with spicy overtones that seemed simultaneously familiar and exotic—I knew I had found my Manhattan. I didn't have to go far. "Spencer's Manhattan," as they call it locally, is a house specialty at the Tavern at The Broadmoor resort in Colorado Springs, where I run my Barbecue University. It was named for Spencer Penrose, who founded The Broadmoor in 1918. What sets it apart is a simple ingredient switch: Drambuie in place of the traditional sweet red vermouth. This makes for a drier, more sophisticated Manhattan with a complex herbal flavor. **Serves 1; can be multiplied as desired**

Ice cubes

2 ounces (4 tablespoons) bourbon, preferably Maker's Mark

½ ounce (1 tablespoon) Drambuie

1 to 2 dashes bitters, preferably Angostura

1 maraschino cherry

The Four Types of Cocktails

▶ Strong drinks: Potent "spirit for-ward" (high alcohol) drinks you're meant to take your time with, for example martinis and Manhattans

▶ Long or tall drinks: Refreshing drinks made with fruit juice and/or mixers; this category includes the collins and the Pimm's cup

▶ Reviver cocktails: Drinks that contain at least three different spirits, for example the corpse reviver and Long Island iced tea; the combination of liquors is said to help revive you from a hangover

▶ Finishing drinks: Your last drink of the evening, these are often sweet or cream-based, like a brandy Alexander or a black or white Russian.

1 Fill a martini glass with ice cubes and add some water to chill it.

2 Place about 1 cup of ice cubes in a cocktail shaker. Add the bourbon, Drambuie, and bitters and stir vigorously with a bar spoon until the shaker becomes painfully cold in your hand, about 30 seconds.

3 Dump and discard the ice and water from the martini glass. Strain the Manhattan into the glass, garnish it with the maraschino cherry, and serve at once.

TATE OLD-FASHIONED

First, do no harm. When it comes to updating classic cocktails, I try to keep this advice from the Hippocratic oath in mind. The old-fashioned is about as classic as drinks get—so classic, it gave its name to a type of cocktail glass. But I've always felt that this vintage combination of whiskey, orange, and bitters could benefit from a whisper of spice. So does John Tate. Founder of Tate's Craft Cocktails in Winston-Salem, North Carolina (a must-visit drinking establishment the next time you're in the area, maybe attending the BookMarks Book Festival), John is something of a mixology reconstructionist, making the old new and the new holy. Cinnamon sugar, orange bitters, and, yes, orange marmalade breathe new life into an old classic. **Serves 1; can be multiplied as desired**

SHOP Tate uses Bulleit rye as his spirit and ginger-flavored Domaine de Canton ginger liqueur as his sweetener. Fee Brothers orange bitters are available at fine liquor stores and online at barproducts.com.

GEAR Your basic bar gear including an old-fashioned glass (what else?), a muddler or a wooden spoon, and a bar spoon, plus a shallow bowl or small dish

WHAT ELSE A purist may wish to omit the cinnamon sugar and orange marmalade.

TIME about 5 minutes

3 tablespoons sugar

1 teaspoon ground cinnamon

1 orange slice (about ¼ inch thick), seeds removed

1 stemless maraschino cherry

1 teaspoon orange marmalade

2 dashes orange bitters or Angostura bitters

2 ounces (4 tablespoons) rye whiskey

1 ounce (2 tablespoons) ginger liqueur, such as Domaine de Canton

About 1 cup ice cubes

1 Place the sugar and cinnamon in a shallow bowl and mix them together with a fork.

2 Run the cut side of the orange around the rim of an old-fashioned glass. Set the orange slice aside. Dip the rim of the glass in the cinnamon sugar mixture to coat it.

3 Place the orange slice and maraschino cherry in the bottom of the glass and, using a muddler or the back of a wooden spoon, crush them well. Continuing to press with the muddler or spoon, work in the marmalade and bitters.

4 Add the rye, ginger liqueur, and ice cubes. Stir well with a bar spoon and serve at once.

DALE DEGROFF

Dale DeGroff takes the stage, cocktail shaker in one hand, guitar in the other, ready to perform in lecture and song the history of the American cocktail. You might say it's his own life story, for if there's one man responsible for the rebirth of the art of the cocktail and the current mixology mania sweeping the world, it's this former Navy brat and English major turned bartender to movers, shakers, and stars.

DeGroff has long had a knack for being at the right place at the right time—the Hotel Bel-Air in Los Angeles, for example, and Joseph Baum's powerhouse restaurants Aurora and the Rainbow Room in New York. At each bar he raised the bar, so to speak, rehabilitating vintage cocktails, popularizing Latin drinks and spirits (think the mojito and the Pisco Sour, page 588),

insisting on fresh herbs and fruit juices, and turning to new technologies and ingredients to make the likes of smoked Bloody Marys (page 596) and kaffir lime gimlets. His books *The Essential Cocktail: The Art of Mixing Perfect Drinks* and *The Craft of the Cocktail* are the only guides most of us will ever need on bartending. If you want additional education, attend DeGroff's BAR (Beverage Alcohol Resource program), a sort of boot camp for aspiring bartenders held annually in New York City. His latest project, the Museum of the American Cocktail in New Orleans, celebrates his lifelong passion for a beverage art America can truly call its own.

Asked why it's important for every self-respecting man to know the rudiments of mixology, DeGroff paraphrases Ernest Hemingway, saying, "A well-made cocktail encapsulates civilization within the bounds of a glass. When you have a martini in your hand, how can you *not* feel as though we've evolved beyond brute existence?"

When did you realize you wanted to become a barman?
When I was eight years old, my grandfather took me to a Red Sox-Yankee game at Fenway Park. It was one of the most glorious days of my childhood, and my overriding memory was the smell of beer and cigars. When I was finally old enough to go to my first bar in New York, I smelled the same aroma of beer and cigars. "My God," I thought. "I'm home."

What was the first cocktail you ever mixed?
A whiskey sour. The sour mix came from a bar gun (one of those pistol-like gadgets that dispense liquids). It was not my proudest moment.

What are the five classic cocktails every man should know how to make?

A martini, a Manhattan, a Negroni, a daiquiri, and a sidecar.

What five modern cocktails should every man know how to make?

A mojito, a margarita, a cosmopolitan, a gin-gin mule, and a whiskey smash [find DeGroff's recipe on page 586].

What's the perfect seduction cocktail?

I can't name a specific drink—that's up to her. But I'd start with tequila—no other spirit is quite as sexy. I'd make the drink spicy and sweet (but not sugary). I'd definitely prepare it in front of her so she can watch my hands.

What's your proudest creation?

There are many, but I'd start with the Ritz cocktail, which I created for my mentor, Joe Baum, at the Aurora restaurant in New York City. I based it on a classic from the Ritz bar in Paris: the Champagne cocktail (Champagne, Cognac, and bitters). I had the idea to add maraschino liqueur for roundness and Cointreau for its bitter orange tang, and we served it in a cocktail glass, not a Champagne flute. The beauty of the Ritz cocktail is that, like Champagne itself, it's perfect pretty much any time of day: before dinner, after dinner, for breakfast, lunch, or as a nightcap.

One drink worth rediscovering?

The daiquiri. The original, which dates back to Cuba at the turn of the last century, contained just three ingredients: rum, lime juice, and sugar. For a lot of young people, it's degenerated

into a sort of alcoholic Slurpee. When you make it with fresh lime juice and a big-flavored Caribbean white rum—perhaps with a whisper of fresh grapefruit juice or maraschino liqueur—it's a revelation.

> ▶ Have fun. It's bartending, not brain surgery.

What do you drink at home?

I love the whiskey smash. I've always found mint juleps a bit boring (too sweet and monodimensional), so I mashed up some fresh lemon with the mint and sweetened the drink with curaçao instead of sugar. The Eastern Standard restaurant in Boston has served more than 25,000 whiskey smashes.

What are the three tools you can't live without?

A bar spoon: It's totally underutilized, but it looks so graceful when you use one, especially when you use a traditional spoon with a long, slender twisted shaft.

A muddler: It's a wooden pestle used for crushing citrus fruit, fresh ginger, and mint and other fresh herbs. There's nothing like a muddler for extracting the fresh juices and aromatic oils, and you can't make a proper caipirinha or whiskey smash without one.

An Aladin smoker: I don't need to tell you, Steven, smoke can add an incredible depth of flavor to a cocktail—just as it does for barbecue. My favorite wood is maple. Insert the smoke hose in the drink for a few minutes, and you wind

up with a smoky Bloody Mary, bloody bull, or Danish Mary you'll never forget.

What are the three most common mistakes guys make when mixing drinks?

Overbuying. A lot of guys will buy an industrial-size bottle of vermouth, for example. But vermouth is a sort of wine and it deteriorates over time, even if you keep it in the refrigerator. You're much better off buying smaller bottles and replacing them often.

Overchilling. Sure, you can store your gin in the freezer and your vermouth in the refrigerator. But that doesn't make a great instant martini. You need to stir the ingredients with ice—indeed, it's the melting ice [water] that rounds out the flavor.

Overconcentrating on measuring. Joe Baum didn't want his bartenders to measure. He wanted the guests to feel like you were pouring a drink for them at your home. Of course, if you're just starting out, use a jigger until you get the feel for a 1½-ounce pour.

Something unexpected you've learned over the years that helped you up your game behind the bar?

Water. Yes, water. You might think it would dilute the other ingredients, but in fact it makes them taste better. It mellows the bite of the alcohol and opens up the flavor. When you shake or stir a cocktail with ice, your goal is to add about one ounce of water.

Parting words of advice?

Have fun. It's bartending, not brain surgery.

DALE DEGROFF'S WHISKEY SMASH

SHOP Use fresh mint—peppermint for a spicier smash; spearmint for a sweeter one. For a more aromatic version of the drink, you could use a Meyer lemon (see page 187 for more about these).

GEAR Your basic bar gear including a cocktail shaker, a muddler or wooden spoon, a bar strainer, and an old-fashioned glass

WHAT ELSE DeGroff uses rye or bourbon or even Canadian whisky—anything but Scotch. The smoky flavor of Scotch, he maintains, would conflict with the citrus and mint flavors.

TIME about 5 minutes

Combine a mint julep with a whiskey sour and you get the whiskey smash. Invented by master barman Dale DeGroff (read about him on page 584), it combines the refreshing acidity of fresh lemon with the mentholated chill of fresh mint. It's hard to imagine a more refreshing cocktail on a hot summer day, but that doesn't mean I don't enjoy it all year long. **Serves 1; can be multiplied as desired**

1 lemon

5 fresh mint leaves, plus a mint sprig for garnish

1 ounce (2 tablespoons) curaçao or Cointreau

2 ounces (4 tablespoons) bourbon or rye whiskey

About 1 cup ice cubes, or more if needed

1 Cut the lemon in half crosswise. Cut a thin round slice off one half of the lemon and set the slice aside for a garnish. Cut the other lemon half into quarters, removing any seeds with a fork. Place the lemon quarters in a cocktail shaker. (Save the remaining lemon half for a future cocktail.) Add the 5 mint leaves and, using a muddler or the back of a wooden spoon, crush them well.

2 Stir in the curaçao or Cointreau, followed by the bourbon or rye and the ice cubes. Cover the cocktail shaker and shake it as hard as you can for about 20 seconds.

3 Strain the whiskey smash into an old-fashioned glass. DeGroff serves his whiskey smash over ice; I like it straight up—add ice if you prefer. Then, make a slit in the reserved lemon slice and press it over the rim of the glass for decoration. Garnish the glass with the mint sprig and serve at once.

DALE DEGROFF'S ESSENTIAL
BARTENDING TECHNIQUES

Dale DeGroff has done more to usher in America's cocktail renaissance than any other barman (read more about his remarkable career and philosophy on page 584). Here are his five essential techniques for bartending.

STIRRING It's something of a lost art, but there are some drinks that taste right only when stirred, not shaken: Think martinis (see page 577 for a recipe) or other cocktails made solely with spirits. Use a long-handled spoon and rotate it fifty times if you're using large ice cubes, thirty times if the ice cubes are small.

SHAKING Any cocktail that contains fruit juices and sweeteners, such as the margarita (page 590) and Pisco Sour (page 588), should be shaken. Your goal is to incorporate air bubbles into the drink, which makes it taste fresh and alive. Use a cocktail shaker—metal if you measure and glass if you free pour (so you can see the ingredient levels). Add the ingredients, close the shaker, and give it ten or fifteen hard, fast shakes. When you do it right, it sounds like a machine gun.

MUDDLING Muddling is using a wooden pestle or the back of a wooden spoon to crush pieces of orange or lemon, mint sprigs, fresh ginger, and/or other aromatics, and often sugar. To do this, you press and grind at the same time, hard and long enough to extract both the juices and the aromatic oils. Examples of muddled drinks are the whiskey smash (facing page) and mojito.

FLAMBEING Start with an oval of lemon or orange zest (one by two inches) cut from a firm fresh fruit. Light a long match or a butane match and hold it one inch above the drink. Hold the piece of zest skin side down between the thumb and forefinger of your other hand about two inches over the flame. Firmly squeeze the zest to send droplets of oil into the flame, where they'll ignite, creating a dramatic flash of fire and dispersing the smoky oils over the surface of the cocktail. Try it over your next martini.

To flambé a cocktail, like a blue blazer, float 151 proof rum on top, then light it.

SMOKING Manhattans and Bloody Marys are awesome smoked. You'll need an instant smoker like Aladin or The Smoking Gun (page 22). Load it with your hardwood sawdust of choice. Insert the rubber smoking tube in the drink to the bottom of the glass and trigger the smoker; normally, three to five minutes does it. Cover the glass with plastic wrap to hold the smoke in.

DARK AND STORMY

SHOP You need real ginger beer, spicier and less sweet than conventional ginger ale. Two good brands are Barritt's Bermuda Stone and Maine Root Ginger Brew. My personal preference for rum is dark Gosling's Black Seal from Bermuda.

GEAR Your basic kitchen gear plus a highball glass

WHAT ELSE To make a Moscow mule (an inferior drink, in my opinion) substitute vodka for the rum.

TIME about 5 minutes

Invented in Newport, Rhode Island, the Dark and Stormy is a traditional cocktail of the sailing crowd, and it also became the official wrap drink of the crew of my *Barbecue University* TV show. We loved the one-two punch of peppery ginger beer and potent rum—eminently refreshing after a hot day at the grill or on a sailboat. **Serves 1; can be multiplied as desired**

Ice cubes

6 ounces (¾ cup) ginger beer

2 ounces (4 tablespoons) dark rum, such as Gosling's Black Seal

1 lime wedge

Fill a highball glass with ice cubes. Pour the ginger beer over the ice. Gently add the rum, floating it on top. Rub the cut side of the lime wedge around the rim of the glass, make a slit in the center of the lime wedge, and then press it onto the rim of the glass. Serve at once.

PISCO SOUR

SHOP To be authentic you need genuine Peruvian pisco—available at well-stocked spirits shops. Two good brands are BarSol and Don César. FYI, lacking pisco one day, I made a pretty interesting sour with grappa.

GEAR Your basic kitchen gear plus a martini glass, a cocktail shaker, and a bar strainer

When the conquistadores invaded what would become Latin America, they brought new ingredients (wine grapes and sugarcane, for example), new cooking equipment (like iron pots and gridirons), and new technologies (such as distillation). In the Caribbean, this gave rise to rum, and in Peru, it blessed us with pisco. This clear aromatic brandy has Cognac's fruit with the bad boy brashness of grappa. Combine it with sugar, lemon juice, egg white, and bitters, shake it like crazy, and you get one of the creamiest, foamiest, most refreshing cocktails in the New World. **Serves 1; can be multiplied as desired**

Ice cubes

2½ ounces (5 tablespoons) pisco

1 ounce (2 tablespoons) simple syrup (recipe follows)

1 ounce (2 tablespoons) fresh lemon juice

1 egg white (see page 39 for separating instructions)

Angostura bitters

WHAT ELSE You need an egg white to achieve the trademark foam atop the sour. If you're queasy about raw eggs, use pasteurized egg whites (see A Guy's Best Friend: Eggs on page 40).

TIME about 5 minutes

1 Fill a martini glass with ice cubes and add some water to chill it.

2 Place the pisco, simple syrup, lemon juice, and egg white in a cocktail shaker with about 1 cup of ice cubes. Cover the cocktail shaker and shake it as hard as you can for about 20 seconds. The mixture should be foamy.

3 Dump and discard the ice and water from the martini glass. Strain the sour into the glass. Shake a dash of bitters on top and serve at once.

SIMPLE SYRUP

Simple syrup is nothing more than equal parts granulated sugar and water boiled long enough to dissolve the sugar. You let the syrup cool, then put it in a clean bottle with a spout. Syrup blends with spirits better than sugar, and it has a mellowing effect you can't achieve with straight sugar.

To make flavored simple syrups, add three strips of lemon or orange zest, three fresh basil leaves, a sprig of rosemary about three inches long, a vanilla bean cut in half, or a cinnamon stick to the water before you bring them to a boil. Remove the flavorings with tongs before bottling the syrup. **Makes 1 cup**

GEAR Your basic bar gear including a funnel and a bottle with a spout and cap, plus a saucepan

1 cup water

1 cup sugar

Bring the water to a boil in a heavy saucepan over medium-high heat. Stir in the sugar and cook just until it dissolves, 1 to 2 minutes. Let the syrup cool to room temperature, then pour it through a funnel into a bottle with a cap and spout. Cover and refrigerate the syrup until ready to use. It will keep indefinitely.

YOUR BASIC MARGARITA

SHOP By law, tequila needs to contain only 51 percent blue agave spirits, but I like a 100 percent agave tequila, like Hornitos or Don Julio Blanco. For the orange liqueur, I prefer the astringency of Cointreau to the mellow sweetness of Grand Marnier.

GEAR Your basic bar gear plus two margarita or martini glasses, a shallow bowl, a cocktail shaker, and a bar strainer

WHAT ELSE Depending on the tequila and the acidity of the limes, you may want to add a little sweetener. To keep things in the cactus family, use agave syrup (a liquid sweetener made from agave cactus).

Tradition calls for salting the rim of the glass. You can certainly omit this step if you don't like salt or it doesn't like you.

TIME about 5 minutes

I could retrace the history of the margarita for you, speculating on the señora who inspired it. I won't. I could list the indignities that have befallen this classic Mexican cocktail over the years, from the sugary bottled sour mix to Jell-O shooters to those tequila-laced slushes known as frozen margaritas. Why bother? I could delve into the arcane debates surrounding the preparation of a proper margarita: *añejo* versus *reposado* tequila, Cointreau versus Grand Marnier, agave syrup versus simple syrup. It wouldn't really help you. The fact is that as long as you use a decent tequila and squeeze your lime juice fresh, the margarita is a pretty hard drink to screw up. I'm constantly tweaking my formula, tinkering with the ingredients and proportions. Here's what I serve these days. **Makes 2 (hey, you shouldn't drink margaritas alone); can be multiplied as desired**

Ice cubes

½ cup coarse salt (kosher or sea)

2 limes (for 2 ounces lime juice)

4 ounces (½ cup) tequila

2 ounces (¼ cup) Cointreau

1 to 2 teaspoons agave syrup (optional)

1 Fill 2 martini glasses with ice cubes and add some water to chill them. Place the salt in a shallow bowl.

2 Cut the limes in half crosswise. Dump and discard the ice and water from the martini glasses. Rub the rims of the glasses with the cut edge of a lime half. Dip the rim of each glass in the salt to coat it.

3 Squeeze the lime halves and measure 2 ounces (¼ cup) of juice. Place the lime juice in a cocktail shaker and add the tequila, Cointreau, and 1 to 2 teaspoons agave syrup, if you like a sweeter margarita. Add enough ice to submerge the liquids by 1 inch. Shake vigorously, and I mean vigorously, for about 20 seconds. Strain the margaritas into the salted glasses and serve at once.

▶ *Left to right: Hemingway Bloody Mary (plus a celery rib), The Berthin Martini, Your Basic Margarita*

A COCKTAIL GAZETTEER

Here are some other cocktails you should be familiar with.

BLACK OR WHITE RUSSIAN An after-dinner drink made with vodka and Kahlúa or another coffee liqueur; to make a white Russian, add cream.

BLUE BLAZER The ultimate pyrotechnic cocktail: hot Scotch with demerara sugar (a brown granulated sugar) and lemon peel, traditionally set ablaze and poured back and forth between pewter cups.

BRANDY ALEXANDER A chocolaty after-dinner drink made with brandy, cream, and crème de cacao.

CADILLAC A margarita made with Grand Marnier instead of Cointreau. Not to be confused with a golden Cadillac—Galliano, an Italian herb liqueur, shaken with crème de cacao and cream.

CAIPIRINHA A classic Brazilian drink made by muddling chunks of lime, sugar, and cachaça, a potent cane spirit.

CAPE CODDER A long drink of cranberry juice and vodka with a squeeze of fresh lime.

COLLINS A tall drink made with gin, vodka, or bourbon, plus lemon juice, simple syrup, and club soda to give it sparkle.

CORPSE REVIVER A reputed hangover remedy consisting of brandy, calvados (or other apple brandy), and sweet vermouth. Other versions veer toward gin, absinthe, orange liqueur, and Lillet Blanc. Some guys drink these to get a hangover, not cure one.

COSMOPOLITAN A colorful combination of vodka, cranberry juice, orange liqueur, and lime juice popularized in the television series *Sex in the City* (which means your girlfriend may like it better than you do).

CUBA LIBRE White rum and Coca-Cola with a squeeze of lime.

DAIQUIRI A vintage Cuban cocktail made with white rum, fresh lime juice, and simple syrup; named for a mining town near Santiago, Cuba.

EGGNOG A creamy holiday drink made with egg yolks, heavy cream, bourbon, brandy, and/or rum, and freshly grated nutmeg.

GIMLET A classic combination of gin and Rose's lime juice. "It beats martinis hollow," wrote the crime writer Raymond Chandler, who insisted that the perfect ratio for these ingredients was equal parts.

GIN AND TONIC OR RUM AND TONIC Two archetypal tall summer drinks based on tonic water, a carbonated drink flavored with a bitter tropical bark with antimalarial properties called quinine.

GIN-GIN MULE A variation on the Moscow mule made with gin, lime juice, simple syrup, and fresh mint.

GLOGG Scandinavian hot mulled wine; Germans and Swiss call it *glühwein*.

LONG ISLAND ICED TEA A potent party drink that combines gin, rum, tequila, vodka, and triple sec with lemon juice, simple syrup, and Coca-Cola.

MINT JULEP The classic cocktail of the Kentucky Derby, made by muddling fresh mint with sugar or simple syrup and adding bourbon and shaved ice.

MOJITO An eminently refreshing combination of muddled fresh mint, rum, fresh lime juice, simple syrup, and club soda.

MOSCOW MULE Ginger beer fortified with vodka and lime.

NEGRONI A pleasingly bitter cocktail comprised of gin, Campari, and sweet red vermouth.

PIMM'S CUP A refreshing combination of a Pimm's No. 1 (an English gin-based aperitif), 7UP or club soda, cucumber, and mint.

SIDECAR A classic cocktail made with Cognac, triple sec or another orange liqueur, and lemon juice.

VESPER James Bond's preferred cocktail, a martini-like combination of gin, vodka, Lillet Blanc, and a twist of lemon. Bond ordered it shaken, not stirred.

WHISKEY SOUR Your whiskey of choice shaken with simple syrup, fresh lemon juice, and an egg white for froth and garnished with an orange slice and maraschino cherry.

BLOODY MARYS
SEVEN WAYS TO SUNDAY

SHOP Most bartenders use Sacramento brand tomato juice, but you might try an organic brand like R.W. Knudsen Family. I like Russian or Polish vodka (these guys invented the stuff), but French, Scandinavian, and American vodkas each have their partisans.

GEAR Your basic bar gear including a large pitcher and a bar spoon, plus a shallow bowl

WHAT ELSE Back in Hemingway's day, blocks of ice were commonplace. Here you'd need a chunk of ice an inch or so narrower than the mouth of the pitcher. Break it up with an ice pick or mallet. Alternatively you can use three to four cups of large ice cubes.

TIME about 5 minutes

The Bloody Mary came relatively late to America's cocktail party (the first written reference appeared in 1939 and was attributed to the actor George Jessel). But we took to this spiced vodka-laced tomato juice big time—in part because brunch would be such a dull meal without it. Ernest Hemingway was an early adopter. You'll find a pitcher of his version here, followed by six of my favorite variations in single servings.

HEMINGWAY BLOODY MARY

Ernest Hemingway offered the following advice on making Bloody Marys: "If you get it too powerful, weaken with more tomato juice. If it lacks authority, add more vodka." Here's how Papa made it. **Serves 4**

Ice	A few dashes of Tabasco sauce
1 pint (16 ounces) vodka	1 teaspoon freshly ground black pepper
1 pint (16 ounces) tomato juice	½ teaspoon celery salt
2 ounces (¼ cup) fresh lime juice, or more to taste	½ teaspoon ground cayenne pepper
1 tablespoon Worcestershire sauce, or more to taste	

Place a large chunk of ice or 3 to 4 cups of ice cubes in a large pitcher. Add the vodka, tomato juice, lime juice, Worcestershire sauce, Tabasco sauce, black pepper, celery salt, and cayenne. Stir to mix, then taste for seasoning adding more lime juice, Worcestershire sauce, and/or Tabasco sauce as necessary.

RAICHLEN BLOODY MARY

When I make Bloody Marys, I skip the vodka debate altogether and proceed directly to gin. Then I add horseradish and Sriracha (Thai hot sauce) to pump up the heat. **Serves 1; can be multiplied as desired**

1 tablespoon Old Bay seasoning or your favorite barbecue rub (mine is on page 285)

1 lemon wedge

¾ cup tomato juice

2 ounces (4 tablespoons) gin

1 tablespoon fresh lemon juice

1 teaspoon prepared or freshly grated horseradish, or more to taste

1 teaspoon Sriracha or other Asian hot sauce, or more to taste

1 teaspoon Worcestershire sauce, or more to taste

Ice cubes

1 rib celery, preferably from the inside of the bunch with leaves still attached

Place the Old Bay seasoning or barbecue rub in a shallow bowl. Rub the cut edge of the lemon wedge around the rim of a highball glass to wet it. Dip the rim of the glass in the seasoning. Add the tomato juice, gin, lemon juice, horseradish, Sriracha, and Worcestershire sauce and stir well to mix; take care not to knock the seasoning off the rim of the glass. Add a few ice cubes and stir to mix. Add the celery rib to the glass (like Mom says, eat your vegetables) and serve at once.

Variations

In all cases, rimming the glass with spices is optional.

Bloody Bull: Make the Raichlen Bloody Mary replacing half of the tomato juice (3 ounces; 6 tablespoons) with beef broth or stock. Add 2 tablespoons of fresh orange juice in place of the lemon juice and garnish with a strip of beef jerky.

Bloody Clam: Make the Raichlen Bloody Mary using Clamato juice in place of the tomato juice. Or use 3 ounces (6 tablespoons) of tomato juice and 3 ounces (6 tablespoons) of bottled clam juice (clam juice is available in supermarkets in the section where they sell canned tuna fish and anchovies). If you're feeling extravagant, add a couple of freshly shucked littlenecks.

Bloody Maria: Make the Raichlen Bloody Mary replacing the gin with tequila, preferably a pure agave tequila. Use sliced pickled jalapeños and some of their juice in place of the horseradish. Substitute a Mexican hot sauce, like Cholula, for the Sriracha.

Smoky Mary: Make the Raichlen Bloody Mary then insert the smoking tube of an Aladin or PolyScience smoke gun and smoke the drink for 3 to 5 minutes, covering the glass with plastic wrap to hold the smoke in. Repeat as needed.

KOREAN MARY

Michael Schwartz of Michael's Genuine in Miami gives his Bloody Mary an Asian twist by adding kimchi, a Korean garlicky pickled cabbage. To get the full effect, you'll need a couple of grilled shrimp to skewer for garnish. **Serves 2**

1 cup tomato juice

¼ cup kimchi with its juices, plus kimchi for garnish

2 tablespoons fresh lime juice

4 ounces (½ cup) vodka

Ice cubes

2 grilled shrimp

Combine the tomato juice, kimchi with its juices, and lime juice in a blender and puree until smooth. Add the vodka and blend just to mix. Pour into 2 highball glasses filled with ice cubes and garnish each with a grilled shrimp and a piece of kimchi on a skewer.

RED BEER

SHOP In keeping with its south of the border origins, start with a Mexican beer.

I'm not much of a partisan of colored beer. But Mexico's *michelada* does the math that any great cocktail should: a net result greater than the simple sum of the parts. In this case those parts include beer, tomato juice, lime juice, and chile powder. It combines the virtues of a Bloody Mary and a cold beer—and it's hard to beat on a hot day. **Serves 1; can be multiplied as desired**

2 tablespoons chile powder

1 lime, cut into wedges

½ cup good-quality tomato juice, such as Sacramento

1 teaspoon Worcestershire sauce

8 ounces (1 cup) cold beer

Ice cubes

Place the chile powder in a shallow bowl. Run the cut side of a lime wedge around the rim of a highball glass. Dip the rim of the glass in the chile powder to coat it. Add the tomato juice, Worcestershire sauce, and beer to the glass. Squeeze in 1 tablespoon of lime juice, setting aside 1 lime wedge for garnish. Stir to mix with a bar spoon. Add enough ice cubes to fill the glass, garnish with the reserved lime wedge, and serve at once.

GEAR Your basic bar gear including a highball glass and a bar spoon, plus a shallow dish

WHAT ELSE Lots of worthy variations here: Clamato juice instead of tomato; *pimentón* (smoked paprika) or even Old Bay seasoning on the glass rim instead of chile powder; a shot of the juice from pickled jalapeños. You get the idea.

TIME about 5 minutes

VODKA OR AQUAVIT
IN A BLOCK OF ICE

Sammy's Romanian is one of the most outrageous restaurants in Manhattan, and even if you're not Jewish you'll find yourself leaping to your feet to dance the hora around the dining room. The food, plate-burying Romanian steaks and pitchers of schmaltz (chicken fat), helps loosen inhibitions; so does the vodka, sold by the bottle and kept icy cold in its own block of ice. An icy presentation that looks, er, cool as all get-out with caviar or smoked salmon—or just by itself. **Makes 1 ice-encased bottle of vodka**

SHOP You probably have your favorite brand of vodka (mine is Wyborowa from Poland.) For aquavit, I like Aalborg from Denmark.

GEAR Your basic bar gear including shot glasses, preferably chilled in the freezer, plus an empty half-gallon cardboard milk carton, rinsed clean, or a small smooth-sided plastic or metal bucket and a clean white cloth napkin for serving

WHAT ELSE For clearer ice, boil and cool spring water before freezing.

TIME overnight

1 bottle (750 milliliters) vodka or aquavit

2 quarts (8 cups) water

1 Place the vodka or aquavit bottle in the center of the milk carton or bucket. Fill the carton or bucket with water to within ½ inch of the top, then place it in the freezer and let freeze overnight.

2 The next day briefly run warm water over the outside of the cardboard carton or bucket. Peel off the paper carton or pull the block of ice with the bottle out of the bucket.

3 Wrap the block of ice in a cloth napkin so you can handle it without freezing your fingers. Pour the vodka or aquavit into iced shot glasses.

SANGRIA FOR GROWN-UPS

SHOP Lambrusco is an effervescent wine from the Emilia-Romagna and Lombardy regions of Italy. (Atria uses Lini Lambrusco.) Domaine de Canton is a ginger liqueur, while St-Germain takes its aromatic flavor from elderflowers. All are available at a good liquor store.

GEAR Your basic bar gear plus a large (at least 2-quart) clear glass pitcher and a wooden spoon for muddling

WHAT ELSE The rum and liqueur base that flavors the sangria should be made ahead of time (the Atria guys do it the day before), but add the Lambrusco just before serving.

TIME 10 minutes preparation time, plus at least 8 hours for macerating the orange

Nothing says party time like a pitcher of sangria. And few guys make it better than chef-owner Christian Thornton and sommelier John Clift at the restaurant Atria in my summer stomping grounds, Edgartown, Martha's Vineyard. The guys start with dark rum and Domaine de Canton and St-Germain liqueurs, which add potency and spice, and they use fresh oranges, not the usual canned fruit cocktail you often find in frat house sangrias. But the real kicker comes from a carbonating agent: the dry Italian sparkling red wine called Lambrusco. **Makes about 4 cups; serves 4 (you probably ought to make a double batch)**

1 orange

2 tablespoons sugar

3 ounces (6 tablespoons) dark rum, such as Myers's

3 ounces (6 tablespoons) ginger liqueur, such as Domaine de Canton

2 ounces (4 tablespoons) St-Germain elderflower liqueur

Ice cubes

1 bottle (750 milliliters) Lambrusco wine, chilled

1 Slice the orange into wedges and, using a fork, remove and discard any seeds. Place the orange and sugar in a pitcher and muddle (mash) them with the back of a wooden spoon.

2 Stir in the rum, ginger liqueur, and St-Germain liqueur and let macerate (steep) overnight in the refrigerator, covered.

3 When ready to serve, add ice cubes to the pitcher. Add the Lambrusco, stir gently, and serve.

TWELVE THINGS YOU NEED TO KNOW ABOUT
COFFEE

1 THREE HUNDRED dollars will buy you a pound of "monkey parchment" (coffee beans chewed and expectorated by rhesus monkeys in India). The process is supposed to give the coffee an inimitable flavor. One hundred and fifty dollars will buy you a pound of *kopi luwak*, beans that have, well, traversed the digestive system of Indonesian civet cats. This process, too, is supposed to impart an inimitable flavor to the coffee.

2 SIX BUCKS will buy you a pound of Café Pilon, a dark roast Cuban-style coffee that meets the criterion in an old Turkish proverb: The perfect cup should be "black as hell, strong as death, and sweet as love." This is our house coffee and no animals were required for its production.

3 THERE ARE six factors that go into brewing a great cup of coffee: the bean, the roast, the freshness, the grind, the brewing technique, and the condiments (milk, cream, sugar—take your pick).

4 FOR ME, the bean matters less than the roast, which I like a few degrees north of burnt.

French roast is dark; Italian roast is darker; espresso roast is the darkest of all, and thus the Raichlen favorite. Freshly roasted coffee beans will be shiny with oils and intensely aromatic. Store them in the freezer, even if the store tells you not to.

5 EVERY MAN should eventually own two coffee grinders: one for coffee and one for spices. Confusing these grinders will ruin both your spices and your coffee.

6 YOU DON'T need to invest in a $1,500 espresso machine that grinds the beans, brews the coffee, foams the milk, washes the dishes, and serenades you with renaissance madrigals while giving you a massage. A $50 electric drip coffee machine produces a respectable pot of coffee.

7 WHEN MAKING drip coffee, use one to two tablespoons of ground coffee per cup of water, depending on how strong you like your coffee (I take mine strong). Make sure you use a drip grind. Too fine a grind will clog the paper filter.

8 EVEN SIMPLER is French press coffee. You place boiling water and ground coffee in a glass beaker, cover, and wait a couple of minutes, then push down the plunger in the lid. The mesh filter pins the loose grounds at the bottom of the beaker. This is a good system for making coffee for one or two people.

9 IF ESPRESSO is your brew of choice, you need a machine that's powerful enough to produce *crema*, a thin layer of tan foam on top of the espresso that results from the pressure of the steam passing through the coffee grounds. (Note for history buffs: The Italian company Gaggia patented the first semiautomatic espresso machine in 1938 and is still a major player in the market.)

There are several things to consider when investing in an espresso machine: First, your budget—prices range from about $100 to $1,000 and beyond.

Next, define the features that are important to you, such as the degree of automation, the ease of use, brew strength controls, whether you want an integrated coffee bean grinder, a frothing wand (for heating and frothing the milk), a hot water dispenser (for making tea), a cup warmer, and so on. A pod-type espresso maker offers the convenience of premeasured plastic coffee capsules, but these cost more per cup and have a greater carbon footprint (while I have one of these machines, I rarely use it).

Finally, consider how the machine looks in the space you've allotted it. You'd rather wake up to a beauty than a beast, right?

10 ONE OF THE COOLEST ways to make coffee is in the style of cowboys and ranchers in South Africa. They boil the grounds in water in a coffee pot over a campfire for a few minutes, then plunge a burning branch into the coffee. The burning branch makes the coffee grounds precipitate to the bottom of the pot and imparts an interesting smoke flavor to the coffee.

11 ANOTHER INTRIGUING method is one used by Greeks, Turks, and Arabs. They start with powder-fine ground coffee (available at ethnic markets) placed in a tall, slender brass pot with sugar to taste and sometimes a cardamom pod. The mixture is brought to a boil three times, and the pot is removed from the heat just before the coffee spills over the edge. You sip the coffee from a tiny cup just until you reach the grounds at the bottom.

12 VIETNAMESE STYLE is yet another way to internationalize your "cuppa Joe." Place a couple of teaspoons of sweetened condensed milk in the bottom of a heatproof glass. Add a shot or two of espresso. Stir before sipping.

Hot Mulled Wine from Quebec
THE CARIBOU

SHOP As with all wine-based drinks and dishes, you don't need a *Grand Cru*, but start with a wine you wouldn't mind drinking straight.

GEAR Your basic bar gear including a zester or vegetable peeler, plus a large heavy saucepan and a ladle

WHAT ELSE Depending on your family tradition or taste, you can fortify the hot mulled wine with brandy, gin, vodka, or another spirit.

TIME about 10 minutes

Ah, the joys of taping a barbecue TV show in Quebec in May. Normally, you'd expect clear skies and warm weather. One morning, we awoke to three inches of snow. So we did what any practical Quebecer would do: brushed off the grills and shoveled off the set, fortifying ourselves with a local cold weather pick-me-up called the Caribou. You start with hot mulled wine, which you reinforce with brandy. It blasts *glühwein* and *glogg* (European mulled wines) off the table, and it just may be one of the reasons French Canadians not only tolerate winter but welcome it. Bring it on! **Makes 8 cups**

1 orange

6 whole cloves

1 lemon

1 piece (2 inches) fresh ginger, peeled and thinly sliced crosswise

4 cinnamon sticks (3 inches), broken in half

2 bottles (750 milliliters each) dry red wine

¾ cup pure maple syrup or honey, or ¾ cup sugar, or more to taste

1 cup Cognac or other brandy, in a measuring cup with a spout

1 Using a vegetable peeler, remove two 1½-by-½-inch strips of zest from the orange, being careful to remove only the orange rind, not the bitter white pith underneath. Stick 3 cloves in each strip of zest. Thinly slice the orange and lemon crosswise. Remove any seeds with a fork.

2 Place the strips of orange zest, orange and lemon slices, ginger, cinnamon sticks, wine, and maple syrup in a large heavy saucepan and bring to a boil over high heat. Reduce the heat and let the wine simmer gently until spicy and richly flavored, about 10 minutes. Taste for sweetness, adding more maple syrup as necessary. Turn off the heat but keep the wine warm in the saucepan.

3 Just before serving, dim the lights. Gently pour the Cognac into the saucepan so that it floats on the wine. Touch a match to the Cognac so it flambés (see page 566). When the flames burn out, stir the Cognac into the wine, then ladle the caribou into mugs. Try to include an orange or lemon slice and piece of cinnamon stick in each mug.

Variation
Hot Mulled Cider

Substitute 2 quarts of apple cider (preferably farm-fresh cider) for the wine and 1 cup of calvados or another apple brandy for the Cognac.

PRAIRIE OYSTER

James Bond gulped one with an aspirin chaser for breakfast. Igor Stravinsky slugged one down daily before he started composing. In the classic P. G. Wodehouse short story "Jeeves Takes Charge," the iconic butler Jeeves proves his worth his first day on the job by administering one to his hungover young ward, Bertie. I speak of the prairie oyster—the infamous cure for a hangover. Why else would anyone gulp a raw egg laced with Worcestershire sauce and Tabasco sauce for breakfast? (There's something decidedly oysterlike about the soft squishy yolk, the viscous white, and the invigorating blast of hot sauce.) I can't promise you that the anti-hangover properties actually work, but legions of guys swear by it. **Serves 1**

SHOP As always, look for organic or pasteurized eggs.

GEAR Your basic bar gear including an old-fashioned glass or a small glass tumbler

WHAT ELSE The classic prairie oyster contains just four ingredients: egg, Worcestershire and Tabasco sauces, and black pepper. I've suggested some additional embellishments that make it taste really good.

TIME about 5 minutes

For the prairie oyster

1 large egg

1 teaspoon Worcestershire sauce

¼ teaspoon Tabasco or other hot sauce

Coarse salt (kosher or sea) and freshly ground black pepper

Add-ins (optional)

A spoonful of prepared or freshly grated horseradish

A squeeze of fresh lemon juice

A splash of red wine vinegar

A sprinkle of pimentón (smoked paprika)

Crack the egg into a glass, taking care not to break the yolk. Add the Worcestershire and Tabasco sauces, a generous sprinkle of salt and pepper, and any of the add-ins you like. Raise the glass to your lips and drink its contents— a lot of us do this in a single gulp.

POWER SHAKE

Our roster of essential guy drinks would be incomplete without a power shake, and this one fortifies you from the first sip. Skim milk and yogurt for protein, banana for potassium, orange juice for vitamin C, and antioxidant-rich blueberries: Think of it as breakfast you drink. **Makes about 2½ cups; serves 1 or 2**

1 cup cold skim milk

¾ cup cold plain or vanilla-flavored Greek yogurt

¼ cup fresh orange juice

½ ripe banana, cut into 1-inch pieces

3 tablespoons blueberries

2 ounces protein powder

Place the milk, yogurt, orange juice, banana, blueberries, and protein powder in a blender.

Blend until smooth, starting the blender on low speed and gradually increasing it to high.

CONVERSION TABLES

Please note that all conversions are approximate but close enough to be useful when converting from one system to another.

OVEN TEMPERATURES

FAHRENHEIT	GAS MARK	CELSIUS
250	½	120
275	1	140
300	2	150
325	3	160
350	4	180
375	5	190
400	6	200
425	7	220
450	8	230
475	9	240
500	10	260

NOTE: Reduce the temperature by 20°C (68°F) for fan-assisted ovens.

APPROXIMATE EQUIVALENTS

1 stick butter = 8 tbs = 4 oz = ½ cup = 115 g

1 cup all-purpose presifted flour = 4.7 oz

1 cup granulated sugar = 8 oz = 220 g

1 cup (firmly packed) brown sugar = 6 oz = 220 g to 230 g

1 cup confectioners' sugar=4½ oz = 115 g

1 cup honey or syrup = 12 oz

1 cup grated cheese = 4 oz

1 cup dried beans = 6 oz

1 large egg = about 2 oz or about 3 tbs

1 egg yolk = about 1 tbs

1 egg white = about 2 tbs

LIQUID CONVERSIONS

U.S.	IMPERIAL	METRIC
2 tbs	1 fl oz	30 ml
3 tbs	1½ fl oz	45 ml
¼ cup	2 fl oz	60 ml
⅓ cup	2½ fl oz	75 ml
⅓ cup + 1 tbs	3 fl oz	90 ml
⅓ cup + 2 tbs	3½ fl oz	100 ml
½ cup	4 fl oz	125 ml
⅔ cup	5 fl oz	150 ml
¾ cup	6 fl oz	175 ml
¾ cup + 2 tbs	7 fl oz	200 ml
1 cup	8 fl oz	250 ml
1 cup + 2 tbs	9 fl oz	275 ml
1¼ cups	10 fl oz	300 ml
1⅓ cups	11 fl oz	325 ml
1½ cups	12 fl oz	350 ml
1⅔ cups	13 fl oz	375 ml
1¾ cups	14 fl oz	400 ml
1¾ cups + 2 tbs	15 fl oz	450 ml
2 cups (1 pint)	16 fl oz	500 ml
2½ cups	20 fl oz (1 pint)	600 ml
3¾ cups	1½ pints	900 ml
4 cups	1¾ pints	1 liter

WEIGHT CONVERSIONS

US/UK	METRIC	US/UK	METRIC
½ oz	15 g	7 oz	200 g
1 oz	30 g	8 oz	250 g
1½ oz	45 g	9 oz	275 g
2 oz	60 g	10 oz	300 g
2½ oz	75 g	11 oz	325 g
3 oz	90 g	12 oz	350 g
3½ oz	100 g	13 oz	375 g
4 oz	125 g	14 oz	400 g
5 oz	150 g	15 oz	450 g
6 oz	175 g	1 lb	500 g

GLOSSARY

I've tried to write this book for guys with all levels of culinary experience. If you're just starting out, you may find some ingredients or anatomical or technical cooking terms in these pages that are not yet familiar to you.

If you don't see an ingredient defined here, please check A Word About the Basic Ingredients on page 25 or Flavor Boosters from A to Z (see page 26).

Agave syrup | A natural sweetener extracted from the cactus that gives us tequila. Some bartenders prefer to use it instead of Simple Syrup (page 589) to sweeten margaritas.

Ancho chile powder | A richly flavored chile powder ground from dried poblano chiles. Spicy but not in the least fiery.

Baste | To brush a meat, seafood, vegetable, or other food with a liquid (often a fat, like melted butter or olive oil) during cooking to keep it moist and add flavor.

Blanch | To plunge into rapidly boiling water for a brief period. Used to parboil (partially cook) vegetables or remove impurities from organ meats.

Blot (as in to blot dry) | To remove excess liquid (as from raw meat or freshly fried food) by patting it with or draining it on paper towels.

Braise | To cook food in liquid in a covered pot at a low temperature. Braising is used to cook tough cuts of meat, like pot roast or lamb shanks, that need penetrating steam to soften the connective tissue and meat fibers.

Brine | A saline solution (salt plus water—and sometimes sugar and spices) used to flavor and cure meats. Also a verb: to soak a food in brine.

Brûlée | "Burned," as in crème brûlée, "burned cream," literally—custard with a burnt sugar crust. Also a verb: to caramelize (see below) with a blowtorch or on a hot *plancha* (see below).

Caramelize | To cook sugar or an ingredient with a high sugar content (like onions or fruit) until golden or darkly browned. This partially burns the sugar (in a controlled manner), which gives it a complex, luscious, candylike flavor. Throughout the pages of this book you'll be asked to caramelize onions (see instructions on page 497). Elsewhere, you'll be asked to caramelize sugar on oatmeal (page 65) or bananas (page 564) to create a hard candy crust.

Cartilage | A gristly white connective tissue found in meats. For example, a triangular white strip of cartilage separates the halves of a chicken breast.

Chile powder | A reddish or brown spice made by grinding dried chiles (for example, dried poblano chiles). Depending on the chile, the powder can be mild (for example, ancho chile powder) or fiery (i.e. *chile de arbol* powder). For the best results, when a recipe in this book calls for chile powder, use a pure chile powder (one free of salt, garlic powder, or other seasonings).

Chipotle chile | A smoked jalapeño pepper from Mexico. Available dried, powdered, and canned. When possible, buy the latter because canned chipotles come in an intensely flavorful sauce called *adobo*.

Chorizo | A Spanish/Latin American pork sausage flavored with paprika, hot peppers, cumin, garlic, and wine. Available fresh (raw) and cooked.

Cold cuts (aka **lunch meats**) | A broad family of hams, sausages, and ground meat loaves thinly sliced and served on deli platters and sandwiches. The short list includes:

▸ **Bologna** | A large, round, finely ground cooked pork or beef sausage modeled on Italian mortadella.

▸ **Corned beef** | Brisket that has been cured in brine and spices, then boiled. Served hot or cold.

▸ **Ham** | Cured pork leg. Can be baked, dried, or smoked, or processed using a combination of these techniques. See Ham entry below for the various types.

▸ **Mortadella** | A giant, round, finely ground pork sausage studded with white chunks of pork fat and pistachio nuts. Originally from Bologna, Italy (the inspiration for American bologna).

▸ **Pastrami** | Brined brisket crusted with black pepper, coriander seeds, garlic, and other spices and smoked. Served hot or cold, thinly sliced.

▸ **Salami** | A cured or cooked sausage (generally beef or pork), most often eaten thinly sliced.

Coppa (aka **capicola**) | *See* Ham.

Cornichons | Tiny sour French pickles. Traditionally served with pâté and other pork products.

Cure | To flavor and preserve meat or sausage using salt, sugar (optional), pepper, and other spices, and often a curing agent like sodium nitrate or Prague powder. Curing was traditionally done to help preserve meats in the age before refrigeration. It's part of what gives bacon and corned beef their inviting reddish hue.

Deglaze | To dissolve the flavorful brown bits (caramelized meat juices) left on the bottom of a pan after you sear meat or poultry. Heat the pan and add a liquid (it will issue an inviting hiss), then bring it to a boil, scraping the bottom of the pan with a wooden spoon. Big flavor. Instant sauce.

Drain | To strain boiled foods (spaghetti comes to mind) in a colander to remove the excess water. Or to blot fried or deep-fried foods on paper towels to remove the excess grease.

Dredge | To dip a moist food, like a fish fillet or chicken breast in flour or bread crumbs. Once both sides are thoroughly coated, you shake the fillet or breast (holding one end with tongs) over the flour bowl to dislodge the excess.

Flambé | To set on fire—usually with alcohol. One purpose of flambéing is to burn off the raw alcohol. The other is to awe your guests.

Fold | To combine ingredients by mixing with a rubber spatula. When done properly, you "fold" the ingredients on the bottom over the top.

Free pour | A bartending term that means to pour spirits directly from the bottle into the glass without measuring the portions.

French | To scrape the end of a bone clean with a paring knife. Done to lamb and veal chops, rack of lamb, prime rib, etc. Legend has it this was done so you could pick up a chop without soiling your fingers.

Grain (as in cutting across the grain) | The prevailing direction of the muscle fibers in a piece of meat. When you slice meat across the grain, you cut perpendicular to these fibers, which shortens them, making the meat more tender.

Ham | A pig's leap to immortality. The leg (specifically the thigh) and occasionally a shoulder roast that is cured with salt or brine, then preserved by drying, baking, or smoking (or sometimes several of these processes).

▸ **Cooked ham** | A brined, baked, or hot smoked pork leg. One example of a great cooked ham is England's York ham.

▸ **Coppa** (aka **capicola**) | An Italian cured meat similar to prosciutto, but made with pork shoulder or neck instead of leg. Available mild or spicy.

▸ **Cured ham** | A pork leg that is cured with salt and spices, then dried for many months or even years. Prosciutto and Smithfield hams are classic examples of cured hams.

▸ **Prosciutto** | Italy's famous dry-cured ham. The best comes from Parma and San Daniele. Prosciutto is also made in the U.S. One especially worthy of note is the Iowan prosciutto made with acorn-fed hogs by La Quercia.

▸ **Smoked ham** | A pork leg that is cured with salt or brined, then smoked. Can be hot smoked (one example is Harrington ham from Vermont). Or cold smoked (salt cured, pressed, then smoked but not cooked). Examples include Italian speck and German Westphalian ham.

▸ **Spanish ham** | Spain makes some of the world's greatest hams. *Jamón serrano* ("mountain ham," literally) is the most basic (and affordable) Spanish ham. *Pata negra* ("black foot," literally), *Jamón ibérico* ("Spanish ham"), *Bellota,* and *Jabugo* are super premium (and super expensive) hams that melt on your tongue like porcine butter.

▸ **Tasso** | Cajun "ham." Spiced, smoked pork shoulder. (True ham comes from the leg.)

Hardwood (as in chips) | Chips, chunks, or logs from deciduous trees (which shed their leaves once a year) used for grilling and smoking and wood-burning ovens. Popular hardwoods include hickory, oak, cherry, apple, and mesquite.

Heritage breeds | Traditional old-time varieties of fruits (for example, apples), vegetables (for example, tomatoes—yes, I know they're fruits botanically speaking, but we eat them as vegetables), and livestock (such as hogs). Heritage breeds have more flavor (and in the case of hogs more fat), but tend to be slower growing (in the case of hogs), less "attractive" (in the case of apples), or have a shorter shelf life (in the case of tomatoes).

Highball | A refreshing summer cocktail often made with a carbonated soft drink or club soda and served in a tall glass.

Lemongrass | One of the defining flavors of Southeast Asian cooking. It looks a little like an overgrown scallion and is endowed with an herbal lemony flavor but no acidity. You can find it in the produce section of most supermarkets (look for it with the packaged herbs), but you'll get bigger, better lemongrass stalks for less money at an Asian market. To trim lemongrass, cut off the green part (the top two-thirds) and peel the outside layer off the cream-colored bottom of the stalk. Because it's so fibrous, lemongrass is either finely minced or cut into large pieces (so you can eat around them) before cooking. Can't find lemongrass? Substitute ½- by-1½-inch strips of lemon zest.

Liquid smoke | A natural smoke flavoring made by burning hardwood (see above), then condensing and collecting the smoke in a still and mixing it with water to make a flavoring. It's strong stuff—a drop or two will do you.

Macerate | To steep. Spices and fruits are often macerated in rum or other spirits to make flavored beverages.

Marinate | To soak in a flavorful liquid (called the marinade). Marinating serves three purposes: to flavor, to moisturize, and to tenderize (the latter requires the presence of an acid, like lemon juice or yogurt, in the marinade).

Multiply | To double, triple, or otherwise increase the quantities of ingredients in a recipe to increase its yield. Note that when you multiply a recipe (particularly significantly), you often need to adjust the proportions of the ingredients.

Nonreactive (as in cookware) | Describing a pot, pan, baking dish, bowl, or other cooking vessel that will not react with acidic or otherwise corrosive ingredients, such as lemon juice or wine. Glass, stainless steel, and ceramic are nonreactive materials.

Parboil | To partially boil an ingredient; that is, to boil it long enough to loosen the skins (as in pearl onions) or otherwise soften an ingredient prior to finishing by another cooking method. *See* blanch.

Plancha | A heavy sheet or slab of cast iron from Spain similar to an American griddle. Great for searing seafood and fruit.

Preheat | To turn on an oven or grill or heat a pan so that it reaches a particular temperature prior to cooking.

Reduce | To boil a liquid to remove excess water and concentrate the flavor. To "reduce by half," for example, means to boil until only half as much liquid remains as when you started.

Sausage | Seasoned ground meat (beef, pork, lamb, poultry, and others) often packed into a tubular casing. Sausages come raw, cured, cooked, and/or smoked.

  ▸ **Andouille** | A cooked, smoked Cajun pork sausage flavored with garlic, paprika, cayenne, thyme, and other spices.

  ▸ **Bockwurst** | A white, finely ground German-style pork sausage that tastes a bit like a hot dog.

  ▸ **Breakfast sausage** | A fresh (uncooked) ground pork sausage flavored with pepper, sage, and other spices and sold in links, patties, or in bulk.

  ▸ **Bratwurst** (aka **brat** or **brats**) | A German- or Austrian-style pork sausage flavored with pepper, mace, and other spices.

  ▸ **Chorizo** | A Spanish-style sausage made and eaten throughout the Hispanic world. Seasoned with paprika, garlic, vinegar, and/or wine. Available fresh (raw) and cooked.

  ▸ **Italian sausage** | A pork sausage sold **sweet** (flavored with fennel and other spices) or **hot** (spiced up with hot pepper flakes). Always sold raw.

  ▸ **Kielbasa** | A garlicky, cooked, smoked Polish-style sausage.

  ▸ *Linguiça* | A garlicky, cooked Portuguese-style sausage similar to **chorizo** (see above).

  ▸ **Soppressata** | A hard, flat, salami-like Italian sausage flavored with garlic and wine.

Sauté | To panfry small pieces of food in hot butter or oil in a frying pan. The term comes from the French word "to jump," which is exactly what the food does in the hot fat.

Score | To make a shallow incision; often done as a series of parallel incisions. You score a flank steak (page 242), for example, to help tenderize it, speed-marinate it, and keep it from curling.

Sear | To brown the exterior of meat or seafood quickly over high heat. Searing helps seal in juices and flavor.

Sesame oil | A topaz-colored oil with an intense smoky, nutty flavor pressed from roasted sesame seeds. One good widely available brand is Kadoya from Japan.

Shaoxing wine | A rice wine from eastern China; available at Asian markets. Sake or dry sherry make good substitutes.

Silverskin | Silvery-white connective tissue that sheathes tenderloins (both beef and pork), ribs, and other large cuts of meat. Trim it off with a paring knife or ask your butcher to do it.

Simmer | To cook a liquid or cook in a liquid at a very low boil (bubbles should barely break the surface).

Sous vide | Cooking food in a vacuum-sealed plastic pouch at extremely low temperatures for a period that can last several days. Sous vide allows you to cook foods to precise internal temperatures while retaining the maximum moistness. You brown the exterior at the last minute in a skillet or fryer or with a blowtorch.

Sushi-quality fish | Fish so fresh you can eat it raw in sushi and ceviche.

Tamari | A super-premium, Japanese or Japanese-style soy sauce containing mostly soy beans. (Lesser soy sauces contain up to 50 percent wheat.)

Tasso | *See* Ham.

Tent | To cover with a sheet of aluminum foil, as in to tent a turkey or prime rib with foil to keep it warm as it rests before carving. Note that when tenting, loosely drape the foil over the meat (or lay it on top). Do not bunch it around the meat or you'll make the exterior soggy.

Warm | To gently heat, as in to warm plates or a platter to keep the food served on them from getting cold. To do this, place the plates in a 250°F oven for 20 minutes. You also warm whole loaves of bread.

Whisk | To stir with a whisk (see page 18), which blends ingredients more effectively than stirring with a wooden spoon or spatula.

Zest | The oil-rich outer rind of a citrus fruit; for example, the twist of lemon zest you use to garnish a martini. Zest is also a verb, meaning to remove the oil-rich outer rind of a citrus fruit with a vegetable peeler, zesting knife, or Microplane grater.

INDEX

(Page references in *italic* refer to illustrations.)

A

Affogato ("drowned" gelato), 560
Agave syrup, 606
Aged meat, wet- vs. dry-, 225–27
The Alsatian (pizza), 525–27
Anchovy(ies), 26, 203
  butter, 230
  grilled cheese sandwich with
    mozzarella, hot peppers, and
    (the Sicilian), 77
  hot tub, 204
  the Sicilian (pizza), 524
  toasts, 202
Andrés, José, 43, 134–35
Appetizers. *See* Starters
Aquavit in a block of ice, 597–98
Artichoke, grilled, dip, 214
Arugula, in green BLTs, 80–81
Asian ingredients:
  fish sauce, 27
  sesame oil, 28
  tamari, 28
  XO sauce, 29
  yuzu, 29
  see also Kimchi; Miso; Soy;
    Wasabi
Asian-style recipes:
  East-West mignonette, 399
  hellfire squid stir-fry, 441–42
  hummus, 215
  lamb vindaloo (fiery Goan-style
    curry), 322–23
  Laotian omelet, 54–55
  maple teriyaki salmon, 373–74

red-cooked lamb shanks, 311–12
soba with spicy peanut sauce,
  462–63
tofu stir-fry with ginger and
  chiles, 475–76
Vietnamese-style coffee, 601
see also Korean; Pac-Rim–style
  recipes
Avocados, 216
  chipotle guacamole, 217–18
  green BLTs, 80–81

B

Baby back ribs, *288*
  with cider rum barbecue sauce
    (on the grill), 283–86, *284*
  indoors (in the oven), 289–90
Bacon, 26
  the Alsatian (pizza), 525–27
  BLT salad, *160*, 161–62
  candied, sundaes, 553–55, *554*
  cheddar quesadillas, 80
  and egg spaghetti, 449
  fat, saving, 555
  green BLTs, 80–81
  grilled cheese sandwich with
    pimento cheese and (the
    Southerner), 74
  loaded potatoes, *492*, 493
  pepper Jack, and jalapeño corn
    bread (PB&J), 514–16, *515*
  prunes or dates wrapped in, 197
  -roasted, cheese-stuffed jalapeño
    peppers (poppers), 195–97, *196*
  roasted brussels sprouts with, 500
  shad roe with capers and, 393–94
  shrimp or scallops wrapped in, 197

Spanglish sandwich (BLT with
  fried egg and cheese), 81–82
  three ways, 67–68
  -wrapped scallops with Scotch
    whisky glaze, 434–35
Bagna cauda (anchovy hot tub), 204
Baking, 9
Baking dishes, *16*, 19
Baking sheets, *16*, 19, *19*
Balsamic vinaigrette, honey poppy,
  183, 184
Baltimore crab cakes, the real deal,
  415–16
Banana(s):
  Foster, deconstructed, 564–66,
    566
  power shake, 604
Bar, home:
  equipment for, *17*, *578*, 579–80
  spirits for, 580
  see also Bloody Marys; Drinks
Barbecue:
  pork burger, 110–11
  rub, made-from-scratch
    (Raichlen's rub #2), 531, *535*
Barbecue sauce:
  cider rum, 286
  dark and stormy, 537–38, *540*
  three-ingredient (Carolina
    mustard sauce), 536–37
Bartending techniques, Dale
  DeGroff's, 587
Basil, *308*, 309
  tomato salsa, 512
Basting, 606
Beakers, 579
Bean(s):
  baked, sweet and smoky, 480–81

bake-fried chiles rellenos, 472–74, *473*

beef and pork chili, really good, *148*, 149–50

black, chorizo soup, 139

black, Meatless Monday tacos with poblano, corn and, 467–69, *468*

breakfast nachos, 58–59

chile, burgers, 471–72

chili sans carne, 153–54

salad, gaucho, 171

shrimp and, Tuscan, 423

white, kale, and kielbasa soup, *136*, 137–38

see also Chickpea(s)

Beef, 223–68

brisket braised with red wine and cognac, French bistro style, 263–65

broth or stock, in bloody bull (cocktail), 595

buying, 225–27

chuck steak, beer-braised, 253–54

cubing, 257

game plan hash, 66–67

grass-fed vs. corn-fed, 225

meatballs with Parmesan and herbs for, 463–64

organic vs. conventional, 225

and pork chili, really good, *148*, 149–50

prime rib, big kahuna, 251–52

Prime vs. Choice, 225

six degrees of doneness for, 229

steak tartare, 267–68

stew with Scotch whisky and lemon, 254–56

tacos, Korean, 244–46

tenderloin, trimming, 251

tenderloin, twenty-minute roast, 250–51

testing doneness of, 228–29

wagyu vs. Kobe, 227

wet-aged vs. dry-aged, 225–27

see also Burgers; Short ribs; Steak(s)

Beer:

-battered fish, *386*, 387–88

-braised chuck steak, 253–54

-braised short ribs, 262

bread, no-knead honey whole wheat, 520–21

brownies, Belgian, 569–70, *571*

red, 596–97

soup with cheddar and stout, 130–31

Beets, roasted, with shallots and walnuts, 499

Belgian beer brownies, 569–70, *571*

Berthin, Gabriel, 577

Beverages. *See* Bloody Marys; Drinks

Big kahuna prime rib, 251–52

Biscuits, drop, 517

Bitters, 581

Bittman, Mark, 471, 482–83

Black and white salad (winter salad of endive, walnuts, and cheese), 176

Black and white tuna seared with sesame seeds and served sushi-rare in the center, 382–83

Black bean(s):

chorizo soup, 139

Meatless Monday tacos with poblano, corn and, 467–69, *468*

Blackened salmon, 380–81

Blackening spice, 381

Black Russian, 592

Blanching, 606

Blenders, immersion, 22

Bloody bull, 595

Bloody clam, 595

Bloody gazpacho, 126

Bloody Maria, 596

Bloody Marys, 594–96

Hemingway, 594

Korean, 596

Raichlen, 595–96

Blowtorches, *16*, 22, 606

Blowtorch oatmeal, 65

Blowtorch salmon, *370*, 371–72

BLT(s):

with fried egg and cheese (*Spanglish* sandwich), 81–82

green, 80–81

salad, *160*, 161–62

salad bruschetta, 162

Blue blazer, 592

Blue cheese(s), 28, 76

dressing, 188

Boiling, 8

Bologna, in "dear" dog, 119–21

Bourbon, 580

-brined roast turkey, 349–51, *350*

Broadmoor Manhattan, 582

brown cow (float), 557

Dale DeGroff's whiskey smash, 586

Bowls, mixing, 15, *15*, *17*

Braising, 9, 606

Brandy Alexander, 592

Brandy-brined pheasants, 357–58

Bratwurst:

grilled cheese sandwich with cheddar and (the Wisconsinite), 74–75

new way with, 116–17

Brazilian-style recipes:

steak house collard greens, 501–2

turbinado, 120

Bread(s), 509–22

bruschetta (the original garlic bread), 511–12

drop biscuits, 517

garlic, in the oven, 513–14

garlic, on the grill, 514

no-knead honey whole wheat beer, 520–21

Hemingway Bloody Mary, 594
Herb(s), *308*, 309–10
   and cheese omelet, 49
   fresh, *chimichurri,* 539–41, *540*
   fresh, ranch dressing, *183,* 185
   mincing, 141
Honey:
   dipping sauce, hellfire, 341
   no-knead whole wheat beer bread,
      520–21
   poppy balsamic vinaigrette, *183,*
      184
Horseradish:
   and prosciutto mashed potatoes,
      498
   sauce, 545
   slaw, creamy, 177
Hot chocolate, Mexican, 574
Hot dogs, 116–22
   advice for, 118
   bratwurst, new way with, 116–17
   "dear" dog, 119–21
   "hot" dog, 121–22
   must-try, from around the world,
      120
Hot mulled cider, 603
Hot mulled wine from Quebec (the
      caribou), 602–3
Hot sauce, 27
Huitlacoche (corn smut), 200
   quesadillas, 80
Hummus, Asian, 215
Hungarian pork chops *paprikás,* 296

I

Ice:
   cubes or crushed ice for cocktails,
      581
   vodka or aquavit in a block of, 597
Ice cream, 27
   "burnt" peaches and, 561–62
   candied bacon sundaes, 553–55, *554*

deconstructed bananas Foster,
      564–66, *566*
Ice cream floats for grown-ups,
      555–57
   bourbon brown cow, 557
   cherry *lambic,* 556–57
   dark and stormy, 556
   rum and Coke, 555–56
Icelandic dog, 120
Immersion blenders, *17,* 22
Immersion circulators, 22
Indian-style recipes:
   curried egg salad sandwiches,
      83–84
   lamb vindaloo (fiery Goan-style
      curry), 322–23
Indirect grilling, 12
Ingredients, 25–29
   basic (how to stock your pantry),
      25–26
   flavor boosters, 26–29
   gathering, 4, 6, 30–31
   measuring, 31–32
   mise en place and, 7, 31
   quality of, 31
   shopping for, 6, 30–31
   substitutions of, 31
Inside-out cheeseburger, 109–10
Instant-read thermometers, 19, *19,*
      20, 229, 276
Italian-style recipes:
   anchovy hot tub (*bagna cauda*),
      204
   bruschetta (the original garlic
      bread), 511–12
   the Caprese (grilled cheese
      sandwich with mozzarella,
      tomato, and basil), 75–77
   Catalonian tomato bread (*pa amb
      tomàquet*), 512
   cauliflower "steaks" Sicilian style
      (with capers, currants, and pine
      nuts), 500–501

"drowned" gelato (*affogato*),
      560
eggs fra diavolo (poached in
      spicy marinara sauce), 56–58
finger-burner lamb chops
      (*scottadito*), *314,* 315
frittata with spring vegetables,
      55–56
hammered veal chops, 268–70
leg of lamb with garlic and
      rosemary, 303–5
porchetta (garlic and herb
      stuffed pork loin), 277–79,
      278
sausage and peppers, 117
the Sicilian (grilled cheese
      sandwich with mozzarella,
      anchovies, and hot peppers),
      77
Tuscan shrimp and beans,
      423
see also Pasta; Pizza; Spaghetti

J

Jalapeño (peppers), 27
   cheese-stuffed, bacon-roasted
      (poppers), 195–97, *196*
   Lone Star pepper steak, 240–41
   pepper Jack, and bacon corn
      bread (PB&J), 514–16, *515*
Japanese-style maple teriyaki
      salmon, 373–74
Jarlsberg cheese, grilled cheese
      sandwich with smoked
      salmon and (the Norwegian),
      78
Jefferson, Thomas, 452–53,
      461
Jepson, John, 146–47
Jiggers, *578, 579*
Juicers, hand, 579–80
Jus, garlic lemon, 335–36